Nothingness in Asian Philc

A variety of crucial and still most relevant ideas about nothingness or emptiness have gained profound philosophical prominence in the history and development of a number of South and East Asian traditions—including in Buddhism, Daoism, Neo-Confucianism, Hinduism, Korean philosophy, and the Japanese Kyoto School. These traditions share the insight that in order to explain both the great mysteries and mundane facts about our experience, ideas of "nothingness" must play a primary role.

This collection of essays brings together the work of twenty of the world's prominent scholars of Hindu, Buddhist, Daoist, Neo-Confucian, Japanese, and Korean thought to illuminate fascinating philosophical conceptualizations of "nothingness" in both classical and modern Asian traditions. The unique collection offers new work from accomplished scholars and provides a coherent, panoramic view of the most significant ways that "nothingness" plays crucial roles in Asian philosophy. It includes both traditional and contemporary formulations, sometimes putting Asian traditions into dialogue with one another and sometimes with classical and modern Western thought. The result is a book of immense value for students and researchers in Asian and comparative philosophy.

JeeLoo Liu is Professor of Philosophy at California State University, Fullerton.

Douglas L. Berger is Associate Professor of Indian, Chinese, and Cross-Cultural Philosophy at Southern Illinois University, Carbondale.

Nothingness in Asian Philosophy

Edited by
JeeLoo Liu and Douglas L. Berger

Routledge
Taylor & Francis Group
NEW YORK AND LONDON

First published 2014
by Routledge
711 Third Avenue, New York, NY 10017

and by Routledge
2 Park Square, Milton Park, Abingdon, Oxon, OX14 4RN

Routledge is an imprint of the Taylor & Francis Group, an informa business

Library of Congress Cataloging-in-Publication Data

CIP data applied for.

ISBN: 978-0-415-82943-4 (hbk)
ISBN: 978-0-415-82944-1 (pbk)
ISBN: 978-1-315-77424-4 (ebk)

Typeset in Times New Roman
by Apex CoVantage, LLC

Contents

Contributors

Douglas L. Berger is Associate Professor of Philosophy at Southern Illinois University, Carbondale.

Arindam Chakrabarti is Professor of Philosophy at the University of Hawaii, Manoa.

Alan K. L. Chan is Dean of the College of Humanities, Arts & Social Sciences, and Toh Puan Mahani Idris Daim Chair Professor of Humanities at Nanyang Technological University, Singapore.

Yasuo Deguchi is Associate Professor of Philosophy at Kyoto University, Japan.

Chris Fraser is Associate Professor of Philosophy at the University of Hong Kong.

Jay L. Garfield is Kwan Im Thong Hood Cho Temple Professor of Humanities at Yale-NUS College, Singapore, Professor of Philosophy at National University of Singapore, Doris Silbert Professor in the Humanities and Professor of Philosophy at Smith College, Northampton, Massachusetts, Professor of Philosophy at the University of Melbourne, Australia, Recurrent Visiting Professor of Philosophy at Yale University, and Adjunct Professor of Philosophy at Central University of Tibetan Studies in Sarnath, India.

Chien-hsing Ho is Associate Professor of Religious Studies at Nanhua University, Taiwan.

Halla Kim is Associate Professor of Philosophy at the University of Nebraska at Omaha.

Gereon Kopf is Professor of Religion at Luther College, Decorah, Iowa, Visiting Lecturer at Saitama University, Japan, Visiting Researcher at the International Research Center for Philosophy of Tōyō University, Japan, and Editor-in-Chief of the *Journal of Buddhist Philosophy*.

John W. M. Krummel is Associate Professor of Religious Studies at Hobart and William Smith Colleges, Geneva, New York.

Chen-kuo Lin is Professor of Philosophy at National Chengchi University, Taiwan.

JeeLoo Liu is Professor of Philosophy at California State University, Fullerton.

Xiaogan Liu is Chair Professor at Renmin University, China, and the Founding and Honorary Director of the Research Center for Chinese Philosophy and Culture at the Chinese University of Hong Kong.

Makoto Ozaki is Emeritus Professor of Philosophy at Sanyo Gakuen University, Japan.

Graham Priest is Distinguished Professor of Philosophy at the Graduate Center, CUNY, and Boyce Gibson Professor Emeritus at the University of Melbourne, Australia.

Rajam Raghunathan is Assistant Professor of Philosophy at the University of Hawaii, Manoa.

Mark Siderits is Emeritus Professor of Philosophy at Illinois State University and Seoul National University.

Koji Tanaka is Senior Lecturer of Philosophy at the University of Auckland, New Zealand.

Sthaneshwar Timalsina is Associate Professor of Religious Studies at San Diego State University.

Zhihua Yao is Associate Professor of Philosophy at the Chinese University of Hong Kong.

Introduction

Conceptions of Nothingness in Asian Philosophy

While the history of Western philosophy began with concerns involving the primary constituents and fundamental nature of *being* and *existence*, the notion of *nothingness* or *emptiness* plays a central role in Asian philosophical traditions from the start. A variety of ideas about *nothingness* gained profound philosophical prominence in a number of South and East Asian lineages of thought in the course of their development, and have remained central for them to this day. In Buddhism, the notion of *emptiness* signifies the underlying nature of the process of change in the impermanent world and the ultimate truth about our transient existence. In Daoism, it is suggested that the word "*wu* (無, nothing or nonbeing)" may best characterize the origin of the entire cosmological order as well as the ontological grounding of our existence. In Hinduism, the ultimate and unitary nature of reality was often described negatively, as "not this and not that" with respect to all the differentiated phenomena that we could speak about, and yet as their shared innermost essence. In the view expressed by philosophers of the Japanese Kyoto School, the idea of *Absolute Nothingness* represents the root of the self and of the world. Furthermore, all these philosophical traditions employed ideas of *nothingness* not only to depict grand metaphysical principles, but also to explain things about everyday life, such as how we experience loss in our temporal and very ephemeral existence, how death is taken to be a form of *nothingness*, how space combined with matter forms physical things, how we can speak in terms of negation, and how we become aware that things are not where we were expecting to find them. The idea of *nothingness* or *emptiness* further develops into a philosophy of life. The philosophies of *nothingness* have, in addition, an ethical import and a transformative power. Once people understand that ultimate reality is *nothingness* or *emptiness*, they acquire levels of insight into their mundane existence that can profoundly change them. This insight, commonly spoken of as enlightenment, enables people to transcend their ordinary concerns in life. In all these respects, the major philosophical traditions of Asia propounded, though in markedly different ways, the view that, in order to explain both the great mysteries and mundane facts about our experience, ideas of *nothingness* and *emptiness* must play a central role.

The collection of essays in this book brings together the work of twenty prominent scholars of Hindu, Buddhist, Daoist, Neo-Confucian, Japanese, and Korean thought to illuminate fascinating philosophical conceptualizations of *nothingness* and *emptiness* in both classical and modern Asian traditions. The collection is, in the current state of scholarly literature, unique in that it brings together a host of accomplished scholars to provide in concert a panoramic representation of the ways in which ideas of *nothingness* and *emptiness* played crucial roles in Asian traditions. These essays offer both traditional and contemporary analyses, sometimes putting various Asian systems of thought into dialogue with one another and sometimes with classical and modern Western philosophers. This combined effort will benefit everyone in the fields of Asian and comparative philosophy who recognizes the great importance of these philosophical resonances of *nothingness*.

As Douglas L. Berger points out in his contribution to this volume that "there was never a homogeneous view of the notion of 'nothingness' in classical Asian thought, and that, instead, the idea was the topic of pointed debate and adjudged from many different perspectives" (Chapter 12). In this volume, we will see formulations as varied as those which depict *emptiness* as the very nature of existence, *nothingness* as a depiction of indeterminacy and formlessness, *nonbeing* as the ontological grounding for being, *nothingness* as the *space* in concrete things, *emptiness* as a psychological state of an ideal moral agent, and *emptiness* as metaphorically represented by the image of *the sky* in our aesthetic appreciation and spiritual elevation. In some cases, the idea of *nothingness* also takes on the role of providing explanations for more common phenomena, such as the absence of things in certain places, or the linguistic forms that make negations function intelligibly in our understanding. Indeed, as the reader peruses these chapters, the wide range of the notion's philosophical significance will become clear. If there is, however, a common theme that emerges from the following essays, it is that *nothingness* is not a *thing* and cannot be conceived to exist in the same manner in which other concrete material substances exist. To make ontological commitment to *nothingness* would be to turn *nothing* into *something*.

Even though not a self-subsisting *thing* or *state of affairs*, *nothingness* is nonetheless a distinctly identifiable constituent of our world, and may be happened upon through empirical, logical, semantic, existential, and reflective approaches. *Nothingness* is, therefore, very much part and parcel of the makeup of the world. The world is not simply "everything that exists," as some contemporary realists take as their starting assumption. In contrast, the views presented in this volume take negative facts, absences, nothingness, and emptiness as furniture of the world. It is this fundamental conviction, that nothingness is both experienced and known by us and is inherent in the very nature of things as well as our own natures, that authors in this collection share. *Nothingness* cannot be posited, but neither should it be dismissed, in our ontology. These essays will help make the traditions they represent valuable participants in the ongoing work of philosophical inquiry and dialogue on the nature of the world.

Chapter Synopses

Part I of this book focuses on the notion of *emptiness* in Brāhmiṇical and Early Buddhist Traditions. The collection opens with Arindam Chakrabarti's "The Unavoidable Void: Nonexistence, Absence, and Emptiness," which offers philosophical reflections on such concepts as *lack*, *absence*, *emptiness*, and *no-self*. Chakrabarti examines the treatment (or suspicion) of *negative facts* in Western and Indian philosophical traditions. He points out that "the observable world around us is replete with real *lacks*": holes, gaps, space, blanks, and the like. In terms of action and event, we also have avoidance, omission, negligence, negation, and inaction. And yet, metaphysicians are reluctant to list absences as part of the furniture of the world. To Chakrabarti, the source of this reluctance to entertain negative facts is that these metaphysicians conflate *not-Being* with those ontologically notorious *nonbeings* such as *the Gold Mountain* or *Pegasus*. Chakrabarti argues that the former expresses a fact of something's *not being there* or *not being the case*, which is nonetheless a part of reality, while the latter, as a creation of the language game, is simply unreal and belongs to the fictional realm. In this chapter, he discusses four arguments against our making ontological commitment to negative facts, and repudiates each. He argues that we must give negative facts their proper status in the world: absences are objectively present in the world, and negative facts have their corresponding truth makers based on positive entities and their relations. As Chakrabarti puts it, the world is simply "the totality of positive and negative facts."

Even though there are absences as negative facts, one should be careful not to allow spurious absences into our ontological landscape. Chakrabarti presents the logic of absence as formulated in the Indian Nyāya school. Nyāya logic takes absence to be delimited and qualified by its counterpart, the present existences of particular things. We can make sense of our discourse of absences, because these real absences are absences of existent things and we can understand them through those existent things. If, on the other hand, we are talking about absences in their own right, such as fictional entities and non-existent things, then such absences are simply *spurious*.

At the end of this chapter, Chakrabarti turns to the psychology of absences—emptying one's self—as discussed by Wittgenstein, Bhattacharya, Descartes, and Bergson. All these philosophers were interested in the phenomenology of the self's *lack*—for example, in the self's lack of a particular experience. Chakrabarti points out that even in negative introspective reports, such as the claim "I have no pain," what is negated is the positive experience—in this case, the experience of pain. There is no positing of any chimerical "no-pain" when one wishes to discuss the absence of pain. In other words, what is being negated, the negatum, is the reference of a negative report. One can speak of the non-existence of something by negating the presence of that *something* without making any ontological commitment to *its absence*. Even in the denial of the self's existence, as proclaimed by nihilism of the self, there is still a full presence of the self as the *locus* of this denial. *The self cannot be annihilated.* Chakrabarti's conclusion represents an underlying theme of this collection: "the idea of absolute naught is a self-destructive pseudo-idea, 'a mere word'."

In Chapter 2, "Semantics of Nothingness," Sthaneshwar Timalsina introduces the prominent Hindu grammarian Bhartṛhari's philosophy of negation. Bhartṛhari takes a linguistic approach to nothingness and focuses on the grammar of sentential negation. Timalsina explains the debate between particularists and wholists in Indian philosophies of language: the former claim that sentential meaning is constituted by the meaning of the words in the sentence; the latter maintain that sentential meaning is primary and indivisible. He groups Bhartṛhari in the wholist camp. According to Timalsina, Bhartṛhari's semantics of negation is that the negative particle *nañ* in Sanskrit functions as a way to *prohibit* what has been postulated by its referent rather than to posit the referent's non-existence. The semantics of negation is crucial to Bhartṛhari's conception of reality because he takes the negative particle to indicate not non-existence but the denial that a particularly existing thing possesses agency in a present case. This is important in the context of the linguistic debates that Bhartṛhari was engaged in because, if the negative particle were understood to have an independent meaning, then its general sense of "non-existence" would create a relation between it and the particular thing that it negates, which can only be identified precisely because it exists. Therefore, associating negation with action and the particularization, in both the compound word and sentential contexts, is not only necessary to explain how sentences can meaningfully negate, but is also essential for Bhratṛhari's metaphysics of being. Bhratṛhari believes that *Brahman*, immutable existence, underlies all things and manifests itself and its differentiations primarily in language. And so, to prevent the implication that some intimation that absolute non-existence could be referred to by the negative particle, it is necessary for us to work out how such a particle does not in fact itself refer to non-existence, but helps, given its semantic function, to particularize non-existence in terms of the things that we know to exist. In general, Bhartṛhari believes that language can truthfully describe a thing-in-itself, and the language of negation always accompanies the thing that is being negated. In other words, negation only negates *something that exists*, not some *non-existent* thing. Timalsina concludes that Bhartṛhari's logic invites us to see negation not as totally negative, but as partial affirmation of something else that exists.

In Chapter 3, "Madhyamaka, Nihilism, and the Emptiness of Emptiness," Jay L. Garfield defends a realist reading of Nāgārjuna, the founder of the Madhyamaka school of Buddhism. Nāgārjuna's core thesis of the emptiness of ultimate existence has often been interpreted as professing nihilism. According to Garfield's reading, however, Nāgārjuna's philosophy reveals a "decidedly realistic attitude" toward worldly phenomena. Garfield's argument is based on a careful analysis of Nāgārjuna's logic—a particular form of Buddhist logic called '*catuṣkoti*', according to which there are four possibilities for the truth value of a proposition: true, false, both true and false, neither true nor false. This logic is of course at odds with the principle of bivalence in classical logic, in which a proposition is either determinately true or false, and nothing else in between. In Nāgārjuna's view, the world is in flux, and cannot be neatly divided into facts and non-facts. We need semantics to capture a wider logical space than what bivalent logic can proffer. The four-value logic reflects the transient and ambivalent nature of things—as soon as something is asserted, it is denied; as soon as someone asserts something, someone else might reject it.

The ultimate goal of Nāgārjuna's teaching, according to Garfield, is to highlight the non-insistence on any ultimate nature, including emptiness itself. If Nāgārjuna were to assert that *emptiness* is the true nature of things, as nihilists do, then the true nature of things would cease to be *empty*, since it now has a designation, a mode of existence. In this sense, 'emptiness' does not really mean unqualified *emptiness*, as nothing can be called "emptiness" itself. Garfield suggests a reading offered by Tsongkhapa, according to which the concept *empty* is parameterized as "empty of." Worldly phenomena are *empty of* intrinsic nature, since their existence is causally interdependent and their natures, or properties, are relational to our cognitive capacities and our linguistic conventions. There is no ultimate reality in addition to our phenomenal world, as our phenomenal world is as real as it gets. Garfield summarizes Nāgārjuna's thesis as: "nothing is ultimately real, not even emptiness." Hence, he calls this view "the emptiness of emptiness."

In Chapter 4, "In Search of the Semantics of Emptiness," Koji Tanaka endorses Garfield's interpretation that 'emptiness' in Nāgārjuna's usage does not mean *nothingness*, and focuses on what it does mean. Tanaka argues that Nāgārjuna's thesis of emptiness is not merely an ontological claim about the nature of existence, but also a semantic thesis about the nature of truth. Nāgārjuna advocates the doctrine of "two truths": conventional truth and ultimate truth. In Tanaka's interpretation, the principle of truth presented in traditional Abhidharma literature adopts something like a modern Russellian approach. Russell takes the object referred to as a component of a proposition, and propositional truth is determined directly in relation to its reference, not mediated through any Fregean *sense*. Any statement about a fictional object, such as "Pegasus has wings," would simply be false since it has no corresponding object as its referent. The *two truths* doctrine advocated by the Ābhidharmikas separates ultimate truth from conventional truth: ultimate truth is about ultimate reality, which to them consists of nothing but the simplest, unanalyzable, partless entities. Conventional truths, on the other hand, are about composite things, which are ultimately unreal, but exist only according to the conventional view. According to Tanaka, Nāgārjuna seems to embrace this reference-based semantic principle of truth when he inherits the two truths doctrine from the Ābhidharmika. If this is indeed the principle of truth to which Nāgārjuna subscribes, however, then there is a paradox of taking about "the emptiness of emptiness" itself: since emptiness is not real, any statement about it must not be true. Nāgārjuna would then be barred by his own principle to speak of emptiness, not to mention from uttering an ultimate truth about emptiness.

We have seen in Chapter 3 that Garfield's solution to this seeming paradox is to attribute a paraconsistent logic to Nāgārjuna, so Nāgārjuna can be saying things that are both true and false, or neither true nor false. Tanaka is not satisfied with this solution. His own solution is to suggest a couple of new semantic theories of truth for Nāgārjuna. The first one is a deflationary theory, which Nāgārjuna's commentator Candrakīrti allegedly endorses. According to the deflationary theory of truth, *truth* is not some special property over and above a statement itself, which says something about the world. If the world is as the statement claims, then that statement is true. Tanaka attributes such a view to Candrakīrti, since the latter claims that what is true is simply "what is acknowledged by the world." Extending Candrakīrti's view of truth to Nāgārjuna's own dilemma of stating truth that cannot be stated, Tanaka argues that Nāgārjuna was not really making any ontological statement about the nature of emptiness. In other words, instead of saying, as Garfield does, that Nāgārjuna's statement about emptiness has multivalent truth values, Tanaka interprets it as having *no* independent truth value. In a related vein, Tanaka suggests that Nāgārjuna could also be employing a pragmatic theory of truth. If the ultimate truth is nowhere to be found, what Nāgārjuna can still do is to use statements about ultimate truth as expedients to make people believe in the nonexistence of ultimate truth. The simple lesson in Nāgārjuna's ontological paradox, according to Tanaka, is thus: Don't worry about the existence of emptiness or how we can make any true statement about things that do not exist. What is said or not said is merely a way to get people to see the operation of *emptiness* in life.

Chapter 5, "Madhyamaka Emptiness and Buddhist Ethics," by Mark Siderits expands the ontological and semantic dimensions of the concept of *emptiness* into ethics. Siderits agrees with both Garfield and Tanaka that Nāgārjuna does not advocate metaphysical nihilism, and he aims to further defend the thesis that moral nihilism should not be attributed to Nāgārjuna either. According to Siderits, the basic teaching of Indian Buddhist ethics is that the suffering of existence originates in our ignorance of the nature of existence. The Mahāyāna further advocate the path of the *bodhisattva*, one who has great compassion for all sentient beings and strives for the cessation of their suffering. If Mahāyāna in general, and Madhyamaka in particular, teaches that all things are *empty* in the sense that all things are devoid of intrinsic nature, then suffering must also be empty. Why should one care about others' suffering if suffering is not ultimately real? In other words, if suffering is empty, then why would a *bodhisattva* be compassionate toward the suffering of others? Hence, theoretically there seems to be a conflict between the Madhyamaka metaphysical claim and its ethical doctrine. Mādhyamikas must therefore establish a connection between emptiness and compassion in order to justify their ethical teaching of *great compassion*. Siderits examines three separate strategies for linking the two concepts, and points out difficulties with each. His own proposal is to appeal to an argument in Śāntideva's (eighth century CE) *Bodhicaryāvatāra*, in which an enduring self is temporally and hypothetically posited even though no such self could possibly ultimately exist. Siderits argues that implicit in this argument is what he calls "semantic contextualism," the view that meaning is contextualized and the same expression could mean different things from context to context. The teaching of *emptiness*, in the metaphysical context, explicates the absence of any intrinsic nature in all phenomena, including suffering. However, in the ethical context or in the context of practical reasoning, an expedient teaching is devised to claim that suffering is *real* and is *intrinsically* bad. Therefore, the Madhyamaka can still preach the emptiness of all things, while at the same time advocating impartial compassion for the "genuine" suffering of all sentient beings. The metaphysical claim and the ethical claim are thus not in conflict on the semantic level.

While Siderits focuses on the connection between the Madhyamaka teaching of emptiness and its ethical teaching of compassion, in Chapter 6, "Emptiness and Violence," Chen-kuo Lin deals with the seeming contradiction between the doctrine of emptiness and the notion of *harm*. According to Lin, Nāgārjuna, his disciple Āryadeva (third century), as well as a later advocate of the Yogācāra-Svātantrika-Mādhyamika school Kamalaśīla (eighth century) all suffered violent deaths. Lin raises the question: how is the issue of violence accounted for in terms of the philosophy of emptiness? Lin suggests that on the realist reading, *emptiness* is taken to be absence of agency, absence of the self, absence of the doer and the doing, and even absence of existence. Therefore, in the case of violent death, both the murderer and the victim are *empty*: there is no one who harms or who is harmed. This interpretation can easily lead to moral nihilism—the good, the bad, the victim, and the assailant, all are empty. As Garfield, Tanaka, and Siderits do in previous chapters, Lin also argues against a nihilist reading of Nāgārjuna's metaphysics and ethics. He points out that what Nāgārjuna rejects is not existence itself, but such notions as *essence*, *intrinsic nature*, *substance*, and *self-nature*.

Lin engages in a comparative study of Nāgārjuna and two Continental philosophers, Derrida and Levinas, in order to highlight a deconstructive reading of the notion of *violence* that is shared by all three philosophers. In Lin's analysis, the ultimate form of violence is not physical, but linguistic—language itself poses the most severe form of violence on all beings since language carves up things, creating dichotomies between selves and Others, this and that, sameness or difference. Language creates distinctions and oppositions, and this is the very foundation of other forms of violence. Lin argues that Nāgārjuna treats language as "empty in itself," which is erroneously assumed to stand opposite to the world, as if it could "match" or "correspond to" the world *as it is*. A direct reference theory, for example, would presuppose a realist picture of the world—names refer to things that exist on their own, separate from everything else. However, under Nāgārjuna's doctrine of *emptiness*, nothing exists independently of anything else. Therefore, to use language to talk about things in the world is already committing violence against things. A second commonality among all three philosophers, according to Lin, is their denunciation of the form of metaphysics that posits substance or transcendental realm. For Levinas, Heidegger's ontological distinction between a transcendent Being and the empirical existents has committed yet another kind of "ontological violence"—a subjugation of individuals to the impersonal. Lin argues that Levinas advocates a return to ethical relationships from abstract ontology, and this would have been Nāgārjuna's main tenet as well. In this hermeneutic context, emptiness is interpreted, not as a metaphysical or ontological thesis of the "true nature" of things, but as an ethical teaching about finding one's *original face*, the naked experience prior to any conceptual proliferation or linguistic differentiation, which is the ultimate form of violence against all things as well as to one's *original face*.

From the negativity attributed to language, we turn to a related topic: how is language possible if its subject matter is empty? The next three papers delve into yet another paradox involving the notion of *emptiness*—how could one possibly speak of *nothing* or *that which is empty*? In Chapter 7, "Speaking of the Ineffable . . . ," Graham Priest examines the paradoxical issue of how one can say what *nothing* is when this very statement would simply turn *nothing* into *something that is*. Furthermore, if the claim is that ultimate reality is *emptiness*, as Nāgārjuna proclaims, or *nothingness*, as Daoism advocates, then one cannot even speak of ultimate reality, or *Truth*, for that matter. *Silence* would then seem to be the only correct path. Priest gives a helpful overview of the ubiquitous difficulty involving the ineffability of *nothingnes*s in some Indian, Chinese, and Japanese philosophies. He also points out how the struggle to deal with the ineffability of ultimate reality is prevalent in Western traditions—in the works of Kant, Heidegger, and Wittgenstein, to name a few. To say that ultimate reality (emptiness, *Dao*, nothingness) is beyond our perception, conception, and description; that it transcends our cognitive capacities; or simply to say that it is ineffable, is already *saying something* about it. The ineffability of the ineffable *ultimate reality* would thus seem to be a problem with no solution.

However, Priest argues that *catuṣkoti* logic (previously discussed in Chapter 3) can be deployed to enable one to speak of the ineffable. In addition to the four possibilities described earlier—that statements are true, false, both, or neither—later thinkers appear to have added a fifth possibility, which seems to be some kind of ineffability, though how this is to be understood precisely is not so clear. Priest provides an understanding using the techniques of contemporary non-classical logic. First Degree Entailment is a well-known four-valued logic in which sentences are assigned one of the values *true*, *false*, *both*, or *neither*. In Priest's reinterpretation, it is states of affairs that are assigned such values. It now makes sense to add a fifth value: the value possessed by a state of affairs that is ineffable. To illustrate how this is possible, Priest relates the issue to contemporary discussions of the paradoxes of self-reference. Paradoxes of denotation, such as Berry's paradox, use the Denotation Schema *Den* ('*t*.' *x*) iff $x = t$ (where t is any noun phrase). Write n for *nothing*; then since *nothing* is no thing (no object), there is no x such that $x = n$, so there is x such that *Den* (‘*n*.” *x*). *Nothing* lacks a name, so one can say nothing about it. But of course, $n = n$, so *Den* (‘*n*.” *n*). Now *nothing* does have a name, *n*, and one can use this to say something about it. We can thus talk of this ineffable thing.[1]

In Chapter 8, “Emptiness as Subject-Object Unity,” Chien-hsing Ho extends the Madhyamaka analysis of the notion of *emptiness* to a Chinese Mādhyamika philosopher, Sengzhao (374?–414 CE). In particular, Ho focuses on the relationship between language and reality in Sengzhao’s philosophy. In correspondence with the “two realities” (the conventional and the ultimate) posited by the Madhyamaka school, Ho distinguishes the *ontic* (designating conventional conceptions) and the *ontological* (designating true nature) levels of existence. On the ontic level, our language and our conceptions inevitably fail to capture the true nature of things, as they carve reality at the wrong joints. Things conventionally conceived are individuated and differentiated; ultimately, however, all things are unified into an indeterminable and undifferentiated whole. In Ho’s analysis, Sengzhao’s conception of *emptiness* is simply “ontic indeterminacy,” as Ho puts it, “to be empty is to be devoid of determinate form and nature.” As soon as we apply any linguistic term to designate a thing, we leave out not only the thing’s unique features but also the thing’s commonality with other things not designated by this term. In this way, not only is *nothingness* itself ineffable, as we see in Priest’s discussion, *everything* is ultimately ineffable. A specific mistake in our conventional linguistic demarcation of things is that we suppose existence and nonexistence to be mutually exclusive, and we embrace the law of the excluded middle. According to Sengzhao, what a thing is and what it is not are interdependent: if we don’t know what it *is not*, we cannot even say what it *is*. In general, opposites have “notional codependence,” as Ho calls it. Given this, we can now see why everything is linguistically and conventionally interdependent and hence lacking a definitive nature. In the sense of not having determinate and definitive existence, all things are *empty*.

On the ontological level, furthermore, even ultimate reality itself is empty. Ho introduces an interesting point that Sengzhao emphasizes: even the designation ‘emptiness’ is itself a conceptual construct, and our enlightened understanding that things are ultimately indeterminate ends up being our conceptual grasp of *indeterminacy* per se. Therefore, what we need to accomplish is not a *different* or even *ultimate* conception of truth; we simply need to return to a “pre-conceptual” state. According to Ho’s analysis, ultimate Truth does not lie elsewhere—there is no separation between conventional and ultimate reality. Ultimate Truth is a state of mind in which there is no longer any distinction between the subject and the object, no interior and exterior, no “mind-independent reality,” and the subject is *one* with the pre-conceptual world as an “amorphous lump,” as Ho puts it. This mental state is termed *nirvāṇa* by Sengzhao. This is the true meaning of *emptiness* in Sengzhao’s philosophy, and yet at the same time it resists being defined as such. *Emptiness* is ineffable, because it simply is the state of *ineffability*.

Chapter 9 by Rajam Raghunathan, “On Nothing in Particular: Delimiting Not Being for Knowing’s Sake,” tackles the assertion of the ineffability of *emptiness* in Madhyamaka philosophy from a comparative standpoint. To highlight the universal difficulty of speaking of *nothing* or *that which is not*, Raghunathan begins her paper with introducing the analysis of not-Being (the negation of being as such) in early Greek philosophy—from Parmenides to Aristotle. Parmenides points out that what does not exist cannot be thought of or spoken about, since there is nothing to think of or to speak about. Taking the verb *is* (*estin*) as the starting point, Parmenides examines the subject of this verb—what can be said to be or not to be, and concludes that the subject cannot possibly be *nothing*. Raghunathan analyzes the verb used in a predicative sense (x is F) and in an existential sense (x *is* or x exists), and suggests different possible scenarios for each sense. A thing could be determinately F or indeterminately F; a thing could definitely or indefinitely exist. For example, a table is determinately a table while a heap of sand is only indeterminately (i.e. vaguely) a heap; President Obama definitely exists while Hamlet only indefinitely exists. According to Raghunathan, Parmenides only acknowledges the possibility of knowledge for that which exists definitely and determinately (what he calls "Being"); that which exists definitely but indeterminately (such as Highway 1 or towns and cities); and that which exists indefinitely but determinately (such as numbers). On the other hand, Parmenides denies that one can possibly know that which exists indefinitely and indeterminately—the negation of "being" (*estin*) in both the predicative and the existential sense is simply "not-Being." In this analysis, we can see, as Raghunathan points out, that Parmenides' conception of *not-Being* is close to Sengzhao's *emptiness* on the ontological level, namely, it is indeterminate and indefinite. The difference is that for Parmenides, we cannot think of, speak about or even have any knowledge of *not-Being*, whereas for Sengzhao, it is only through knowing beings as indeterminate *not-Beings* that we gain enlightenment. Raghunathan also examines Parmenides' categorical rejection of the possibility of speaking of the ineffable in the comparative framework of Nāgārjuna's and the *Vimalakīrti Sūtra*'s methods of resolving the paradox of speaking of that which is unspeakable. This comparative study, she suggests, may open the door to deeper reflections on a common approach to the notion of *not-Being* and of *emptiness*: the ultimate reason for our inability to speak of or know about *not-Being* lies in its formlessness, indefiniteness and indeterminacy.

Chapter 10 by Zhihua Yao, "The Cognition of Nonexistent Objects," continues to investigate the possibility of knowledge of *nonbeing* according to the Yogācāra school; in particular, he lists five arguments developed by the Yogācāra Buddhists in support of the claim that one can know or have consciousness of nonexistent things. Nonexistent things, from the Yogācāran perspective, include macro-objects composed of existing elements, as well as conceptual entities (thought, ideas, etc.) that are not graspable by the five senses. Argument one deals with the past and the future, which do not exist according to the Yogācāras. Yao argues that the Yogācārins embrace *presentism*, the view that only the present is real. Since they also acknowledge that the mind can have consciousness of past and the future phenomena, they are asserting the possibility of the *knowledge* of nonexistent things. In his reformulation of Yogācāra's second argument, Yao explains that since the mind's consciousness can have nonexistent things as its intentional objects, and intention presupposes cognition, the mind can cognize such things even though they do not exist. In both these arguments, Yao identifies "consciousness" or "cognition" with "knowledge" and concludes that the mind can therefore *know* nonexistent things. The third argument deals with no-self and impermanence. Yao explains that, according to the Yogācārins, the mind can comprehend both the fact that the substantial self does not exist, and the fact that a permanent entity does not exist. Inferring from the claim *there is no self*, the mind can derive the concept of *no-self*; based on the claim *all phenomena are impermanent*, the mind can thereby be consciously aware of *impermanence*. Argument four is based on the received view that only basic elements of sensible things truly exist, which Yao calls "atomistic realism," and concludes that ordinary macro-objects such as food and drink do not truly exist. The Yogācārins acknowledge that the mind can have consciousness of food and drink; hence, by implication, the mind can cognize these non-existent things. Finally, argument five is made to distance Yogācāra philosophy from nihilism, which would deny all existences. Yao interprets Yogācāra's theory of truth as a correspondence theory, for which the correctness of judgments is what matches existent things. And yet, he argues, the Yogācārins allow for cognition, and hence knowledge, of nonexistent things. Yao concludes that the Yogācāra theory of knowledge is more suitably viewed as a theory of intentionality, which gives the mind and its consciousness a more active role than in the traditional theory of perception.

Part II of this book includes essays on Chinese Daoism, Korean Buddhism, Japanese Zen Buddhism, and the philosophy of the Japanese Kyoto School. A common theme that emerges in several chapters in Part II is that *nothingness* is to be rendered as the absence of determination, of designation, of limitation, of boundary; in general, it is to be *formless*. As John Krummel writes in his contribution to this volume, Nishida's observation of the East-West philosophical orientations is that "reality for the West is grounded in *being qua form*, while reality for the East is grounded in *the nothing as formless*" (Chapter 18). If *formlessness* is a core theme in the philosophy of *nothingness*, then 'nothingness' does not denote any entity or any particular state of affairs; rather, it is descriptive of an ideal state that can be manifested in the world at large as well as in human existence. Hence, the concept of *nothingness* in these schools is inextricably tied up with human existence located in various sociopolitical contexts and the impermanent world. The discussions in these essays focus less on the paradoxical nature of the realness of nothingness, the semantics of speaking of the ineffable, or the epistemology of perceiving what is imperceptible. Instead, we have the ethics of nothingness, the psychology of forgetting the self or the embodiment of nothingness, the cultivation of a mental void in which one becomes *thoughtless*, the mutual determination of the self and the world in existential negation as well as the affirmation of meaning, and the mental release derived from the appreciation of the image of the sky, which symbolizes *emptiness*. *Nothingness* is immanent in our world and a mode of our existence; it should further be incorporated into our mental lives and become a paradigm of ethical practice.

In Chapter 11, "The Notion of *Wu* or Nonbeing as the Root of the Universe and a Guide for Life," Xiaogan Liu gives a detailed analysis of the concept *wu* (non-being or nothing) in the *Daodejing* and summarizes four major senses of *wu*. According to Liu, in the *Daodejing*, the concept of *Being* (*you*) could denote some primary and general stuff of existence, and he thinks this stuff is *qi*. The concept *wu*, on the other hand, denotes nothingness or non-being, from which *Being* emerges. Liu suggests that in the *Daodejing*'s usage, *wu* in the sense of designating the initial status of the universe could be identified with *Dao*. In another usage, however, *wu* represents one aspect of *Dao*—the aspect of imperceptibility, ineffability, and incomprehensibility from the human perspective. We might call the former the cosmological sense of *wu* and the latter the epistemic sense of *wu*. The third sense of *wu* applies to the presence of space or vacancy in the empirical world. Without an internal empty space, a room cannot be a room and a vessel cannot contain anything. The functions of *wu* are multifold in material things. Liu points out that this sense of *wu* is neither metaphysical nor epistemic. We may call it the *relative* sense of *wu*. Last but not least is the sense of *wu* as denoting the ultimate *Dao* that is both transcendent and immanent. Liu argues that WANG Bi introduced this sense of *wu* in his commentary on the *Daodejing*, while the original author(s) may not have intended *wu* in this sense. Under WANG Bi's philosophical development, *wu* came to signify an abstract *Non-being*, which stands both as the grounding and the origin of the universe. *Non-being* in WANG Bi's philosophical reconstruction of the *Daodejing* takes up an ontological dimension, as the original state and the post-existence state of any concrete thing. However, Liu thinks that the temporal phases between concrete things and their non-being should not be seen as transitions in a physical process, but should be taken spiritually and metaphorically. The concept of non-being in WANG Bi's philosophy denotes the ontological grounding for existence—being must be grounded in non-being, since multiplicity is not possible without a unifying *One* and nothing can exist without an underlying *Non-being*.

Liu further points out that despite the various usages and connotations of the concept *wu* in the *Daodejing*, the *Daodejing*'s overarching aim is to construct an ethics based on this notion. Liu describes it as an ethics of a negative direction but with a positive ideal. The negativity is aimed at contemporary social practices and values, and Liu argues that both Laozi as the author of the *Daodejing*, and WANG Bi as its most innovative commentator, were very much social critics, cultural reformists and spiritual idealists. The ethics based on the concept of *wu* in the sense of negation teaches us to look beyond our mundane affairs and trivial concerns. If things are fundamentally derived from, and will ultimately return to, the state of nothingness or non-being, then our temporary existence along with its sorrows and joys should no longer be our primary concern.

In "The Relation of Nothing and Something," Douglas L. Berger focuses on the concept of *wu* in Chapter 11 of the *Daodejing*, as this conception offers the most applicable rendition of nothingness in human life. Using Xiaogan Liu's analysis in the previous chapter, we can say that the concept *wu* in this chapter of the *Daodejing* is the relative sense of *wu* in the empirical world. Nothingness (*wu*) in this context is part of the physical world, and as Berger puts it, nothingness is "literally built into the structure of physical phenomena." However, this brief Chapter 11 of the *Daodejing* has received multifarious interpretations both historically and in the contemporary world, making it one of the most controversial chapters in the whole text. Berger selects two representative analyses of Chapter 11 given by WANG Bi and ZHONG Hui, both prominent Daoists in the third-century CE. According to Berger, both of them take the sense of *wu* (nothingness) in the empirical world to signify *space*, and their shared interpretation enables us to see how the concept of nothingness could be employed in our physical construction and appreciation of concrete things. On the other hand, however, Wang and Zhong differ in their understanding of the connection between nothingness (*wu*) and existence (*you*): whereas Wang is a foundationalist, Zhong takes a relational approach, and Berger argues for the latter conception.

According to Berger, WANG Bi takes *nothingness* to be the foundation of concrete existence—this sense of *nothingness* is what Xiaogan Liu calls "the ground" in the previous chapter. The particular space within each concrete thing, where nothing is located, is what grounds the particular thing and its functions. Berger explains that we typically think of matter as constituting material things, and WANG Bi's point is that without the spaces in between matter, material things cannot have their functions. Therefore, particular nothingness, namely, space, is the foundation of the usefulness of concrete things. In WANG Bi's philosophy of nothingness, according to Berger's analysis, the particular nothingness is connected to the cosmological sense of *wu*, namely, the infinitely indeterminate *Nothingness* that is the originary state of all existence. Therefore, existence, or the generation of *something*, does not wipe out *nothingness*; it merely dissects nothingness, confining it into local spaces. Nothingness is thus foundational for both the universe and particular things. This analysis seems to agree with the overall theme of the *Daodejing*. Interestingly, however, WANG Bi's contemporary ZHONG Hui came up with a different analysis of the relationship between concrete matter and particularized nothingness. Berger explains that ZHONG Hui gives a contextualist reading of the usefulness of a thing—a particular thing's functions depend on its conventional economic and social values rather than merely on its internal structure. Under Zhong's reading, both the constitutive matter and the particularized nothingness (the space in concrete things) have to depend on each other for a thing to be useful. Thus, nothingness is not foundational, but is rather reliant on the concrete *you* (being) as an interdependent and mutually supportive pair. This second interpretation of the role of particularized nothingness, in Berger's assessment, gives a more cogent account of the empirical placement of *wu*. Nothingness is no longer a mysterious abstract construct, but an in-the-world necessity in the material construction as well as practical functions of concrete things. This conception of particularized nothingness as *space*, according to Berger, renders space as a "mode of nothingness." Understanding *wu* in this way may help us better understand the connection between the Daoist notion of *nothingness* and the Buddhist notion of *emptiness*, since both 'space' and 'emptiness' are expressed by the Chinese word *kong*.

In Chapter 13, "Was There Something in Nothingness?" JeeLoo Liu focuses on the cosmological sense of *wu* in classical Daoists texts. Liu argues that the Daoist cosmology is fundamentally based on its theory of *qi*, and since *qi* is something, albeit a formless something, classical Daoist texts such as the *Daodejing* and the *Zhuangzi* do not posit a cosmic void as the initial state of the Universe. Using contemporary philosophical analysis, she also argues that neither Laozi nor Zhuangzi makes an ontological commitment to *nothingness*. WANG Bi, on the other hand, turns the cosmogonic speculation of *wu* into an ontological foundationalist theory of *wu*, which in this context denotes an overarching *Nonbeing*. Liu explains that even though traditionally Neo-Confucians take themselves to oppose the Daoist theory of *wu*, what they actually oppose are the ethical implications derived from WANG Bi's conception of *nonbeing* rather than the *Daodejing*'s conception of *nothingness*. In terms of their cosmogonies, Neo-Confucian *qi*-theorists such as ZHOU Dunyi and ZHANG Zai, and ancient Daoists in the *Daodejing* and in the *Zhuangzi*, have nothing but a terminological dispute about whether formlessness should be called "*wu*." At the end of this chapter, Liu engages in an analytic philosophical critique to suggest that WANG Bi's ontological commitment to *Nonbeing* is ill-grounded.

In Chapter 14, "Heart-Fasting, Forgetting, and Using the Heart Like a Mirror," Chris Fraser probes the ethical as well as the psychological dimensions of the philosophy of *emptiness* in the *Zhuangzi*. Fraser takes "ethics" in a Foucauldian sense, according to which ethics is more than a set of normative directives regarding one's lifestyle and conduct; rather, it involves the agent's self-constitution and self-realization. Fraser argues that the ideal self in the *Zhuangzi* would be one entertaining the psychological state of emptiness—without preconceptions, without insistence, and with total equanimity as well as spontaneity that flows with situational demands. Such a psychological state, according to Fraser, is partly due to the agent's cognitive as well as affective identification with nature and the changing conditions in life. Fraser also stresses the connection between the concept of *qi* and the Zhuangzi's notion of *emptiness* (*xu*), and he too argues that *emptiness* does not refer to nothingness, non-existence, or an absolute void. He thinks that in the Zhuangzi, *emptiness* (*xu*) should be understood as the absence of fixed forms. In cultivating the psychological state of emptiness, one is to emulate the fluidity and the insubstantiality of *qi* in one's response to daily affairs and external objects. This is the virtue of *receptivity*, which has the loss of self-insistence and even self-awareness as a prerequisite. In this way, the way to self-cultivation is actually to *empty* the self—in the

Zhuangzi's terminology, it is to have the mind be "like a mirror," responding to things as they appear but leaving no trace after things pass. As Fraser points out, the ethics of emptiness in the *Zhuangzi* is not psychological nothingness, but is grounded in practiced skills. The aim is to cultivate a greater sensitivity to changing circumstances and to deal with things with open-minded composure. This philosophy of life can help us become more receptive to unforeseen turns of events, alternative possibilities, and diverse ethics. In this way, the Daoist ethics of emptiness does not need to recommend a life of negativity and passivity as we have seen in Wei-Jin Daoists; rather, it can affirm multiple ethical spaces for individuals.

In Chapter 15, "Embodying Nothingness and the Ideal of the Affectless Sage in Daoist Philosophy," Alan K. L. Chan continues the discussion on the Daoist ethics of nothingness. Chan calls a Daoist sage someone who "embodies nothingness," and explains that the embodiment of nothingness is manifested in multiple ways: in the *Daodejing*, it is the absence of desire as well as the absence of active striving (*wu wei*, 無為); in the *Zhuangzi*, it is manifested "affectless" (*wu qing*, 無情)—the absence of emotions or affective responses to things. However, in this chapter Chan focuses on the third century CE Wei-Jin Neo-Daoists' views for his detailed analysis of "the sage's embodiment of nothingness." In HE Yan's conception, the ideal agent, the sage, is endowed with a special disposition to be free from affective disturbance of the mind. This special disposition, inborn in the sage, is marked by a perfect "harmony (*zhonghe*, 中和)" of all emotions and affective responses. In other words, the sage does not *lack* emotion; he or she simply has the perfect balance of emotions, not achieved through effort but is inborn by nature. The sage is thus one born with the "undifferentiated completeness" of affective responses to the world. Sagehood becomes an unreachable ethical goal, a trait that is *given*, but not accessible to others through self-cultivation.

Chan explains that to HE Yan's contemporary, WANG Bi, the possibility of becoming a sage through self-cultivation must be affirmed. WANG Bi portrays the sage's embodiment of nothingness as a spiritual luminosity, which is a heightened state of perfect harmony of desires and emotions. In a later Neo-Daoist GUO Xiang's conception, the sage's embodiment of nothingness is achievable through an active oblivion of attachments. The sage "forgets," as it were, not as the result of any deliberate effort in suppressing emotion or desire. Rather, forgetting affectivity is an intellectual feat, resulting from the abandonment of judgments of what is right or wrong for oneself. In other words, in GUO Xiang's philosophy of emotion, emotion is a derived state from one's judgment based on self-interest. Thus, if one can stop making these judgments, one's affective states would not be so easily aroused. If affectivity stands in the way of one's embodying nothingness, then emotion is not the culprit; rather, judgment is. Hence, to forget affectivity is not to eradicate natural emotions, but to check one's aroused emotions derived from self-interested judgments. This state of sagehood is much more obtainable, albeit still an exceptional accomplishment.

In Chapter 16, "Nothingness in Korean Buddhism: The Struggle against Nihilism," Halla Kim turns our attention to the notion of *nothingness* in Korean philosophy. Kim focuses on three Korean Buddhist philosophers from the seventh to the fourteenth centuries, Wŏnhyo, Chinul and T'aego Pou. As Garfield argues against the nihilistic interpretation of Indian Madhyamaka school of Buddhist philosophy, Kim too argues that the Korean Buddhist notion of *nothingness* should not be taken to represent nihilism. According to Kim, "nothingness" signifies the absence of self-independence; hence, to say that things are empty means that they have a dependent-arising nature. In other words, our self-nature is empty, but this does not mean that our existence is empty. To embrace the philosophy of nothingness, one does not need to terminate daily activities; however, one does need to recognize the transient and interdependent nature of all things.

In Kim's exposition, all three Korean philosophers share the belief that intellectual discernment of the true nature of existence is achievable for everyone. What makes enlightenment possible is the inborn luminosity of the mind—our Buddhahood. To attain enlightenment, for Wŏnhyo, one needs to retrieve one's original true nature through the realization that one is ultimately *nothing*. "Nothing" in his conception is not to be understood as non-existence; rather, it means being empty of permanent self-dependent nature. His attitude about the phenomenal world is very anti-nihilistic: we should not be preoccupied with the concept of nothingness and forget our worldly responsibilities. Hence, his methodology of contemplating *nothingness* does not involve inaction or the renunciation of engagement with the world. Enlightenment is achievable simply by seeing that the greatest seed of enlightenment is already inherent in one's nature. In contrast, Chinul placed his emphasis on individuals' mental cultivation. In Chinul's usage, the word '*mu*' (nothingness) can be used as a weapon that "destroys wrong knowledge and wrong understanding." Correct knowledge and understanding, on the other hand, is the realization that one's true nature, one's Buddhahood, is fundamentally *nothing*. According to Chinul's method of self-cultivation, one needs to obtain a psychological state of "thoughtlessness," which is when the mind stops making discrimination of things and their values. This psychological state is in a sense a form of "void," through which the agent can obtain a special kind of knowledge that Chinul calls "numinous awareness." The mental voidness is the positive aspect of his concept of nothingness, since according to him, only in this voidness can the mind achieve the fullness of insights and wisdom. One needs to study sūtras, practice meditation, and gradually develop one's *numinous awareness*. The cultivation of this mental state may be gradual and torturous; however, the final awakening could be suddenly available to us—if only we could see that we are all inherently Buddhas to begin with. Finally, for T'aego Pou, the access to Buddhahood is not gained through studying sūtras, but through practice. He abandons Chinul's teaching of gradual cultivation, and advocates both sudden awakening and immediate cultivation. In his analysis, the word '*mu*' does not mean non-existence or nothingness; rather, it designates the practitioner's mental state of emptying thought, such that one no longer has any conscious thought—not even the thought of "not-to-think." The concept of *nothingness* thus turns out to be the depiction of an ideal mental state, not a designation of any ultimate reality external to the human mind. In all three philosophers' conceptions of *nothingness*, Kim concludes, there is not an inkling of nihilism.

In Chapter 17, "Zen, Philosophy, and Emptiness: Dōgen and the Deconstruction of Concepts," Gereon Kopf argues that the thirteenth century founder of Sōtō practice in Japan offers the most highly developed "blueprint" for a consistent non-dualistic philosophy. Dōgen achieves this by taking the foregoing philosophical commitments of Madhyamaka *śūnyavāda* (the doctrine of emptiness) and the sayings and writings of Chan Buddhism to their most "radical" conclusions. Kopf provides an extensive analysis of how the notion of *emptiness* is treated and developed in a sprawling history of Buddhist texts, from the *Prajńaparamitā* literature to Nāgārjuna's treatises, from the *Diamond Sūtra* to the *Platform Sūtra* that holds the former in such high esteem, to the works celebrating the dramatic teachings of China's Tang and Song masters of Chan and the *kōan* collections that developed from them, and finally to the synthetic treatises of Korea's Sōn thinkers.

Dōgen, in his seminal work *Shōbōgenzō* (*The Treasury of the True Dharma Eye*) formulates a "hermeneutics of emptiness" that "deconstructs" a perilous dichotomy that had developed even within the history of Buddhist reflection. On the one hand, we have a line of Buddhist thought that follows the *Heart Sūtra*'s dictum that "form is emptiness, emptiness is form" and is championed by certain Chan Buddhist mottos like Mazu's "the ordinary mind is Buddha," which would tend to suggest that emptiness can be found in concrete experiences, expressions, and acts. On the other hand, there is an equally compelling argument made first by the Madhyamaka philosophers, who are thoroughly represented in this volume, that the compulsion to give a genuine description of *emptiness* will lead us only to paradoxes and eventually silence. Dōgen, Kopf maintains, dissolves this dichotomy through the advocacy of a kind of "linguistic practice" that at once "destabilizes" language, thus halting its natural urge to essentialize through distinctions, and yet enables language to express the real ambiguity in the relationships between things and persons as well as awakening and delusion. Through his exposition of Dōgen's formulations of "*dharma* positions," that is, the stages of belief that Buddhist practitioners pass through on their journeys of realization, and his dialectical playfulness with the oppositions that language presents us with, Kopf makes the case that "ambiguity," "continuous practice," and the intersubjectivity of expression and action are hallmarks of a truly non-dualistic philosophy of emptiness.

East Asian philosophical explorations of *nothingness* are not merely a vestige of ancient or medieval thought—they have been reignited by the profound and provocative works of the twentieth century founders of the Kyoto School of thought. The historical, political, and intellectual circumstances within which the works of the major thinkers of this school were produced ensured that they would engage both Western and traditional Asian philosophical resources in subtle, complex, and incredibly rich ways. The three Kyoto School authors covered in this volume, Kitarō Nishida (1870–1945), Hajime Tanabe (1885–1962) and Kenji Nishitani (1900–1990), bring traditional Buddhist conceptions of *emptiness* and Daoist conceptions of *nothingness* to bear on their own insightful readings of Western systems of thought, the fate of contemporary civilization, and the existential challenges of human life. Their works guaranteed that Asian formulations of *nothingness* would be for us not merely a matter of antiquarian or cross-cultural reflection, but of vital and ongoing philosophical significance in areas as diverse as dialectics, sociopolitical philosophy and existentialism.

In Chapter 18, "Anontology and the Issue of Being and Nothing in Kitarō Nishida," John W. M. Krummel illustrates how the founder of the Kyoto School, over the course of thirty years, came to articulate the idea of "nothingness" (*mu*, 無) as a groundless and formless "place" (*basho*, 場所), within which the manifest "beings" of the world can exist and become differentiated from one another. This conviction, Krummel demonstrates, does not merely derive from what Nishida drew upon in East Asian thought, but also from the works of Western Neo-Kantians such as Lotze and Lask, belying an all-too-simplistic dichotomy that would see "Western" thought as exclusively motivated by the search for "being" and Asian thought by the quest for "nothingness." In the writings of his early philosophical career, Krummel argues, Nishida's sense of "nothingness" is thematized in terms of both various considerations of epistemological formality, subject-object duality, as well as reflections on the experiences of fluidity and interiority. Eventually, Nishida comes to the realization that both the "implacement" of things and the positing of self-consciousness lead us to comprehend the "place" of absolute nothingness as well as the processes through which things and individuals in the world positively and reciprocally determine one another. We must not, however, suspect that Nishida, in the articulation of his mature thought, was merely creating another ontology that replaced "being" as the ground of existence with "nothingness." Instead, Krummel claims, Nishida, through his simultaneous focus on the groundlessness of nothingness and his attempts to understand how that very nothingness serves as the place of the world's process, offers us not ontology, but an "anontology."

In the following chapter (Chapter 19), "Tanabe's Dialectic of Species as Absolute Nothingness," Makoto Ozaki highlights how Tanabe, Nishida's successor as the chair of the Philosophy Department at Kyoto Imperial University, attempts to remove the notion of nothingness from the rarified theoretical heights of Nishida's system and place it within our historical lives. In his "triadic logic of species" that deals with universality, particularity, and individuality, Tanabe understands nothingness to be "eternity." However, this "eternity" is not a static *being*, but rather the ongoing "negation" of the past by the present and then the present by the future. Moreover, this ongoing "negation" is primarily experienced by the self, in the forms of uncertainty, finitude, and repetition or renewal. The political state, on the other hand, also plays a crucial role in the historical unfolding of nothingness insofar as it, on the one hand, "negates" the individual and groups her into a mere genus and, on the other, attempts to unite the individuals within itself as well as all other states. Both the individual and the state can, in attempting to preserve an illusory aspiration for their own unmediated existences in the face of their differential resistances to mediating negativity, turn to evil, and even "radical evil." They are both, therefore, ever in need of repentance and conversion, which itself is a manifestation of the work of nothingness in human practices. Ozaki's essay argues emphatically that Tanabe's philosophy of nothingness is indispensable for us today. Tanabe's philosophy situates nothingness within the historical world of religion, politics, and individual practice, and acknowledges that radical evil is a necessary condition of existence in that very world. It envisioned a dialogue between Buddhist, Christian, and Marxist thought that would foreground nothingness, repentance, and sociopolitical reform all at once, a "syncretic" dialogue that places religion in a finally appropriate role of helping to achieve "the salvation of humanity."

Finally, in Chapter 20, Yasuo Deguchi turns our attention toward the existential significance of the experience of nothingness in his essay, "Nishitani on Emptiness and Nothingness." In a careful analysis of the early and late works of Kenji Nishitani, Deguchi uncovers how a personal "reconciliation" with nihilism can be made possible through the experience of emptiness. In his early thought, Deguchi argues, Nishitani constructed merely intellectual grounds for justifying the superiority of traditional Mahāyāna Buddhist conceptions of emptiness over both foregoing Theravāda and Western existentialist ideals, as well as Western philosophical lionizations of subjectively constituted reason. This superiority was seen by Nishitani as lying in the resistance of Mahāyāna Buddhists to either objectify the self and its immutability or objectify nihility and make of the self a center of defiantly triumphant will. Insofar as this is the case, Mahāyāna enables us to "overcome" the nihilism in which modern existentialism has dead-ended us. In this early work, Deguchi maintains, Nishitani makes no substantive distinction between the Buddhist notions of "nothingness" and "emptiness." However, in his later reflections, Nishitani is compelled by the realization that nihilism, though it cannot be completely overcome, may be amenable to our acceptance, in our "reconciliation." This acceptance, however, requires that our emotions and will be "captured" by an experience that enables us to embrace nihility. Such an "emotive-volitional" reconciliation can only be achieved by a special sort of *image* experience. It is here where the decisive distinction between the traditional Buddhist ideas of "nothingness" and "emptiness" appears, since, as Nishitani argues, while there is no archetypal image of nothingness available to us, emptiness does present itself to us in the image of the sky. In classical Chinese, the term for "emptiness" (*kong*, 空) also meant "sky." Since we can be immersed in aesthetic rapture at the sky's infinity in everyday experiences as well as be drawn to it by art forms such as traditional circle calligraphy and paintings, we can effectively, like the sky itself, envelop the infinite expanse of nihility within us. In Nishitani's mature thought then, Deguchi argues, East Asian Buddhist expressions of nothingness and emptiness—aesthetic ones and not merely those of the doctrinal variety—can come to our own aid in living as finite creatures in the world.

JeeLoo Liu
Douglas L. Berger

Note

1 We wish to thank Graham Priest for help with this paragraph.

Part I

Emptiness in Brāhmiṇical and Early Buddhist Traditions

1 The Unavoidable Void

Nonexistence, Absence, and Emptiness

Arindam Chakrabarti

CORDELIA: Nothing, my lord.
KING LEAR: Nothing!
CORDELIA: Nothing.
KING LEAR: Nothing will come of nothing: speak again.
—Shakespeare[1]

What is Nothing?

Philosophically, the Nāsadīya Hymn of Beginning (*RgVeda* X.129) remains by far the richest poem in the Vedic Indian literature. "Not nothing was" are the first three words of this difficult text, which has been copiously commented upon in the last two thousand years. Out of those three words, the last two appear to propose a prima facie theory of the origin of everything, which the first word negates. Where did this universe come from? Before this universe (anything) existed, what was there? If "the universe" means all that exists, the logical answer should be "nothing." But that answer, the hymn tells us, must be mistaken: "*asad āsīt ādau iti (cet) na*"—if you say, "In the beginning, there was nothing," that is not acceptable. It cannot be true that nothing was there, before anything was there, for in sheer nothing no world can originate; as King Lear warns Cordelia, nothing will come out of nothing. That seems to be the line of thought captured in those three cryptic words "*na*," "*asat*," and "*asīt*." Yet, as Bergson (1911) remarked with uncanny precision, the deepest philosophical question, why is there something rather than nothing at all, inexorably pushes us to the notion of "naught," as if all positive entities that exist have to make room for themselves by pushing out a bit of the ontologically prior omnipresent mud of nothing. But what is this nothing?

There has been much woolly thinking about "nothing" between the time when Parmenides cautioned philosophers against diving into that bottomless swamp and when Heidegger recklessly disregarded the warning. Based on some well-established clarifications and debates in Indian metaphysics, this paper will draw attention to some important distinctions, ignoring which has led to part of the woolliness.

In cosmology, the possibility that the universe might not have existed at all seems to make sense to some philosophers even in recent times (see Parfit 1998; Holt 2012). In ontology and semantics, the questions of whether negative facts exist, and if the meaning of the expression "nothing," or truth conditions of the statement that nothing exists, can be coherently conceived of or articulated has never lost its importance. All of this, of course, sprouts from the presence of negation in all languages. Whether negation devices would have existed if humans never committed an error that needed to be corrected is a seductive but idle thought experiment to conduct. Correction of mistakes seems as ingrained in human language and thinking as the drive to get it right. And correction, like the physical act of scratching through or striking out a written word or sentence, amounts to negation. Neither the negation nor what is negated has any touch of unreality, or fictionality, about it. If I say "Obama is Jewish," my statement would be real but false. Corresponding to the falsity of my statement, once it is corrected, we can discover the unremarkable fact that Obama is *not* Jewish. That fact is as real as the fact that he is the current president of the United States. Independent of the negation devices in our thinking and language, certain things or features are missing in certain places. There are no snakes in Hawaii, and no nitrogen in pure water. These lacks are absences. Neither the snakes nor nitrogen need to be nonexistent like Santa Claus or his elves in order to be absent in a place. In Sanskrit, absences are called "*abhāva*-s" (literally: not-being-s). They are real; for example, the fact that there is no wine in my fridge, is existent, a real fact, unlike nonexistent entities (e.g. the fortieth planet in the solar system) which would be termed "*asat*" or "*alīka.*" Turtle-hair is a typical *asat*. But the real *abhāva* of real hair on a real turtle-shell is not *asat* (unreal) but *sat* (real). What if one takes this notion of absence and applies it to the universal set of things? Could we make sense of "nothing" as the absence of all things? We shall see in what follows that every absence requires both an absentee and a locus, or site. One problem about the absence of everything would be that it could not be hosted by any site, since all things are its absentees. The other problem—somewhat epistemic and phenomenological—is that we cannot imagine the absence of everything. The only nagging worry about this second objection against the idea of pure nothing is that if we commit some item to unimaginability, don't we need to first have at least a concept of the thing in order to know that the thing is unimaginable? In that case, the absence of all things seems to have some kind of conceivability. Nothing may be unimaginable (though images, like a totally blank canvas or an entirely cloudless sky, suggest themselves) but it surely has to be conceivable insofar as we know what it is we are supposed to try and fail to imagine.

Utterly different from both total nonexistent(s) and absences, is the currently much-celebrated Buddhist *śūnya* and its abstract cousin *śūnyatā* (emptiness). Emptiness could be achieved by a reasoned rejection of all positions and disputations in philosophy (by thinkers like Nāgārjuna or Śrīharṣa, for example), or through the contemplative, nonconceptual, ineffable experience of "being no one," or the transcendental experience of merging into cosmic pure consciousness, or identifying with the emptiness beyond the four logical options of real, unreal, real-and-unreal, and neither. We need, therefore, to distinguish very clearly between absences, nonentities and emptiness.

Besides these very large issues of metaphysics, verging on soteriology (some form of "experience of emptiness" is supposed to be liberating), there is a simple phenomenon of a felt lack of feeling. Expressed in negative introspective reports, for example, "I am not in pain" or "the excitement is gone," a happy relief or a lamentable lack is often felt, which is of great importance for our ontology and phenomenology of the self. Indeed, just before he drank hemlock, in *Phaedo* 60c, Socrates describes the simple absence of the pain of the chains on his legs as a pleasure following pain. The positive claim of this sort of "feeling of a lack of feeling" is what I would like to discuss at the very end of this paper. In that context, we shall switch gears and dwell on the contemplative phenomenology of "thinking or feeling or imagining nothing at all," going back to Bergson's and K. C. Bhattacharya's (1976) description of attempted imagination of such an absence of not only of this or that introspectable feeling, but even the lack of an introspecting self.

Real Not-Beings: The Logic of Lacks

Let me begin by drawing some distinctions. Distinctions, by the way, are themselves negative things. Sheldon's being distinct from Penny consists in Sheldon's not being Penny. This is true of both type distinctions, like the distinction between ants and antelopes, as well as numerical or token distinctions, like the distinction between one ant and another ant. The only difference between the two kinds of distinctions (if we ignore, for the moment, the complication about distinction between distinctions) is that in the first, the otherness (*anyonyābhāva*) resident in the antelope is delimited by the generic property of anthood, whereas the otherness of each ant is determined by the haecceity of the other individual ant.

To come back to absences, lacks are not-beings, not to be confused with nonbeings, because lacks are there whereas nonbeings are simply not there. My bedroom lacks a television. The television's not-being there is a bit of reality, not a bit of unreality. I can artificially or imaginatively cook up a nonbeing out of this absence and call it "the television in my bedroom." That is roughly how all nonbeings are "manufactured" in language and in imagination. You take a concept like the concept of a mountain and combine it with another concept, say of gold, when you know the intersection set generated by the extensions of the two concepts is the null set. The combined concepts such as that of a golden mountain, a rabbit horn, or turtle wool, would be distinct conceptual modes of presenting pure nullity. Often in this manner are constructed the intentional objects of our unfulfilled, sometimes unfulfillable, desires. If I have the desire to own a dog as a pet, but also have the conflicting desire that my pet must sing and have wings, then I end up desiring a winged, singing dog, a nonexistent entity, a nonbeing (unless facing both the desires I cancel out one with the other). A not-being—to be clearly distinguished from a nonbeing—is either not-being-there, such as the actual absence of the Statue of Liberty in Pakistan; or not-being-the-same, such as Obama's not being Bush. The present (2013) Queen of the United States, on the other hand, would be neither an absence (there is nothing negative about this fictional woman, unless she is described as non-blonde or powerless) nor a non-identity (she, in a fictional plot, may be very distinguished, but she is not a distinction). She would simply be a nonbeing, a creature of fiction, a figment of imagination, a wisp of unreality. The absence of color in air is not such an imaginary fictional nonentity. The only "reason" why someone may think that such an absence is imaginary, is—alas a very common—confusion between the absence and the absentee, what it is an absence of. That absence is real rendering air colorless.

Indian metaphysicians spent a lot of defensive and offensive argumentative energy on the nature, varieties, and objectivity of such gappy realities. They are most generally called "*a-bhāva*-s," which I have literally translated as "not-being," although once it was fashionable to translate that word as "negation." Bimal Krishna Matilal called his book on *abhāva Navya Nyaya Doctrine of Negation*, and before him Gopinath Bhattacharya wrote *The Category of Negation* (see Kellner 2006, 530–533). I do not approve of that old-fashioned translation because it makes the absence or not-being sound like something we do, like denying or negating. It is very hard to imagine even such realists as the Naiyāyika-s insisting that negations are there in the objective external world, just as one cannot imagine them being realists about disjunctions. Denying and considering two states of affairs as alternative scenarios are cognitive acts a conscious being with linguistic and representational capacity does. But the negative fact that there is no water in large stretches of the Sahara desert is not something we do by our thinking or speaking. We cannot *do* facts. We can assert that fact by negating or contradicting someone's false claim that the Sahara is full of water everywhere, but our asserting or negating does not make the desert arid.

The closest that early (Western) analytic philosophy came to sorting out the issue of the ontological status of lacks was when Bertrand Russell and the young Ludwig Wittgenstein engaged in the controversy regarding negative facts (later on in the seventies, there was an erratic discussion on the ontological status of holes, which has been revived in more recent times by Casati and Varzi [1995]). In a letter to Lady Ottoline Morrell (November 2, 1911), Russell complained: "My German Engineer, I think, is a fool . . . . I asked him to admit that there was not a rhinoceros in the room, but he wouldn't." After rummaging under all his furniture and not finding a rhinoceros, when Wittgenstein would still not confess to seeing this plain negative fact that there is no rhinoceros in the room, he was not being obstinately skeptical as Russell thought. Given Wittgenstein's puzzlement, in this period, with the "mystery of negation" (G.E.M. Anscombe reported that Wittgenstein was obsessed with the problem of our judgment about nothing first raised by Plato in *Theaetetus* 189a), we can surmise that at least part of his problem was ontological. It had to do with his deep suspicion that, on top of Russell's furniture, books, and so on, it would be extravagant to posit an item of reality called the absence of a rhinoceros in the room, just to account for the truth of the negative statement that there was none. Simply the falsity of the sentence "there is a rhino in this room" should be enough. The absence of food on an empty plate need not be anything over and above the bare plate. This economical strategy of keeping one's ontological commitment confined to positive things was also attempted by a school of practical realists in classical Indian philosophy, as we shall soon find out.

Russell himself was no less troubled by such logical specters as, for example, the fact that renders "Socrates is not alive" true in the twentieth century. He proudly reminisced in 1918 how, four years back while lecturing in Harvard, he "nearly produced a riot" by provocatively maintaining that negative facts are parts of the furniture of the world. Then he painstakingly rebuts Mr. Raphael Demos's three strong objections (both in "The Philosophy of Logical Atomism," 212–215, and in "On Propositions," 288–289) and concludes that negative facts are not reducible to anything positive (Russell 1956). But in his later work, *Inquiry into Meaning and Truth* (1940), he gets rid of negative facts by practically embracing Demos's point of view (to be explicated later). So we see that he changed his mind on this issue, as on many others—and might have been speaking of his own deep qualms when he prefaced his pro-negative fact campaign with the following flamboyant remark:

> There is implanted in the human breast an almost unquenchable desire to find some way of avoiding the admission that negative facts are as ultimate as those that are positive. (Russell 1956, 287)

However, these gappy entities seem to be unavoidable in an ontology that stays faithful to commonsense and ordinary language. Even in the metaphysics of actions, which would be deeply connected to our sense of responsibility-attribution and agency-ascription for reprehensible or laudable acts, omissions, or non-doings seem to claim equal status as doings. Indeed avoidance itself is a form of negative act. There is a practical void, an act of desisting, in "a-void," so to say! We give credit for *avoiding* civilian killings to a soldier charged with bombing some "terrorists" out of a hideout.

In some salient schools (Nyāya and Bhāṭṭa Mīmāṃsa) of Indian philosophy, lacks are considered real—although not a member of the inner circle of privileged substantial particulars, properties, or relations—in the face of formidable objections from Buddhist and Prābhākara Mīmāmsaka foes of negative facts.

As we started by remarking, lacks are not-beings. The Taj Mahal is not in Glasgow. Glasgow lacks the Taj Mahal. Instead, it has the absence of the Taj Mahal. There was no rhinoceros in Russell's Trinity College room at Cambridge. The room possessed the lack of rhinoceroses. These Indian realists posit this extra type of entity called a *not-being* (*to be carefully distinguished, as shown above, from nonbeings*). Not-beings come, mainly, in two forms: **x's *not***

being in **y** and **x's *not being*** **y**. Just as being itself can be either being-in, which is residence, or it could be being-the-same-as, which is identity, not-being can be either lack of residence or lack of identity. The former is called absence (*samsargābhāva*) and the latter, somewhat misleadingly, mutual absence or mutual negation. The latter (x's not being y) is simply *otherness*. That the Taj Mahal is not in London is an absence; that the Taj Mahal is not the Big Ben is otherness. That John Searle is not in the Sahara desert is a kind of not-being-in (*atyantābhāva*), that he is not Jacques Derrida is a kind of not-being-the-same-as (*anyonyābhāva*). For perspicuity, let us call lack of residence *absence* and lack of identity *otherness*. Otherness, like its counterpart sameness, has its own maddening problems. Strict monists in India have tried to prove that otherness between any allegedly distinct objects can never be logically or epistemologically intelligible. Everything is one and the same as anything else, because there is no difference or duality in reality. In response, commonsense realists and pluralists have pointed out with a vengeance that in every simple piece of awareness, some otherness or other must figure as part of the content.[2] From now on, I shall only speak of absences as lacks and forbear mentioning otherness. Difference—real or not, and our knowledge of difference, deserves a more elaborate treatment than we have space for here.

Absences Everywhere

Holes, silences, intermissions, omissions, gaps, recesses, waits, blanks, voids, bald patches, clearings, slits, gaping apertures, the eye of the needle—the observable world around us is replete with real *lacks*. Yet why do metaphysicians find these so hard to stomach? Why do they hesitate to list lacks in a catalog of real things? One commonly alleged reason, errant of course, is an elementary confusion between not-being with nonbeing. 'Nonbeing'—against which Parmenides warned philosophers—can itself be used in two different senses. First as a count-noun: Pegasus is *one* nonbeing, Sherlock Holmes is *another*. The Statue of Liberty in Pakistan is *another*. Since none of them exists, they can be, in a second sense, said to enjoy the same phony property, namely nonbeing or unreality, shared as it were by all nonbeings in (should we not say "outside of") the world! But Quine (1963) has cautioned us that there can never be any legitimate individuation criterion for such fictional entities. We do not know how many flying horses there are because, as Russell said about unicorns, if they cannot be admitted in Zoology, they cannot be any more welcome as objects in Logic either. There remains, of course, the nagging worry that the different stories from which the flying horse and the flying man emerge would not permit us to count Pegasus and Batman as the same null entity. But nonbeings are, undoubtedly, metaphysically messy. While existence can be permitted to be a universally shared property of all existent things, nothingness cannot be taken seriously as an ontologically permissible universal.

Now, what I call 'a lack' has nothing to do with these nonbeings, unreal entities or their shared nullity. In a manner of speaking, such things as color-of-air—a nonexistent—can be said to be absent from the face of the world (even then, its absolute absence would not itself be a nonexistent). But this, to say the least, is a very misleading manner of speaking. A much saner description would be: "the absence of color in air." We have been duly warned by Parmenides against these artificially manufactured absolute absentees. In another section of this chapter I shall try to prove that a nonexistent object cannot be made either the *locus* or the *absentee* of a genuine *absence*. Neither does Pegasus lack existence nor does reality lack Pegasus. In order to lack or be lacked, things need to be real somewhere, at some point of time. Pegasus is unreal, hence cannot be the absentee or site of a real absence. Wings and horses can be.

So lacks are not creatures of "Meinong's jungle." They are plainly such things as I discover when I look into the fridge and see *that there is no milk in it*, or such gaps as I lament when I miss my consumed candy bar, or what we find in a child's mouth when he loses a tooth thanks to having had too many candy bars.

It would be noticed that we have already introduced three little bits of jargon: locus, absentee and absence. Suppose the cap of my ballpoint pen is missing; the pen lacks a cap. Three things must be distinguished: the pen, which I call it the *locus* of absence; the cap, which I call it the *absentee*; and the pen's not having a cap or the pen's lack of a cap, which I call the *absence*. All three are real. Even if the missing cap is now destroyed, it has not been reduced to a figment of imagination. It has just been pushed back to the pure past. It is absent, not nonexistent. My father is dead, but I cannot state that fact by saying that I have no father, which would impute immaculate conception to my mother. The cap and the pen bereft of the cap, of course, both have to be real. Finally, there is this fact involving these two, or this feature of the pen: that the cap is missing from the pen. My claim is that it is a third and distinct entity: a real lack, or in this case, an absence. Whenever I come back and *see* that my wife is not at home, or infer correctly from the look of a paper bag that there is no puppy inside it or know by being told that it is not snowing in New York City now—I come across a fact of the form "x is not in y" or "x does not bear the relation R to y" (or "x is no longer in y" or "x will be in y" or "x is not yet in y"). It is obvious that such pieces of veridical awareness do not represent presences, but neither do they fail to represent. Except in idiomatic uses, such as "Madonna has a stage presence," a *presence* can be identified with *what is present*. But an absence, obviously, cannot be identified with *what is absent*. That is why it is monstrously mistaken to identify a negative fact with *what is not the case*.

What is not the case is a nonexistent state of affairs—and I believe that there *are none* such in the world. That there is no elephant in this room, on the other hand, *is the case*: the state of affairs is very much existent. Unlike an elephant, its walking, or its skin color, its absence in this room is not a basic particular—that is, it is not a substance, event, or unrepeatable quality. Absences are not universals either. As their representations in language and awareness reveal, they are complex entities individuated by what they are absences of: absentees, locations, and the relation and property that delimits the relevant absenteehood. Quickly, to make clear the notion of *limitor of absenteehood*: I may come to class and notice Amit's absence. Amit, then, is the absentee, as Amit. But I may be looking for the only student who can read both Chinese and Sanskrit and find him absent. If Amit satisfies that definite description, then he is again the absentee of this absence, but not *qua* the person called "Amit." The limitor of his absenteehood has changed from "being Amit" to "being the only student who can read both Chinese and Sanskrit."

Though it makes sense to call absences negative facts, if only the *presence* of a relation between objects and properties counts as a fact, then absences should not count as facts. Even Russell, while giving the strongest defense of negative facts, warns us that "it must not be supposed that the negative fact contains a constituent corresponding to the word 'not'" (Russell 1956, 287). The negative fact that makes the sentence "the Taj Mahal is not in London" true has only the *Taj Mahal*, the city of *London*, and the *relation of being located in* as its constituent items. But the Taj Mahal figures as an absentee whose absenteehood in the locus London is delimited by the relation of being located in. Negation, we must insist, is not another object or item participating in the absence; it is just the way these three are placed with respect to each other that makes it the case that this great city lacks that great building as something locatable in it.

Analytic philosophers writing in English in the twentieth century, and Indian philosophers writing in Sanskrit in the eighth to thirteenth centuries have come up with four powerful arguments against the admission of negative facts into ontology. The four arguments are: (1) the proposal that absence as a category is ontologically redundant because it can always be reduced to the bare locus; (2) the argument that absence is imperceptible, hence only a creature of conceptual construction; (3) the argument (by Russell's opponent Demos) that the absence of any *x* can always be reduced to the presence of some *y* which repels *x*; and (4) the argument (by Bradley) that absences are subjective, appearing to be there due to the thwarted expectations of some mind.

The Bare Locus Theory

First: the bare locus theory. Anticipating David Lewis's move of reducing the holes in cheese to the cheese itself and generally all holes to their surrounding walls or linings, Prabhakara, an Indian philosopher of the ritual-hermeneutic school who lived sometime in the seventh century CE, proposed that the lack of a pot on the floor is nothing but the bare floor—the bare locus. To see the holes in cheese is to see the cheese as perforated. To see that the chairman is not on the chair is just to see the chair; the so-called absence of the chairman is no additional entity apart from its bare locus. This, naturally, provoked a quick rejoinder from pro-absence realists: If the floor or chair by itself constitutes the absence (or the object of the negative awareness), then even when the floor has a pot or the chair has the chairman on it, we should be still perceiving the absence, because it is the same floor or chair. To block this absurd consequence, the reductionist has to articulate what it means by the "*bare* locus." It is not the floor or chair as such, but *only* the floor or chair *without* the man in it that constitutes the absence. But isn't it obvious that this "only" or "without" are negative words reintroducing the abstract element of lack into the picture? So we have to perceive the floor plus its potlessness, the chair plus its unoccupiedness, in order to perceive the absence. Thus the bare locus theory fails to avoid the positing of real lacks. As Brendan Gillon (1997) comments cleverly, mocking the Prābhākara Mīmāmsaka, "If my office-mate's absence is identical with . . . his chair, then anytime I perceive the chair, which includes the times that my office-mate is in his chair, I should know that my office-mate is absent."

In a larger context, this problem surfaces in Wittgenstein's concept of *the world* in the first sentences of the *Tractatus*. In a sense, all positive facts put together make up the world. In an inventory of the world, we do not need to mention negative facts or lacks. But in order to close the inventory, we have to add that these are the *only* facts; no other states of affairs obtain. But "that's all" means "nothing else remains to be listed." Those are the *only* facts. As Bradley (1922) remarked at the end of his discussion of negative judgment:

> Our sober thinkers . . . I wonder if ever any of them see how they compromise themselves with that little word 'only'. (1: 125)

To give a limit to positive fact—which you need to do if you are to describe *all* that is the case exhaustively—is to transcend that limit and allude generally to the big negative fact that no other combination of objects obtain. Richard Taylor (1952), one of the clearest and boldest defenders of negative facts in the twentieth century, makes this point. But in representing the opponent's position—perhaps deliberately—he commits the typical blunder of conflating the absence with the absentee: "We can now ask . . . whether negative facts should have to be included in such an inventory or whether, as seems more reasonable, they should be excluded on the ground that they are essentially absences: i.e., *things which are not*." Later on he gives as examples "the ink bottle that is not on the table, the eraser which the pencil lacks" (441). He should have said instead "*that* the ink bottle is not on the table, *that* the pencil lacks the eraser." The question is not whether the absent ink bottle or eraser should be counted as part of the world (obviously they should not be counted as items in a purely fictional world, for they do show up elsewhere in the real world, maybe even on my own mantelpiece); the question, rather, is whether *their absence* (that is, the absentees) should be documented as part of the world. And the answer to that is "yes," because unlike the absentees which are not there, the absences *are* there, characterizing their loci and rendering them bare in this specific respect.

The reduction of absence to the bare locus also violates the verdict of direct awareness that the absence of the man is *in* the chair; there is a sense of locatedness, or residence, between the lack and the locus. The hole is in the cheese—hence, it cannot be the same as the cheese. Compare the following bit of dialogue between Argle, the reductionist, and Bargle, the realist, about holes:

ARGLE: I say the hole-lining *is* the hole.
BARGLE: Didn't you say the hole-lining surrounds the hole? Things don't surround themselves. (Lewis & Lewis 1970, 209)

In response, Argle, who is quite good at drastically *revising* commonsense and finding fault with ordinary usage, says that "surrounds" in the case of holes means "is identical with." This reminds us of Gangeśa's exclamation:

> Oh! What skill at explaining things! Even what is obviously experienced is being cleverly explained away! (Matilal 1968, 174)

The Repulsion Theory of Absence

Next: let us consider Demos's repulsion theory of absence (which in some form is anticipated by Dharmakirti [1985] in his *Nyāyabindu*, ch. 2): The lack of the color purple in a buttercup is reducible to the presence of yellow which repels purple in it. To take Dharmakirti's example, we feel *lack of warmth* because we feel coldness, which is incompatible with warmth in the same locus. In the case of missing milk in the fridge, the causal conditions of perception we know to be such that if there were milk I would have seen it; the fridge light is on, yet I do not see milk—instead I see other things—hence, I infer the absence of milk. The latter story of course uses the language of lacks in two unusual places, both in stating the ground of the inference—lack of perception of milk, and in stating its conclusion—lack of milk. Even if we agree that all alleged cases of perception of absence are cases of nonperception of the absentee, it only pushes back the absences to the epistemic level; at least there are nonperceptions, that is, *lacks* of perception, in the mental realm!

Still, for Dharmakirti, reducing so-called "experience" of absence to a fact of inference served a purpose, because for a Buddhist Sauntrantika, what is directly perceived without conceptualization is real, what is inferred or perceived indirectly with the help of analytical construction is, in the ultimate analysis, merely a *vikalpa*—conceptual fiction.

To come back to Demos's theory: To assert that a rose is not purple is to assert the positive disjunctive fact that it is either white or red or yellow or pink and so on. Its not being purple amounts to its being of some purple-repellent color. This repulsion theory of lacks, however, has the following profound weakness: First, as Richard Taylor (1952) observed, I can know that its being yellow entails its not being purple only if I know the fact that it cannot be both, which is a negative fact. Second, very often we have not the foggiest idea about the so-called "positive and repellent" quality of an object, and yet we can know for sure some negative property fit. Thus, without any idea about who it will be, one could say in 1991 that the would-be president of America in 1993 does not have a pierced earring in one ear. Of course, the repulsion theory could still be true, because in fact what makes true the fact that Bill Clinton's ears have their lobes intact is incompatible with his having pierced ears. But let us not get involved with holes, however minute, once again.

The real point of the repulsion theory of Demos is, as Russell saw it, to make the relation of opposition and incompatibility (between predicates or propositions) ultimate and understand lacks and negation in its terms. Thus, the truth of "John is not in" consists in John's being out because "in" and "out" are incompatible, when incompatibility somehow remains undefined or at least allegedly not defined in terms of "not." In order to show the absurdity of this theory, Russell (1956) constructs this imaginary exchange:

DEMOS: '~*p*' just means 'it is the case that *q*, and *p* & *q* are opposites.'

RUSSELL: But is not '*p* & *q* are opposite' just equivalent to 'It is not the case ever that *p* & *q* are both true'?

DEMOS: No. They are opposites because an opposite of '*p* & *q*' is true.

RUSSELL: But suppose someone obstinately says, I believe *p*, I believe *q*, and I also believe that an opposite of '*p* & *q* can both be true'. How will you make this fellow realize his inconsistency?

DEMOS: I'll tell him that this is impossible: if the opposite of '*p* & *q* are compatible' is true then you cannot truly believe that *p* and also truly believe that *q*.

RUSSELL: But how will you say that in a negation-free language just by talking about *opposites*?

The obstinate "positivist" would go on forever admitting opposites but refusing to make any concessions for objective counterparts of negations. But without objective negatives, there are no incompatibilities or oppositions. There will always be the negation in the logical prohibition "you can*not* assert both." Thus there is an obviously vicious circularity in trying to define away negations in terms of logical opposition when the latter itself has to be eventually defined in terms of two things *not* being true together. Thus the repulsive theory of lacks fails.

Subjective Thwarted Expectation Theory

Finally, there is Bradley's (1922) view that *negation is subjective* which, after all, he recognized as a mistake in the second edition of *Principles of Logic*. The view, however, was very widespread and has a considerable grip over philosophers even now. Lacks cannot be objective, the argument goes, because they are posited by human imagination and language only to express a thwarted expectation, a rejected suggestion, a denied false belief—each of which are subjective states of cognizers and describers of reality, but would not be there if human thought did not try to represent the world. It is undeniable that the sentence "the Taj Mahal is not in London" gets its psychological and conversational significance from the error that someone might commit of thinking that the Taj Mahal *is* in London. Hence, negative facts are looked on as second-order comments on the truth value of an affirmative one, and therefore are never on a par with the latter. To use Bradley's words:

> The reality repels the suggested alteration, but the suggestion is not any movement of the fact, nor in fact does the given subject maintain itself against the actual attack of a discrepant equality. The process takes place in the unsubstantial region of ideal experiment. (120)

Now, as far as the psychological/conversational contrast is concerned, the occasion for a negative assertion can be simply a question to be answered, rather than an error to be exposed: If the fact that "Trafalgar Square is in London" is most commonly stated in answer to a query—"Where is Trafalgar Square? Is it in London?"—does it render the content of the affirmative judgment subjective? There is no reason on earth why the fact that the question, "Where is the Taj Mahal? Is it in London?," which is quite normally answered by, "It is not in London. I can't recall where it is though," should render the content of the negative judgment subjective. My failure to recall the exact place name may be subjective, but the Taj Mahal's failure to be in London is the Taj Mahal's, not mine!

The point is this: in one strict Kantian sense, wherever there is predication and judgment, there is some combination of thought and theory, and it is not raw, unconceptualized "sensed" reality that we encounter. Ascription of a predicate to an object is one sort of conceptual processing of the data of experience, and rejection of a predicate with respect to an object is another sort of processing. If we regard the lacks as man-made holes in a nonporous reality because negative awareness—whether introspective like, "I don't feel any *p*" or truth-functional, as "it is false that p"—is qualificative rather than nonconceptual awareness, then we have to dismiss most of our positive pictures of objective reality and finding of positive facts as subjective. But facts should not be confused with finding of facts. In facts, objects fit into each other like the links of a chain, precisely because the possibilities of such combinations are etched into them as their formal properties. Facts are not man-made constructions. They are the stuff that the world is made of. If the world were not *in itself* the totality of positive and negative facts, then it would not be a totality of facts at all—it would be just a jumble of things.

The fact that we have to recall or think of the absentee before our knowledge of its absence in a site can arise does not show that the knowledge is inferential or indirect. Any particular perceptual judgment, even affirmative ones, is usually mediated by our mastery or memory of the word or concept by which we identify the perceived object. That does not necessarily render the judgment nonperceptual. (In that case only pre-conceptual nonjudgmental sensation would count as *perception*, as Buddhist epistemologists arguably hold as their austere view). So perception of absence is no less perception than any other qualificative perception. Here again, somewhat in the spirit of Quine, the Buddhist asks: what distinguishes one absence from another? Suppose you say, it is the difference between their absentees that distinguishes the absences. Absence of a cup on the table is distinct from the absence of the pencil on the table, because a cup is not a pencil. Now, the positive things are distinguished by mutual absences or lacks (of identity), and the lacks are distinguished by the positive things: isn't this circular? This charge is not as formidable as it looks, really. The absences are distinct because their absentees are distinct, not because of the absentees themselves. If distinctions are responsible for further distinctions, that is not circular. The following section gives a sample of how sophisticated and technical the logic of absences becomes in the hands of thirteenth to seventeenth century Nyāya analysts.

Heterologous Absences: Constraints on Real and Spurious Absences

Unlike the familiar structure of Western logic, which uses sentences called "premises" and a "conclusion," Indian Logic is more a logic of things and their properties. One infers from the reason-property H (*probans*), to the presence of the target-property (*probandum*) S, in the site P, on the basis of the invariable concomitance or universal co-location informally formulated as "wherever there is H, there is S, as in the corroborating instance U." If there is wetness on the street, for example, there must have been rain, or a garden sprinkler, on the street because wherever there is wetness, there has been some kind of shower in the recent past. The problem in logic then is to define this rule of invariable concomitance—a required feature of a good reason (*saddhetu*).

If invariable concomitance (*vyāpti*) is defined as "*not* occurring in places where the target-property is *absent*," we run into a difficulty in counting as valid those inferences that involve universally present target properties, because a universally present property is nowhere absent. "This must be nameable because it is knowable" is such an inference. The inference relies on the invariable concomitance between knowability and nameability, both of them omnipresent properties, with null exclusion range—everything that exists is knowable and nameable. If something like this cat is knowable, it must be nameable as well. The definition given in terms of absence of the prover property will be inapplicable to (invariable colocation rules grounding) such good inferences, thus suffering from under-coverage.

Provisionally, to solve such problems, it has been proposed that we construct absences even of omnipresent properties like existence and knowability. But how can we find the absence of even an omnipresent property? Let us remind ourselves first of a common phenomenon: we sometimes lose a wallet and find it absent even when it is lying right there on the table because we have somehow in our false memory switched its features with something else; we are (erroneously) looking for a brown wallet when the wallet we have "lost" is black. Similarly, we can talk even about a present (never-absent) thing as absent if we delimit the absenteehood of the absentee by a property that does not belong to the absentee. Existence, which is found in everything that exists, is still not a color. Existence could be missing from any particular existent thing if we search for it under the wrong sortal, say, for example, as a shade of grey![3] Nothing—not even existent grey things—possesses existence-as-a-hue, just as hours cannot be four meters long. Thus, even where horns are present, such as in a buffalo, horns as being organic rabbit limbs are absent. Even if red color is present in a cranberry, red color, *as related by contact*, is absent in it, because a color cannot be in contact with anything. Analogously, since knowability does not technically *inhere* in what is knowable, even in things that possess knowability, we can miss that feature, find it absent, *as an inherent property*. Such an absence of something whose absenteehood is delimited by a demarcator property non-colocated with the absenteehood (that is to say, a specifier property which is not located in the actual absentee where absenteehood is located) is called "heterologous absence."

Gangeśa (twelfth/thirteenth centuries CE) (Ramanujatatacharya, 1999) rejects such heterologous absences as artificial and redundant. Our cognition of absence, according to him, always has a doubly qualified content. If a copper pot is missing from the cupboard, then the cupboard has (is characterized by) an absence. The absence in turn is qualified by the pot's absenteehood, which is again delimited by the property of being made of copper. If the qualification of the pot with the property of being made of copper is an error or make-believe, then our awareness of such an absence is also an error or make-believe, corresponding to which no real absence can exist. Heterologous absences do not exist because their absentees are necessary nonentities. This shows how absences have to be absences of real things and properties, and unicorns or six-tusked elephants are not even absent.

Raghunatha (1477–1547) (Ramanujatatacharya, 1999) distils out Gangeśa's reason for throwing out such absences, even though they would have solved some problems in the definition of the rule of universal concomitance between the prover and the probandum (target property) in case of never-absent target properties. Our statement or judgment of an absence does not have three independent constituents: the absence, the absentee, and the (de)limitor of absenteehood. It is only as a qualifier of the absentee, not on its own right, that we recognize the limitor of absenteehood. For example, we need a property really riveted to a horse (such as being white and being a stallion) in order that we can take that property to be the limitor of absenteehood when we speak of or locate an absence of a white stallion in a stable. Being winged is not such a riveted property for a horse. By artificially importing wingedness from birds and butterflies, we can—playfully—construct the absence of a horse as winged or absence of a winged horse, but that would not be one of those gappy bits of reality as the posthumous absence of a living white stallion in a stable when the only white stallion dies.

This investigation should have shown us one suggested but unpopular non-Meinongian way in which Navya-Nyāya could handle our (somewhat elliptical and rhetorical) *talk* about the nonexistence of fictional or impossible objects, such as rabbit horns, sky flowers or squared circles, without getting committed to their shadowy existence in some fictional realm. The underlying connection between logical insight, phenomenological evidence, and ontological decision-making gets clearer through this abstruse technical debate at the heart of the logic of invariable concomitance.[4]

However, flouting all such strictures on what can and cannot be coherently meant by a negation, *Yogavāiṣṭha* (*Mokṣopāya*)—a philosophical text that uses "narrative logic" to slacken our sense of unchangeable objective external reality—dares all logicians to listen to this illogical lullaby about three impossible princes:

> In a city which did not exist there were three princes, two of whom were unborn and one had not yet been conceived. When all their kith and kin died, they set out on a summer day to seek their fortune in a foreign land. Exhausted by the heat, they took shelter in the shade of three trees of which two were non-existent and one had not been planted. They bathed in three rivers two of which had dried up and the third had no water in it. After that, they entered a city which was about to be built and were charmed by the city's future grandeur and beauty. In wall-less and un-built palaces they cooked ninety nine minus one hundred pounds of rice, and invited two bodiless and one mouthless holy men to eat . . . (Venkateshananda 1985, pp. 98–100)

It is quite amazing that we *are* able to follow this logic-lambasting storyline. That extremely idealist text teaches us that our conviction of the reality of a common mind-independent physical world out there is no securer than our conviction that we can visualize the absurd plot of that child-entertaining tale of impossibilities.

In his path-breaking study of Indian literary and philosophical theories of imagination, David Shulman (2012) remarks about this particular narrative:

> At the bottom of a progression that has no bottom lies the satisfaction proper to a subtle internal space *empty of objects, hence utterly full*. This same space is the locus of imagination, as the text proceeds to explain. (111, my emphasis)

We shall see in the very last section of this essay that Bergson arrives at the same idea of the vibrant fullness of the void, not by the narrative but by the phenomenological method of strenuously trying to empty the mind of all images and memories and ideas. But first we must give another chance to the absolute skeptic who whispers to us that we cannot eliminate the possibility that nothing whatsoever is real, that everything could be nothing.

Ancient Nihilism: From Exclusion to Universal Unreality

In *Nyāya Sūtra* 4.1.37, Gotama (Jha, 1999) poses, as the opponent's view, that nothing exists, a nihilist position similar to the extreme skepticism Sextus Empiricus from which distances himself. "All is non-being," this ancient nihilist contends, "because in every being one can find (establish) the non-being of another." Determinations are negations. Insofar as things are differentiated and excluded from one another, all entities are negations of one another, and hence nonentities. Everything is simply not another thing. What is interesting is that in this nihilistic position we hear a vague anticipation of a powerful exclusion (*apoha*) theory of meaning that later on would become the foundation of Buddhist nominalism and negative semantics in the hands of Dignaga and Dharmakirti. To indulge in the irresistible Greek comparison, it is as if the first and third version of the absolute skepticism of Gorgias of Leontini, summarized by Sextus Empiricus (1949, vii, 65–87): that nothing exists; and that even if something exists it is impossible to speak about it, are being rehearsed by these pre-Buddhist ancient Indian nihilists.

The context, in the fourth book of Gotama's *Nyāya Sūtras*, is the refutation of several un-commonsensical extremisms (e.g. "everything is one," "everything is many," "everything is unknowable"). This is one of those sweeping universalizations of a certain "revisionary metaphysics": Everything is a non-being, because in beings we can establish the nonbeing of each other. Gotama rejects this view with the following running argumentation:

First, the proposition to be proved is patently self-refuting. There is something positive called "everything." (Remember Quine's one word answer to the deepest ontological question "What is there?") Here is a two-thousand-year-old definition of universal quantification. "For all x" means "for a plurality of x's without any remainder." Many x's and no x left behind, that's what "all x's" means. So the nihilist extremist's own word "all" means many real entities. How then could the presence of these many reals, exhaustively enumerated, be equated with absolute absence of everything? Surely there is no plurality, let alone remainderless plurality, in zero!

Second, even if we somehow make sense of the conclusion to be proved, the reason proffered is incompatible with the thesis to be proved. If the *bhāva*-s, and all of them, have mutual otherness or exclusion among themselves (which is the prover-reason), then they are *bhāva*-s—positive entities, which is inconsistent with the conclusion that they are all nonentities.

Gotama (Jha, 1999) proceeds in 4.1.38 to put forward his own positive thesis: Every positive entity is not nothing or nonbeing, because entities have their own identity, their own being or own nature, own reality. If you try, perversely, to look upon a cow as a bird, then it may look "nothing like a bird," but when you see it as a cow, it very much exists as what it is. If you see a spade as a spade, it is a spade—it is real and has the being of a spade.

Now the nihilist shifts ground. Anticipating Nāgārjuna's famous soteriologically motivated (no-view) view that things are not void, but only devoid of any own-nature or essence, the nihilist contends that the so-called positive things cannot be said to possess any being because they exist only relatively or dependently to other beings. Long things depend upon shorter things, and short things on longer things, in order to exist as long or short. Because of relative and dependent nature (*āpekṣikatva*), there is no proof of own-being of entities. Now the thesis of universal nonbeing boils down to the relativity of all things. Just as there is no real redness in a colorless crystal but the redness of a hibiscus placed next to it is superimposed on it, everything comes to "borrow" some (what has been called "Cambridge properties," such as grandfatherhood or being taller than) features in relation to other things, and these features are not real because they are superimposed.

Gotama answers this objection with an intricate reasoning in 4.1.40. The main points of that reply are two. First, even in case of relational or relative properties such as "short" or "long," no comparison is possible without an objective standard. If a cat is smaller than a tiger only relatively, then the tiger's size cannot again reciprocally depend upon the cat's size. Second, it is our knowledge of smallness, bigness, and so forth, which are relative and mutually dependent upon the context of comparison, not the actual size of things. For example, the cat will not grow in size if, instead of comparing it to a tiger, we compare it to an ant. The absolute skeptic or relativist, typically, is superimposing the relativity of human judgment onto the objective nature and existence of things judged. Third, not all properties are subject to such relativity, even if shortness and largeness are. That a cat is a cat does not change if we compare it with a larger cat or a smaller mouse.

Finally, the sub-commentator Uddyotakara (c. sixth century CE) brings four major charges against any relativism or absolute negativism of the above sort:

1. If anyone is trying to give a proof, adducing a source of certain knowledge, of his nihilistic conclusion, then at least he is committed to the existence of that proof. Hence he cannot claim that nothing exists, for at least the proof has to *be there*.
2. If the nihilist expects his sentence "All is non-being" to have a meaning, then the being of his own sentence-meaning must be a counterexample to his own claim, unless he is happy to be saying (like early Wittgenstein) that his own statements are senseless.
3. If the nihilist admits the existence of a speaker and a hearer of his assertion, then he is not seriously saying that no entity whatsoever exists.
4. If the nihilist does not wish to take the sentence "everything is nonexistent" and the sentence "everything is existent" to be synonymous, then the distinction between their meanings exists, in which case "nothing exists" must be false. If the distinction between their meanings does not exist, then the "none-ist" could very well pass for an "all-ist," and the nihilist ends up agreeing with his radical opponent, who says, "All things are real" (under *Nyāyā Sūtra*, 4.1.37–38, in Jha, 1999).

From Essencelessness, Positionlessness, to Emptiness of Emptiness

In a famous set of verses in MMK XV,[5] Nāgārjuna invites us to consider what makes something the essence or own intrinsic nature of something. Burning, we say, is the own nature of fire, while wetting is the own property of water. When water is heated, we call its hotness extrinsic or adventitious because this foreign property is borrowed by water from fire, which causes the high temperature. But even the hotness of the fire is caused by the fuel which is causally responsible for the fire. "Genuine," "intrinsic," and other variants of "essentially own" and "real" nature of things, thus, crumbles into other-dependent, description-dependent and framework-relative properties that we arbitrarily divide into own and not-own properties. That does not mean that, like the ancient nihilists did, we should call everything "other than itself" or unreal. Everything is neither essentially real, nor essentially unreal, and they cannot be essentially both real and unreal, nor can they be essentially neither real nor unreal. But this fourfold negation itself should not be treated as "the correct view" of things. Even the middle way should not be fixed into an ontological permanent address. The even more ancient *Samādhirāja sūtra* quoted here by Candrakīrti (sixth century CE) says it beautifully:

> "Exists" is one edge, "doesn't exist" is another edge, purity and impurity these are both extreme edges. Therefore avoiding both edges, the wise ones do not even place themselves in the middle . . . by engaging in disputes suffering does not ameliorate; suffering is cured when one attains non-disputes. (Nāgārjuna, 1983)

Emptiness itself has to be emptied out of its disputative edge.[6] Even if "repudiation of all metaphysical disputes" was the purpose of Nāgārjuna's argumentation about the natureless nature of emptiness, his ancient Brahminical opponents, as well as some contemporary Western supporters, take his logic of emptiness to be one that drops the basic law of non-contradiction. The logical dispute over whether the Mādhyamikas Buddhist is a dialetheist (contradiction-welcoming) or whether he rejects the third ontic option (it is real and unreal) precisely because he wants to avoid self-contradiction shows no sign of subsiding.[7] But behind all this negative dialectics, one detects a contemplative purpose: to see the limits of egoless thinking. This is what we would like to conclude by exploring.

Mind the Gap: The Role of Absences as Contents of Negative Introspective Reports and a Deeper Phenomenology of Negation in Frege, Wittgenstein, K.C. Bhattacharya, and Bergson

In his *Philosophical Remarks*, Wittgenstein (1975) keeps coming back to a negative introspective report as an illuminating analysandum. " 'I haven't got stomach-ache' may be compared to the proposition 'These apples cost nothing.' The point is that they don't cost any money, not that they don't cost any snow or any trouble." (110)

We know that Wittgenstein was a very careful reader of Frege, while at the same time eager to prove that the self is a non-object. It is entirely possible that his inspiration for this preoccupation with negative introspective reports could have been this suggestive but small passage in Frege's (1967) classic essay, "The Thought: A Logical Inquiry":

> I am not my own idea, and if I assert something about myself, e.g. *that I do not feel any pain at this moment*, then my judgment concerns something which is not a content of my consciousness, is not my idea, that is me myself. (33, my emphasis)

Now, Wittgenstein first explains this negative introspective report in terms of exposure of falsehood of a proposition: " 'I have no pain' means: if I compare the proposition 'I have a pain' with reality, it turns out false" (Wittgenstein 1975, 92). The point he makes is logical: the negation of pain, talk of zero pain, is still talk about pain. "The zero is the zero of *one* scale. 'I haven't got a pain' does not refer to a condition in which there can be no talk of pain, on the contrary, we are talking about pain" (110). Already the emphasis has shifted. In Frege, "I have got no pain" was supposed to show that the self is distinct from its feelings and ideas. In Wittgenstein it has become a phenomenological illustration of the logical point that the negatum must be referred to in a negative report. In the thought of a senior contemporary of Wittgenstein, K. C. Bhattacharya (1875–1949)—who does not seem to have read any Wittgenstein—the same introspective report of a relief from pain figures as crucial evidence for a progressively meditative phenomenology of the self's freedom from a feeling, from a desire for a wanting feeling, and eventually even from the agency to this introspective act of feeling the lack of feeling.

Following the work of K. C. Bhattacharya, I would like to conclude by hinting at the deep significance of the feeling of an absent feeling for jettisoning the dispute between self-ism and no-self-ism. The self cannot be reduced to a flow of feelings, since we seem to be able to catch it as a locus of absence of a feeling. If, for example, one day I find that my passion for someone or something is simply gone, through the window of that experience I seem to have an encounter with my bare self, as Frege was claiming. But then, digging deeper, I may find that even this introspector self can be thrown out as a philosophical or grammatical construct. Nevertheless, there would still not be complete hollowness, but a rich impersonal ownerless consciousness of subjectivity without a subject. Bhattacharya describes the first steps of this progressive thought experiment in the following passage:

> The feeling of not having a feeling is not an uncommon experience. The awareness of wanting a feeling—whether sense-enjoyment, aesthetic satisfaction

> or spiritual serenity—is itself a feeling. All desires involve a present feeling of not having a feeling, an awareness of the 'inferiority' of the anticipatory pleasure to the actual feeling that is to come. It is not simply one feeling due to the want of another feeling but the feeling of the want of its own being or actuality. Nor is it yet the disinterested awareness of the want, a detachment from it such as introspection would imply. It can only be characterized as the *feeling of a feeling*, with which are bound up interesting spiritual attitudes like sentimentalism on the one hand which confuses the felt want with the actual feeling[8] that is wanted and the experience of the want on the other as a pain that miraculously ends in a fulfillment. (Bhattacharya 1983, 440)

In a passage in the Third Meditation, Descartes tries to witness the self in a similar exercise of shedding sensory and cognitive content one by one:

> I will now close my eyes, plug my ears, and withdraw all my senses. I will rid my thoughts of physical objects—or, since that is beyond me, I shall write those images off as empty illusions. Talking with myself and looking more deeply into myself, I'll try gradually to know myself better. (Descartes 2003, 79)

Almost following the same recipe of emptying one's mind of all sensory or intellectual impressions and ideas, Henri Bergson (1911) describes the following contemplative Yoga-like thought experiment (perhaps it should be called a "no-thought experiment"):

> Let us then see what we are thinking about when we speak of 'Nothing.' To represent "nothing" we must either imagine it or conceive it. Let us examine what this image or this idea may be. First, the image.

> I am going to close my eyes, stop my ears, extinguish one by one the sensations that come to me from the outer world. Now it is done; all my perceptions vanish, the material universe sinks into silence and the night,—I subsist, however, and cannot help myself subsisting. . . .[9] How can I suppress all this? How eliminate myself? I can even, it may be, blot out and forget my recollections up to my immediate past; but at least I keep the consciousness of my present reduced to its extremest poverty, that is to say, of the actual state of my body. I will try, however, to do away with this consciousness itself. I will reduce more and more the sensations my body sends in to me: now they are almost gone; now they are gone. . . But no! At the very instant that my consciousness is extinguished, another consciousness lights up—or rather, it was already alight—it has arisen the instant before, in order to witness the extinction of the first. . . . I see myself annihilated only if I have already resuscitated myself by an act which is positive, however involuntary and unconscious. (302–303)

In diagnosing, similarly, the step-by-step production of the concept (rather than the image) of absolute nothingness, Bergson (1911) ends up with the following, Upanishad-like conclusion:

> *The representation of the void is always a representation which is full* and which resolves itself on analysis into two positive elements: the idea, distinct or confused, of a substitution, and the feeling, experienced, or imagined, of a desire or regret. (304, my emphasis)

So, the idea of absolute naught is a self-destructive pseudo-idea, 'a mere word.' Emptying the mind, as a Yogic or phenomenological exercise, may reach its climax with getting rid even of this idea of this last desire or regret: the desire to get rid of all thoughts, or the regret that one has not quite been able to get to the empty heart of things. Overcoming this desire or regret has been achieved, it seems, by Nāgārjuna with his crowning claim of the emptiness of emptiness, after rejecting even the *position* of essencelessness reached by the reasoned refutation of all logically contradictory positions. Such mutual cancelling out gets us on to the middle way that consists in emptiness of emptiness. The *Mahtābhārata* instructs this in a wonderful move: "Give up both dharma and adharma, truth and falsehood, and then give up that by which you give up" (Book XII, chap 329, verse 40).

In the end, the world of ordinary objects and conventional truth is left undenied as an object of non-attached double-denial, wherein one denies the denial of the world of ordinary experience. One lives, with a wonderful lightness, without any interest in world-affirmation or world-denial. As Abhinavagupta instructs us: "Don't renounce anything, don't possess anything, just stay as you are and enjoy" (Baumer 2011, 296–298). But such throwing away of the ladder of logic befits only those who have painstakingly argued their analytic way, rung by rung, up and down, ascending and descending, M. C. Escher-like, to that depth/apex of fullness that is at the heart of the seductive void we cannot avoid as thinking/feeling beings.[10]

Notes

1 King Lear, Act 1, Scene 1. The dialogue begins as follows.

King Lear: Which of you shall we say doth love us most?
That we our largest bounty may extend . . .

. . . .

Cordelia: [Aside] What shall Cordelia do? Love, and be silent.

. . . .

King Lear: . . . Now, our joy,
although the last, not least . . .
. . . what can you say to draw
A third more opulent than your sisters? Speak.

2 *na sā dhī yatra bhedo na bhāsate*—Śankara Miśra. *Bhedaratnam*, "The Jewel of Difference" (Varanasi: Samparnanand Sanskrit University, 2003).

3 This is not a very plausible example because it is highly unlikely that we would make such a category mistake, but other category mistakes, we shall see soon, are not that uncommon.

4 For more details, see Arindam Chakrabarti, *Denying Existence* (Dordrecht, Netherlands: Kluwer Academic Publishers, 1997), 235–243.

5 Nāgārjuna. *Mūla-madhyamaka-kārika*. Full text at http://indica-et-buddhica.org/repositorium/nagarjuna

6 A "lucid exposition" of the nuances of Nāgārjuna's self-deconstructing view of viewlessness is to be found in the first five chapters of Jay Garfield, *Empty Words: Buddhist Philosophy and Cross-Cultural Interpretations* (New York: Oxford University Press, 2001).

7 See papers by Garfield, Priest, and others in Koji Tanaka, ed. "Buddhism and Contradiction." Special issue, *Philosophy East and West*, vol. 63, no. 3 (2013).

8 One wants, that is, feels the lack of, the feeling of the presence of a loved one so strongly that one feels as if one is already in the presence of that person (my illustration).

9 Here we stumble against the same unimaginability of the nonbeing of the self, the thinker, that Samkara, Al Ghazali, Descartes, Frege, and indeed Freud, have all stumbled against, and a powerful insight that the contemporary Buddhism-inspired "I am no one" thinkers and psychologists seem to duck.

10 My graduate research assistant, Ian Nicolay, and one of the editors of this volume, JeeLoo Liu, helped me make the chapter tighter, shorter, and more readable.

2 Semantics of Nothingness

Bhartṛhari's Philosophy of Negation[1]

Sthaneshwar Timalsina

Introduction

Bhartṛhari (fl. 450 CE) is one of the foremost philosophers of classical India. While there are many narratives relating the story of his life, that he was a king-turned-hermit, the author of three hundred stanzas, and so on, one thing is certain: he was the author of the masterpiece, the *Vākyapadīya* (VP). There are very few texts in the history of Indian philosophy that have had as penetrating an influence as this one. Although the text primarily relates to the philosophy of Sanskrit grammar, the first section on the Brahman (*brahmakāṇḍa*) discusses the metaphysics of, and provides the philosophy for, non-dualism, with the introduction of terms such as 'transformation/false projection' (*vivarta*) that became pivotal to subsequent philosophers, such as Śaṅkara (700 CE). Bhartṛhari's thought can also be seen unmistakably on the works of another prolific classical Indian philosopher, Maṇḍana Miśra (700 CE).[2] The depth to which Bhartṛhari has shaped Indian philosophy has yet to be properly appreciated, as scholars are coming to recognize that even the Pratyabhijñā school of Kashmiri non-dualism is largely derived from Bhartṛhari's philosophy of language.

After the "linguistic turn" in the latter half of the twentieth century, philosophers in the West have been more open to exploring the possibility of solving philosophical problems by understanding more about language.[3] It would not be an exaggeration to say, by way of contrast, that philosophical speculation in India has linguistic origins. Early Brahmanical thinking is heavily ritualistic and relies on analyzing Vedic sentences. Classical philosophers primarily derive their conclusions from an exegetical analysis of the *Upaniṣads* or the *Sūtra* literature. The philosophical debate among Hindus, Buddhists, and the Jains oftentimes goes back to linguistic issues. The linguistic philosophy of Bhartṛhari needs to be addressed in his milieu. His speculations about the nature of language and his analysis of Sanskrit both transcend the boundaries of language and relate to metaphysics, epistemology, and ontology.

Since understanding some of the most pivotal issues in the history of Indian philosophy, and particularly those issues involving debates about nonbeing and being, are so dependent on traditional Indian philosophy of language, understanding how classical Indian thinkers understood negation and how it functions linguistically is fundamentally important. This paper will therefore examine what the seminal grammarian Bhartṛhari had to say about negation, particularly in debates with rival philosophers and schools. Reading Bhartṛhari's philosophy of negation is therefore not restricted to merely analyzing Sanskrit syntax. While he was an original thinker, many of his ideas have evolved historically, and we cannot address Bhartṛhari's philosophy without seeing it in the context of his predecessors. This, however, is not to indulge in only history of philosophy, but only to point out that history of ideas should not be ignored while exploring answers to philosophical questions.

Negation: From Patañjali to Bhartṛhari

Patañjali (150 BCE) is one of the earliest scholars to explicitly describe two types of negation: *prasajya* and *paryudāsa*,[4] generally translated as nonimplicative and implicative negations. The first one is used to simply negate the existence of X (there is no X), while the other refers to negation of X in Y (a Y that is not X). This twofold schema of negation is used in Indian philosophy for morphological analysis (as in Patañjali's *Mahābhāṣya*), sentence analysis (primarily in the tradition of Mīmāṃsā), and metaphysical analysis (both in the Nyāya tradition and in the Mādhyamika of Nāgārjuna). However, the way negation has been analyzed and applied varies from one school to another. Around the same time as Patañjali, Jaimini (200 BCE) explored primarily the sentences used in ritual injunction and systematized a framework of threefold negation, including the injunction of an alternative by means of negation.[5] Semantically, both forms of negations are expressed by the negative particle *nañ*,[6] and both are addressed in the semantic and morphological analysis of Patañjali and Bhartṛhari. This paper is limited to the meaning of negation in the work of these two grammarians. I will also briefly engage the views of negation of both Jaimini and Śabara and analyze some of their crucial positions in an attempt to expand upon the semantic analysis of *nañ*.

It has already been mentioned that there are implicative and nonimplicative forms of negation. The implicative negation affirms something (y) by means of negating one entity (x). By contrast, the nonimplicative type of negation simply negates a purported fact. Sanskrit grammarians often cite the following verse to identify these forms of negation:

> If the negative particle corresponds with the final term [in a compound], this should be known as implicative negation. If the negative particle corresponds with the verb [in a sentence], this should be considered the nonimplicative negation.[7]

Fritz Staal writes nonimplicative negation as ~F(x) and implicative negation as F(~x) (1962; see also 1988, 260). The most oft-cited example of implicative negation is *abrāhmaṇa*, where the term is not used in negating a *brāhmaṇa* but in the affirmation of someone else who bears some of the characteristics of a *brāhmaṇa*. While all classical discussions on negation can be categorized as word-negation and sentence-negation, the position of Bhartṛhari favors sentence negation, as words are not independently meaningful in his paradigm of the non-divisible sentence, *sphoṭa*. In this metaphysics, whether expressions are made in words or sentences, they all stem from speech (*vāc*) identified with the Brahman, and no form of negation can negate this foundation. Evidently, even the word used for negation is nonetheless a word.[8]

Bhartṛhari's Analysis of Sentential Negation

The word '*na*' is used in the Sanskrit language for both implicative and non-implicative negation. In compounds, the particle '*nañ*' or its derivative (*an*, if followed by a vowel) expresses the concept of negation. Commentators suggest that twofold negation is implicit in Pāṇini's (fourth century BCE) *Aṣṭādhyāyī* (AA).[9] George Cardona synthesizes this position by accepting two types of negation in Pāṇini's rules, where one is constructed with the nominal following the negative particle in the compound (e.g. "non-X" or F(~x)), and the other is linked with the verb (e.g. ~F(x)). He further explains that the first is the positive rule, as it provides operation in the domain restricted by the negative particle and the second negates operation, thereby stopping an operation that has already been given by other rules (Cardona 1967).

In Indian philosophy, grammarians primarily focused on morphology, with words being their immediate concern. Mīmāṃsakas, the ritualist philosophers from classical India, fulfilled the need of contemplating upon sentential meaning. In order to advance the analysis of sentence negation in Sanskrit grammar, I will briefly explore examples from the Mīṃāṃsā school, although a detailed study of this aspect would require a much larger space. Below are three examples they give of sentential negation:

1. One should <u>not</u> eat *kalañja*.[10]
2. [The phrase] '*ye yajāmahe*' is cited during sacrifices <u>except for</u> the Anuyājas.[11]
3. [The sacrificer] does not hold the *ṣodaśi* vessel in the Atirātra.

The first is an example of imperative negation, which I will set aside, as it demands a separate treatment. Something positive is derived from the second sentence, while the third sentence simply negates a fact. In the Sanskrit language, the way negation is linked, whether with the antecedent term or with the verb, determines which type of negation is used in a sentence. For instance:

*phalaṃ**nā**sti* |
S neg. V.

1. There is no fruit.
2. [This] is not a fruit.

In the above example, the sentence can be understood either way. In the first translation, negation corresponds to the verb, negating the existence of fruit. In the second translation, negation corresponds to the subject, while the object under consideration, such as a plastic replica, is not a fruit. This distinctive understanding evokes the classical debate between the particularists, those who maintained that sentence meaning is gleaned from the meanings of the words in the sentence, and the wholists, who maintained that sentence meaning is indivisible.

Whether the sentential meaning is derived from words that independently express meaning, or whether meaning is a collective or unitary expression of a sentence, is one of the classical debates involving multiple schools in Indian history. The wholists, such as Bhartṛhari and the Prābhākaras, and the particularists, such as Naiyāyikas and the Bhāṭṭas, wrestled over what the term '*na'* negates. Even when we engage the position of the particularists who state that negation relates to specific terms in a sentence, there are various ways in which the negative particle can be analyzed. For instance, (1) what we negate is the cognition of the existence of what has been negated; (2) negation affirms the falsity of cognition; (3) negation not only denotes itself but also its substratum; and (4) negation in a sentence indicates the sense communicated by the word with which the negative particle is linked.

These are therefore the four possible analyses of '*na*' according to the particularists:

1. Negation in a sentence negates the existence of the referent linked with the negative particle *nañ*. The sentence would be "There is no fruit" in the above example.
2. Negation makes known the falsity of cognition. The sentence, then, is "This is not a fruit" (but a plastic replica).
3. The negative particle denotes both negation and the substratum of that negation. In an example, "There is no book on the table," the substratum of the negation, the table, is also referred to by this negation. In this manner, the referent of the negative particle is not the table but the book, but the table is implicitly referred to as existent.
4. The negative particle is not independently meaningful. Since it means something by being affiliated with other words, it is therefore 'coreferential' (*dyotaka*). Negation, in this sense, is intrinsic to the meaning of the word itself, as is affirmation. For instance, the word 'table,' when articulated, has the potential to both affirm and negate the table. That is, negation is already there as a potential within the term, and the negative particle only brings to the spotlight what is already there as the meaning of the term.

Although Bhartṛhari maintains a holistic approach, he does not reject some of the arguments discussed above. In particular, he addresses at length the fourth point. This approach highlights his broader agenda to synthesize all the existing positions as far as possible. Returning to our example, the term 'table,' for instance, can mean both the being and absence of table, and the negative particle simply highlights negation. This, however, is not to say that Bhartṛhari surrenders to the particularists, as he rejects their viewpoint and concludes that words such as 'asymmetry' cannot be broken into parts and analyzed separately. This position of Bhartṛhari tallies with that of Wittgenstein: "The positive proposition necessarily presupposes the existence of the negative proposition and vice versa" (T 5.5151). For Bhartṛhari, both assertion and negation rest on speech (*vāc*), equated with the highest universal (*mahāsāmānya*) that involves all that exists. For Wittgenstein, both positive and negative facts are "facts." Negation is crucial for Bhartṛhari not just for comprehending sentence meaning, but also because it represents his primary strategy for describing reality: both of the terms that he uses in the first verse of VP to describe the absolute that is identical to speech are constructed in the negative form (*anādinidhanam* and *akṣaram*). This negation, however, does not go all the way, because for Bhartṛhari, the absolute is the Brahman, or the *Śabda-tattva*, a positive entity.

This analysis of the negative particle needs to be read in light of the ways classical philosophers have assigned meaning to it. There is not one single position, even among the grammarians, regarding the role of *nipātas*, a class of word elements of which the negative particle is a member. Whether these particles are the signifiers (*vācaka*), or the cosignifiers (*dyotaka*) is another question where the classical philosophers differ. For grammarians such as Bhartṛhari, these particles appear to be merely cosignifiers. This needs to be understood within the context that 'meaning' in Bhartṛhari's philosophy is understood in terms of 'primary' and 'secondary.' Cosignifiers bring the secondary meaning to the spotlight. In words such as 'asymmetry,' if *negation* of symmetry were the primary meaning, the negative particle /a/ would be the signifier and not cosignifier. Grammarians such as Bhaṭṭoji Dīkṣita (seventeenth century), however, maintain that the particles are both the signifiers and cosignifiers. The Nyāya philosophers, in yet another variation, maintain that select particles in the group of '*pra*' that are prefixes are only cosignifiers and the other particles in the group of '*ca*' are only signifiers. Grammarians reject this position (VSM 1977, 56).

Although these positions may appear to be merely linguistic, philosophy in India is closely intertwined with linguistic issues such that one cannot be addressed without the other. Whether there is a primacy of the particle (i.e., negation, rather than an affirmation of something positive) or not can change the course of ritual for the ritual philosophers, the Mīmāṃsakas. One of the central categories of the Advaitins is ignorance or *avidyā*, a negative term, and the difference in understanding leads to the position of one sub-school or the other. The school of logic, Navya-Nyāya, advances its argument to counter the Sautrāntika-Mādhyamika arguments of negation. And even within the Mādhyamika school of Buddhism, the division of Svātantrika and Prāsaṅgika primarily rests on how to interpret negation. Therefore, linguistic speculation about negation is a gateway to enter the many schools of classical Indian philosophy.

Bhartṛhari addresses negation at length in two different sections of his writings, first when establishing sentence meaning (VP 2.240–45), and second in the last section of his *magnum opus* when addressing compounds (VP 3.14.248–315). In the first instance, Bhartṛhari deals with the issue of negation when addressing sentence meaning, maintaining that meaning cannot be reduced to single words and that a sentence gives a unitary meaning and must be read as a whole. In Sanskrit, one can place the negative particle at the end. For instance, *aśvatthaś chedanīyo na* (one should *not* cut the ficus tree). Bhartṛhari argues that, if each word were to independently give rise to meaning, the sentence could be considered complete before the negative particle appears, enjoining one to cut the tree (VP 2.240). If words were to independently convey meaning, in sentences such as *vṛkṣo nāsti* (tree, there is not), one would have in mind first the existence of tree as affirmed by the term 'tree,' and the negative particle would deny its existence (VP 2.241). It then would mean that a single sentence gives rise to two contradictory concepts. Puṇyarāja (1000 CE) adds in his commentary an interesting argument: if something exists, it cannot be denied, and something that does not exist does not need to be negated. Either way, the negative particle is meaningless.[12] This argument is given to negate the particularist's position that each word in a sentence gives meaning independently. If the meaning is given by sentence holistically, on the other hand, the aforementioned consequence will not ensue.

One can argue that the positive terms in a sentence give rise to the object in the mind, and the negative particles negate only what exits in the mind and not the external reality. Bhartṛhari at this point states that it is not the cognition but the real object that is denoted by the negating term (VP 2.242). Puṇyarāja's commentary upon this verse is crucial:

> The particle *nañ* negates the meaning expressed by the word. A concept is not denoted by a word. The word denotes an external object. Concept, dependent upon [external] object, cannot be referred to by a word. This being the case, how can this concept {*sā*} be negated by [the particle] *nañ*?[13]

Embedded within this position is the thesis that language describes reality. The opposite position is that language only expresses our concepts and therefore cannot describe the thing-in-itself. For Bhartṛhari, the word principle itself is the Brahman, the absolute. Language, in his metaphysics, has a higher status and is capable of describing the object, not just its concept. Bhartṛhari is explicit in the following verse: "If the [negative particle] *nañ* establishes that the concept that arises [by hearing negation] is false, [in that case] the [negative term] *nañ* will have a separate operation [and] how can [its] absence be comprehended?" (VP 2.243) With this meaning of negation, when one says 'not a tree' one would be only negating the idea of a tree, not the tree as such. Puṇyarāja also adds in the commentary that since the objective of the verb is to simply negate existence, the negation in '*nāsti*' is of the nonimplicative (*prasajya*) type. Bhartṛhari rejects the argument that a negative particle does not correspond to any object or the substrate that it is negating. The argument is that negation always accompanies something that is being negated. If negation were generic, in the sense that what it negates is the substrate and not the particular object, the terms that accompany negation would lack referential meaning other than the substrate of negation (VP 2.244). Whatever its position in the sentence, on this view, the negative particle would be referring to both negation and its substrate and the words that accompany the particle would be irrelevant.

Another alternative is that instead of finding an independent reference for the negative particle, it is read as coreferential. This would allow one to escape from the above dilemma and the meaning could still be broken into words. The question is, does this particle *nañ* refer to its meaning directly (*vācaka*) or is it coreferential (*dyotaka*)? If the particle is merely a coreferent, this would mean that both 'tree' and 'negation' would be identified by the first term, '*vṛkṣa*,' and the particle *nañ* would only be coreferring to what has been established by the first term, or this negative term would simply be dangling, having no independent meaning of its own. It would then be merely delimiting, that it is not-tree (VP 2.245). Bhartṛhari thus reaches the conclusion that sentential meaning is indivisible and words do not have independent meaning.

Compounds with Negative Particles and the Metaphysics of Negation

An oft-cited passage identifies six different meanings of the negative particle:

> The negative particle has six different meanings: similarity with and contradiction to X, otherness and diminution, reproach and absence (*Śabdakalpadruma*, Vol II, p. 818).

Accordingly, the negative particle expresses the following meanings, depending upon the context:

1. Similarity: e.g. the term *anaśva* (non-horse) refers to an animal that is similar to but exclusive of a horse, such as a mule, donkey, or zebra.
2. Contradiction: e.g. the term *apuṇya* (non-virtue) refers to vice.
3. Otherness: e.g. *abrāhmaṇa* (non-Brahmin) refers to Kṣatriyas, etc.
4. Diminution: e.g. *anudarā* refers to a girl with a slim waist.
5. Impropriety or reproach: e.g. *apaśavaḥ* (non-animals) used to refer to the animals that are not to be sacrificed.
6. Absence: e.g. *abrāhmaṇo grāmaḥ* (a village without Brahmins) demonstrates the absence of Brahmins in a village.

Opinions vary about which meaning is primary. Kauṇḍa Bhaṭṭa maintains that only the final one, absence, is the primary meaning of the negative particle, the rest being secondary (Coward & Raja 1990, 288). According to Naiyāyikas, both contradiction and absence are the primary meanings of the negative particle. Patañjali's commentary on the *Aṣṭādhyāyī* (AA) 2.2.6 also raises issues relevant to understanding the meaning of negation in a compound term. A section in *Vṛttisamuddheśa* (VS 248–315) reads as a commentary upon Patañjali's MB (AA 2.2.6).[14]

Patañjali argues that the term *abrāhmaṇa* can be explained in three different ways, being dependent upon the primacy of the second term (or *brāhmaṇa*), an external term (someone else being referred to by this term), or the first term (the negative particle).[15] When reading Patañjali, it becomes clear that he considers the second term to be primary and he also defends the position that, in different contexts, even the negative particle can be primary. The position that an external term is primary has here been abandoned altogether. Bhartṛhari's treatment of negation in a compound (VS 248–315) primarily rests on these assumptions. We should not, however, conclude that all grammarians maintain the same position.[16]

The issue of which among the parts of a compound is primary in comprehending its meaning is broadly philosophical, and what has been addressed by classical philosophers about negation rests on their underlying metaphysics and epistemology. However we interpret negation, all the interpretations provided lead to the question of whether negation negates something that exists or whether it negates something nonexistent. In his attempt to resolve the apparent paradox, Bhartṛhari goes back to the absolute *vāc*, the reality-constituting-speech, and argues that even when negation is affirmed, the affirmation represents the foundation of all epistemic and ontological considerations. When we say, "There is no book on the table," the negation relates to the book that has no existence while the application of the term 'book' affirms its categorical existence. Negation can negate only things that exist, and at the time of negation, there is no existence: a paradoxical situation. It would, however, be too hasty to draw further parallels. Sanskrit grammarians escape the paradox by adding one level to existence: the superimposed existence (*upacārasattā*).[17] The existence of what has been negated, accordingly, is superimposed upon what is being negated. Rather than *nañ*, the negative particle that has its own reference, the negative particle becomes a coreference (*dyotaka*),[18] indicating that the term 'book' refers both to its existence and nonexistence, and the particle indicates negation that is linked with the term 'book.' This position relates to the earlier argument regarding the primacy of the terms if compounded with *nañ*, with an application that the negative particle does not have an independent meaning.

The tradition of the Sanskrit grammarians weighs the primacy of the second term in a compound with the negative particle.[19] The issue, however, is how can something that does not exist (e.g., a *brāhmaṇa* in the case of *abrāhmaṇa*) be primary? When even the primacy of the first or second term in the compound is called into question, the primacy of an external term is impossible. Unlike sentential negation, this negation cannot give meaning by corresponding to the verb either. When, for instance, we say, "There is an asymmetrical pattern on the wall," we cannot derive the meaning that there is the absence of a symmetrical pattern, but rather that there is existence of a pattern that is asymmetrical.

Bhartṛhari argues on this ground that this negation can only correspond to the subject and not to the verb (VS 251). This suggestion of the grammarians that the negative particle has only coreferentiality further distances them from the way Parmenides understood negation. Rather than accepting negation as a case of paradox, the approaches of the grammarians appear to resolve it by advancing different epistemic and ontic structures.

This position, however, does not satisfy Bhartṛhari, who instead invites further scrutiny. If *nañ* is just coreferential, the issue of it having three different positions with regard to the primacy of meaning in a compound would not even arise.[20] If the argument is that the action that is subordinate to the agent in a compound, such as *pācaka*, is what the negative particle corresponds to when in a compound, since there is not even a subordinate action expressed by the term *brāhmaṇa*, the negative particle in the compound *abrāhmaṇa* would not corefer to anything (VS and VSṬ 252). Helārāja (980 CE) concludes on this ground that in the case of compounds (and not in sentences), the particle has to be understood as referring directly to something.[21] What is directly negated then, when in a compound, is the existence of its referent (given that this existence is superimposed).

It has been postulated that being (*sat*) is given with every single term and what a term 'book' means, for instance, is 'a book exists.' Bhartṛhari presents a position that rejects this understanding and instead maintains that the term *nañ* does not express nonexistence (*asattā*) but only prohibits (*niṣedha*) what has been postulated by its referent. This position of the negative particle referring to prohibition, rather than negation, stems from the following reasoning:

1. Existence is embedded with all terms (as all terms refer to something that exists).
2. The term existence (*sattā*), if the above position is correct, then refers to the existence of existence (as existence is given to all terms including the term 'existence' itself).
3. The negation of existence (*asattā*), then, would mean the negation of the existence of existence, a tautology (VS 253).

In Sanskrit, one can make compounds where the suffix expresses repetition of action, and so the meaning of the suffix is similar to that conveyed by the verbal root. Verbs, it must be noted, convey process. However, negation can be linked only with what can be negated, and if the negative particle is to be understood as nonexistence, there would be no relation between it and the referent term. The conclusion, then, is that the negative particle, instead of meaning nonexistence, only means negation.[22] By relying on the above-mentioned argument that words directly refer to reality, Bhartṛhari escapes the tautology that the term 'existence' refers to the existence of existence.

The above argument, however, is not applicable in the case of *abrāhmaṇa*, where existence is part of the base term (*brāhmaṇa*) and what exists cannot be negated. This raises a bigger issue. One can make the same argument regarding the terms *asan* or *akṛtvā*, as they both refer to a positive nature (*bhāva*). This leads to the argument that the negative particle is merely coreferential rather than having its own primary meaning. Helārāja points out that there are two options, even when the particle is understood as coreferential:

(1) *nañ* is understood as revealing an object which is the substratum of a particular action.
(2) It is understood as revealing an object which is the substratum of objects in general (Iyer 1974, 240).

The problem is, if the first position is maintained, a compound with the negative particle would not be possible, as there would be no semantic connection. Even if some connection is maintained, the three possibilities of interpreting negation will not arise. In the second alternative, if the action in general coreferred to by *nañ* is linked with the second term expressing only the objects in general, this will lead to an infinite regression. It cannot be linked to the second term that is expressive only of a particular. If the particle is considered to be coreferring, it will be linked with the meaning that is coreferred (*dyotya*) to, and there will only be primacy of the second term. Either way, the possibility of three alternative meanings of negation will not arise in this case. Only when negation is considered as having its own independent meaning among the terms that have come in the compound word would it make sense to argue whether the negative particle or the second term is primary.

Relating to the previous conversation, whether *nañ* refers to nonexistence or negation, Bhartṛhari maintains that even when the meaning of the particle is maintained as nonexistence, there will be no consequence in examples such as *asan* or *akṛtvā*. Bhartṛhari argues:

> The negative particle relates to the generic substrate of the agency of action. Due to this, [the particle] is [also] linked with particular substrates such as *brāhmaṇa* [in the example *abrāhmaṇa*]. (VS 255)

When the negative particle is explained as referring to nonexistence, absence is explained in terms of its substrate. Since the particle is explained as referring to the substrate, existence in general, there will be no consequence in the example *asan*. Since the verb √*as* is intransitive, the instrument (*sādhana*) that accomplishes this action is the very agent itself. Accordingly, absence is explained in terms of its substrate (i.e., absence is the absence of something). The particle, then, is negation in general. The words that accompany the particle particularize negation. As Iyer summarizes, "In a compound, the negative particle is expressive of the substratum in general, colored by non-existence, of the action of existence. So the meaning of *nañ* amounts to *nāsti* = 'it does not exist'" (Iyer 1974, 241). Accordingly, in terms such as *abrāhmaṇa*, the negative particle expresses the nonexistence of the substrate in general and the term *brāhmaṇa* refers to a particular substrate.

From this emerges the crux of the problem: when two meanings are combined, which meaning is primary, the particle referring to the substratum in general, or the second term referring to the particular? The issue is this: if the particle is interpreted as prohibition, three possibilities (of the primacy of the second term in a compound, the primacy of the external term, and the primacy of negation or the particle itself) would not arise. When negation in general is linked with a particular entity, with negation referring to its substrate, or when the substratum is negated, this raises the issue of the primacy of the terms in a compound. That is, shall this be understood as $\sim(P)$, or $P(\sim)$, or $\sim P(Q)$, where Q stands for an external term?

It needs to be explained how the particle corefers in a sentence while directly referring to something in a word. Bhartṛhari adds that particles do not just negate; they also involve action. For instance, when one uses the term '*niṣkauśāmbiḥ*' (one who has exited out of Kauśāmbi), the prefix *niṣ* does not simply stand for negation but also for the act of exiting (VS 256). The particle here does not just denote nonexistence, but existence. If the particle here were to simply negate existence, it could not combine with the second term that refers to being. It is therefore reasonable to say that the compound term denotes the agent of the action of exiting from Kauśāmbi. This leads to the issue of which meaning is primary. It is commonly seen that when there are multiple qualifiers, it is upon the speaker to decide which among them is primary.[23] This makes the discussion of three alternative ways of describing negation relevant. We shall now turn to these three possibilities.

(1) The Primacy of the Final Term in a Compound

A significant section in VS (259–315) focuses on the primacy of meaning among terms when a term is combined with a negative particle.[24] In this discourse, Bhartṛhari first examines the case where there is a primacy of the final term. In the example "non-Brahmaṇa" (*abrāhmaṇa*), while the negative particle refers to nonexistence, the second term describes a positive entity. When primacy is given to the second term, this means 'someone in whom the quality of being a *brāhmaṇa* does not exist.' While the particle *nañ* refers to nonexistence in general, *brāhmaṇa* particularizes this nonbeing. Bhartṛhari compares this negation with any other qualifier. If we say, "a fair lady," the term 'fair' makes explicit what is implicit in the lady, and the term 'fair' does not invent something what is not in the lady.

One can argue that if the very existence of *brāhmaṇa* has been denied by the particle, why would someone utilize the positive term that also contains the meaning of existence? Bhartṛhari addresses this question by maintaining a distinction between language and reality. In language, we do use *san brāhmaṇa*, where existence that has already been affirmed by the term *brāhmaṇa*, is twice affirmed by the use of the qualifier *sat* (VS 261). Along these lines, the negative particle as a qualifier and that which is being negated are thus inherently related and inseparable. When we say, "a blue lily," there is no such thing as 'blue' that is distinct from the lily. In language or in conceptualization, however, this distinction is obvious. When a compound with a negative particle is used, Bhartṛhari argues, a mistaken identity is corrected (VS 262). When we say, for instance, "This dairy is non-organic," we are correcting a mistaken identity (or a presumed mistaken identity) that the dairy was organic.

A problem, however, still remains. In terms such as *abhāva*, nonexistence, what is comprehended by negation is not "some other entity similar to existence" (*bhāva*). Rather, a simple negation of existence is comprehended. In such instances, Bhartṛhari maintains that the meaning is comprehended by assuming a cognitive entity even in the absence of its external reference (VS 263). This explanation of negative compounds rests on "superimposed existence," rather than the real entity. In other words, every word, when pronounced, gives a mental presence of the entity, and negation denies the entity having a real reference. Here, Bhartṛhari deviates from Patañjali, who maintains that a word, *brāhmaṇa* for instance, refers to a constellation of properties, and by means of referring to the constellation of properties, it also stands for the particular properties.[25] Bhartṛhari does present this position (VS 264), albeit as an alternative to what he has presented before. The negative particle *nañ*, along these lines, reveals the absence of those properties, and accordingly, the term *abrāhmaṇa* describes the lack of the properties of a *brāhmaṇa* in someone other than the *brāhmaṇa* (VS 264). In other words, in the term *abrāhmaṇa*, the term *brāhmaṇa* stands for the partial qualities of a *brāhmaṇa*.

A question emerges: if the negative particle refers to the absence of properties in its substrate, how can it be connected with the term in making a compound? The question is, the part that has been negated is what has not even been described by the second term. When we say *abrāhmaṇa*, the *nañ* is negating the properties that do not exist in its referent, *kṣatriya* (a warrior) for instance. Bhartṛhari responds to this by saying that when something is half-accomplished, both terms are used to denote it, as accomplished and not accomplished (VS 265). What he means is, when we use the term '*abrāhmaṇa*,' it refers to someone who is neither a *brāhmaṇa* nor someone that entirely lacks the properties of a *brāhmaṇa*.

This response, however, invites further problems. Even the term *brāhmaṇa* would then refer to *abrāhmaṇa*, for there may be some expected properties lacking in any individual *brāhmaṇa*. Furthermore, there will be no distinction between the tasks that have been fully accomplished and those half-accomplished, if the term 'accomplished' is used in such a loose sense (VS 266). Bhartṛhari responds to this objection by showing how a term can be used in both a primary and secondary sense. *Brāhmaṇa*, for instance, is used to denote a person with a particular blood lineage, and to describe the person's tendency to ascetic practices and studies. There is a secondary use of the term to describe someone with a tendency of austerities and studies. Bhartṛhari says that the term *abrāhmaṇa* is used to negate the primary meaning in a subject who has some qualities of a *brāhmaṇa* (VS 267). This exposition is required particularly when the compound is interpreted with respect to the primacy of the second term. If the negative particle were to negate the meaning of the second term, the particle could not be considered an attribute, because it does not reject its substrate but only qualifies it. Along these lines, a negative particle only negates a part of the attributes among those expressed by the second term in a generic sense and thus the remaining attributes describe the referent (VS 268). When we use a term 'non-chemical' to refer to something, the entity being referred to does not have a total absence of chemical properties. Instead, it only lacks certain properties, such as toxicity.

Another problem arises. There may be a lack of one or another property in every *brāhmaṇa*. The above interpretation of the term *abrāhmaṇa* with a negative particle presumes that the term *brāhmaṇa* refers to one with all the properties assigned to a *brāhmaṇa*, and its negation will relate to someone with only some of such properties. In the absence of such *brāhmaṇas* that have all the assigned properties, this negative particle will be meaningless (VS 269–70). Bhartṛhari responds, when in a compound, the term loses its primary meaning and is used only in the secondary sense. As has been described earlier, Bhartṛhari maintains that both existence and nonexistence are embedded in the terminal meaning and the negative particle only underscores nonexistence that is intrinsic to the word meaning. He further explains that the same is found in other compounds, such as a 'king's officer,' where the qualifier stands for something that already exists in what is qualified (VS 271–2).

However, a problem still persists. How can a term be used to refer to something that has only partial properties?[26] Bhartṛhari responds to the objection by saying that a word in a compound cannot exclude both its primary meaning and the reference by the negative particle that is identified by the term (VS 277–8). Independent of external referents, words convey the meaning that is linked with their concepts, and negation, along these lines, limits the scope of meaning of the word only to the negative aspect (VS 279).

Bhartṛhari claims, following a similar argument, that the term *aneka* can also be explained where the second term means 'one,' and the compound stands for 'many.' If the second term were not primary, he argues, the term would not be declined similar to the term *eka*, and the formations such as *anekasmai* would not be possible (VS 281–3). Bhartṛhari explains that, just as *abrāhmaṇa* describes some qualities ascribed to a *brāhmaṇa*, oneness is superimposed in what is more than one (VS 284). This passage is an explicit reference that describes a superimposed concept on the primary meaning. What the negative particle represents in such instances, according to Bhartṛhari, is the removal of the error that has superimposed oneness onto something that is more than one. This negation, therefore, does not negate the word 'one' but rejects the erroneous cognition of oneness (VS 285). In his understanding, the negative particle in a compound *aneka* is similar to its use in a sentence: such as, "This is not one," where the term 'one' refers to other than one due to its association with 'not' (VS 286). Although the meaning of the term 'one' is not what is derived from 'not-one,' the second term is used only to reject what has been superimposed on a substrate that is not one. Just as the term 'non-white' refers to something that is of any color but white, so does the term '*aneka*' refer to something that is not singular (VS 287–8).

This conversation reinforces Bhartṛhari's underlying philosophy that terms directly refer to concepts rather than external entities. When one term is uttered, all possible meanings have the potential to manifest, and the negative particle restricts meaning, limiting it only to what has been meant. When one says "Seat them all," the first term, 'seat,' does not express the scope of the imperative. In the same way, *anekam āsaya* (seat no-one) restricts the scope of the injunction (VS 289). A mere negation of number cannot be the meaning of *aneka*, as the term is understood in the meaning of the number that is more than one. Accordingly, this cannot be interpreted as the nonimplicative (*prasajya*) type of negation (VS 290). Whether in a sentence or in a compound, this category of negation needs to be explained along these lines (VS 294). When one says, "I do not take sugar," he may still take a sugar substitute. If what is meant is a total rejection of all that is sweet, that is, a nonimplicative negation, the negation would be different from when a substitute is comprehended through negation, a case of implicative (*paryudāsa*) negation.

(2) The Primacy of the External Term

Having extensively addressed the argument that a compound with a negative particle places primacy in the second term, Bhartṛhari addresses the position that there can also be primacy in an external term in a compound with a negative particle (VS 296–315). Although it does have a certain logical appeal to it, this alternative seems to have been abandoned by Patañjali as well as by Bhartṛhari. The argument in favor of the primacy of the external term goes along these lines. The term *abrāhmaṇa* has been analyzed in earlier conversation by accepting that the second term in the compound denotes the superimposed meaning, rather than the meaning of the term itself. This is to say that the term *kṣatriya* (or one like it) is understood to be superimposed on the term *brāhmaṇa*, and when the terminal meaning is derived, there is still the primacy of the second term in a negative compound. However, if the negative particle is interpreted as a qualifier, with the second term being qualified by it, the meaning derived is something external. Accordingly, the term *abrāhmaṇa* would be interpreted as "someone who lacks the properties that qualify a *brāhmaṇa*." In this unique situation, although the negative particle in general denotes nonexistence, it denotes the same external object as does the second term that is positive in essence, and thus the negative particle and the positive term both have the same substrate, affirming the primacy of an external term.[27] In this regard, this compound functions similarly to a relative or adjectival compound.

If the view that words refer to a class and not particular entities is adopted, its negation relates to a particular entity external to both terms in the compound when the second term refers to the class (VS 302). When this position is followed, a clear distinction can be made between a compound with a negative particle and a relative compound. In Sanskrit, there are two ways a compound with the negative particle can be made:

(1) If the term is referring to someone who lacks cows, the compound will be *agu* (a case of the *bahuvrīhi*).
(2) If the term is referring to an animal that is not a cow, the compound will be *agau* (a case of the *tatpuruṣa*) (VS 303).

This is to show that the primacy of the external entity cannot be confused with that of the second term in compounds.

(3) The Primacy of the Negative Particle

Bhartṛhari eventually addresses the position that, in a compound, primacy belongs to the negative particle which is the first term. If this position is followed, the positive term, for instance *brāhmaṇa*, would qualify the negative particle, since the meaning would be derived with the primacy of negation (VS 305). An interlocutor raises the question: if negation is considered the terminal meaning, how can it be linked with action, the verbal meaning, as in the case of 'feed the non-*brāhmaṇa*'? Bhartṛhari replies, that what is considered as nonexistent also exists in another way. In other words, while negation is primary, the verb still relates to something existent, a case of implicative negation (VS 306).

Bhartṛhari points out that there should be no confusion over the issue of the primacy of negation in a compound, as the Sanskrit language offers two different types of compounds that explicitly highlight this difference.[28] Words have innate power, but unlike in a sentence where a negative particle can simply negate something, they denote what has been negated when applied in compounds, and thus what has been negated has primacy over the particle or negation as its meaning. Because of this, the compound terms follow the gender and number of the final term (VS 308). Furthermore, if they are not related to verbs, there would be no grammatical applicability of such terms, and sentences such as "bring a non-*brāhmin*" would have no meaning (VS 309).

The objection regarding the gender of the term, that the term should be indeclinable if the negative particle is primary, is also not tenable, as the gender, following Sanskrit grammar, is considered inherent to words themselves (VS 310). The genders of name-words, along these lines, are not necessarily congruent with the objects they identify, since gender in Sanskrit is grammatical and not natural. The term *dāra*, referring to wife, for example, is in the masculine. The term *kṣātra* has a neuter gender and possesses the same meaning as the term *kṣatriya* (warrior) in the masculine. Accordingly, the nonexistence that is expressed by the negative particle is comprehended in the form of some positive substrate, along with the gender and the number which correspond to the substrate (VS 312). Bhartṛhari concludes by maintaining that the terms that refer to two distinct entities refer to a single object in a compound, and since the negative prefix represents all the deviations from the second term, there is primacy of the first term (VS 313). The second term, *brāhmaṇa* in the aforementioned example, is only coreferring to what is meant.[29] Consequently, the second term expresses the particular from among what have been generically referred to by the first term.

Bhartṛhari assimilates the position that there is primacy of an external term within the perspective of the primacy of the first term, arguing that the primacy of negation also accommodates the arguments for the primacy of the external term (VS 314). Helārāja expounds on this by saying that the notion that the external term has primacy in negation arises due to error.[30] If the immediate term after a compound is a noun, the primacy of that noun is assumed due to association, and in cases where it is not, a pronoun is superimposed. In either case, the primacy of the external term does not stand a chance. The issue regarding gender and number is followed in this case with a meta-rule (*atideśa*) of negation according to which negation implies a superimposition of the properties of an associated term.

Bhartṛhari points out that the same problems regarding gender and number that forced one alternative to be dropped solidify the alternative that there is primacy in the first term. Following this argument, if the second term is not predominant, the number and gender of the compound cannot be regulated (VS 315). The argument is, in the absence of the compound term qualifying a second term, the term should be referring to something generic, and when there is no particular as a referent, the term should be used in neuter gender singular.[31] Helārāja explicitly concludes on this ground that the only supportable position to be maintained is that there is primacy in the second term.[32] He also rejects that gender and number are understood with superimposition. He gives an example in which both the cases of the external term being in neuter and masculine, the compound term remains in the masculine (VSṬ 315). This argument, however, does not counter the argument that gender and number are inherent with the term. On this ground, Helārāja, returning to the primacy of the first term, maintains that even this position should not be abandoned.[33] He also points out that Patañjali has supported this argument by refuting the objections against it.[34] This, then, allows the declination of the compound term with a pronoun.[35] Helārāja's final word on this matter is that the primacy of the first term is established.[36] Therefore, it would be wrong to countenance that there is only the primacy of the final term in the particular compound under consideration and not a primacy to negation.

Conclusion

This discussion of Sanskrit semantics has multiple philosophical implications. Bhartṛhari's treatment of negation as ultimately grounded on being, and his assertion that there is no absolute negation of speech, removes it from the paradox that underlies negating something. This speech, or *vāc*, of Bhartṛhari is not just a means of communication though. When speech is identified with the absolute, the Brahman, the consequence is that no negation of the foundational being is possible, a rejection of the Nāgārjunian approach.

Bhartṛhari's treatment of sentence negation and word negation further illuminate other issues. It has been discussed above that negation in a sentence relates to the verb and negation in compounds relate to the second word. The consequence is that word negations do not simply negate something. Bhartṛhari's logic rests on three-tiered negation:

$$\sim P = Q$$
$$\sim P = \sim$$
$$\sim = P'$$

(Where P' stands for something that is neither identical to P nor is absolutely different from it, in the sense that P' shares many of the constituents of P but not all.) While Bhartṛhari rejects the position that $\sim P = Q$, this is only in the context of the compound terms. His analysis of three-tiered negation (which stems from Patañjali's analysis) still has relevance in understanding negation in the issues outside of semantics.

The consequence of Bhartṛhari's conclusion is that $\sim P = P'$ leaves negation as affirming something existing. For the Advaitins, 'ignorance' (*avidyā*) is of the essential character of being (*bhāvarūpa*). This understanding of ignorance as something phenomenal (while not having its own intrinsic being) would be semantically impossible had not the philosophy of language allowed such interpretation. Along the same lines, the Svātantrika-Prāsaṅgika discourse on negation also stems from the semantic issue of whether the negative terms simply negate being or affirm something else. The discourse on language is therefore pivotal to understanding a wide range of philosophical issues that originated in classical India. Although I have restricted myself to the philosophy of Bhartṛhari, his answers to the issues regarding negation are relevant for a wider discourse not only on language but also epistemology.

Abbreviations

AA = Aṣṭādhyāyī
MB = Mahābhāṣya of Patañjali
MS = Mīmāṃsāsūtra
T = Tractatus Logico-Philosophicus
VP = Vākyapadīya
VPṬ = Vākyapadīyaṭīkā of Helārāja
VS = Vṛttisamuddeśa (Vākyapadīya 3.14)
VSM = Vaiyākaraṇasiddhāntamañjūṣā
VSṬ = Vṛttisamuddeśaṭīkā of Helārāja

Notes

1 I am thankful to Drs. JeeLoo Liu, Douglas Berger, Madhav Sharan Upadhyaya, Diwakar Acharya, David Buchta, and Boris Marjanovich for their valuable insights. I am equally thankful to Mrs. Mary Hicks for reading an earlier draft of this chapter.

2 See Timalsina (2009a and 2009b).

3 I am directly referring to Rorty (1992, particularly the Introduction pp. 1–39).

4 Patañjali's MB on AA 8.4.47. According to Kaiyaṭa, this reading is corrupt due to a copier's error. Even in his suggested reading, both terms of negation are present. Cf. AA 8.4.47.

5 Jaimini's terminology for threefold negation is *pratiṣedha*, *vikapa*, and *paryudāsa*. For a detailed analysis of negation in Mīmāṃsā, see MS 10.8.1–22. See Staal (1962, 52–71) for the Mīmāṃsā and Vyākaraṇa exegeses of negation. Staal (1962, 61) analyzes two types of *paryudāsa*: 1) "the door should be unlocked"; and 2) "another door should be locked," basically expanding upon the concept of *vikalpa* and *paryudāsa*. While *pratiṣedha* and *vikalpa* are spelled in MS 10.8.1, *itaraparyudāsa* is mentioned in MS 10.8.15. That Pāṇini does consider *vikalpa* as a type of negation is affirmed by '*na veti vibhāṣā*' AA 1.1.44.

6 While the particles *mā*/*māṅ* refer to negation, this imperative negation requires a much wider discussion that involves the ritual theory of Mīmāṃsā, and due to limitation of space, I am not addressing this aspect of negation in this paper. In English, besides 'not' and 'no,' the varied appearances of negation in compound words such as unimaginative, non-reliable, atheist, incomplete or dysfunctional can be included in Sanskrit *nañ*.

7 Cited in *Mīmāṃsānyāyaprakāśa* (262, Niṣedha section). For *prasajya* and *paryudāsa*, see also VP (2.84). A slight variant of this verse is cited by Staal (1962).

8 What underlies Bhartṛhari's argument is that all negation rests on something positive as its foundation. Nyāya philosophers argue that the absence of a jar, for instance, is located on the surface upon which the jar is negated. Advaita Vedantins argue that Brahman is the foundation upon which entities are affirmed or negated but which in itself cannot be negated. Bhartṛhari here appears to counter the Buddhist doctrine of emptiness, particularly the one grounded on Nāgārjunian arguments that rest on negation. Bhartṛhari's discussion of sentential negation also has a great relevance for the historical analysis of the Svātantrika and Prāsaṅgika arguments of negation.

9 When Pāṇini gives a rule that *prātipadika* is any meaningful word that is exclusive of the verb and the suffix (AA 1.2.45), implicative negation is implicit. In another rule (AA 8.4.47), Pāṇini states that all the consonants except for /*h*/ that are subsequent to a vowel can be optionally duplicated, and so both formations (e.g., *kḷpta* and *kḷppta*) are correct. However, this rule does not apply to those consonants if there is a vowel subsequent to it. This negation is nonimplicative, and in this case the sentence is divided into two when analyzing meaning.

10 The Sanskrit sentence is: *na kalañjaṃ bhakṣayet* | It is likely that *kalañja* meant the red garlic. For discussion, see Edgerton (1986, 164n213).

11 For a detailed treatment of this sentence in the context of negation, see Staal (1962, 59).

12 This argument, evident in the following verse cited by Puṇyarāja, resonates the position of Dharmakīrti:

satāṃ ca na niṣedho 'sti so 'satsu ca na vidyate| jagaty anena nyāyena nañarthaḥ pralayaṅgataḥ || *Pramāṇaviniścaya* 226.

Cited by Puṇyarāja in his commentary (VP 2.241).

13 VP 2.242.

14 Most of the philosophical issues raised by Bhartṛhari while addressing negation are seminally present in MB in AA 2.2.6. There is a stylistic difference in their presentation though. Patañjali first addresses the primacy of the second term, and with a brief objection, goes on to address the sides of the primacy of the external and the first terms. Bhartṛhari, on the other hand, addresses the central position, the primacy of the second term, and then addresses the positions of the primacy of external and first terms.

For a summary of this section, see Iyer (1992, 390–401). For this discussion, I have primarily relied on Helārāja's commentary for understanding the VP passage. I have also utilized Iyer (1974, 236–271) in summarizing the concepts.

15 See MB (AA 2.2.6) for discussion.
16 This is visible in Nāgeśa's statement. See Uddyota on MB (AA 2.2.6).
17 Helārāja uses the term in this particular context: (*upacārasattā* VP 3.14.250).
18 See VP 3.14 250cd.
19 Pāṇini reads *nañ* (AA 2.2.6) as an independent *sūtra* in the sequence of addressing *tatpuruṣa*, a type of compound where the second term is primary. Patañjali's elaboration upon the passage maintains the same position, demonstrating the primacy of the second term.
20 VP 3.14.250.
21 VP 3.14.252.
22 In the case of terms such as *akṛtvā*, the particle simply negates what is denoted by the verbal root, and so the relation between the negative particle and the referent term is established. Based on VS 254 and Helārāja's Ṭīkā thereon.
23 For discussion, see VS 257–258.
24 Bhartṛhari raises a wide range of issues, primarily inspired by the MB, with regard to the meaning of the negative particle in a compound. For the primacy of the final term in a compound with a negative particle, see VS 259–295; for the primacy of the external term, see *Saṃbandhasamuddeśa* 296–304; and for the primacy of the first term or the negative particle, see VS 305–315.
25 Mahābhāṣya on AA 2.2.6. This passage is read with 'hi' instead of 'ca' in VSṬ 264.
26 The situation is even worse with terms that are used in two opposite senses. For instance, the term *ārāt* is used to refer to both 'near' and 'far' (VS 273–5). Bhartṛhari clarifies his position by adding that, while the base words have a wide range of meanings, particles exclude certain aspects. In this sense, a negative particle only highlights what is already there in the term itself. He gives an example of the root √*sthā*, which has both the meanings of staying and going away, but the second meaning is manifest only when the term is combined with the prefix *pra* (as in *prasthāna*) (VS 276).
27 See Helārāja's exposition for illustration. VP 3.14.296.
28 Bhartṛhari addresses the problem with an acceptance of the above position as follows. When the negative particle is primary in a compound, the formation would be '*abrāhmaṇya*,' which is an indeclinable (*avyaya*), while a formations such as *abrāhmaṇāḥ* etc. would not be possible.
29 VSṬ 313.
30 VSṬ 314.
31 Although verse VS 315 comes in a sequence of arguments rejecting the position that there is primacy in the external term, in the discussion initiated in VS 314, Helāraja expands on this and also defends the position that there is a primacy of the first term. Helārāja provides several examples in the list where the gender of the qualifier does not match that of the qualified. See VSṬ 315.
32 VSṬ 315.
33 VSṬ 315.
34 VSṬ 315.
35 In consequence, formation of the terms such as *asarvasmai* remains possible.
36 *tasmād upapannaṃ pūrvapadārthaprādhānyadarśanam* | VSṬ 315. Noteworthy in this context is that Iyer (1974, 270–1; 1992, 399–40) considers that grammarians maintained only the position of the primacy of the final term. This understanding not only contradicts Helārāja and in contemporary times, the commentator Raghunātha Śarmā, this goes explicitly against Patañjali's defense of this position by maintaining that the gender and number of the terms are innate and not controlled by any external terms.

3 Madhyamaka, Nihilism, and the Emptiness of Emptiness

Jay L. Garfield

Introduction

Nāgārjuna (c. 200 CE) is the founder of the Madhyamaka school of Buddhist philosophy, and after the Buddha himself, easily the most influential philosopher in the Mahāyāna Buddhist tradition. Despite the great consensus on his philosophical and doctrinal importance, there is little consensus regarding the interpretation of Nāgārjuna's work, either in the canonical Buddhist and non-Buddhist literature of India, Tibet and East Asia, or in the contemporary secondary literature of European and Asian Buddhist Studies. In virtue of his distinctive doctrine that all phenomena are *empty* (*śūnya*), nothing exists ultimately (*paramārtha*), and that things only exists *conventionally* (*vyvavahāra/samvṛti*), he has often been accused of defending nihilism (see Matilal 2002 and Wood 1994). Indeed, he says in *Mūlamadhyamakakārikā (Fundamental Verses on the Middle Way)* and in *Vigrahavyāvartanī (Reply to Objections)* that he defends no thesis. This claim and his willingness to deny all four limbs of certain tetralemmas (*catuṣkoṭi*) add fuel to this fire.

In this chapter, I will argue that this nihilistic reading of Nāgārjuna is unjustified, and that Nāgārjuna is in fact a robust realist, offering an *analysis*, not a *refutation*, of existence. On his analysis, to exist is to exist conventionally, and ultimate existence is in fact an incoherent ontological fantasy. I focus on what many take to be the sharpest case for extreme nihilism, Nāgārjuna's negative *catuṣkoṭi*. The *catuṣkoti* (four corners or *kotis*), or tetralemma, is a standard figure in early Buddhist logic that portions logical space into four possibilities: truth, falsity, both truth and falsity, and neither truth nor falsity. It is deployed in both positive and negative forms. In the positive form, each of the four limbs is asserted; in the negative form, each is denied. The fact that Nāgārjuna sometimes deploys the negative *catuṣkoti* has been taken by his Indian and Western critics as evidence that he is an arch-nihilist. I will argue that this is far from the case, and that the negative *catuṣkoti* when properly understood in fact undermines, rather than provides evidence for, a nihilistic reading of Madhyamaka.

The Negative Tetralemma in Mūlamadhyamakakārikā XXII: 11

In the chapter of *Mūlamadhyamakakārikā* entitled *Examination of the Tathāgata*, Nāgārjuna asserts one of the more challenging and paradoxical of his famous tetralemmas:

> We do not assert "empty."
> We do not assert "nonempty."
> We neither assert both nor neither.
> They are asserted only for the purpose of designation. (Quoted in Tsongkhapa 2006, 447)

Tsongkhapa (fourteenth and fifteenth centuries CE), following Candrakīrti (sixth century CE) closely, comments as follows:

> We do not say that because the Tathāgata is *empty* he is *nonexistent*, because that would be to commit the error of deprecating him. Moreover, the Tathāgata has been shown to be essenceless. Because we aspire to present the undistorted meaning, nor do we say that he is *nonempty*—that is, that he exists *inherently*.
>
> We do not assert both of these; nor do we assert neither that he exists nor does not exist because *ultimately*, none of these four alternatives can be maintained. On the other hand, if we did *not* assert these *conventionally*, those to whom we speak would not understand us. So, from the standpoint of the conventional truth and for conventional purposes, we say "empty" and "non-empty," "both empty and non-empty," and "neither empty nor non-empty." We say these having mentally imputed them from the perspective of those people to whom we are speaking. Therefore, we simply say that "they are asserted for the purpose of designation." (Tsongkhapa 2006, 448)

This tetralemma might seem to be about as nihilistic as one can get, denying not only the possibility of asserting anything, but also the possibility of denying anything.[1] On the other hand, Candrakīrti and Tsongkhapa, in commentary, take some of the sting out of this reading by substituting a *positive* tetralemma in its place (that which we can say "from the standpoint of the conventional truth and for conventional purposes"), and distinguishing between two philosophical perspectives: an ultimate perspective and a conventional perspective.

In brief,[2] the conventional perspective is that of ordinary human consciousness, filtered through conceptual thought, language and our collective and individual modes of taking up with the world. The ultimate perspective is that of a fully awakened being—a buddha—from which all things appear as empty of any intrinsic identity or essence, as interdependent, and independent of their presentation by conceptual thought, or as described by social or linguistic conventions. While Candrakīrti and Tsongkhapa argue that we can't say anything at all from the ultimate perspective in virtue of its transcendence of the discursive, it is agreed that there is quite a bit that we can say from the conventional perspective. The fact that we can say so much, and that we can make so much sense of truth from the conventional perspective undermines a nihilistic reading of Nāgārjuna's project and of the negative tetralemma in particular. Understanding why Madhyamaka is a rejection, not an embrace, of nihilism requires us to attend to the two truths, as Candrakīrti and Tsongkhapa suggest, but also to much else, a great deal of which can be examined through the prism of this verse.

In what follows, I will show how Madhyamaka ideas about logic and about the nature of metaphysical dialectic allow us to unpack this tetralemma, to understand its relation to its positive shadow, and to thereby reveal a decidedly realistic attitude emerging from the rhetoric of emptiness. The analysis I offer here is not new, and owes much to Candrakīrti and Tsongkhapa.[3] But the refraction through the prism of this particular tetralemma and its commentary offers a new perspective, and may allow us to see how different colors in the Nāgārjunian spectrum combine to illuminate emptiness as an affirmation, not a denial, of the actuality of the world.

This essay is not intended to provide an introduction to Madhyamaka thought in general, or even to the thought of Nāgārjuna in particular. I will have to presuppose a basic familiarity with this landscape. The interested reader is directed to the more general presentations I cite in this paper. I do expect, however, that even for those readers to whom Madhyamaka is *terra incognita*, some of this will make sense. If so, I hope that it will provide a stimulus to venture further into the world of Indian and Tibetan Madhyamaka, a philosophical world that repays its visitors with rich insights.

Madhyamaka and Four Valuations

As noted above, in a Madhyamaka logical framework, sentences can be (just) true, (just) false, *both* true and false, or *neither* true nor false. Nāgārjuna's concern was not the semantics of conditionals, per se, but was closely related to the concerns that led to a four-valued semantics for relevant logics. In particular, Nāgārjuna was concerned with the possibilities of presuppositional failure, as well as the possibility of a deeply paradoxical reality and the need to reason in these logically challenging environments.[4]

We often see in Nāgārjuna's work the *catuṣkoṭi*, or four-corners, a partition of logical space with regard to a proposition into four possibilities: true, false, both or neither. Nāgārjuna's approach to the tetralemma is distinctive in that he does not always see these as four *alternatives*. We see instances in *Mūlamadhyamakakārikā* in which all four *koṭis* are affirmed (such as that in chapter XVIII, in which it is said that the self exists, does not exist, both does and does not exist, and neither exists nor does not exist), and instances in which they are all denied, as in the verse on which we focus here. In this case, as we have seen, while all are denied in the root verse, the commentary explains that joint denial through an implicit joint affirmation in a different register.

The joint denial indicates the perspective of ultimate truth, the standpoint from which all phenomena are apprehended as empty. From that perspective, Nāgārjuna argues, nothing at all can be said, since language itself implicates reification, the imputation of intrinsic identity to its putative referents. There are several ideas at work here, and to develop them all would take us far afield. But quickly: In chapter XXII, the context of the negative *catuṣkoti* under consideration, Nāgārjuna is concerned with the Tathāgata (an epithet used for the Buddha, literally meaning *thus-come* or *thus-gone*, depending on how the compound is parsed), and so with how the world appears from the perspective of full awakening. He is asking first what is *ultimately true*. The answer is, "nothing." When we assert anything, we implicate the reality of the referent of the subject term, and the qualification of the subject term by a property. But ultimately, nothing exists, and properties, from a nominalist Buddhist perspective, are all fictional. So, from the ultimate standpoint, every sentence we utter is misleading.

Furthermore, even to say that the Tathāgata is *neither empty nor non-empty* is ultimately impossible, since for him to be *ultimately neither empty nor non-empty* would be for the state of being neither empty nor non-empty to be his ultimate or intrinsic nature, and that would undercut Nāgārjuna's insistence that emptiness is the emptiness of *any* intrinsic nature. This is an important issue. Earlier in the text (XV: 7, 8), Nāgārjuna reminds us that emptiness is the relinquishing of all views, and that anyone for whom emptiness becomes a view is hopeless. In his careful gloss of this verse, Candrakīrti compares someone who takes emptiness to be the intrinsic nature of things to someone who, upon hearing that a shopkeeper has nothing to sell, asks for some of that nothing. On this reading, emptiness really is the lack of any intrinsic nature, or any nature that things have ultimately, not an ultimate nature to replace others.

On the other hand, as Candrakīrti and Tsongkhapa emphasize, from the conventional perspective, we can *assert* all four *koṭis*. We can say that the Tathāgata is empty—after all, he lacks any intrinsic nature; that he is non-empty—that is, emptiness is not his intrinsic nature; that he is both empty and non-empty—that is, he lacks intrinsic nature, but does not do so intrinsically; and that he is neither empty nor non-empty—neither intrinsically empty nor actually non-empty.

Note the use of parameterization at the conventional level, contrasting with the univocal nonassertability at the ultimate level. That is, at the conventional level, each of the four *koṭis* is asserted in a slightly different voice, with qualifiers such as "intrinsically" or "not intrinsically" implicitly qualifying the predicate *empty*. At the ultimate level, on the other hand, there is no such need for these insertions. Note also that at the conventional level the *catuṣkoṭi* does not involve us in paradox—the four assertions, suitably parameterized, are mutually consistent—while at the ultimate level the tetralemma takes us straight to paradox, since we are forced to say what we cannot say.[5] The elegance of Nāgārjuna's analysis consists in the demonstration that these tetralemmas in fact encode identical ideas and that the consistent conventional truth is identical with the paradoxical ultimate truth. This insight indeed is Nāgārjuna's most profound contribution to ontology, and explains why his analysis of reality as empty is realistic, not nihilistic.

The Importance of Identifying the Object of Negation

As I said above, the charge of nihilism is not a new indictment for Madhyamaka. It was leveled against Madhyamaka by classical orthodox Indian philosophers. Indeed, even Buddhist philosophers who subscribed either to the realistic and reductionist Śrāvakayana schools regarded Madhyamaka as nihilistic, as did the idealist Yogācāra. In each case, their critics accused Mādhyamikas of nihilistically denying the reality of obviously real entities (fundamental dharmas to which all of reality reduces, or consciousness, respectively) in virtue of the doctrine that all phenomena are empty. We will return to Nāgārjuna's own reply to this charge in *Mūlamadhyamakakārikā* below. But for now, it may be instructive to introduce Tsongkhapa's approach to rebutting this charge. Tsongkhapa was a major Tibetan commentator (fourteenth and fifteenth centuries) on Nāgārjuna and Candrakīrti whose interpretation of Madhyamaka is developed in several of his important treatises, including *Great Exposition of the Path to Enlightenment* (2000), *Ocean of Reasoning* (2006) and *Elucidation of the Purport of Madhyamaka* (not available in a Western language, see Tsongkhapa 2009).[6]

"Emptiness," Tsongkhapa emphasizes, requires a parameter. We must specify that of which an empty thing is empty. For example, the room in which I write is indeed empty of elephants, but it is not empty of people. When I leave, the room will be empty of people, but not of furniture, and so on. If I were to remove all of the furniture, it would still not be empty of air. To assert simply that something is empty is hence not to assert anything at all. We must add what Tsongkhapa calls "a qualifying phrase" in order to complete the assertion. He emphasizes that emptiness is a negation, indicating the absence of something—and the kind of negation relevant to emptiness in the Mādhyamika's sense is an external, or nonimplicative, negation, not projecting an alternative property or entity of which the empty thing is full.[7] In order to understand the claim that something is empty in Nāgārjuna's sense, we must identify what Tsongkhapa calls "the object of negation (*dgag bya*)" or the property that is denied to inhere in the subject in question. The opponent who regards Madhyamaka as nihilistic, Tsongkhapa argues, misidentifies the relevant object of negation as *mere existence*. If this were the object of negation, then to say that all phenomena are empty would be to say that all phenomena lack even mere existence, and that would of course to say that everything is nonexistent, a nihilistic position if ever there was one. But, Tsongkhapa argues, this is a misreading of Nāgārjuna and his followers. The correct object of negation, he urges, is not *mere existence*, but rather *intrinsic existence*.

The Sanskrit word here is *svabhāva*, and translation into English is a notorious can of worms. I have often used *essence* to capture its meaning, but that is not ideal. Others have used *substance*, *substantial existence*, *self-nature*, *self-being*, *own-being*, *essential existence*, and so forth. A widely accepted translation now is *intrinsic nature*. But no English expression captures the Sanskrit perfectly. The idea is this: to have *svabhāva* is to exist independently, to have a property (a *svabhāva*) that makes the thing the thing it is, to be capable of existing as that thing independently of anything else. Tsongkhapa argues that the primal confusion that Buddhists regard as conditioning attraction and aversion—and hence as the very root of the existential suffering Buddhism aims to eradicate—consists principally in the projection of this kind of existence onto entities. The mistaken attitude includes the attribution of this kind of existence to our selves and to all objects of our experience, as well as to any fundamental constituents in which we might believe that these entities consist. Emptiness as articulated by Nāgārjuna, Tsongkhapa argues, is the absence of *this* kind of intrinsic existence.

To be empty of intrinsic identity, according to Candrakīrti and Tsongkhapa, is hence not to be nonexistent, but rather to exist interdependently, relationally, nonessentially, conventionally. To assert that things are empty, then, is not to assert that they are nonexistent, but to assert that nothing has any essence, any intrinsic identity or reality, that to see the world in terms of substantially existent phenomena is a fundamental metaphysical error. This insight in turn grounds Nāgārjuna's doctrine of the two truths or two realities—conventional and ultimate truth/reality.[8]

Conventionally, there are people, dogs, tables, and chairs, and each of these things has countless properties, prosaic and profound. These things exist dependently upon one another, on other entities, and on their constitutive parts. Their status as entities as well as their properties further depend upon our cognitive and sensory apparatus and social, cognitive, and linguistic conventions. Since they are dependent, these things and properties do not exist ultimately. To exist conventionally is hence precisely to be empty of ultimate reality. The ultimate truth is that everything is empty; that nothing is ultimately real, not even emptiness. Emptiness too, is only conventionally real; it is only the emptiness of empty things. If emptiness were more real than that, then conventional reality would indeed be a less than full reality, since it would be a second-grade existence contrasting with a possible first-grade existence. But with no such contrast, conventional existence is the only kind of existence that is possible.

Mūlamadhyamakakārikā XXIV: 18–19

Before returning to the tetralemma with which we began, it is instructive to examine two other well-known verses of *Mūlamadhyamakakārikā*, verses that many take to be the very heart of the text, and indeed the heart of Madhyamaka philosophy itself. The eighteenth and nineteenth verses of chapter XXIV, the investigation of the four ennobling truths, appear as the climax of a response to an interlocutor anticipated in the opening verses of the chapter.

This interlocutor is clearly a Śrāvakayana Buddhist, who Nāgārjuna imagines charging him with nihilism. In verse one, we hear the opponent complaining:

> If all this is empty,
> There would be neither arising nor ceasing.
> And for you, it follows that
> The four noble truths do not exist. (Quoted in Tsongkhapa 2006, 472)

After a cascade of *reductio* consequences, the opponent concludes at verse six:

> Hence you undermine the fruits
> As well as the profane:
> The Dharma itself
> And all mundane conventions. (Quoted in Tsongkhapa 2006, 476)

The opponent's position here is clear. Madhyamaka is nihilism, and Nāgārjuna's philosophical position is not merely inconsistent with Buddhist doctrine; it flies in the face of ordinary reason, making a hash of everyday life and common sense. It is in the context of this charge that we encounter verses eighteen and nineteen:

> That which is dependent origination
> Is explained to be emptiness.
> That, being a dependent designation
> Is itself the middle way.
>
> There does not exist anything
> That is not dependently arisen.
> Therefore there does not exist anything
> That is not empty. (Quoted in Tsongkhapa 2006, 503, 505)

These verses repay careful reading and contemplation. In the first, Nāgārjuna identifies dependent origination and emptiness, and by implication, conventional and ultimate truth. He then asserts that this identification is itself merely conventional, and hence empty, and that it, and its emptiness, constitute the middle path between reification and nihilism he is at pains to limn. Let us consider each point in turn.

First, to be dependently originated—to exist in dependence on causes and conditions, in relation to other things, and to have an identity dependent on conceptual designation—is what it is to be empty. Note that to exist dependently is *not* to be nonexistent; instead, for a Mādhyamika, it is the only way to be *real*. When we consider things carefully, Nāgārjuna suggests, that is how everything exists. Emptiness, then, is *not* nonexistence.

Second, even though emptiness is the ultimate reality of things, it is no *more* real than any conventionally real thing. Emptiness is a dependent designation—merely a verbal formula; dependent origination is merely a dependent designation, and even the fact of the identity of emptiness and dependent origination is merely a dependent designation, a way of taking things. Hence, all are empty of intrinsic identity. Emptiness is only the emptiness of empty things, not a self-subsistent universal. It, too, is therefore merely conventionally real. The conventional reality of things is their emptiness, and hence their ultimate reality. And so, the two truths—conventional and ultimate, the world of dependent arising and the emptiness that is ultimate reality—are identical.

The identification of the two truths, Nāgārjuna asserts, is the *middle way*. To take emptiness to be distinct from dependent origination or to take emptiness to be ultimately real while taking everything else to be merely conventionally real, would be, as Tsongkhapa felicitously puts it, to fall into both extremes simultaneously. Emptiness would be reified as an ultimately existent phenomenon, and conventional reality would be deprecated as a second-class existence, as illusion. We would then be stuck with an inaccessible real world and an illusory world we are condemned to inhabit. Only by understanding the real world as empty of intrinsic reality, by understanding the emptiness of intrinsic reality to be interdependence, and so by understanding reality to be causally and conventionally interdependent, can we take reality, ourselves, and our analysis of being itself seriously. Emptiness is not on this view an *alternative to* existence, but an *analysis of* existence. This is the true spirit of the middle way.

Two Ways to Read the Negative Tetralemma and Its Positive Counterpart

So, let us return to the tetralemma with which we began and consider two ways of reading it in the context of this understanding of emptiness. Let us recall the tetralemma.

> We do not assert "empty."
> We do not assert "nonempty."
> We neither assert both nor neither.
> They are asserted only for the purpose of designation.

There are two ways to read the verse and its positive image, and each is illuminating. First, we can think of the verse itself straightforwardly in terms of presupposition failure. On this reading, when Nāgārjuna recuses himself from each of the four *koṭis* of the *catuṣkoṭi*, he does so to indicate that he is speaking from the ultimate perspective (or at least attempting to do so, indicating the impossibility of *actually* doing so). As we noted at the outset, since all language is conventional, and since it can only designate what exists conventionally, any assertion can at best be conventionally true. The last line affirms this. Conventionally, we can say any of these things; ultimately, we can say none, because the presuppositions of assertion—the reality of referents and the possibility of instantiating properties—are not satisfied from that perspective. This is the reading with which we began.

But there is a second, slightly deeper, way to take this tetralemma and the positive shadow to which Candrakīrti and Tsongkhapa direct our attention. I have argued that this is the reading that takes us closer to the heart of Madhyamaka and dispels once and for all any nihilistic reading. This reading illuminates the deep paradox Nāgārjuna finds at the heart of reality. When Nāgārjuna says "we do not assert 'empty'," he indicates that to say that phenomena are empty is fundamentally contradictory: it is to say that they have no intrinsic nature at all, but since to exist is to be empty, nothing can exist without being empty, and so emptiness *is* the intrinsic nature of anything that exists; hence the intrinsic nature of things is to lack intrinsic nature (see Garfield and Priest 2003). However, Nāgārjuna does not assert "non-empty" either. To do so would also be contradictory. It would be to assert that things have intrinsic nature, which, for a Mādhyamika, is incoherent. Each of the first two *koṭis* is thus, in some sense, nonassertible, or at least, not *consistently* assertible.

To assert *both* is a plain contradiction, as is to assert neither, since they are mutually exclusive and exhaustive. So, on this reading, the negative tetralemma indicates the fact that ultimate reality is deeply paradoxical. To say anything about it, to maintain any of the four alternative positions, lands us in a paradox. Silence would then appear to be the only way to maintain consistency. But even silence can only achieve consistency if it is *articulate* silence—the silence of Vimalakīrti, who replies to Mañjuśrī's request to explain nonduality, despite the fact that that all language is dualistic by remaining silent. It is not the silence of Śāriputra, who earlier in the *Vimalakīrti-nirdeśa-sūtra* replies to the goddess's request to explain a difficult philosophical point by remaining silent and citing inexpressibility as an excuse. But even Vimalakīrti's silence, if it is articulate at all, lands us in a paradox. For it says both that nothing can be said, and *that*. Silence, that is, if it is to be articulate, is a kind of speech; and when taken as speech, it lands us back in the paradox it seeks to avoid.

On the other hand, the fourth line still indicates the positive shadow tetralemma. *Conventionally* we do assert all four of these, and each, from a conventional standpoint, is entirely unproblematic. That positive version might *appear* to be the contradictory tetralemma; after all, its first two *kotis* are the negations of one another, and the third and fourth are explicit contradictions. But, in virtue of its straightforward parameterization, it is in fact consistent. Conventionally, we can certainly assert that all phenomena are empty—after all, they are dependently arisen; we can assert that all phenomena are not empty (ultimately), both conventionally empty and ultimately non-empty, and neither ultimately empty nor ultimately non-empty. Conventional reality, the only reality we inhabit, is the domain of speech and of all truth.

But as the fourth line of the root verse indicates, and as XXIV: 18, 19 explain, the assertible positive tetralemma is just the other side of the nonassertability of any limb of the negative tetralemma. It is because emptiness is dependent origination—because the ultimate truth and the conventional truth are in the end identical—that it is true conventionally that all things are empty, that it is true that their emptiness is the ultimate truth; and that ultimately that cannot be true, simply because *nothing* is ultimately true.

It is because we can say nothing from the ultimate standpoint that the conventional is the only standpoint we have. The conventional is thus the only framework within which truth is possible, including this truth. It is for this reason that we need all four possibilities represented in the *catuṣkoṭi*. We need to be able to talk about getting it right, getting it wrong, speaking when only contradictions can reveal the truth, and when all speech fails. The *catuṣkoṭi* is therefore not a mere rhetorical flourish in Nāgārjuna's hands; it is a reflection of the structure of emptiness and its relationship to reality. It is the only logic adequate to a Madhyamaka metaphysics, the only logic that can express that metaphysics in a way that reveals both its paradoxical character and its thoroughgoing realism.

Conclusion: Conventional Existence is Real Existence

The negative tetralemma is taken by most critics of Madhyamaka as the most decisive evidence for that reading. After all, it does seem to say explicitly that nothing whatever is true. We have seen not only that it provides no evidence for that reading, but that when unpacked, the negative tetralemma is in fact a profound logical and rhetorical device for exploring the positive ontological significance of the Madhyamaka doctrine that all phenomena are empty of intrinsic nature.

In reading the tetralemma this way, we have also seen that the negative tetralemma is equivalent to the positive tetralemma it projects. Everything that is unsayable from the ultimate perspective is assertible from the conventional perspective, and not accidentally so. It is emptiness that makes sense of conventional reality, and conventional reality that explains emptiness. A proper understanding of emptiness thus entails the identity of the two truths. But if that is so, to take the emptiness of all phenomena seriously is to take the conventional reality of all phenomena seriously. And to take reality seriously is precisely to deny nihilism. From the standpoint of Madhyamaka, to be empty is hence not to be nonexistent, but rather is the only possible way to exist.

Notes

1 Nāgārjuna certainly has been read that way, both by his classical Indian interlocutors, especially the Nayāyikas, and by such contemporary commentators as B. K. Matilal (2002) and Thomas Wood (1994).

2 See Cowherds (2010); Garfield (1995, 2001); Newland (2011); and Westerhoff (2010) for more detail.

3 I have also defended much of this both on my own in numerous essays, and with the Cowherds in our recent polygraph *Moonshadows* (Cowherds 2010).

4 As Richard Routley noted a few decades ago (Meyer and Routley 1972, 1973; Plumwood and Routley 1982), Nāgārjuna scooped Meyer and Dunn (1972) by a few millennia in proposing a four-valued approach to logic (or at least a four-way valuational approach, as the set of truth *values* remains binary—only the assignment function goes quarternary. A similar approach, and similar concerns, of course, motivates the Meyer-Dunn semantics for Relevant Logic, and the gappy and glutty worlds it requires.

5 See Garfield and Priest (2003) for more on these paradoxes.
6 The Cowherds (2010) develop this idea in detail in *Moonshadows*, but we can sketch the important points here in short compass.
7 Indian logic recognizes two kinds of negation, external, or nonimplicative negation, and internal, or implicative negation. The former is a sentential negation, and the latter a predicate negation. When I say, for instance that I have no brown horse (external) I do not implicate that I have a horse of a different color; when I say that my horse is not brown (internal) I do.
8 The Sanskrit *satya* denotes either truth or reality, and different readings may be appropriate in different contexts.

4 In Search of the Semantics of Emptiness

Koji Tanaka

Emptiness

In one of his key texts, *Mūlamadhyamakakārikā* (MMK), Nāgārjuna famously expounds the thesis of *emptiness*.[1] This thesis is the core of the Madhyamaka ('Middle-Way') school of Buddhist philosophy, and the MMK is considered to be a foundational text for the Mādhyamikas.[2] The thesis can easily be stated: anything which exists is empty of *svabhāva*. (I will leave the Sanskrit term '*svabhāva*' untranslated for now.) What the thesis means is a hotly debated question by traditional and modern commentators. One thing that is clear from the discussion of Garfield in his contribution to this volume (Chapter 3) is that Nāgārjuna was not a nihilist. That is, the thesis of emptiness does not mean that nothing exists. Emptiness in Nāgārjuna's sense is not the lack of everything, or nothing.

In order to work out what it does mean, we first need to examine the notion of *svabhāva*. Westerhoff (2009, § 2.1) has usefully identified three senses of *svabhāva* that Nāgārjuna employs in his argumentation (at least according to the sixth-to-seventh century commentator Candrakīrti, whose interpretations were in the margins in India but became very influential in Tibet). First, '*svabhāva*' is sometimes used to mean *essential property*. An essential property is what gives an object its numerical identity. It is something that an object cannot lose without becoming something else. For example, if heat is an essential property of fire, something is a fire so long as it possesses heat. In other words, it is heat as an essential property that makes it a fire. If heat were removed from a particular fire, that fire would be extinguished. Second, '*svabhāva*' is sometimes used to mean *independence*. In this sense, to have *svabhāva* is to exist independently of everything else. This means that an object with *svabhāva* can exist in a possible world that is otherwise unpopulated by any other things, since the existence of an object with *svabhāva* does not depend on the existence of anything else. To say that an object exists independently of everything else is not just to say that it is the sole occupant of an otherwise empty world, but also to say that it is not composed of anything. If the object with *svabhāva* has a mereological relation (part-whole relation) to its parts, then it exists in a way that depends on those parts. *Svabhāva* in the sense of independence also implies that the object is not constituted by things that are more basic or simple.

So, an object with *svabhāva* is unconstructed, not causally based on anything else and not mereologically based on its parts.

If an object with *svabhāva* exists independently of everything else, any successful analysis of it can't be done in terms of anything else because *svabhāva* gives an object an independent existence. Furthermore, it can't be analyzed away by positing more basic entities since it has no parts and therefore can't be decomposed any further. Thus, *svabhāva* is what we are left with when an analysis of a thing reaches its limit. *Svabhāva* is what we aim to identify as the end point of a thorough analysis and it must not disappear during the process of analysis. The third sense of *svabhāva* is then that it *withstands any (logical) analysis*.

Strictly speaking, Nāgārjuna mostly employs the second sense of *svabhāva*, and we hardly see him using its other senses (Westerhoff 2009, § 2.1). It should be noted in this context that the Ābhidharmikas, against whom Nāgārjuna's argument is partly directed, argue for a different view of *svabhāva*. In the Abhidharma literature, which contains an early exploration of Buddhist philosophy based on the teachings of the Buddha, we see arguments to the effect that it is only parts which are real and the whole is unreal. Using the example of the chariot from the popular text *Milindapañha* (*The Questions of King Milinda*),[3] the relevant ontological view can be presented such that when certain "parts" (a pole, an axle, wheels, the body, the flagstaff, a yoke, reins, and a goad) are put together, there is nothing other than the parts themselves. When there is a collection of parts, that is all there is. There is no entity that is distinct from or even identical with a collection of the parts other than the collection itself. To think otherwise is to think that there is a collection of parts and, in addition, a chariot. Such a view, according to the Ābhidharmikas, is incoherent. In his influential *Abhidharmakośa*, considered a compendium of Abhidharma literature, Vasubandhu presents this Abhidharma view in terms of particulars which we perceive and universals which we conceive. Putting aside the epistemological dimension of his presentation, Vasubandhu elucidates several mereological arguments for the view that only particulars are real and universals are unreal. According to Abhidharma ontology, there are no universals of which the particulars are instances or which supervene on the particulars.[4] When this mereological analysis is applied to the parts themselves, the resulting view is that it is only the simple, partless entities (the ultimate 'parts') that really exist. It is these ultimate simple entities that are considered to have *svabhāva*. But for most Ābhidharmikas, these ultimate simple entities are considered to be causally efficacious. An object with *svabhāva* arises from other objects with *svabhāva* based on causation. So *svabhāva* is, for their theory, dependent on causes. This shows that, for the Ābhidharmikas, *svabhāva* does not have an independent existence. Nāgārjuna is thus arguing against the notion of *svabhāva* that can be found in the Abhidharma literature.[5]

In any case, if *svabhāva* has the three characteristics described above, then Nāgārjuna's thesis of emptiness can be restated as follows:

> Anything which exists is empty of any essential property that is independent of anything else and that withstands any (logical) analysis.

In the MMK, Nāgārjuna presents several arguments for this thesis. His arguments proceed by showing that we can't identify the essential and independent nature of anything that exists by means of a thorough (logical) analysis.

After presenting his arguments for the thesis, in Chapter XXIV of the MMK, often considered to be the most important chapter of the text, Nāgārjuna turns his attention to explaining how to understand his thesis of emptiness. He does so by invoking ultimate and conventional realities. If we understand the essential property that is independent of everything and that withstands analyses to give the status of ultimate existence to an object, then the thesis of emptiness implies that nothing ultimately exists. This means that nothing can be subjected to an ultimate analysis that establishes its independent and essential properties. No analysis can show the ultimate existence of anything.

What does exist is explained by Nāgārjuna in terms of conventional existence. What exactly this means is a hard question to answer. However we try to answer it, we must not forget that emptiness is not just an ontological thesis revealing what exists, but also a semantic thesis. The word Nāgārjuna uses to introduce two 'realities' as an explanation of emptiness is '*satya*'. In MMK XXIV.8, Nāgārjuna writes:

> The various buddhas' teaching of the Dharma [buddhas' teaching] relies upon two *satye* [dual form of *satya*]: the conventional truth of the world and what is true from the ultimate perspective. (Translated in Cowherds 2011, ch. 3)

The word '*satya*' can mean 'real' or 'existence'. It can thus be used as an ontological category. But it can also mean 'truth'.[6] Despite the fact that semantics (or language) receives very little attention from Nāgārjuna, we must examine the semantic aspect of emptiness in terms of two *truths*. As I will show, it is the semantics behind the two truths that is crucial to understanding emptiness.

The Two Truths

The notion of the two truths did not originate with Nāgārjuna. We can find the two truths doctrine in Abhidharma literature. According to the Ābhidharmikas, only simple, partless entities exist and everything else, such as chariots, doesn't exist. Given that simple, partless entities are real, we can talk about them truthfully. Moreover, since those entities are the ultimate reality, a statement about them is ultimately true when it describes them accurately.[7] So, for the Ābhidharmikas, there are statements which can be said to be *ultimately* true.

When we analyze ultimate truth in this way, we are presupposing that there are things that are referenced by the statement. A statement is ultimately true so long as it corresponds to the ultimate way in which the referents exist. A helpful way to understand the semantic principle underlying ultimate truth is to think of it as Russellian (as opposed to Fregean). Early in his career, Russell argued that true propositions (expressed by sentences) were facts, and facts were constituted by objects standing in certain relations to one another. Russell (1904) says thus:

> People imagine that if *A* exists, *A* is a fact; but really the fact is '*A*'s existence' or 'that *A* exists'. Things of this sort, *i.e.* 'that *A* exists' . . . I call *propositions*, and it is things of this sort that are called *facts* when they happen to be true. (492)

If this were not the case, we would not know anything (objective) about objects. As Russell (1904) writes in response to Frege:

> I believe that in spite of all its snowfields Mont Blanc itself is a component part of what is actually asserted in the proposition 'Mont Blanc is more than 4,000 metres high'. We do not assert the thought, for this is a private psychological matter: we assert the object of the thought, and this is, to my mind, a certain complex (an objective proposition, one might say) in which Mont Blanc is itself a component part. If we do not admit this, then we get the conclusion that we know nothing at all about Mont Blanc. (169)

Despite the fact that Russell presents his view in an epistemological context, it is not only knowledge about the world but also (true) propositions that get this Russellian treatment. Thus, Russell treats truth purely extensionally. That is, for Russell, truth is only a matter of reference. A consideration of truth is thus a consideration of what exists.

We can similarly understand the nature of the Abhidharma semantic principle behind ultimate truth. Russell can be seen as collapsing the distinction between existence and truth. The word '*satya*' itself does not make such a distinction. An ultimate truth is thus just what ultimately exists. For the Ābhidharmikas, what ultimately exist are simple, partless entities and nothing else. An ultimate truth is just the (ultimate) way in which these simple, partless entities exist.

In Abhidharma literature, the same semantic principle underlies conventional truths. At least, there is no evidence to suggest that conventional truths are based on a different semantic principle. If an ultimate truth is concerned with what ultimately exists, then a conventional truth is concerned with what conventionally exists. But what are the things that conventionally exist? A chariot can be analyzed further into its parts. So, from an Ābhidharmika's point of view, a chariot is constructed out of simple, partless entities. But the chariot is unreal, it does not really exist because only its parts really exist. A chariot is thus a "fictional" object. It is just a figment of our imagination. Hence, the statement "a chariot is in the backyard" can't be an ultimate truth even if its parts can be said to ultimately exist. Nonetheless, uniformity demands that conventional truths are given the same semantic treatment as ultimate truths. Moreover, the Ābhidharmikas do not present a different semantic principle to deal with conventional truths. So, it would seem to follow that a conventional truth is concerned with a conventional reality where chariots and everything else can be said to exist albeit only conventionally.

The semantics Ābhidharmikas adopted were the orthodox account in Indian philosophical circles around the time of Nāgārjuna.[8] While arguing against the ontology of Abhidharma, Nāgārjuna does not seem to introduce a new semantic principle. In the context of arguing against the notion of *svabhāva*, one might say that his semantics is also Russellian. Nāgārjuna does not invoke anything like a Fregean sense that mediates between the truth-bearer and its referent. He, like the Ābhidharmikas, appears to assume a reference-based semantic principle. That is, Nāgārjuna seems to account for the truth of a sentence in terms of reference.

Even though Nāgārjuna's semantics can be seen to be continuous with previous philosophical developments, it poses some difficulties for understanding his thesis of emptiness. The main difficulty is that ultimate reality is empty for Nāgārjuna. Nothing exists with *svabhāva* according to his thesis of emptiness. Given that it is *svabhāva* that bestows ultimate existence, this means that nothing ultimately exists. But if nothing ultimately exists, then there can't be ultimate truth either, per the semantic principle that Nāgārjuna inherits from the Abhidharma literature. According to Abhidharma semantics, a statement is ultimately true if it corresponds to the ultimate way in which things exist. For Nāgārjuna, however, there is no ultimate way in which things exist and, hence, there is nothing to which a statement can correspond. Hence his semantics, together with his ontology, deliver no ultimate truths; that *there are no ultimate truths* can't be an ultimate truth either, since there is nothing to which it can correspond.

The trouble is that it is now unclear what the truth-value of Nāgārjuna's statements is. Do his statements express ultimate truths or conventional truths? If they express only conventional truths, the Ābhidharmika can reject them because, for them, conventional truths are about fictional entities. If they express ultimate truths, however, his statements are contradictory because Nāgārjuna must also subscribe to the existence of ultimate truths, which is impossible given everything else he says about the emptiness of ultimate truth. How then are we to understand his statements?

Semantic and Ontological Paradox

It was the contemporary commentators Garfield and Priest (2003) who thematized the paradoxical nature of Nāgārjuna's thesis of emptiness. After showing that there are no ultimate truths for Nāgārjuna, Garfield and Priest point to a paradox of expressibility. Since there are no ultimate truths, an ultimate truth can't be expressed. Yet, it *is* expressed by Nāgārjuna. For example in MMK XXIV.19, he writes:

> Something that is not dependently arisen
> Such a thing does not exist.
> Therefore a non-empty thing
> Does not exist. (Quoted in Garfield and Priest 2003, 11)

According to Garfield and Priest, this passage is concerned with ultimate reality, and Nāgārjuna is asserting an ultimate truth. If this is right, then Nāgārjuna is squarely in the realm of paradox.

As Garfield and Priest argue, the paradox Nāgārjuna presents us with is not only about expressibility but also about ontology. To see this, we must remember that Nāgārjuna adopts a reference-based semantics. Under this semantics, to think of his thesis as an ultimate truth is to think that there are things which ultimately exist. But that is exactly what Nāgārjuna sets out to refute. According to Nāgārjuna's ontology, ultimate reality is empty in the sense that there is no ultimate way in which things exist. So the paradox of expressibility permeates through his ontology by means of his semantics. For Nāgārjuna, ultimate reality is and is not empty, according to Garfield and Priest.

Traditional commentators did not embrace the paradoxes and the contradictions that they entail. The traditional Mādhyamika (and Buddhist) attitude toward contradictions is clear: just reject them. In fact, Nāgārjuna seems to be aware of the contradictory implication of his statements and tries to defuse it. In the *Vigrahavyāvaryanī* (VV), he says:

> If I had some thesis the defect would as a consequence attach to me. But I have no thesis, so this defect is not applicable to me. (Quoted in Westerhoff 2009, 183)

As Westerhoff explains, Nāgārjuna makes this dramatic statement in response to his opponent (real or imagined) who accuses him of being committed to contradictions or ineffectualness. According to the opponent, if his statements are not empty, they contradict his thesis of emptiness; but if his statements are empty, they are ineffectual for refuting the opponent's view. Nāgārjuna does not consider accepting the first horn of the dilemma. Instead, he accepts the second horn of the dilemma and holds that his statements are empty. He nevertheless rejects the consequent that his statements are ineffectual. In order to do this, Nāgārjuna claims that his opponent's statements are empty too. He then considers the opponent's complaint that the alleged ineffectualness of the opponent's statement is due to Nāgārjuna's thesis of emptiness. In response to this, Nāgārjuna claims that he has no thesis of his own (Westerhoff 2009, § 9.2).

It is important to note for our purpose that Nāgārjuna's opponent presupposes a reference-based semantics and assumes that the norms embodied in statements come from references. If Nāgārjuna's statement of no thesis is effectual as a response to this opponent, one of the things that he needs to articulate is a different semantics. He does not formulate such a semantics even in the VV, however. It is thus not clear how we are to understand his semantics, a semantics that is forced upon him by his opponent.

Semantics for Mādhyamikas

The Mādhyamika can either replace the orthodox reference-based semantics by another account (the situation Nāgārjuna seems to be forced into) or keep the orthodox account but deflate its problematic consequences.[9] For the second option, one can deflate the problematic consequence by adopting a deflationary account of truth. A deflationalist can accept a reference-based semantics so long as it is not metaphysically charged. According to the deflationary account, the statement <*s*> is true iff *s* (the T-schema). If we think of *s* on the right hand side of the biconditional as a fact or a state of affairs, it contains objects that are referenced by the statement <*s*>. Yet, the referential relation does not have to determine the truth of the statement. All there is to the notion of truth is the T-schema. There is no need to assume that it is the reference relation that guarantees the biconditional. The Prāsaṅgika-Mādhyamika Candrakīrti presents an account that can be described along these lines. He accepts the view that what is true is only "what is acknowledged by the world (*lokaprasiddha*)." In his *Prasannapadā Madhyamakavṛtti*, he approvingly cites a passage of the *Ratnakūṭa* (one of the collections of the Buddha's teachings):

> The world argues with me. I don't argue with the world. What is agreed upon in the world to exist, I too agree that it exists. What is agreed upon in the world to be nonexistent, I too agree that it does not exist. (Quoted in Cowherds 2011, 151)

Thus, according to Candrakīrti, all we can do in search of truth is simply "read off the surface," leaving no room for (logical) analysis, as Siderits (1989, 244) puts it.[10]

Given the small philosophical success Candrakīrti had during his lifetime, it is not clear how widespread his view (or a view like his) was in India. Other Mādhyamika philosophers criticized him for his radical view, however. For example, the eighth-century Svātantrika-Mādhyamika philosopher Kamalaśīla argued against the view of Candrakīrti (or someone like him) by showing that the *lokaprasiddha* account of truth reduces 'truth' to mere beliefs and thus is unreliable (*Sarvadharmaniḥsvabhāvasiddhi*, p. 312a 8–312b 6).[11] Kamalaśīla emphasized the importance of (logical) analysis in accounting for truths because simply referring to people's opinions is not tantamount to truth. The problem with a deflationary account for the Mādhyamika, according to Kamalaśīla, is that it is no longer clear in what sense it provides an account of *truth*. Because a deflationalist tries to account for truth by deflating the world-statement relation, the importance of 'reality' gets lost. What is left for an account of truth might then be just beliefs and opinions that people happen to have. As Tillemans suggests, Candrakīrti's *lokaprasiddha* account faces exactly this problem (Cowherds 2011, ch. 9).

The Mādhyamika might respond by proposing a fictionalist account. If there are no ultimate truths, all we can do is to adopt a make-believe attitude toward truth without assuming that fictional ontology does heavy metaphysical lifting. One way to cash out such a fictionalist account is to appeal to Carnap's distinction between internal and external questions.[12] We can think of a belief as a consequence of setting a framework which contains a mechanism to regulate what is admissible within the framework. It is only within a framework that beliefs can be meaningfully talked about. To ask whether reference relations can account for truth, however, is to step outside of the framework. So no such question can be meaningfully raised. This is not to deny the existence of reference; instead, this shows that such a Carnapian account can explain the working of deflation in a fictionalist account.

If we go for a Carnapian account, however, we are already moving away from the reference-based semantics to a pragmatic account of truth. For Carnap, the question about truth comes down to our practice. It has to do with the "planning and optimization of the future of the species" (Carus 2004, 349). The Svātantrika-Mādhyamikas such as Śāntarakṣita and Kamalaśīla may be adopting the pragmatic account of truth espoused by Dharmakīrti (see Cowherds 2011, 145–146).[13] As Finnigan and Tanaka suggest, by adopting a pragmatic account of truth, the Mādhyamika can accommodate norms embodied in Nāgārjuna's statements in terms of practical efficacy. There may not be a theoretical explanation of the norm's effectiveness. Unlike a reference-based semantics, a pragmatic account doesn't specify the ontological basis for determining the truth-values of statements. The Mādhyamika can, nevertheless, point at the practice where the effectiveness is observable. By adopting a pragmatic account of truth, the Mādhyamika can respond to the charge of ineffectiveness in the thesis of emptiness raised by Nāgārjuna's opponent (Cowherds 2011, ch. 11).

Conclusion

Despite the fact that there are several options that Mādhyamikas can take as their semantic account, it is not clear that they have a settled position about semantics. How to make sense of Nāgārjuna's claim of having no thesis is a live question. The debates surrounding the no-thesis position were transmitted to Tibet. Two of the most influential philosophers in Tibet, Tsongkhapa and Gorampa, seem to have engaged with this very issue. As we can see from Garfield and Priest's (2003) identification of paradoxes within Nāgārjuna's system, how best to understand Nāgārjuna's thesis of emptiness is still debatable.

Whatever we can say about Nāgārjuna's semantics embedded in his thesis of emptiness, one thing is clear: we can see the difficulty of making sense of emptiness once we consider the semantics that must underlie it. We can all agree on Nāgārjuna's ontology. Even then, we can disagree about his semantics. The realization of emptiness thus depends on the attainment of a semantics that can accommodate it.

Notes

1 An English translation of the text can be found in Garfield (1995) from the Tibetan translation, Kalupahana (1986), and Siderits and Katsura (2013).
2 I adopt the modern convention of using 'Madhyamaka' for the thought or school and 'Mādhyamika' for the thinker.
3 This text is usually not considered to be canonical. However, it is a useful text in explaining Buddhist metaphysics and modern scholars often refer to it.
4 An English translation of Chapter 9 of *Abhidharmakośa* where Vasubandhu presents an argument for this ontology can be found in Duerlinger (2009).
5 See a discussion by Mark Siderits in Cowherds (2011, ch. 10).
6 See a discussion by Guy Newland and Tom Tillemans in Cowherds (2011, ch. 1).
7 I mainly talk about statements here as truth-bearers. Nothing I say here depends on this, however.
8 See Garfield (1996) and Westerhoff (2009, ch. 9). Garfield claims that this orthodox account is Fregean. Given that it does not posit anything intermediary between the statement (or the thought expressed by the statement) and the referents, that is, *sense*, the orthodox semantics cannot be Fregean.
9 For the options discussed in this section, see a discussion by Graham Priest, Mark Siderits and Tom Tillemans in Cowherds (2011, ch. 8).
10 See also a discussion by Tom Tillemans in Cowherds (2011, ch. 9) for this interpretation of Candrakīrti.
11 An English translation of this passage can be found in Cowherds (2011, 153–154).
12 For an application of Carnap's distinction to the two truths, see a discussion by Bronwyn Finnigan and Koji Tanaka in Cowherds (2011, ch. 11). For other fictionalist accounts in the context of Candrakīrti's *lokaprasiddha* account, see a discussion by Tom Tillemans in Cowherds (2011, ch. 9).
13 Whether or not Dharmakīrti was a pragmatist is a hard question to answer. For a discussion, see Dreyfus (1997, ch. 17).

5 Madhyamaka Emptiness and Buddhist Ethics

Mark Siderits

Mahāyāna Buddhists claim that all things are empty (*śūnya*), and that we are obligated to exercise compassion (*karuṇā*). Given that these two claims are central to Mahāyāna identity, it is natural to suspect that they are connected. But recent attempts at finding a connection have had mixed results. Indeed there are those who see a conflict between them: emptiness would, they believe, preclude the grounding of any normative claim. The present chapter will investigate the consequences of emptiness for Buddhist ethics. The understanding of "emptiness" we shall be working with is specifically that of the Indian Madhyamaka school, but just what "Buddhist ethics" might be will be left somewhat more open.

Earlier chapters by Garfield and Tanaka have discussed the central Madhyamaka claim that all things are empty or devoid of intrinsic nature (*niḥsvabhāva*). But they disagree about just what this claim means, so some discussion is called for. Here it helps to begin with the Abhidharma background to the claim.[1] In explicating the Buddha's teachings, Buddhist philosophers of the Abhidharma schools distinguished between conventional and ultimate truth—between how the world ordinarily and usefully says things are, and how things objectively are independently of considerations of our interests and cognitive limitations. The point of the distinction was to explain how our sense of there being an "I" might be virtually universal and yet still erroneous. This distinction turns out to require that there be truth-makers such as facts or states of affairs for ultimately true statements, and that these consist of things that have their natures intrinsically. The result is a two-tier ontology consisting of the ultimately real, namely, those entities (the *dharmas*) that are the way they are *anyway* and so have their natures intrinsically, plus the merely conventionally real, things usefully treated as existing but lacking in natures not dependent on human conceptual construction. Crucially, the purported object of the "I"-sense, the person, belongs in the second category, being constructed out of a causal series of sets of impersonal impermanent psychophysical elements.[2] Now, Ābhidharmikas say that the person, as well as other composite objects, is empty or devoid of intrinsic nature. This is precisely why they say that such entities exist merely due to conceptualization (are *prajñaptisat*): their existence depends on a certain way of conceptualizing things that has proven useful but does not correspond to the intrinsic natures of things. But Madhyamaka extends this claim to the *dharmas*, which are likewise said to lack intrinsic nature. If the arguments for their claim are sound, then it seems there can be nothing that is ultimately real. The question is what to make of this.

Opponents of such a view, be they Ābhidharmikas or Mahāyāna Buddhists of the Yogācāra school, see this as equivalent to metaphysical nihilism, the absurd claim that nothing whatsoever exists.[3] It is easy enough to see why these opponents drew this conclusion. If the only things that could, strictly speaking, be said to exist are things with intrinsic natures, and nothing can have an intrinsic nature, then metaphysical nihilism follows. Madhyamaka does embrace intrinsic nature as the criterion of ultimate existence, so it is difficult to see how they escape this *reductio* on their core claim. One attempt at a more charitable reading has them saying that the ultimate nature of reality is inexpressible, but this interpretation is difficult to square with other things Mādhyamikas say. In Chapter 3 of this volume, Jay Garfield argues that the lesson we are to take from this is that the natures of existing things are extrinsic—dependent on how other things are and on how things are conceptualized by sentient beings like us. This reading generates a paradox, but Garfield avoids the route from this paradox to equating emptiness with mystical inexpressibility by embracing a paraconsistent logic that allows for true contradictions. In Chapter 4, Koji Tanaka agrees that Madhyamaka is not metaphysical nihilism, but rejects the claim that Madhyamaka embraces paradoxical assertions. He suggests that the many seeming paradoxes in Madhyamaka texts may instead be designed to force us to abandon the very idea of ultimate truth, of how things are *anyway*. Tanaka thus favors a semantic interpretation of emptiness (the point is to get us to think differently about what it means for a statement to be true) where Garfield gives a metaphysical interpretation (the reals are interdependent and reality is paradoxical). Even so, there is some agreement. Both reject the metaphysical nihilist interpretation, and they agree that emptiness is incompatible with metaphysical foundationalist projects.

We shall be examining a number of different views about the consequences of emptiness for ethics, some holding that emptiness supports certain moral claims, others saying that emptiness undermines those claims. When it comes to understanding what emptiness itself is, I am inclined to side with Tanaka.[4] But our differences will not matter when it comes to assessing the claim that emptiness creates difficulties for Buddhist ethics. Since all three of us agree that Madhyamaka is anti-foundationalist and is not metaphysically nihilist, we can also agree that a Mādhyamika needs some response to moral nihilism, the view that nothing is morally wrong, and that this response cannot depend on there being ultimately real things with intrinsic nature. Where the competing interpretations of emptiness may make a difference is in strategies for responding to the challenge of moral nihilism by seeking a positive ground for compassion. Those who prefer a metaphysical reading may look to metaphysics for (non-foundationalist) answers. But the semantic reading turns emptiness into a variety of anti-realism, or perhaps a quietism. Anti-realism is the rejection of the view that a statement's truth consists in its correspondence to some mind-independent state of affairs, while a quietist is someone who is skeptical about the ability of philosophical theorizing to address real problems. Since both anti-realists and quietists reject the idea of there being such a thing as how things really and ultimately are, the road of appealing to metaphysics to support normative claims is closed to them. Consequently, we will eventually need to look at some of the evidence concerning the competing interpretations of emptiness.

There is broad agreement among the different schools of Indian Buddhism concerning the basics of Buddhist ethics. Here are some things that all schools of Indian Buddhism accept: The ideal state for sentient beings is nirvāṇa, the cessation of suffering. Suffering arises as a result of ignorance of the three general characteristics of existence: suffering, impermanence, and non-self. Suffering is perpetuated through the three defilements, or afflictive habits: desire, aversion, and delusion. Due to these deeply ingrained psychological mechanisms, we respond to stimuli in such a way as to reinforce our ignorance about how things truly are, thereby setting the stage for yet more suffering in the future. Cessation of suffering is accomplished by following the path taught by the Buddha. This involves a variety of practices that overcome delusion by developing insight into the true nature of reality, and uproot desire and aversion by cultivating virtues that are their antidotes. Two such virtues are of particular importance here: loving kindness and compassion. A practitioner is instructed to develop an all-embracing wish for the welfare of all sentient beings, as well as the wish that all suffering everywhere cease. When these virtues are fully developed, they disrupt such personal reactive attitudes as partiality, jealousy, and resentment.[5] These attitudes perpetuate one's own suffering by reinscribing false belief in an "I." They do so by, for instance, making it seem natural for me to prefer that I and my nearest and dearest benefit more than others, and making it seem normal for me to wish for the suffering of those who have harmed me. The virtues of loving kindness and compassion serve to disrupt some of the processes whereby the defilements perpetuate suffering-inducing ignorance about the fact of non-self. When, for instance, I wish for the well-being of someone who has harmed me, this blocks the automatic response of anger, a response that reinforces belief in an "I" that is the victim of the harm.

While virtually all schools of Indian Buddhism agree on these basics, Mahāyāna Buddhists claim that their teachings are ethically superior to those of the Abhidharma schools in that they advocate the career of the bodhisattva as opposed to that of the *arhat*. The *arhat* is someone who, having followed the path taught by the Buddha, attains cessation of the defilements and thereby achieves liberation from suffering. Residual karma from this and previous lives may generate continued existence in this liberated state for some finite duration. But because the *arhat* creates no new karma, when this residue is exhausted their series of rebirths ends. This results in the state known as "cessation without remainder," death without rebirth. The bodhisattva, by contrast, intentionally stops short of the state that would make cessation without remainder inevitable. Their motive is to continue to undergo rebirth so as to develop the talents of a buddha, someone who is highly skilled at helping others attain the cessation of suffering. What those who think Mahāyāna is ethically superior claim is that the path of the *arhat* is ethically inferior to the path of the bodhisattva, insofar as the former aims at the cessation of only their own suffering whereas the goal of the latter is the cessation of the suffering of all sentient beings. This is sometimes put as the charge that the *arhat* is selfish.

If this criticism of Abhidharma is warranted, then there would be reason to suspect that emptiness plays a role in explaining the bodhisattva's "great compassion" (*mahākaruṇā*).[6] Even though Mahāyāna advocates the path of the bodhisattva, Mahāyāna texts do not portray the path leading to *arhat*ship as hopelessly misguided. Instead, they commonly relegate the practices making up this path to a relatively early stage in the long career of the bodhisattva. One might then suspect that the other signature doctrine of Mahāyāna, emptiness, must play a role in diverting the practitioner from the *arhat* path to the bodhisattva path. But we must exercise caution here. It is not entirely clear just how different these paths would actually be. Mahāyāna claims they are different. We can see this in their use of "great compassion" to describe the virtue of the bodhisattva. All Buddhist schools hold that cultivation of compassion—the wish that all suffering everywhere cease—is a necessary part of the path. Mahāyāna apologists charge that for those seeking *arhat*ship, compassion is merely of instrumental value. Their charge is that if one develops an attitude of concern for the suffering of others just in order to bring about the cessation of one's own suffering (by countering the defilements), then one does not really disvalue the suffering of others in itself. They argue that the bodhisattva's compassion is "great" precisely because it takes the suffering of others to have intrinsic disvalue. Is this a fair characterization of those who seek *arhat*ship?

How one answers this question will depend in part on how seriously one takes the claim that someone might intentionally follow the career of a bodhisattva over many lives. Suppose we did not believe that there is rebirth, so that the comparison were between the post-liberation life of the *arhat* and of the equivalently accomplished aspiring bodhisattva over the remaining years of the present life in which full realization of non-self occurs. Further, suppose we grant that its being cultivated for instrumental reasons makes the aspiring *arhat*'s compassion different from that of the aspiring bodhisattva. But consider what becomes of the aspiring *arhat*'s compassion once the goal of cessation has been achieved and *arhat*ship attained. Since the *arhat*'s own suffering has been stopped, compassion can no longer be instrumental in bringing about that cessation. Is there any reason to believe the *arhat* will become indifferent to the suffering of others? Not only is there no reason to believe this is true, there is actually reason to believe it is false. If we are to believe what we are told in the *Nikāyas*,[7] at least some of those *arhat*s who were disciples of the Buddha devoted their post-liberation lives to helping teach the Dharma. It seems plausible to suppose that this was motivated by the wish to ameliorate suffering wherever it occurs.

We began with the question of whether emptiness might explain the bodhisattva's great compassion. But the present line of thought takes us in the opposite direction. Since the *arhat* does not hold that all dharmas are empty, if the *arhat* also possesses great compassion, that is, continues to be compassionate after attaining their own liberation, this cannot be due to insight into emptiness. Is there any reason to think that emptiness and compassion are linked? We are now ready to explore various proposals, some for a positive link, others for a negative link. One popular proposal is that realization of emptiness fosters a sense of interconnectedness among all sentient beings and thereby promotes fellow-feeling.[8] The thinking here begins with the point that Mādhyamikas sometimes claim the emptiness of all *dharma*s follows from the fact that they all originate in dependence on causes and conditions. But the emptiness of something consists in its not having its characteristic nature independent of how other things are. So, it is claimed, if all is empty because all is dependently originated, then everything must get its nature in dependence on how other things are. From this it is said to follow that my being who I am depends on how other things are, so I am no island and my welfare is intimately bound up with that of others. Consequently, egoism is not rationally justifiable. This idea of interconnectedness is often expressed by the analogy of Indra's net: an immeasurably large web, at each node of which is a mirror reflecting light from mirrors at the other nodes.[9]

However, while this Indra's net view is widely represented as the basis of Mahāyāna ethics, it is not without difficulties. First, the normative conclusion that one ought to be compassionate toward others appears not to follow from the metaphysics invoked in its defense. The Holocaust survivor may well be the way they now are due to their treatment at the hands of Nazis, but it does not seem to follow from this *alone* that they ought to promote the welfare of Nazis. The most that might be said to follow from the alleged fact of interconnectedness is that one should adopt a strategy of enlightened self-interest: if my fate and the fates of others are interconnected, then perhaps I can best promote my own welfare by promoting that of others. But this is something quite different from the impartial benevolence of the bodhisattva.[10] Second, the metaphysics itself is problematic. Abhidharma says that a *dharma* must have a nature that is intrinsic or wholly its own. Causation is commonly thought to involve necessary connection between cause and effect. Suppose we agree that there can be no necessary connections between things with intrinsic nature. It would then follow that if causation does involve necessary connection, no *dharma* could be dependently originated. It would not follow from these assumptions that everything is internally related to other things. The implication might be that we were wrong to think that causation involves necessary connection, and the causal relations that hold among *dharma*s do not involve necessary connections, or it might be that the contradiction deriving from *dharma*s' being dependently originated serves merely as a *reductio* to disprove the very idea that there are ultimately real entities, and so says nothing about relations among things that are only conventionally real.

Of course if the Mādhyamika were to say that their intention was to show just that there could be nothing answering to the description "ultimately real," they would be accused of metaphysical nihilism. The Mādhyamika would reply that there are, after all, existents in relations of dependent origination, namely, conventionally real entities: tables and chairs, rocks, trees, and so on. From what has been said so far, nothing at all follows concerning how dependent origination might obtain among conventionally real existents. It might be that conventional reals have intrinsic natures (albeit not in the manner in which *dharma*s were thought to have them), but that (as Humeans claim) causation does not involve necessary connection. Or it might be that while the dependent origination that obtains among intrinsically characterized conventional reals does involve necessary connection, no contradiction actually follows from the holding of necessary connections among conventional reals with intrinsic natures. This would be so if conventional reals are real precisely insofar as they are "not subjected to analysis" (*avicāryamāṇa*). It is, after all, philosophical analysis that leads to the claims that only *dharma*s could be, strictly speaking, real, and that they must be innocent of all internal relations. If, as some Mādhyamikas claim, it is a mistake to subject conventionally real entities to philosophical analysis, then there cannot be said to be a contradiction in holding both that such entities have natures wholly their own, and that they enter into the sorts of producer-produced relations that the Humeans criticize as involving necessary connections.[11] So it is not clear that the metaphysics of Indra's net follows from the emptiness of all *dharma*s.

The last possibility does, however, suggest a second possible strategy for building a connection between emptiness and compassion. As we just saw, Madhyamaka is likely to respond to the allegation of metaphysical nihilism by championing realism about our folk ontology, our commonsense theory about what exists. On the other hand, the Abhidharma ontology of *dharma*s that Madhyamaka rejects is nothing at all like our folk ontology. Central to its philosophical project is the reduction of the person to a causal series of impersonal impermanent entities and events. It might be said that this Abhidharma reductionism robs compassion of its natural object, the person, and thus subverts the path of the bodhisattva.[12] And Madhyamaka's reinstatement of our folk ontology could then be said to restore persons to the place they require for the practice of compassion. This would not amount to a grounding of compassion in emptiness, but at least emptiness would then play some role in explaining the bodhisattva's conduct. The rejection of Abhidharma's "cowboy metaphysics"—its ontology of things with "lonely" natures, natures that might be had while unaccompanied—is seen as tantamount to a rejection of an associated "cowboy ethics"—the rugged individualism of the egoist.

There are, though, two difficulties with this strategy. First, it is not clear that cowboy ethics does follow from cowboy metaphysics. We will shortly be looking at an argument that actually uses such metaphysics to support compassion, the antithesis of cowboy ethics. If this argument is sound, then the reduction of persons to impersonal entities does not undermine the bodhisattva path. Second, it is not clear that a Mādhyamika would want to reinstate that part of our folk ontology that gives persons pride of place.[13] The model Madhyamaka quietist Candrakīrti (seventh century CE) is quite vehement on the point that it is the sense of an "I" possessed by all but the enlightened that must be extirpated.[14] It is difficult to see how this attitude could be squared with the acceptance of conventionally real persons that is central to the present strategy for connecting emptiness with compassion. The claim behind this strategy was that the exercise of compassion requires taking the object of compassion as a distinct subject of experience: "someone having their own feelings, just like I have." Given the Buddhist orthodoxy that cessation of suffering requires overcoming the "I"-sense, if this claim were true, then no enlightened person could exercise compassion.

At this point one might be led to conclude that rather than helping foster impartial benevolence, emptiness instead obstructs it. This third proposal for a link between emptiness and compassion is thus not positive, like the first two, but negative. The route to this negative conclusion is quite simple. One thing Tanaka and Garfield agree on is that Madhyamaka is committed to metaphysical anti-foundationalism, the view that the truth of ordinary claims about ordinary things does not require grounding in states of affairs involving things with intrinsic natures. It follows from this that normative claims lack grounding in how things ultimately are—a view that seems tantamount to moral anti-realism. The idea is that if morality is not based on facts about the world, then there are no moral facts, such as the fact that murder is wrong. And if, as the moral anti-realist holds, there are ultimately no moral facts, then there can ultimately be no moral obligation for the enlightened person to alleviate the suffering of others. Of course, one might point out that the bodhisattva is not responding to a moral obligation when they exercise compassion—that they simply express their nature when they so act. But even if this were so, there is still the necessity of grounding the normative claim that one *ought to* choose the bodhisattva path over that of the *arhat*. Since unenlightened people do not naturally exercise "great compassion," some obligation seems to be involved in this choice, and the "ought" here cannot be one of instrumental rationality. It is supposedly the *arhat*, not the bodhisattva, who cultivates compassion for merely prudential reasons.

It might be further argued in response, however, that if emptiness does entail moral anti-realism, it is not the typical sort, so the usual reasons for taking some form of moral skepticism to follow from moral anti-realism do not apply here. The typical moral anti-realist denies that there are moral facts on the grounds that they would be "ontologically queer," that is, not the sort of thing that could be found in the natural world.[15] As the queerness complaint brings out, the typical moral anti-realist takes alleged moral facts to compare unfavorably to "natural" facts, such as the fact that fire is hot. Typical moral anti-realism is thus a form of *local* anti-realism: while certain kinds of claims (in this case, the claims of moral discourse) lack realist truth-conditions, other kinds of claims (e.g., those of the natural sciences) are made determinately true or false by facts that obtain independently of the concepts we happen to employ. However, if the Mādhyamika is a moral anti-realist, this is because they espouse *global* anti-realism: there being nothing that could count as ultimately real, there cannot be objectively real truth-makers for any form of discourse, be it normative or descriptive. As a result, under this view our moral claims and our claims about the natural world are actually in the same boat.

True, that boat might capsize and sink. This is what critics of global anti-realism allege. What we now see is that the stock charge of nihilism against Madhyamaka must encompass both metaphysical nihilism and moral nihilism. This, in turn, suggests that a Madhyamaka approach to answering the charge of metaphysical nihilism might be used to answer the allegation of moral nihilism as well. We have already noted that Garfield and Tanaka both reject the charge of metaphysical nihilism against Madhyamaka. Their strategies for answering the charge differ,[16] as would any strategies adapted to respond to the charge of moral nihilism. The point here is that the existence of ways to counter the first charge gives some reason to suppose that there may be ways of answering the second as well. Since both descriptive and normative discourses are in the same boat, the strategy that rescues the Mādhyamika from metaphysical nihilism might work for moral nihilism as well.[17] That Madhyamaka emptiness entails a kind of moral anti-realism need not be grounds for convicting Madhyamaka of moral nihilism.

So far we have failed in the search for connections, whether positive or negative, between Madhyamaka emptiness and compassion. It is time to widen our scope and seek support for compassion in something common to Madhyamaka and other Buddhist schools, namely, the teaching of non-self. As was pointed out earlier, the fact of non-self is also described as a kind of emptiness or lack of intrinsic nature, namely the person's lack of intrinsic nature. The idea here is that the person is a mere conceptual construction, since its nature is wholly borrowed from the parts on whose existence it depends. Different Buddhist schools share the view that ultimately there is no person; what they disagree on is whether there is anything that does possess intrinsic nature. Let us put this disagreement to one side and see if compassion can be grounded in this more specific form of emptiness, that of the person. At first glance, it might seem obvious that compassion and non-self are connected. We do, after all, describe a compassionate person as altruistic, and altruism is commonly said to be "selfless". But caution is called for here. The person described as selfless typically puts the welfare of others above their own, but this is perfectly compatible with having a robust sense of self. What is unusual about such a person is just the relative importance he or she attaches to the question of whose welfare is at stake. If there is a connection between compassion and emptiness of the person, some argumentation is needed to bring it out.

As a matter of fact, such an argument is suggested by a passage in an important Madhyamaka work, Śāntideva's *Bodhicaryāvatāra*. This passage may be seen as the response to a moral skeptic, someone who accepts the force of prudential (self-regarding) reasons for action but fails to see why they should be moved by moral (other-regarding) reasons. Here is the argument:

> 97 If one says that the suffering of other persons does not harm me, hence efforts need not be made to prevent it,
>
> Then since the suffering of a future body does not harm me, why should efforts be made to prevent it?

98 "Because that too is *me*;" if this is one's thought, that is a mistaken construction,

For it is one set of elements that dies and another that is born.

99 If it is thought that it is the suffering that belongs just to oneself that is to be prevented,

The suffering of the foot does not belong to the hand, why should it be prevented by that [hand]?

100 If it is said that while this is mistaken, still one behaves out of the "I"-sense,

[We reply that] one should try as hard as one can to stop what is mistaken in oneself and others.

101 The series and the collection are illusory, like a queue, an army and the like,

Since that does not exist to which suffering belongs, of whom will that come to be one's own?

102 Ownerless sufferings are all devoid of distinction [between mine and other].

Because it is suffering, it is to be prevented; how can this be restricted?

103 If it were asked why suffering is to be prevented, it is agreed upon without exception by all that it is.

Thus if it is to be prevented, then indeed all of it is to be prevented, if not then one's own case is just like that of other persons. (BCA 8.97–103)

The argument may be seen as proceeding in two stages. In the first stage (verses 97–98), the moral skeptic invokes the principle that suffering provides a reason for action only for the subject that is its owner. The occurrence of pain gives its owner a motivation to act so as to make the pain stop, but pain is motivating for others only to the extent that its occurrence will have negative consequences for them. In other words, the moral skeptic holds that people are all egoists and will not act to alleviate suffering for others unless they see it as in their self-interest to do so. In response, Śāntideva points out that one cares about the suffering of one's future body, even though one is not presently being harmed. Therefore, there is an asymmetry in the moral skeptic's scheme of practical reasoning: temporal neutrality (no bias in favor of the *now*), but a bias in favor of the *here*. The moral skeptic replies that this asymmetry is rationally grounded, in that prudential reasons concern the interests of a subject that exists equally in the present and in the future, so that whether the pain is presently occurring or only envisioned as occurring in the future, it is equally *mine* and consequently equally motivating for *me*, its owner. Śāntideva's response is that such grounding requires the existence of an enduring self, something that in fact is not to be found. What we find instead is a causal series of sets of psychophysical elements, each existing for a while but then ceasing to exist while causing a new set of elements to come into existence. Such a series is a mere conceptual construction, so not the sort of thing that could ultimately justify the asymmetry. In verse 101ab, Śāntideva gives the example of a queue in support of the claim that the causal series of elements is not ultimately real. While we might ordinarily say that there was a line in front of the theater between 7:00 and 7:30, for example, we generally concede that strictly speaking there was just a succession of individual patrons making up the queue from one time to the next. The term "queue" is merely a convenient way of designating this ordered succession. The same should go for the term "person" as applied to a causal series of psychophysical elements. So the asymmetry in the moral skeptic's position lacks rational ground.

The second stage begins with the moral skeptic trying to restore symmetry between the temporal and the locational by adopting an equal bias with respect to the *here* and the *now*. The resulting view might be called Punctualism, given its core claim that the person exists for only a moment; when the presently existing psychophysical elements go out of existence and are replaced by the new elements that are their effects, it is someone else who comes into existence. Punctualism restores symmetry to the position of the moral skeptic by confining the scope of self-interest to the present moment.[18]

Śāntideva, though, is having none of the Punctualist's position. This is the point of the example of the hand and foot in verse 99. Suppose there is pain caused by a splinter in the foot. The foot cannot itself stop the pain by removing the splinter; this requires action by the hand. But the hand is elsewhere than where the foot is, so by the Punctualist's principles, only the foot and not the hand has a reason to act. Of course, the Punctualist will claim that it is I, the owner of both foot and hand, who has the pain and so has a reason to act to stop the pain. The difficulty is that this presently existing "I" is just as much a fiction as the enduring "I" that the moral skeptic sought to invoke in the first stage. The "I" is merely a collection, like the presently existing army mentioned in 101ab—an aggregate of simultaneously existing elements such as hands and feet arranged in a certain way and so functioning as to make it useful for us to have a convenient designator for the collection.[19] Given this result, the Punctualist moral skeptic lacks all grounds for their bias in favor of the here and the now. Because all pain is, strictly speaking, ownerless (verse 102ab), the moral skeptic is left with a dilemma: either acknowledge that suffering is to be prevented regardless of when and where it occurs (be it now or in the future, "mine" or "another's"), or else hold that there is no reason to stop any pain. Since no one is likely to choose the second option ("it is agreed upon without exception by all that it is to be prevented"), it follows that impartial benevolence is rationally required.

This argument involves interpreting Buddhist ethics as a form of consequentialism, the view that the moral status of an action or policy depends on its consequences. Some find this surprising, but there is good reason to classify Śāntideva as a consequentialist.[20] The real difficulty with his argument is that it relies on the premise that suffering has an intrinsic nature, badness, or to-be-preventedness (*vāryatva*). The argument supports impartial benevolence by exploiting a difference in ontological status between person and suffering: the person is empty and so not ultimately real, while suffering is ultimately real and so non-empty. When the argument claims that suffering is bad but ownerless, the grounds for this have to be that suffering is ultimately real and ultimately bad, while the person that we think of as the owner of the suffering is merely a conceptual construction and so not ultimately real. This would be perfectly acceptable to an Ābhidharmika, but it seems to conflict with the core claim of Madhyamaka that all things are devoid of intrinsic nature. What then are we to make of the fact that Śāntideva seems to have given such an argument? One option is to say that he did not intend it as an argument, but instead just as a useful device for meditators trying to cultivate compassion.[21] This might be a way to resolve an apparent inconsistency in Śāntideva's text, but it does not answer our core question: can Madhyamaka use an argument like this to support impersonal benevolence? I would suggest that the appearance of inconsistency can be avoided if we make use of the doctrine known as semantic contextualism, according to which an expression has meaning only in a determinate context. This results in a kind of "semantic insulation" between statements occurring in different contexts, so that apparent inconsistencies are dissipated. If we then understand the claim that all things are devoid of intrinsic nature and the claim that suffering has the intrinsic nature of badness as occurring in distinct contexts for different purposes, then since they are semantically insulated from one another, they need not conflict.

The claim that all things are empty is made in a context in which the Mādhyamika is addressing someone who has followed the Abhidharma path up to full realization of non-self. Because such a person has used the distinction between the two truths in order to rid themselves of the "I"-sense, they are unlikely to realize that the very idea of an ultimate truth—of there being how things are *anyway*—can itself constitute a subtle source of appropriation and thus self-affirmation, and so can represent one last obstacle to liberation. The cure for this final vestige of clinging is Madhyamaka emptiness. To see that all things are empty is to see that the very idea of ultimate truth—something that has proven useful on the path so far—is actually incoherent, and is just another useful teaching device. The claim that suffering is intrinsically bad (and so impartial benevolence is obligatory) is made in the very different context in which someone is wondering what reason there might be to prevent suffering in others. Mādhyamikas are on record as holding that there are contexts in which it is not appropriate to assert that all things are empty.[22] The second context, the context of practical reasoning, may well be one of them. It may well be that in that context it is not true that suffering is empty of intrinsic nature, but it is true that suffering has the intrinsic nature of badness.

This contextualizing strategy would make it safe for a Mādhyamika to endorse the argument for impartial benevolence. There remains the question whether Madhyamaka emptiness makes any positive contribution to the resulting ethic of great compassion. If we accept the semantic interpretation of emptiness, then perhaps we might say that realization of emptiness promotes a kind of moral humility that is important to the practice of compassion. Here is how. On the semantic interpretation of emptiness, the point of establishing emptiness is to show that the very idea of ultimate truth is incoherent and should be abandoned. Its soteriological role is to help the aspirant overcome a final hurdle to cessation of suffering, the subtle sort of self-affirmation that comes with the metaphysical realist conception of truth, a self-affirmation characteristically revealed in the gesture of pounding the table. (See Siderits 2003b.) Now the aspirant for whom the teaching of emptiness is intended has presumably already understood the reasons for the practice of compassion and has overcome those affective habits (the *kleśa*s or "defilements") that stand in its way, for realization of emptiness does not play a role in those achievements. So the aspirant may well have begun the practice of compassion before coming to a full realization of emptiness. But just as, on the epistemic side, the Abhidharma path to full realization of non-self can lead to the table-pounding of the metaphysical realist, so on the ethical side a grasp of the reasons for impartial benevolence can lead to the overweening stance of the moral fanatic. Someone who is newly convinced, by an argument like Śāntideva's, that moral judgments do have a ground may be prone to finger-pointing, the moral equivalent of table-pounding. Realization that there is no such thing as the ultimate truth can help here, just as it can help on the epistemic side. To know that the conclusions of practical reason, like those of theoretical reason, are always contextually determined and provisional in nature is not to give way to the impotence of moral relativism. It is instead to embrace the thought that there can be better without a best. This can inform the bodhisattva's practice of compassion in two ways. First, it can prevent one from falling into the arrogance of the moral absolutist by instilling a healthy sense of irony about one's own practical reasoning. Second, the knowledge that there is no best but there can always be a better may trigger greater spontaneity and creativity in one's search for useful ways to prevent suffering.[23] In Madhyamaka thought, there are said to be two principal perfections in the path of the bodhisattva. The full realization of the emptiness of all *dharma*s is referred to as the "perfection of wisdom" (*prajñāpāramitā*); great compassion is the second of the two. On the present understanding of the role of emptiness in the path of the bodhisattva, while Madhyamaka emptiness does not provide a rationale for the bodhisattva's compassion, its perfected realization may nonetheless contribute significantly to this second perfection.

We have now looked at four proposals concerning the supposed link between emptiness and suffering. Each of the first three has its difficulties, either lack of textual support or inability to stand up to critical examination or both. The fourth at least has some textual support: Śāntideva does give such an argument, and Mādhyamikas do make use of contextualist semantics. Whether it can also stand up to further philosophical scrutiny I shall leave to the reader to judge.[24]

Abbreviations

BCA	=	*Bodhicāryāvatāra of Śāntideva with the Commentary Pañjika of Prajñākaramati*, edited by P. L. Vaidya. Dharbanga: Mithila Institute, 1960.
MAV	=	*The Madhyamakāvatāra of Candrakīrti, (chapter VI with the author's* bhāṣya *reconstructed from the Tibetan version)*, edited by N. Aiyaswami Sastri. Madras: Madras Oriental Series vol.4, 1929.
MMK	=	*Mūlamadhyamakakārikā* of Nāgārjuna
LVP	=	Louis de la Vallée Poussin, ed., *Mūlamadhyamakakārikās (Mādhyamikasūtras) de Nāgārjuna avec la Prasannapdā Commentaire de Candrakīrti*. Osnabrück: Biblio Verlag, 1970.
NMW	=	*Nāgārjuna's Middle Way: The Mūlamadhyamakakārikā.* Translated, with commentary and introduction, by Mark Siderits and Shōryū Katsura. Somerville, MA: Wisdom, 2013.

Notes

1 I use the term "Abhidharma" to refer to those schools of Indian Buddhism, such as Theravāda, Vaibhāṣika, Sautrāntika, Mahāsaṃghika, and the like that developed out of the teachings of the Buddha ("early Buddhism") before the rise of the Mahāyāna. Others use the term *Śrāvakayāna* or "Hearers" with the same intent. To be avoided is the pejorative term "Hīnayāna"; to call an Ābhidharmika such as the Sautrāntika philosopher Vasubandhu a "Hīnayānin" is equivalent to calling Aquinas a "Papist."

2 For more on how all this is supposed to go, see Siderits (2007, 32–68).

3 The claim is absurd because it is performatively self-refuting: when one wonders whether metaphysical nihilism might be true, at least the one thought must exist.

4 My reasons are given in Siderits (2013).

5 The term "reactive attitudes" stems from Strawson (1974), where it is used to cover a variety of affective responses (such as such as gratitude or resentment) that one might have when treated in a certain way by another.

6 It has become standard to translate *karuṇā* as "compassion" and *mahākaruṇā* as "great compassion," and I shall for the most part follow that practice. But there are two difficulties with this rendering. First, compassion is ordinarily thought of as a personal reactive attitude, and the enlightened person presumably lacks such attitudes. Second, "compassion" suggests an exclusive and self-sacrificing focus on the welfare of the other, whereas enlightened persons act so as to maximize overall well-being regardless of whether it is others or themselves or both who benefit. For this reason, "impartial benevolence" might be a better translation, and I shall sometimes use that term instead.

7 The *Nikāyas* are the discourses of the Buddha and his immediate disciples.

8 For a survey of attempts to use this as the basis of a Buddhist environmental ethics, as well as a critique, see Ives (2009).

9 The idea is that the god Indra has created and hung an infinitely large net that encompasses all of space, and placed a mirror at each juncture of the strands making up the net. Each mirror is positioned so that it reflects light from all other mirrors

while each other mirror reflects light from this mirror as well. The point is presumably that one cannot then distinguish between the light of any one mirror and the light of other mirrors.

10 A similar point is made in James (2007); see especially sec. 4.

11 This is the sort of thing that the quietist interpretation of Madhyamaka might have them say. Quietists think that philosophical theorizing should only be used for therapeutic purposes, such as helping people overcome their over-intellectualizing tendencies.

12 Something like this was claimed in Williams (1998).

13 Tillemans (2010) claims that a Mādhyamika of a quietist bent can still resist the conclusion that there are epistemic resources available to the Mādhyamika for fending off the worst sort of flattening of truth into whatever is accepted by the folk. The question of whether understanding emptiness according to the semantic interpretation allows a Mādhyamika to avoid the "dismal slough" of relativism about truth is debated in Cowherds (2011, 151–188).

14 See MAV VI.141: *paśyann ahiṃ chidragataṃ svagehe gajo 'tra nāstīti nirastaśaṅkaḥ | jahāti sarpād api nāma bhītim aho hi nāmārjavatā parasya ||*

15 For a catalog of the different forms that the "ontological queerness" objection can take, see Cuneo (2007, 90–101).

16 See chapters 8–13 in Cowherds (2011) for a variety of suggestions on how to answer this charge.

17 Among the more popular strategies that have been tried in the realism-anti-realism debate in metaphysics are minimalism, deflationism, and quietism. To this list I would add the use of contextualist semantics—the idea that a word has meaning only in a specific context—that is deployed toward the end of this paper.

18 Many people today think the point of Buddhism's denial of a self is to advocate "living in the here and now." What this interpretation misses is the fact that the Buddha rejected as extreme views both eternalism—the view that the person continues to exist when the present psychophysical elements cease to exist—and annihilationism—the view that the person ceases to exist when these elements cease. Punctualism is a radical form of annihilationism. For more on this view see Siderits (2003a: 37–39, 42–43).

19 I here pass over the argument meant to show that all such aggregate entities are mere conceptual fictions. The interested reader should consult MMK X.14 (translated at NMW 118) and MMK XVIII.1 (translated at NMW 195). Further discussion is in Siderits (2007, 105–111).

20 For evidence that Śāntideva is a consequentialist, see Clayton (2006); Goodman (2009, 89–103); but also see Davis (2013) for an interesting partial dissent. For evidence that early Buddhism and Theravāda are likewise consequentialist, see de Silva (2007).

21 I also made this claim about a different passage in BCA that also appears to express an argument, that at 6.22–32, in Siderits (2008); but see Goodman (2002), which takes the passage to express an argument.

22 See MMK XXII.11 (translated at NMW 247–249), and Candrakīrti's comments on the verse, at LVP 444–445.

23 For more on this see Goodman (2009, 129–130); Siderits (2003a, ch. 9).

24 I want to thank the editors of this volume for their many thoughtful and useful suggestions. I have also profited greatly from discussing the topic of this paper with my fellow Cowherds.

6 Emptiness and Violence

An Unexpected Encounter of Nāgārjuna with Derrida and Levinas

Chen-kuo Lin

> [I]n a world where the face would be fully respected (as that which is not of this world), there no longer would be war. In a world where the face no longer would be absolutely respected, where there no longer would be a face, there would be no more cause for war.
>
> —Derrida 1978, 10

Introduction

Inspired by Jacques Derrida's reading of Emmanuel Levinas in "Violence and Metaphysics," this chapter attempts to bring Nāgārjuna into a dialogue with these two European philosophers, showing how the issue of violence is viewed differently in both traditions. Although some might doubt the feasibility of arranging such a meeting for both sides, I would rather believe that a face-to-face talk between strangers will bring about rewarding surprises.

In daily usage, "violence" means to use force to break a law or rule, to assault sexually, to desecrate something sacred, and so forth. Violence in this sense never stops crying in the darkness of history. At the heart of violence, however, language always loses its voice. Aharon Appelfeld writes in the *New York Times* about what happened in Auschwitz in January 1945:

> The few people left alive describe the prevailing silence as the silence of death. Those who came out of hiding after the war—out of the forests and monasteries—also describe the shock of liberation as freezing, crippling silence. Nobody was happy. The survivors stood at the fences in amazement. *Human language, with all its nuances, turned into a mute tongue.* Even words like horror or monster seemed meager and pale, not to mention words like anti-Semitism, envy, hatred. (Appelfeld 2005, italicization mine)

In such a silent situation, how could violence be brought into language, not to mention philosophy, when we are faced with "a past that has never been present"?[1] This is the question striking us in the first place.

Nevertheless, the limitation of language shall not completely prevent us from meditating on this problem. The first step of the investigation in the following is to look into how violence is told in the hagiographical narratives in the Madhyamaka Buddhist tradition. Then I will try to see how violence is tacitly treated in Mādhyamika philosophy; Levinas and Derrida will be taken as interlocutors to bring to the surface some hidden insights. The reason why I place Nāgārjuna, Levinas, and Derrida together is that all of them distrust the metaphysics of the same. They all try to find the exit, the opening space, by which oppression in the metaphysics of identity can, with hope, be overcome.

Murder, Death, and Narratives

The death of Nāgārjuna was reported differently in Chinese and Tibetan sources (Walleser 1922). According to the *Biography of Bodhisattva Nāgārjuna*, the cause of his death was attributed to the conspiracy of a Hīnayānist who was deeply upset by Nāgārjuna's radical refutation of all other religious and philosophical schools. Knowing his agony, old man Nāgārjuna asked this Hīnayānist: "Is it your wish for me to have long life in this world?" The Hīnayānist replied: "It is truly not my wish." Hoping to fulfill the antagonist's wish, Nāgārjuna locked himself in room and was found dead some days later (Kumārajīva, T.50.2047:185.a-b).

In this Chinese source, no explicit evidence points to the death of Nāgārjuna as a case of murder. According to a Tibetan Buddhist scholar Bu-ston's (1290–1364) account, however, Nāgārjuna was murdered by Prince Shaktiman, who tried to take the power of the crown. It is said that Nāgārjuna stood on the side of the king in the rather nasty royal politics of the time. Due to conflicts in the court, Prince Shaktiman cut off Nāgārjuna's head with a blade of Kusha grass (Bu-ston 1931, 127–128).

A similar fate also happened to Nāgārjuna's disciple Āryadeva (third century CE), who was killed by a Brahmin. According to the *Biography of Bodhisattva Āryadeva*, a young Brahmin, who felt deeply humiliated by Āryadeva's severe criticism toward his teacher, vowed to revenge, saying: "As far as you embarrassed me with an empty knife, I will return you a real knife." When Āryadeva took a walk after sitting meditation, this young Brahmin jumped forward and stabbed him to death (Kumārajīva, T.51.187.b-188.a).

Kamalaśīla (740–796), an advocate of the Yogācāra-Svātantrika-Mādhyamika school who engaged in debates with a Chinese monk belonging to the Chan lineage was also famously murdered. The debate was held in the presence of the king at the Tibetan court. It is reasonably believed that the debaters had been involved with political rivalry. Tibetan Buddhists were split into two parties. One part, the Chan followers, was siding with China and the Buddha-nature doctrine, while the other was with India and the Mādhyamika view of emptiness. According to the Tibetan records, Kamalaśīla's side won the debate. The Chan monks were driven back to China and their teachings were prohibited. Sadly, as reported by Bu-ston, four Chinese butchers, sent by the Chinese Chan monk, brutally squeezed Kamalaśīla's kidneys to death (Bu-ston 1931, 196; Williams 1989, 193–197).

All three of these prominent Mādhyamika philosophers died as a result of religious violence. As stated in the above narratives, the question concerning us is how the issue of violence is accounted for in terms of the philosophy of emptiness. According to the Madhyamaka teaching, all beings, including self and things, are empty in themselves. The same teaching also applies to the case of murder—the one who kills is empty in himself, and the victim who is killed is also empty in himself. Even the killing itself is empty in itself. This is therefore the same as saying that murder is empty in itself. There is no one who kills, nor one who is killed. *Then, who needs to mourn? Who is in need of mourning?* (These are ethico-religious questions that will be addressed later in this article.) It is just like what Ārydeva told his disciples at the moment of his death:

> In light of reality, who is wrongly accused? Who is treated cruelly? Who cuts? Who kills? *In light of reality, there is no victim, nor the one who harms*. Who loves? Who hates? Who steals? Who hurts? You cry because you are attached to the wrong views deluded by the poison of ignorance. It causes evil karma. As a matter of fact, he harms not me, but his own retribution through karma. (Kumārajīva, T.50.187.c)

A nihilistic reading of the notion of emptiness might easily suggest that, according to the above Madhyamaka account, the whole event of murder is nothing but a mere fiction. If this reading were accepted, the religion will inevitably be defeated by its own nihilistic consequence.[2]

Emptiness in the Accusation of Nihilism

Obviously, Nāgārjuna is fully aware of the accusation of nihilism. In Chapter XXIV of the *Mūlamadhyamakakārikā*, an opponent accused Nāgārjuna of destroying everything sacred and profane in his claim that all beings are empty in themselves. The criticism can be summarized as follows. If everything is empty in itself, there is nothing either arising or ceasing. If there is nothing either arising or ceasing, there is no causation. If there is no causation, then it follows that there are no Four Noble Truths, for the Four Noble Truths are also guided by the principle of causality: the Second Truth is taken as the result of the First Truth, and the Third Truth as the cause of the Fourth Truth. If the Four Noble Truths do not exist, then knowledge, relinquishing the cause of suffering, cultivation, and realization of *nirvāṇa* would all be impossible. Consequently, no Sangha, Dharma, or Buddha exists. "Speaking in this manner about emptiness, you contradict the Three Jewels, as well as the reality of the fruits, both good and bad, and all such worldly conventions" (*Mūlamadhyamakakārikā* [MK].XXIV.5–6; Kalupahana 1986, 330). In short, the opponents claim that if everything is emptiness, then the law of causality will be untenable, because causation is possible only if it occurs in the relation of A and B, where A and B must not be empty. These realists thus argue that the theory of emptiness is not compatible with the theory of causation. Only if the theory of causation is firmly established can ethics and religion be securely grounded. For realists, such as the Sarvāstivādins, ethics and religion must be grounded in the metaphysics of essence/substance (*svabhāva*).[3]

In response to this criticism, Nāgārjuna points out that the realists have wrongly understood the concept of *emptiness* to be mere *nonexistence*. As for Nāgārjuna himself, he takes "emptiness" to mean "absence of essence" (*niḥsvabhāva*). He denies the notion of *svabhāva* (essence, substance, existent-in-itself, intrinsic nature),[4] but never reject the notion of existence (*bhāva*). Hence, Nāgārjuna claims that he did not destroy anything, including Buddhist teachings and the order, religion, or ethics. What he destroys is the *metaphysics* of essence/substance. Nāgārjuna goes further to argue that, on the contrary, ontologically speaking, everything is established by virtue of emptiness. If there were no emptiness, nothing would be established (MK.XXIV.14).[5] In other words, everything can be said to exist in emptiness. This statement will not be difficult to understand, if the notion of emptiness is understood in terms of *existence in causation* without presupposing the notion of *svabhāva*.

On the other side, those philosophers known as Sarvāstivādins (of the Sarvāstivāda school) classify all existences with categories that, in the final analysis, are based on the notion of *svabhāva*. Although the Abhidharma realists firmly refute the notion of self, they nevertheless assume the existence of elementary factors that exist with *svabhāva*. That is, the notion of *svabhāva* is accepted by the Buddhist realist as the metaphysical foundation upon which all beings and their activities (*kāritra*) can be made intelligible. It is precisely this metaphysical essentialism that prompts Nāgārjuna to oppose the Abhidharma realists.[6]

It is worthy of note that, in his analysis of the notion of *svabhāva* (MK.XV), Nāgārjuna does not explicitly claim to negate the existence of *svabhāva*.[7] On the contrary, Nāgārjuna goes on to question the Abhidharma distinction of ontological categories: ultimate existence (*paramārtha-sat*) and conventional existence (*saṃvṛti-sat*). According to Abhidharma realists, ultimate existence refers to any element that cannot be further analyzed, viz., something that has its own *svabhāva*, whereas conventional existence refers to that which is composed of elementary factors. For instance, while a person is regarded as a conventional existence, the aggregates of the person, such as bodily form, consciousness, feeling, etc., are considered to be ultimate entities that exist in themselves (Hirakawa 1990, 143–144). For the Abhidharmika, the reason why the notion of *svabhāva* is introduced in this context as an ontological substratum is to prevent the entire edifice of personhood from falling apart. On the side of Nāgārjuna, however, the metaphysics of *svabhāva* as such serves nothing but as illusive comfort, because it conceals the bare reality of dynamic causation which functions without any need to presuppose the metaphysical notion of *svabhāva*.[8]

It is quite clear that Nāgārjuna deliberately denied the metaphysics of *svabhāva*. However, in MK.XV Nāgārjuna claims that, following Katyāyana, while "existence" implies grasping after essentialism, "nonexistence" implies taking the side of anti-essentialism. Without exception, both extremes are confined within the metaphysical discourse of *svabhāva*. They are different only in the manner of affirming or negating the notion of *svabhāva*, which is *conceptually* assumed in each system. As for Nāgārjuna, neither essentialism nor anti-essentialism should be accepted. In the final analysis, the metaphysical distinction between essentialism and anti-essentialism, or *svabhāva* and *niḥsvabhāva*, should be called into question, because even the latter has been caught up into the notion of *svabhāva*.

Nāgārjuna rejects any metaphysical differentiation, knowing that the saṃsāric life-world is constituted by defilements of action (*karma-kleśa*), while the latter in turn results from conceptual differentiation (*vikalpa*) and discursive construction (*prapañca*) (MK.XVIII.5; Kalupahana 1986, 266–267). According to Candrakīrti's (sixth century CE) commentary, "discursive construction" refers to

> the beginninglessly recurring cycle of birth and death, which consists of knowledge and objects of knowledge, words and their meanings, agents and action, means and act, pot and cloth, diadem and chariots, objects and feelings, female and male, gain and loss, happiness and misery, beauty and ugliness, blame and praise. (Sprung 1979, 172)

The whole world of life and death is constructed by the weaving of conceptual and psychological discriminations. Within the conceptual system, beings are ontologically hypostatized and categorized as "female" or "male," "object" or "subject," and so on, instead of as being in themselves. For Nāgārjuna, *it is exactly in this metaphysical hypostatization that "violence" occurs.*

Violence as Inscribing within Difference

But what is the violence inscribed in metaphysics? Following Nietzsche and Heidegger, Derrida (1978) treats violence as a metaphysical act that attempts to reduce the irreducible to something more essential. Beings are made intelligible within a system of metaphysics structured by the categories of duality and hierarchy. For instance, with the ontological distinction of "transcendental" and "empirical," beings are often explained in terms of a reduction from the "empirical" to the "transcendental." A typical example is Platonism, in which the "transcendent" is considered more fundamental than the "empirical" in terms of truth and value. However, such metaphysical differentiation and reduction finds no deeper ground other than itself for justification. Moreover, metaphysical reduction has always been done in a conspiracy of suppression and domination. For Derrida, violence is always already immanent in all forms of metaphysics, such as logocentrism, ethnocentrism, phallologocentrism, and so forth, which excommunicate the Other in the system of the Same.

In Derrida's discussion of violence, two articles published in 1967 need to be read carefully: "The Violence of the Letter: From Levi-Strauss to Rousseau"

(Derrida 1974) and "Violence and Metaphysics: An Essay on the Thought of Emmanuel Levinas" (Derrida 1978). In the former, Derrida brings out a "genealogy" of violence in three "stages" (Beardsworth 1996, 22–23). First, Derrida places violence in the context of writing/naming:

> The structure of violence is complex and its possibility—writing—no less so . . . . There was in fact a first violence to be named. *To name, to give names that it will on occasion be forbidden to pronounce, such is the originary violence of language which consists in inscribing within a difference, in classifying, in suspending the vocative absolute.* To think the unique *within* the system, to inscribe it there, such is the gesture of the arche-writing: arche-violence, loss of the proper, of absolute proximity, of self-presence, in truth the loss of what has never taken place, of a self-presence which has never been given but only dreamed of and always already split, repeated, incapable of appearing to itself except in its own disappearance. (Derrida 1974, 112, italicized mine)

The originary violence appears in the act of naming the unnamable, the proper, the self-presence, *which has never taken place*. In using the notion of "the proper" and "self-presence," Derrida carefully warns us not to fall into the metaphysics of the Same, or *svabhāva*, if we are allowed to bring Nāgārjuna into dialogue here. For Derrida, even the "self-presence," the "proper," or the "absolute proximity" cannot be hypostatized as something permanent and fixed. That is, when they are pronounced, they are already imprinted in violence. However, this does not mean that Derrida naïvely believes that one can be free from metaphysics and consequently free from violence. As he claims, wherever there is arche-writing, there is arche-violence. That means, to borrow a phrase from Heidegger, human beings *always already* exist in language as the matrix of metaphysics. It is in language that things are named and defined *within the system*. It is also in language that good and evil are divided *within the system*, that world is constructed *within the system*. Language itself is a *system* where the unnamable proper is inscribed.

As for Nāgārjuna, language itself is devoid of intrinsic nature, and is empty in itself. Like anything else, language is dependently originated. Just like an artificial person interacting with another artificial person, both of which are devoid of *svabhāva*, linguistic interactions also occur in the daily world without any necessity of presupposing the notion of *svabhāva* as metaphysical substratum (Bhattacharya 1986, 108). On the other side, the opponents—Naiyāyikas and Sarvāstivādins—contend that the meaning of a word exists in the corresponding/referring relationship between a name (*nāma*) and things (*vastu*). In order to secure the certainty of meaning, both the name and the thing must be real in the sense that they are innately endowed with *svabhāva*. In other words, the metaphysics of *svabhāva* is introduced again to endorse a realist semantics of language.[9] For Nāgārjuna, however, precisely due to the conspiracy of language and metaphysics, there arises ignorance that leads to the karma of violence.

Following arche-violence, as Derrida continues to point out, the second stage of violence appears as an institution of moral and juridical law. In other words, the possibility of law as the second violence, as well as the possibility of the third violence, commonly called evil, war, indiscretion, rape, and so on, is also rooted in the same conspiracy of language and metaphysics. Here we see that Derrida confronts this last violence seriously.

> This last violence is all the more complex in its structure because it refers at the same time to the two inferior levels of arche-violence and of law. In effect, it reveals the first nomination which was already an expropriation, but it denudes also that which since then functioned as the proper, the so-called proper, substitute of the deferred proper, *perceived* by the *social* and *moral consciousness* as the proper, the reassuring seal of self-identity, the secret. (Derrida 1974, 112)

In this passage, which "is dense and demands very careful reading" (Beardsworth 1996, 23), Derrida interprets empirical violence as the effect of the previous levels of violence, as the consequence of "the first nomination which was already an expropriation," and as the denudation of the so-called "proper," which is nothing but a metaphysical construct. Violence was already seeded in the soil of psycholinguistic construction (i.e., *prapañca*, a key word in Madhyamaka philosophy). It can be traced genealogically to the naming of the first thing. To name something is therefore the same as to classify something as something, to make something capable of being possessed, and therefore to dominate something. To name something is the same as to label something for a purpose other than merely naming. Here we see the Nietzschean motif of the will to power in Derrida's deconstructive thinking.

In Buddhist philosophy, this process of naming, classification, and discrimination is also called *vikalpa*. As Paul Williams (1980) explains lucidly, "the use of '*vikalpa*'—as expressed by the divisive prefix 'vi-'—is to place emphasis on the creation of a referent through the ability of language to partition and create opposition, to divide a domain into mutually exclusive and contradictory categories" (27). This usage of *vikalpa* reminds us of what Derrida just said about "the originary violence of language which consists in *inscribing within a difference*, in *classifying*, in *suspending the vocative absolute*" (Derrida 1974, 112, italicized mine).

Irreducibility of the Other as Face

Let us now turn to Derrida's "Violence and Metaphysics." In the following discussion I will not touch on Derrida's double reading of Levinas, "which . . . shows, on the one hand, the impossibility of escaping from logocentric conceptuality and, on the other, the necessity of such an escape arising from the impossibility of remaining wholly within the (Greek) logocentric tradition" (Bernasconi & Critchley 1991, xii). Here I am not concerned with Derrida's strategy of deconstruction. Nor will I discuss Levinas directly, although in this article he is always a face of absence looking at us from above.

In “Violence and Metaphysics,” Derrida (1978, 82) reads Levinas as one who “summons us to a dislocation of the Greek logos, to a dislocation of our identity, and perhaps of identity in general.” This stance looks quite similar to Nāgārjuna’s attempt to escape from the essentialist ontology exemplified in Nyāya logic and Sarvāstivāda realism. In his plan of escape, Levinas seeks after the “naked experience,” which is said to

> liberate from the Greek domination of the Same and the One (other names for the light of Being and the phenomenon) as if from oppression itself—an oppression certainly comparable to none other in the world, an ontological or transcendental oppression, but also the origin or alibi of all oppression in the world. (83)

A similar account has been seen in Heidegger’s critique of Western metaphysics that, as the origin of ontological or transcendental oppression, this “Same,” “One” or “Being” has different names in the history of Western philosophy: *Physis*, *Logos*, *Hen*, *Idea*, *Energeia*, Substantiality, Objectivity, Subjectivity, the Will, the Will to Power, the Will to Will, and so on (Heidegger 1969, 66). Each of those names represents a particular metaphysical system within which being is present to us. A pressing problem for all Heideggerians, including Levinas and Derrida, is that the truth in any form of metaphysics can be possible only at the expense of concealment and domination within totality.[10]

As to Nāgārjuna’s similar response to the onto-theological tradition in India, which is mainly characterized by the metaphysics of *svabhāva*, we also see a strong yearning for liberation from ignorance and suffering rooted in the metaphysics of the Same. For Levinas, Derrida, and Nāgārjuna, the most serious problem of their respective reflections is precisely this ontological violence rooted in the metaphysics of the Same or *svabhāva*.

For Levinas, the agonism between the Greek (Hellenism) and the other of the Greek (Hebraism) reveals a perennial conflict between ontology and ethics. On the side of the Greek is Heidegger’s ontology, which is, as Levinas and Derrida remark, always confined in subjectism,[11] a stance contradicting Heidegger’s own intention, for “Being is inseparable from the comprehension of Being” (Levinas 1969, 45). Being reveals itself in the existent’s *understanding* of Being. It is important to note that, as Levinas points out, a *violent* priority has been found in Heidegger’s ontological distinction between Being (ontological) and existent (ontic).[12] To quote Levinas’ own words:

> To affirm the priority of *Being* over the *existent* is, indeed, to decide the essence of philosophy; it is to subordinate the relation with *someone*, who is an existent (the ethical relation), to a relation with the *Being of the existent*, which, impersonal, permits the apprehension, the domination of the existent (a relationship of knowing), subordinates justice to freedom . . . the mode of remaining the same in the midst of the other. (Levinas 1969, 45)

It is very clear that, for Levinas, the subordination of the *existent*, the individual person, for example, to the *Being of the existent*, the impersonal Existence, is violence—ontological violence. The same violence is also depicted as the subordination of ethics to ontology, of ethics to theoretism, and of the Other to the Same. With such subordination, the neutral, impersonal character of Being neutralizes the Other as a same neutral, impersonal being. This kind of ontology is, to quote Levinas and Derrida again, "a philosophy of power," "a philosophy of the neutral, the tyranny of the state as an anonymous and inhuman universality" (Derrida 1978, 97). This accusation, with its strong political implication, is very serious, reminding us as it does of the controversial relationship between Heidegger and Nazism. Although it is not our purpose here to make any judgment on the controversy, the above comments do express Derrida and Levinas's concern with the conspiracy between ontology and phenomenal violence.[13]

To escape from the Greek to the Hebrew means a return to ethics from ontology. As Levinas claims, ethics should replace ontology as the first philosophy. In this replacement, the recovery of the nonviolent relationship, the relationship "neither mediate nor immediate," is, according to Derrida, Levinas' true concern (Derrida 1978, 90). "[His] thought calls upon the ethical relationship—a nonviolent relationship to the infinite as infinitely other, to the Other[14]—as the only one capable of opening the space of transcendence and of liberating metaphysics" (Derrida 1978, 83). The infinite Other we encounter should not be taken as the object, particularly the object of *theoria*. Regarding the latter, Levinas attacks the imperialism of theoretism because it "predetermined Being as object" (Derrida 1978, 85). Whether or not philosophical discourse is able to escape from the "violence of light" in theoretism is not our concern at this moment. (To this question, Derrida does give a deconstructive answer.) What concerns us is Levinas' ethical aim to lead us back to the "naked experience" characterized by what is found "face-to-face." For Levinas, violence, in both the ontological and ontic senses, will occur to the *object* only, but not to the Other as face.

But what is face? In many places Derrida repeats the description of face in the style of phenomenology:

> The face is not only a visage which may be the surface of things or animal facies, aspect, or species. It is not only, following the origin of the word, what is seen, seen because it is naked. It is also that which sees. Not so much that which sees things—a theoretical relation—but that which exchanges its glance. The visage is a face only in the face-to-face.
>
> For reasons now familiar to us, the face-to-face eludes every category. For within it the face is given simultaneously as expression and as speech. Not only as glance, but as the original unity of glance and speech, eyes and mouth, that speaks, but also pronounces its hunger . . . The other is not signaled by his face, he is this face: "Absolutely present, in his face, the Other—without any metaphor—faces me." The other, therefore, is given "in person" and without allegory only in the face.

> The face does not signify, does not present itself as a sign, but *expresses itself*, offering itself *in person*, in itself, *kath'auto*: "the thing in itself expresses itself." (Derrida 1978, 98, 100–101)

Above all, face is naked, not covered by sign, not signified by metaphor or allegory. It is that which exchanges its glance. Face is face-to-face.

It is interesting to note that Levinas's "face" is reminiscent of Chan Buddhist's "original face." The phrase "original face" (*benlai mianmu*, 本來面目), as seen for the first time in the Zongbao edition of the *Platform Sūtra of Huineng*, refers to that which is beyond the inscription of good and evil (Zongbao, T.48.2008: 349.b). In its later usage in Chinese Buddhism, this phrase has often been used as a synonym of "original mind," "original scenery," and "original nature." These expressions are better employed to denote the "naked" experience without conceptual and ontological contamination. As a matter of fact, they should be regarded as nothing but the existential expressions of emptiness.

Violence in Discourse and Its Exit

The notion of the "original face" was invented in Chinese Buddhism to lay down an existential meaning of emptiness. For Nāgārjuna, the Other as face is purely ineffable. It can be understood only in light of negative theology. That is, no existents can be reduced to other categories (e.g., five aggregates, *saṃskṛta/asaṃskṛta*, etc.) characterized by *svabhāva* (sameness, self-identity). True existents are beyond conceptualization and verbalization. In Mahāyāna Buddhism, they are called *paramārtha* (transcendence), *dharmatā* (thingness), *tathatā* (suchness) or *śūnyatā* (emptiness). As illuminated by Nāgārjuna:

> When the sphere of thought (*citta-gocara*) has ceased, that which is to be designated (*abhidhātavya*) also has ceased. Like *nirvāṇa*, the nature of things (*dharmatā*) is neither arising nor ceasing. (MK.XVIII.7)

The "original face" can be seen only when it ceases to be the object of consciousness as well as when it ceases to be the object of designation (Kalupahana 1986, 268). On the other hand, violence to the Other as face arises right in the discursive construction (*prapañca*) when the Other is reduced to be an object. Here, *prapañca* is always diagnosed in Buddhism as the main cause for the arising of defilement and suffering. Regarding the meaning of *prapañca*, the most puzzling, yet crucial, philosophical term in Mādhyamika philosophy, for the sake of convenience, I will quote Paul Williams's lengthy exposition:

> I suggest that the word "*prapañca*" in the Madhyamaka seems to indicate firstly the utterance itself, secondly the process of reasoning and entertaining involved in any articulation, and thirdly further utterances which result from this process. "*Prapañca*" therefore designates the tendency and activity of the mind, weakly anchored to a (falsely constructed) perceptual

> situation, to proliferate conceptualization beyond its experiential basis and therefore further and further removed from the foundation which could lead to a correct perception via impermanence. *Prapañcas* are thus language inasmuch as language forms their 'substance,' but since their content is heavily loaded with contextual suggestion so they are caused by language, that is, they always stretch beyond themselves in implication of other conceptual structures. (Williams 1980, 32)

Prapañca, as the process of designating, uttering, reasoning, entertaining, desiring, imaging, proliferating, and constructing, is reminiscent of what is called by Derrida *différance*, which is also called "arche-writing." Derrida introduces *différance* as the temporization and spacing through which

> the movement of signification is possible only if each so-called "present" element, each element appearing on the scene of presence, is related to something other than itself, thereby keeping within itself the mark of the past element, and already letting itself be vitiated by the mark of its relation to the future element . . . . (Derrida 1982, 13)

For Derrida, precisely due to this *différance* as arche-writing that originary violence occurs. It is in this sense, for Derrida, that originary violence cannot be erased, because language is not possible without *différance*. As long as we need to use language, we will be unable to avoid violence. Violence is right in language. Put in Madhyamaka vocabulary, violence seats right in *prapañca*. Only following this line of meditation can we understand why Nāgārjuna defines "*nirvāṇa*" as "the serene coming to rest of *prapañca*" (*sarvaprapañcopaśama*) (Sprung 1979, 33).

One last, though certainly not the least, problem remains to be further pondered. For Nāgārjuna and Derrida, is it possible to eliminate *prapañca/différance* in the process of searching for liberation? If *prapañca/différance* cannot be eliminated forever, then it seems that violence will never cease. For Derrida, strategically speaking, there is no exit, no once and forever solution. As such, what can be done is to practice deconstruction ceaselessly in the history of metaphysics. As for Nāgārjuna, however, he seems to suggest that final liberation (*nirvāṇa*) can be realized only in *saṃsāra*, the world of suffering and violence. Without *saṃsāra*, there is no *nirvāṇa*, and vice versa. By the same token, without *prapañca*, there is also no elimination of violence.

Finally, we come to Levinas by asking him the same question. From the perspective of Derrida's (1978) reading, Levinas seems to hold a messianic eschatology within which hope is still possible:

> Truthfully, messianic eschatology is never mentioned literally: it is but a question of designating a space or a hollow within naked experience where this eschatology can be understood and where it must resonate. This hollow space is not an opening among others. It is opening itself, the opening

of opening, that which can be enclosed within no category or totality, that is, everything within experience which can no longer be described by traditional concepts, and which resists every philosopheme. (83)

I would like to conclude my paper here, which is based on this accidental dialogue among Nāgārjuna, Levinas, and Derrida, with the above quotation, suggesting that we read the Buddhist term "*śūnyatā*" (emptiness, voidness) in the sense of that "hollow space," "opening," "the opening of opening," within which the face of the Other will never be humiliated.

Notes

1 "A past that has never been present: this formula is the one that Emmanuel Levinas uses, although certainly in a nonpsychoanalytic way, to qualify the trace and enigma of absolute alterity: the Other" (Derrida 1982, 21).

2 To say that murder is a fiction is different from proposing a fictionist account. A fictionist would further qualify the first statement as "*the conventional knowledge of* murder is fiction," which means that to say "X kills Y" always conceals the causal complexity of the event by merely reducing it to the battle of verbal labels.

3 Jan Westerhoff (2009) distinguishes two usages of *svabhāva* in Mādhyamika philosophy: (1) *svabhāva* as essence and (2) *svabhāva* as substance. Essence-*svabhāva* refers to the specific property of an object by which an object is distinguished from the other objects. Substance-*svabhāva* is employed as an ontological notion, meaning "primary existent" in the sense that it is free from the causal law. It is the permanent foundation of the impermanent phenomena. Westerhoff concludes that "the elaborate Mādhyamika criticism of the notion of *svabhāva* is directed against this stronger notion of substance-*svabhāva* rather than against essence-*svabhāva*" (19–29). However, I would like to emphasize that the ontological notion of substance-*svabhāva* should not be separated from the epistemological notion of essence-*svabhāva*. This issue has been subject to dispute in the Madhyamaka tradition in regard to whether the notion of essence-*svabhāva* can be endorsed without qualification at the conventional dimension (*saṃvṛti*).

4 See also Chapter 4 for a detailed analysis of the notion *svabhāva*.

5 Here I adopt Kumārajīva's Chinese translation, which is different from the Sanskrit text. Also see Bocking (1995, 344). Among many English translations from the Sanskrit text, I favor Nancy McCagney's translation for the same verse: "Because openness works, therefore everything works. If openness does not work, then everything does not work" (McCagney 1997, 201).

6 Shōryū Katsura (2011, 267–275) also explains two usages of the Abhidharma notion of *svabhāva*, which correspond to the "loose" usage and the "strict" usage. The loose usage of *svabhāva* is applied to the category of *dharmas*, while the strict usage of *svabhāva* is applied to individual *dharma*. The former refers to the intrinsic nature shared by a group of *dharma*s that are classified into the same category. In this sense, *svabhāva*s means category or genus. The latter refers to the intrinsic nature of *dharmas* which determines each individual dharma *qua* individual dharma.

7 In the *Vigrahavyāvartanī*, Nāgārjuna criticizes Nyāya's theory of negation (*pratiśedhā*) (Bhattacharya 1986, 130–131).

8 In the MK.XV, Nāgārjuna defines "*svabhāva*" as "not created nor dependent on anything other than itself" (verse 2cd). In Candrakīrti's commentary, "*svabhāva*" is explained as "the one which exists of and for itself (*sva bhava*); it is the unique, ownmost nature (*ātmiya rūpa*) of anything" (Sprung 1979, 154).

9 For the debate between Nāgārjuna and the Nyaiyāyikas on the theory of negation, see Bhattacharya (1986, 101–106).

10 Ironically, in the Winter Seminar of 1933–34, "On the Essence of Truth," Heidegger asserted the necessity of violence in the path from the cave to liberation: "The *liberation is violent*. It involves acts of violence, and thus a resistance on the part of the man; he does not want to leave his old situation at all" (Heidegger 2010, 113).

11 'Subjectism' refers to the metaphysics of subjectivity to which Heidegger's critique is directed. For Heidegger (1977a, 229), "Man is never first and foremost man on the hither side of the world, as a 'subject', whether this is taken as 'I' or 'We'."

12 Krell provides a clear explanation of Heidegger's ontological distinction:

> "Ontological" refers to the Being of beings (*onta*) or to any account (*logos*) of the same; hence it refers to a particular discipline (traditionally belonging to metaphysics) or to the content or method of this discipline. On the contrary, 'ontic' refers to any manner of dealing with beings that does *not* raise the ontological question. Most disciplines and sciences remain "ontic" in their treatment of beings. (Krell 1977, 53–54)

13 Regarding the Heidegger/Nazism controversy, it is well know that Derrida stands on the side of Heidegger. At the end of "Violence and Metaphysics" (Derrida 1978) where "nationalism" is discussed, Derrida quotes Heidegger's critical comments on nationalism: "On the metaphysical plane, every nationalism is an anthropologism, and as such, a subjectivism" (319n80).

14 French '*autrui*' (the personal Other, the you) is translated by 'Other', while '*autre*' by 'other'. See Derrida (1978, 12, translator's note).

7 Speaking of the Ineffable . . .

Graham Priest

Introduction

Nothing(*ness*) is an important, difficult, and tantalizing concept.[1] Many philosophers, both East and West, have held it to be of central importance. On the Western side of the ledger, Hegel, Heidegger, and Sartre come immediately to mind. On the Eastern side of the ledger, there are a number of Buddhist philosophers who will be our focus in what follows.

Many philosophers who speak about nothing make the further claim that it is ineffable: one can say nothing about it. They even explain why this is so. Here, for example, is Heidegger:

> What is the nothing? Our very first approach to the question has something unusual about it. In our asking we posit the nothing in advance as something that 'is' such and such; we posit it as a being. But that is exactly what it is distinguished from. Interrogating the nothing—asking what and how it, the nothing, is—turns what is interrogated into its opposite. The question deprives itself of its own object.
>
> Accordingly, every answer to the question is also impossible from the start. For it necessarily assumes the form: the nothing 'is' this or that. With regard to the nothing, question and answer are alike inherently absurd. (Heidegger 1977b, 98ff.)

Our Buddhist philosophers are in the same situation, as we shall see; they take nothing to be ineffable, and explain why.

Clearly, there is a contradiction involved in speaking about the ineffable in this way. What is one to make of the situation? Here, the Buddhist tradition has resources not available, historically, to Western philosophy. A principle of Buddhist logic, the *catuṣkoṭi*, allows for the possibility that some contradictions are true. Perhaps this is just one of them. Of course, modern Western readers, heavily indoctrinated by Aristotle on the law of non-contradiction, may be skeptical of the coherence of such a possibility; however, it can be made perfectly precise and rigorous using the techniques of contemporary non-classical logic, particularly paraconsistent logics—logics in which contradictions do not imply everything. In this paper I will show how.

In the first two sections of the paper I will explain the notion of nothingness as it arises in Buddhist philosophy, by looking at its historical development. Then, after a brief interlude comparing Eastern and Western perspectives on the ineffable, we will look at a formal development of the *catuṣkoṭi*, and how this may be deployed to handle speaking of the ineffable. It might yet be thought that treating ineffability in this way—allowing that it may be spoken about—is something entirely alien to Buddhist thought. It is not. In the last section of the paper, we return again to Buddhist texts: this time the *Vimilakīrti Sūtra*. A central concern of this *sūtra* is exactly the ineffable and the significance of speaking about it.

Indian Buddhism

So let us start by going back to the origins of Buddhist philosophy. One of the most significant philosophical doctrines of early Buddhism is *anātman*, the doctrine of no-self.[2] All there is to a person is a bunch of physical and mental parts (*skandha*s) that constantly come into existence, interact causally, and go out of existence. A person, to the extent that she exists at all, is just a conceptual construction out of these—in much the way that, one might think, countries are not real, but arise from imposing conceptual distinctions on geographical terrain. There was nothing special about persons in this regard: the same story was applied to all partite objects. What does exist in reality is a bunch of ultimate parts, *dharma*s. These have self-being (*svabhāva*): each is what it is quite independently of any other thing. Everything else, and in particular, the objects of phenomenal reality, like tables and stars, is a conceptual construction out of these. Thus arose the doctrine of two realities, *satyas*:[3] an ultimate reality of self-standing elements, and a conventional reality which is merely a conceptual construction out of these.

When Māhāyana Buddhism arose, this picture of reality was severely attacked. In particular, the claim that there is an ultimate reality comprising *dharmas* with self-being was subjected to fierce criticism. The main architect of this critique was, arguably, Nāgārjuna (c. first or second century CE). In the *Mūlamadhyakamakārikā* (MMK) he mounted many arguments to the effect that no thing has self-being. Everything has its being by relating to other things, including its causes and effects, its parts, and our language/concepts. One might then expect him to have jettisoned the doctrine of two *satya*s. But he did not. Nāgārjuna (MMK XXIV.8–10) says:[4]

> The Buddha's teaching of the Dharma/ Is based on two truths:/ A truth of worldly convention/ And an ultimate truth.
>
> Those who do not understand/ The distinction between these two truths/ Do not understand/ The Buddha's profound truth.
>
> Without a foundation in conventional truth/ The significance of the ultimate cannot be taught./ Without understanding the significance of the ultimate/ Liberation cannot be achieved.

How, now, to understand the doctrine of two realities is a difficult and contentious question (see Cowherds 2011). It is clear that everything has the same ontological status, namely being empty (*śūnya*) of self-being. In that sense there is only one reality. But one must understand this reality as having two poles: One pole is our conventional reality, a world infused with conceptual construction. The other is the world *an sich*, the world as it is without such conceptualization: emptiness (*śūnyatā*). (Though note that this, like all things, must be empty. That is, it must be what it is only in relation to other things—in this case, to conventional reality. Conventional and ultimate reality are like different sides of the same coin.) We meet here, the origin of the Buddhist notion of nothing.

But what is this emptiness, the world *an sich*, like? Almost by definition, one cannot say. It is what remains when one strips away all human imposition, and that means all language. Nāgārjuna makes the point explicitly. MMK XXII.11–12 tells us that:

> 'Empty' should not be asserted./ 'Nonempty' should not be asserted./ Neither both nor neither should be asserted./ They are used only nominally.
>
> How can the tetralemma of permanent and impermanent, etc.,/ Be true of the peaceful?/ How can the tetralemma of the finite, infinite, etc.,/ Be true of the peaceful?

We meet here the *catuṣkoṭi* (Greek: tetralemma; English: four corners) for the first time, so let us pause to look at it more closely. The *catuṣkoṭi* is a logical trope, a sort of principle of excluded fifth, which goes back to the earliest days of Buddhism.[5] Given any two situations, there are, in general, four possibilities: that one (but not the other) holds, that the other (but not the one) holds, that both hold, and that neither holds. In the standard Buddhist thinking of the time, this applied just as much to being true and being false: statements may be true (only), false (only), both true and false, or neither true nor false.[6] An exhaustive examination of any situation must, therefore, consider all four cases.[7]

Given all this, the above verses can be interpreted as saying that something (the peaceful) is such that one can say no thing of it; the something in question is ultimate reality.[8] This does not mean that this reality cannot be experienced. It can (with appropriate training). But a grasp of it can be had only with knowledge by acquaintance, not knowledge by description. All one can do, as it were, is to point at it. It is a simple thatness (*tathātā*).

Nāgārjuna effectively founded the Madhyamaka school of Māhāyana Buddhism. A somewhat different perspective on the matter at hand appeared when the other Indian school of Māhāyana Buddhism, Yogācāra, took shape a few hundred years later. The idealistic spin of Yogācāra comes out clearly in the *Trisvabhāvanirdeśa* (TSN) of Vasubandhu (fourth century CE). According to Madhyamaka, an object has two aspects, conventional and ultimate. Yogācāra splits the first of these into two, making three aspects, or natures, in all. The first nature of an object of phenomenal reality is its *imagined* (*parikalpita*) nature. A tree, for example, appears to be a mind-independent object existing outside of consciousness, but it is not. That is its imagined nature. Its second nature is its (*other-*) *dependent* (*paratāntra*) nature: the object exists only in dependence upon the cognizing intellect, which constructs it out of concepts, and projects it onto an "outside" world.

The tree's ultimate aspect is its *consummate* (*parinispanna*) nature. For Yogācāra, this ultimate reality is just as ineffable as in Madhyamaka, and for the same reason: the very use of language produces an object of conventional reality. Says Vasubandhu (TSN 25):[9]

> The imagined is entirely conventional./ The other-dependent is attached to convention./ The consummate, cutting convention,/ Is said to be of an entirely different nature.

What Yogācāra most significantly adds to this picture is an emphasis on non-duality (TSN 13):

> Since it is the non-existence of duality./ And exists as non-duality/ The consummate nature/ Is said to have the characteristic of existence and non-existence.

There are no dualities in the consummate. This, in fact, entails that it cannot be described. To attribute any property to it would presuppose a duality between an object, *qua* bearer of properties, and the property borne. (How, then, one might ask, can it be characterized as both existing and not existing? We shall see in due course.)

One duality is particularly important for the Yogācārins: that between (cognizing) subject and object. Because conventional objects have no mind-independent reality, one cannot have an object without an act of consciousness directed toward it. But conversely, of course, an intentional mental state must be directed toward some such object. In conventional reality, then, there is always a duality of subject and object: the two go together. By contrast, there is no such distinction in the consummate. Ultimate reality, then, transcends even this duality.

Out of these considerations comes a revised notion of emptiness. In Madhyamaka, to be empty is to be empty of self-being. For Yogācāra, it is to be empty of all duality (as well), especially subject/object duality. Emptiness (*śūnyatā*) is beyond all such things.[10]

Chinese Buddhism

Next, to China. When Buddhism entered China at around the turn of the Common Era, it encountered the indigenous philosophies of Daoism and Confucianism; and the former, in particular, was to exert a profound influence on its development. The foundational text of Daoism is the *Dao De Jing*, a text of uncertain origin, probably written or compiled sometime around the fifth century BCE. Its gnomic utterances can be interpreted in various ways. But one particular sort of interpretation is relevant here.[11]

Phenomenal reality is in a constant state of change. All things have both a positive and a negative aspect, *yang* 陽 and *yin* 陰; as one waxes, the other wanes, until matters are reversed. Beneath the flux, however, there is a metaphysical ground, the *Dao* 道 (Wade-Giles: '*Tao*'). The myriad objects of phenomenal reality are its manifestations. Just as one cannot have manifestations without the thing of which they are manifestations, one cannot have the thing without its manifestations.

The Dao, however, is ineffable. As the famous opening lines of the *Dao De Jing* say:[12]

> The Tao that can be talked about/ is not the true Tao./ The name that can be named/ is not the eternal Name./ Everything in the universe comes out of Nothing./ Nothing, the nameless, in the beginning./ While Heaven, the mother, is the creatrix of all things.

The Dao cannot be described because, to give any description, one would have to say that it is a *this*, rather than a *that*. The Dao is not a being: it is behind all beings. Indeed, there are passages in the *Dao De Jing* which suggest that it is the application of language which constructs the phenomenal world: "the Tao has no name; it is a cloud that has no shape. . . . Things have been given names from the beginning" (Chapter 32).

Because Dao cannot be described, it is common for it to be referred to as *wu* 無, nothing, nonbeing. This contrasts with *you* 有, the beings of phenomenal reality. Some care is needed here, however. *Yin* and *yang* are opposed pairs (day/night, male/female, cold/hot), and one of these pairs is *being* and *nonbeing*. These are categories that apply to the things of the phenomenal world. This sort of nonbeing is a *relative* nonbeing, on a par with being. The *Dao*, by contrast, is *absolute* nonbeing (nothing), behind both.

The similarities between the Buddhist ultimate and conventional realities, on the one hand, and the Dao and its manifestations, on the other, are obvious. Indeed, so much so, that in China, at first, Buddhism was taken to be an exotic form of Daoism. Though it is not, the similarities were such as to ensure a substantial Daoist influence on the development of Chinese Buddhisms (see Priest 2010a). In particular, a concept of ultimate reality as nothing emerged from the fusion of the Indian Buddhist concept of *śūnyatā* with the Daoist concept of *wu*.[13]

Nothing plays a very important role in what is perhaps the most distinctive of Chinese Buddhisms, Chan (called Zen in Japanese).[14] The very name of this kind of Buddhism already says something very important about it. 'Chan' is a phonetic corruption of the Sanskrit *dhyāna*, meditation; and 'Zen' is a phonetic corruption of this. In Indian Buddhism, a major function of meditation was to provide a phenomenological experience of *tathāta*, ultimate reality. Various

Chan masters developed these meditative techniques, and augmented them with other notable techniques, such as shouting, eccentric behavior, striking, and other shock tactics. One of the most important devices in the context was the *kōan*, which is a puzzle given to students to solve. They struggle with it, only to discover that it has no coherent solution. The puzzle is generated by the fact that language is an inadequate vehicle for describing (ultimate) reality. Realizing this can trigger the veil of language to fall away.

The ineffable nature of ultimate reality is expressed by perhaps the greatest Zen theoretician, Dōgen (twelfth century, Japan). In one of his lectures to his monks, he says the following (note that '*Dharma*-nature' is just one of the many names used for ultimate reality):

> when people who call themselves twenty- or thirty-year veterans witness discussion of the *Dharma*-nature, they stumble on through life in blank oblivion. They climb upon the [master's] round wooden chair, claiming to have become satisfied with monastic life, but when they hear the sound '*Dharma*-nature' or catch sight of '*Dharma*-nature,' their mind-and-body, object-and-subject, usually just blob into a pit of confusion. Their state is such that they deludedly imagine that after the triple world and the ten directions[15] which we are experiencing in the present have suddenly dropped away, then the Dharma-nature will appear, and this *Dharma*-nature will be other than the myriad things and phenomena of the present.[16] The true meaning of the *Dharma*-nature can never be like that. This universe of things and phenomena, and the *Dharma*-nature, have far transcended discussions of sameness and difference, and have transcended talk of disjunction or union. Because they are beyond past, present and future, thought, action, and consciousness, they are *Dharma*-nature. (Nishijima and Cross 1994–1997, III: 126.)

The irony of this passage is that it comes from a lecture entitled *Hosshō*, Dharma-nature. Dōgen's claim that nothing is ineffable is embedded in a whole lecture about what it is. Dōgen, just as much as Nāgārjuna, Vasubandhu, and the Daoists, is speaking of the ineffable.

Ineffability East and West

The Buddhist traditions we have been looking at, then, seem committed to speaking of the ineffable. Indeed, they do so in explaining why nothing is ineffable. This is, in fact, not an uncommon phenomenon in the history of philosophy, the West just as much as the East; for instance in the work of Heidegger, as we have already noted. The same thing happens for Wittgenstein in the *Tractatus*. According to him, the form (of a fact, of a proposition) is not an object, and one can speak only of objects. Hence form is ineffable—the rub is that all this is explained in the *Tractatus*. In the *Critique of Pure Reason*, Kant is at pains to explain why the categories cannot be applied to *noumena*. Any statement about something deploys the categories. So one cannot make statements about *noumena*—the rub, again, is that all this is explained in the *Critique*.[17] (And before one runs away with the idea that this happens only in way-out metaphysics, it should be noted that exactly the same sort of thing happens in a number of the logical paradoxes of self-reference. More of this anon.)

Of course, the Western philosophers in these apparently contradictory situations have often suggested ways to defuse them. However, they have met with no great success in this regard. This is not the place to survey the matter, but let us take just one example. In the famous penultimate proposition of the *Tractatus*, Wittgenstein famously bites the bullet, and declares most of the *Tractatus* meaningless. This, however, saws off the very branch on which he was sitting. If what the *Tractatus* says is meaningless, we have been given no reason to suppose that form is ineffable—or even that there is such a thing.

Now, what do our Buddhist writers make of the predicament in which they find themselves? Perhaps surprisingly, they often don't mention it. (Why this might be, we will come to in a moment.) When they do, they tend to deploy the same sorts of evasive maneuvers as their Western colleagues—with the same degree of success.

Take, for example, the fifteenth century Tibetan Māhāyana philosopher Gorampa. He is as clear as his Māhāyana predecessors that the ultimate is ineffable. He says in his *Synopsis of Madhyamaka*:

> The scriptures which negate proliferations of the four extremes [cf. of the *catuṣkoṭi*] refer to ultimate truth but not to the conventional, because the ultimate is devoid of conceptual proliferations, and the conventional is endowed with them. (Kassor 2013, v. 75)

But he also realizes that he is talking about it. Indeed, he does so in this very quote. Gorampa's response to the situation is to draw a distinction. Kassor describes matters thus:

> In the *Synopsis*, Gorampa divides ultimate truth into two: the nominal ultimate (*don dam rnam grags pa*) and the ultimate truth (*don dam bden pa*). While the ultimate truth . . . is free from conceptual proliferations, existing beyond the limits of thought, the nominal ultimate is simply a conceptual description of what the ultimate is *like*. Whenever ordinary persons talk about or conceptualize the ultimate, Gorampa argues that they are actually referring to the nominal ultimate. We cannot think or talk about the *actual* ultimate truth because it is beyond thoughts and language; any statement or thought about the ultimate is necessarily conceptual, and is, therefore, the nominal ultimate. (Kassor 2013, 406)

It does not take long to see that this hardly avoids contradiction. If all talk of the ultimate is about the nominal ultimate, then Gorampa's *own* talk of the ultimate is about the nominal ultimate. Since the nominal ultimate is clearly effable, Gorampa's own claim that the ultimate is devoid of conceptual proliferations is just false.

In fact, the situation played itself out again 300 years later in Kant's *Critique of Pure Reason*. To try to avoid the apparently contradictory situation in which he finds himself with respect to talking of the ineffable, Kant drew a distinction between an illegitimate positive notion of a noumenon and a legitimate negative, or limiting, notion. This does not help, however: according to Kant, the negative notion is there to place a limit on the domain in which we can apply thought/language. But to say that there is a domain to which we cannot apply thought/language is clearly to say something about this domain, and so apply thought/language to it.[18]

Indeed, the Gorampa/Kant/Wittgenstein predicament is inevitable. If one wishes to explain why something is ineffable, one *must* refer to it and say something about it. To refer to something *else*, about which one *can* talk, is just to change the subject.

How, then, is one to proceed if one is to make sense of the situation?

Formalizing the Catuṣkoṭi

A strategy that recommends itself is simply to endorse the contradiction involved! After all, the Buddhist thinkers were working in the context of the *catuṣkoṭi*, the third *koṭi* of which is precisely that of a true contradiction. (Perhaps this is why many of the Buddhist thinkers we have met did not appear to be troubled by the contradiction.) But how is one to make sense of this, precisely?

It might be thought that the idea is entirely incoherent. It is not. The *catuṣkoṭi* can be given a rigorous formulation by applying the techniques of contemporary paraconsistent logic. Deploying these, one may see exactly how some things can be true of the ineffable. I now show how.

We will proceed in four stages. The first is a simple formalization of the *catuṣkoṭi*. First Degree Entailment (FDE)[19] is a system of paraconsistent logic that can be set up in many ways, but one of these is as a four-valued logic whose values are exactly: *t* (true only), *f* (false only), *b* (both), and *n* (neither). The values are standardly depicted by the following diagram—called by logicians a 'Hasse diagram':

$$\begin{array}{c} t \\ \wedge \\ b \quad n \\ \vee \\ f \end{array}$$

The four corners of truth and the Hasse diagram seem like a marriage made for each other in a Buddhist heaven! (as observed in Garfield and Priest 2009). The four corners (*koṭis*) of the diagram are exactly the four corners of truth.

Sentences are assigned *one* of these values. If a formula, *A*, has the value *t*, its negation, ~*A* (*it is not the case that A*) has the value *f*. If a formula has the value *f*, its negation has the value *t*. The negation of a formula with value *b* is itself *b*; and the value of a formula with value *n* is itself *n*. The value of a conjunction of two formulas, $A \wedge B$ (*A and B*), is the greatest lower bound of the values of *A* and *B*; that is, the greatest value that is less than or equal to both of them. (So if *A* has the value *t* and *B* has the value *b*, the conjunction has the value *b*; and if *A* has the value *b* and *B* has the value *n*, the conjunction has the value *f*.) The value of a disjunction of two formulas, $A \vee B$ (*A or B*), is the least upper bound of the values of *A* and *B*; that is the least value that is greater than or equal to both of them.

A valid argument is one that preserves truth, in some sense. In many-valued logics of the kind we have here, the values to be preserved are called *designated values*. In the present logic, the designated values are *t* and *b* (true only, and both true and false). So an inference is valid just if whenever all of the premises take one of these values, so does the conclusion. (In particular, then, the inference from *A* and $\neg A$ to B is invalid, since *A* and ¬A can take the value *b*, while *B* takes the false *f*.)

As formulated, FDE gives us an account of *truth*. But what we need is a theory that explains how certain states of affairs are ineffable. In other words, we need, not a theory of truth, but a theory of *reality*. This is obtained by reinterpreting the semantics in a natural way. This is the second stage of our procedure.

We now think of the bearers of semantic values, not as sentences, but as states of affairs. Connectives generate complex states of affairs. Thus, if *A* and *B* are states of affairs, then $A \wedge B$, $A \vee B$, and $\neg A$ are the corresponding conjunctive, disjunctive, and negative state of affairs. As for the values themselves: A state of affairs that receives the value *t* exists, and its negation does not. A state of affairs that takes the value *f* is such that its negation exists, and it does not. A state of affairs that receives the value *b* is such that both it and its negation exist. A state of affairs that receives the value *n* is such that neither it nor its negation exists.

Now that we have machinery to talk about states of affairs, we can represent the thought that some of these are ineffable. This is the third stage of the construction. We do this by adding a fifth value to the values of the *catuṣkoṭi*, *e* (emptiness).[20] This is the value of a state of affairs that is ineffable. It cannot be described. *A fortiori*, it neither exists, does not, both or neither. Clearly, a state of affairs is ineffable iff (if and only if) any complex state of affairs involving it is. (Thus, e.g., you can describe the state $\neg A$ iff you can describe the state *A*—by adding or removing a negation.) This means that the truth functions for the connectives should be extended to handle *e*, by requiring that a state of affairs take the value *e* iff one of its parts does. Nothing else in the machinery, including the designated values, changes.

We now need to accommodate the possibility that a state of affairs can be ineffable, *and* that one can say something about it—that is, that it can take the value *e and* one of the other value. This is done with the fourth, and most crucial, stage of the construction. We turn the logic into plurivalent logic.[21] In the usual semantics of a logical system, including the ones we have been dealing with so far, the bearers of semantic values (formulas or states of affairs) take *exactly* one semantic value. In a plurivalent logic they can have *more* than one. So technically, value-bearers are evaluated not by a function, but by a relation. Every bearer relates to at least one of our five values, but possibly to more than one.

$\neg A$ relates to some value, v, just if v can be obtained by negating (in the old sense) some value of A. $A \wedge B$ relates to some value, v, if this can be obtained by conjoining (in the old sense) some value of A and some value of B. Similarly for disjunction. A valid inference is now one such that whenever every premise has at least one designated value, so does the conclusion.[22]

With this, our aim has been achieved. The crucial point, for present purposes, is that a state of affairs can have the value e (ineffability), but it can have one of the (other) values of the *catuṣkoṭi as well.*

The Paradox of Speaking of the Ineffable

Given these technical details, we can now return to speaking of nothing. A state of affairs that receives the value e is ineffable.[23] If a state of affairs receives one of the other values, it exists or it does not, and its negation exists or does not. *A fortiori*, it is effable, since we can say true and false things about it.[24] A state of affairs can therefore be both ineffable and not ineffable.

The fact that one can say true things about a state of affairs might well be thought to render its ineffability—the assignment of e to it—otiose: an idle wheel. That would be a mistake. The fact that one can say something about nothing does not undercut the fact that one cannot. We are, after all, in the context of the *catuṣkoṭi*, where the falsity of a statement does not necessarily rule out its truth. But what, then, grounds the assignment of the value e?

We may answer this question by noting how paradoxes of ineffability arise in modern logic, in connection with some of the paradoxes of self-reference—notably, those that concern the notion of definability. Take König's paradox, for example. There is an absolute infinity of ordinals, but only a countable number that are definable: that is, such that there are names (non-indexical noun phrases) that refer to them. Hence, there must be a least indefinable ordinal. Since it cannot be referred to, one cannot say anything about it. But the phrase "the least indefinable ordinal" refers to it, so one can say something about it, such as that it is indefinable.[25]

So it is with nothing. Let us write '**n**' for 'nothing'. The symbol '**n**' is certainly a name for nothing. To see this, note that the natural principle governing the predicate 'denote' is the Denotation Schema:[26]

- Den ('t' , x) iff $x = t$

That is, 't' denotes an object x iff $x = t$ (e.g., 'John' denotes x iff x = John). In particular:

- *Den* ('**n**', **n**) iff **n** = **n**

Since it is a logical truth that **n** = **n**, it follows that *Den* ('**n**', **n**). That is, '**n**' denotes *nothing*.

But nothing is not an object; it is behind all objects. So no object is **n**. That is, for every object, x, $x \neq \mathbf{n}$. Hence, if 't' is any name of an object, $t \neq \mathbf{n}$. By contraposing the Denotation Schema, it follows that ¬ *Den*('t' , **n**). Thus, **n** has no name—not even '**n**'.

Therefore, '**n**' behaves exactly as does the name 'the least indefinable ordinal'. It refers to something that cannot be referred to—nothing—and so this cannot be spoken of. But it does, so it can.

The Transcendence of Duality

It might be thought that this kind of maneuver, though it be at home in modern logical paradoxes, is alien to Buddhism. Let me therefore conclude my discussion by looking at one of the most important Māhāyana texts, at least in the Chinese tradition, the *Vimilakīrti Sūtra*. This text is much concerned with the transcendence of dualities, including that between the effable and the ineffable, and it shows exactly how one can, indeed must, talk about the ineffable.

At one point in the *sūtra*, a goddess appears in the room. When the somewhat hapless Śāriputra tries to brush off the flower petals she scatters around, a dialogue ensues. This turns to the question of how long Śāriputra has been enlightened. We then read:

> "Venerable sir," said the goddess, "how long has your attainment of emancipation been?"
>
> Shariputra was silent and did not answer.
>
> The goddess said, "With your great wisdom, venerable sir, why do you remain silent?"
>
> Shariputra replied, "Emancipation cannot be spoken of in words. Therefore I do not know what I can say to you." (Translation from Watson 1997, 87)

The emancipated state (grasping nothing) is ineffable, so one can say nothing of it. Śāriputra then receives a sharp rebuke:

> The goddess said, "Words, writing, all are marks of emancipation. Why? Because emancipation is not internal, not external, and not in between. And words, likewise, are not internal, not external, and not in between. Therefore, Shariputra, you can speak of emancipation without putting words aside.

> Why? Because all things that exist are marks of emancipation." (Watson 1997, 87)

One can, then, speak of the ineffable. If all things have the nature of emptiness, then so do words. Words are not things over and above nothing. They are in nothing.

If one left matters at this, one might just think that the *sūtra* is simply rejecting ineffability. It is therefore important to take the preceding passage in conjunction with another concerning silence that occurs a little later in the *sūtra*. The topic at this point is the nature of transcending duality. Vimilakīrti asks a host of bodhisattvas what it is to transcend duality. Each bodhisattva notes a duality and says what it is to transcend it. The dualities are things such as: good and not good, perception and object perceived, self and other. For example, the bodhisattva Good Eye says:

> The unique in form and the formless constitute a dualism. But if one understands that the unique in form is in fact the formless, and then does not seize on the formless but sees all as equal, one may in this way enter the gate of nondualism. (Watson 1997, 104)

At the end of the sequence, Mañjuśrī himself (the Bodhisattva of Wisdom) is asked for his answer. He says:

> To my way of thinking, all *dharma*s are without words, without explanation, without purport, without cognition, removed from all questions and answers. In this way one may enter the gate of nondualism. (Watson 1997, 110)

Finally, Vimilakīrti, the real hero of the *sūtra*, is asked what he thinks:

> Then Mañjuśrī said to Vimilakīrti, "Each of us has given an explanation. Now, sir, it is your turn to speak. How does the bodhisattva enter the gate of non-dualism?"
>
> At that time Vimilakīrti remained silent and did not speak a word.
>
> Manjushri sighed and said, "Excellent, excellent! Not a word, not a syllable—this truly is to enter the gate of non-dualism. (Watson 1997, 110)

Effable/ineffable is itself a duality. If all dualities are to be transcended, then so must this one be. The goddess has shown how to speak about nothing. Vimilakīrti shows how not to. What Mañjuśrī appreciates is that, in conjunction with what has already been said, Vimilakīrti's silence—unlike his own words—manifests the transcendence of this duality.

Non-duality, then, *requires* that one talk about the ineffable; the techniques of paraconsistent logic show how to make precise sense of this idea.

Notes

1 In English, 'nothing' may be a noun phrase or a quantifier phrase. In this essay, I shall use it solely as a noun phrase, reserving 'no thing' for the quantifier phrase.
2 For a general introduction to Indian Buddhism, see Siderits (2007).
3 '*Satya*' can also mean 'truth'. Unfortunately, it is standardly translated this way, which is often most misleading.
4 Translations from the MMK are from Garfield (1995).
5 Thus, for example, in some of the *sūtras*, we find interlocutors of the Buddha employing it. For discussion, see Priest (2010b).
6 Note, in particular, that something's being false is *not* the same as it not being true, since it can be both true and false.
7 Jaina thought, developing around the same time, took there to be not just four, but seven, possibilities on any given topic. See Priest (2008a).
8 In fact, the above claim is made about a Buddha, someone who has achieved liberation. But we are told just a few lines later that a Buddha and (ultimate) reality have the same nature. Indeed, it is a common view in Buddhism that the Buddha has three distinct embodiments, one of which is just reality itself, the *Dharmakāya* (reality body).
9 Translations are taken from Garfield (2002b).
10 See Garfield and Priest (2003, esp. Secs. 5 and 7).
11 For an account of Daoism, see J. L. Liu (2006, chs. 6, 7).
12 Translations are many and varied. The following come from Kwok, Palmer, and Ramsay (1993).
13 Much of this is made by Watts (1957).
14 On Zen, see Kasulis (1981).
15 Sc.: the directions of time and space.
16 Recall that these are aspects of the one reality.
17 For more on these matters, see Priest (2005).
18 See Priest (2002, sec. 5.5).
19 For full details of FDE, see Priest (2008b, ch. 8).
20 For what follows, see Priest (2010b), where the logic is called FDE^e.
21 For the technical details of what follows, see Priest (2014).
22 It can be shown that these semantics determine exactly the same inferences to be valid as FDE^e.
23 Strictly speaking, here and in what follows, what is said is with respect to a particular assignment of semantic values.
24 Is to be ineffable to be such that one can say no *true* thing true about it, or no *true or false* thing about it? These, in fact, come to the same thing. If one can say no true or false thing, one can say no true thing. And if one can say no true thing, one can say no false thing either. For if one could say something false, one could say something true by negating it.
25 On König's and related paradoxes, see Priest (2002, secs. 9.3, 9.4).
26 See Priest (2005, sec. 8.2).

8 Emptiness as Subject-Object Unity

Sengzhao on the Way Things Truly Are

Chien-hsing Ho

Introduction

The notion of emptiness figures prominently in both Indian and Chinese philosophy. In India, Nāgārjuna (c. 150–250 CE), founder of the Madhyamaka school of Mahayana Buddhism, propounded a philosophy of emptiness, according to which, since all things are dependently originated, all things are empty (*śūnya*) in the sense of having no independent and unchanging existence or nature (*svabhāva*). He set forth a doctrine of two truths/realities (*satya*) to the effect that things are empty and illusory from the perspective of ultimate truth (*paramārthasatya*), but are real from that of conventional truth (*saṃvṛtisatya*). In the Madhyamaka school, ultimate truth is equated with emptiness (*śūnyatā*). However, there are wide disagreements on how best to construe the notion of ultimate truth.

With the introduction of Buddhism into China during the early centuries of the common era, the notion of emptiness (*kong*, 空) soon became a focus of attention among Buddhist thinkers. In the Wei-Jin period (220–420 CE), Chinese philosophers were typically preoccupied with the trend of thought known as "arcane learning" (*xuanxue*, 玄學), which laid great emphasis on the Daoist classics the *Laozi* and the *Zhuangzi* and the notion of nothingness (*wu*, 無). In this intellectual milieu, while Chinese thinkers were less likely than their Indian peers to dismiss the notion of emptiness as nihilistic, even those of Madhyamaka leanings might interpret it in the light of Daoist views.[1]

One naturally wonders, given the strong Daoist presence in the Wei-Jin period, how anyone from the period would construe the notion of emptiness and take the myriad things to be empty. As a way of illuminating this issue, I shall, in this paper, turn to Sengzhao (僧肇, 374?–414 CE), a prominent Chinese Mādhyamika philosopher, to explore his exposition and modification of the Indian Buddhist doctrine of emptiness.[2] Sengzhao exerted a considerable influence on later Chinese Buddhist thinking, so our exploration will shed light on the general Chinese reception of the doctrine. In addition, it will be seen that Sengzhao's notion of emptiness is philosophically interesting in itself, in terms of its relevance for ontology and the relationship between language and reality.

For the sake of conceptual analysis, let us distinguish the level of the myriad things *qua* individuals from that of the way things truly are. We shall call them, respectively, the *ontic* and the *ontological* levels. These two levels correspond to conventional and ultimate truth/reality as understood by Sengzhao. For Sengzhao, the myriad things constitute conventional truth (*sudi*, 俗諦), and their ontic status is exposed as that of being empty or void. Meanwhile, he equates the way things are at the ontological level with ultimate truth (*zhendi*, 真諦), supreme void (*zhixu*, 至虛), emptiness, the way (*dao*, 道), nirvana, and even non-attachment. Herein, I use the term 'emptiness' principally to indicate the way things are at the ontological level. However, it should be noted that Sengzhao eventually affirms the sameness or non-duality of the two truths. Hence, the distinction between the two levels is primarily conceptual rather than substantive, because the myriad things at the ontic level are, at the bottom, the same as emptiness at the ontological level.

In light of the foregoing, we need to explicate the ontic status of the myriad things and the ontological notion of emptiness, as well as the relationship between the myriad things and emptiness. In this paper, I read Sengzhao as dismissing the idea that reality has a mind-independent structure that comprises discrete entities waiting to be captured by concepts. I shall show that his notion of emptiness points to a subject-object unity wherein both the subject and the myriad objects are conceptually undifferentiated. Moreover, for Sengzhao, to be empty is to be devoid of determinate form and nature, so for him, the emptiness of the myriad things is related to their indeterminacy. On his view, the nature of each of the myriad things is indeterminate in itself, and taken together, the true nature of the myriad things is to form a conceptually indeterminable and undifferentiated whole.

In what follows, I will provide a philosophical analysis and rational reconstruction of Sengzhao's philosophy of emptiness. In the second section, I discuss the sense in which the myriad things are, for Sengzhao, empty, and ascribe to him a thesis of ontic indeterminacy. In the third section, I explore his conception of emptiness *qua* subject-object unity and explicate its relationship with the myriad things. In the fourth section, I draw out some implications of Sengzhao's philosophy and suggest its relevance for contemporary philosophical reflection.

The Status of the Myriad Things at the Ontic Level

Why, and in what sense, are the myriad things at the ontic level said to be empty? For Sengzhao, they are empty because, first, they are not real, and second, their status is intrinsically the same as that of emptiness at the ontological level. Later, we shall add provisos to this account, to accommodate certain subtleties in Sengzhao's thought; for now, we will focus on the ontic status of the myriad things as not real.

For a proponent of Madhyamaka, things arise, change, and cease, completely dependent on various causes and conditions. They are dependently originated and thus never self-existent. Further, things are thoroughly impermanent and ever-changing. Thus, things are empty of any independent and unchanging existence or nature. They are then not substantially existent. Consequently, Indian Madhyamaka holds that things are empty and illusory. On similar grounds, Sengzhao speaks of the myriad things as not real and as empty.[3] However, he offers a further reason for the myriad things' not being real: they are devoid of determinate form and nature and thus cannot ultimately or exclusively be determined as such and such.[4] As a result, they are not definitively existent in the way that is suggested by their seeming verbal determinability. This issue warrants closer inspection.

We are accustomed to discriminating between things and determining them as definitively this or that, say, as cats or dogs, blue or yellow, desirable or undesirable, and so forth. For Sengzhao, however, such determination is based on conceptualizations that are inevitably inaccurate, indeed delusional, and does not accord with true states of affairs.[5] For example, one may take a green tree to be definitively such. Yet, the tree may be green only in respect of the surface of its young bark and leaves, not elsewhere; furthermore, even the green surface will look differently to a color-blind person, to a dog, or under a microscope. Moreover, what a villager takes to be a tree may be just food for tree-eating bugs, a post ablaze for some meditating yogis, or a great mass of wave-particles of indeterminate nature for a stubborn quantum physicist.[6] Therefore, the tree is not definitively a green tree.

From the human perspective, it may not be erroneous to conventionally or expediently determine a particular tree to be a tree. Even if we dismiss any universal property, such as treeness, in virtue of instantiating which all trees are trees, the tree has a number of features that distinguish it from dissimilar things, namely non-trees, such that one is justified in calling it a tree. However, this does not mean we can use the word 'tree' or other, similar terms to have a complete determination of the tree. In its use of general terms, such as 'tree' and 'maple', language operates on the grounds of resemblance or commonness. It relies for its operation on the application of a general term to many particular objects that are held to be subsumed under the concept that corresponds to that term. For example, the word 'tree' does not by itself designate only one particular tree, but can be used, on the ground of different trees' resemblance to one another, to refer to any one tree or all trees. Yet, features that are truly specific to a particular tree do not fall within the semantic range of the word. It will not help if we appeal to more specific words such as 'maple' or 'sugar maple', because they, as general terms, also function on the grounds of resemblance. Then, such features can themselves be so concrete, specific, and fine-grained that the tree evades *complete* conceptual or linguistic determination, which must be abstract, generic, and coarse-grained.

The ontic level is the conceptual level at which we conceptually cognize things as distinct individuals and, generally, we tend to take them to be determinate. Nevertheless, we can also recognize, right at this level, that things are ontically indeterminate on the grounds of their being devoid of determinate form and nature. In light of the foregoing, we attribute to Sengzhao this thesis of ontic indeterminacy: given anything X, no linguistic term can truly and conclusively be applied to X in the sense of positing a determinate form or nature therein.

For Sengzhao, the way things appear to us is typically conditioned by concepts. As we shall see in the next section, for him, reality is somehow amorphous; it becomes (conceptually) structured into a world of distinct objects only when it is conceptually articulated and cognized by us. In today's terminology, he would agree that there is no ready-made mind-independent world with a determinate structure that empirical investigation can reveal to us; a world that houses properly sliced *res* waiting to be labeled accurately by linguistic terms. We may even suggest that much of what things are *taken* to be, as such and such, is only relative to the observer's conceptual scheme and perspective; there is no ultimate, perspective-free determination of things as what they are.[7]

Let us now consider the issue of ontic indeterminacy in relation to the use of language. After arguing that words do not match anything real, Sengzhao contends as follows:[8]

> As the *Zhonglun* puts it, "things are neither this nor that." Yet, one person takes this to be *this* and that to be *that*, while another takes this to be *that* and that to be *this*. This and that are not determined by one word ['this' or 'that'], but deluded people think they must be so. Then, this and that are originally not existent, whereas to the deluded they are existent from the beginning. Once we realize that this and that are not existent, is there anything that can be deemed existent? Hence, we know that the myriad things are not real; they have for long been provisional appellations [*jiahao*, 假號]!

A thing may be referred to by 'this' and taken by the speaker as *this*. However, it would be the referent of 'that' and taken as *that* in respect of another speaker some distance away. The thing can be referred to by both 'this' and 'that', but is not fittingly determined by either. Though it can provisionally be said to be *this* or *that*, it is not definitively either. This observation is made only with respect to indexicals. However, Sengzhao extends the point to apply it to all referring expressions and their referents, whether the expressions are indexical or not. The argument implicit here is shaky, in that Sengzhao shifts the ground from indexical expressions to expressions that people conventionally think to have a fixed reference. It might be that he views demonstratives or indexicals as primordial among all nominals and so capable of representing other nominals. In what follows, we shall, utilizing some other ideas of Sengzhao's, try to reconstruct an argument in support of his view that things do not have any determinate form that the use of any words whatsoever may tend to superimpose on them.

Just as we may, mistakenly in the eyes of Mādhyamikas, take the myriad things to be mutually independent, we may also treat individual words as independent of other words. We may further *entify* and reify the referents of nominal words, taking them to be self-identical, real, and distinctly demarcated entities. It is then a short step to believing that things, as referents of linguistic expressions, are endowed with determinate forms or natures. Nominal words are supposedly connected to, and properly matched with, their referents; in their literal uses, they, via definite meanings, direct our attention straight to the referents and identify determinate properties therein. Hence, we believe that something that can reasonably be expressed by the word 'existent' is definitively existent, while that expressed by 'nonexistent' is definitively nonexistent. We may further suppose that existence and nonexistence are mutually exclusive and jointly exhaustive, such that a given thing must be either existent or nonexistent, but not both or neither.[9]

This whole picture of the way referring expressions function is arguably flawed. Many words, and their correlated concepts, are interdependent and complementary, forming such pairs as 'high' and 'low', 'life' and 'death', 'something' and 'nothing', and so on. In such cases, one cannot introduce one concept without simultaneously introducing another for its opposite. Surely, for Sengzhao, the demonstratives 'this' and 'that' form a codependent pair of opposite concepts. Indeed, given any nominal word 'X', we can always coin a word, say, 'non-X', to form a codependent pair of concepts. Let us term such codependence "notional codependence." In light of notional codependence, it seems that we can cognize something as existent, as being something of which the concept of existence can be predicated, only when we are aware of nonexistent items of which the concept of nonexistence can be predicated. In this sense, the existent and the nonexistent, as objects of conceptual cognition, are interdependent. We can then appreciate Sengzhao's claim that there is no existence without nonexistence, and no nonexistence without existence.[10]

In general, the word 'X' can refer to the thing X only by depending on the word 'non-X' and non-X things. It follows that X cannot be identified and fixed by 'X' or the correlative concept independently, without regard to non-Xs. For example, the word 'cat' can refer to something and make us think of it as a cat only in relation to the category of non-cats, namely, things other than cats. A cat cannot be identified and fixed by 'cat' independently, without any regard to non-cats. A cat is a cat only in relation to non-cats. Moreover, due to the fact that X, the intended referent of 'X', cannot be identified independently of non-Xs, it is not what we may think of as a determinate X; that is, it is not an X as something fittingly determined, with an identifiable determinate form, by 'X', and thereby definitively differentiated from all non-Xs. Using the same example as above, we say that a cat is not something fittingly determined by 'cat' and definitively differentiated from non-cats. It is not endowed with a determinate cat-form identified by the word 'cat'. Put paradoxically, X is not definitively X and not definitively different from non-Xs.

In light of the foresaid, we can appreciate Sengzhao's view implied in the above quotation that things conventionally referred to by the word 'X' are not fittingly determined by 'X'. They are not definitively Xs, not things endowed with a determinate X-form. This constitutes his thesis of ontic indeterminacy. In addition, there is no sharp demarcation between Xs and things referred to by the word 'non-X'. Under a different context or conceptual scheme, the Xs may well be designated by 'non-X'.

As noted above, the myriad things are considered not real partly because they cannot ultimately or exclusively be determined as such or such. Just as the verbal referentiality of a thing induces us to reify it, similarly, its seeming verbal determinability leads us to attribute to it definitive existence. Now, if a given thing cannot be fittingly determined by its designating expression, it, *qua* a thing designated thereby, is not *existent* in the sense of having a definitive existence that people associate with its verbal determinability. It is not definitively existent. Since the myriad things cannot be fittingly determined by words, they are then said, in the earlier quotation, not to be real.

From the recognition that the myriad things are not real in the sense of being substantially and definitively existent, Sengzhao concludes that they are empty. It is critical to appreciate that emptiness here does not mean sheer nothingness. Sengzhao, as a good Mādhyamika, contends that as things originate dependently and are endowed with various forms and features, they are *not* nonexistent. Their non-reality stems from their lacking substantial (inherent and unchanging) and definitive existence, but not from their being mere nothings. The non-reality of the myriad things also stems from their being objects of conceptual experience, and not being the way things truly are.

For Sengzhao, the myriad things are neither existent nor nonexistent, though they can provisionally be said to be existent and/or nonexistent.[11] Here, all words are for him *provisional* because they do not denote the real, and are used to express their referents without positing any determinate nature therein. Consequently, one and the same thing can be expressed simultaneously by both 'existent' and 'nonexistent', insofar as the two words are understood provisionally; namely, such that their use does not ascribe to the thing singly determinate and mutually exclusive properties.

So far, I have discussed Sengzhao's claim that the myriad things are empty because they are not real. In the next section, we turn to his second reason for saying that the myriad things are empty: that their status is intrinsically the same as that of emptiness at the ontological level.

Emptiness *qua* the Way Things Truly Are at the Ontological Level

In addition to the considerations of the preceding section, according to Sengzhao, the myriad things are empty because they are intrinsically the same as emptiness *qua* the way things truly are. After all, if a thing is of the nature of, and intrinsically the same as, emptiness, it can reasonably be said to be empty. In fact, even emptiness itself is empty,[12] for it is neither substantially or definitively existent nor conceptually determinable. With a view to clarifying this crucial notion of emptiness, I now attend to the ontological level and Sengzhao's ideas on ultimate truth and nirvana.

To begin, consider this passage:[13]

> Though the myriad things are widely diverse, they are one in their true nature. They should not be taken [definitively] as things, yet neither are they nothings. When they are taken as things, names and forms spread out diversely. When they are not taken as things, they are themselves the real [*zhen*, 真]. Hence, sages do not take things [definitively] as things, nor do they take things to be nothings.

For Sengzhao, Buddhist sages can, like the rest of us, conceptually take the myriad things to be things, cognize forms therein, and use words to designate them. The myriad things *qua* individuals constitute the world of conventional truth, which cannot to be ignored or discarded, because it is the world of experience in which we live as human beings. The myriad things are not nothings; they form the framework of our world. However, given Buddhist sages' knowledge of what we call ontic indeterminacy, they do not delusionally take them *definitively* as things. The myriad things are devoid of any determinate thing-form. The fact of their being intrinsically the same as the real *qua* the way things truly are also indicates that they are not definitively things.

A Buddhist sage, indeed an enlightened buddha, can also approach things without conceptualization, in that he can experience things pre-conceptually in their conceptually undifferentiated and unconstructed state. Things in such a state are here known as the real, which is none other than the way things truly are, namely, emptiness. By contrast, not only do we, the unenlightened, normally experience things conceptually, but we also tend, delusively with a mind of attachment, to take them to be determinate. Then, when we learn that the myriad things are indeterminate, we further tend to take them to be *definitively* indeterminate. Since determination is a function of conceptualization, the best way for one to break away from such tendencies would be to eschew any conceptualization and attain a pre-conceptual experience of emptiness. Ultimately, emptiness can only be realized when the myriad things are not conceptually taken as things.

What is realized only pre-conceptually is without any conceptually identifiable form. Given the correlation of language and concepts, if an item lacks a conceptually identifiable form, it is not directly and properly expressible. Since emptiness is realized pre-conceptually, it is, in an appropriate sense, formless and nameless. Here, while the myriad things, being conceptually accessible, are, in principle, directly expressible, emptiness is not.[14] It cannot be represented adequately by words. Hence, emptiness as the way things truly are is *ontologically* indeterminate, in the sense that it lies beyond any conceptual identification and linguistic representation.

The difference between emptiness and the myriad things *qua* individuals corresponds to that between ultimate truth and conventional truth, a distinction drawn by Nāgārjuna. Here, one may be tempted to view "ultimate truth" as a metaphysical notion that refers to some underlying ineffable reality as the ground of the myriad things. However, Sengzhao emphasizes that verbal difference between the two truths by no means predicates that they are two *types* of thing. Ultimate and conventional truths are intrinsically one and the same actuality. Their difference concerns two different ways in which the myriad things can be presented in experience, namely, the pre-conceptual and the conceptual. We shall return to this issue later.

Nāgārjuna is widely read as holding that emptiness is itself empty, and that there is, ultimately, no difference between ultimate and conventional truths. Based on this reading, several contemporary philosophers of Indian Madhyamaka have adopted a broadly semantic interpretation of ultimate truth to the effect that the ultimate truth is that there is no ultimate truth. On one view, this means that the truth that must be grasped in order to attain full enlightenment is that there is no statement that corresponds to the ultimate nature of mind-independent reality. On another view, it means that the truth that must be grasped is that there cannot exist anything that is what it is in separation from everything else.[15] In either case, the point made is that there is *no* such thing as the way things truly are.

Irrespective of which stance Nāgārjuna might have taken on this issue, the above interpretation does not tally with Sengzhao's notion of ultimate truth. For Sengzhao, the teaching of ultimate truth highlights the idea that the myriad things are not definitively existent, and that when not taken as things, they are themselves the real. Truly, there is no true statement that corresponds to the ultimate nature of mind-independent reality. However, this is because there is, in a sense, no *mind-independent* reality, and, even if there is anything ultimate, it lies beyond the grip of words and concepts. Ultimate truth is ineffable; it is not a propositional fact that one can grasp conceptually and formulate in words. In addition, one cannot attain enlightenment by grasping the fact. And yet, for Sengzhao, as for Mahayana Buddhists in general, the direct realization of ultimate truth would effectively lead to the attainment of enlightenment.

Meanwhile, some may want to adopt a pragmatic interpretation of Sengzhao's notion of ultimate truth.[16] Indeed, on one occasion Sengzhao equates ultimate truth and conventional truth, respectively, with nonacquisition (*wude*, 無得) and acquisition (*youde*, 有得).[17] Since nonacquisition is a state of mind, it would seem that, for Sengzhao, nothing is ontologically real and the notion of emptiness is simply a soteriological expedient that is meant to empty one's mind of cravings and to suggest that enlightenment comprises freedom from any attachment whatsoever. However, this pragmatic interpretation does not appear to concord with the work of Sengzhao, who refers approvingly to emptiness or ultimate truth and takes them to be realized by a sacred mind. For Sengzhao, it is not that no reality is truly real; the fact is, rather, that the real is realized only by a mind of non-attachment.

If all these alternatives fail to account for Sengzhao's notion of ultimate truth, what option is there left for us? I think we need to look at his conception of nirvana, for it concerns what is considered ultimate in his philosophy, and he cites approvingly a line from an unspecified sutra to the effect that ultimate truth is nirvana.[18] Sengzhao discusses nirvana at some length, so we are in a good position to investigate his view on ultimate truth and emptiness. In this context, the following passage is the most noteworthy:[19]

> Things [in reality] have no form of existence or nonexistence. Sages have no knowledge of existence or nonexistence. . . . There is no figure in the exterior, no [objectifying] mind in the interior. Both the [exterior and interior] are quiescently ceased; both things and oneself are harmoniously one. Being tranquil and traceless, this state is termed *nirvana*.

In this passage, it is clear that Sengzhao takes nirvana to be a state of quiescent emptiness in which external things and oneself, forms and the mind, become one. The myriad things are rid of any conceptually cognizable forms (of existence, nonexistence, etc.) and sharply demarcated identities. This state of nirvana is a quiescent subject-object unity, in which the interior and the exterior cease to be divided, in that they no longer have conceivable separate forms.

On the ontic level, the myriad things are conceptually cognized and demarcated, but Sengzhao exposes their nature of being codependent, indeterminate, and without sharp demarcation in between. On the ontological level, emptiness is realized pre-conceptually, and enlightened beings apprehend how things are independent of our conceptual scheme and any concepts we happen to employ. On the one hand, it is advisable to refer to emptiness as the way things truly are, for it is what the myriad things are in the absence of conceptual differentiation and structuring. On the other, since emptiness cannot be represented by words, there are no true statements that represent how it is independent of the concepts we employ in trying to express it. Being devoid of conceptually imposed structures, emptiness *qua* reality is somewhat like an amorphous lump,[20] to be carved up using our conceptual scheme into the things that we take to be constitutive of our world.

In emptiness, Xs are not yet Xs, and Ys not yet Ys. However, although the myriad things are not yet conceptually taken as things, as this or that, they are not completely nonexistent. For Sengzhao, the notion of emptiness implies a quiescence of conceptual differentiation (and this is one reason why emptiness is called 'emptiness'), but not the elimination of pre-conceptual (non-human-made) differences and features. Indeed, he takes emptiness to embrace the multiplicity of the myriad things while transcending all conceptual differentiation and determination.[21]

Now, if, for Sengzhao, emptiness transcends all conceptual differentiation, then by implication it must transcend the conceptual differentiation between the subject and the object. As a matter of fact, the subject-object divide is the most fundamental and enduring conceptual differentiation in our conscious life. Our daily experiences involve an experiencing subject and an object that is experienced. We think that external things are objective and separate from the mind. However, in emptiness *qua* reality, the subject is not yet the subject, and the object not yet the object. In recognition of this, in the quoted passage, Sengzhao speaks of oneself and objects as being quiescently one. Moreover, our discussion above about notional codependence enables us to see that the subjective and objective are interdependent, such that there cannot be one without the other. Their interdependence at the conceptual (ontic) level indicates their indeterminacy and non-reality, the knowledge of which may induce one to relinquish attachment to either the subjective or the objective and to seek to go beyond the conceptual divide. We then have subject-object unity at the pre-conceptual (ontological) level.

In the pre-conceptual experience of emptiness, the subject and objects are not yet conceptually differentiated. Clearly, emptiness as the way things truly are cannot be characterized as either subjective or objective. It is both and neither. For Sengzhao, emptiness is not a mind-independent objective reality, because what we conceptualize as mind at the ontic level is *part* of it. He would suggest that there is no such reality: when we see mountains as mountains, streams as streams, both of them as things external to our mind, they cease to be *real* things. Correlatively, the mind is not separate or independent from the things either. There is no real pure subjectivity.

As noted at the beginning of the paper, the distinction between the ontic and ontological levels is conceptual rather than substantive. The distinction is indeed *conceptual*, for, as mentioned above, the difference between ultimate and conventional truths concerns two different ways in which the myriad things can be presented in experience, namely, the pre-conceptual and the conceptual. The point is that the difference between the two levels is primarily that between the myriad things, the subject included, as conceptually individuated on the one hand and as realized pre-conceptually on the other. At the ontic level, the myriad things are conceptually differentiated; at the ontological level, the very same things form an ineffable intermingled whole. That being so, emptiness and the myriad things *qua* individuals are not intrinsically different. They are the same thing as experienced in two different ways, the pre-conceptual and the conceptual.[22]

The view that emptiness and the myriad things *qua* individuals are intrinsically one and the same actuality accords with Sengzhao's statement that the two truths are not two types of thing. However, this does not mean that emptiness and the individual things are *identical*. If they were identical, there would be no difference between the pre-conceptual and the conceptual, and an unenlightened person would be a buddha in every respect, which is absurd. While this is an intricate issue, we shall, for our purposes here, adhere to the *conceptual* distinction between the two levels concerned.

On Sengzhao's view, the myriad things are empty, indeterminate, and without any sharp demarcation between them. All this is reinforced by his acknowledgement of emptiness as their true nature. The myriad things are empty partly because they are of the nature of emptiness. Their ontic indeterminacy is strengthened by the ontological fact that emptiness cannot be conceptually determined. Moreover, the fact that, in emptiness, all things are conceptually undifferentiated strengthens the view that the myriad things are not definitively distinct from one another. From this, we see the intimate relationship between emptiness and the myriad things.

Correspondingly, as one recognizes that the myriad things are codependent and should not be taken definitively as this or that, one may refrain from attaching oneself to any of them while comprehending that things are interrelated and not truly mutually distinct. One may then turn toward the ontological level, wherein the myriad things are not conceived as things at all.

Sengzhao's Philosophy of Emptiness for the Contemporary World

As discussed in the preceding section, Sengzhao's ontological notion of emptiness implies the quiescence of conceptual differentiation and structuring as well as formlessness and ineffability. The subject-object divide is also quiescent, and emptiness entails a subject-object unity. Thus, in a line reminiscent of the *Zhuangzi*, Sengzhao writes, "Heaven and earth have the same root as me; the myriad things and I are one body."[23] Emptiness, indeed, is the common root for all things exterior and interior. Far from being sheer nothingness, it embraces the multiplicity of the myriad things in their pre-conceptual state.

Adopting Sengzhao's notion of emptiness, we can view this world in a new and enriched light. Instead of taking the myriad things to be clearly demarcated and independent, we may now see them as interdependent, interwoven, and deeply equal. The world does not distance itself from us; rather, it is we humans who distance ourselves from the world. As we learn to feel ourselves as one with the myriad things and begin to appreciate the intimate connections between ourselves and other humans, other living beings, and the environment, we may develop increased compassion and an increased motivation to care for these things. This would surely make for a better world to live in.

Significantly, Sengzhao's articulation of emptiness is of direct relevance for contemporary philosophical reflection. He would concur with a number of contemporary philosophers in rejecting the ontological realist views that objects and properties exist independently of our mental access to them, and that the world is as it is independent of what we think about it. This does not mean, however, that for Sengzhao there is no such thing as the way things truly are. Nevertheless, emptiness as the way things are is somehow amorphous; it is transformed into a world of individual things when it is conceptually cognized and structured by us. Even though the myriad things are not real, they are not nothings either. Being constitutive of conventional truth, and as direct referents of provisional words, the myriad things may be said to have conventional and provisional existence. In addition, they are deemed to be real when they are not conceptually taken to be things.

If contemporary philosophers who reject the above realist views acknowledge the prevalence of notional codependence, they may appreciate the thesis of ontic indeterminacy that we ascribe to Sengzhao. Some of them may agree that the myriad things are *empty* in the sense of lacking substantial and definitive existence. Nonetheless, it would be difficult for contemporary philosophers to swallow Sengzhao's ontological notion of emptiness. Many of them, believing that all awareness is a conceptual or linguistic affair,[24] would readily dismiss as impossibility any concept-free experience that reveals a subject-object unity.

Our conscious experience is normally laden with concepts. One could even argue that concepts are prerequisites for our daily experience, in that the ways the myriad things appear to us are fundamentally conditioned by them. However, it is doubtful whether *all* seeing involves propositions and concepts, such as seeing that (X is *F*, for any *F*) or seeing as (X as *F*), such that, for any subject S, if S sees X, then S has the concept *F* and applies it in her awareness of X. It is one thing for one to have the concept *F*, but quite another for one to apply it in one's awareness of things. It seems to be neither phenomenologically evident nor logically necessary that our conscious experience always involves the application of concepts.

The genuine experience of emptiness is even less likely to involve concepts than any other nonconceptual experience, if any. Sengzhao would claim that such experience could be had only by those extraordinary beings who have attained enlightenment. In experiencing emptiness, one perceives the world without making conceptual differentiation between oneself and the world or between this and that object. While such an experience can easily be taken to be a kind of mystical experience with soteriological significance, it is unlike other mystical experiences in that it does not obliterate the myriad things and dissolve the subject in an utterly undifferentiated vacuity.

To defend Sengzhao's view, we can say that once we concede that the myriad things lack substantial and definitive existence and cannot be taken definitively as X or non-X, it is only one step further to recognize that they are in their true nature conceptually indeterminable. In addition, conceptualization may bring in subjective coloring and structuring that obscure the way things truly are. Consequently, the best way to know the true nature of the myriad things is to resort to pre-conceptual experience. As stated earlier, what is eventually realized in such experience will involve a realization of subject-object unity. In any case, the point for us to note is that the notion of emptiness is in tune with the dismissal of a purely objective, mind-independent reality.

Even though emptiness is indicated previously as somewhat like an amorphous lump, this does not mean that the various ways in which we could possibly carve up reality are equally valid with regard to the texture of reality, or that we can rationally carve up reality according to whatever perspective we please. In Sengzhao's philosophy, there is a reality beyond people's conceptual constructions. Reality is devoid of conceptually identifiable forms. Still, it comprises pre-conceptual differences. While conceptualization tends to preclude the presentation of reality as it is, some conceptual differentiations are better than others in reflecting the differences. Likewise, while words cannot properly represent reality, some ways of indirectly expressing the differences are better than others. For example, on a clear shiny day, the statement "the sky is clear" is conventionally true, while "the sky is full of rain clouds" is not. Even if the statement "the sky is clear" is *conventionally* true, it is *not* true by convention. We can say that it is conventionally *true* because it somehow correctly, though indirectly, expresses the pre-conceptual differences related to the sky. Similar points can be made about conceptual differentiations. Thus, when it comes to carving up reality, it is not the case that any conceptual scheme or perspective works as well, or as badly, as any other. Sengzhao's philosophy, then, would not collapse into an incoherent relativism to the effect that no one perspective—relativism included—is any truer than any other perspective.

Correlatively, the myriad things on the ontic level are endowed with concrete and specific features that evade complete conceptual determination. For instance, from our human perspective, a tomato is sense-perceived with such and such concrete features that the perceiver is justified, given the relevant convention, in calling it a tomato, but not a ball or an orange. The perception cannot be reduced to conceptual determination, let alone the perceiver's whim, but has to be regulated by the features of the perceived object. That being so, when it comes to our perceptual access to the world, it is also not the case that any conceptualization works as well, or as badly, as any other.

We have previously suggested that much of what things are taken to be, as so and so, is relative to the observer's conceptual scheme, and that people of different cultures and languages have different conceptual schemes. Still, this does not mean that different conceptual schemes are equally suitable (or equally unsuitable) as means for carving up reality. This is indeed a complicated issue, and we should just concern ourselves with two situations. First, people in different societies somehow perceive things differently, which contributes to the difference in their conceptual schemes. The Inuit reportedly have numerous words for different kinds of snow and ice. We may agree that their perception of snow/ice is more finely grained than ours, and that their conceptual scheme in *this* respect is more in tune with the pre-conceptual differences of snow/ice than our scheme. Second, the difference in our conceptual schemes affects how we further classify a perceived object: say, one society may classify a tomato as a fruit, another as a vegetable, a third one both a fruit and a vegetable. In the first situation, we should be able to find reasons for judging that a given conceptual scheme is more suitable than others for revealing a certain aspect of the reality. In the second situation, we are probably unable to judge between different conceptual schemes, yet this inability is not of much significance. Overall, while the world as we know it is conceptually structured by us, the structuring is not entirely a matter of social convention, much less of personal discretion.

For Sengzhao, objects and properties in our world do not exist independently of our conceptual access to them, though at the same time they are not merely conceptual constructions. Concepts are interdependent and incapable of fully determining the intended referents. This recognition should induce one to look for the way things truly are before all conceptual processing. In his philosophy, the ontological notion of emptiness represents precisely the way things are before conceptualization, which is not a structured world of discrete objects, but a quiescent subject-object unity. This notion, together with the correlated indeterminacy thesis, comprises a theory of emptiness that is coherent and philosophically interesting. Irrespective of its soteriological import, the theory itself constitutes a viable alternative in the ongoing debate between realism and anti-realism. It provides a refreshing and challenging perspective on how we may perceive the world and understand our relationship to it.[25]

Notes

1 Concerning the charge of nihilism leveled against Indian Madhyamaka, see Jay Garfield's contribution to the present volume (Chapter 3).
2 Sengzhao's main works are the *Zhaolun* and the *Zhu Weimojiejing*, which are here cited according to the *Taishō Shinshū Daizōkyō*, henceforth abbreviated as T.
3 In *Zhaolun* (T 45: 152c16–20), Sengzhao implies that as things do not really arise (out of themselves), they are not substantially existent, that they are not nonexistent either, and that, consequently, they are not real and can be said to be empty and illusory.
4 *Zhu Weimojiejing* (T 38: 377a7–10, 386b18–20, 389b21–22). Such a view is not clearly evident in Indian Madhyamaka, although Matilal (1971a, 155–159) had long ago construed 'emptiness' as meaning the indeterminacy of all things in the world.
5 The word 'delusional' is added to designate the kind of conceptualization that grasps things with attachment and take them to be definitively such and such. Such conceptual activity is present in greater or lesser degrees in all unenlightened people. Because an enlightened Buddhist sage can, and indeed needs to, make use of conception to identify things and communicate with others, not all conceptualization is delusional. Cf. *Zhaolun* (T 45: 152c24–27, 153c8–10, 154b3–8).
6 Sengzhao's own example is exotic: just as a goddess can, with her divine power, turn a man into a woman, so a person does not really have a determinate male or female form. See *Zhu Weimojiejing* (T 38: 389c9–11).
7 For a criticism of the notion of a ready-made world, see Putnam (1982). By "conceptual scheme," I mean a network of basic concepts and propositions by which people of a society organize, classify, and describe their experience. People of different cultures and languages have different (though often overlapping) conceptual schemes.
8 *Zhaolun* (T 45: 152c23–28). The *Zhonglun* is Kumārajīva's Chinese translation of Nāgārjuna's *Mūlamadhyamakakārikā* and Piṅgala's commentary thereon.
9 Some similar views are repudiated in *Zhaolun* (T 45: 153c15–22, 159a17–23).
10 *Zhaolun* (T 45: 159a27–b3), and *Zhu Weimojiejing* (T 38: 332c29–333a1).
11 *Zhaolun* (T 45: 152b1–7, b18–c20, 156b11–13); *Zhu Weimojiejing* (T 38: 332c27–29). In Sengzhao's view, to say provisionally that X is existent is to show that X is *not* nonexistent; to say provisionally that X is nonexistent is to show that X is *not* existent.
12 Editors' note: see Chapter 3 where Garfield analyzes the emptiness of *emptiness*.
13 *Zhaolun* (T 45: 156b8–11). For Sengzhao's emphasis on the intrinsic sameness of the myriad things and the real, see also *Zhaolun* (T 45: 152b1–4, b11–18, 153a1–5).

14 If emptiness is ineffable, the question arises as to how words can be used to gesture toward it. One cannot even *say* that emptiness is unsayable, because in doing so, one would have made it *sayable*. In his contribution to this volume, Graham Priest points out the predicament and contradiction of speaking of the ineffable. His strategy for resolving the predicament is to endorse the contradiction (see Chapter 7). By contrast, I have, in Ho (2006), attempted to resolve the predicament by proposing a strategy that does not require us to accept a statement of ineffability as both true and contradictory. Consequently, I shall assume that this issue does not constitute a serious problem for our approach.

15 See Siderits (2007, 202) and Arnold (2010, 394), respectively, for the two views.

16 For this interpretation in relation to Chinese Madhyamaka, see Cheng (1984, 53, 98–99) and Liu (1994, 103).

17 *Zhaolun* (T 45: 152b11–16). In Sengzhao's writings, the word 'acquisition' signifies conceptual obtention of something that is taken as real and determinate and is an object of attachment. The word 'nonacquisition', by contrast, signifies a state of mind without such an obtention. Cf. *Zhu Weimojiejing* (T 38: 377c9–26) and *Zhaolun* (T 45: 161b1–4). We can treat 'nonacquisition' and 'non-attachment' as interchangeable.

18 *Zhaolun* (T 45: 159a25–27; cf. 159b27–29). It is here stated that conventional truth consists of existent and nonexistent things, which, for Sengzhao, should mean the myriad things *qua* individuals.

19 *Zhaolun* (T 45: 159c8–11; cf. 161a7–19, 161b7–9). All these passages come from the essay titled "Nirvana Is Nameless," the authenticity of which has been questioned by some modern scholars. The bulk of modern scholarship, however, seems to regard the essay as penned by Sengzhao himself. That Sengzhao affirms a state of subject-object unity can also be seen in *Zhu Weimojiejing* (T 38: 372c19–24).

20 For the picture of reality as an amorphous lump, see Dummett (1981) and Eklund (2008).

21 In *Zhaolun* (T 45: 154c6–10), Sengzhao refers to the myriad things as being real and formless. Immediately afterwards, he indicates that, on the ontological level, things are implicitly different, but are not yet conceived as different.

22 This situation confers on the myriad things a paradoxical character. They are intrinsically unitary, real, formless and nameless, yet appear to be divergent, non-real, and endowed with forms and names.

23 *Zhaolun* (T 45: 159b28–29). The corresponding line in the *Zhuangzi* reads, "Heaven and earth were born together with me, and the myriad things are one with me" (*Zhuangzi yinde* 5/2/52–53). The influence of the *Zhuangzi* on Sengzhao's philosophy of emptiness is unmistakable. On the other hand, Sengzhao's notion of emptiness differs from the classical Daoist conception of nothingness as the cosmogonic origin of all things. Emptiness does not causally give rise to the myriad things.

24 See, for example, Sellars (1963) and McDowell (1996).

25 The author would like to thank JeeLoo Liu, Douglas Berger, and Wren Akasawa for their valuable comments and suggestions on earlier drafts of this paper.

9 On Nothing in Particular

Delimiting Not-Being for Knowing's Sake

Rajam Raghunathan

Introduction

How is it that we are able to know, to say or to think anything about nothing? Aristotle, in the *Metaphysics*, tries to sort out some of the difficulties that are involved in talking about "what is not." The failure to distinguish between different senses of not-being across the different categories, according to him, ends in a fundamental indeterminacy stemming from the predication of all possible contraries at once:

> For if anyone thinks that the man is not a trireme, evidently he is not a trireme; so that he also is a trireme, if, as they say, the contradictory is true. And we thus get the doctrine of Anaxagoras that all things are mixed together, so that nothing really exists. They seem then, to be speaking of the indeterminate, and, while fancying themselves to be speaking of being, they are speaking about non-being; for that which exists potentially and not actually is in the indeterminate. But they must predicate of every subject every attribute and the negation of it indifferently. (*Metaphysics* 1007b, 22–30)

We can say, in other words, that a particular subject lacks a particular attribute, or is what it is in virtue of not-being in some limited and specific way, rather than having to accept that it is all contraries at once and, hence, is indeterminate in nature. Similarly, though things are said to be in many ways—as privations, affections, comings-to-be, passings-away, relatives—this is always in reference to substance; negations, then, are always negations of "of some of these things or of substance itself. It is for this reason that we say even of non-being that it *is* non-being" (*Metaphysics* G2 1003b10–11).

Aristotle's various attempts to define not-being constitute a reinterpretation of the understanding of not-being introduced by Parmenides in "On Nature." For post-Parmenidean thinkers in the Greek tradition, the need to reinterpret not-being arose not only due to the unappealing conclusions to which the Parmenidean position tended, such as the denial of belief and opinion, but also in view of the challenge to the potential for knowledge which it subsequently inspired. Despite the controversy surrounding interpretations of Parmenides's poem, I will argue that there is a coherent sense of *not-being* as indefiniteness and indeterminacy which we can discern. In showing why, for Parmenides, the way of 'is-not' must be rejected in order to stake a claim to the prospect of knowledge, I hope to provide a context for appreciating the discussion of these same issues in Asian philosophy: to better understand the innovative nature of the philosophical contributions made by Asian thinkers, including Nāgārjuna and Sengzhao, a clear picture of the historical and philosophical development of the difficulties surrounding nothing and not-being is essential.

Interpreting Parmenides's "On Nature"

In order to get a handle on the sense of *not-being* at issue in Parmenides, we must first examine the difficulties surrounding the interpretation of Parmenides's poem. We are introduced to the central problem of the poem through the device of a journey it describes. The daughters of the sun bear the poet along a "much famed road" (*'odon poluphēmon*) (fr. 1, ln. 2)[1] to the "House of Night" (fr. 1, ln. 9), where he meets the Goddess—his interlocutor during the rest of the poem. The Goddess bids him to "learn all things" (*chreo de se panta puthesthai*), both the way of truth and the opinions of mortals in which there is no true conviction or trust (*ouk eni pistis alēthēs*). She presents two ways of inquiry or thinking:

> *ē men opōs estin te kai ōs ouk esti mē einai* (fr. 2, ln. 3)
> The former, is and is not possible for {it}[2] not to be.
> *Ē d' 'ōs ouk estin te kai 'ōs chreōn esti mē einai* (fr. 2, ln. 5)
> The latter, is not and is necessary for {it} not to be.

Of these two options, however, the Goddess reveals that only one is a viable path toward knowledge: the latter route is "utterly inscrutable," both because we mortals cannot gain an understanding of "what-is-not"[3] and because "what-is-not" cannot be pointed out or indicated. She further rules out a third possibility (6.8–9), a route of confusion and ignorance that mortals wander confounded, wherein *to be* and *not to be* are considered to be both the same and not the same. The poet is counseled to steel himself against the force of habit which quickly leads us to hear and speak along the lines that are proscribed, and instead to employ reason to judge the challenge (*krisis*) which Truth has issued (7.3–6).

Presented with these alternatives, the main question emerges as to what exactly the two initial "ways of inquiry" are, and the grounds on which the Goddess proscribes the second way. First, we can inquire into the subject of the verb *estin*. Taking our cue from the poem that describes a journey in which knowledge is revealed to the poet, we can understand the subject of *estin* as the object of thought and speech, exemplified in Burnet's translation of the two roads: "[*W*]*hat can be spoken of and thought of* must exist, because it can, whereas nothing cannot" (Burnet, quoted in Owen 1982, 15, emphasis added).

The nature of the two alternatives presented by the Goddess hinges on how we must read the verb *estin*. Those who would take the *estin* in its existential sense, as advocated by Furley (1989), Gallop (1984), and suggested in remarks by Owen (1982),[4] see the Goddess as presenting an exclusive choice that reduces to the strong disjunction that *something* exists or does not exist (Gallop 1984, 67). From this interpretation of *estin*, we can understand the purpose of the Goddess's arguments in terms of ruling out two of the possible answers to the question "does it exist or not?": an "unqualified 'no'" and a "qualified 'no'," leaving only the third of an exhaustive list, an "unqualified 'yes'" (Owen 1982, 11). The dismissal of the way of not-being, the first wrong road represented by the "unqualified 'no'," is quick, on the basis that what does not exist could not be thought of or spoken about (B. 2.7–8). The first incorrect road, then, represents an incoherent position of absolute nihilism. Parmenides's treatment of it amounts to nothing more than a formality; it is quickly crossed off the list of exhaustive possible answers to the central question, leaving the more problematic possibility of the second incorrect road, the "Blind Alley" of mortal opinion, introduced by the Goddess in fragment six. This is the route of confusion where the answer to the question is "either yes or no depending on what one is talking about, and when and where" (Owen 1982, 11). What is alluded to here, according to Owen, is the tendency of mortals to want both *einai* and *ouk einai* as determined by kind or contingent circumstance: in speech and thought, we try to distinguish existent things from nonexistent things by making claims, such as, "horses exist but unicorns do not," or "there is snow on the mountain but not here." However, in trying to draw distinctions between such instances, we cannot help but identify them, on some level.

The second reading of the verb *estin* that I will consider here, is that which understands the verb chiefly *predicatively*. This reading is offered by Alexander Mourelatos (1976) in "Determinacy and Indeterminacy, Being and Non-Being in the Fragments of Parmenides." Mourelatos understands the verb as a bare copula whose subject and predicate complement are "deliberately suppressed." The two ways, thus, represent sentence frames which characterize the subject in positive and negative terms: '_____ is _____' or Φx, and '_____ is not _____' or ~Φx (46). Under this reading, Mourelatos suggests, the negative way is too vague and would be without termination: like being told to go to 'not-Ithaca,' the way of '_____ is not _____' would entail a journey whose object cannot be correctly "determined, fixed or encompassed." In other words, negative specification must be relinquished from the start since it can go on *ad infinitum* without actually telling us anything. Mourelatos attributes Parmenides's desire to avoid the indeterminacy latent in the negative way, on the one hand, to a kind of psychological aversion to the "horrors of the *apeiron*," which he posits as "closer to Parmenides' philosophic consciousness than worries about the ontological status of non-existent entities or negative facts" (50).

On the other hand, Parmenides lacks, according to Mourelatos (1976), a conception of the world as "logos-textured," in which every concept has a privative that delimits negative predication to a distinct domain of meaning, which it is allowed to specify (51). For example, the expression "not-Athena" is unhelpful and vague without an understanding of the context in which it is employed, viz., in the absence of "an analysis of proper names in terms of definite descriptions" that could point to "relevantly contrastive relationships" among concepts, delimiting the range of possibilities to which the expression applies (53). If Pegasus, Diotima, Ithaca, Hera, and Aphrodite can all be described as "not-Athena," then the sentence "Paris gave the apple to not-Athena" tells us very little in the absence of further information about context and an understanding of the privative function of 'not-Athena,' viz., an understanding of the scope of the negation. For instance, is "not-Athena" a goddess other than Athena, a female other than Athena, or a divine being other than Athena?

Using this analysis of the way of 'is not' in light of the predicative sense of the verb, Mourelatos (1976) distinguishes between two senses of 'not-being' in the poem. Not-being as the opposite of 'what-is' emerges as limitless indeterminacy, which reveals itself epistemologically as an "incurable vagueness" (54). This is the "inscrutable" and uninformative track that must be avoided for knowledge to be possible. Not-being, however, also exists in more limited contexts, in the "relatively bounded" not-being present in judgments of mortal opinion (*doxa*): " 'Doxa' posits pairwise dependent incomplete things each of which has a character that can only be defined by negative reference to its paired 'other' " (59). The disjunction here is not an absolute one, since there is a mixing of opposites. Mourelatos takes up the imagery of the text to show how it parallels the two senses which he describes. He contrasts the directed "pointing out" of Truth, which he characterizes as "centripetal and target-oriented," whose object is what-is, to the wandering vagaries of Doxa, described in terms of "un-targeted [cf. B7.4 *askopon omma*, untargeted eye] and centrifugal" (59), which meanders toward the indeterminate and inchoate. Mourelatos's reading is explained in detail and carefully defended in several of his texts, but it is important to note as reason to give pause that such an impersonal use of the verb is without parallel in Greek (Kahn 1968/1969, 709n12). Furley (1989) points out, in a similarly problematic vein, that those described in the sixth fragment as *eidotes ouden* "are surely men who know nothing, not men who know 'the so-and-so which really is not such-and-such' or the 'such-and-such that so-and-so really is not' " (36). In other words, there are instances within the poem itself where Mourelatos's (1976) preferred reading of the verb is frustrated by the implied meaning of the passage, which demands an explicitly existential understanding of the verb. While Mourelatos's predicative reading of the verb suggests a subtle, psychological answer to why the way of "is-not" must be rejected as unthinkable and unknowable, textual concerns regarding his reading the verb in an exclusively predicative sense, to which I have merely gestured here in passing, must give us pause.

Fused *estin*: A Possible Reading

The interpretative difficulties that arise when we try to take the verb as exclusively existential or predicative recommend an understanding of *estin* as 'fused'.[5] On this account, existential uses of the verb remain the same, while predicative or copulative uses of it can be rephrased in existential terms; hence, statements such as *tauta esti* should be understood as "these things are the case" or "these things exist," while "this is sweet" could be construed as "there is sweetness here" (Furth 1968, 123–124). Accepting that the verb admits both predicative and existential senses allows us to distinguish two levels of description when it comes to the being in question: determinacy versus indeterminacy from the predicative sense of the verb, and definiteness versus indefiniteness from the existential sense of the verb. We can define these descriptive continua as follows:

> **Determinacy**: Conveyed by the predicative sense of the verb, determinacy consists in the existence of a thing as it constitutes a subject for predication and an object of language and thought.

What is determinate admits of being predicated and specified and, thus, is knowable and semantically distinct. The indeterminate, conversely, cannot be specified in conception and speech, thus emerging, as Mourelatos speculates, as a kind of semantic vagueness. We can think of determinate objects like a robin's egg about which we can make specific claims, such as "this robin's egg is fifteen millimeters in diameter," and "this robin's egg is a lovely shade of blue"; conversely, we can make some claims about indeterminate objects, such as "the crowd today was larger than yesterday's," and "the pile of socks in my room is growing"; but often, the ability to make such claims is undermined by the amorphous nature of the indeterminate thing as a subject for predication. For example, it is difficult to say exactly *what* a distant rumble "sounds" like.

> **Definiteness**: Conveyed by the existential sense of the verb, definiteness specifies the existence of a thing viewed from the perspective of its ontological distinctness.

That which is definite is most real and exists most truly. That which is indefinite has less real, perhaps only conceptual existence. Definite things include those that we bump up against in the 'real' world—the Statue of Liberty, a persimmon, my mother. Indefinite things, on the other hand, occupy a continuum of reality, ranging from a movie projection and time zones to mermaids, unicorns, and imaginary friends.

From the two levels of existence emerge four possible combinations:

1. The definite and determinate.
2. The indefinite and determinate.
3. The definite and indeterminate.
4. The indeterminate and indefinite.

It is these four possibilities that underlie Parmenides's specification of the possible ways of knowing. The first, the definite and determinate describes that which exists most definitely and distinctly and most admits of being known. For Parmenides, this, most properly, is Being. The last of the four possibilities, the indefinite and indeterminate, characterizes not-Being: as pure negation, it lacks distinctness and has no ontological status; while as utter indeterminacy, it is recalcitrant to being captured in speech and thought. The two middle alternatives can be inferred as the objects of *doxa*, representing—as Owen (1971) says—"qualified not-Being." The indefinite and determinate constitute nonexistent, conceptual entities which can still be the object of language and thought; hence, we can tell vivid tales about unicorns and mermaids, but are hard pressed to produce either one at the dinner table. The definite and the indeterminate, on the other hand, describe existent things, those with more than just conceptual existence. We do not attach predicates and attributes to these, either because we cannot do so—the thing lacks any defining characteristics besides the fact that it is indistinguishable—or, because it does not merit such specification, the thing is not identical with anything that we consider important or worthy of attention. Examples of the definite but indeterminate can be drawn from the use of "nothing" when it is not meant to dispute the existence of the thing in question:[6] if I hear a distant humming and ask, "What is that?" the reply, "Nothing," does not deny the existence of the sound but denies that it could be *of* anything in particular, it is just some indeterminate rumble; or, "nothing" in this context could also mean, 'It is not anything of importance or concern to us," or "No, it's not an axe-murderer. It's just the wind. Go back to sleep."

Of the four possibilities, Parmenides explicitly entertains only two: the definite and determinate, and the indefinite and indeterminate. The former, the way of *estin*, is held out as the way to knowledge by the Goddess. The way of 'is' is knowable and thus, determinate to the fullest degree: it can be specified inasmuch as it is studded with "sign-posts" evincing its nature as "ungenerable, unperishing, a whole of a single kind, unmoving and perfect" (8.3–4).[7] Being is also characterized in terms of what is ontologically most distinct and definite: the Goddess asserts the eternal, immutable nature of Being in light of the fact that it cannot come-to-be out of anything else; its perfection is embodied in the sphere, which is fully self-contained. The latter way, by contrast, is proscribed; it is not a "true way" to knowledge precisely because of its utter indeterminacy and lack of existence. The eighth fragment poses the decision between the two routes in terms of a strong disjunction, "it is or it is not" (8.16), but the Goddess adds that "it is judged—as it necessarily must—that the latter option remain unthinkable and without name (for it is not a true path), while the former one remains and is true" (8.16–18). Hence, the injunction of the Goddess in the sixth fragment is barring the poet—and through him, all mortals—from pursuing the route of nothing: *nothing* does not exist and cannot be thought, nor will it ever be the case that the things which are not will be (6.1). Therefore, no inquiry into them should be attempted. On the other hand, it is appropriate for us to say and to think of what-is, because it can exist and can be the object of thought and inquiry.

On this reading, the purpose of Parmenides's rejection of not-being, understood in terms of indeterminacy and indefiniteness, is to defend the possibility of human knowledge and philosophical inquiry. This point becomes clearer if viewed in light of Parmenides's dialogue with Xenophanes. An older contemporary of Parmenides, Xenophanes denied the possibility of human knowledge of the divine, contending that we could, at best, have belief (fr. 34, 35).[8] Parmenides is staking out a claim for the possibility of human knowledge and this claim rests on shutting down anything that infringes upon and dilutes this possibility. Hence, the way of is-not must be rejected by Parmenides: lacking all limits and boundaries, the indeterminate nature of 'what is not', along with its indefinite existence, eludes our epistemic grasp. Not-being "is not a true way," since it essentially negates the existence and knowability of things, obviating the possibility of knowledge.

By extension, however, the way of mortal opinion must also be rejected—by falling short on the scale of either determinacy or definiteness, the way of belief admits that its objects may not even fully exist or may be recalcitrant to thought. Qualified not-being is based on the assumption that determinacy and definiteness operate on a continuum, such that there are degrees of being and, hence, degrees of knowing. Given this assumption, it becomes increasingly difficult to say at what point something "exists" or is "known." Parmenides's rejection of the "blind alley" of mortal opinion is designed, then, to rout the kinds of challenges that arise from considerations of vagueness, both from a semantic perspective and from an ontological perspective. He thus inverts Xenophanes's claim that knowledge of things is impossible and human beings can only hope for belief regarding divine things. Belief, for Parmenides, is a manifestation of the confusion that arises in mortals when they try to pursue both what is and what is not—when they direct their attention to those things whose very being is indefinite and that only admit of incomplete and indeterminate awareness. Knowledge, on the other hand, is possible of determinate and definite reality, "what-is," the only subject of which knowledge is possible.

If we are to understand Parmenides as trying to lay claim to the possibility of human knowledge by excluding the boundless indeterminacy and indefiniteness which not-being at any level involves, it is, perhaps, ironic that his legacy should fall partly into the hands of the Megarians, whose paradoxes based on indefiniteness and indeterminacy of language and conceptual thought challenged dogmatic attempts to solve philosophical problems. Euclid of Megara (430–360 BCE), a disciple of Socrates, is described as deeply influenced by Parmenides and became the founder of the Megarian school. Though none of his writings are extant, his successor Eubulides of Miletus is credited with the invention of logical puzzles like the *sorites* paradox, which problematizes dogmatic attempts at answering philosophical questions by appeal to semantic and ontological vagueness.

Calling upon the indeterminacy of a conceptual category, such as 'heap', and the indefinite and ambiguous nature surrounding such a fact in the world, the Megarians appeal, at some level, to the Parmenidean analysis of not-being understood as indeterminacy and indefiniteness, casting doubt on the possibility of a stable reality that forms the object of cognition. While this may be overstating the case—since Euclid and Eubulides seem to be interested in raising problems for those who would presume to defend some philosophical view rather than systematically undermining the intelligibility of reality proper—the material point remains that the arsenal they employ in their assault is Parmenidean in nature.

If we are correct in identifying the dual continua of definiteness and determinacy as specifying two levels of reality and being, we can better understand the claim that only 'what-is' can be spoken of, thought, or known as a claim about the nature of the object of speech or knowledge. A definite and determinate thing can be the proper object of what is called knowledge. Anything falling short of that, either in terms of definiteness or determinacy, might be taken up as an object of reflection or speech, but could never be adequately captured by either, since it would fail to be adequately "real." The two continua allow us to specify in what way exactly the object in question falls short. The inheritors of the Parmenidean legacy seem to have adopted and adapted these continua in their own struggles against philosophical dogmatism. The Megarians, in the puzzles that have come down to us, clearly draw on the concepts of indeterminacy and indefiniteness to question the philosophical intuitions of their contemporaries. It is this continued application of the Parmenidean insight into not-being that lays the gauntlet for all subsequent Greek thinkers. For philosophical thought to be possible, these thinkers must all struggle with and find some way of responding to the challenge of Parmenides's two ways.

Ineffability, Change, and the Possibility of Knowledge: A Comparative Dialogue with Parmenides

Post-Parmenidean Greek thinkers like Plato and Aristotle contend with the consequences of Parmenides's two ways by attempting to mitigate and qualify Parmenidean not-being, suppressing the understanding of not-being as limitless indeterminacy. They interpret not-being, instead, in terms of not-being-a-something in order to recover the possibility of philosophical knowledge. By way of contrast, I will show that both ineffability and indeterminacy as the condition of possibility for complete human emancipation are arguably embraced in several textual traditions of Indian and Chinese Buddhist philosophy. In this section, I will first outline the Platonic response to Parmenidean not-being. I will then compare this view to the understanding of emptiness and not-being as ineffable and nonconceptual in Indian and Chinese Madhyamaka philosophy, as treated by Priest and Ho (Chapters 7 and 8 in this volume), respectively. I argue that while both Plato and the Asian thinkers considered herein concur that conceptual, philosophical knowledge depends on some determinate, definite understanding of not-being, they implicitly embrace some further notion of not-being that lies beyond the purview of concepts and thought. The dual continua identified in Parmenides's poems can further help us to better understand the nature of this implicit not-being in both cases.

First, let us look at Plato's response to the Parmenidean challenge. Plato illustrates the confusion that attends the discussion of not-being in his dialogue, *Sophist*. The interlocutors—the visitor and Theaetetus—are plagued by perplexity in their initial attempts to sort out "what-is-not", which is said to be unutterable, unthinkable, unformulable, and resistant to predications of quantity or quality. Yet, in virtue of speaking of "not-being" they cannot help but attach *being* to it in speech by characterizing it in terms of its qualities or quantities, thereby resulting in contradictions (239a1-b3). The nature of perplexity, here, stems not from the incurable vagueness of not-being inasmuch as it is recalcitrant to any attempt to characterize it, but from the contradiction to which it gives rise given the kind of thing it is—not-*being*, that is, not the kind of thing of which any attribute can be predicated. In other words, the perplexity and confusion surrounding not-being are no different from the difficulties that attend talking about nothing. The point to note is that in the interlocutors' quick dismissal of not-being based on our inability to talk about it or conceive of it without falsifying it, the nature of not-being is circumscribed in light of our understanding of being and beings that admit of predication, quantification, and qualification rather than in light of any sense of not-being as something indeterminate, without limit, or indefinite.

Plato goes on to identify the principal difficulty he sees with the Parmenidean conception of being and not-being: there is no conception of what is different from being without its lapsing into not-being (*Sophist* 244d2–8). In other words, Plato thinks that Parmenides never explores the distinction between *not-being* as different from a something or different from what exists and *not-being* taken absolutely. He tries to show how Parmenides's view leads to absurdities on both the semantic and ontological levels (244c–e). He further points out how Parmenides's views negate generation and corruption.

To mitigate these absurdities, Plato elaborates on the nature of the "different" as a relational term, through which whatever is different "has to be what it is *from* something that's different" (*Sophist* 255c), hence stands in relation to that something. All other things which participate in the *different* are different from *that which is*, hence the description "different" makes each of them not be; yet, they are all still beings, so they also share in *that which is* (256e5–257b2, 258b2–3). On the other hand, *that which is not* is different from those beings, hence it is "itself," pure negation and not-being; but it is also part of those things as limited not-being (257a4–6). From this, Plato (via the visitor) concludes that denial does not signify a contrary; rather, negations such as 'not' and alpha privatives such as "non-" point us to something other than the things signified by the words following these negatives (257c). In the case of *that which is*, what is different from it is precisely *that which is not* (25b7–8), which must exist, since it is so related to *that which is*. Hence, according to the visitor, their discussions have not only contravened Parmenides by showing that that which is not is, but also have manifested the form and true nature of *that which is not*:

> Since we showed that the nature of *the different* is, chopped up among all beings in relation to each other, we dared to say that *that which is not* really is just this, namely, each part of the nature of the different that's set over against *that which is*. (258d4–e3)

Here, Plato effectively makes a corrective sweep at Parmenidean not-being: it cannot be the indeterminate limitlessness whose very nature makes contemplation of it impossible. Rather, not-being is "not-being-a-particular-something" in virtue of being different from it; like the flip side of a coin, not-being is simply the "reverse side" of *that which is*. Since *that which is* also shares in the different, it is different from many other things, each of which not only *is* in many ways, but also *is not* in many ways too (259b1–5). Hence, not-being is "scattered over all those which are" (260b6).

The converse of the Platonic view is evident in Madhyamika philosophy, in its Chinese interpretation, as a point of comparison. As Chien-hsing Ho explains in Chapter 8 of this volume, it is precisely the indeterminate nature of the myriad beings that constitutes their emptiness of substantial existence. While reality may be divisible into ontic and ontological levels—the former constituted by the myriad of empty beings, the latter, absolute emptiness, supreme void, the way, and *nirvāṇa*—the two levels are actually fused, given the impossibility of locating determinate beings even on the ontic level. The radical momentariness of beings contributes to the inability to confer determinate form or definite boundaries on beings. According to Ho, Sengzhao's understanding of emptiness can be characterized in terms of ontic indeterminacy. That is, things are empty of substantial existence (that is Being) even on the ontic level of the myriad phenomena because they are devoid of determinate form and cannot be delimited or determined to be such. The myriad things, in other words, do not correspond in a definite way to the linguistic designations that refer to them. It is this referentially indeterminate reality that we clumsily carve up by concepts to suit our conventional purposes and needs.

Under Ho's explanation, Sengzhao's ultimate or ontological level comes closest to Parmenidean not-Being. Being indefinitely indeterminate, in contrast to the definite indeterminacy of the ontic level of the myriad of empty things, supreme void or absolute emptiness is pre-conceptual and inexpressible. The ineffability and uncognizability of this emptiness resonates with the Parmenidean point that the way of not-Being is unthinkable, unknowable and inexpressible. While Parmenides eschews this in order to make philosophical reflection possible and to rescue the human intellect from perplexity, the Madhyamika Buddhists advocate the soteriological potential of this reality. Comparing supreme void with ultimate truth, Ho articulates this claim:

> Ultimate truth is ineffable; it is not a propositional fact that one can grasp conceptually and formulate in words. In addition, one cannot attain enlightenment by grasping the fact. And yet, for Sengzhao, as for Mahayana Buddhists in general, the direct realization of ultimate truth would effectively lead to the attainment of enlightenment. (Chapter 8, this volume, 111)

One can ask, here, what this "direct realization" would look like. It cannot be conceptual, linguistic, discursive, rational, or, as Ho goes onto explain, even pragmatic. Citing the *Zhaolun sūtra*, which Sengzhao discusses approvingly, Ho suggests that *nirvāṇa*, thc attainment of enlightenment by the direct realization of the ultimate truth that is supreme emptiness (*kong*), would be one of conceptual quiescence. Additionally, Ho points to the erasure of the distinction between subject and object that must also necessarily occur in the experience of ultimate reality, that is, supreme void.

The discussion of the ontological level of supreme void and the characterization of it in terms of *nirvāṇa* and conceptual quiescence raise a familiar paradox: if ultimate truth is pre-conceptual and without subject-object distinction, how can we say anything about it at all? Does not any discussion of the nature of ultimate not-being necessarily misrepresent it purely in virtue of expressing it? Graham Priest's essay "Speaking of the Ineffable . . ." (Chapter 7 of this volume) presents us with a provocative response to this challenge. Confronting head on the contradiction involved in speaking about the ineffable, Priest marshals the conceptual resources of the Buddhist tradition, specifically the *catuṣkoti*, and contemporary paraconsistent logic in order to rigorously defend how one can express the ineffable. Priest begins with a historical look at the development of the concept of nothingness in Buddhism, which we see as culminating with the view of Nāgārjuna, who makes a corrective sweep at the Abhidharma tradition and distils the preceding Mahayāna *sūtra* tradition in his *Mūlamadhyamakakārika* (MMK). Everything is empty of self-existence and has being in virtue of its relation to other things, viz., causes and effects, its parts, concepts, and language. Nāgārjuna also embraces and reinterprets the doctrine of two truths, where emptiness is the nature of the world as it is ultimately, devoid of conceptual interpretation, while conventional reality is the converse side of it, replete with linguistic and conceptual proliferation. As such, one cannot express the ultimate nature of reality (MMK XXII.11–12). Priest clarifies that one can have knowledge of it by acquaintance, but not via description. Despite this admission, Buddhist philosophers, like their Western counterparts, as Priest points out by way of comparison, appear committed to speaking of the ineffable.

One way to interpret this contradiction is to defuse it by making a distinction. This seems to be the strategy of Gorampa, who distinguishes, Priest tells us, between a nominal and an ultimate ultimate. Any statement about the ultimate, then, applies to the nominal ultimate, while the ultimate ultimate is, by definition, ineffable. Priest critiques this strategy, however, by saying that this would make Gorampa's own talk of the ultimate ultimate about the nominal ultimate, so the contradiction stands.

Priest, instead, advocates the use of the *catuṣkoti*, articulated and formalized through the techniques of paraconsistent and plurivalent logic, to endorse rather than defuse the contradiction. Paraconsistent logic echoes the third limb of the *catuṣkoti*, which is a true contradiction. Plurivalent logic sets up a system wherein we can designate a state of affairs, e, as ineffable, illustrating that "[t]he fact that one can say something about nothing does not undercut the fact that one cannot" (Chapter 7, this volume, 100). Priest shows how contraposing the denotation relation specifies that variable **n** has no name, not even 'n'. While this technique formalizes the claim that ineffability is describable, it is the *Vimalakīrti Sūtra*, to which Priest draws our attention, which suggests yet another approach to the problem. The Goddess's admonishment to Śāriputra provides an interesting counterimage to the Goddess of Parmenides's poem, which the ineffable can and must be expressed because words are not anything distinct from nothing, but are empty as well and manifest its nature. The concluding "expression" of nonduality by Vimalakīrti points to the fact that the ineffability of nonduality can be expressed precisely in relation to an expression of duality. Priest describes the technique: "Non-duality . . . *requires* that one talk about the ineffable; the techniques of paraconsistent logic show how to make precise sense of this idea" (Chapter 7, this volume, 102). Though Parmenides would certainly take issue with the concept of emptiness and relational being, as would Plato, we can use the dual schema of determinacy and definiteness to help us understand the conceptual move that Priest identifies in the *Vimalakīrti Sūtra*. Adopt *definiteness* and *determinacy* as axes *x* and *y*. Of the four quadrants created, the upper right quadrant would plot *definite* and *determinate* things, the upper left all *determinate* but *indefinite things*, lower right all *definite* but *indeterminate* things, and lower left the *indeterminate* and *indefinite*. Given the nature of the *indefinite* and *indeterminate*, we can assume that the lower left quadrant remains unpopulated. We can identify, however, what belongs there precisely in virtue of the fact that the remaining three quadrants are populated. In other words, expressing nothing requires that we attempt to give expression to it—what we end up expressing, perhaps best captured by Gorampa's nominal ultimate, serves as a sign pointing beyond itself to some ultimate ultimate. To appreciate Vimalakīrti's expression of nonduality, in other words, we require Mañjuśri's characterization of it.

Conclusion

There is an original sense of not-being in Parmenides, understandable in terms of a set of logical alternatives that are inherent in his characterization of the ways of inquiry. Of these alternatives, the sense of not-being as indeterminacy and indefiniteness that informs them is seized upon by Megarian followers of Parmenides who adopt his fundamental conceptual categories, but without the attendant commitment to defending the possibility of human knowledge.

The sense of not-being which is inherent to Parmenides's account is covered over, to some extent, by other interpreters. Plato is more interested in reversing some of the absurd conclusions to which Parmenides's analysis lends itself. On the other hand, by comparison with Madhyamaka treatments of emptiness and ineffability in the Indian Buddhist and Chinese Buddhist traditions, we can begin to see a dialogue emerge about the nature and limits of not-Being, whether understood in terms of Parmenidean *indeterminacy* and *indefiniteness* or in terms of the Buddhist notion of emptiness. The other values on the four-value scale of interpreting Parmenides, *definite determinacy*, *determinate indefiniteness*, and *definite indeterminacy*, may also prove to be an effective tool in parsing the different senses and levels of emptiness that thinkers such as Sengzhao and Nāgārjuna and his commentators employ. The direct realization of emptiness is taken to be without concepts and inexpressible in some sense, though this remains a matter of interpretation, as Priest suggests. The philosophical discussion of emptiness and the articulation of the path to its direct realization, however, requires concepts and language, which might lead us to distinguish, as Ho articulates in Sengzhao's philosophy, two levels through which to understand the emptiness or not-Being of things: an ontic level that endorses distinctions and an ontological one that erases them. Despite their distinctly different starting points, Plato, Sengzhao, and Nāgārjuna adopt a strikingly similar attitude toward not-being, though for vastly different reasons. Regardless of these differences, on some fundamental level, these thinkers seem to concur that recovering the possibility of philosophical knowing depends on delimiting and defining not-being in terms of some particular nothing. We may not be able to know everything, but to grasp anything we must know nothing in particular.

Notes

1 There is some disagreement in the critical literature as to how to translate this expression. Gallop (1984) reads it as a "much-speaking route" (49), but this seems nonsensical. While Scott Austin (1986) renders it as "a significant road" (156). In conversation with S. Menn, it was pointed out to me that "much famed road" seems like the simplest meaning; in addition, *poluphemon*, recalling the Cyclops in Homer's *Odyssey*, highlights Parmenides's use of epic vocabulary and imagery in his poem.

2 I employ {} to indicate that the 'it' supplied by me in the translation of this passage is a matter of some contention in the critical literature—there may be no subject of the *esti*, or it may have to be supplied, as discussed further later on.

3 Sider (1986) notes that the *mē* has a "generalizing force," hence '*what*-is-not' or 'not-being' (12).

4 I do not mean to suggest here that Owen (1982) propounds this view; rather, remarks of his against a cosmological understanding of the poem are taken up by Gallop (1984) in his defense of the existential reading of the verb. I point to Owen's remarks, here, in order to reconstruct the case as lucidly as possible.

5 The argument for a fused *esti* is advocated and defended expertly by Furley (1989) and Furth (1968, 123ff.).

6 I am indebted to examples presented in Mourelatos (1979, 319–329). Mourelatos introduces these examples to support a distinction he draws between uses of 'nothing' and 'nobody': the existential use, which I interpret as the indefinite but determinate, and the characterizing use, which I conceive of as the definite but indeterminate.

7 Many commentators note the prevalence of negative language in the Goddess's own speech as a remarkable feature of the poem. See Austin (1986), who contends with this problem.

8 Fragment 34: "No man knows, or ever will know, the truth about the gods and about everything I speak of: for even if one chanced to say the complete truth, yet oneself knows it not; but seeming is wrought over all things [*or* fancy is wrought in the case of all men]" (Sextus *Adversus Mathematicos* VII, 49).
Fragment 35: "Let these things be opined as resembling the truth" (Sextus *Adv. Math.* VII, 110).

10 The Cognition of Nonexistent Objects

Five Yogācāra Arguments

Zhihua Yao

Introduction

Ever since Leibniz, the fundamental question of metaphysics has been: "Why is there something rather than nothing?" But before we can start to ponder this problem, we should have some sense of the meanings of the terms "being" (or "what there is") and "nothing" (or "what there is not"). Philosophers throughout history have devoted themselves to these two subjects by developing the field of ontology. If, however, we are not satisfied with traditional speculative metaphysics, we should ask a more fundamental question, that is, "How do we know what there is or what there is not?" While the question "How do we know what there is?" makes perfect sense and has helped to plant the fruitful field of epistemology, the question "How do we know what there is not, or nonbeing?" encountered skepticism from the very beginning. A natural and even more fundamental question is: "Can we know what there is not?" or "How is it possible to know what there is not?" In other words, we need to ask whether we could possibly know nonbeing.

A group of Western and Asian philosophers answered "no" to this question. They denied the possibility of knowing nonbeing by claiming that "thought and being are the same" (Parmenides) or "whatever that is knowable (*jñeyatva*) is existence or being (*astitva*)" (Vaiśeṣikas, Sarvāstivāda Buddhists). This extreme view that expels nonbeing or nonexistence from the realms of knowledge and ontology has been influential in the history of Western and Eastern philosophy and developed into various different varieties.

An apparent alternative answer to the question of whether we can know what does not exist is "yes." A quick assertion to support this answer is that whatever that is knowable includes both being and nonbeing, hence thought equals being plus nonbeing. In this way we have made knowablity (*jñeyatva*), or potential intentional objects, a more fundamental ontological concept than being or nonbeing. On this view, we can know nonbeing, or what there is not, as well as we know being or what there is. But the issue is how to prove this assertion. Meinong had famously justified the ontological status of nonbeing by distinguishing thus-being (*Sosein*) from being (*Sein*). According to him, one can meaningfully talk about or know the thus-being or characteristics of a nonexistent object without committing oneself to the being or existence of this object.

Several Buddhist philosophical schools also attempted to prove this view of the knowability of nonexistents by developing various arguments against the extreme views of their main opponents, the Sarvāstivādins. Elsewhere I have discussed the Mahāsāṃghika (Yao 2008) and Dārṣṭāntika-Sautrāntika arguments (Yao *forthcoming*; see also Cox 1988). In this chapter, I will focus on the five arguments developed by the Yogācāra Buddhists in support of the knowability of nonexistents, and evaluate how successfully they have established their object view of intentionality.

Thesis: "Mental Consciousness Takes Nonexistents as Objects"

The sources that I am going to deal with are some sections of the encyclopedic *Yogācārabhūmi* (YBh) that discuss the concepts of the awareness of nonexistent objects (*asadālambanabuddhi*) or the consciousness of nonexistent objects (**asadālambanavijñāna*). Before examining these arguments, we should formulate the thesis that they are attempting to prove. However, this turns out to be not an easy task. The shorter first section (text A) under discussion is from the most ancient layer of YBh. In this section, the key point is to establish the concept of the awareness of nonexistent objects with a major and a minor argument, but it does not explain what this awareness (*buddhi*) is. Nor does it explicitly state the thesis they try to prove. The second, longer section (text B) under discussion is from the *Viniścayasaṃgrahaṇī* section of YBh, which is apparently a commentary and elaboration on text A. In this section, two major and five minor arguments are developed to prove the following thesis:

> **[Thesis 1]** "Therefore, it is known that there is the mental consciousness (*yishi*, 意識, *yid kyi rnam par shes pa*) that takes nonexistents as objects." (YBhc, CBETA, T30, no. 1579, p. 585, b4–5; YBht, Derge 4038: zhi18a3)[1]

Here the key concept is the mental consciousness of nonexistent objects. Elsewhere a similar thesis is stated: "Hence we know that mental consciousness in the same way takes nonexistents as objects" (YBhc, CBETA, T30, no. 1579, p. 585, a7–8). The Tibetan translation, however, simply has "*yid*" (mind, mental) instead of "*yid kyi rnam par shes pa*" (mental consciousness) (YBht, Derge 4038: zhi17a4). In the established Yogācāra doctrinal system, mind (*manas*) and mental consciousness (*manovijñāna*) become two distinctive concepts. But in the earlier Yogācāra and Abhidharma sources, mind (*manas*, *yi*, 意, *yid*) is normally used in the way that covers both the sense of mental organ (*manas*) and mental consciousness (*manovijñāna*). As the passage under discussion is drawn from the early Yogācāra work YBh, it is therefore justified to interpolate "consciousness" (*shi*, 識), as Xuanzang (玄奘, 602–664 CE) did in his Chinese translation. So the two statements express the same idea: mental consciousness takes nonexistents as objects.

In another concluding remark, there seems to be a different thesis stated:

> [**Thesis 2**] "One should also know that there are further rational discourses of a similar kind that fully establish the consciousness (*shi*, 識, *rnam par shes pa*) of nonexistent objects." (YBhc, CBETA, T30, no. 1579, p. 585, b5–6; YBht, Derge 4038: zhi18a3–4)

Here the more general term "consciousness" (*vijñāna*) instead of the specific "mental consciousness" is used. In an alternative Chinese translation of the *Viniścayasaṃgrahanī* by Paramārtha (449–569 CE), it is stated even more explicitly as follows: "For this reason, it is definitely known that all consciousnesses (*zhu shi*, 諸識) take nonexistents as objects" (JDZL, CBETA, T30, no. 1584, p. 1022, c29-p. 1023, a1). The term "consciousness" or "all consciousnesses" covers not only mental consciousness, but also the five sense-consciousnesses, which, in the Indian philosophical tradition, refer to visual, auditory, olfactory, gustatory, and tactile sensations. Does this mean that the Yogācāras try to prove that visual and auditory consciousnesses can also take nonexistents as objects? Do they believe that we can actually see or hear nonexistents? If so, they would have a much greater theoretical burden than simply proving the mental consciousness of nonexistent objects.

In Paramārtha's translation, a brief dialogue is inserted by Paramārtha to explain this point. A question is raised: "If visual consciousness cannot take nonexistents as objects, how can mental consciousness (*xinshi*, 心識, **manovijñāna*) take nonexistents as objects?" (JDZL, CBETA, T30, no. 1584, p. 1022, c9–10) Here the opponent explicitly denies the possibility of having visual consciousness of nonexistent objects, and in turn questions the proponent's thesis of the mental consciousness of nonexistent objects. In his reply, the proponent does not object to the denial of the visual consciousness of nonexistent objects. He simply states that mental consciousness can take nonexistents as objects because it can penetrate objects of all three times, namely the past, present and future.

Based on both Paramārtha's and Xuanzang's translations, we can safely assume that thesis two is not intended to establish the sense-consciousness of nonexistent objects. Instead, it is only meant to express a more general concept of the consciousness of nonexistent objects, which, in the same way as the concept of the awareness of nonexistent objects implies, only refers to the more specific mental consciousness of nonexistent objects. So we can treat both thesis one and two as proving the same view: mental consciousness takes nonexistents as objects. In other words, the Yogācāras try to prove that one can think or know nonexistents, but not see or hear them.

Argument One: The Past and the Future

As mentioned earlier, there are a major and a minor argument in text A and two major and five minor arguments in text B. For our analysis, I will group them into five major arguments. Among these, the first argument deals with the past and the future. The Yogācāra and Sautrāntika concepts of the cognition of nonexistent objects were developed against the backdrop of the Sarvāstivādins' epistemological argument for the existence of the past and the future. This epistemological argument can be formulated in the following simple way:

1. Whatever is knowable is existent.
2. The past and the future are knowable.
3. Therefore, the past and the future exist.

However, the Yogācāras and other major Buddhist philosophical schools committed themselves to a view of presentism, that is, only the present exists; the past and the future do not. Under their view of presentism, the Yogācāras would surely reject the conclusion. However, they accept premise two, and, in turn, they would have to reject premise one. By formulating the Yogācāra view against the existence of the past and the future, we arrive at their argument for the cognition of nonexistent objects:

1. Mental consciousness can know past and future objects.
2. Things in the past or the future do not exist.
3. Therefore, mental consciousness can know nonexistent objects.

For someone committed to presentism, premise two is unproblematic. The contentious statement is premise one. To support premise one, the Yogācāras came up with the following argument: "Because it is evident that mental consciousness takes the past and the future consciousnesses (*shi*, 識, *rnam par shes pa*) as objects" (YBhc, CBETA, T30, no. 1579, p. 584, c26–27; YBht, Derge 4038: zhi16b7). A *sūtra* passage quoted in text B also supports this argument by saying: "Depending on the past phenomena (*saṃskāra*), there arises mind (*manas*); depending on the future phenomena, there arises mind" (YBhc, CBETA, T30, no. 1579, p. 584, c18–19; YBht, Derge 4038: zhi16b3). In other words, the argument is that mental consciousness, or mind, can take the past and the future consciousnesses or phenomena as objects, and since objects of the past and the future are under the purview of past and future consciousnesses, they become objects of the present mental consciousness as well. The key to understanding this point is that mental consciousness is believed to be able to penetrate objects of all the three times, that is, past, present and future, even though the five sense-consciousnesses can only take their respective present objects as objects.

The second key point to be kept in mind is that the objects of mental consciousness are believed to comprise *all* dharmas.[2] What are all *dharmas*? Text A refers to a presumably Abhidharma view that holds: "All [*dharmas*] etc. refer only to the twelve sense spheres (*āyatana*)."[3] The twelve sense spheres include five sense organs (eye, ear, nose, tongue, and body) and their respective objects (form, sound, smell, taste, and tangible things) plus mind and its object *dharma*. These twelve sense spheres are believed to be the basic elements (*dharma*) from which the whole phenomenal world is built. The phenomenal world can be considered illusory because of its compounded and finite nature, but its building blocks are real existents. In the same passage, the existence of all these *dharma*s is emphasized: "All *existents* etc. refer only to the twelve sense spheres."[4] This traditional Abhidharma view takes the object of mental consciousness ("all *dharmas*") to be the twelve sense spheres, which cover all the real existents. Therefore, we should take "*dharma*" here to mean "real existents." If this is the case, then past and future consciousnesses, as mentioned in the supportive argument of the Yogācāras, are apparently not included in the twelve sense spheres, so they are examples of nonexistent objects. Past or future consciousnesses here are considered to be nonexistent probably because they are *of* the past or the future, for the same reason that we would consider all the past or the future phenomena as nonexistents.

However, it is self-contradictory to say that the objects of mental consciousness, which are real existent (*dharma*), are nonexistent. The Yogācāras think that the problem is due to a narrow understanding of the term *dharma* as "real existents" only. They believe that there is a hidden meaning of the Buddha, according to which, "Mind can grasp whatever object (*don gang*) that is not the object-field (*gocara*) of five [sense] consciousnesses, which is metaphorically designated as *dharma* by the Buddha" (YBhc, CBETA, T30, no. 1579, p. 584, c23–24; YBht, Derge 4038: zhi16b5–6). In other words, mental consciousness not only takes as objects the *dharma* as sense spheres (*fachu*, 法處, *chos kyi skye mched*) or real existents, but also whatever that is beyond the object-field of five sense consciousnesses, which is the designated or conceptualized *dharma* (*jiashuo ming fa*, 假說名法, *chos gdags pa*). Although the past and the future consciousnesses are not real existents as the sense spheres are, they are designated or conceptual *dharma*s, therefore they can be the objects of mental consciousness. The same applies to all the past and the future phenomena. In his commentary on YBh, Kuiji (窺基, 632–682 CE) adds that even the "sky-flower," an extreme case of a nonexistent object, can also be designated as a *dharma* and be cognized by mental consciousness.[5] This implies that he takes the designated or conceptual *dharma*s as nonexistent objects.

If the notion of *dharma* is expanded to cover not only the *dharma*s as sense spheres, that is, real existents, but also the designated *dharma*, or nonexistents, then it would not be self-contradictory to say that the objects of mental consciousness (i.e., *dharma*s) can be nonexistent. However, we are then confronted with another problem. If *dharma* includes both existents and nonexistents within itself, then what is this *dharma*? This issue is addressed in the second argument.

Argument Two: Existents and Nonexistents

The second argument is based on a radically new interpretation of the concept of *dharma* proposed by the Yogācāras. According to them, *dharma* is derived from the verbal root √*dhṛ*, literally meaning "to hold, bear, or maintain." Hence an existent *dharma* means something that bears the characteristics of existence; similarly, a nonexistent *dharma* means something that bears the characteristics of nonexistence. Both existence and nonexistence are therefore included in the notion *dharma*. "*Dharma*s with the characteristics of existence bear the characteristics of existence; *dharma*s with the characteristics of nonexistence bear the characteristics of nonexistence. Hence [both existence and nonexistence] are called *dharma*."[6] In other words, *dharma* can be understood literally as something held in mind, the knowable, or as a potential intentional object. As we have discussed earlier, this concept is more fundamental than such concepts as existence or nonexistence, being or nonbeing. The prevailing understanding and interpretation of *dharma* in terms of existents, or elements of existence, was posited by the dominant Sarvāstivāda ontology, which expels nonexistence or nonbeing from its realm and suggests that only that which exists is knowable. The Yogācāras argue against this dominant view by establishing the cognition of nonexistent objects. Their arguments can be analyzed in three steps. The first step is:

1. "With regard to existents (*youxing*, 有性, *yod pa*), one can establish existent objects and grasp existent objects; with regard to nonexistents (*wuxing*, 無性, *med pa*), one can establish nonexistent objects and grasp nonexistent objects." (YBhc, CBETA, T30, no. 1579, p. 584, c28–29; YBht, Derge 4038: zhi17a1)

Rephrasing this in contemporary philosophical terms, we may say: with regard to what there is, we can establish existent objects and take them to be intentional existent objects; with regard to what there is not, we can establish nonexistent objects and take them to be intentional nonexistent objects. This way both existent and nonexistent objects are established and they are both taken to be intentional objects.

The second step is concerned with the subjective side:

2. "Because mental consciousness, with regard to existents, if it can establish a certain [existent] object, then it can cognize this very [existent] object; with regard to nonexistents, if it can establish a certain [nonexistent] object, then it can cognize this very [nonexistent] object." (YBhc, CBETA, T30, no. 1579, p. 584, c29-p. 585, a3; YBht, Derge 4038: zhi17a1–2)

Here it is clear that on the subjective side, mental consciousness is responsible for and is capable of cognizing both existent and nonexistent objects. If it can intend a certain existent object, it can cognize this very existent object; if it can intend a certain nonexistent object, it can cognize this very nonexistent object. In other words, intention presupposes cognition.

After discussing both the objective and subjective aspects of the issue, the Yogācāras conclude their second argument with the third step:

3. "If the two kinds [of mental consciousness] do not cognize these two kinds of [existent and nonexistent] objects, then it is unreasonable to say that mind can take all objects as objects and grasp all objects." (YBhc, CBETA, T30, no. 1579, p. 585, a3–5; YBht, Derge 4038: zhi17a2–3, corrected after the Peking edition)

The two kinds of mental consciousness refer to those that cognize existent and nonexistent objects respectively. They belong to one and the same mental consciousness. If this mental consciousness can cognize only existent but not nonexistent objects, then it should not be said that mental consciousness takes all *dharmas* as objects. By reinterpreting *dharmas* more broadly as intentional objects, the Yogācāras establish their concept of the cognition of nonexistent objects. This view does not violate the doctrine that mental consciousness takes all *dharmas* as objects, which is accepted by all the major Buddhist philosophical schools.

One might question whether the three steps in this argument clearly constitute a valid argument. Let me therefore reformulate this argument in the following five step form:

1. Mental consciousness takes all *dharmas* as intentional objects.
2. All *dharmas* include both existent and nonexistent objects.
3. Therefore, mental consciousness takes both existent and nonexistent objects as intentional objects.
4. Intention presupposes cognition.
5. Therefore, mental consciousness can know both existent and nonexistent objects.

In this reformulation, premise one restates what is implied in step three, a commonly accepted thesis in Buddhism. Premise two is a reformulation of step one. Premise three is drawn from one and two. Premise four is the central idea of step two. Finally, we arrive at the conclusion, step five, with an apparently valid argument.

Moreover, yogic practice is invoked in text A to explain this argument. "If otherwise, that is, the yogic practitioners only know existents but do not know nonexistents, then they should not be those who intimately observe the *dharmas* as objects. But this is unreasonable."[7] Text A also refers to a *sūtra* passage to support this view: "Again the world-honored one said: 'My disciple of non-deceit, as I have taught, the correct practice is that with regard to existents, one knows existents, and that with regard to nonexistents, one knows non-existents."[8] This quote shows that not only in theory, but also in practice, the Yogācāras should know both existents and nonexistents through their mental consciousness. Otherwise, they are not carrying out the correct practice, nor do they correctly observe the *dharmas* as objects.

Argument Three: No-Self and Impermanence

We have seen that the first argument concerns the past and the future and the second argument deals with existents and nonexistents. In text A, there is a brief discussion on no-self, which can be formulated as the third argument. The text says:

> If it [i.e., the awareness that grasps nonexistents] does not arise, then there would not be the awareness that grasps no-self, the horn of a rabbit, the son of a barren woman, etc. But this is unreasonable.[9]

In text B, after presenting the main arguments that we have analyzed as arguments one and two above, five additional arguments are introduced that are called the five rational discourses of *vaipulya* (*guangda*, 廣大, *yangs shing rgya che ba*).[10] The first and fourth rational discourses of *vaipulya* are related to the topic of no-self:

1. "As the Buddha has elegantly said, 'There is no-self inside, outside and in between the two.' This selflessness is not included in the conditioned [*dharma*s], nor is it included in the unconditioned [*dharma*s]. Regarding the conceptual cognition (*yongs su rtog pa*, **parikalpa*) of universals (*sāmānyalakṣaṇa*), it is not the case that the consciousness of this object [of selflessness] does not arise.[11] This is the first rational discourse." (YBhc, CBETA, T30, no. 1579, p. 585, a10–13; YBht, Derge 4038: zhi17a5–7)
2. "Again, all phenomena (*saṃskāra*) are not permanent, stable or eternal. The very nature (*xing*, 性, *nyid*) of impermanence, unstableness and the non-eternality of all phenomena is not included in the conditioned [*dharmas*], nor is it included in the unconditioned [*dharma*s]. Regarding the conceptual cognition of universals, it is not the case that the consciousness of this object [of the very nature of impermanence, unstableness and non-eternality] does not arise.[12] . . . This is the fourth rational discourse." (YBhc, CBETA, T30, no. 1579, p. 585, a22-b2; YBht, Derge 4038: zhi17b5–18a2)

All these arguments rely heavily on the concepts of no-self and impermanence, two foundational Buddhist teachings. Both concepts can be rephrased into negative judgments: "The substantial self (*ātman*) does not exist," and "The permanent entity does not exist." The key to understanding this set of arguments lies in the relationship between linguistic and logical negation and ontological nonexistence. In other words, the issue being addressed here is whether or not negative judgments have to be based on an ontological commitment to nonexistence. If they do, it is easier to explain negation and any kind of negative cognition, but there is a danger of reifying a nonexistent object or entity, which sounds like a self-contradictory concept. If they don't, we do not have to multiply unnecessary entities, and can limit negation and negative cognition to the scope of language or cognition. But this way, negation and negative cognitions become only secondary and derivative as compared to affirmation and positive cognitions. The second option seems to be popular among Western philosophers, who tend to avoid the ontological commitment to nonexistence and try to limit negation and negative cognitions to the scope of language and cognition (Horn 1989, 45–79). The Yogācāras seem to favor the first option and believe that negative judgments associated with no-self or impermanence are based on an ontological commitment to selflessness or the very nature of impermanence. Because there is no self in the first place, we can then say that "there is no self" and derive a concept of no-self. Because all phenomena are impermanent in reality, we can then state that "all phenomena are impermanent" and have a concept of impermanence.

What, then, is the ontological status of this selflessness and the very nature of impermanence? The Yogācāras say that they are not included in either conditioned or unconditioned *dharma*s. In the metaphysical framework that is accepted or presumed by the major Buddhist philosophical schools, there are two basic types of *dharma*s or existents. One is the conditioned existents that are governed by causal relations, which comprise material form (*rūpa*), mind (*citta*), mental activities (*caitta*), and the elements that are neither material nor mental (*cittaviprayuktasaṃskāra*). The other is the unconditioned existents that go beyond causal relations; this class of things mainly consists of *nirvāṇa*, the final goal of all Buddhist practices. Different Buddhist schools developed various schemes to classify these main types of existents, but none of them would include selflessness in their classification of existents. So selflessness should be similar to the case of the horn of a rabbit or the son of a barren woman and be classified as nonexistent. The same applies to impermanence. In his commentary to YBh, Dunnyun (遁倫, active during the seventh century) confirms this point by quoting a definition from the *Bodhisattvabhūmi* (BBh) section of YBh, which says: "Here the conditioned and unconditioned [*dharma*s] are called existents; self (*ātmā*) or mine (*ātmīya*) are called nonexistents."[13]

Having made it clear that selflessness and the very nature of impermanence enjoy the ontological status of nonexistence, the Yogācāras move on to their subjective aspect. With what kind of cognition can one cognize selflessness or impermanence? The Tibetan translation states: "Regarding the conceptual cognition of universals, it is not the case that the consciousness of this object [of selflessness] does not arise" (YBht, Derge 4038: zhi17a6–7). Xuanzang's Chinese translation conflates "cognition" with "consciousness" and reads: "The consciousness of universals does not arise without taking this object [of selflessness] as object" (YBhc, CBETA, T30, no. 1579, p. 585, a11–12). So it is the conceptual cognition (**parikalpa*) or consciousness (*vijñāna*) of universals (*sāmānyalakṣaṇa*) that is responsible for the cognition of selflessness. In his commentary to YBh, Dunnyun quotes a view attributed to his contemporary Huijing (惠景, active during the seventh century) who explained the observation of no-self, or impermanence, in three different stages. In the stages of learning and thinking, one observes no-self or impermanence as abstract universals through inference (*anumāna*). In the further stage of practice, one is supposed to observe the particular characteristics of no-self or impermanence through direct realization (*abhisamaya*), which is a cognition or perception (*pratyakṣa*) of particulars (*svalakṣaṇa*). But in YBh, the observation of no-self or impermanence is called the cognition of universals, regardless of the different stages of learning, thinking, and practice. Why is this? Dunnyun quotes again Huijing's views to explain this discrepancy. One view holds that although in reality the cognition of no-self in the stage of practice is a cognition of particulars, it is convenient to call it the cognition of universals despite its appearance in different stages. However, this reasoning of convenience is not convincing. Another argument holds that although particular objects (*zixiang jingjie*, 自相境界) are observed in the stage of practice, these particular objects can be called universals because each individual phenomenon is no-self and impermanent, and hence all phenomena are universally no-self and impermanent. Each particular is a manifestation of the universal. Therefore, even the observation of no-self in the stage of practice can be called a cognition of a universal.[14]

Even with this discrepancy, the strength of the current argument is not weakened. Although the observation of no-self and impermanence in the stage of practice can be considered a cognition of particulars, hence a perception, it is not a regular type of sense perception like seeing or hearing, but rather a yogic perception, which is still a capacity of mental consciousness rather than sense-consciousness.[15] In the stages of learning and thinking, the cognition of no-self and impermanence is attributed to inference, which is surely a capacity of mental consciousness. So both cases would support the thesis to be proved: mental consciousness can cognize nonexistent objects such as selflessness and impermanence.

Argument Four: Food and Drinks

The fourth argument corresponds to the second rational discourse of *vaipulya* and is concerned with food and drinks, which are assumed to be not really existent according to major Buddhist schools. It is stated in text B:

> Again, food, drinks, vehicles, clothes, ornaments, house, army, and forest etc. are metaphorically designated upon the bases of form, smell, taste and tangible things, which arise, change and are established this and that way. These food and drinks etc. do not exist at all apart from form and smell etc. Their very nature of nonexistence (*wu you xing*, 無有性, *med pa nyid*) is not included in the conditioned [*dharma*s], nor is it included in the unconditioned [*dharma*s]. Regarding the cognition of particulars, it is not the case that the consciousness of this object [of the very nature of nonexistence] does not arise.[16] This is the second rational discourse. (YBhc, CBETA, T30, no. 1579, p. 585, a13–17; YBht, Derge 4038: zhi17a7–b2)

To make sense of this argument, we have to understand the nominalist position that was accepted or presumed among major Buddhist philosophical schools. According to this received view, the real existents are the five classes of conditioned and unconditioned *dharma*s that we have mentioned in the last section. Form, smell, taste, and what is tangible are covered in the class of material form (*rūpa*), which also includes the rest of the six elements, that is, sound and the five senses (eye, ear, nose, tongue, and body).[17] In other words, this view assigns existence to the constituents of sensible objects and physical organs alone. The entire material world is built upon these basic elements. They arise, combine, change, and are sustained in various different ways, which produce the colorful world that we experience. This picture is rather similar to the worldview as advocated by contemporary scientific realism, which takes the fundamental reality of the material world to be the interactions between various particles and basic forces. As a matter of fact, the Buddhists and the scientific realists shared the common heritage of atomism as developed in both ancient India and Greece.

Under this atomistic realism, food and drinks are said not to exist at all apart from form and smell, because they are metaphorically designated upon the bases of these existent elements. Food and drinks are called universals, whereas form and smell are particulars. Now do these universals exist or not? There are two existing views. One is to take them to exist in the manner of designated or conceptual existents (*prajñaptisat*), and this is the view of the Sarvāstivādins. The other view holds that they do not exist precisely because they are designated and conceptual, and this view was advocated by the Sautrāntikas. In this context of discussing the cognition of nonexistent objects, the Yogācāras seem to adopt the latter view, as they hold that food and drinks, being nonexistents, are not included in the categories of either conditioned or unconditioned existents. In his commentary to the *Nyāyapraveśa*, a work of Buddhist logic, Kuiji states that "if [universals] exist, then this would disprove the cognition of nonexistent objects" (CBETA, T44, no. 1840, p. 138, c23–24). For Kuiji, universals do not exist, and one knows universals through his or her conceptual cognition, hence there is the cognition of nonexistent objects. If, however, universals exist, then the knowledge of universals only proves the cognition of *existent* rather than nonexistent objects. This implies that the Yogācāras have to treat universals as nonexistents if they accept the cognition of nonexistent objects.

Nonetheless, the Yogācāras still conceive the possibility of cognizing food and drinks. What kind of cognition is involved with nonexistent food and drinks? Text B says that it is the cognition or consciousness of particulars. This is problematic because food and drinks are universals, rather than particulars. Moreover, the cognition of particulars would be a sense perception; for instance, visual perception can perceive an existent visual object, but not nonexistent food or drinks. Kuiji tries to explain away the problem by insisting that the particulars here are not the objects of sense perception, nor are they in contrast to universals; instead, they only refer to food and drinks *themselves* (CBETA, T43, no. 1829, p. 181, c3–5). The cognition of the nonexistent food and drinks themselves is therefore not sense perception, and it is still the function of *mental consciousness*. The alternative Chinese translation by Paramārtha simply takes it to be the cognition of universals (*zongxiang*, 總相, **sāmānyalakṣaṇa*) (JDZL, CBETA, T30, no. 1584, p. 1022, c17–18), which is also the function of mental consciousness. Without the Sanskrit original, we cannot determine which solution is justified. But in either case, it would support the thesis to be proved: mental consciousness can take as objects the nonexistent objects, such as food and drinks.

Argument Five: Heretical Views

The fifth and final argument corresponds to the third rational discourse of *vaipulya* and is concerned with the heretical view of nihilism.[18] It is stated in text B:

> Again, the heretical view of the nihilists holds that there is no donation, no wish, and no worship . . . . Suppose that the very nature of the nonexistence of donation, wish, worship etc. really is an existent,[19] then such views as [that there exist soul and person][20] would not be heretical views. Why?[21] Because it would be a correct view and a correct assertion. But if [their very nature of nonexistence] does not exist, for those who hold heretical views, their consciousness of such an object would not arise.[22] This is the third rational discourse. (YBhc, CBETA, T30, no. 1579, p. 585, a18–22; YBht, Derge 4038: zhi17b2–5)

The heretical view under discussion is labeled nihilism. In the eyes of its opponents in the Indian tradition, Buddhism is often viewed as a school of nihilism that negates everything. Major Buddhist philosophical schools, however, try to maintain a "middle way" position that goes beyond the extremes of nihilism and eternalism. In the context of discussing the cognition of nonexistent objects, it is especially important for Buddhist philosophers to distance themselves from nihilism, because the ontological commitment to nonexistent objects can easily lead to the impression of opponents that Buddhism really does represent an extreme form of nihilism.

The heretical views are said to deny donation, wish, and worship, which sounds like a kind of ethical or religious version of nihilism. These views are extensively discussed and refuted elsewhere in YBh, where it points out that ethical or religious nihilism is based on a metaphysical nihilism, which claims that "all things with all characteristics do not exist."[23] If Buddhism also holds that all these things really do not exist, then the nihilists who hold that they do not exist would be expressing a correct but not heretical view.

On the Yogācāra view, however, it is not the case that all things do not exist. Some things exist, some things do not. A correct cognition consists of two aspects: the cognition of existents as existents, and the cognition of nonexistents as nonexistents. The nihilists, according to the Yogācāras, made a mistake by taking existents as nonexistents. Since donation, wish, and worship do exist, there would not arise any cognition of their nonexistence. If the nihilists still believe that they do not exist, they hold a wrong and heretical view.

From this reasoning, we can infer that the difference between the correct and wrong views lies in their correspondence to reality, and that the Yogācāras here would embrace a correspondence theory of truth. A correct view of existents corresponds to relevant existent objects, and a correct view of nonexistents corresponds to relevant nonexistent objects. In contrast, a wrong view of either existents or nonexistents does not have a corresponding existent or nonexistent object. So the cognition of nonexistent objects that the Yogācāras try to prove here would be a correct view. Accordingly, a cognition of nonexistents without corresponding nonexistent objects as advocated by the nihilists would be a wrong view.

Conclusion

In this chapter I have examined each of the five Yogācāra arguments for the cognition of nonexistent objects in their historical context. Now let us evaluate how successful these arguments are for the purpose of establishing an object view of intentionality. In the history of philosophy, the main rival of the object view is the existent-object view, which is the view shared by Parmenides, Vaiśeṣikas, Sarvāstivādins, and many other Western and Eastern philosophers that I mentioned in the beginning of the chapter. On this view, all the knowables, or potential intentional objects, are existent objects, either in the forms of abstracta, mental concreta, or possibilita, depending on different versions of this theory to which one may subscribe. To argue against this dominant view, the main agenda of the object view is to introduce and establish the concept of the cognition of nonexistent objects. This approach also distances itself from a more recent but popular rival—the adverbialist theory of intentionality, which tends to rid philosophical discourse of intentional objects altogether, either of the existent or nonexistent variety.[24]

There are two logical steps to establish the cognition of nonexistent objects. First, nonexistents are *the objects of cognition*; second, these objects of cognition are *nonexistents*. On the first step, the Yogācāras had repeatedly made it clear that mental consciousness can take as objects nonexistent objects (argument two), the past and the future (argument one), no-self and impermanence (argument three), and universals such as food and drinks (argument four). Regardless of the variety of these objects, they are all unproblematically objects of mental consciousness.

Now on the second step, we can use the popular fourfold classification of nonbeing or nonexistence (*abhāva*) among Indian philosophers as a benchmark. In argument two, the general concept of nonexistent objects is contrasted to existent objects. In argument one, the past and the future correspond respectively to two basic types of nonexistence, specifically, posterior nonexistence (*dhvaṃsa*), that is, the nonexistence of something after it has ceased to exist, and prior nonexistence (*prāgabhāva*), the nonexistence of something before it has come into existence. In argument three, no-self and impermanence are treated on par with such things as the horn of a rabbit and the son of a barren woman, two famous examples of the third type of nonexistence—absolute nonexistence (*atyantābhāva*). In argument four, universals such as food and drinks are taken to be nonexistents. However, they do not directly correspond to the final type of nonexistence—mutual nonexistence (*anyonyābhāva*). In argument five, the Yogācāras argue for a general object view of intentionality and distance themselves from a heretical view without corresponding objects, which can be seen as a version of the adverbialist theory of intentionality.

Therefore, I conclude that the Yogācāras have, to a great extent, successfully established their concept of the cognition of nonexistent objects, and strengthened the object view of intentionality against its rivals. This study has shown the great variety of the Buddhist theories of intentionality and mining these theories and arguments can greatly enrich the ongoing research on this subject.[25]

Notes

1 Due to the constraint on the length of these essays, I have omitted the Chinese and Tibetan texts, while only providing the Sanskrit originals when they are extant.

2 How to understand and interpret the term *dharma* will be crucial to the second argument. For now, we can simply understand it as the object of mental consciousness.

3 *Sarvam iti yāvad eva dvādaśāyatanānīti* / YBhs, p. 127, 10.

4 *Sarvam asti yāvad eva dvādaśāyatanānīti* / YBhs, p. 127, 13–14.

5 See Kuiji's commentary on the *Yogācārabhūmi* (CBETA, T43, no. 1829, p. 181, b10–11).

6 *Sallakṣaṇā api dharmāḥ sallakṣaṇaṃ dhyārayanti / asallakṣaṇā api dharmā asallakṣaṇaṃ dhārayanti tasmād dharmā ity ucyante* / YBhs, p. 127, 15–17.

7 *Anyathā tu sato jñānād asataś ca ajñānād yogino na nirantarajñeyadharmaparīkṣā syād iti na yujyate* // YBhs, p. 127, 17–18.

8 The Sanskrit text of this passage is missing in YBhs. Its Chinese translation is found in YBhc (CBETA, T30, no. 1579, p. 305, a16–18); and its Tibetan translation is found in *rNal 'byor spyod pa'i sa* (Derge 4035: dzi64a3).

9 *Sa ced apravṛttiṃ / tena yā nairātmyagrāhikā śaśaviṣāṇavandhyāputrādigrāhikā buddhir naivāstīti na yujyate* / YBhs, p. 127, 12–13.

10 The term vaipulya could refer to one of the twelve divisions of the Buddhist canon. Alternatively, it could refer more generally to the Mahāyāna sūtras. It could also be associated with the Vetulyakas, and therefore linked to the Mahāsāṃghikas. But in my study of the scattered Mahāsāṃghika sources on the cognition of nonexistent objects (Yao 2008), no parallel was found between their arguments and these five arguments.

11 Here I follow closely the Tibetan translation. Xuanzang's translation (YBhc) conflates "cognition" with "consciousness," and reads: "The consciousness of universals does not arise without taking this object [of selflessness] as object."

12 Here I follow closely the Tibetan translation. Xuanzang's translation (YBhc) conflates "cognition" with "consciousness," and reads: "The consciousness of universals does not arise without taking this object [of the very nature of impermanence, unstableness and non-eternality] as object."

13 *Tatra saṃskṛtam asaṃskṛtaṃ ca sat. asad ātmā vā ātmīyaṃ vā*. BBh, p. 276, 17–18. See Dunnyun's commentary on the *Yogācārabhūmi* (CBETA, T42, no. 1828, p. 610, a7–8).

14 See Dunnyun's commentary on the *Yogācārabhūmi* (CBETA, T42, no. 1828, p. 610, a6–16).

15 For the relationship between yogic perception and other types of perception, see Yao (2004).

16 Again, I follow the Tibetan translation. Xuanzang's translation (YBhc) reads: "The consciousness of particulars does not arise without taking this object [of the very nature of nonexistence] as object."

17 The Sarvāstivādins accept one more material element called "unmanifested form" (*avijñaptirūpa*), while the Yogācāras accept instead five more kinds of material form called "material thought-objects" (*dharmāyatanikāni rūpāni*).

18 I did not get a chance to discuss the fifth and final rational discourse of *vaipulya*, which says:

> Again, the future phenomena have not arisen yet, how can there be their cessation? But it is not the case that the sagely disciples do not abide in observing the arising and cessation of future phenomena. This is the fifth rational discourse. (YBhc, CBETA, T30, no. 1579, p. 585, b2–4; YBht, Derge 4038: zhi18a2–3)

Since it discusses future phenomena, it can be taken as part of argument one.

19 The Tibetan translation reads: "Suppose that the non-existence-ness (*med pa nyid*) of the nonexistence (*med pa*) of desire, worship, etc. really is an existence" (*gal te 'dod pa dang mchod sbyin la sogs pa med pa'i med pa nyid gang yin pa de yang dag par yod pa nyid yin na ni*). The omission of "donation" supports an alternative edition of Xuanzang's translation (YBhc) which also skips "donation."

20 The interpolation of "that there exist soul (*puruṣa*) and person (*pudgala*)" (*skyes bu gang zag*) is based on the Tibetan translation.

21 The Tibetan translation omits this interrogation.

22 This is the best way I can formulate this difficult sentence. The Tibetan translation seems to suggest the arising of the non-arising of the heretic's consciousness: "*ci ste med na ni log par lta ba rnams kyi de la dmigs pa'i rnam par shes pa yang 'byung bar mi 'gyur ba zhig na 'byung ste*".

23 *Sarvaṃ sarvalakṣaṇena nāstīti* / YBhs, p. 151, 21; *nāsti sarvaṃ sarvalakṣaṇena iti* / YBhs, p. 153, 3.

24 For further discussions on the adverbialist theory, the object view, and the existent-object view of intentionality, see Kriegel (2008).

25 This work was supported by the Academy of Korean Studies (KSPS) Grant funded by the Korean government (MEST) (AKS-2012-AAZ-104).

Part II

Nothingness in Early and Modern East Asian Traditions

11 The Notion of *Wu* or Nonbeing as the Root of the Universe and a Guide for Life

Xiaogan Liu

The term *wu* 無, or nonbeing, is a concept particular to the *Laozi* and the Daoist tradition. This article will analyze the four meanings of *wu* based on the *Laozi* and WANG Bi's (226–249 CE) annotation of that text. In addition to textual and philosophical discussion, I will also introduce *wu*'s significance in social and political life as suggested by the *Laozi* and Wang's theories.

Background

In modern Chinese, the word "*wu*" 無 means there-is-not, nothing, or non-being; it denotes the opposite of the word "*you*" 有, there-is, substance, or being. *Wu* usually functions as a negative particle, just like "not" in English phrases such as "there is not," "have not," or "do not." As a negative form, *wu* is inevitably and frequently used in the language of everyday life, but not as a philosophical concept in the modern world. It is notable then that *wu* is an important philosophical concept in ancient Daoist texts. It is critical not only in a metaphysical sense, but also as an idea that can guide human social and political life, as well as individual self-cultivation. Although the idea of *wu* was only popular in ancient times thanks to the historical preeminence of Daoist thought, it may still exercise a positive function in today's world if we understand and reinterpret it properly.

The idea of *wu* originated with a text known as the *Laozi* or the *Daodejing*, which is conventionally attributed to a senior contemporary of Confucius, Lao Dan, who was revered as Laozi, the suffix *zi* indicating something like "master."[1] The thought laid out in the *Laozi* was spread broadly through numerous commentators and their interpretations, among them the youngest-ever philosopher, WANG Bi, who lived for only twenty-three years. WANG Bi's work has remained the most influential annotation on the *Daodejing* since he has dramatically developed its ideas, bringing them into a new form that was relatively systematic, coherent, logical, and well-defined—though perhaps not in the modern academic sense. In this chapter, we will discuss both the original meanings of *wu* in the *Laozi* and the clearer ideas about this concept developed by Wang in his annotation.

In Wang's version of the *Laozi*, we count a total of 101 references to *wu*. This frequency is significant considering that the word *dao* gets only 76 references and the whole text has only about 5,400 words. However, this is not an entirely fair comparison because in most instances *wu* just plays the role of a negative particle and cannot be understood as a philosophical term like *dao*. Still, among the 101 references there are six places in three chapters where *wu* is used as a noun,[2] and is clearly one of the essential ideas of the *Laozi*. In Wang's annotation, there are 304 references to *wu* in numerous chapters, and among them twenty-six in nine chapters are nouns,[3] four times more than in text of the *Laozi*. The reason we present this statistic data is that nouns are much more significant in philosophical discussion than other classes of words, such as verbs, adjectives, and adverbs.

In philosophical narrative and discussion, concepts are the major foci for theoretical analysis, and these are framed in nounal forms that may denote general, universal, or abstract meanings. For example, if we want to discuss the characteristic feature of various religions, we need the term religiosity, which is obviously different from merely generically qualifying something adjectivally as religious. In other words, nominalization is a primary step that is standard in the formation of philosophical concepts. Chinese is an analytical language, rather than an inflected one, like many European languages are. This means that in Chinese, whether a word is a verb, noun, or adjective depends on its function with respect to a sentence's other words and word order, instead of on an identifying suffix. Thus, we cannot tell what part of speech a given Chinese word may be based merely on its form; instead, we have to analyze its position and function to decide its word class.

Elsewhere I have proposed four standards for judging whether or not a Chinese word indicates a philosophical concept in a text.[4] 1) It has a fixed form, namely, its meaning and form are associated consistently. This refers to compounds, such as *wu-wei* (nonaction, 無為) and *wu-si* (unselfish, 無私). 2) It must be used as a noun. This is a primary principle for a philosophical concept; in other words, not all important and representative words and terms may be considered philosophical concepts. For example, in the *Laozi*, *wu-wei* (nonaction, 無為) is used as a noun, but *wu-si* is not. Accordingly, *wu-si* cannot be counted as a philosophical concept, though it is meaningful in Laozi's thought. 3) A noun can be used in sentences as either a subject or object or both. This may be the most convenient way to determine whether or not a word is used as a noun. 4) Its content must concern general or universal issues or situations, not only specific cases. The first three standards concern linguistic formalities, while the last one is about the content of a term. The latter is obviously a necessary condition for a philosophical term. According to these standards, we can find four philosophical senses of the concept *wu* in the *Daodejing* itself and in Wang Bi's annotations of the *Daodejing*: *wu* as the origin of the universe, *wu* as a feature of *Dao*, *wu* as relative to *you* in particular things, and finally, as introduced by Wang Bi, we see *wu* as representing a transcendent and immanent *Dao*. We shall turn to these four senses next.

Wu as the Origin of the Universe

The most important sentence about *wu* appears in Chapter 40 of the *Laozi*, which states:

> Reversion is the action of Dao.
> Weakness is the function of Dao.
> All things in the world come from *you* [being, 有].
> And being comes from *wu* [nothingness or nonbeing]. (Chan 1973, 160)[5]

The first two lines reveal the features and attributes of Dao's operation and function. As for our topic, *wu*, the last two lines are critical. The myriad things in the universe come from *you*, which denotes something primary and general, a kind of substance, like *qi* (material and vital force, or elementary matter); we may use *being* as a token for *you*. The *Laozi* contends that *you* arises from *wu*, which denotes nothingness or the original state of the universe when nothing has emerged. For convenience, we can use *nonbeing* as merely a symbol for *wu*. We should not think being and nonbeing are literally equal to *you* and *wu*, because the *Laozi* did not give us a clear definition or description of them, and neither gets one specific meaning across the whole text. Therefore, we should not expect a perfect translation of Laozi's philosophical terms, though we should keep exploring possible accurate meanings as historical approach that differs from contemporary approaches pursuing new interpretations for improving or enriching the modern philosophical arsenal. Here being and nonbeing are just convenient and acceptable as tokens for the various meanings of *you* and *wu* in the *Laozi*; we should not suppose that *you* and *wu* have in all cases the same meanings as being and nonbeing in certain Western philosophies. One thing is clear, however, that both *you* and *wu* are here used as nouns with general and abstract meanings, distinct from most other occurrences of *you* and *wu*, which function more grammatically than philosophically.

The statement that "being comes from *wu*" suggests that *wu* is the primal root, origin, or first phase of all beings. Therefore, *wu* has the status of the ultimate origin or the primary condition of the whole universe. Is *wu* then equal to Dao?

It is worth noting that the *Laozi* never explicitly states that *wu* is Dao or Dao means *wu*, though similar ideas may be inferred if we compare and connect Chapter 42 with Chapter 40. In Chapter 42, Laozi claims:

> Dao generated the One [*sheng yi*, 生一],
> The One generated the two,
> The two generated the three,
> And the three generated the myriad things. [my compilation][6]

In this passage, Laozi clearly claims that Dao is the source and origin of all things in the universe. Compare this with Chapter 40, where Laozi states that all things come ultimately from *wu*. So it is easy to infer from these two chapters that Laozi believes Dao is *wu* in the sense that Dao is the final source of the universe, though he does not say that explicitly. However, we should not over-infer and conclude that Laozi's Dao is *wu* in a general sense, because we can find no textual evidence to support this idea. This point will become clearer after we discuss Chapter 1 in the next section.

Wu as a Feature of Dao

To understand Chapter 1, we have to pay attention to the three excavated versions from the Han dynasty: two well-known silk versions and a more recently published bamboo-slip version (Beijing Daxue Chutu WenXian Yanjiusuo [BJDX] 2012). Because the earlier Guodian bamboo-slip version has no text of Chapter 1, these three Han versions are important as the earliest ancient versions, which can be supposed to be closer to the original text than any received versions. Intriguingly, the three versions of the following passage are identical, though different from all the received versions, which read:

> The *nameless* (*wu-ming*, 無名) is the beginning of *Heaven and earth* (*tiandi*, 天地),
> The *named* (*you-ming*, 有名) is the mother of *myriad things* (*wan-wu*, 萬物). [my compilation]

According to these statements in the received versions, the nameless and the named seem to be two stages of generation, of Heaven and earth and of the myriad things respectively. The meanings of "beginning" and "mother" represent two distinct cosmological phases. However, this reading has been seriously challenged by the excavated Han versions, which state:

> The *nameless* is the beginning of *myriad things* (*wan-wu*),
> The *named* is the mother of *myriad things* (*wan-wu*). [my compilation]

The critical difference of these newly discovered but oldest versions is the repetition of *myriad things* (*wan-wu*) in both lines. This repetition suggests that the nameless (*wu-ming*) and the named (*you-ming*) are used to describe the same thing: the generation of the myriad things (*wan-wu*), so they are two aspects of the character of the generator of myriad things, instead of designating two temporal phases. Here the words "beginning" (*shi*, 始) and "mother" (*mu*, 母) are synonyms, indicating the earliest state or origin of universe. In the *Laozi*'s dictionary, *shi* and *mu* are not in chronological sequence. For example, Chapter 52 states: "There was a *beginning* of the universe, which may be called the *mother* of the universe." Both "beginning" and "mother" denote Dao, the very initiating phase of the universe. Similarly, Chapter 25 argues: "There was something undifferentiated and yet complete . . . it may be considered the *mother* of the universe. I do not know its name; I style it Dao" (Chan 1973, 152). Here, mother is also the very Dao.

Thus, if we accept the conclusion that Dao is the ultimate origin and source, then we should understand that both the nameless and the named are two characteristic aspects of Dao, the source and origin of the universe. The named and nameless are not two stages of cosmological evolution. This understanding fits better with the theme of Chapter 1, namely the features and functions of Dao.

Similarly, *you-yu* (having desires, 有欲) and *wu-yu* (having no desires, 無欲) in the next couplet should not be read as *you* (being) and *wu* (nonbeing). According to the silk versions, a particle *ye* 也 immediately follows *you-yu* and *wu-yu*; thus, in the phrases "*wu-yu ye* (無欲也)" and "*you-yu ye* (有欲也)," *you* and *wu* cannot be read as *being* and *nonbeing* according to the grammar rule. The silk versions read:

> Therefore, always be without desire [*wu-yu ye*, 無欲也,] so as to see their subtlety,
> And always have desire [*you-yu ye*, 有欲也], so as to see their margins. (Lynn 1999, 51, with minor modification)

However, some philosophers prefer a rather different reading initiated by Wang Anshi 王安石 (1021–1086), who reinterpreted the compounds *you-ming* 有名 and *wu-ming* 無名. He read *you* and *wu* as single-word nouns and *ming* 名 as a verb and he read the next two lines similarly; that is to say, he read *you* and *wu* as single-word concepts as in *you-yu* (having desires, 有欲) and *wu-yu* (having no desires, 無欲), wherein *yu* 欲 serves as a particle. Thus the four sentences, on this construal, read:

> *Wu* (nonbeing) names [*ming*, 名] the beginning of *Heaven and earth* [*tiandi*, 天地],
> *You* (being) names [*ming*, 名] the mother of *myriad things* [*wan-wu*, 萬物].
> Therefore, be with constant *wu* (non-being), so as to perceive its subtlety,
> Be with constant *you* (being), so as to perceive its margins. [my compilation]

This reading effectively turns the terms *you* and *wu* into being and nonbeing, making them more conceptual, and the text more philosophical, in comparison with ancient thought. Generally speaking, in the Song Dynasty, scholarship, represented by Neo-Confucianism, paid more attention to conceptual analyses. This is the reason why some modern philosophers favor Wang Anshi's reading. Unfortunately, the excavated versions have undercut this reading and proved that the ancient text need not satisfy later philosophers' desires and needs. However, since we aim to approximate the true form and the original meaning of the text, we have to relinquish this more conceptual and philosophical reading for the earliest, less ideal versions.[7] In this way, we can observe the development of the *Laozi*'s thought through WANG Bi's theories, and get a sense of the early evolution of this ancient thought.

According to the Han bamboo and silk versions, the *Laozi*'s Dao could be *wu* as the source and origin of the universe, but it does not mean that Dao is *wu* or nonbeing in a general way. In Chapter 1, Dao is given the characteristics of both the named and the nameless. What is named suggests nameability, while what is nameless suggests unnameability; which in turn suggests that Dao's perceptible features are equal to *you* or being, and its incomprehensible features are equal to *wu* or nonbeing. These two aspects refer to the human faculty of recognition of a metaphysical being and have nothing to do with the empirical world.[8] The description of Dao in Chapter 21 helps us to better understand these two attributes:

> The all-embracing quality of the great virtue [*de*, 德] follows alone from the Dao.
> Dao as a thing is but dim, is but dark.
> Dark, oh, dim, oh, but within it some image is there.
> Dim, oh, dark, oh, but within it something is there.
> Abstruse, oh, indistinct, oh, but within it the essence of things is there.
> Its essence is most authentic, for within it authentication occurs. (Chan 1973: 150; Lynn 1999, 86, with my compilation)

Here, words such as *dim*, *dark*, *abstruse*, and *indistinct* describe the incomprehensible aspect of Dao, pointing to *wu* or nonbeing; while words such as *image*, *something*, *essence*, and *authentication* suggest Dao's perceptible aspects, pointing to *you* or being. The general feature of Dao combines both *you* and *wu*, though not straightforwardly. So there is no textual evidence for the claim that the *Laozi*'s Dao is only *wu* or nonbeing. All descriptions of Dao seem to be *wu*, in the sense that human beings cannot grasp it because it is not any concrete thing humans can know. Chapter 14 describes it this way:

> We look at it and do not see it, its name is the invisible. We listen to it and do not hear it, its name is the inaudible. We touch it and do not find it, its name is the subtle (formless) . . . . Infinite and boundless, it cannot be given any name [unnameability.] It reverts to *wu-wu* [nothingness, 無物.] This is called shape without shape, image without entity . . . (Modification of Chan 1973, 146)

So this chapter also describes characteristic aspects of Dao as *you* and *wu*. Again, *wu* is a feature of Dao, distinct from *wu* as the initial status of the universe.

Wu and *You* in the Empirical World

How might notions of *you* and *wu* operate in the empirical world? Chapter 11 in the *Laozi* argues:

Thirty spokes are united around the hub to make a wheel,
But it is on its *wu* (nothingness) that the utility of the carriage depends.

Clay is molded to form a utensil,
But it is on its *wu* (nothingness) that the utility of the utensil depends.

Doors and windows are cut out to make a room,
But it is on its *wu* (nothingness) that the utility of the room depends.

Therefore, regard *you* (being) as advantage, and regard *wu* (nothingness, non-being) as utility. (Modification of Chan 1973, 144–145)

Here *wu* and *you* are mutually dependent. '*You*' indicates the concrete part of objects, while '*wu*' is their vacant part. *Wu* in the first three verses is just emptiness, or the spaces in an entity, and these instances are used to introduce the last verse, in which *wu* and *you* are more general and abstract concepts. Though *you* and *wu* are a pair that cannot be separated, this chapter's larger purpose is to promote awareness of and reverence for *wu*, and to correct the common mistake among people ignorant of or forgetting its function and utility in the world. *Wu* and *you* in this chapter of the *Daodejing* have nothing to do with the metaphysical kingdom, and are very different from *you* and *wu* as Dao's two aspects. There is a similar case made in Chapter 2:

You (being) and *wu* (non-being) bring about each other;
Difficult and easy complete each other;
Long and short contrast with each other;
High and low distinguish each other;
Sound and voice harmonize with each other;
Front and back follow each other,
Therefore the sage manages affairs without action [*wu-wei*, 無為],
And spreads doctrines without words [*bu-yan*, 不言] . . . . (Chan 1973, 140)

Some points should be noted: 1) *You* (being) and *wu* (nonbeing) are seemingly equal in a pair, and either side can bring about the other. 2) In this chapter, every line is concerned with affairs in the mundane world; there is nothing related to Dao or metaphysical concerns. 3) Obviously, the relationship of mutual transition between *you* and *wu* is not suitable to Dao or a feature of Dao. Dao, as the source of the universe, cannot be *you*, and the named and nameless sides of Dao cannot be transformed into each other. 4) In the mutually dependent relation of *you* and *wu*, as well as that of the other oppositions, people are used to seeing and pursuing the positive sides (being, easy, long) and are inclined to neglect and avoid the negative sides (nonbeing, difficult, short). Therefore, the author's emphasis on oppositional dependence and transformation is actually intended to promote the negative aspect, and this introduces a special way to deal with social and political issues—the *wu-wei* (nonaction) and *bu-yan* (no-words) that are principles of operation for Daoist sages.

Wu as the Transcendent and Immanent Dao

The fourth form and meaning of *wu* was produced by WANG Bi about six or seven centuries after the *Laozi* gained currency. Wang provides an important development, supplement, and even logical completion of the *Laozi*'s philosophy, especially with regard to the theory of *wu*. His philosophy was expressed through his famous annotation of the work, and he was the first to establish the convention that an annotator may build a new philosophical system through formal commentaries (Liu 2008–2009, 23–33; Liu 2009b, 131–156). Wang's dramatic development of the *Laozi*'s theories made Daoism more conceptual and philosophical. He transformed the term *wu* as *nonbeing* into a more abstract, universal, and coherent concept that denoted both the ground and source of the universe.

Wang introduces three new premises related to *wu*. The first is that Wang states literally that Dao equates with *wu* or nonbeing, which is a hidden idea in the *Laozi*. Wang takes this for granted in his annotation on the *Laozi* without serious argument to support it, but he does argue for it in his "Outline introduction to the Laozi" (*Laozi zhilue*, 老子指略) (Lynn 1999, 30–47). Chapter 8 of the *Laozi* highly praises the attributes of water:

> The highest good is like water.
> Water is good at benefiting myriad things and competes for nothing.
> It dwells in [lowly] places that all disdain,
> This is why it is so near to Dao. (Chan 1973, 143 with modification)

This passage does not mention *wu* or nonbeing, but in his annotation Wang introduces nonbeing as Dao's essence: "Whereas Dao [is] *wu* (nonbeing), water [is] *you* (being), thus [the text] says [it is] 'so near to Dao.'"[9] Wang's annotation is so brief and terse that it omits the "be" verb in the statement "Dao is *wu*"; even though such an omission is not an uncommon practice in classical Chinese, this brief assertion suggests that Wang doesn't think there is any need to argue the point in his commentary. The statement that "Dao equals nonbeing" is a critical statement that establishes a clear and general connection between Dao and *wu* (or nonbeing) in the history of Daoist philosophical developments. This is a point the *Laozi* itself never actually reaches.

Wang proposes a second premise about *wu* in his annotation of Chapter 40:

> That all beings in the world come into existence is due to being, but the origin of being takes nonbeing as its *ben* [root, 本]. If one wants to keep the

> wholeness of all beings, one must return to nonbeing [*wu*]. (Lynn 1999, 40, with my compilation)

Ben 本 originally and literally denotes the root part of a plant, in opposition to *mo* 末, the branches, twigs, and leaves. So we may translate *ben* as 'root'. However, *root* is merely a metaphor that suggests the association of a plant temporally growing from a seed into a tree or from nothing into something. But this is not precisely the thrust of Wang's theory. As early as in the *Analects*, the word *ben* had shed the original image of a plant root and was used in an abstract and general sense as the most important foundation of something.

According to Wang's doctrine, all beings come from their *ben*, namely nonbeing, and each one must return to nonbeing to realize its completeness. The term nonbeing negates the temporal and physical association of the *root* image. One's returning to nonbeing is not meant in a temporal or physical sense, but at a spiritual and intellectual level; it means transcending earthly attractions and the mundane life to preserve one's wholeness. Therefore, it is better to render '*ben*' as *grounds* or *foundation* instead of *root*. Both *ben* and nonbeing denote the grounds of the universe and human life, much akin to Dao; thus, people should constantly turn their minds to nonbeing or Dao, so they will not lose sight of their life's direction and become entangled in the twigs and leaves, that is, in life's trivial affairs.

WANG Bi's equation between nonbeing and Dao is critical. Dao as nonbeing suggests that the whole universe and all human beings are based on the final grounds, *wu* or nonbeing, for their existence. This means that nonbeing as Dao denotes both the origin and grounds of the universe and the human world. While the term "origin" implicates cosmological theory, "grounds" suggests ontological issues. Wang actually occupies the gap between the two. Or more likely, he did not notice the difference between cosmology and ontology, which, after all, as philosophical concepts he would never have encountered. This explains his ontological interpretation of Chapter 42, in which, the statement that Dao generates the one, two, and three is apparently a process of universal temporal evolution. The meaning of "generate" (*sheng*, 生) is simple if we read it straightforwardly, but this easy passage has produced conflicting readings and much argument (see note 6 to this essay). These have been partly inspired by Wang's commentary, which reads:

> Although the myriad things exist in myriad forms, they all revert to the One [*qi gui yi ye*, 其歸一也]. Why do they all ultimately become One [*heyou zhiyi*, 何由致一]? It is due to *nonbeing* [*wu* 無]. Because One comes from *non-being*, can One still be called *non-being*? Because we already call it "One," how can there not be a word for it? Because we have this word and because we have the One, how can there not be two? Because we have the One and have these two, this consequently gives birth to three . . . (Lynn 1999, 135)

Wang's expressions *guiyi* 歸一 (revert to the One, reduce to the One, or return to the One) and *zhiyi* 致一 (become One) are apparently not about the origin of the universe, and as such, are irrelevant to the *Laozi*'s original expression *shengyi* 生一. According to Wang, the *Laozi*'s claim that Dao generated the One, two, and three does not necessarily describe a physical process of universal evolution. Wang's explanation is more like an intellectual inference and language game influenced by the school of logic (*mingjia*, 名家) of the late Warring States period. We can say that Wang's exegesis is closer to ontological theory than cosmological hypothesis. TANG Yong-tong 湯用彤 (1893–1964) has suggested that Laozi's philosophy is cosmological, and that it was WANG Bi who first formulated Chinese ontological theories, taking *wu* 無 or nonbeing as *ontic* (Tang 1983, 195, 214).

Wang's theory of *wu* as the grounds of the universe not only combines the cosmological and ontological issues, but also eliminates the gap between the metaphysical and mundane realms. In other words, under his interpretation, *wu* as Dao is both transcendent and immanent. The best illustration is the statement that all beings take nonbeing as their universal grounds, thus all beings should return to nonbeing to realize their completeness. In light of this, Wang's third premise straightforwardly presents guidance for human beings. Wang argues: "If one preserves the child by holding fast to the mother and makes twigs [*mo*, 末] flourish by enhancing the roots [*ben*, 本,] form and names will all exist, but anomalies will not occur" (Lynn 1999, 183). Here the key statement is *chong-ben-ju-mo* 崇本舉末, to venerate or promote the root so that branches and twigs will flourish accordingly.[10] In this usage, *ben* is the ground for both the universe and myriad things, and equal to Dao and *wu*. Hence, the premise is both a metaphysical claim and a practical direction for human beings to achieve success in both great enterprises and trivial affairs.[11]

The Ethics of Nothing: *Wu* as a Guide for Life in Society

We have analyzed four different meanings of *wu* in the *Laozi*. But the *Laozi* is not purely theoretically focused and neither is the concept of *wu*. The *Laozi* contains the author's concern and reflections about the tendencies of human civilization, and it manifests his worry and his hope for human societies and life. This point is supported by the late preeminent philosopher LAO Siguang 勞思光 (1927–2012), who made a brilliant remark about the function and features of Chinese philosophy. Lao points out the general idea that Chinese philosophy is "philosophy as proposal," whose function is to present an orientation for the world and human life. Thus, Chinese philosophy might have less explanatory power, but it is strong in its "orientating power" (Lao 2003, 9, 20). Certainly, Daoism must be counted as a key thread of Chinese philosophy. The phrases "philosophy as proposal" and "orientating power" are perfectly suited for the wisdom in the *Laozi*. This point liberates us from the simplistic demarcation that Daoism is "naturalist" while Confucianism is "humanist."

Indeed, Daoist theory seems to draw more on the natural world and explore more metaphysical topics than Confucianism does, but its essential concerns still focus on human life and destiny. The "naturalist" impression, moreover, is partly caused by the common misreading of another key term, *ziran* 自然, as the Nature or the natural world (Liu 2009a, 226–233). We will come back to this point later.

To discriminate between *wu*'s different meanings is necessary and significant. But as far as practical functions are concerned, the different meanings of *wu* work together coherently and indicate the same direction: toward better social goals and order. Specifically, the *Laozi*'s *wu* is a negative measure that is recommended in achieving a positive ideal. The negative direction connotes reflection and criticism of mainstream values and styles of human social and political life. The positive direction suggests advocacy of transcendent pursuits and yearning for order and harmony in the world. Although the negation perspective is a distinctive feature of the *Laozi*'s philosophy, it is neither the whole nor the last of it. The more important perspective lies in its ideal of an inclusive peaceful world operating in natural harmony. This positive and constructive aspect of the *Laozi*'s thought has been neglected for a long time.

The negative aspects of *wu* make it distinct: as a negative particle, it exercises a negating function in many sentences and many expressions, such as non-action (*wu-wei*, 無為), no-name (*wu-ming*, 無名), no-affair (*wu-shi*, 無事), not-selfish (*wu-si*, 無私), no-knowledge (*wu-zhi*, 無知), no-desire (*wu-yu*, 無欲), no-self body (*wu-shen*, 無身), no-taste (*wu-wei*, 無味), and no-army (*wu-bing*, 無兵), and so on. All these *wu*-combinations are used to criticize mainstream actions and pursuits, including being aggressive in profit-driven activities, endlessly pursuing fame, knowledge, self-interest, or victory in war. Furthermore, another negative particle, *bu* 不, is also used frequently, in expressions such as not-competing (*bu-zheng*, 不爭), not-daring (*bu-gan*, 不敢), not-speaking (*bu-yan*, 不言), not-claiming (*bu-shi*, 不恃), not-humane (*bu-ren*, 不仁), not-initiating (*bu-wei-shi*, 不為始), and not revering worthies (*bu-shang-xian*, 不尚賢). Still another negative particle, *wu* 勿, forms compounds such as not being supercilious (*wu-jing*, 勿矜), not being haughty (*wu-jiao*, 勿驕), and not showing strength (*wu-qiang*, 勿強), just to name a few (Liu 1997, 111). These many negative compounds present weak or strong criticisms of rulers' thoughts and actions, and on the common people's habits and goals in life. At the same time, they suggest a more natural, peaceful, and leisurely way to live.

Although Laozi's criticism was leveled as a general negation of prevailing trends in ancient Chinese societies, some scholars are inclined to limit it to a more narrow sense. They interpret *wu-wei* as critical of only wrong-doing, wild behavior, or actions generally against natural laws. According to this view, the *Laozi* is merely a book of common sense for children, because few adults, especially those in power, think they are doing wrong even if their actions result in terrible disasters. In fact, however, the *Laozi*'s wisdom is based on a radical observation of the movement of the universe and human civilization: everything has its opposite, and everything moves toward or brings out that opposite; what is normal and even good is necessarily tied to its other extreme. Only people who recognize and admit the existence of this oppositional transformation may be able to prevent or reduce the effects of this process by controlling desires and activities. This general negation is supported by Dao, which is both equal to *wu* as the root of the universe and integrates *wu* as characteristic of its features.[12] Thus, we may understand why Wagner renders *wu* as "negativity" (Wagner 2003, 257), though "negativity" may not give a completely adequate account of *wu*. It is perhaps impossible to translate a Chinese philosophical term across history and cultures into another single word that carries all of the original term's resonance.

What, then, are the constructive and positive aspects of *wu* in the *Laozi*'s philosophy? To get to this we must backtrack a bit. The most distinctive idea in the *Laozi* is *ziran* 自然 (naturalness),[13] which represents transcendence from regular values and ideals. The last passage of Chapter 25 reads:

> Man takes his models from Earth [*ren fa di*, 人法地],
> Earth takes its models from Heaven [*di fa tian*, 地法天],
> Heaven takes its models from the Dao [*tian fa dao*, 天法道],
> and the Dao takes its models from *ziran* [*dao fa ziran*, 道法自然]. (Lynn 1999, 96, with my modification)[14]

The assertion that "Dao takes its models from *ziran* 自然" puts *ziran* in the highest position, though it does not posit *ziran* as an entity, but as an idea or principle. Here, *ziran* cannot mean the natural world or human nature, since these ideas cannot be mapped into ancient Chinese thought. Like many ancient Chinese philosophical terms, *ziran* does not have a singular meaning, and it is very difficult to find a proper counterpart for it in either English or modern Chinese. Therefore, we will use naturalness as a token for it. *Ziran* is a good result that comes from the negation of mainstream or deviant policies and strategies. The *Laozi* argues that the principle of naturalness or natural harmony can reduce levels of unhealthy transformation and avoid the disasters caused by regular competition and strife. Comprehensively, then, we can say that *ziran* is the central value, highest principle, and the ideal state of human societies in the universe (Liu 2009a).

Too much could be said about how to realize *ziran* or naturalness. Since space is limited, we will briefly introduce one term, *fu* 輔, from the Guodian bamboo *Laozi* (A):

> And so the sage is *able* to *assist* the myriad things' *naturalness*,
> but is *unable* to *act* [in the common manner] [*shigu shengren neng fu wanwu zhi ziran er funeng wei*, 是故聖人能輔萬物之自然而弗能為.] (my compilation)

This earliest version foregrounds the contrast between "able" and "unable," which in turn illuminates the relation between *fu* (assisting, 輔) and *wei* (acting, 為). We can make out that the *Laozi* does not intend "*assisting* the *naturalness* of the myriad things" to be the usual sort of "action," but rather a *wu* version of action. Here, *fu*, or assisting, is promoted as a special kind of behavior that proceeds in accordance with the principle of *naturalness*. In other words, the sage is able to advance the prosperity of the myriad creatures and things, but not by the usual means. Thus, *fu* carries the senses of assistance, aid, or support. It is better understood as the middle of the spectrum where one extreme is restraint, manipulation, interruption, interference, exploitation, control, and oppression, while the other is pampering, spoiling, indulgence, permissiveness, and over-protection. In this way, '*fu* (assist)' as a positive term depicts a principle that arises between two common modes of action and behavior that are usually negated by the *Laozi*'s philosophy of *wu*.

Both these negative and positive sides are significant and intended to help correct a prevailing tendency in the human world, where people pursue certain values blindly, endlessly, and purposelessly. Paul Tillich (1886–1987) once criticized modern people for competing mindlessly with the line "better and better," "faster and faster," "more and more" (Tillich 1987, 2). The *Laozi*'s idea of *wu* can help us recognize and correct this unhealthy social trend. The principle of a different course of engagement with things, such as assisting (*fu*), deserves to be adopted by all modern people, but especially those in higher positions.

Through his concept of nonbeing, WANG Bi has also successfully fused his metaphysical theory and instructions for human life, creating a rich and coherent system. It applies equally to the explanation of the origin and development of the universe, as well as serving as a guide for people's political and social life and their moral cultivation. Wang argues in his annotation of Chapter 38:

> How is virtue to be attained? It is to be attained through Dao. How is virtue to be completely fulfilled? It is through non-being as its function. As non-being is its function, all things will be embraced. Therefore, in regard to things, if they are understood as non-being, all things will be in order, whereas if they are understood as being, it is impossible to avoid the fact that they could not avoid [adversity] with their life. (Chan 1973, 322)[15]

This is a full fusion of transcendent nonbeing and humans' political, social, and moral life. Wang's theories may seem mystifying and distant from the concerns of the modern world, but if we understand nonbeing as a negation of common values, which promotes a transcendent level of human consciousness, his philosophy can be inspiring and enlightening.

Conclusion

In this chapter we have examined four meanings of *wu*. 1) *Wu* is the source of the universe, or the state before anything has emerged. This meaning of *wu* is more like *nothingness*. As a concept, this *wu* relates to cosmology and has nothing to do with affairs of the mundane world. 2) *Wu*, together with *you*, expressed as nameless and named, reflect the conceivability and incomprehensibility of Dao. In this sense, *wu* and *you* are two aspects of Dao. Neither of the two is directly related to issues of the physical or the human world. 3) *Wu* is a notion or phenomena opposite to *you* in the empirical world. At this level, *wu* and *you* transform from and into each other; this relationship should not be applied to the two above-mentioned metaphysical levels. 4) These three meanings of *wu* belong to different realms, but WANG Bi fused all these meanings of *wu* into one abstract and universal concept, as nonbeing and Dao, the origin and grounds of the universe and human societies. Wang's theory is an early peak of abstract thought, with both coherence and comprehensiveness, in the history of Chinese philosophy.

Some people may be dissatisfied with these itemized analyses of the *Daodejing*'s usage of *wu*. As philosophers, they prefer to latch onto a single meaning of *wu* that is suitable for the whole text and good for interpreting the *Laozi*'s philosophy systematically. This preference—a common approach and practice—relies on the assumption that the *Laozi* is a consistent philosophical treatise. Obviously this is not the case: the *Laozi* is neither a treatise in the modern academic sense, nor a miscellaneous collection of aphorisms and proverbs. Thus, to faithfully understand it, we must take considerable care to analyze *wu* in each chapter and verse according to its specific context. Certainly, one can consciously reform and improve the *Laozi*'s thought for modern consumption, but that is a different project from regular interpretation. Methodological issues in Chinese philosophical studies are significant and difficult, and demand sustained thought and discussion.

Notes

1 There are controversies about the *Laozi*'s author and date. This essay will not be concerned with this issue. Readers who are interested in the author's position and arguments about the text's origins are invited to consult Liu (2009a) for a brief discussion in English and Liu (1997) for a Chinese discussion.
2 See Chapters 2, 11, and 40 of the *Daodejing*.
3 Chapters 1, 11, 14, 16, 21, 38, 40, 58, and 64 of the *Daodejing* or the *Laozi*.
4 This is the first time I discuss these four standards for a Chinese philosophical term in English. The first Chinese version was published in 1988 and reprinted in 2010 (Liu 2010, 138).
5 All translations, no matter from whom, are modified according to my understanding and for narrative smoothness. I have consulted many translations, including Chan (1973), Lynn (1999), Henricks (1991), Lau (2001), Ivanhoe (2002), and Wagner (2003).
6 There are controversies about the translation of the word *sheng* 生 in this context. Fu, following Mou Zongsan, argues:

> the passage about "Dao generates One" should be re-rendered philosophically as "Dao (metaphysically) comes before One . . . Three (metaphysically) comes before all things." Taking the ontological version of Laozi's cosmological thinking, I would maintain that Dao is the ontological ground of all things in the non-conceptual, symbolic sense. (Fu 1973, 378)

Nevertheless, in the most straightforward reading, *sheng* just means to generate, produce, or bring about, though not necessarily as a mother's giving birth to a baby.

7 I have argued that there are two essentially different orientations in the study of Chinese philosophy, namely, 1) textual and historical orientation for approximating the possible truths of ancient thought; and 2) modern and constructive orientation that presents new ideas for contemporary and future societies. Both orientations are significant and crucial to quality research. Scholars of Chinese philosophy should consciously differentiate these two kinds of tasks for better research outcomes. See Liu (2008–2009) in English and Liu (2009b) in Chinese.

8 Therefore, the theme of Chapter 1 is about the human faculty of recognition of a metaphysical being, not the Dao itself. This reading is different from popular impressions of the chapter.

9 Citations of Wang in this essay are adapted from translations in Lou (1980), Lynn (1999), Wagner (2003), and Chan (1973).

10 Here, *chongben jumo* 崇本舉末 is from Wang's commentary on Chapter 38. In his "*Laozi* zhilue" 老子指略 (Outline introduction to the *Laozi*), Wang uses *chongben ximo* 崇本息末 instead. The word *xi* 息 can denote both *tingxi* 停息 and *shengxi* 生息, namely to cease and to grow; the two meanings are in opposition. Some reasonable textual evidence exists for reading it as "cease," but since it always appears together with *shoumu cunzi* 守母存子, *xi* should be read as "grow." This reading is in accordance with Wang's commentary on Chapter 38.

11 In the context of Chinese philosophy, "metaphysics" cannot be understood in a Platonic or essentialist sense, since Dao is also imminent in all the myriad things.

12 The term "oppositional transformation" was suggested by Prof. Douglas L. Berger in a personal communication.

13 Based on extant literature, we are able to say that the word *ziran* was first coined and used in the *Laozi*. In central early texts, such as the *Shangshu* 尚書, *Shijing* 詩經, *Zuozhuan* 左傳, the *Analects* 論語, and the *Mencius* 孟子, there is no reference to this term. The *Guanzi* 管子 refers to it once; the *Mozi* 墨子 twice; in the *Xunzi* 荀子 there are two references, in the *Zhuangzi* 莊子 six, and in the *Hanfeizi* 韓非子 eight.

14 Lynn (1999) translates *ziran* as "the Natural", p. 96.

15 The meaning of the last sentence is not clear. The word "adversity" is added according to my analysis and understanding of the context.

12 The Relation of Nothing and Something

Two Classical Chinese Readings of *Daodejing* 11

Douglas L. Berger

Introduction

Chapter 11 of the Chinese Warring States classic, the *Daodejing*, has provoked profound and far-reaching interpretations, from seminal Daoist commentators such as Guo Xiang (郭象 252–312 CE) to twentieth century Western philosophers and architects like Martin Heidegger and Frank Lloyd Wright.[1] The brief text of the chapter is as evocative and mysterious as it is suggestive about how things in the world lend themselves to human arrangement and use, and do so precisely to the degree that their "nothingness" makes them amenable to being employed for specific functions. Ultimately, this chapter argues, "nothingness" is not some utterly mysterious metaphysical doctrine that inspires mystics and confounds philosophers, but is instead something we encounter every day in our engagements with things. Simple and compelling examples are offered by the text to illustrate that, if it were not for the spaces, the "nothings" (*wu*, 無) found in common implements like wheels, vessels, and dwellings, we could not use them for their intended purposes. These everyday encounters, not just with sheer "nothingness," but with the ways in which "nothingness" is literally built into the structure of physical phenomena, should attune us to the fundamental significance of "nothingness" in our lived experience and in the natural order as a whole.

This chapter of the *Daodejing* and its many different readings in subsequent centuries try to tease out the relation between "nothingness" and the physical objects in which it is found. We see in these variant readings, as well as in the entire collection of essays in this volume, that there was never a homogeneous view of the notion of "nothingness" in classical Asian thought, and that, instead, the idea was the topic of pointed debate and adjudged from many different perspectives. This chapter will review the readings of two contemporary third-century Chinese advocates of "Dark Learning" (*xuan xue*, 玄學), namely Wang Bi (王弼 226–249 CE) and Zhong Hui (鍾惠 225–264 CE), in order to highlight perhaps the most consequential philosophical problems that the *Daodejing* raises. Those problems concern how we are, if at all, to properly conceive of the notion of "nothing" (*wu*, 無) in its relation to the cosmological order as a whole and how, if at all, we encounter "nothing" at work in the unfolding of the world. In light of this review, I will argue that, even though it is more difficult to square with other passages in the *Daodejing*, ZHONG Hui's relational understanding of "nothing" makes greater sense out of this fascinating chapter than WANG Bi's more foundational one. Furthermore, Zhong's reading provides us with a powerful insight into at least one significant way in which "nothing" plays an active role in the things we experience and use. However, I will also point out that despite their different conceptions of *nothing* (*wu*), WANG Bi and ZHONG Hui share the view that spatiality is one manifestation of nothingness. Their reading of *nothing* (*wu*) illustrates how it both helps constitute and contribute to the usefulness of things. The spatiality reading of *wu* aids us in understanding one of the most prevalent and important convictions about "nothing" in the Daoist philosophical tradition, namely that nothingness is commonly manifested in everyday experience as *space*.

Initial Textual Puzzles

One of the great and rich ambiguities of Chapter 11 derives from the sheer grammatical puzzle of the text itself. Different textual readings offer various perspectives for comprehending the stated relationship between *wu* 無 and *you* 有, the latter of which we may understand as the "presence" or general "existence" of concrete things. The Chinese text of the chapter, according to the most common reading and punctuation, along with my enumeration of the lines for easy reference, follows.

1.	三十輻共一轂;	Thirty spokes join at a hub;
2.	當其無, 有車之用.'	In its nothing (*wu* 無), there is (*you* 有) the use of the cart.
3.	埏埴以為器;	Mixing clay produces a vessel;
4.	當其無, 有器之用.	In its nothing (*wu* 無), there is (*you* 有) the use of the vessel.
5.	鑿戶牖以為室;	Cutting doors and windows produces a room;
6.	當其無, 有室之用.	In its nothing (*wu* 無), there is (*you* 有) the use of the room.
7.	故有之以為利;	Thus, its something (*you* 有) produces benefit.
8.	無之以為用.	Its nothing (*wu* 無) produces use.[2]

While this is an entirely plausible and indeed the generally favored construal of the stanza, as we shall see, it is neither the only possible reading nor, according to some, even the most sensible one. The reading would have us treat the notion of "nothing" (*wu*, 無) as a self-standing term and associate it with the spaces in various things, such as wheels, vases, and rooms, in such a way as to explain their "usefulness" (*yong*, 用). However, even without any assistance from traditional commentaries, an attentive reader will notice that one difficulty of this rendering is the sudden nominal treatment of *you* 有 as another independent term meaning "something," and its multiple identifications in this short text. It is in a noun-form and identified as the basis of "benefit" (*li*, 利) in the seventh line, while in lines two, four, and six it has been treated as a verb that means roughly that there "is," or one "has" the usefulness of things "in (*dang*, 當)" their respective "nothings." Why is the nominalized term *you* suddenly linked with "benefit" when its foregoing verbal forms were indicative of usefulness? The final two lines in the text present a summary of the contrast between *you* and *wu*, and yet they do not seem to follow in any obvious way from what has preceded them. And indeed, early commentaries on this chapter in the Chinese literature such as the one written by ZHUANG Zun (莊遵) (83 BCE–6 CE) and the Xiang 'Er (想爾) (written between approximately 190 and 220 CE) seem to have taken their primary explanatory task to be elucidating how people came to associate "benefit" with mere matter, for the text itself leaves this issue unresolved (Wagner 2000, 231–237). Wagner's exposition shows that ZHUANG tried to disambiguate the verse by explaining that mere matter does not produce either benefit or usefulness, and "nothing" had to be fashioned by intelligent innovators. For its part, the Xiang 'Er takes the whole chapter to be a metaphor for the need of *qi* cultivation in following *dao*, as the latter would not be possible were we to simply rely on physical form alone.

One way to address this difficulty is simply to reconstruct the relationship between *wu* and *you* by changing the punctuation of this chapter.

1.	三十輻共一轂;	Thirty spokes join at a hub;
2.	當其無有,車之用.	In its nothing (*wu*) and something (*you*) is the use of the cart.
3.	埏埴以為器;	Mixing clay produces a vessel;
4.	當其無有,器之用.	In its nothing and something is the use of the vessel.
5.	鑿戶牖以為室;	Cutting doors and windows produces a room;
6.	當其無有,室之用.	In its nothing and something is the use of the room.
7.	故有之以為利;	Thus, its something produces benefit.
8.	無之以為用.	Its nothing produces use.

Here, it is the combination of *wu* and *you* that constitutes things and gives them, respectively, their matter and usefulness. Consequently, this treatment gives rise to the possibility that each of the terms, the "nothing" and the "something" of things, may be analytically separated out in all the things in the world, enabling the two terms to be linked with "benefit" and "function" in the closing sentences. This reading renders the chapter more coherent than the first reading. But it too has interpretive difficulties. First, if we read it this way, the stanza seems to be saying something that, while insightful, is relatively uncontroversial, namely that things can be made useful through, as it were, an art of crafting them that arranges their matter and their spaces in ways that best suit their intended purposes. Furthermore, if that is the case, then what precisely is the rationale for attributing usefulness solely to the "nothing" of things in the final line, since the latter has been explicitly identified with both "something" and "nothing" in this version of sentences two, four, and six?

I will return to the difficulties of internal coherence with which each of these two readings presents us later. For now, we shall turn to the two Chinese commentators who are the subjects of this paper, Wang Bi and Zhong Hui. These two thinkers, roughly contemporaneous, capture the import of the two alternative fashions of parsing the chapter outlined above, with Wang defending the first reading and Zhong the second, with great subtlety and far-reaching alternative philosophical consequences. Wang Bi's reading illustrates how taking "nothing" as the sole source of the usefulness of things may prompt one to see in the idea of "nothingness" some foundational metaphysical priority, not only in the structure of things, but in their ultimate emergence into existence as well. For Zhong, on the other hand, it is the relation of "nothing" and "something" in the makeup of phenomena that, while indissoluble, may teach us something about the relatedness of all things to one another, a relatedness that cannot be understood without a proper consideration of "nothingness." This contrast of views is therefore not only philosophically instructive for us in the larger sense, but is also at the heart of Daoist debates that took place within a movement in which both Wang and Zhong were participants. In the context of these discussions that occurred in the Wei-Jin school of "Dark Learning" during the third century, the question of how to grasp the relationship between *wu* and *you* was placed within the framework of the purported relationship between *wu* and *Dao* 道, understood as the "course" or "path" of the world's unfolding. In the Dark Learning philosophers' alternative hermeneutic approaches, to properly grasp the relationship between something and nothing in our daily experience, one must first have the correct understanding of cosmology and the natural order. The different views of Wang Bi and Zhong Hui were contested as early as in the third-century commentarial literature, and contemporary scholars such as Rudolph Wagner and Alan Chan have also paid special attention to these divergent views. We now engage Wang Bi's and Zhong Hui's interpretations of this chapter.

Wang Bi's Interpretation

Wang Bi gives the following explication of *Daodejing* 11.

> 轂所以能統三十輻者, 無也. 以其無能受物之故, 故能以實統眾也. 木埴, 壁之所以成, 三者而皆以無為用也. 言無者, 有之所以為利, 皆賴無以為用也. (Wagner 2003, 154)[3]
>
> That which is able to unite (*tong*, 統) thirty spokes in the wheel is nothing (*wu*, 無).
>
> Because its nothing is able to receive (*shou*, 受) things (*wu*, 物), it is able, by means of what is concrete (*shi*, 實), to unify everything. Wood and soil are that by which the mortar is completed (*cheng*, 成), but these three things accord with (*yi*, 以) nothing to produce usefulness. It is said, regarding a thing's nothing (*wu zhe*, 無者), that though the something of a thing (*you zhi*, 有之) produces benefit, nonetheless in all cases, its nothing produces usefulness.

WANG Bi's interpretation of this chapter moves from the specific to the general. From analyzing the relationship between the nothing and the something that make up particular things such as a wheel, a vessel, and a room, he summarizes the connection between nothing and matter in all things. In his analysis, the nothing that can be found in the wheel is what enables it to be unified (*tong*, 統), presumably meaning the nothing, or the empty hole, at the hub that allows the wheel to rotate along the axle and so function as a wheel with a unified purpose. In a more general sense, the nothing, as it is found in particular things, serves as the internal space that is able to receive or make room for the material configuration. Having the requisite matter to construct things is then necessary for those things to benefit us, as we could, presumably, do nothing if we only had nothing at hand. However, in a more general sense with regard to physical things, once there is concrete matter that has been shaped or crafted by either the natural circumstances or by human intentions, then the spaces in it, the "nothing" of the things, is what makes them useful. That is why, WANG Bi argues, usefulness is entirely the production of nothing. There is then in any given thing, on WANG Bi's account, a definite relation between concrete material (the something) and the nothing in it, but given this relation, the usefulness of a thing does not come from its physical constituents themselves, but is instead entirely attributable to its nothing.

Wang's exegesis of Chapter 11 is derived from his understanding of the cosmological primacy of *wu* in the formation of the entire natural order. The famous first chapter of the *Daodejing* articulates the relationship between the "course (*Dao*, 道)" of the world's unfolding and how we are to "name (*ming*, 名)" the source or origin of the natural world and its subsequent emergent phenomena, and, as he explains, "all things begin in nothing.[4] The theme emerges in his interpretation of a number of other pivotal chapters as well. With reference to Chapter 4, for example, Wang claims that *Dao* can be considered the "inexhaustible" source of things precisely because the infinite varieties of those things could only have been made possible if they emerged from a shapeless "nothing" that was an infinitely accommodating source (Wagner 2003, 131–132). Wang also lays great emphasis on Chapter 40, which is capped with the phrase: "the ten thousand things are generated from what is (*you*, 有), and what is (*you*, 有) is generated from what is not 無 (*wu*)." In his commentary, he connects the notion of "nothing" to that of the "root" of the world.

> 天下之物皆以有為生，有之所始，以無為本，將欲全有，必反於無也. (Wagner 2003, 257)
>
> The things (*wu*, 物) under heaven all accord with something (*you*, 有) in being generated, but as for the originary state (*suo shi*, 所始) of something, that accords with nothing (*wu*, 無) and takes it as its root (本 *ben*). If one wishes to complete things (*quan you*, 全有), one must return (*fan*, 反) them to nothing (*wu*, 無).

The idea that "nothing" is the formless and nameless source of the material world is reinforced in Wang's commentary on other related chapters as well. For instance, in his explication of Chapter 39, *Dao* is called "one" and thus said to be the origin of all numbers and things, and in Chapter 42, *Dao* is said to generate oneness, and from oneness consequently emerges the basic configurations of *qi* and by extension the ten thousand things.[5]

With Wang Bi's interpretation, we are entitled to ask: how does the claim that "nothing" lies at the foundation of the general existence of material things help us understand his assertion in the commentary to Chapter 11 that "nothing" is the sole source of the usefulness of particular material things? He seems to be making an implicit inference that "nothing," as the "root" (*ben*, 本) of things, is what material things "accord with," or are ultimately "produced by" (*yi wei*, 以為) in their original formation. That is to say, while the "something" that constitutes material things can, in the order of material production and reproduction (*sheng*, 生), be "in accord" with other material things, the originary state (*suo shi*, 所始) of all things must have been infinitely indeterminate in a way that could facilitate the production of the myriad things. Once produced, that indeterminate "originary state" of things, the so-called "nothing," was not simply superseded and, as it were, replaced or filled up by the concrete materiality of things. Instead, that originary "nothing" still inhabits things and continues to be a causal source of their interaction in the world. As Wang sees it, the specific way in which the "nothing" of particular things contributes to their relation in the world is that each of the nothingnesses produces (*wei*, 為) the usefulness of a particular thing. This relationship between nothingness and the functions of particular things is what Wang captures in his commentary on Chapter 11. As the original text of Chapter 11 points out, were it not for the empty spaces in things, things would have no unity of purpose. Without space, the matter out of which a thing is constituted can have no such capacity to lend things unity of purpose, for concrete matter cannot "receive" (*shou*, 受) or make room for other concrete matter. This explains why Wang Bi attributes usefulness in its entirety to the "nothing" of things.

In summary, Wang Bi connects nothingness in a cosmological sense to the nothingness in particular things. In a grander sense, only the limitless can accommodate the infinite space that things inhabit as well as the infinite number of ways things can take shape. In the particularized existence of a thing, on the other hand, both the configuration and serviceability of each particular thing must be derived from the "nothing" that is found there or built into them. Nothingness is thus foundational both in the overall scheme of the cosmos and in particular things.

Zhong Hui's Interpretation

Even though Zhong Hui's reading of the *Daodejing* as a whole is, along with many other third century "Dark Learning" commentaries, also devoted to developing a thoroughgoing understanding of *wu*, his exegesis of Chapter 11 deals with the stanza as a self-standing unit (Wagner 2000, 242). He attempts to make more detailed sense out of the relationship between the material and the spaces of a thing.

> 舉上三事, 明有無相資, 俱不可廢. 故有之以為利, 利在於體. 無之以為用, 用在於空. 故體為外利, 資空用以得成. 空為內用, 藉體利以得就. 但利用相藉, 咸不可亡也. 無賴有為利, 有藉無為用, 二法相假. (Chan 2003, 117)[6]
>
> The above three matters are raised to illuminate the fact that *you* and *wu* support (*zi*, 資) one another, and neither can be diminished. 'Thus, its something produces benefit' means that benefit is found in the physical substance (*ti*, 體). 'Its nothing produces use' means that use is found in the empty space (*kong*, 空). Thus, in order for the physical substance to produce external (*wai*, 外) benefit, it is supported by use to obtain its completion. In order for the empty space to produce internal (*nei*, 內) use, it is indeed by means of the benefiting physical substance that it is attained. Therefore, benefit and use are a means (*jie*, 藉) for one another and neither can be eliminated. Nothing relies (*lai*, 賴) on something to produce benefit, something uses the means of nothing to produce use; the two models (*fa*, 法) borrow (*jia*, 假) from one another.

In Zhong Hui's analysis, the relationship between something and nothing, or we can say the matter and empty spaces in a thing, is not one of ultimate generation as we saw in Wang Bi's analysis, but of mutual dependence in the production of both benefit and use. As his commentary points out, benefit is itself something external (*wai*, 外), while use is something associated with the inside (*nei*, 內) of a thing. The external-internal contrast had some important currency in Han and Wei-Jin philosophical debates in China, as these notions not only point to the physically outer and inner constituents of a thing, but also connote, respectively, that which is only seen on the outside, the surface, and potentially superficial visible features of a thing, and what is, as it were, at its heart or in its "essence." Consequently, Zhong Hui means that benefit is measured in terms of the socially accepted, and thus artificially constructed, value of the physical material that meets the eye and can be handled. Use, on the other hand, is "internal" to a thing, in the sense that the spaces that belong to a thing are inside it, essential to its structure, and it is the structure of a thing that makes it useful in the ways it is.[7] This has the implication that benefit and use are not two wholly separable features of a thing, but are merely features whose significance is determined with respect to the context and the makeup of a thing respectively. How highly a thing is valued and how useful it is are inextricably related to both its context and its makeup, as the less structural integrity and coherence a thing has, the less useful it will be, and the less useful it is, the less socially valuable it will be. In notable contrast to Wang's assessment, in Zhong Hui's conception of "nothing," although it is the primary source of a thing's use, also contributes to the creation of benefit by relying (*lai*, 賴) on a thing's material. Likewise for the material constitution (*you*, 有) of particular things: though it is the primary source of a thing's benefit, it also contributes to the production of the thing's use, but only by means (*jie*, 藉) of the spaces that are incorporated within it. Benefit and use are thus mutual means (*xiang jie*, 相藉) to one another's attainment, just as something and nothing are mutually supporting (*xiang zi*, 相資) in the constitution of a thing.

Since we only have a total of about twenty-four chapters of ZHONG Hui's commentary, which is fragmentarily cited in independent works, it is a speculative enterprise to gauge how well Zhong's extrapolation of Chapter 11 fits in with his larger understanding of the import of the whole *Daodejing* (see Chan 2003, 114, 150–151).[8] Chan conjectures that, given the contrast between the thematic approaches of ZHONG Hui and WANG Bi, the former might be a "transitional" figure in the school of "Dark Learning," for the reason that Zhong's focus on unpacking the meaning of individual lines and stanzas precedes Wang's commentarial practice of seeing a philosophical coherence in the whole work (150). These textual-historical considerations are among the reasons that we find in WANG Bi's exegesis a far tighter tie between the treatment of *wu* in Chapter 11 and its interpretation in the rest of the entire work, while in ZHONG Hui's case we find more attention paid and greater effort directed to understanding this chapter on its own terms.

All this being the case, there are a number of reasons to believe that Zhong's philosophical account of the chapter under discussion is more convincing than Wang's, and provides us with a more tenable picture of how "nothing" interacts with the things in our world. We shall turn to this philosophical comparison next.

Nothingness: Foundational or Interdependent?

Let us recall the questions that the two distinctly punctuated renditions of Chapter 11 left us with at the beginning of this paper. If, according to the first translation, we understand *wu* and *you* in the last two lines to be wholly distinct terms, and *wu* as both the originary basis of things and the sole source of their use, then we are left with the puzzle as to why benefit is introduced in the penultimate line and identified with concrete things (*you*). WANG Bi lays out the claim in his reading that the concrete matter of a thing must "accord with" (*yi*, 以) that same thing's "nothing" in order to create benefit. Now, even though there is no discernible argument on the level of the already existing thing showing how or why this is the case, that claim might lead us to expect Wang to conclude that benefit and use depend precisely on the interrelation of the nothing and something in things. Wang does write regarding this matter that it would not be possible for a thing to have benefit or use were it not for its concrete matter (*shi*, 實), for otherwise, no product or thing could be complete (*cheng*, 成). But then, at the close of his commentary on the verse, benefit is said by Wang to solely derive from a thing's materiality. In this respect, then, WANG Bi's exegesis leaves the puzzle of benefit posited by the text of *Daodejing* 11 unsolved. This is so because what Wang hints at with regard to the "accord" between benefit and use in the balance of what he writes would seem to preclude us from inferring that benefit is the exclusive production of a thing's matter.

There is another difficulty with WANG Bi's interpretation of this chapter. Even if we concede that Wang has gone to great lengths to connect the notion of "nothing" in this chapter with how it can be understood in the rest of the text, the content of that connection does not explain the claim that "nothing," as the originary state of things, contributes to their present causal capacities. Wang affirms the assertion of the last line of the chapter that "nothing" produces use. Note that, in its fullest sense, "nothing" according to Wang is not only identifiable with the spaces in a thing that have the ability to "receive" its material and make it a unified whole, but it is also the root (*ben*, 本) or originary state (*suo shi*, 所始) of things, insofar as all forms had to have their possibility based in an infinitely encompassing formlessness. Even if one were to accept that this representation of *wu* could be found in the other chapters of the *Daodejing*, it yet remains quite unclear as to how the receptivity found as the spaces within a thing is related to the infinite receptivity of originary cosmic formlessness with respect to the production of a specific thing's usefulness. In other words, let us assume with Wang that the physical universe emerged out of a state of formlessness, and, now that the former has evolved into concrete, multifarious things, that originary formlessness has itself become dispersed into the structures of each individual thing. We still do not know the how, the causal mechanics, through which the particularized nothings in things, on their own, "produce" the thing's usefulness. The mere conviction that *wu* was the foundation for the emergence of the cosmos because of its infinite formlessness does not tell us anything about how it works in individual things, much less how it could be solely responsible for the thing's serviceability to human needs. If, therefore, there is a discernible relation between the particular "nothings" of things and the more foundational "metaphysical" root of the originary "nothing" in the causal emergence of the usefulness of individual things, Wang has not informed us about that relation.[9]

By contrast, one of the virtues of ZHONG Hui's explanation of *Daodejing* 11 is precisely that it directly addresses, in a fairly compelling way, one of the basic ambiguities highlighted by the second possible translation of the chapter. If we understand both the concrete matter of a thing and its "nothings" or spaces to be mutually involved in rendering a thing useful, then why does the last line of the text claim that use is exclusively the production of the thing's "nothing?" Zhong clarifies that the use of a thing emerges from its "internal" (*nei*, 内) structure, for if there were not a hub at the center of a wheel, a space on the inside of a vessel, or doors in a room, none of these things could be used for their distinct functions. The "nothing" that belongs to a thing and that makes it what it is cannot be found on the "outside" of it, and so in this regard, the chapter is justified in emphasizing that use is particularly indebted to the constitutive role that a thing's "nothing" plays in its structure. That does not mean, however, that "nothing" is exclusively productive of use, for the use of a thing must also depend on its concrete materiality. The chapter is also justified, according to Zhong's reading, in laying special emphasis on the fact that the "something," the matter of a thing, is especially important in yielding its benefit, since benefit is an "external" (*wai*, 外) feature of a thing insofar as the materials out of which a thing is made have different conventional economic and social values. At the same time, the benefit of a thing does not rely solely on the value of its material constituents, but also on its "nothing," insofar as the specific configurations of space in a thing make it in varying ways and to varying degrees serviceable.

To elaborate on Zhong's helpful qualifications a bit more clearly, let us consider the first example of a thing deployed by *Daodejing* 11, namely a wheel. Zhong argues that the chapter is right to emphasize that usefulness would be utterly impossible without the "nothing" or the space at the hub through which the axle runs, for without that space, the wheel couldn't rotate and thus could not perform its function. Furthermore, that "nothing" or space that renders the wheel serviceable for its intended purpose is found in its internal structure, not outside of it. But the fact that the chapter points out in its final line the direct relation between usefulness and the spaces found on the inside of a thing, as Zhong sees it, is merely a point of emphasis and not of exclusion. That is to say, what has been emphasized about the importance of "nothing" for usefulness should not lead us to infer that usefulness depends only and entirely on a thing's internal "nothing." After all, both the text and common sense should prompt us to conclude that, in order to be useful, the "nothing" of a thing must be incorporated into its concrete matter in the right way, and different for different things like vases and rooms. In like manner, the seventh line of the chapter, on Zhong's account, is right to emphasize the necessity of concrete matter in making a thing beneficial, for a thing's matter gives it shape and makes it possible to handle, and its constituent materials may furthermore make it more or less valued as a commercial item. Matter and commercial value are degrees of a thing's "externality," its surface features and social assessment. But again, the chapter's emphasis on the connection between externality and benefit as especially deriving from a thing's matter is merely that, an emphasis, and not a reason to deny that a thing's matter contributes to its use too. And so, with Zhong Hui's distinctions, we get a fairly straightforward and plausible account of how both the concrete exterior matter of a thing and its internal spatial features and arrangement interdependently offer both its benefit and usefulness.

But what of the remaining possible objection leveled against the second construal of the verse above? While the observation this reading makes about how a thing's "nothing" makes it useful may be insightful, may call our attention to the non-material features of a thing that might otherwise escape our notice, isn't the observation, once understood, more or less noncontroversial, even perhaps trivial? Of course both a thing's matter and the way it is fashioned or structured determine the degree to which it can be used and its monetary and social worth. Is there any substantive philosophical import to this insight, or may it just be a realization of a more ordinary and commonly agreeable sort? Speaking to the commonalty and ordinariness that this objection may target, these in fact might indeed be strong support for the insight into things that *Daodejing* 11 is offering us, for they would lend great corroboration and soundness to the stanza's claim that "nothing (*wu*, 無)" plays a palpable rule in our everyday experiences and actions, despite how initially counterintuitive that claim may appear. However, I would argue there is yet another aspect of what is being asserted about "nothing" in the chapter that, far from being philosophically trivial, is argued for not just by the text of *Daodejing* 11 but by both the commentaries of WANG Bi and ZHONG Hui, despite their significant differences. I turn to this dimension of significance in the final section.

Space and Spatiality as Nothingness

According to the text of Chapter 11, "nothing" can be found to be both inside things and in various ways productive, or at least causally efficacious, when it comes to employing things toward their intended purposes. In a structural sense, the "nothing" in things is identified with the spaces inside of them, the area where there is no material substance present, but where space pervades in such a way as to make the material configuration serviceable to human needs. As the *Daodejing* has it, it is the hub at the center of the wheel that makes space for the axle, the space between the internal sides of a vessel that allows one to place things in it, and the openness that doors create in rooms that allow us to enter and exit them. Despite their disagreement about the foundational or relational nature of "nothing" in the workings of the thing and the unfolding of the cosmos, Wang and Zhong both overtly identify our experience of "nothing" in our everyday experience with these spaces that are built into things in ways that make them useful. They therefore depict space and spatiality as nothingness, and this formulation not only becomes extraordinarily influential in the history of East Asian thought beyond the Daoist tradition, but also lays the groundwork for many different ways in which we may understand "nothingness" as cosmologically and even practically significant.

Both of our commentators take note of the fact that the "nothing" under discussion in the examples of a wheel, vessel and room can be encountered in their "empty spaces." WANG Bi points out that the "nothing" we find in the internal structure of things "receives" (*shou*, 受) the concrete matter (*shi*, 實) that constitutes each thing, and in virtue of this receptivity, the wheel, vessel, and room cited in the chapter are unified (*tong*, 統) both in terms of structure and purpose. This way of formulating the relationship between the "nothing" and the "something" of a thing represents the former as providing the space within which different kinds of matter can be brought together, joined, as happens with the thirty spokes of a wheel, the various kinds of clay in a vase and the different slabs of wood used to construct a room. Just collecting spokes, for example, does not make a wheel, nor does merely throwing different kinds of clay together haphazardly give us a vase. Instead, it is how these material things are arranged around "nothing," or, more concretely, how spaces are built into them, that makes them into identifiably functional things.

Zhong's vocabulary is yet more direct, as he refers to the "nothings" found in a wheel, vase and room their "empty spaces" (*kong*, 空), which are distinct from the matter that makes up a thing's "physical substance" (*ti*, 體). In Zhong's construal, usefulness, though it must be attributed to the completed thing as a whole and not merely with its "nothing," is nonetheless especially facilitated by the empty spaces that are "inside" (*nei*, 內) the thing's configuration. Insofar as Wang and Zhong concur that "nothing" is found in our everyday encounters with things, specifically in their respective empty spaces, they witness together to the conviction of "Dark Learning" thought that space and spatiality should be understood as a prevalent way in which nothingness is found in the world. For them, that is, space is a manifestation of nothingness.

This philosophical insight into nothingness offered by the *Daodejing* and its classical readers has multiple levels of significance to both thought and action. I will trace a few of these out briefly in conclusion. The first has to do with the grounds for the claim just made that "nothingness" in *Daodejing* 11 is taken by its commentators' not merely to refer to particularized spaces in individual things, but with spatiality as such. If nothingness is about spatiality and not just individual spaces, then it has precisely the kind of cosmological import that is so significant for Daoism as well as other traditions of East Asian thought. Let us recall, to begin with, the term ZHONG Hui uses to identify the "nothing" in things, namely "empty space (*kong*)." Even in its earliest overt definitions from dictionaries such as the *Shouwen Jiezi*, the Chinese term *kong* 空, while it does have a variety of associations with "hollowness" or "emptiness" as these can be observed, for instance, in a "hole" or "cave" (*xue*, 穴) as well as existential senses of "emptiness" like "vanity." Nothing also can refer to the empty and open "air" or "sky," and so does not exclusively have a privative meaning, but also can suggest expansiveness and limitlessness. Now, with respect to individual things, it is perhaps the privative meanings of *kong* that prompt Zhong to deploy the concept in his analysis of them, for it is the emptiness in things, around which their matter is configured, that makes them useful. However, the positive senses of the concept, which have to do with expansiveness and infinity, would seem also to play into the grander cosmological role of *Dao*, as on Zhong's view, the generation of all things in nature is mutually dependent on the interrelation of their "nothing" and "something," which would imply that, in order for *Dao* to produce the ten thousand things, it must pervade everywhere. Even WANG Bi, who aligns the notion of *Dao* more closely with the privative and negative senses of *wu* or "nothing" as well as with the specific hollow or empty spaces of individual things, lays a great deal of emphasis on the use of the term *xu* 虛 in the *Daodejing*, which also can mean "empty" or "vain" but often denotes expansive empty spaces like the sky as well. The pervasiveness of "nothing" in the form of space then is not only found in the arrangement of individual things, but in the spatiality of the whole cosmological order, conceived as both the space from which the totality of things can emerge as well as the space in which the things of the world interact. This expansiveness of things was surely fundamentally important for the articulation of Buddhist thought in East Asia, particularly in view of the fact that *kong* became the standard translation of the Sanskrit term *śūnyatā* or "emptiness." While in Buddhist texts composed in Sanskrit, the notion of *śūnyatā* was most of the time associated with the "absence" or "nonexistence" (*abhāva*) of a fixed and abstract "essence" (*svabhāva*) in things, East Asian Buddhists, through their rendition of "emptiness" as *kong* or "empty space," also foregrounded the cosmological pervasiveness of "nothingness," a theme which several other papers in this volume explore in more detail. Both the specific spaces in things and the spatiality of the whole natural order then are seen here to be modes of nothingness.

It may be possible from a contemporary perspective to quibble with the examples the *Daodejing* solicits to make its envisioned point about "nothing." After all, might we not say that the spaces inside a wheel hub or a vase or a room are not really "empty," but are instead themselves constituted by minute forms of matter that, though invisible, are chemically or physically amenable to various kinds of interaction with other matter? But such a question may force us only to change the scale of the examples and not the substance of the claim. We might today speak of the "empty" space, in the form of different "spins," between the orbits of electrons inside an atom or the state of degenerate matter in stars, but we would still confront questions of fundamental forms of spatiality, however it may be translated into alternative terms, as constitutive of the nature of things. On the other hand, it might be unnecessary to be so literal about the translation of the notion of *wu* 無 into the modern categories of physics. After all, space and spatiality are still pervasive enough structures of our experience of the world as a whole, and as individual things within it, that we have abundant justification for reflecting on the fashions in which "nothing," "absence," and "receptivity" function positively in experiences and in the world as a whole.

Furthermore, as the text of the *Daodejing* and its commentators attempt to illustrate, we do not merely encounter "nothingness" in the makeup of particular things or in our abstract considerations of spatiality, but we also use it. A craftsperson must know how to build space into the implements she designs, both in order to make specific tools like wheels or vessels according to the respectively appropriate designs, but also to skillfully make them in order to optimize the usefulness of her products. Such an insight is hardly confined to the pages of the *Daodejing*, but other texts from the period that in time became associated with the Daoist tradition make some conspicuous and well-known reference to the artful navigation of space and how this can make a person superlatively skilled, even sage-like, at their livelihood. The second chapter of the collection of texts known as the *Zhuangzi* notes how the famed butcher Ding, in contrast to other butchers, rarely had to sharpen his knife, because instead of being driven though knotted flesh in cutting up an ox's body, Ding's knife found the gaps between the sinews, which were inside of the "natural structure" (*tian li* 天理) of that very body, and so could unravel it quickly and efficiently (see Ziporyn 2009, 22–23). Similar stories are told in the collection about swimmers finding the right way to peel through torrential waters and travelers navigating dense forests, precisely by finding the right paths (*dao* 道) of access through them. For both WANG Bi and ZHONG Hui, then, one of the most significant details about *Daodejing* 11 is that its examples, namely a wheel, a vessel, and a room, are all products of human intention and design, and therefore demonstrate how any virtuously plied art appropriates "nothingness" very directly and concretely into the things that are meant to fulfill human ends. Nothingness, therefore, both encountered in everyday experience and solicited in our crafting of a livable environment, is not met with only in rarified metaphysical speculation or elevated mystical experience. Instead, nothingness is found in the spaces of things and in the world, and is one of the most important ways in which those things can be what they are.

Notes

1 Heidegger, of course, thought that the chapter confirmed one of the major themes of his later career, that nothingness provided the opening or clearing that enabled beings to appear. Wright, for his part, drew some inspiration from the chapter, believing that what it asserted about the usefulness of space corresponded to basic principles of functionalism in architecture.

2 This and the following full translations of *Daodejing* 11 are my own.

3 Citations from the Chinese text of WANG Bi's commentary have been drawn from Wagner (2003), in the case of the present passage from p. 154, but the English translations are my own.

4 凡有皆始於無 (*fan you jie shi yu wu*) (Wagner 2003, 119). It is interesting that Wang reads the chapter in this manner despite the fact that the way he parses lines three and four has them saying that there is a distinction to be made between the primordial time when things have no names (*wu ming*, 無名) and a later state in which they have names (*you ming*, 有名). An alternative, and perhaps more coherent, understanding of these two lines would make *wu* 無 and *you* 有, or "nothing" and "something," the sole topics of each line; *ming* 名 in each case would function as the verb, so the lines together would read: " 'Nothing' is called the beginning of heaven and earth. 'Something' is called the mother of the ten thousand things." As has been pointed out by a number of other commentators from the Song Dynasty to modern times, this reading would make the reference of the expression "these two things" (*ci liang zhe*, 此兩者) a few lines later explicit, denoting the "nothing" and "something" previously mentioned (Robinet 1999, 138–140). WANG Bi solves this problem to his own satisfaction by asserting that the "two" things being referred to are "beginning" of things, which lies with the "nameless" and the "mother" of things, which lies with that which "has a name," and both of these in their turn have their origin in what is dark (*xuan*, 玄), something without form, which generates the universe.

5 Alan Chan (2003, 130–131) has argued that the notion of *wu*, rather than making "nothing" a sort of "metaphysical entity" that lies at the foundation of the world, received a more "radical" formulation by WANG Bi, in whose hands it should be understood as "non-being" (*wu-you*). Apart from the philological uncertainties surrounding this rendering, the overtly Heideggerian language employed as the hermeneutic should inspire some caution, and prompt us to look for ways to understand the concept that are both linguistically and contextually appropriate while still enabling us to capture the philosophically unique aspects of WANG Bi's construal of *wu*.

6 Again, the Chinese text is quoted from Chan (2003), but the translation is my own.

7 Chan (2003, 138) adds that philosophers of the early Wei period frequently saw the outer-inner distinction in terms of another distinction between mere "names" and

"actuality," where the latter comprised the real essence of a thing, which could belie its outer reputation, especially in the case of political officiants. There could thus be detected in the outer-inner distinction some connotations for which the latter could enjoy preference, but not in all cases, and sometimes with the important caveat that outer and inner could ideally mutually reinforce one another's value.

8 Chan speculates that Zhong's commentary centers on the relationship between actuality and mere names cited in the note above, but is also able to more easily harmonize *wu* and *you* because of his conviction that everything within the "course" of *dao*'s unfolding is a transformation of *qi* or psychophysical energy. While Chan's reconstruction is surely possible, it is hard to say for sure what the overall aim of Zhong's *Laozi* commentary was with only 24 extant chapters.

9 In her recent study on Heidegger, Lin Ma criticized Heidegger's reading of *Daodejing* 11 by arguing about diction. In classical Chinese, Ma claims, *you* 有 meant "having" something or the "presence" of something, while nothing (*wu*, 無) similarly denotes a thing's "absence," and since therefore *you* and *wu* cannot be understood as anything like "being" and "non-being," a "metaphysical" reading of *Daodejing* 11 is simply not permissible (Ma 2008, 137–138). She therefore defends something like the second translation of the chapter featured at the beginning of this essay. It seems to me, however, that Wang Bi has a rather thoroughgoing metaphysical reading of Chapter 11 insofar as the distinctions he makes between "something" and "nothing" have profound cosmological and even spiritual significance, even if there are important ways in which Wang's reading is different from Heidegger's. Therefore, it's not that there are no "metaphysical" readings of the *Daodejing* in the Wei-Jin commentarial literature; indeed both Wang's and Zhong's readings are, despite their disagreements, metaphysical readings. It's just that Wang's specific conception of *wu* as producing the usefulness of things both in terms of its "originary state" and its manifestation as the "spaces" in particular things is not satisfactory.

13 Was There Something in Nothingness? The Debate on the Primordial State between Daoism and Neo-Confucianism

JeeLoo Liu

Introduction

The question "Was there something in nothingness?" is an attempt to clarify the nature of the primordial state of the universe. There is now a growing consensus in modern cosmology that the universe did not come out of nothing. In the initial state, the vacuum was never completely empty, but was "a bubbling quantum soup where virtual particles of matter and antimatter pop in and out of existence and give rise to energy" (Royal Swedish Academy of Sciences 2011, 6). In other words, there was never absolute *nothingness*. If we want to answer the question "Why was there something rather than nothing?" we may reply that there is *something* exactly because there was never *nothing*. This paper argues that in both the classical Daoist and the Neo-Confucian conceptions, there was no primordial absolute nothingness.

The difference between Neo-Confucian and Daoist cosmogonies has been taken to be founded in their conjectures of whether the world has always existed or there was absolutely nothing at the beginning. Daoist cosmogony is traditionally interpreted as advocating the idea that being emerges out of nothing (*wu zhong sheng you*). In this paper, I argue that despite this construal of the Daoist cosmogonic principle, ancient Daoists were committed to *qi*-cosmology, and the debate between Neo-Confucians and Daoists should be framed as a debate centering on the initial state of *qi*, which is often called "primordial *qi* (*yuanqi*)," in some Daoist texts as well as in some Confucian texts and historical records beginning in the Han dynasty (206 BCE–220 CE). Primordial *qi* is supposedly the state of *qi* before its split into *yin* and *yang*. It is the original, undifferentiated, formless, invisible *qi*.[1] In Daoist texts, "primordial *qi*" typically designates the state of *qi* before the formation of heaven and earth. This state is referred to as "chaos (*hundun*)," a nebulous state of infinite space and formless *qi* that preceded the existence of the ordered cosmos. Since it existed before the separation of heaven and earth, and without any distinctions between objects and things, it is a unified, singular *One*. I shall argue that both the *Daodejing*'s and the *Zhuangzi*'s conceptions of nothing (*wu*) should be understood as a depiction of the nature of primordial *qi*—that it is a formless *something*. Therefore, Daoist cosmogony, at least in its original version,[2] does not endorse the hypothesis that there was initially an absolute cosmic void. I will show how Neo-Daoists such as WANG Bi turned the debate into an ontological issue with ethical ramifications. When Neo-Confucians rejected the Daoist theory of nothingness, they were responding to the ontological conception of nothing established by WANG Bi. In terms of cosmology, both Daoists and Confucians embrace the theory of *qi*, though they differ in their understanding of the nature of the initial state of *qi*. Neither view, accurately understood, endorses the conjecture that *something* could have emerged out of absolutely *nothing*.

In what follows, the paper will first trace the development of the concept of *wu* in classical Daoist texts to argue against the received interpretation that Daoism advocates that *being* comes from *nothingness*. It will show that the early Daoist conception of *wu* as signifying the origin of the universe depicts *formlessness* rather than *nothingness*. It will then explain how the posit of a primordial *nothingness* became the standard interpretation of Daoist cosmogony since Neo-Confucianism.

"Nothing$_1$": From *Formlessness* to the Epitome of *Absence*

According to a traditionally revered lexicographer Xu Shen (許慎58?–147? CE), the etymology of the Chinese word '*wu*' has three origins and thus the word has three possible meanings: (1) *wu* 亡, gone; (2) *wu* 無, meaning what seems to be nothing but is actually something; and (3) *wu* 无, the original void. Even if his analysis is not without contention, this etymology shows that, in as early as the Han dynasty, the word '*wu*' was already ambiguous. In this paper I shall show how the word '*wu*,' when used as a noun in the *Daodejing* and in the *Zhuangzi*, connotes the second sense. A contemporary scholar PANG Pu 龐樸 (1995) explains that the Chinese word '*wu*, 無' (in the second sense) depicts what is formless, shapeless, invisible, and imperceptible.[3] Pang argues that the written form '*wu*, 無' and the Chinese word for dance '*wu*, 舞' have the same origin and are closely related in a historical context: primitive people danced in religious ceremonies as a tribute to the invisible, unknowable realm, as well as to whatever spirits that might grant them good fortune. Therefore, dance (*wu*, 舞) is a way to communicate with the invisible *something* (*wu*, 無). This state of *wu* is therefore still *something*. It can be further interpreted as a *something* that encompasses all, and is the master of everything (see Pang 1995, 277–278). I shall argue that this is the sense in which the *Daodejing* uses this word.

To begin with, the word 'nothing (*wu*) used by the *Daodejing*'s attributed author Laozi[4] does not refer to an absolute cosmic void. We see this from the *Daodejing*'s narrative of the beginning of the world. According to the *Daodejing*, everything is generated by *Dao*, which seems to be ontologically and temporally prior to the formation of heaven and earth as well as the myriad things. The *Daodejing* says, "*Dao* gives rise to the One, One gives rise to Two, Two gives rise to Three, and Three gives rise to the myriad things" (Chapter 42).[5] Since the *Daodejing* also says, "The myriad things are generated by

Being (*you*, 有); Being is generated by Nothing (*wu*, 無)" (Chapter 40), many scholars identify the *Daodejing*'s *Dao* as *Nothing*. However, Chapter 25 of the *Daodejing* clearly states that *Dao* is *something*: "There is *something* (*youwu*, 有物) undifferentiated and yet complete, which existed before heaven and earth" (Chapter 25, modification of Chan's translation, Chan 1973, 152). In the *Daodejing*, Chapter 21, *Dao* is also depicted as a "thing (*wu*, 物)": "The *thing* that is called *Dao* is eluding and vague. Vague and eluding, there is in it the form. Eluding and vague, in it are things. Deep and obscure, in it is the essence. The essence is very real; in it are evidences" (Chan 1973, 150). In both passages, the *Daodejing* uses the word "thing[6]" to describe *Dao*; in ancient Chinese philosophical works, the word "thing" depicts actually existing things.[7] This shows that Laozi's *Dao* should not be interpreted merely as an abstract, purely spiritual, metaphysical posit.

How do we understand this *thing* that is tentatively named '*Dao*' in the *Daodejing*? I argue that this thing is *qi* itself, and *Dao* should be understood in the framework of *qi*-cosmology. Laozi mentions *qi* in several chapters, and in Chapter 42, he links it to *Dao*'s generation of the myriad things: "Everything carries *yin* and embraces *yang*. *Qi*'s mutual agitation constitutes harmony." It is likely that the author of the *Daodejing* endorses the view that *qi* produces all things, which is a common view expressed in pre-Qin philosophical works.[8] It is reasonable to suspect that Laozi's conception of *Dao* is derived from his conception of *qi* in its initial state, and based on the text, we may further argue that his notion of *Dao* could be an idealized conception of the nature and operation of *qi*.[9] We find that many descriptions of *Dao* in the *Daodejing* are likely descriptions of *qi*. For example, the *Daodejing* depicts *Dao* as "containing the form and essence of things" (Chapter 21), as "soundless and formless" and "circulating incessantly" (Chapter 25), as invisible, inaudible and intangible (Chapter 14), as agitating and inexhaustible (Chapter 4), as continuous and connected (Chapter 14), as overflowing left and right (Chapter 34), and as moving in reversal (Chapter 40). If *Dao* is understood as a spiritual metaphysical entity, then these descriptions are difficult to interpret. However, once we understand the initial cosmic state as *qi*'s initial state, these descriptions become intelligible. The *Daodejing* further describes "the root of heaven as earth" as "continuous as if existing, while its use is inexhaustible" (Chapter 6). This description also becomes intelligible once it is seen as a reference to *qi*.

N.J. Girardot argues that in Chapter 1 as well as Chapter 25, the *Daodejing* makes reference "to the fact that *Dao* is a living thing: it moves, changes, pervades, gives birth yet paradoxically remains whole by constantly regenerating itself without alteration, without consumption or exhaustion" (Girardot 2008, 43). Once we adopt this reading of *Dao* as a living thing, and as I suggest, as the primordial state of *qi*, *Dao* is no longer the mystifying concept that has been traditionally attributed to Laozi. Under this reading, the *Daodejing*'s cosmogonic claim is that, in the beginning, there was *qi* in its primordial state, and this formless primordial *qi* is what the *Daodejing* refers to as "*nothing* (*wu*, 無)" when it says that something is generated by *nothing*.

Using this analysis of the *Dao-qi* correlation in the *Daodejing*, I argue that the text's conception of nothing (*wu*) is further derived from the notion of *formlessness* (*wu xing*).[10] The notion of *form* plays a significant role in Chinese philosophers' understanding of the physical realm. In the *Yijing*, for example, there is a distinction made between *Dao* and concrete things (*qi*, 器): "What is beyond form (*xingershang*, 形而上) is called *Dao*; what is with form (*xingerxia*, 形而下) is called concrete things" (*Xici*, Part I; see Wilhelm & Baynes 1977, 323, my translation here). In the history of Chinese philosophy, this distinction has since been taken to be the standard criterion for separating the metaphysical realm from the material world. The *Daodejing* did not place *Dao* "beyond form," however. It depicts *Dao* as soundless and formless (Chapter 25), and declares: "The greatest sound cannot be heard; the greatest image has no form. *Dao* is hidden with no name" (Chapter 41). Thus, the distinction between *Dao* and things made in the *Daodejing* is that between *being formless* and *being with form*. Before anything was generated, there was no form. Thus, the *formless* (which the *Daodejing* calls *Dao*) precedes the myriad forms. The formless is one, while the myriad forms are many. We may further explain how the One generates the many: through the division and individuation of forms.

Before any concrete thing comes into existence, the primordial state of *qi* is of course without any concrete physical form. However, in ancient Chinese texts, form (*xing*, 形) is not just physical form, but includes any determination of quality, shape, scope, definition, and so on. All qualities of particular things can be called "form," and in the *Daodejing*'s conception, the absence of definition and determination—having no shape, no sound, no form, no name, and no concrete things—depicts *Dao*. The theme of *formlessness* permeates the *Daodejing*'s philosophy. We can understand that form materializes and concretizes things; however, it at the same time restricts things. Anything with a fixed diameter is thus limited in space. Only the absence of all detectable measurements can be infinitely expansive. Formlessness (*Dao*) is therefore *great*. The *Daodejing*'s notion of *nothing* can thus be extended to signify the epitome of the absence of definition and determination. As *absence*, the state of nothing exists before things with definition emerge. It is not an active negation of qualities after distinctions are made; rather, it stands for the initial state of the absence of determination. This is why the *Daodejing* advocates a "return" to the original state (Chapter 16). According to this reading, in the *Daodejing*, the notion of "nothing (*wu*)," when used to represent the initial cosmic state, does not connote *nonbeing* or a "negation" of all existence, but merely the "absence" of particularity and determination. This would explain why the *Daodejing* describes this initial state as vague, indistinct, undifferentiated, inscrutable and indescribable. No names could possibly be attached to this state of indeterminacy, because any name would simply take away the indeterminacy itself. We can also understand why the *Daodejing* refuses to give this initial state a name and only reluctantly addresses it as "Dao" (Chapter 25).

While the theory of *qi* in its primordial state is implicitly referred to in the *Daodejing*, in the *Zhuangzi* it is explicitly embraced and defended. To the attributed author Zhuangzi,[11] the initial, pre-ordered state of the universe is a state of "chaos (*hundun*)." *Hundun* is introduced symbolically as "Emperor *Hundun*" in Chapter 7 of the *Zhuangzi*. According to N. J. Girardot (2008), this allegory represents an underlying theme of "returning to the beginning" in the *Zhuangzi* (64).[12] Under this cosmogony, the whole universe is simply the result of the transformation of *qi*, which begins with chaos. In the depiction of the *Zhuangzi*, individual life forms emerge out of the formless chaos as well: "The initial state of indiscernible, imperceptible chaos transforms into *qi*, *qi* transforms into shape and form, shape and form transform into life" (*The Zhuangzi* 1961, 612). This primeval state of chaos is the amorphous indiscernible state of *qi*, which fills up space; or better yet, since there is nothing outside of this primordial state of *qi*, it is simply identified with space itself. In the *Zhuangzi*'s depiction, order and determination are both derived states, not the initial cosmic state, which is nothing but the formless chaos.

As in the *Daodejing*, the *Zhuangzi* also uses "form" to distinguish *qi* and the emergence of things: the formless *qi* came before concrete things, and *Dao* is identified with the formless: "What is explicit and bright is born from the high and dim space (*mingming*); what has order came from formlessness (*wuxing*). . . . All things generate one another with forms"[13] (*The Zhuangzi* 1961, 741). On the other hand, in the *Zhuangzi*, what characterize concrete things are their forms, while "heaven and earth are simply the vastest among forms"[14] (913). Since *Dao* has no form, it also has no borders, and is thus called "borderless (*wuji*)." Chapter 22 of the *Zhuangzi* says,

> That which makes beings beings is not separated from beings by any border. So the borders that the beings themselves take on—these are merely borders from the side of the beings. The borders that do no bordering, the borderlessness that nonetheless borders—this is what fills and empties beings, what decays and kills them. What which fills and empties them is not filled or emptied, what which decays and empties them is not decayed or emptied, that which roots and branches them is neither rooted nor branched, that which congeals and scatters them is neither congealed nor scattered" (The *Zhuangzi* 1961, 752. This is Ziporyn's translation, see Ziporyn 2009, 89).

If we understand this passage to be depicting the state of primordial *qi*, then it is perfectly intelligible why this creative force itself is borderless, inexhaustible and indestructible.

There is plenty of textual evidence to suggest that the *Zhuangzi*'s conception of *Dao* is closely related to its theory of *qi*. In some passages, the transformation of *Dao* in the production of things is simply the transformation of *qi*: the existence of concrete things is marked by the consolidation and dissolution of *qi*. Furthermore, the attributes of *Dao* in the *Zhuangzi* are frequently derived from the attributes of *qi*. The *Zhuangzi* says, "*Qi* is vacuous (*xu*) in its dealing with things. *Dao* is simply the accrual of vacuity" (The *Zhuangzi* 1961, 147).

Since *qi* is real, the *Zhuangzi* says, "*Dao* has realness and dependability. It does not act and has no physical form [i.e., it is formless]. . . . Before there were heaven and earth, *Dao* perdures from time immemorial" (246–247). Since Zhuangzi takes *Dao* to be ever-present, he would not embrace the hypothesis that there had been any time when *Dao* was nonexistent. The world has always been, as "*Dao* has no beginning nor end" (584).

Under this premise, we can analyze the *Zhuangzi*'s conception of nothing. The comment, "At the very beginning (*taichu*) there was nothing (*wu*); there was no existence and no name" (*The Zhuangzi* 1961, 424), has often been interpreted as an acknowledgement of the primordial void. However, what the *Zhuangzi* calls "the very beginning" is standardly taken by Daoists to refer to the beginning state of *qi*. We have seen that the *Zhuangzi* depicts it as an indiscernible, imperceptible chaos. This state exists before the split of *yin* and *yang*, and this is what is meant by "chaos," a nebulous state of infinite space and formless *qi*. We should understand that it is *nothing* simply in the sense of having no *things*.

Ultimately, however, in the *Inner Chapters* Zhuangzi rejects the whole investigation on whether there had been a "beginning," or whether something comes from nothing: If we say there was a beginning, then we must trace it all the way to the time before the beginning and further beyond. If we say there is something and there is nothing before something, then we will have to go back to the time before *nothing* and further beyond.[15] This is a vicious regression to no end. This comment may have been directed at Laozi. On the *Daodejing*'s remark that "There was something undifferentiated and yet complete, which existed before heaven and earth" (Chapter 25, Chan 1973, 152), Zhuangzi asks:

> If there is something before heaven and earth, could it be some specifiable *thing*? What produces things is not itself a *thing*. If we are considering the origin of things, we cannot put a thing before things. We can only say that it is *as if* there was something. This seeming something continues unfalteringly. (*The Zhuangzi* 1961, 763, italics mine)

To posit a *thing* before the beginning of all things would just lead to an infinite regress. We can deduce that for Zhuangzi, *qi* is not a *thing*. However, *qi* is not nothing either. This may be why the *Zhuangzi* uses the pair "*wuyou*" (无有, "nothing-something," or, taking the *wu* here as negation, "non-being") to signify the origin of everything, and calls it "the Gate of Heaven" (Chapter 23, *The Zhuangzi* 1961, 800). It is conceivable that Zhuangzi's aim is to break down the dichotomy between being and nothing. He thus rejects the possibility that *nothing* could have an actual existence. In an allegory in Chapter 22, a friend asked a fictional person named *Wuyou* (literally, "nothing-something") whether he was something or nothing, and did not get any response. The friend realized from the silence that, even though he could recognize *nothing*, he had not yet reached the level of negating the existence of *nothing*

(*The Zhuangzi* 1961, 759). This shows that ultimate understanding compels us to see *nothing* not as something real.

Both the *Daodejing* and the *Zhuangzi* thus assert that at the beginning, there was something, the primordial *qi*, which permeated space from the start. Things came into existence because of the transformation of *qi*. Therefore, being did not come out of an absolute nothingness. I conclude that for both the *Daodejing* and the *Zhuangzi*, the word '*wu*' used in the cosmogonic context is a *descriptive* rather than a *denoting* term. It signifies the absence of qualification, classification, and determination, but it does not denote an initial void.

"Nothing$_2$": From *Nonexistence* to *Nonbeing*

The concept of *wu* became *the* major theme in the philosophical developments during the Wei and Jin Dynasties (220–420 CE). The philosophical pursuit at the time went beyond speculating on the origin of the universe, and started investigating the substance, or the fundamental essence, of all things (Tang 2001, 43–44). The debate on being and nonbeing in Wei-Jin philosophy was primarily a dispute in two dimensions, over the ontological foundation of the phenomenal world and the ethical application of the adopted ontology. It was not a pursuit of the cosmogonic origin or cosmological foundations of the world as it was manifested in the *Daodejing*.

In commenting on Laozi's *Daodejing*, WANG Bi (226–249 CE) inherited Laozi's concept of *wu*; however, he gave it an ontological dimension and turned Laozi's nameless, formless *something* into a named *Nonbeing*. WANG Bi thought that Laozi was after all still someone who focused on *being*, and thus Laozi's theory was not complete.[16] WANG Bi established a meontology beyond Laozi's scope and became one of the two leaders of the School of Venerating Nonbeing (*Chongwu*). WANG Bi's *wu* has multiple connotations: formlessness,[17] empty space,[18] the total absence of distinctions and discrimination,[19] and the absence of existence—Nonbeing. The last sense is WANG Bi's own development and our focus here. Whereas the word '*wu*' in the *Daodejing* is, as I have argued, a descriptive term, in WANG Bi's usage it is a denoting term. It denotes ultimate reality, which is "quiet, deserted, without form and body" (Wang 1980, 63). WANG Bi identifies *Dao* with Nonbeing; however, he uses 'nonbeing' as a name and '*dao*' as a designation: "Nonbeing *names* the origin of heaven and earth"[20] while "*Dao* is the *designation* for Nonbeing. There is nowhere that Nonbeing cannot penetrate and there is nothing that does not follow Nonbeing. It is therefore metaphorically designated as '*Dao*'"[21] (624, emphasis mine). For WANG Bi, the difference between a name and a designation is that "a name affirms the object while a designation follows the speaker's intention. Name is based on the object while designation is subjectively given. Therefore, when we want to refer to *that which* all things must follow, we designate it as *Dao*" (197, emphasis mine). This shows that it was WANG Bi's deliberate choice to use '*wu*' as a name and '*dao*' as a designation, and the word '*wu*' is treated as a denoting term.

In his commentary on the *Daodejing*'s Chapter 40, WANG Bi (1980) writes: "All things in the world have a beginning of their existence. The beginning of being is *grounded in* nonbeing, and to complete its existence, the being must return to nonbeing" (110, italics mine). In other words, for each particular thing, it was *nonbeing* before the thing came into existence, and *nonbeing* after it goes out of existence. Nonbeing sets the determination of the temporal boundary of the existence of particular things: each existing thing has its own pre-existing state and its post-existence state. Nonbeing is the original state as well as the end state of each existence. Particular things would only be a temporary stage that breaks away from nonbeing. Nonbeing is thus the ontological foundation for each particular being: "Everything cannot avoid having nonbeing as its substance" (94). In this sense, nonbeing is relative to each particular being.

From the *nonbeing* essential for individual things, WANG Bi further introduced an all-encompassing *Nonbeing* as the foundation of all things. This Nonbeing is not just an undifferentiated *something* like the *Daodejing*'s *Dao*; rather, it is nonbeing in the absolute sense since it is the negation of all existence. He writes, "The ten thousand things have ten thousand different forms but ultimately they are one. How did they become one? By virtue of *wu*" (Wang 1980, 117). The explanation offered here about the relation between *wu* and One, "by virtue of (*youyu*)" (also rendered as "because of (*yin*)" in another version of the text collected in the *Daozang Ji*, see WANG Bi 1980, 118), is of course open to different interpretations. How does the *wu* generate the One? I propose that *wu* in this context designates the ultimate negation. If we can grasp the truth that ultimately things do not exist, then all things would merge into *One*. The *One* is Nonbeing—the negation of all existence and all forms.

WANG Bi's Nonbeing is primarily a product of the intellect. The intellect traces the existence of things to their root to derive the notion of *Nonbeing*, because Nonbeing itself is incomprehensible: "Nonbeing cannot be explicated with nonbeing; hence, we must appeal to being. Reaching the ultimate end of beings, we comprehend the origin of all beings" (Wang 1980, 548).[22] In other words, the notion of *Nonbeing* is the product of our intellect's retrospective reflection on existing things. The intellect also negates the existence of all things to derive Nonbeing: "So in regards to things, if one negates its existence, then everything will be in order" (93). The intellect's understanding unifies all things into Nonbeing: "In all movements, if one *understands* that it fundamentally does not exist, then one can penetrate everything" (109, italics mine). We can conclude that WANG Bi's *Nonbeing* is beyond space and time because it is an abstract construct.

However, WANG Bi further developed the abstract Nonbeing into an ontologically subsisting entity. His Nonbeing can be *grasped* or *comprehended* by the intellect, but to him it is not *created* by the intellect. We have seen that he uses the word '*wu*' to denote Nonbeing, and his *Dao* is merely a depiction of the function of Nonbeing. WANG Bi (1980) calls Nonbeing "the beginning of heaven and earth" and "the source of being" (1, 2). Nonbeing to him is something *real*. In contemporary jargon, we could call him a realist with regard to Nonbeing. The historical record *Jin Shu* even interprets his Nonbeing as a super-entity that has efficacy: "This Nonbeing is what penetrates everything and accomplishes all affairs. There is nowhere that it *does not exist*" (see WANG Bi 1980, 647, italics mine). If this view attributed to WANG Bi is reliable, then WANG Bi is ontologically committed to the existence of Nonbeing. However, WANG Bi's Nonbeing is not an actual cosmic state, but the ultimate reality of the phenomenal world. The world of being is the function, or the appearance, of the ultimate reality. As LOU Yulie 樓宇烈 concludes in his introduction to the collected works of Wang Bi, WANG Bi's philosophy of Nonbeing is "fundamentally a negation of an objective material world along with its movement and change" (Wang 1980, 7).

WANG Bi not only turns the *Daodejing*'s cosmological speculation into an ontological analysis of the underlying foundation for all exiting things, but also elaborates on the ethical application of the notion *wu*. To experience *nonbeing* is to negate discrimination, judgment, and intervention. If the ultimate truth of reality is Nonbeing, then to be cognizant of ultimate reality, one must empty one's mind and obtain the virtue of *wuwei*, literally, doing nothing. The shift from a philosophical speculation on the state of nonbeing to an ethical advocacy of negating discernment and distinction had serious social ramifications. Situated amidst political turmoil and vicious persecution, Wei-Jin intellectuals were seeking ways out of their precarious predicament. The doctrine of nonbeing and negation gave them an excuse to abandon social bounds and conventional values. This kind of negativity became associated with the Daoist notion of *wu*. It was primarily for this reason that Neo-Confucians turned against the Daoist cosmology.

The Initial Cosmic State in Neo-Confucianism: The Boundless and Vacuous *Something*

Neo-Confucians harshly criticized the School of Venerating Nonbeing for advocating *nonbeing* as the fundamental state of things, and they thought the root of this philosophy lay in Laozi's conception of *nothing* as the primordial cosmic state. Hence, Neo-Confucians, beginning with ZHOU Dunyi (1017–1073 CE) and ZHANG Zai (1020–1078 CE), rejuvenated the cosmology of *qi* derived from the *Yijing* to explain the original state of the universe.

ZHOU Dunyi's cosmological thought is condensed and obscure, and his terse text has stirred up controversial interpretations in the history of Chinese philosophy.[23] A noted contemporary scholar CHEN Lai (2005) argues that ZHOU Dunyi's cosmology is a form of *qi*-monism and Zhou regards *Taiji*, the Supreme Ultimate, as one homogeneous *qi*—before *yin* and *yang* were divided (40). According to this interpretation, which I embrace, ZHOU Dunyi's conception of the Supreme Ultimate (*Taiji*) is very close to primordial *qi* even though Zhou himself did not use this term.[24] Zhou depicts the origin of the Universe as traceable "from the Boundless (*wuji*, 無極) to the Supreme Ultimate (*taiji*, 太極)" (Zhou 1975, 4). In the *Yijing*, the Supreme Ultimate is posited as the primordial state and it has always existed. In Zhou Dunyi's description, the Supreme Ultimate has motion and rest: the Supreme Ultimate generated *yang* and *yin* through its movement and rest; *yin* and *yang* further generated the five basic elements that constitute concrete things. Hence, in Zhou's conception, the primordial state is not a vacuum.

The Chinese term for the Universe is '*yuzou*,' which means space and time.[25] If we consider the fact that the spacetime framework itself "depends on what it frames,"[26] then we can imagine it as without limits and without boundaries when there were no concrete things in space and time. It is reasonable to speculate that the spacetime framework came into existence after the myriad things were formed and divided—their existences mark space because they were separated, and their existences mark time because they come into existence, go through change, and then go out of existence. Before heaven and earth were separated and concrete things formed, the *pre-myriad-thing Taiji* could be infinitely expansive while at the same time infinitely minute. There was nothing inside it or outside it; hence, it was without bounds. This may be the reason why Zhou Dunyi calls it "the Boundless (*Wuji*)." We can also understand why Zhou Dunyi would say, "*Wuji* and then *Taiji*; *Taiji* was initially *Wuji*" (Zhou 1975, 4). Under my analysis, Zhou Dunyi's *Wuji* is not absolute nothingness, but a state of indeterminacy, full of potentiality and possibilities.[27] The myriad things would eventually emerge out of this infinite primordial *qi* because *qi* itself is active and potent.

Zhou Dunyi may have started a new direction for Neo-Confucian cosmology based on the notion of *qi*; however, the real founder of Neo-Confucian *qi*-cosmology was Zhang Zai. Zhang Zai explicitly argues that there was never a time, nor any cosmic state, in which there was absolute nothingness or an undifferentiated primordial *qi*.

Zhang Zai (2006) refers to the initial cosmic state as "the Supreme Vacuity (*taixu*)," and he takes the Supreme Vacuity and the presence of *qi* to be concurrent from the start. We have already seen that the word 'vacuity (*xu*)' was used to depict *qi* and *Dao* in the *Zhuangzi*, where vacuity could be taken to mean emptiness. Zhang Zai explicitly points out that in his own usage, the word "vacuity (*xu*)" does not mean void or emptiness; rather, it means the opposite of "solid (*gu*)" (64). Zhang Zai further argues that the Supreme Vacuity contains *qi*, and since *qi* is real, the Supreme Vacuity is not an absolute void: "When one knows that the Supreme Vacuity is simply *qi* itself, one sees that there cannot be *nothingness* (*wu*)" (8).

According to Zhang Zai (2006), there has never been real nothingness, even in the state of Supreme Vacuity, because *qi* permeates all of space: "The Supreme Vacuity was already seething with *qi*, which incessantly moves upward and downward" (8).[28] It is obvious from the depiction of *qi*'s having movement that Zhang Zai takes *qi* to have real physical existence. In Zhang Zai's conception, vacuity (*xu*) is no more than *formlessness* (*wuxing*). This initial state was *vacuous* simply because there were no concrete forms. However, there is potential for forms, and for Zhang Zai, potential forms are nonetheless real: "Whatever *could* have a form is really existent (*you*); whatever exists is an image (*xiang*), and whatever has an image is *qi*" (63). Under ZHANG Zai's conception, the initial state of the cosmos is not *nothing* but *something*—an ever-present *qi*.

ZHANG Zai conceives *Dao* as the constant interaction between *yin* and *yang*, as he repeatedly cites the *Yijing*'s saying, "once *yin* and once *yang* is the so-called *Dao*" (*Xici*, Part I, Chapter 5; for ZHANG Zai's analysis, see Zhang 2006, 187). To say that *Dao* generates things is simply to describe the production of *yin* and *yang*. This is why ZHANG Zai says: "from the transformations of *qi* derives the name for *Dao*" (2006, 9). He takes the initial formless state to be the expansive and mobile *qi*, with two opposing forces constituting its movement. *Qi* carries energy with it; hence, even before concrete things were formed, the state of *qi* (i.e., the Supreme Vacuity) was still seething with energy and not a complete vacuum. *Qi* changes from a thin, vacuous state into a state filled with concrete things; in time, concrete things will dissolve into nonexistence and *qi* will then return to the state of the Supreme Vacuity. In other words, ZHANG Zai's cosmology can be seen as a cyclical development of *qi*. Under this view, the world has always existed—be it empty of, or filled with, concrete things. ZHANG Zai's contribution to *qi*-cosmology is to point out that *qi* and concrete things are not ontologically distinct categories. From vacuous *qi* to concrete things, there is no *ontological leap*.

ZHANG Zai would have agreed with the *Daodejing* and the *Zhuangzi* that the initial cosmic state was *formless*. However, he argues that what is formless is still *something*, and cannot be called '*wu*'. In other words, ZHANG Zai thinks that Daoists made a mistake in calling the formless *qi* "nothing (*wu*)." The difference between cosmos and pre-cosmos is not the difference between *something* versus *nothing*, according to ZHANG Zai, but the difference between manifest and hidden, perceptible and imperceptible (Zhang 2006, 8, 182). Therefore, Laozi's mistake in ZHANG Zai's assessment would be terminological. ZHANG Zai and Laozi share a similar cosmological view, but they disagree on whether that initial formless state should be called '*nothing*'. Their disagreement is a "verbal dispute," namely, a disagreement not really about the domain of concern—cosmology, but one based on linguistic issues.

Thus far, I have argued that the key to deciphering the concept of *wu* in both Daoism and Neo-Confucianism is the notion of *formlessness* (*wuxing*), not *void* or absolute *nothingness*. At the end of this chapter, I would like to examine whether these philosophers make any ontological commitment to things that do not exist.

Ontological Commitment to the Formless and Nonbeing

The Chinese term for formless, '*wuxing*,' means being invisible, imperceptible, and literally, without a concrete form. Compatible with Chinese usage, the predicate "is formless" can literally mean several things:[29]

1. *x* is formless if it has no definite form; or
2. *x* is formless if it is invisible and intangible; or
3. *x* is formless if it does not have material existence.

Something can be formless in the first sense without being formless in the second sense. Something can be formless in the second sense without being formless in the third sense. We can say that a cloud or fog is formless in the first sense, while air is formless in the second sense. Spirits or ghosts would be formless in the third sense. When *x* is formless only in the first two senses, *x* can be considered as having material existence. We shall thus use a bound variable for it: there is an *x*, which has no definite forms, or which is invisible and intangible. I think both Daoists and Neo-Confucians would agree that *qi* is formless in the first two senses, but not in the third sense. *Qi* has material existence in that it constitutes material things and has actual effects on material things. *Qi* is therefore real. When formlessness is considered in the third sense, on the other hand, whether we want to grant the existence of *x* depends on the kind of ontology we embrace. According to at least one traditional interpretation, Laozi may have posited *Dao* as formless in the third sense, but since he takes *Dao* to be some *thing*, his ontology could also include immaterial existence. In this paper, however, I have analyzed his notion of *Dao* as derived from his conception of *qi*. The *Daodejing*'s cosmogony of *Dao*'s generation of things is simply an abstract narrative of *qi*'s generation of things. In the *Zhuangzi*'s cosmology, the possibility of *Dao* as an abstract *entity* is ruled out by Zhuangzi's refusal to call it a *thing*. On the other hand, Zhuangzi seems to be ontologically committed to the existence of *qi*.

In the above analysis, the negation of form is predicated of a thing. However, the negation of form can also be read as "wide scope," in which case "formlessness" is understood as "it is not the case that there is any form." This reading would be compatible with the claim that "there is nothing." If "nothing" means simply "no concrete things," then both ancient Daoists and Neo-Confucians would be in accord. What the *Daodejing* calls "nothing" in this context would be the same as what ZHANG Zai calls "the Supreme Vacuity." Both would agree that in the initial state of *qi*, there was simply no concrete existence. What exists in that state is the disorderly undifferentiated primordial *qi* in Laozi's and Zhuangzi's conceptions, and the harmoniously interacting *yin* and *yang* in a thing-less state in ZHANG Zai's conception. Nevertheless, when we say: "there is nothing," we do not make any existential claim about anything, least of all to the thing called "nothing." Therefore, in all three views, there is no ontological commitment to *nothingness*.

The case is different with the notion of *Nonbeing* introduced by WANG Bi. WANG Bi derives Nonbeing from the negation of existence. However, to say that it is ~x before x and it is ~x after x ceases to exist does not entitle us to derive the existence of ~x. As Alex Orenstein (1995) raises the question concerning *vacuously true existential generalizations*: "How can a denial of existence all by itself imply an affirmation of existence? How can it follow from the sole fact that one thing doesn't exist, that something else does exist?" (96) To derive the existence of nonbeing from the negation of being would be committing the fallacy of what Quine (1948) calls the "old Platonic riddle of nonbeing": "Nonbeing must in some sense be, otherwise what is it that there is not?" (2)

Quine's targeted reasoning is this: If I claim that nonbeing does not exist, my claim is about something such that it does not exist. However, if I make a claim about something, then I am making an ontological commitment to that thing. Quine thinks that it is this kind of thinking that leads philosophers to make false ontological commitment to nonexistent things. WANG Bi derives nonbeing via a similarly fallacious route: he gets nonbeing not from denying the existence of nonbeing, but from asserting the nonexistence of being. From asserting that a thing does not exist before it materializes, WANG Bi concludes that the thing's *nonexistence* precedes (or is logically prior to) the thing's existence. Nonbeing thus becomes primary, as the foundation of existence. Furthermore, from having the intellect trace back the origin of all existing things to their root, WANG Bi derives an all-encompassing Nonbeing: ($\sim x$ & ~y & ~z . . . & ~n). This move can be seen as a "logical creation *ex nihilo*" (Orenstein's [1995] phrase, 97), deriving something out of nothing. However, since Nonbeing simply *negates* all existence, there is no existing thing that we could pick out as "Nonbeing." Therefore, as a denoting term, WANG Bi's '*wu*' is an *empty name*.

To avoid the fallacious move of logical creation *ex nihilo*, we can rewrite WANG Bi's deduction with the negation operator in the wide scope:

1. There is an *x*, and *x* exists from time t_1 to t_2.
2. At time t_0, it is not the case that *x* exists.
3. At time t_3, it is also not the case that *x* exists.
4. Therefore, there is no *x* at time t_0 and t_3.

This deduction does not have existential force and would not get us to the existence of ~x. In a similar fashion, we can also avoid deriving the existence of the collective ($\sim x$ & ~y & ~z . . . & ~n).

There are further problems with WANG Bi's all-encompassing Nonbeing as the negation of all existence, however. I shall list two problems here:

1. **The Problem of the Logical Dependence of Nonbeing:** First of all, WANG Bi's Nonbeing cannot be the logical foundation of beings, but must be logically dependent on the existence of all particular things. Recall that this Nonbeing is produced by the intellect's *retrospective* deduction, from existing things back to their original nonexistence. Therefore, Nonbeing would have to be the collective individual nonbeings: ($\sim x$ & ~y & ~z . . . & ~n). In this way, Nonbeing as a conceptual construct has to come *after* all beings.
2. **The Problem of the Fuzzy Boundary of Nonbeing:** Furthermore, if Nonbeing is derived from existing things, then it ends up having multiple scopes. If the world of existence had been in any way different, then we would have Nonbeing_2 = ($\sim x$ & ~y & ~z . . . & ~n−1), or Nonbeing_3 = ($\sim x$ & ~y & ~z . . . & ~n+1), and so on. This possibility generates the paradox of having both $\text{Nonbeing}_1 \neq \text{Nonbeing}_2 \neq \text{Nonbeing}_3$ because of their different scopes, and $\text{Nonbeing}_1 = \text{Nonbeing}_2 = \text{Nonbeing}_3$ because they

are simply *the* Nonbeing. Following Quine's (1957) precept, "no entity without identity" (20), we should not postulate entities that have no clear identity criteria. I thus conclude that Wang Bi's Nonbeing does not have any ontological merit.

Conclusion

The traditional interpretation of the main difference between the Daoist cosmogony and the Neo-Confucian cosmogony is that they take different positions on whether the world originated in nothing or something. In this paper, I have reframed this debate in terms of the theory of *qi*. I have argued that the Daoist notion of *nothing* (*wu*) was originally derived from *formlessness* (*wuxing*), and does not denote complete nothingness. The Neo-Confucians' attack on the Daoist conception of *nothing* (*wu*) was primarily a reaction against the ethical teachings of the Wei-Jin School of Venerating Nonbeing. Neo-Confucians and classical Daoists actually share a cosmological worldview based on the conception of *qi*. Neither school acknowledges an absolute cosmic void or a primordial absolute nothingness. So, how does *something* come out of *nothing*? On their answers, it would be because there was always *something* in *nothingness*.

Notes

1 The term "primordial *qi*" (*yuanqi*) was allegedly first seen in the early Daoist text *Heguanzi* (exact dates unknown): "Heaven and earth are composed of primordial *qi*, while the myriad things rely on heaven and earth [for their existence]" (*Heguanzi* 2004, 255). The word '*yuan*' has many connotations, but in conjunction with *qi* as in *yuanqi*, it means primordial, elemental, originating, and *single*. In the context of Chinese medicine, there is another important usage of *yuanqi* to stand for individual health, spirit, or vitality. Here we only consider the cosmological sense of *yuanqi*.

2 Other Daoist texts, such as the *Liezi*, the *Huainanzi*, and the writings of Eastern Han astronomer Zhang Heng (78–139 CE), added a stage before the emergence of primordial *qi*, and this added stage may have incorporated the notion of a cosmic void.

3 Pang Pu (1995) argues that the word '*wu*' has three written forms, which represent these three possibilities.

4 For simplicity's sake, I shall use "Laozi" here as the placeholder for the author(s) of the *Daodejing*.

5 Unless otherwise noted, the translations are my own.

6 Though sounding the same as the word form for nothing (無), this word form is 物. There are no connections between the two words.

7 This is according to a famed intellectual historian, Zhang Dainian, in his preface to Cheng Yishan's (1986, 1) *Theories of Primordial Qi in Ancient China*.

8 In pre-Qin conception, *qi* is an amorphous substance that constitutes concrete things. When *qi* transforms into concrete things, it is no longer viewed as *qi*. See Cheng Yishan (1986, 19–20). Later Neo-Confucians, starting with Zhang Zai, would view concrete things as *qi* as well.

9 The *Daodejing* does not use the phrase "primordial *qi*," but its identifying *qi* as "the One" (e.g., Chapter 42) shows that under this view, initially *qi* has not yet

divided into *yin* and *yang*. Recently the interpretation of the *Daodejing* as based on the theory of *qi* has gained more support among Chinese scholars. Contemporary Chinese scholars such as LIU Youming (2009), and others have argued convincingly that Laozi embraces the theory of *qi*.

10 In WANG Bo's (2011) "The Discovery and Establishment of *Wu*," he also writes:

> Lao Zi has never understood wu as emptiness. "Looked for but not seen," "listened for but not heard," "grabbed for but not gotten" all merely describe its formlessness (Chapter 14). However, this formlessness still exists, and the form of its existence is the image (*xiang*). "The Great Image is formless" and only insofar as it is formless is it called *wu* (Chapter 41). (14)

11 Many chapters in the *Zhuangzi*, especially in the *Outer Chapters* and the *Miscellaneous Chapters*, are likely authored by different people. Here for convenience's sake, I shall simply refer to the joint authorship in the *Zhuangzi* as Zhuangzi.

12 According to Girardot (2008), the concept of *hundun* is already implicitly employed in the *Daodejing*. He identifies *hundun* as the pervasive cosmogonic theme in Daoism. For detailed discussion, see Girardot (2008, Chapter 2).

13 This interpretation is also supported by Girardot's (2008) reading. Girardot analyzes this chapter in the following way: "The *Dao* as the 'source' and 'root' of life is that which in chapter 22 is said to be 'chaotic, dark, or hidden . . . and 'without form'" (79).

14 According to Ziporyn's (2009) translation, this passage says:

> If we calculate the number of things, it does not stop at ten thousand, and yet we set a limit by calling them the "Ten Thousand Things"—this is just to speak of them with a provisional name due to their great quantity. So "Heaven and earth" just means the vastest among forms, "*yin* and *yang*" just means the vastest among forces, and the "Course" [Ziporyn's translation of "*Dao*"] just means what is most unbiased among all activities. (110)

15 This is a condensed quote from the *Zhuangzi*'s Chapter 2. I take the *Zhuangzi* here to be pointing out a *reductio ad absurdum*. The *Huainanzi*, however, took this passage literally and turned it into a cosmogonic narrative.

16 This remark of WANG Bi on Laozi is recorded in a biography of WANG Bi written by He Shao (?–301 CE). See Wang (1980, 639).

17 WANG Bi frequently uses "not yet with form (*wei xing*)" in place of "without form (*wu xing*)."

18 This usage of '*wu*' occurs in WANG Bi's commentary on Chapter 11 of the *Daodejing*, where Laozi presents the utility of *wu* in the example of the cart and wheels.

19 This sense of '*wu*' is used in his speaking of the sage's mentality: "The sage has *wu* as his fundamental mental state" (Wang 1980, 639).

20 This brief quote is from the *Daodejing*, Chapter 1, "Nonbeing names the origin of heaven and earth; being names the mother of the myriad things." With alternate punctuation, the original quote has also been rendered as "The nameless is the origin of heaven and earth; the named is the mother of the myriad things." Here WANG Bi breaks the sentence after the word '*wu*' and explains that Laozi's point is to declare that all beings originate in nonbeing. (Wang 1980, 1).

21 The Chinese word for '*Dao*' originally means "the path" or "to follow."

22 This is a quote from WANG Bi by HAN Kangbo in his commentary on the Great Appendix (Xici) of the *Yijing*. Han's whole commentary is collected in Wang (1980).

23 The controversy surrounds how to interpret ZHOU Dunyi's opening line in his *The Exposition of the Taiji Diagram* (*Taiji tushuo*): "From the Boundless to the Supreme Ultimate (*Wuji er taiji*)." It is beyond the scope of this paper to go into the various interpretations of this line.

24 According to contemporary scholars CHEN Lai and CHENG Yishan, the *Supreme Ultimate* as depicted in the *Yijing* refers to the undifferentiated *qi*, and Confucians in the Han dynasty typically understood "*Taiji*" as primordial *qi* (see Chen 2005, 39; Cheng 1986, 27).

25 The analysis of *Yuzou* is: the four directions (front, back, left, and right) plus the two dimensions (up and down) are called '*yu*'; from the ancient and the past to the present and the coming is called '*zou*'. This analysis originally came from Wenzi, allegedly a disciple of Laozi and a contemporary of Confucius. It was recorded in Duan's annotations to XU Shen's *Shuowenjiezi*, and is now an established analysis of the term.

26 This is Roy Sorensen's (2009) description of Einstein's conception of space.

27 A fuller defense of this analysis is in Chapter 1 of my forthcoming book on Neo-Confucianism: *Neo-Confucianism: Metaphysics, Mind and Morality* (forthcoming, Wiley-Blackwell).

28 In CHEN Lai's explanation, "the supreme vacuity" originally refers to space itself, but in ZHANG Zai's conception of space, there is no absolute void because space is filled with an imperceptibly thin *qi* (Chen 2005, 47).

29 We have also seen how "formless" can be used metaphorically as signifying without determination.

14 Heart-Fasting, Forgetting, and Using the Heart Like a Mirror

Applied Emptiness in the *Zhuangzi*

Chris Fraser

Introduction

Bohun Wuren had such unshakeable composure that he could lecture the Daoist worthy Liezi on personal cultivation while standing with his heels over the edge of a precipice (21/57–61). His students included even Zichan, chief minister of Zheng, among the most renowned political figures of the age (5/14). Ai Tai Tuo was astonishingly ugly and possessed no special power, wealth, knowledge, or initiative. Yet he projected such charisma that people found him compellingly attractive and trustworthy; less than a year after he arrived at court, Duke Ai of Lu appointed him prime minister (5/31–49). Wang Tai was a one-footed ex-convict who attracted half the state of Lu as his followers. Confucius himself resolved to become his disciple. Without any explicit teachings, he set others aright; people "went to him empty and returned full" (5/1–13). Dongguo Shunzi was a man so authentic he could enlighten others and change their intentions merely by adjusting his bearing. "Clear and tolerant of things," he had "the looks of a person but the emptiness of Nature." Just hearing about him left the ruler of Wei speechless and transfixed (21/1–7).

These and other depictions of ethical adepts in the classical Daoist anthology *Zhuangzi* 莊子 illustrate a eudaimonistic ideal focused on developing and applying distinctively human virtuosity (*de*, 德). In previous publications (see, e.g., Fraser 2014; Fraser 2011, 102–103), I have argued that for many of the writings collected in the *Zhuangzi*, the exercise of virtuosity (*de*) in a mode of activity the texts call "wandering (*you*, 遊)" constitutes the fullest expression of human agency. Unlike pursuit of a single, fixed *dao* 道 (way, course, path), wandering (*you*) involves meandering through life without a fixed destination—discovering, exploring, shifting between, and playing along various paths, flexibly adapting to circumstances and "riding along with things" (4/52–53) without depending on any one thing in particular (1/21). In this essay, I apply an analytic framework introduced by Foucault (1988) to focus on dimensions of these Zhuangist ethical ideals that have received relatively little attention. Foucault distinguishes between three aspects of what he calls "morality" (25–28): a moral code, or substantive values and norms; the actual conduct of persons living under some moral code; and what he calls "ethics," namely "the set of attitudes, practices, and goals" by which agents guide their self-fashioning activities as subjects committed to the moral code in question (O'Leary 2002, 11). "Ethics" for Foucault's purposes is thus a subset of morality dealing with questions of practice, self-cultivation, and self-constitution rather than directly with normative issues.

Much research on the *Zhuangzi*—my own included—has focused on the substantive content of Zhuangist views: What positions, norms, or values do various writings in the anthology critique or defend? What *dao*, or way of life, do they present or endorse? What are the grounds for their stance? In Foucault's framework, these questions concern "morality" but not "ethics." Here I will temporarily set aside such questions to inquire instead into what Foucault would consider the "ethical" side of Zhuangist thought: How does the *Zhuangzi* depict the ethical adept's process of self-constitution? By what course or regimen does an agent become a *dao*-virtuoso like the idealized figures described above? How can agents who commit to the Zhuangist path employ or develop their virtuosity (*de*) so as to engage in a life of wandering (*you*)? In light of this volume's theme, one might propose—only partly tongue-in-cheek—that Zhuangist ethics, in Foucault's sense, revolves around *nothing*. More precisely, I will suggest that the crux of the practical process by which one becomes a Zhuangist adept lies in attaining a blank, clear, or open psychological state, typically denoted by the word "*xu* 虛" (empty, blank, insubstantial). The chief technique for attaining emptiness (*xu*) is "forgetting" (*wang*, 忘). Agents who successfully "forget" and attain the empty (*xu*) state are able to apply their heart "like a mirror (*ruo jing*, 若鏡)." This mirror-like functioning facilitates a life of virtuosity (*de*) and wandering (*you*).

The first section below introduces Foucault's analytic model and sketches how it might be applied to a version of Zhuangist ethics. The following section explores a Zhuangist version of one particular element in the Foucauldian framework, the "ethical work." In particular, I consider accounts in the *Zhuangzi* of the practices, techniques, and processes by which an agent may become an ethical adept. The subsequent section briefly compares and contrasts Zhuangist emptiness with the concept of "flow" in positive psychology. The final section considers potential shortcomings of this picture of ethical work given Zhuangist ethical ends. I will suggest that, provided we remain aware of the limitations of the Zhuangist approach, it is likely to prove fruitful for its intended purpose.

The Foucauldian Framework

Foucault (1984, 1988) identifies four major elements implicated in the activity of constituting ourselves as ethical agents. These are the ethical substance, the mode of subjection, the ethical work, and the *telos*.[1] The "ethical substance" refers to the part of the agent that is the object of ethical work or training. This object could be one's desires, feelings, acts, or motives, for instance. The "mode of subjection" refers to the manner in which agents see themselves as relating to moral norms. Agents could see themselves as subjects of a divine command, for example, or as rational beings who act from respect for duty as determined by the Kantian categorical imperative. The "ethical work" refers to the practices or techniques by which agents transform themselves to achieve conformity to moral norms and become ethical adepts. The "*telos*" of an ethics is the ideal toward which the ethical work is directed—the goal of the agent's self-cultivation.

Before attempting to apply this framework to Zhuangist ethics, I should clarify a methodological point. The *Zhuangzi* is a diverse collection of writings. Passages with implications concerning the objects, grounds for, processes, and outcomes of ethical self-development are scattered throughout its many constituent texts, and these very probably present a variety of distinct ethical standpoints. This observation holds not only for texts that are fairly obviously doctrinally heterogeneous, but even for regions of the anthology that some scholars consider relatively homogenous, such as the seven "inner" books.[2] A thorough study of the *Zhuangzi* would meticulously explore the doctrinal similarities and differences between its various parts, but such a detailed treatment is beyond the scope of this essay.[3] What I will attempt instead is to explicate and critically examine a hypothetical Zhuangist position constructed from prominent themes—such as virtuosity (*de*), wandering (*you*), emptiness (*xu*), and forgetting (*wang*)—that appear repeatedly across a selection of doctrinally related passages drawn mainly from the "inner" books (Books 1–7) and the cluster of six books (17–22) that Graham (1981) dubbed the "School of Zhuangzi" writings (28). I make no claim that the resulting set of views constitutes *the* unique, overarching Zhuangist standpoint, captures all the relevant ideas in the *Zhuangzi*, or represents the best interpretation of each text considered. Nor do I contend that these ideas were intended by the original writers and editors to fit together in precisely the way I suggest. I claim only that the resulting position is one interesting, plausible way to assemble an ethical outlook from *Zhuangzi* material.

Applied to Zhuangist thought, then, Foucault's model might yield an account roughly like the following. The most conspicuous candidate in the *Zhuangzi* for the "ethical substance"—the part of ourselves that we attempt to modify, train, or develop through ethical practices—is probably the heart or mind (*xin*, 心). In classical Chinese thought generally, the heart (*xin*) is the organ of cognition, the locus of emotion, and above all the part of the agent that guides action. Other aspects of the agent are clearly also of concern in Zhuangist ethical practices. For instance, emotional equanimity is a distinctive feature of the person of virtuosity (*de*) (see Fraser 2011 for details). Passages valorizing skills or addressing the challenges of political service make it clear that efficacious action is another focus. However, *Zhuangzi* discussions of both of these topics typically revolve around the operations of the heart (*xin*). Moreover, key passages describing ethical adepts emphasize their distinctive way of "applying the heart" (5/5, 7/32, 21/63), while others treat the heart as a focus of ethical development (4/26, 4/42–43, 19/62–64, 21/34–35). Still others identify improper use of the heart as a cause of ethical difficulties (1/42, 2/21–27, 4/24). The heart is thus manifestly an important ethical substance for *Zhuangzi* writers and may well be the primary one.

Exposition of the second and third Foucauldian elements in Zhuangist thought will be facilitated by first discussing the fourth, the "*telos*." Elsewhere, I have presented a detailed treatment of a Zhuangist eudaimonistic ideal that, borrowing the texts' own terminology, I label "wandering" (*you*) (Fraser 2014), along with an account of the emotional equanimity characteristic of wandering (Fraser 2011, 102–103). A distinctive characteristic of human agency is the capacity to discover, appreciate, and explore a plurality of distinct *dao* (ways or paths) within the totality of facts and processes that constitute the holistic *Dao* of the cosmos. "Wandering" refers to the mode of activity in which we employ this capacity effectively. It amounts to a second-order *dao* by which we explore the various first-order *dao* open to us—a meta-*dao* of recognizing and taking up potential paths presented by the interaction between agents' personal capacities and motivation and their objective circumstances. Virtuosity (*de*) is in effect agents' proficiency in resiliently, skillfully, and harmoniously wandering through the *dao*.

Wandering (*you*) is marked by cognitively aware, affectively calm, adaptive, and generally enjoyable or zestful activity (see Fraser 2014). Cognitively, the "wanderer" or Zhuangist virtuoso appreciates the order and patterns of nature, recognizing the vastness and duration of the cosmos, the continual transformation of things within it, and the contingency and causal dependence of each thing upon others. Accordingly, the wanderer regards any path or project as conditional and limited in nature. Affectively, such a person maintains equanimity regarding his or her contingent, transitory circumstances. This equanimity is partly the product of cognitive and affective identification with the whole of nature and the process of change. These attitudes in turn yield an ability to adapt fluidly, creatively, and efficaciously to changing conditions, such that agents spontaneously find effective paths to follow, which they undertake in a spirit of ease and playfulness. Although the *Zhuangzi* rejects morality *per se* as a guide to action, what we think of as morally right courses of action will often be endorsed in the guise of fitting or efficacious responses to circumstances.

The *telos* of Zhuangist ethics, I suggest, is to fully develop our virtuosity (*de*) by realizing the wandering ideal through whatever concrete course of action comes spontaneously to us. An agent might be a woodcarver, a butcher, a diplomat, a ferry helmsman, a tutor—a wide range of activities can serve as fields for Zhuangist ethical achievement. Practitioners might strive simply to improve psychophysiological health and excel at daily tasks, or they might eventually become sages or spiritual teachers, depending on their abilities and circumstances. The texts suggest no single vision of the good life. To the contrary, the implication is that different agents, with different capacities, may flourish in a variety of ways. Whatever the specifics of the practitioner's situation, he or she can engage in wandering as a mode of activity that various passages portray as central to psychophysiological health, personal flourishing, and judicious, efficacious action.

Foucault's second element, the "mode of subjection," answers for a particular ethical system the question of *why* the agent should engage in the work of reforming the ethical substance (O'Leary 2002, 13). In the context of Zhuangist ethics, the mode of subjection is in effect the self-conception that explains why agents should seek to reform their heart (*xin*) so as to realize the wandering life of virtuosity (*de*). The mode of subjection is probably partly aesthetic or attractive, in that wandering, virtuoso activity is depicted as admirable and efficacious, and partly teleological, in that it is depicted as best fulfilling our capacities and maintaining psychophysiological health (Fraser 2011, 108). In the *Zhuangzi*, wandering is a conception of flourishing activity that emerges from reflection on a world of constant, uncontrollable flux, without absolute or universally applicable values, and the conviction that our creative ability to adapt calmly and efficaciously to changing circumstances is the finest, most distinctive feature of human agency. The human condition and natural environment are such that no single, fixed path is always appropriate, no fixed action-guiding distinctions are reliably efficacious, and events may not proceed as we expect. Against this background, wandering is considered an effective way of finding one's place in the cosmos—an approach to "nurturing our center" (4/53), or maintaining the inward ease and harmony characteristic of proper psychophysical hygiene, while smoothly responding to natural patterns and processes and "overcoming things without injury" (7/31–33). For the *Zhuangzi*, the mode of subjection involves neither obligation nor imperatives of human nature, however. Pursuing the ethical *telos* is not a duty, nor is it essential to human life. An agent who rejects or ignores the project of training the heart may live a suboptimal life or behave foolishly but does not thereby violate a moral requirement or fail to be fully human. Indeed, one passage implies that nature may place the ethical *telos* beyond the reach of some agents (5/31).

The remaining element in the Foucauldian scheme is the "ethical work." By what processes of training or cultivation do adherents seek to reshape themselves so as to approach the ethical *telos*? Zhuangist ethical ideals concern broad traits such as responsiveness, openness, and equanimity, rather than concrete judgments, habits, or conduct. Hence the texts generally do not spell out a specific ethical regimen or curriculum of personal cultivation, as some Ruist (Confucian) texts do, for instance. The relevant conception of ethical work does not yield particular steps, exercises, or formulae; it is more a process of training oneself to become more open-minded, spontaneous, or attentive. However, numerous passages do address ethical development, and some explicitly discuss how to overcome obstacles and make progress in self-cultivation. A shared theme of many such passages is that development ensues from clearing out the heart to attain a state of emptiness or blankness (*xu*), which both facilitates achievement of the ethical *telos* and is partly constitutive of it. The next section explores this conception of ethical work in detail.

Zhuangist Ethical Work

The most prominent depiction of ethical work in the *Zhuangzi* is "heart-fasting (*xin zhai*, 心齋)," a task that a fictional Confucius assigns his student Yan Hui as a corrective to the latter's ambitious, elaborate strategies for reforming the headstrong, reckless tyrant of Wei.[4] Yan first proposes a straightforward, aggressive approach, which Confucius rejects as forced and likely to invoke resistance. He next suggests an indirect, passive strategy, which Confucius rejects as ineffectual. Both approaches, Confucius remarks, amount to "taking the heart as instructor (*shi xin*, 師心)" (4/24). In both cases, Yan is self-consciously preparing to deal with the tyrant according to fixed formulae determined in his heart, the organ that in classical Chinese thought was typically assumed to guide action. To move beyond these inadequate strategies, Confucius assigns Yan an explicit task of ethical work: he is to "fast" the heart to empty it of any preformed content. Confucius explains "heart-fasting" as follows:

> Unify your intent (*zhi* 志). Listen not with the ears but with the heart; listen not with the heart but with *qi* 氣 (breath, ether). Listening stops at the ears; the heart stops at tallies. As to *qi*, it is what is empty (*xu*) and waits on things. Only take as your *dao* [the path of] gathering emptiness. Emptiness is the fasting of the heart. (4/26–28)

In response, Yan reports that before receiving this task, he solidly took himself to be himself, but after this assignment, it is as if he has never existed. Confucius responds that this loss of self is precisely what he intends by "emptiness" (*xu*). He then encourages Yan to "wander in the tyrant's cage" without responding to his use of names. If the opportunity arises, Yan is to speak, but otherwise not. He should neither shut himself off nor force things along, but instead unify himself and dwell in "the inevitable (*bu de yi*, 不得已)." Rather than knowing by means of received knowledge, he is to know by means of lacking knowledge, allowing his senses to connect directly within him and putting himself outside the heart's cognitive processes.

The conceptual link the passage establishes between *qi* (breath) and emptiness (*xu*) has important implications for our interpretation of the latter. In early Chinese metaphysics, *qi* was the fluid-like "ether" from which everything was thought to be constituted. Objects were regarded as "solids" or "stuff" (*shi*, 實) formed from coagulated or consolidated *qi*. Since *qi* is empty (*xu*), we can infer that emptiness (*xu*) does not refer to nothingness, nonexistence, or utter vacuousness, the absence of anything whatsoever. Instead, it refers to the absence of completed "formation (*cheng*, 成)" of things into solid, fixed forms. "Emptiness (*xu*)" is better interpreted along the lines of what is open and receptive, plastic or fluid, and unformed or insubstantial than what is vacant or nonexistent. The directive to fast the heart thus entails abstaining from fixed, fully formed preconceptions that might guide action. Yan is to concentrate on the situation, but not by means of normal sense perception or the heart, which "stops at" or "fixates on" tallies. An ancient Chinese tally (*fu*, 符) was a symbol of a covenant or of authority. Tallies were divided into two halves that fit together like puzzle pieces. To enforce or change the covenant or to verify one's authority, the holder of one piece of the tally had to match it to the other. Metaphorically, the implication is that the heart functions by using preformed signs that tally with exactly one sort of object, thus impeding the agent's ability to respond adaptively to a variety of objects. By contrast, *qi* is fluid or insubstantial and thus responsive to all things—it "waits on" them before flowing one way or another. To sum up, Yan should clear his heart of preconceived plans, attend fully to the situation, and let his *qi* respond to the concrete circumstances, yielding attuned, intuitive responses that issue not from the heart but from the person as a whole. Rather than relying on prior know-how to recognize and respond to things, he should employ an unformed, open receptivity to generate spontaneous responses to novel cases. A mark of this receptive, unformed state is a loss of conscious self-awareness.

As an instructive contrast with "heart-fasting" and "listening with *qi*," consider the story of Huizi's (Hui Shi 惠施 c. 380–c. 310 BCE) ineptitude at using his giant gourds (1/35–42). Having raised a crop of huge gourds, Huizi found them too big to make dippers and too heavy and unwieldy to be water containers. Concluding they were useless, he smashed them. His friend Zhuangzi ridicules his inability to see beyond the two most common uses for gourds, asking why he didn't make them into floats and go drifting on a river or lake. He attributes Huizi's lack of imagination to his "weed-choked" or "overgrown" heart. Unlike an empty heart, an "overgrown" one is incapable of creative adaptation to novelty.

A well-known passage about the perfected person's (*zhiren*, 至人) use of the heart develops the concept of emptiness (*xu*) and clarifies the mode of activity supposed to issue from this psychological state.

> Do not be the incarnation of a name; do not be a storehouse of schemes; do not undertake affairs; do not be a master of knowledge. Embody the limitless while wandering where there are no tracks; exhaust what you receive from nature without any thought of gain—just be empty (*xu*), that's all. The perfected person's employment of the heart is like a mirror, neither sending off nor welcoming things, responding without storing. So he can overcome things without being harmed. (7/31–33)

This passage instructs us to set aside names or titles, schemes, ambitions, and received knowledge. We are to wander without boundaries or fixed labels for things, simply realizing our nature-given capacities without any thought of profit or achievement. The ensuing mode of agency is "like a mirror" in directly responding to the flow of events without welcoming them before they arrive, sending them away, or following after them when they depart. This mirroring characteristic purportedly yields practical efficacy.

The mirror metaphor can easily be pushed too far. The text does not imply that the perfected person has simply become a mirror, which automatically, objectively, yet passively reflects its environment without exercising agency or any input of its own. The passage primarily concerns the mode of the ideal agent's action, not the content. The content of the response will depend on the material of the mirror and the circumstances reflected: a bronze mirror in twilight reflects differently from a glass one at noon, a convex mirror differently from a concave one. The emphasis of the metaphor here seems instead to be that the virtuoso responds to situations spontaneously, from a blank, fluid mindset, without fixating on or forming attachments to things. Because no ambitions, preferences, or fixed "limits" or "tracks" obstruct his heart, he can respond flexibly and fittingly. A mirror aptly symbolizes emptiness (*xu*) in that it reflects only if its surface is clear of dust and grime, it is always ready to reflect, and it neither anticipates nor binds itself to objects—when there is no object, there is no reflection.[5] By analogy, emptiness (*xu*) supposedly allows us to employ nature-given capacities without conscious ambition or distraction, clearing the heart so that we can respond promptly and directly to changing circumstances. The point here is how emptiness enables an open, "reflective" response that allows our capacities to function at their fullest.[6] Just what those capacities are and the content of their response will depend on our particular character, education, and abilities.

How exactly are we to empty the heart and allow it to respond freely and instantaneously, as a mirror does? Two further passages that explicitly treat ethical work provide hints about specific approaches. Assigned a risky, high-stakes diplomatic mission that could place his life in danger, Master Gao, the Duke of She, finds himself physically overcome with stress and consults Confucius, his mentor. Confucius notes that we all face inescapable decrees of fate and duty. Fate mandates that we be born into a family and care about our parents; duty entails that wherever we go, we find ourselves living under some political authority. Besides this service to kin and state, however, there is also self-cultivation, one's "service" to oneself:

> As to serving your own heart, without sorrow or joy alternating before you, to know what you can't do anything about and be at peace with it as with fate, [this is] the ultimate in virtuosity (*de*). In being a political subject or son, there are bound to be things that are inevitable. Act on the reality of the situation and forget yourself. What leisure will you then have for delighting in life and hating death? (4/41–44)

Confucius goes on to offer detailed advice about managing communication and rivalry. He urges Master Gao to proceed with caution, neither compromising his assignment nor rushing to complete it, since compromised assignments and rushed completions are dangerous, while fine accomplishments take time (4/51–52). The "ultimate" is to "let your heart wander (*you*) by riding along with things, and nurture your center by entrusting yourself to the inevitable" (4/52–53).

These instructions constitute a brief but rich depiction of the Zhuangist ethical *telos* and ethical work. Master Gao is to learn to recognize "the inevitable (*bu de yi*)" and accept it, finding his peace with it as he does with unchangeable features of his fate, such as his age, height, or birthplace. An outcome of this work will be emotional equanimity, a core aspect of virtuosity (*de*). By accepting and riding along with the inevitable, he can preserve his psychophysiological equilibrium and maintain a clear, empty heart, which is ready to respond spontaneously, in no fixed direction, much as a mirror does. The specific technique by which to pursue this *telos* is to proceed according to the "facts" or "reality" (*qing*, 情) of the affair in which he is engaged and "forget (*wang*, 忘)" himself.

This guidance meshes well with that of the passages just considered. Each alludes to concentrating attention on the task at hand, accepting "the inevitable," and fluidly responding to changing circumstances. Each alludes to a process of emptying oneself of the preconceptions, concerns, and ambitions that typically drive action. Each depicts a form of "nurturing one's center," maintaining a loose, responsive equilibrium. A consequence of "heart-fasting" and blank, unstructured "listening" to things for Yan Hui was a loss of conscious self-awareness. Master Gao is explicitly told to forget about himself so that worries about self-preservation do not stress him and he can focus on his mission, responding freely to circumstances.

The theme of forgetting appears repeatedly in *Zhuangzi* passages dealing with ethical work. Another dialogue between Confucius and Yan Hui implies that forgetting is a concrete technique for achieving emptiness (6/89–93). Yan announces that he has made progress: he has forgotten moral goodness and duty (*ren yi*, 仁義), two central Confucian virtues. Confucius approves but indicates his work is still unfinished. At their next meeting Yan declares further progress: now he has forgotten rituals and music, two major concrete guidelines in Confucian ethics. Again Confucius approves but urges him to continue. On still another day Yan reports he has advanced again: "I sit and forget . . . I let my limbs and torso fall away, dismiss hearing and vision, depart from bodily form and expel knowing, and assimilate to the Great Connection (*da tong*, 大通)."[7] Confucius praises him for identifying with the totality of natural transformations and thus having no preferences or constancy, being ready to adapt to anything. Yan has forgotten his originally professed values, the concrete norms of conduct he was trained in, and in the end even his own distinct existence apart from the flow of the cosmos. No self-awareness or concerns distract him from absorption in the ongoing course of events.

In another anecdote, Yan Hui admires a ferryman for his preternatural boat-handling. Confucius explains that a good swimmer or diver can easily become an adept helmsman, as he "forgets the water" (19/24). He is as at home on water as on land, so the fear of capsizing does not enter his heart (19/25), which can thus remain empty. When we are distracted by fears, extraneous concerns, or the stakes of our actions, our performance suffers:

> Playing for tiles, you're skilled. Playing for silver buckles, you get the shakes. Playing for gold, you're a nervous wreck. Your skill is the same,

> but [in the latter two cases] there's something you care about; this is putting weight on something outside yourself. Anyone who puts weight on what's outside gets clumsy on the inside. (19/25–26)

By implication, then, "forgetting" here refers to emptying the heart of worries about or distractions from the "outside" so that we can maintain inward equilibrium and act freely and adeptly, without impediments. Yan Hui sits and forgets, removing preconceptions that might interfere with the appropriateness and efficacy of his responses; Master Gao and the ferryman forget concerns that might disrupt the smooth functioning of their abilities. The woodworker Qing, who sculpts bell-stands of unearthly beauty, explains that before starting a new piece he fasts to still his heart until all thoughts of praise or reward, rank or salary, honor or disgrace, and skill or clumsiness vanish. Ultimately, he too forgets even his limbs and body. His skill concentrated and outside distractions having drained away, he is able to discern wood of exceptional quality and match his unadulterated natural powers with the natural grain of the wood (19/54–59)—presumably an instance of a mirror-like response to things. This anecdote again emphasizes concentrating on a task, eliminating distractions, losing self-awareness, and responding efficaciously to circumstances.

"Forgetting" is not a prescription for utter mindlessness, however. Some *Zhuangzi* passages criticize agents for forgetting points that *should* guide their actions—for "hiding from nature and spurning reality, forgetting what one has received" (3/17) or for "forgetting oneself" (20/66) and "forgetting one's genuineness" in pursuit of profit (20/67). What distinguishes appropriate from inappropriate forgetting? A further passage offers a suggestion that ties together several of the themes examined so far:

> The artisan Chui drew curves and angles that surpassed those made with the compass and set square. His fingers transformed along with things and he did not check them with the heart, so his soul platform (*ling tai*, 靈臺) was unified and unfettered. Forgetting your feet—this is your shoes fitting. Forgetting your waist—this is your belt fitting. Your cognition forgetting *shi* (right) and *fei* (wrong)—this is your heart fitting. Neither alternating inwardly nor getting drawn along outwardly—this is affairs and encounters fitting. To begin by fitting and never to have not fit—this is fitting so well that you forget all about fit. (19/62–64)

Chui performs efficaciously because his embodied skills transform along with the things he encounters, requiring no conscious monitoring from the heart. Hence he is psychologically unified and unobstructed. By implication, the hallmark of the right sort of forgetting is practical efficacy, as indicated by a relation of "good fit" between the agent and the circumstances. Good fit both enables forgetting and identifies the appropriate sort of forgetting. It obtains when things are functioning smoothly and unobtrusively, causing us to forget them. Consciously attending to something indicates that activity is not proceeding smoothly; the heart is engaged in "checking" or "monitoring" and thus is no longer "empty." As virtuoso walkers, normally we need not attend to our shoes in order to stroll down a path. Similarly, the passage implies, if we are acting with virtuosity (*de*), we need not attend to *shi* (right) or *fei* (wrong) to determine what to do. Indeed, when all is functioning smoothly, we tend to "forget" things to the extent that distinctions between them vanish. The shoe that fits is not noticed as distinct from the foot; the normally functioning foot is not noticed as distinct from the leg or body. Indeed, the agent interacting adeptly with the environment often ceases to notice the body or self as distinct from the surroundings and so "forgets" self-awareness, as Yan Hui does when he "sits and forgets."

The passages cited treat different dimensions of forgetting. Some focus on how what is forgotten ceases to have any role in conscious action guidance. Master Gao is to forget himself so that worries about his safety no longer hinder his job performance. Yan Hui forgets ritual and music, which will no longer guide his social interactions. Other passages focus on how forgetting results from good fit. A belt that fits well is unobtrusive and thus forgotten. These two dimensions intersect, in that factors that are forgotten because of their good fit thereby also play no role in consciously guiding action, while conscious concerns, strategies, norms, and so forth that are better forgotten may prevent us from finding a good fit with our circumstances. The interplay between these dimensions is illustrated by the swimmer or diver who can helm a boat because he "forgets the water." Worries about the water—fear of capsizing and drowning—are wholly absent from his heart precisely because of his good fit with the water—how at ease he is with it.

This example introduces a third dimension of forgetting: competence or mastery. The good swimmer or diver forgets the water because his swimming competence allows him to find an efficacious fit between his movements and the wet environment. Chui draws perfect curves and angles without his heart consciously verifying his movements because his craftsmanship enables his fingers to "transform along with things" and find the perfect fit. In mastering a skill, we both forget the explicit rules or steps by which we learned it and achieve an efficacious good fit with the objects of our skill—a fit so good that extraneous worries melt away. The empty mirror provides an apt analogy for both the seemingly automatic, instantaneous way a skilled virtuoso responds to her context and the blank, receptive state of "forgetting" from which her actions issue.

Skill mastery also helps to explain precisely how Zhuangist ethical work proceeds. The idea of ethical work as forgetting concerns and emptying the heart raises an obvious practical problem. Directly working at forgetting or emptying is a self-contradictory enterprise. Consciously, deliberately attempting to empty our attention or to forget something merely causes us to notice more acutely whatever it is we are doing or seeking to forget. Yet the emptiness, forgetting, and good fit the *Zhuangzi* depicts are familiar from the experience of learning and mastering skills. So just how do we forget? We can cultivate forgetting and emptiness by concentrating on challenging, world-guided skills that fill our attention and provide immediate performance feedback. Skilled tasks present us with "inevitable" conditions that lie beyond our control yet within which, with sufficient sensitivity and responsiveness, we can find openings to proceed. We begin with explicit steps or movements in mind but eventually "forget" these and learn to act from a blank, empty state in which we concentrate on the task at hand without focusing on any one thing in particular. We come to experience action as a spontaneous response to our context, rather than the result of self-conscious cognition and deliberation. As the masterful butcher Cook Ding says, "I encounter the ox with my spirit, rather than looking with my eyes. Perceptual knowing ceases, while spirit-desire proceeds" (3/6).

To wrap up this section, my interpretive proposal is that for a major thread of Zhuangist thought, the concrete ethical work, in Foucault's sense, lies in training ourselves to attain a state of "emptiness" (*xu*) by regularly engaging in challenging, world-guided activities in which we "forget" rules, distractions, concerns, and even our own identity while seeking "good fit" between our actions and the environment. To help achieve such emptiness, we might try "sitting and forgetting"—probably a form of apophatic meditation—under a garden tree or while floating in a raft on a lake. We might reflect on the rhetoric of the *Zhuangzi* itself, such as the many aporetic arguments or the stories depicting diverse, uncommon perspectives. Above all, we can learn and exercise skills, which offer ready, concrete opportunities to apply emptiness, forgetting, and spontaneous, mirror-like responses to practical challenges.

Emptiness and Flow

The "empty" state I have been describing, along with its relation to skills, brings to mind the "autotelic" or intrinsically rewarding state of total absorption in challenging, goal-directed activities that Csikszentmihalyi (1990) has dubbed "flow." Indeed, Csikszentmihalyi himself discusses the *Zhuangzi* and the example of Cook Ding the butcher (150). Flow for Csikszentmihalyi is the crux of what he calls "optimal experience" and hence a cornerstone of a well-lived life. I have been suggesting that attaining emptiness constitutes the major ethical work leading to the Zhuangist ethical *telos*. Elsewhere I have also proposed that it is a substantive element of the Zhuangist conception of the good life (Fraser 2008, 132–135). To what extent do Csikszentmihalyi's concept of flow and the Zhuangist notion of empty, "forgetful," yet fitting activity converge?

Csikszentmihalyi identifies several key factors characteristic of "flow."[8] It is an intrinsically rewarding or enjoyable state involving intense concentration on the present instant, a loss of reflective self-consciousness, a fusing of action and awareness, an altered experience of time (which may seem to pass more slowly or quickly than usual), and a sense of control over one's situation.

Preconditions for flow are that the agent be engaged in an activity with clear goals, which provide straightforward, immediate performance feedback, and that the challenges of the activity balance the agent's competence, such that the agent can realistically be confident of success. The activities I have suggested constitute Zhuangist ethical work clearly involve deep concentration, loss of self-awareness, and the agent's merging with her actions and environment. At least some are intrinsically rewarding—Cook Ding, for instance, mentions the satisfaction that ensues from his work (3/11).

However, the Zhuangist stance on the role of control, confidence, and goals seems nearly antithetical to Csikszentmihalyi's account of flow. For Csikszentmihalyi, flow experiences are a way for agents to impose a satisfying, self-fulfilling order on psychological chaos. In the *Zhuangzi*, by contrast, emptiness, forgetting, and discussions of skill seem directed at acknowledging and accepting chaos, whether psychological or external to the agent. We are to learn to accept and cope with unforeseeable change and "the inevitable," or circumstances over which we have no control (see also Jochim 1998, 64–65). Rather than bring order to chaos, we give up our presuppositions about order and adapt fluidly to change. Some passages depict the ethical work as leading to a state of psychological constancy—a "constant heart (*chang xin*, 常心)" (5/9). But this constancy is achieved by relinquishing our sense of a self that controls its own fate and pursues its own fixed goals. It arises from maintaining an empty, responsive state that depends on nothing in particular (1/21) and by identifying with the totality of the course of nature (5/7–8, 21/31–35). For the *Zhuangzi*, the human condition is that we continually face uncontrollable, unpredictable processes of "creation and transformation (*zao hua*, 造化)," which may cause existing skills to lose purchase or previously defined goals to evaporate. The point of emptiness and mirroring is that they prime us to spontaneously find a new "fit" even when we cannot be confident that any of our existing values, goals, or skills will remain applicable.

Critical Reflections

Emptiness (*xu*) and mirroring are metaphorical, not literal notions. "Heart-fasting" and "forgetting" can of course never fully purge the agent of assumptions and habits, nor take us beyond registering things by means of some aspect of the system of "tallies" we have learned to employ. At most they can only loosen the grip of received habits of thought or action and prime us to modify or replace them. They may help us achieve a more transparent state of consciousness, in which attention is directed more fully and sensitively toward our context, while plans, distractions, and self-reflexive awareness fade away. They do not really empty us out entirely, however, or we would lack the resources by which to register and respond to things. A wholly empty mirror would be a hollow frame, unable to reflect at all. Nor are mirror-like responses pure reflections. Our intuitions and skills continue to guide action, albeit unconsciously and with a heightened sensitivity to novel, creative paths. Our responses are not passive "mirrorings," but reactions, grounded in tacit interpretations of what we encounter. Zhuangist emptiness (*xu*) is not wholesale psychological nothingness, but a state similar to that of a jazz player improvising a solo, both taking cues and inciting responses from the other musicians. Self-awareness and self-conscious cognition—aspects of our psychology attributed to the *xin* (heart, mind) and *zhi* 知 (knowing, understanding, cognition)—are absent or marginalized. But deeper, unconscious sources of agency continue to function, denoted by terms such as *qi* (breath), *shen* 神 (spirit), or *ling tai* (soul platform). Indeed, the *Zhuangzi* highlights how intelligent, adept action often springs chiefly from such other aspects of the agent.

A further respect in which this cluster of metaphors might mislead concerns the objects "reflected" in the heart's mirror-like functioning. As Wenzel (2003) observes, the circumstances the Zhuangist agent must be aware of include not only what is outside the agent, but also the agent's own dispositions, abilities, and possibilities for action (122). The most fitting path for Cook Ding to slice up the ox or for the phantom-like whitewater swimmer to navigate the rapids (19/49–54) is determined partly by the natural structures they face, partly by their relation to those structures and their ongoing movement. To find an effective course, the empty, mirroring heart must respond in ways that stem partially from an awareness of the self and its relation to the environment, even if this awareness is unconscious. The virtuoso's activity thus cannot simply be a reflection of or response to her context. It must be partly a projection of her self-understanding and goal-directedness—albeit a fluid, responsive self-understanding and directedness, not the rigid, predetermined attitudes supposedly purged through "heart-fasting."

Hansen's (1992, 300–302) analysis helps to clarify these points. In the performance of advanced skills, self-conscious, deliberate decision-making vanishes, since it would only interfere with performance. Complex sequences of activity become compressed into a single basic action. We become so at ease performing a skill that we forget the discrete, constituent actions by which we learned it. We no longer think about moving our fingers one by one to strike the keys; we simply perform the sonata. We no longer concentrate on rotating our legs to link a series of turns; we just ski down the trail. Phenomenologically, our actions can come to seem like spontaneous reflexes triggered by the environment, reflections in an empty mirror. In fact, however, as Hansen points out, we are experiencing the high-level functioning of an advanced skill structure.

These reflections raise the question of whether Zhuangist ethical work can truly be effective in achieving the ethical *telos* of wandering (*you*) with virtuosity (*de*). Wandering entails a creative openness to a plurality of ways of going on, some of which might be radically different from what we are accustomed to. Perhaps immersion in skills to the extent that we perform them automatically or unconsciously might instead lock us into habits and preconceptions, breeding cognitive sclerosis or blindness to anything that does not fit neatly into the existing framework of our skill. If spontaneous responses issuing from the empty (*xu*) state are actually grounded in habit, prior training, and our existing self-understanding, how can we distinguish insensitive, heedless responses from sensitive, adaptive ones? How can an agent confirm she is not being guided by baseless or suboptimal prejudices?

One possible criterion for these distinctions is practical efficacy. On reaching a knotty juncture, Cook Ding pauses, concentrates, and allows his intuitive skill structure to spontaneously move the knife through the ox's body, thus advancing beyond his original level of skill. Supposedly, his response is appropriate because he succeeds in slicing up the meat. Yet perhaps a more fitting response would be to recognize that he has encountered this obstacle only because he is mutilating the corpse of a fellow creature, one who would surely have preferred to remain alive and in one piece. Efficacious as his response may seem, a more adroit reaction might be to change careers and stop killing harmless animals. Efficacy does not ensure that a course of action is fitting, since we can question whether the task at which an agent is so successful is one he should be performing at all.

This line of critical questioning highlights a genuine challenge, but one I suggest the Zhuangist conception of ethical work has the resources to cope with, provided we clarify its aims and purposes. The texts we have examined do not imply that empty mirroring is an end in itself or that the recipe for attaining the ethical *telos* is simply to master one or more skills. Nor do they suggest there is some general "skill of life" that one can master in the way the ferryman has mastered boat handling or the cicada-catcher has acquired the trick of plucking cicadas from trees with a pole (19/17–21). They do not promise easy or direct solutions to thorny practical questions, such as whether to slaughter oxen or become a vegetarian. To the contrary, several passages—such as the discussion of Master Gao's mission—underscore the difficulty and complexity of practical issues. Identifying and overcoming ethical blind spots is a persisting challenge, to which neither the *Zhuangzi* nor any other ethical approach can ensure a solution.

The implication is rather that learning how to approach a challenging assignment such as Master Gao's or to master a skill such as Cook Ding's illustrates key elements of ethical work and thus "how to cultivate life," as Lord Wen Hui, Ding's employer, remarks (3/12). This ethical work is an ongoing process of developing greater sensitivity to our circumstances, cultivating a calm, centered constitution that allows us to notice and respond to opportunities rather than force things along, and allowing room for novel, effective responses that shatter existing biases, assumptions, and limitations. The process offers no guarantees. But it seems plausible that continued ethical work along these lines can help us become more sensitive, responsive, and creative and thus make incremental progress toward the ethical *telos*. Indeed, since the Zhuangist approach encourages practitioners to look beyond received paths of thought and conduct and consider alternatives, it seems at least conducive to greater ethical awareness. Cook Ding may not have appreciated that oxen would prefer to live in peace, but elsewhere in the *Zhuangzi* a ritual priest observes that his pigs would rather munch chaff and bran in their pen than dine on choice grain only to later be slaughtered as sacrificial offerings (19/35–38). All one can do is persevere in the ethical work, treating life as a field not just for performing skills but for continually extending, refining, and challenging them.[9]

Notes

1 For a detailed discussion, see O'Leary (2002, 12–13).

2 The ethical ideal of the "authentic man" depicted in the opening lines of Book 6 (6/1–20), for instance, may well diverge from the "cultivating life" ideal presented in the story of Cook Ding, who follows *dao* through his work as a butcher (3/2–12).

3 For a study that contrasts several distinct uses of *xu* (emptiness) in the *Zhuangzi*, see Fraser (2008).

4 The dialogue is at *Zhuangzi* (4/1–34). For a detailed discussion, see Fraser (2008). This dialogue and several other passages bearing on ethical work cast Confucius as the writers' spokesman—a role that seems at least partly ironic, since the ideas presented are not typically associated with Confucianism and in some cases may be antithetical to it.

5 On "binding" as a hindrance to virtuoso action, see Fraser (2011, 103).

6 Fox (1996) plausibly links the fasting of the heart to the metaphor of the axis or hinge of *dao* (*dao shu*, 道樞) in Book 2 of the *Zhuangzi* (2/30–31). The text states that the axis of *dao* is achieved when the action-guiding distinctions between *shi* 是 and *fei* 非 (this and that, right and wrong) cease to stand in opposition. The pivot can then rotate freely, "responding without end," such that anything can be deemed *shi* or *fei* temporarily for practical purposes. Fasting the heart, Fox proposes, amounts to clearing out the "socket" in which the hinge of *dao* rotates, allowing for unimpeded responsiveness. The text also links this responsiveness to light metaphors, such as "illuminating things with *tian* (sky, nature)" (2/29) and "applying illumination/understanding (*yi ming* 以明)" (2/31), thus drawing the discussion of the features and limitations of *shi-fei* distinctions into the same metaphorical space as the image of the clear, reflective mirror. Indeed, in the heart-fasting dialogue, Confucius implies that the empty heart gives off light, as a clear mirror does (4/32). Oshima (1983, 78) aptly calls attention to how the sage's relationship to *dao* parallels the mirror's association with light.

7 The "Great Connection" could be an alternative way of alluding to the all-encompassing "Great *Dao* (*da dao*, 大道)" of the cosmos, since the two phrases are linked conceptually: whereas "*dao*" refers to a path or way, "*tong*" can refer to connecting things by means of some path. Elsewhere, *Zhuangzi* writings refer to *Dao* as "connecting (*tong*) things as one" (2/35) and to the agent "connecting (*tong*) with *Dao*" (13/64) or "connecting (*tong*) with what creates things" (19/12).

8 For analytic characterizations of "flow," see Csikszentmihalyi (1990, 49) and Nakamura and Csikszentmihalyi (2009, 195–196).

9 I thank the editors of this volume, JeeLoo Liu and Douglas Berger, for helpful comments on an earlier draft.

15 Embodying Nothingness and the Ideal of the Affectless Sage in Daoist Philosophy

Alan K. L. Chan

Introduction

The concept of "nothingness (*wu*, 無)" forms a central thread in Daoist philosophy. At the ethical level, which encompasses spirituality in this context, it translates into a vision of an ideal "sage (*sheng ren*, 聖人)" who "embodies nothingness (*ti wu*, 體無)" in his being and as such is "without affects (*wu qing*, 無情)." This seems to distinguish the Daoist conception of the sage sharply from that of Confucian philosophy. However, just as there are competing views of the sage in the Confucian tradition, notwithstanding family resemblances, the embodiment of nothingness and the nature of the sage find diverse interpretation in the equally contested Daoist hermeneutic landscape.

Indeed, this is only to be expected. Terms like Daoism and Confucianism are abstractions; while they pick out certain perceived commonalities, they do not imply a tradition that is hermeneutically uniform or monolithic. The question of the affectless sage is central to the Daoist imagination. From its first appearance prior to the founding of the Qin dynasty in 221 BCE, it draws successive generations of scholars into the world of Daoist learning and compels fresh hermeneutic engagement. The construal of the sage, in other words, affords insight into an important facet of the dynamic development of Daoist philosophy. From Laozi and Zhuangzi to the *Xuanxue* movement—"Learning of the Profound," or "Neo-Daoism" as the term is often translated—in the Wei-Jin period from the third to the fifth century CE, the main lines of interpretation emerged. This will form the focus of the present discussion, although I will conclude with some observations on later developments in both Daoist and Confucian philosophy.

Hermeneutics of Nothingness and the Problem of Desire

The concept of *wu* features prominently in the *Laozi* and the *Zhuangzi*, and through them, though there were of course other contributors, it came to represent a major theme in Daoist philosophy. The graph *wu* appears over one hundred times in the current *Laozi*. Not all of the occurrences are philosophically significant—*wu* is a common word of negation meaning, most basically, "not having" something; for example, the phrase "*wu dao*" in Chapter 46 of the current 81-chapter version of the *Laozi* means simply "there is no *dao*." But some occurrences are significant. In particular, Chapter 40 of the *Laozi* states: "All things in the world are born of something (*you*, 有); something is born of nothing (*wu*)."[1]

The fact that this statement is found in all the excavated or recovered early texts of the *Laozi*—that is, the Guodian version, the Mawangdui version, and the recently published *Laozi* bamboo slips in the collection of Peking University—suggests that it formed a part of the text from an early stage.[2] What it means, however, cannot but invite interpretation and debate. In English, *wu* has been translated variously as "nothing," "nothingness," and "non-being," to cite but the more common ones, each of which reflects a particular reading of the *Laozi*.

While the concept of *wu* may be interpreted differently, there is no disagreement that it serves to explain the concept of *Dao*, the "Way," which in Daoist philosophy opens up a fertile semantic field, including the sense that *Dao* represents the "beginning" of all things. In this context, the more intuitive reading probably would be a cosmological one, taking *Dao* as a formless and therefore nameless source of generative power that engenders the yin and yang *qi* 氣, the energy-like substance that constitutes "heaven and earth" and all beings.[3] *Dao* is "something undifferentiated and complete," as the *Laozi* also intimates (Chapter 25). As such, although one might call it "*Dao*" in view of the suggestiveness of the term, technically nothing can be said about it and in that sense, it can be said to be *wu* or "nothing."

However, it is also possible that *wu* seeks to convey a sense of radical transcendence; that is, not just the absence of discernible characteristics or properties of being, but not being at all. Such noun phrases as "no-thing (*wu-wu*, 無物)" (Chapter 14) and "that which does not have any limit (*wu ji*, 無極)" (Chapter 28) found in the *Laozi* can easily be seen to lend support to this view. In this sense, *wu* does not refer to a formless and nameless something but rather absolute nothingness. It is a metaphysical concept. These readings are familiar to students of the *Laozi*. The point here is not to adjudicate between them, but to see how they inform interpretations of the sage in the subsequent unfolding of Daoist philosophy.

At the ethical level, the concept of *wu* finds expression in a mode of being characterized by the absence of desire (*wu yu*, 無欲) and the absence of active striving (*wu wei*, 無為). These are negative descriptions, though they assert positive outcomes. Positively, the *Laozi* emphasizes quietude and simplicity. This seems to be the concrete meaning of "embodying nothingness." Yet the text also seems to allow a more radical reading, as suggesting a state of mystical oneness with a transcendent *Dao*. In either case, *wu* at the ethical level presupposes the view that many of the most troubling problems confronting the world can be traced to a desire-driven mode of being.

These themes figure prominently also in the *Zhuangzi*, where we find clearer hermeneutic directions. Human beings are born with certain affective interests and the capacity to generate emotions in response to phenomena. This is constitutive of human "nature (*xing*, 性)," which is seen to have been endowed naturally by "heaven." Problems arise when desire becomes rampant or excessive and comes to dominate the "heart-mind (*xin*, 心),"—literally "heart," but understood as the seat of both cognitive and affective functions—and harm one's nature. How does desire work and what is the solution?

The *Liji* (*Records of Rites*) defines *yu* 欲, desire, as the movement of *xing*-nature when aroused by things.[4] This may be regarded as a baseline reference in the history of Chinese philosophy. The concept of *xing* describes generally the constitution and predispositions of human beings, whereas operationally it is the heart-mind that activates the affective interest and capacity that is inherent in human nature. As the heart-mind comes into contact with phenomena through the senses, its affective capacity, or *qing* 情, is aroused, and through the movement of *yu*-desire, gives rise to the various differentiated affective responses, from sensations such as cold and hunger to higher-order emotional states such as pleasure and anger involving cognitive function.[5]

More specifically, there is some consensus in the early literature that human beings are essentially constituted by *qi*-energies. Breath is a basic meaning of *qi*. The blood that courses through one's body, the internal organs, the workings of the body as a whole, and the natural endowments of each person—these are all made up of and powered by *qi*. At a basic level, this reflects but a general understanding of the life process. As the *Zhuangzi* puts it, "The coming to be of a person is a matter of the amassing of *qi*."[6] The *Laozi* also explains that when "the heart-mind exercises its *qi*—this is what is called assertion" (Chapter 55). The word translated here as "assertion (*qiang*, 強)" also connotes strength and the application of force or even violence, and it is usually so translated; but in this context the critical point is to realize how the heart-mind's exercise of *qi* results in self-assertion, which in the eyes of the mundane world may represent a sign of strength, but in reality, according to the *Laozi*, can only lead to self-exhaustion and bring violence, both in language and in action, to other human beings and the environment. In any event, it should be easy to see how willful or reckless expenditure of *qi* could ruin both mental and physical health.

Coming back to the problem of desire, when the heart-mind comes into contact with external stimuli, it rouses and becomes animated, which is to say that its *qi*-based affective *qing*-capacity is set in motion. The movement of that arousal is what is meant by *yu* (desire), as the *qi* of the heart-mind charges in a certain direction, which leads to the subject's "liking (*hao*, 好)" or "disliking (*wu*, 惡)" certain things, and which in turn generates the differentiated emotions such as pleasure and anger, depending on whether the liking or disliking is satisfied. The differentiated emotions are also collectively designated by the term *qing*, and sometimes the word *yu* may also reference particular desires. Nevertheless, it is important to pinpoint their precise philosophical meaning. In this philosophical framework, although there may be different views about the predispositions of *xing*-nature, the heart-mind is always in motion, animated by *qi* and interacting constantly with the world. Being alive, put simply, means that the heart-mind is always moving and is moved by external influences. As such, the possibility of excessive desire must also be recognized. As a solution, for example, the *Mencius* puts forth the idea of "a heart-mind that cannot be moved (*budong xin*, 不動心)," on the strength of its moral focus (see especially *Mencius* 2A.2, Yang 1984). What is the Daoist position and that of the *Zhuangzi* in particular?

Relying on rituals or other external controls to curb one's desire may work, but it is obviously not the Daoist response. On the *Liji* passage cited above, the Han scholar ZHENG Xuan (127–200 CE) comments that if *xing*-nature does not come into contact with things, there would not be any desire (*Liji zhengyi* 1963, 37.3a). This, too, does not seem to be what the *Zhuangzi* is getting at, if it involves artificial effort in cutting off contact with the world. In a separate study (Chan 2009), I have argued that two lines of argument in response to the problem of desire can be discerned in the *Zhuangzi*, even within the so-called "inner chapters," that is, Chapters 1–7, often traced to the historic Zhuangzi. Both center on the idea of an ideal sage who is "affectless," *wu qing*. However, they present a different understanding of *wu qing*, which I will only summarize briefly here.

The first type of argument focuses on the ideal of abiding by or realizing the "true" state of one's nature, which includes the naturally endowed capacity to generate affective responses. Logically, this view will have to assume that one's inborn affectivity is inherently measured and in its pristine state not given to excesses; otherwise, abiding by one's true nature would have disastrous ethical consequences. As the *Liji* also states, prior to the arousal of desire, human beings are tranquil by virtue of their heaven-endowed nature (*Liji zhengyi* 1963, 37.3a). There is a cosmological dimension to this, as the ideal *qing*-state is seen to mirror the patterns of heaven. Unlike the common people, whose nature has been corrupted and whose heart-mind operates habitually on a high level of desire, the sage is simple and quiet. To use a crude analogy, the sage is like a car idling at ease, whereas the common people are constantly on a high-revving drive mode, which if unchecked would inevitably result in serious damage. In this sense, the *Zhuangzi* describes the sage as "having the form of a human being, but not having the affective responses of human beings" (Chapter 5; Guo 1985, 1: 217; cf. Watson 1968, 75).

Although the sage embodies nothingness, it is not the case that he lacks the capacity of *qing* to generate affective responses. Rather, his nature is such that the *yu*-desire movement of his heart-mind remains still; consequently the heart-mind is not overrun by the emotions. Thus, Zhuangzi also says that by the phrase *wu qing*, he means that the sage "does not let his liking and disliking harm his body on the inside" (Chapter 5; Guo 1985, 1: 221; cf. Watson 1968, 75). From this perspective, the important ethical point is that one should "pattern the *qing*-capacity of liking and disliking, and harmonize the measure of pleasure and anger" after the order of heaven. If one could accomplish this, then one would become free of the "burden (*lei*, 累)" of insatiable, ever-demanding desire (Chapter 31; Guo 1985, 4: 1031; cf. Watson 1968, 349). Outwardly, indeed, the sage may behave in ways that the mundane world would consider highly improper or even outrageously shocking, like celebrating at funerals. Inwardly, however, the heart-mind of the sage is always calm and at ease. There are many such examples in the *Zhuangzi*. This is one type of interpretation of the sage's embodying nothingness and being without affects.

The second line of argument offers a stronger reading of *wu qing* as the cessation of all affective activity. From this perspective, when the *Zhuangzi* describes the heart-mind of the sage as being like "dead ashes," it means exactly that.[7] It is not saying that the ashes are still smoldering imperceptibly, leaving open the possibility of their being reignited; rather, there is absolutely no fire at all. Only in this way can one speak of the mind of the sage as being like a clear mirror, which simply reflects the true nature of phenomena but does not respond to them.[8] Thus, when YAN Hui, Confucius' prized disciple, suggests that the sage follows the patterns of heaven in his heart but outwardly conforms to the ways of the world, Confucius (i.e., in Zhuangzi's portrayal) makes clear that even that seemingly exalted state falls far short of the ideal mark resulting from the "fasting of the heart-mind," because it still takes the heart-mind as the guide for being and action (Chapter 4; Guo 1985, 1: 143–145; Watson 1968, 57). As "Knowledge," the protagonist in another memorable *Zhuangzi* story, found out in his northward journey, the *Dao* can be found only in the mystic silence of the true sage (Chapter 22; Guo 1985, 3: 729; Watson 1968, 234). As Liezi also found out from his teacher, absolute transcendence is more than being in harmony with the patterns of heaven (Chapter 7; Guo 1985, 1: 297ff; Watson 1968, 94ff). The best exemplar of the ideal of embodying nothingness should be Hundun, a symbol of primordial chaos, whose total lack of sensory receptivity means that his heart-mind simply cannot be aroused.[9]

These two types of interpretation have their own internal logic and are not easily reconcilable. I believe they are both present throughout the current thirty-three chapters of the *Zhuangzi*, a composite work with different layers of material and points of editorial intervention. Once desire is recognized as problematic, *wu qing* comes into the ethical picture as a remedy. How it is to be interpreted would depend on the prior understanding of the concept of *wu* and the possibility of embodying it. In a general sense, of course *wu qing* can be rendered as "without emotions," but the point is to explain what that means, and there is more than one way of interpreting it in Daoist philosophy. During the Wei dynasty (220–265 CE), building on the early explorations in not only the *Laozi* and the *Zhuangzi* but also the *Yijing*, the question of embodying nothingness once more propelled fresh debate, in the so-called "Neo-Daoist" movement that dominated the intellectual scene of early imperial China.

Nothingness and the Nature of the Sage

The term "Neo-Daoism" is perhaps not quite apt, because the movement, known as *Xuanxue* in Chinese sources, is not about reviving any particular school of thought but rather aims at disclosing the "mystery (*xuan*, 玄)" of *Dao*, by reinterpreting the entire tradition of classical learning. Profoundly deep and in that sense "dark," as the word *xuan* literally suggests, the concept of *Dao* does not belong to any one school but represents the supreme discernment of sages past. Not reducible to anything and yet responsible for everything, this is the mystery of *Dao*. At the ethical level, it became increasingly apparent that embodying *Dao* in one's being, which is the hallmark of the ideal sage, cannot be understood apart from one's endowed nature. Is it possible to learn to embody nothingness and be free from the dictates of desire? Is it possible, indeed, to become a sage? A key figure in this development is He Yan (d. 249 CE), one of the most influential thinkers of the third century.

According to the *Sanguo zhi* (*Records of the Three States*), "He Yan believed that the sage does not have pleasure and anger, or sorrow and joy; his arguments are very cogent" (1982, *juan* 28, 795n1). The sage embodies *Dao*; *Dao* is defined in terms of *wu*, and the embodiment of nothingness manifests itself as *wu qing*. While the logic seems clear, in what sense can the sage be said to be without emotions? Fundamentally, for He Yan, the sage is endowed with a special inborn nature that precludes the possibility of affective disturbance.

Human beings may be endowed with a nature of different "grades (*pin*, 品)." This view has a long history and can be traced to the *Laozi*, Confucius and other pre-Qin philosophers. It is usually understood in terms of the quantity and especially quality of *qi* that a person is endowed with, which accounts for his or her physical, intellectual, affective, and moral capacities. What requires further explanation is whether such differences are of kind or degree. In He Yan's "Discourse on *Dao*" (*Dao lun*), he explicitly defines *Dao* in terms of its "completeness (*quan*, 全)."[10] On this view, the sage is able to embody *Dao* in his being by virtue of his special nature, which is categorically different from that of the ordinary person. Formed by exceptionally pure and abundant *qi*, the inborn sage nature is marked by perfect "harmony (*zhonghe*, 中和)," which mirrors the complete and undifferentiated nature of *Dao*. As such, when He Yan argues that the sage "does not have" (*wu*), or does not experience, pleasure and anger, sorrow and joy and by extension other emotions, he is not saying that the sage is *wu qing* in the sense of lacking in affective capacity. The sage is perfectly endowed and thus not lacking in any way; however, because the nature of the sage is undifferentiated and complete, it does not generate differentiated emotions in response to external stimuli. The concept of harmony in this sense is better understood as having been derived from insight into the art of cooking, pointing to a state in which all the ingredients are perfectly blended and thus indistinguishable, as opposed to a musical reading of harmony in which the lead note and the complementing sounds, while performing in unison, remain distinct. These two interpretations of harmony can both be found in Chinese philosophy (see Chan 2011).

From this perspective, the nothingness of *Dao* should not be taken to mean pure absence, but rather boundless presence beyond description. Put differently, the nothingness of *Dao* reflects but the fullness of *qi*. However, it is difficult to imagine how this conception of ideal harmony would be embodied in actual ethical practice, except that absolute impartiality would be a characteristic of the sage, reflecting his special nature marked by undifferentiated completeness. Perhaps the being of the extraordinary sage—whose "virtue," to quote a common refrain in the Chinese philosophical literature, "merges with that of heaven and earth"—points to a mystical state. Be that as it may, because on this view sages are born rather than made, full embodiment of *Dao* and thus nothingness in the sense of perfect harmony remains beyond the reach of the common people. In this context, HE Yan declares provocatively, "*Dao* cannot be embodied."[11]

It is not possible to achieve "sagehood" through learning or practice if "sageness" is defined in terms of an inborn sage nature. Such sages are extremely rare, and to HE Yan and many of his contemporaries, Confucius was the last great sage. There is a sense in which the sage has been promoted upstairs, so to speak, in the ethical arena, so much so the ideal has become largely irrelevant. Theoretically, it is of course possible that a true sage may arise, and there were sages who ruled the world under heaven in the past, but in the "real" world, it is the "near-sages" or "great worthies" who provide an achievable ethical model. A classic example would be YAN Hui, who according to HE Yan (1963) is "close to the way of the sage" (commentary to *Lunyu* 6.3 and 11.19, 51–52, 112) and whose *qing* (affective) responses are never excessive and always accord with the patterns of heaven. For such individuals, while they are not without emotions, they are unaffected by them; their heart-mind is always tranquil and they are therefore able to make impartial judgments and serve as a guide for the people. One might learn to become like YAN Hui, or if even such near-sages and worthies are beyond reach because they, too, are blessed with an uncommonly fine nature, then the argument would follow that these gifted individuals should be entrusted with the task of governing the people, and that the latter should be made to submit to them.

HE Yan's view drew a strong critique from WANG Bi, his junior contemporary and one of the most important *Laozi* and *Yijing* commentators in Chinese history. WANG Bi counters that the sage is the same as everyone else in having differentiated emotions such as pleasure and anger, and is different only in his "spiritual luminosity (*shen ming*, 神明)" (*Sanguo zhi* 1982, 28, 795n1).

To WANG Bi, the difference between the sage and the common people cannot be traced to inborn nature. The capacity to generate distinct emotions is part of human nature and common to all. The sage is no different in that respect, but the heart-mind of the sage is pervaded by a spiritual luminosity, which translates into a profound perspicacity, allowing him to rise above the clamoring calls of desire. On this basis, the sage could therefore respond to things without being burdened by them, thereby attaining nothingness in the sense of being without self-interest or partiality. This is how the sage embodies harmony (*Sanguo zhi* 1982, 28, 795n1).[12] Unless one assumes that *shen ming* is also inborn, forming a part of the nature of a select few, one must conclude that it is a heightened state of the heart-mind to be attained or recovered. On this view, the possibility of becoming a sage through self-cultivation must also be affirmed.

Commenting on the *Analects* (*Lunyu*), Wang Bi also seems to take the position that *Dao* cannot be embodied (7.6; Lou 1980, 624). However, Wang's point is that "*Dao*" is but "the designation of *wu*," and as such must not be taken to signify anything with form or substance—not even an original undifferentiated life-forming stuff that does not have specific form itself and therefore cannot be named. Literally, there is *nothing* to embody. The concept of *wu*, on this view, points rather to a radical "otherness" or transcendence as the conceptual ground of being, for being ultimately cannot engender itself and thus can only be accounted for philosophically by its "other," or "not-being."

However, in another sense Wang also asserts that "the sage embodies nothingness" (*sheng ren ti wu*) (*Sanguo zhi* 1982, 28, 795n1). Because *Dao* does not have any referent, the possibility of embodying *Dao* leading to the state of spiritual luminosity (*shen ming*) cannot be traced to an external source. Wang Bi also emphasizes that the *Laozi* defines *Dao* in terms of "naturalness" or more precisely, what is "self-so (*ziran*, 自然)," which should be understood properly as a term for the "ultimate" or "that which has no designation" (Lou 1980, 65, commentary to *Laozi* 25). Without going into details here, suffice it to say that the emphasis on *ziran* signals an inward turn and points to an assumed originally pristine nature that is tranquil and simple, not burdened by the excessive movement of desire. Recovering the *xing* that is naturally so (*ziran zhi xing*) or the "authenticity (*zhen*, 真)" of being (e.g., commentary to *Laozi* 16, 28, 32) is thus vital to realizing spiritual luminosity. On this basis, Wang Bi argues that so long as the affective activity of the heart-mind conforms to the pristine nature (*xing qi qing*, 性其情), it would naturally find the right measure, reflecting the tendency of *xing* toward stillness (Lou 1980, 631–632, commentary to *Lunyu* 17.2). This is the concrete meaning of embodying nothingness. In this same sense, Wang Bi also emphasizes the need to "honor the root and calm the branches."[13]

From the perspective of philosophical hermeneutics, interpretation is always guided by certain lead insights and bound by the rules of coherence. The conception of the ideal sage in He Yan and Wang Bi rests on their prior understanding of the meaning of *Dao* as *wu*. On the one hand, if one takes nothingness in the context of the genesis of *qi*, one would more readily arrive at a view of the sage as being privileged by a special inborn sage nature. This would in turn shape one's understanding of the place of affectivity in the nature of the sage. This is the interpretive path that He Yan seems to have taken. On the other hand, if one takes *wu* conceptually as "not being," not any formless and nameless generative force but a logically necessary ground for being-as-such, the embodiment of nothingness can only be located within an imagined pristine inborn nature that is common to all. This seems to be Wang Bi's position, which shares certain features, albeit with greater philosophical clarity, with one of the interpretations in the *Zhuangzi* outlined above.

Xuanxue scholars were adept in argumentation. In attempting to lay bare the mystery of *Dao*, they engaged in rigorous debates that brought to the fore some of the most fundamental questions in Chinese philosophy: Are there different "grades" of human nature? Can sagehood be attained? What is the relationship between human nature and capacity? How can the constant emotional disturbances of the heart-mind be overcome? When placed in a philosophical framework of *Dao* as *wu*, these issues would then shape the interpretation of the ideal sage as embodying nothingness and being free from the burden of desire and emotions in a state of *wu qing*. During the Wei-Jin era, these questions came into sharper focus and there was yet another interpretation of the affectless sage that proved particularly influential in the subsequent development of Daoist philosophy. This has to do with the idea that the sage is oblivious to, or "forgets," the emotions (*wang qing*, 忘情).

Embracing Nothingness in Affective Oblivion

Although in some contexts the word *wang* may figure in the basic sense of *wu* as "not having," it represents a unique approach to the question of embodying nothingness in Daoist philosophy. The fifth-century work *Shishuo xinyu* (*New Accounts of Tales of the World*) reports that when WANG Rong's (234–305 CE) son died, he was inconsolable. When someone questioned whether his grief was excessive, WANG Rong replied,

> Sages are oblivious to their emotions (*sheng ren wang qing*). People of the lowest kind are incapable of having (genuine, heart-felt) emotions. It is precisely in people like us that intense emotions find their place. (*Shishuo xinyu* 17.4, in Xu 1987, 349; cf. Mather 1976, 324)

Elsewhere, the *Shishuo xinyu* (2.51) relates that GU He (288–351 CE) took his two grandsons, ZHANG Xuanzhi and GU Fu, to visit a Buddhist temple in which there was a visual representation of the Buddha entering into *nirvana* attended by his disciples. GU He asked the two boys why some of the disciples were weeping and some were not. Whereas Zhang ventured that those who were crying must have been favored by the Buddha, GU Fu saw a deeper reason: "This must have been because some of the disciples had forgotten their emotions and thus they did not weep; the others could not forget their emotions and thus they were weeping" (Xu 1987, 61; cf. Mather 1976, 55). These examples indicate the prevalence of this interpretation in early medieval China. The idea of Daoist oblivion is already present in the *Zhuangzi*, and not surprisingly this view finds eloquent support in GUO Xiang (d. 312 CE), arguably the greatest *Zhuangzi* commentator in Chinese history.

It should be clear that this kind of oblivion or "forgetfulness" is entirely natural and does not involve any deliberate or suppressive effort. For GUO Xiang, the "person of ultimate attainment (*zhi ren*, 至人)," which is another way of describing the sage, is indeed *wu qing*, without affects,[14] but this cannot be explained in terms of a special nature characterized by undifferentiated harmony as HE Yan does. GUO Xiang does recognize that human beings are born with different *qi* endowments, and as such the possibility of a few individuals like Confucius, the sage par excellence, being endowed with a perfect sage nature must be admitted (e.g., see Guo 1985, 1: 13, 194, commentary to *Zhuangzi*, Chapters 1 and 5). However, this does not preclude the possibility of those who are less favorably endowed reaching full self-realization. Whatever the *qi* endowment, a person's inborn nature is complete in and for itself and has the capacity to attain spiritual enlightenment. As is well known, for Guo Xiang, the term "sage" means fundamentally someone who has fully realized his nature (Guo 1985, 1: 22, commentary to *Zhuangzi* 1). What, then, does *wu qing* mean in this context?

Guo Xiang could have followed Wang Bi's approach in emphasizing the authenticity of being. However, he was critical of Wang Bi's understanding of *Dao* as *wu*, arguing that it remains an abstract concept and cannot bring to light the processes of "transformation (*hua*, 化)" that constitute the Daoist world (Guo 1985, 1: 50, commentary to *Zhuangzi* 2). Rather than assuming a pristine nature that naturally gravitates toward stillness, as Wang Bi does, Guo Xiang focuses on the workings of *qing* as rooted in judgments. Sorrow and joy, for example, are born of one's sense of "loss and gain," respectively (Guo 1985, 1: 129, commentary to *Zhuangzi* 3). More generally, differentiated emotions are derived from one's liking or disliking certain things, which in turn arise from self-interest. The calculus of gain and loss is further traced to judgments of what is "right (*shi*, 是)" or "wrong (*fei*, 非)" for oneself. Regarding those who do not harbor judgments of right and wrong, and therefore do not have likes and dislikes, Guo Xiang says, though they are human in every way, their heart-mind is never ruled by the emotions (Guo 1985, 1: 222, commentary to *Zhuangzi* 5). In this sense, they can be said to embody the nothingness (*wu*) of *Dao*.

Wu qing in this interpretive framework does not hinge on the absence of affective activity. The argument is rather that once the discriminating function of the heart-mind comes to rest, the affective life will no longer be a source of ethical problems. In other words, the affective function remains intact, but the responses that issue from a calm and pacified heart-mind are qualitatively different from the emotions experienced by ordinary people. In the state of *wu qing*, as Guo Xiang puts it, one rests in utmost "equanimity (*ping*, 平)" (Guo 1985, 1: 215, commentary to *Zhuangzi* 5). In this sense, Guo Xiang also speaks of the "*qing of wu qing*," "affectless affects" or less awkwardly, the affective life stemming from a heart-mind that is oblivious to external influences, cannot be aroused and is consequently not driven by the sway of emotions (Guo 1985, 1: 247, commentary to *Zhuangzi* 6).

The heart-mind of the sage may indeed be likened to "dead ashes," but this does not entail eradication of *qing* in the sense of affective capacity. To Guo Xiang, what Zhuangzi means is that if one fully realizes one's inborn nature, one would be able to become oblivious to all *shi-fei* judgments, understood as self-interested right and wrong distinctions (Guo 1985, 1: 44, commentary to *Zhuangzi* 2). Whereas a mystical reading may arrive at a position in which all judgments are extinguished, what is postulated here is that when free from the burden of desire, the heart-mind, like a clear mirror, would then be able to discern the "true" *shi-fei* of things and affairs. It is futile and foolish to try to emulate someone else, even when that someone is a sage, or to impose a single standard on the multitude. When one understands the relativity of self-interested judgments, one comes to abide by one's own nature.

Like WANG Bi, GUO Xiang seems concerned with the exclusivity of HE Yan's thesis, given that it closes all avenues to attaining sagehood. Nevertheless, he would concur with HE Yan, and for that matter the majority of *Xuanxue* scholars, that sages like Confucius must have received a special *qi* endowment that made them incomparably superior. Mediating between these positions, GUO Xiang argues that the immutability of *xing*-nature and the attainability of sagehood are not mutually exclusive. The way to sagehood, to embodying *Dao* in one's being, is not to reduce diversity to unity, as WANG Bi seems to have done, but to understand the processes of transformation and consequently realize the futility of self-serving judgments, thereby becoming oblivious to desire and attaining equanimity. There is perhaps a keener appreciation of the power of enlightened consciousness in GUO Xiang, when compared with HE Yan and WANG Bi.

Later Reverberations

The argument that one can be oblivious to desire and that there is a totally equanimous "*qing* of *wu qing*," an affectivity that is not driven by self-interest, is not an easy one to make. At first glance, it seems akin to asserting that there can be an "X that is not X." But there is a hermeneutical reason for GUO Xiang to pursue this more complex interpretive course; otherwise, to him certain questions about the sage's ability to embody the nothingness of *Dao* cannot be answered. The views of HE Yan, WANG Bi, and GUO Xiang crisscross at certain points, but they each reflect careful critical deliberation and hermeneutical sensitivity. I will conclude with a brief analysis of how this same issue is addressed by the Tang Daoist thinker WU Yun (d. 778 CE), and the Neo-Confucian scholar CHENG Hao (1032–1085 CE).

WU Yun is a major figure in Tang dynasty Daoism. In his *Shenxian kexue lun* (*Discourse Affirming the Possibility of Becoming a Divine Immortal*), Wu acknowledges that there are individuals who attained the state of the perfected, which meant ascending to the rank of "immortals (*xian*, 仙)" in the religious Daoist belief system at that time, not on account of their learning and practice, but because they have been allotted an extraordinary *qi* endowment. However, he also recognizes that there are others, indeed the majority, who must first devote themselves to spiritual cultivation before they can achieve that goal.[15] In another essay, *Xingshen kegu lun* (*Discourse Affirming the Possibility of Rendering the Body and Spirit Perfectly Firm*), WU Yun argues that in principle, human beings should enjoy everlasting life, because like heaven and earth they, too, come to be through the transformation of the "one *qi*" that engendered the cosmos (1992, 19). However, desire and the resultant affective disturbances get in the way. As Wu states in his major work, *Xuangang lun* (*Discourse on the Principal Features of the Profound Mystery of Dao*), "That which gives me life is *Dao*, and that which extinguishes my life is *qing*."[16]

The argument thus far seems straightforward enough, but the idea of *wu qing* as the implied solution needs explication. For Wu Yun, like Guo Xiang before him, *wu qing* cannot mean simply the cessation of all affective activity. This is because of the basic premise that immortality, which is a mark of transcendence, can be learned and achieved by the common people. If the focus is on the exceptional few who are born with a special affectless nature, and if it is assumed that immortality cannot be taught, not much needs to be said except to offer homage to them. For these exceptional individuals, categorically different from the common people, perfect being is an expression of their nature, and *wu qing* could presumably mean complete absence of affectivity. But if the concern is with the majority, whose nature necessarily involves affectivity, and if the possibility of embodying *Dao* is to be affirmed, then Wu Yun would have to reconcile the emphasis on stillness in Daoist teachings with the pervasive influence of *qing* in human affairs.

On the one hand, like Wang Bi, Wu affirms that human nature is modeled after *Dao* and is in its root form not burdened by desire (XL 7, 25). On the other hand, he must also acknowledge that affectivity forms an integral part of *xing*-nature; in fact, Wu defines *qing*, the inborn affective capacity to generate emotions, simply as the movement of *xing* (XL 5). Although the arousal of affectivity will inevitably upset the stability of *xing*, it cannot be argued that the Daoist remedy lies in cutting off the capacity of *qing*. This is because the workings of *xing* and *qing* is ultimately a function of *qi*. Cutting off *qing* would amount to extinguishing the flow of *qi*, which spells the end of life itself. What is envisioned, rather, is an ideal state in which "the heart-mind is quiet and *qi* moves about" smoothly and calmly (XL 6), or "the body is active but the mind is quiet." This is also what Wu describes as the ideal mode of being in which "*qing* is forgotten" (XL 15).

In principle, the stillness of inborn nature entails a state of equilibrium in one's internal *qi*-operations, and this equilibrium predisposes the heart-mind to function in repose. However, the heart-mind naturally responds to phenomena. How does one preserve the stillness and tranquility of the heart-mind? As Wu observes, one must not allow even "small pleasure and anger, and (assertions of) right and wrong, and what is acceptable and what is not. These are the constant affective manifestations of human beings, and they are extremely difficult to guard against" (XL 18). Forceful suppression of desire, by means of asceticism for example, may be ruled out (XL 13). The *Xuangang lun* also dismisses ritual and worship as ineffective and counterproductive in this context (XL 20). The way to embodying nothingness through sagely forgetfulness lies rather in "training in quietude (*xi jing*, 習靜)" (XL 25), which encompasses both ethical and spiritual practices. This is a large topic, and Wu Yun is well known for his contribution to establishing "inner alchemy (*nei dan*, 內丹)," which includes complex meditative practices, as the mainstream in Daoist practice, but for this discussion it is sufficient to outline the logic of his argument. Training in quietude, in the final analysis, should lead to "utmost understanding (*zhi ming*, 至明)" (XL 15). The emphasis on intellectual discernment calls to mind Guo Xiang's approach to the question of embodying nothingness and the affectless sage.

The last point I would like to make is that embodying nothingness is not a partisan Daoist problem, but one that permeates the entire spectrum of Chinese philosophy. Confucian scholars, too, were keen to bring to light the mystery of the affectless sage, although they may not employ the language of nothingness. For most Confucians, meaning and value reside in a relational universe; the presence of affectivity is required to explain filial affection and humaneness, and to assure right and timely responses to the affairs of the world. Though desire and emotions are a potential ethical liability, an affective harmony may be brought about by rites and music, as well as Confucian learning at large. This is a powerful vision. Nevertheless, Confucian scholars must also address the nature of the sage, the attainability of sagehood, and other related issues, which would compel them to account for the role of *qing*.

The Tang scholar Li Ao (ca. 774–836) offers a good example in this regard. In his *Fuxing shu* (*Essay on Returning to Original Nature*), like Wu Yun, Li Ao labors to explain the seemingly contradictory proposition that "although (the sage) has *qing*, he actually never has *qing*" (1990, 1.3b, 2850).[17] While a fuller discussion cannot be offered due to space constraints, Li's point is that although the sage has the capacity of *qing* to generate affective responses, he does not suffer the experience of being burdened by *qing* in the sense of affects linked to likes and dislikes.

The influential Neo-Confucian thinker Cheng Hao took up the same issue in his *Dingxing shu* (*Essay on Stilling One's Nature*). Cheng Hao's main thesis is that the sage may be likened to "heaven and earth": "Now, it is the constancy of heaven and earth that they use their heart-mind to benefit all things but are without self-interest or partiality (*wu xin*, 無心); (in the same way) it is the constancy of the sage that he uses his *qing* to enable the flourishing of all things but is without *qing*" (Huang 1966, 319). The claim that heaven and earth "use" or effect change with their "heart-mind" sounds jarring to the modern ear, but the translation here seeks to preserve the parallelism in the original. Is Cheng Hao thinking of a special inborn "harmonious" sage nature that is undifferentiated and complete; is he appealing to a universal authentic nature that is inherently still; or is he arguing for a kind of profound understanding of the workings of *qing* that would free the sage from all self-referential "right and wrong" distinctions?

Human beings are unable to abide by *Dao* because their *qing* are clouded, Cheng Hao next observes. Concentrating their intellectual capacity on self-gain, they are unable to discern the true state of things and affairs. To reverse this is the task of stilling one's nature. However, this is not to say that one should devote oneself exclusively to cultivating the inner realm of the heart-mind. "Rather than repudiating the external and affirming the internal, it would be far better to forget both the internal and the external," CHENG Hao writes (Huang 1966, 319). Once they are both "forgotten"—that is, no longer a factor in the operation of the heart-mind—the heart-mind would no longer be troubled by any stirring of desire or external influences, as if a veil has been lifted. Without self-interest, the heart-mind becomes still. In stillness, the heart-mind becomes illuminated and perspicacious (*ming*). With such clarity, there should be no concern that the heart-mind would become burdened by things when it responds to them.

The pleasure and anger of the sage, CHENG Hao continues, invariably accord with what ought to be the case. The sage's emotions have nothing to do with self-interest and thus do not deceive or manipulate. Yet, how can one be sure that one is responding to phenomena in the right way? Anger is quick to rise and difficult to control, CHENG Hao recognizes. What is needed is that one "forgets" one's anger at the point when it arises and examines the principles of the case, the reasons that caused the heart-mind to stir in anger. The sage thus certainly experiences emotions, but in discerning the rightness of things he responds in impartiality and is in this sense, *wu qing*. Though only an outline can be given here, in emphasizing not only the need to rectify one's heart-mind but also discern the objective principles of things, CHENG Hao seeks to provide a clearer account of the problem of desire than the views previously discussed in this chapter.

The idea that the sage embodies *Dao* in his being furnishes a powerful vision and guides the development of Daoist philosophy. Once it is assumed that *Dao* can only be understood as *wu*, the possibility of embodying nothingness comes to define the Daoist hermeneutical agenda. The question gains sharper focus in the ideal of a mode of being free from the burden of desire. While the total absence or cessation of affectivity may be in some sense an easier argument to make—the sage is special, like Hundun, and that's all—it is for good reason that the majority of Daoist philosophers focus on a heart-mind that is capable of generating *qing*-responses and yet not ruled by the emotions. Although the concept of nothingness does not feature in any significant way in Confucian discourse, it is clear that the question of *wu qing* equally informs the Confucian interpretive horizon.

There are other views as well. For example, the Jin dynasty (265–420 CE) recluse GUO Wen argues that emotions arise from memory, and so long as the latter is not exercised one would not be troubled by the former.[18] During the Tang dynasty, the scholar and poet LIU Mian (d. 805 CE) simply dismissed the whole idea that the sage is *wu qing*, for *qing* is part and parcel of heaven's order and both "sages and worthies are within the realm of *qing*." The sage never "forgets" his emotions; one only needs to think of Confucius's heartfelt grief when YAN Hui died.[19] Nevertheless, the issue for many Daoist and Confucian thinkers, as this chapter hopes to have shown, remains not so much the sage's affective capacity, which should be recognized, as the nature of the sage's affective responses. In different ways, notwithstanding the similar language and certain assumptions such as the role of *qi* they share, they struggle to explain the meaning of *wu qing*, which is also to say that the concepts of nothingness and affectivity should not be reduced to any single interpretation. They are seminal ideas, which fuel the philosophical imagination and constantly invite fresh interpretation.

During the Jiajing period (1522–1566) of the Ming dynasty, HU Song (1503–1566) lectured on CHENG Hao's *Dingxing shu* in the Capital, which attracted an audience of over 5,000 (Huang 1966, 320). I mention this in closing not so much to highlight the influence of CHENG Hao's essay as to underscore the hermeneutical character of Chinese philosophy. HU Song had his own contribution to make, just as CHENG Hao did not simply "follow" WU Yun and other scholars before him in formulating an account of the ideal sage, especially with respect to the problem of desire. Although the nuances of their arguments cannot be fully captured in a short chapter, I hope it is nonetheless clear that regardless of their philosophical persuasion, whether they may be branded "Daoist" or "Confucian," they each had to come to terms with a host of interrelated questions about the sage ideal that already surfaced in the pre-Qin philosophical literature. Some of the ideas presented such as divine immortality may seem distant today, but there is little reason not to believe that the question of embodying nothingness and the affectivity of the sage will continue to play a critical role in contemporary Daoist and Confucian reflections. The idea of embodying nothingness seems to fly against conventional wisdom that tends to favor the full flowering of being, and the idea of *wu qing*, not having emotions, seems counterintuitive in a world that cherishes affection. Moreover, the envisioned clarity and equanimity of the heart-mind is not easy to explain, especially as ethics crosses into spirituality in the Chinese context. Nevertheless, the figure of the affectless sage strikes a powerful chord and no doubt will continue to resonate where the idea of transcendence still holds meaning. Perhaps more pertinent to the present discussion, the interpretation of the sage ideal should also provide useful insight into certain basic philosophical problems. In particular, the analysis of affectivity, especially the way in which affects and judgments are shown to form an integral whole, should be of some interest to contemporary discussions of ethics and moral psychology.

Notes

1 For a general introduction to the *Laozi*, see Kohn and LaFargue (1998). See also the chapters by Xiaogan Liu, Douglas Berger, and JeeLoo Liu in this volume. Quotations from the *Laozi* are based on the standard version that accompanies the commentary by WANG Bi (226–240 CE); translations are my own unless stated otherwise. Xiaogan Liu (2006) provides a comparison of five different versions of the *Laozi*, including the Mawangdui and Guodian versions. The two Mawangdui silk manuscripts of the *Laozi* were discovered in 1973, whereas the Guodian *Laozi* fragments written on bamboo slips were unearthed in 1993. The Guodian slips are generally dated to around 300 BCE, and the Mawangdui manuscripts, around 200 BCE. The article "Laozi" in the online *Stanford Encyclopedia of Philosophy* (Chan 2013) offers a general discussion of the textual traditions. Lau (1983) presents a useful bilingual edition, combining the author's earlier Penguin translation with a new translation based on the Mawangdui manuscripts. Readers unfamiliar with

the Daoist tradition may also consult the article on "Daoism" in the online *Oxford Bibliographies*.

Earlier generations of sinologists generally made use of the "Wade-Giles" system when transliterating Chinese terms, whereas the *Hanyu pinyin* system is preferred in more recent studies. The latter is used here, except for names and titles romanized in the former in the original.

I would like to thank JeeLoo Liu and Douglas Berger for their helpful comments on an earlier draft of this chapter.

2 There are minor variants in the wording, but they do not affect the interpretation of this statement. For a translation of the Mawangdui *Laozi*, see Lau (1983) and Henricks (1989). For the Guodian text, see Henricks (2000), and Ames and Hall (2003). The Peking University text is dated to the early Han dynasty, around 140 BCE, and was recovered from overseas. See Han (2012).

3 On the concept of *qi*, see Chapter 13 by JeeLou Liu in this volume.

4 *Liji*, "Yueji" (*Record of Music*), in *Liji zhengyi*, with commentary by KONG Yingda (574–648) (1963, 37.3a). The text reads: "Affected by things and stirring into motion, this is the (operation of) desire of human nature." References to the *Liji* are all taken from this edition.

5 The chapters in Eifring (2004) provide a helpful introduction to the concept of *qing*.

6 *Zhuangzi*, chapter 22; in *Zhuangzi jishi* (1985), edited by GUO Qingfan, 3: 733). All citations from the *Zhuangzi* are from this edition. Cf. Watson (1968, 235).

7 This metaphor appears in *Zhuangzi*, Chapters 2, 22, 23, and 24.

8 On this metaphor, see *Zhuangzi*, Chapters 7 and 13, and Chris Fraser's discussion in Chapter 14 of this volume.

9 *Zhuangzi*, Chapter 7; Guo (1985, 1: 309); Watson (1968, 97). The story of Hundun should suffice to make the point: his two friends, who appreciated the way in which Hundun treated them and wanted to repay him, reckoned that since Hundun did not have the seven sensory openings for seeing, hearing, eating and breathing like everyone else, they should create them for him. "Each day they bore one opening, and on the seventh day, Hundun died."

10 HE Yan's *Dao lun* is preserved in a quotation by the fourth-century scholar Zhang Zhan in his commentary to the *Liezi*; see YANG Bojun (1980, 10).

11 HE Yan 1963, 64; commentary to the *Lunyu* (*Analects*) 7.6. Though HE Yan was only one of the compilers of the commentary, it is generally accepted that his views are represented in the work. See Makeham (2003) for a study of this text.

12 The reference to harmony directly addresses HE Yan's concern. While there is no disagreement over the desired outcome, for WANG Bi it is not necessary to assume inborn sageness, which rules out the possibility of attaining sagehood.

13 For example, see WANG Bi, Commentary to *Laozi*, chapter 57, in Lou (1980, 149). This is a key theme in WANG Bi's *Laozi* commentary.

14 Commentary to *Zhuangzi*, Chapter 3, Guo 1985, 1: 128. Subsequent references to GUO Xiang's *Zhuangzi* commentary are all from this edition and will be cited in the text.

15 WU Yun, *Shenxian kexue lun*, in his collected works, *Zongxuan xiansheng wenji* (Shanghai, 1992), 13. All references to Wu' writings are from this edition. For a detailed study of WU Yun, see De Meyer (2006). The question whether one could learn to become an "immortal" (*xian*) also has a long history. The influential view of JI Kang (223–262 CE) that immortality cannot be achieved through effort but depends on an exceptionally endowed nature provides a backdrop to WU Yun's discourse. Though there are significant differences between the conception of the *xian*-immortal and that of the sage, they must equally confront the problem of desire and the meaning of *wu qing*.

16 *Xuangang lun*, section 7. This work is contained in Wu (1992, 36–48). It is divided into 33 short sections. For ease of reference, citations from this work, abbreviated "XL" hereafter, will be identified by their section number.

17 In Li Ao (1990), page 2850 appears after page 2908 due to a misprint). For a study and translation in English, see Barrett (1992).

18 This is reported in the *Jin shu*, *juan* 94 (Beijing, 1982), 2441. The *Sui shu* also mentions that during the Liang dynasty (502–556 CE), there was a "Discourse on the Sage's Not Having Emotions" (*Sheng ren wu qing lun*). Unfortunately, the work has not survived; see *Sui shu* 1982, *juan* 34, 1002.

19 See *Tang Wencui*, *juan* 84.3b (Shanghai: Shangwu, 1937), p. 1335.

16 Nothingness in Korean Buddhism

The Struggle against Nihilism

Halla Kim

Introduction

Around the turn of the fifteenth century, Korea witnessed an unusual and remarkable political upheaval during which there was a dynastic transition from Koryŏ (918–1392) to Chosŏn (1392–1910). This transition also represented a major shift in state ideology, a shift in which Neo-Confucianism replaced Buddhism as the leading political influence. Chŏng Tojŏn (1337–1398), a Neo-Confucian scholar and statesman who helped make this transition possible, says in his *Treatise against the Buddha* (*Pulssichappyon*)[1] as well as in *The Three Treatises on the Mind, Ki Force and the Principle* (*Simkiri sampyon*)[2] that Buddhism is fundamentally mistaken from the very outset. According to him, Buddhism, as a doctrinal thesis, necessarily falls into the trap of nothingness (*kong*, 空) because of its false depiction of the mind (*sim*, 心).[3] In a sequel to these works, Kwŏn Kŭn (1352–1409), a contemporary of Chŏng who was also a Confucian statesman, concurs that the kind of nihilism entailed in Buddhism is partially but decisively to blame for the downfall of the Korean society.[4] This anti-Buddhist view in fact echoes the sentiment of many leading literati in Korea at the time. It then appears that Neo-Confucian intellectuals in general conceived the notion of nothingness as an integral—and dangerous—part of the Buddhist tradition in Korea, and believed that this very notion would lead to the most severe form of nihilism.

In this article, I examine the notion of nothingness in the thought of Wŏnhyo (元曉 617–686 CE), Chinul (知訥 1158–1210 CE), and T'aego Pou (太古普愚 1301–1381 CE), three important Buddhist philosophers in Korea, and trace its historical development. I conclude that, even though the *Mādhyamaka* system of thought—the family of the view that *kong* (nothingness) is at the foundation of various phenomena—never took root in Korea as an independent school, its central notion of nothingness played a significant role in various schools of Buddhism, especially in Wŏnhyo's philosophy of interfusion and the *Sŏn* (Chan or Zen) philosophies of Chinul and T'aego Pou. In the process, it will be shown that nothingness thus conceived does not lead to nihilism. Rather, it is an active and dynamic principle that is at the heart of Buddhist practice. The ideas of these philosophers all show a strong tendency to overcome the nihilistic pitfalls of the principle of nothingness by way of promoting and engaging practices of various types.

Wŏnhyo

Even though Buddhism originally arose in India, and the concept of nothingness or emptiness is also found in early Buddhism, the form of Buddhism that made inroads to Korea in the fourth century was a highly sinicized form of Mahāyāna, the most emphatic expression of which can be found in Nāgārjuna's (now sinicized) doctrine of the middle path (*madhyamā-pratipad*). According to his masterpiece *Mūlamadhyamaka-kārikā*, all things are empty (*śūnya*), for they are devoid of intrinsic self-nature (*svabhāva*). They are thus impermanent because of the necessary lack of self-nature (*nihsvabhāva*).[5] Things are devoid of intrinsic self-nature because they causally depend on other things for their existence. This of course stems from the familiar Buddhist doctrine of interdependent arising. Nāgārjuna's suggestion, then, is that the nature of reality is the very absence of self-nature in all entities.[6] As a matter of fact, the concept of nothingness represents the middle path that we can take, steering clear of extremes. This is a development of the historical Buddha's original insight about enlightenment, which he saw as lying between the extremes of self-mortification and sensual indulgence. Nāgārjuna's view seems to be far from nihilistic, because it is emptiness or nothingness that makes possible the existence of all entities.[7] That these entities are empty does not mean that they don't really exist. On the contrary, it means that they exist as dependent-arising, without *svabhāva*. Nothingness in Nāgārjuna must then be another way of pointing to the Buddhist Middle Way between eternalism (i.e., the metaphysical belief in an eternal self) and annihilationism (the denial of the eternal self) but in a way that is more systematic.

Whereas the vast majority of his contemporary exegetes in China practiced doctrinal classification (判教), that is, the method of systematically ranking various Buddhist schools of thought, Wŏnhyo became known as a practitioner of something called "*hwajaeng* (和諍)" or "harmonization of disputes." Through *hwajaeng*, Wŏnhyo took the differing, even apparently conflicting, positions of various schools or masters, thoroughly investigated the presuppositions and motivations that they brought to their work, pinpointed the very source at which their variance occurred, and, finally, showed how, when these backgrounds were fully understood and elaborated, the Mahāyāna Buddhist system could still be seen as an integrated whole. It is an acknowledgment of this contribution that he was posthumously honored with the title of "National Master of the Harmonization of Disputes."[8]

In two of his major works, the *Autocommentary on the Awakening of Mahāyāna Faith* (hereafter *Autocommentary*) and the *Exposition of the Vajrasamadhi Sūtra* (hereafter *Exposition*), Wŏnhyo argued that One Mind (一心) is the ultimate nature of reality. One Mind is not only the source of all beings but it also permeates them. In this respect, it is no different from *tathatā* (suchness).

It is also called "original enlightenment (*pon'gak*, 本覺)." But this does not mean that all things have their own fixed nature. Rather, everything in the world can be characterized as nothingness (*śūnyatā*). As Wŏnhyo himself puts it in *First Division of Contemplation Practice of the Exposition*,

> All the characteristics of the mind originally have no origin and originally have no original focus; they are void and calm, producing nothing. If the mind produces nothing, it then accesses void calmness. At that ground of the mind (*cittabhumi*), where all is void and calm, one then attains nothingness of mind. . . . The characteristics of mind are originally unproduced; therefore, it says, "they are void and calm, producing nothing."[9]

Note that his remark is not to be understood purely negatively. In particular, it does not mean that nothing exists in the world. It rather means that all is empty or devoid of any distinct or permanent nature. This is also true of humans. As conscious beings who temporally participate in an ever-developing reality, we have our nature that may be viewed as participating in "acquired enlightenment (*sigak*, 始覺)."[10] This nature of ours can also be described as nothingness, but here that term expresses the possibility of liberating our minds from the shackles of the mundane, material world. As Wŏnhyo puts it in the *Exposition*, "when one who cultivates contemplation practice penetrates to the [nothingness], he emerges from existence and accesses nothingness."[11] Furthermore, when one "accesses nothingness, he also does not cling to the nature of nothingness; and, although he does not cling to nothingness, he also does not abandon nothingness."[12] In other words, Wŏnhyo in effect suggests that we can only fulfill nothingness when we are not preoccupied with it. Again, this nicely shows Wŏnhyo's way of steering the middle way between two extremes in the spirit of the early Buddhism.

Wŏnhyo's conception of nothingness is far from implying the attitude of despair and inaction entailed by nihilism. Simply because one obtains and realizes nothingness, one does not suddenly stop engaging in any practice. Calling this practice "the *samadhi* [i.e., concentration] of nothingness,"[13] Wŏnhyo claims that "[in] accessing nothingness, there are no remaining practices, but one also does not neglect any action."[14] What he means is that in contemplating nothingness, we are completely liberated from the shackles of the world yet without forsaking it. As Wŏnhyo puts it: "In accessing nothingness through the contemplation of principle, there are no remaining subjects or objects, one does not neglect the actions of the six perfections, etc."[15] Wŏnhyo even compares nothingness to "a superb medicine" as opposed to mundane "existence [which] instantly gives rise to disease."[16] In other words, he views our daily existence as a potential cause of our sufferings, and it is only through contemplating the nothingness of our existence that we can be liberated.

Wŏnhyo's conception of ultimate reality thus reveals the character of nothingness as the epitome of the middle path that Nāgārjuna, indeed, the Buddha himself, emphasized. In being all-encompassing, yet without forsaking various perspectives in the spirit of interfusion,[17] nothingness is neither absolute nor relative. Wŏnhyo's conception thus not only goes beyond the doctrine of the three treatises school, with its emphasis on the unconditioned and thus absolute nature of reality (historically represented by the Korean monk Sŭngnang, 450–520 CE), but also the Consciousness-Only school with its emphasis on the conditioned and subjective nature of reality (represented by the Korean-Chinese exegete Wŏnch'ŭk, 613–696 CE). Following the author of the *Awakening of Faith*, Wŏnhyo calls such an ultimate reality "One Mind (一心)."[18] It is now clear that for Wŏnhyo One Mind is neither a subject, nor an object, nor a mind, nor a body. It is a sublimated form of these pairs of opposites—it denies yet affirms both in a higher sense. Resorting to a passage in the *Vajrasamadhi Sūtra*, Wonhyo suggests that "there are neither self nor objects-of-self, neither subject nor object views" and goes on to claim that "one leaves behind all the defiled characteristics that are associated with views, the characteristics that are affiliated with self and object-of-self."[19] As contemporary commentator Pak Chong-hong explains, Wŏnhyo's view of One Mind "neither advocates an extreme nor tries to merge such views together by adopting a median position."[20] The One Mind allows the "interfusion of two contrary positions," but without obscuring the independence of those positions, either. It posits nothing itself, and yet there is nothing that it does not posit, because it transcends all limitations.[21]

We can thus clearly see that Wŏnhyo not only aimed to unify various trends including the three treatises school and Consciousness-Only school in his syncretic form of Buddhism, but also carried out a practice of harmony in person in the community to which he belonged. The ideal of Buddhism in Wŏnhyo consists in its profound soteriological effect on the individual, freeing his mind from its limited, myopic perspectives and leading to liberations. For Wŏnhyo, the act of believing is the most important element in our practical life. Meditation is important, doctrinal studies are crucial, but without the basic, genuine act of faith, we get nowhere. One can attain enlightenment only if one first believes in the scriptures. But the ultimate source of this faith lies in meditation on reality, that is, the reality of the Buddha or One Mind, "where one is all, all is one, where nothing stays but nothing does not stay, where nothing is done but nothing is undone."[22] In One Mind, the *samsara* (i.e., the ordinary world) and *nirvāṇa* (i.e., the enlightened state) are interfused, the form (*rupa*) and nothingness (*śūnyatā*) are intertwined, and the essential nature and its manifested characteristics are interwoven with each other. Indeed, in his philosophy there is a dynamic interaction between faith and practice. In many of his treatises, Wŏnhyo confesses his own sins in acts of contrition. He further moves on to an advanced meditation on the reality of things, leading to the ecstasy arising from the realization of reality. The underlying assumption in his teaching is that enlightenment begins with faith. Only when one has faith in the scriptures can one eventually attain enlightenment upon completing the necessary training.

But in order to realize the essential interfusion in various pairs of opposite positions, we have to achieve a distinctive, superior standpoint from which we can view things comprehensively. This is provided by Wŏnhyo's view of *enlightenment*. We live in the world of transient existence. But underlying this changing, limited world lies a non-changing reality, a true metaphysical realm. In the *Autocommentary on the Awakening of Mahāyāna Faith*, this underlying reality is called "original enlightenment (*pon'gak*)."[23] The whole of reality consists of original enlightenment, which is in the continual process of self-realization. The world we see now is an expression of everlasting enlightenment.[24] The entire web of relations among different living beings is then founded on the ultimate eternal reality which is beyond time and space, and which makes enlightenment possible for humans. Wŏnhyo also calls this true reality "pŏpsin" (*dharmakāya*, i.e., the essential body of Buddha) because it is the eternal being beyond everything.[25] But this reality is not separated from the common, banal mind. Indeed, the common mind has a seed by which it can reach the ultimate. The ultimate reality is *eo ipso* the ultimate mind, that is, what Wŏnhyo calls "One Mind."

In Wŏnhyo's view, the prospect of enlightenment is something innate to the mind itself and inherently accessible to all living creatures. Since original enlightenment is ubiquitous, even the common people can obtain enlightenment by way of purifying their mind. Like many East Asian Mahayanists, Wŏnhyo thinks that in each of us there is a unique and untainted nature that serves as the foundation for becoming a Buddha. This is the doctrine of the womb (or embryo) of Buddhahood (*tathāgathagarbha*). Even deluded ordinary beings possess in their very makeup the capacity to achieve enlightenment. As he sees it, our mind is intrinsically luminous even though, in actuality, because of adventitious defilements, it can become easily dulled. Thus, the mind is not intrinsically ignorant, but only contingently and yet universally so. This inborn luminosity within the mind is what Wŏnhyo calls "Buddhahood."

According to Wŏnhyo, even though we may not be clearly conscious of ultimate reality (*pŏpsin*), we can reach for it. He calls the developing state of mind, in which enlightenment is partially and gradually exemplified, "acquired enlightenment (*sigak*)." It is enlightenment in its actual realization. As a seed becomes a tree, the mind is on the way to the finite end, the fruit, of the *original enlightenment*. The seed in the mind (i.e., the womb of the Buddha, or Buddhahood) is in the mind only as a potentiality. When the seed is discovered, the reality is also understood. Moreover, this reality can be revealed by the active work of *tathāgathagarbha* through the process of *acquired enlightenment*.

In Wŏnhyo's conception, the One Mind, which is at the fountainhead of all reality, has two aspects, and they are different from, yet complementary to, each other.[26] The One Mind has an absolute, ultimate aspect, the aspect of true thusness (*chinyŏ*). This aspect is itself twofold: It can be *empty* of either self-nature or defilements, but it also can be *full* of the myriads of wholesome qualities that contribute to enlightenment.[27] The absolute aspect of the Mind as being empty and full is the same as Buddhahood, which can be active in enabling sentient beings to attain enlightenment, but which can also be passive in that it can be concealed by the defilements. In the One Mind, there is also a conventional, "production-and-extinction (*saengmyŏl*)" aspect, which is in the realm of existence that is subject to continual birth and death. This conventional aspect is associated with the *ālaya-vijñāna*, or storehouse consciousness, which serves to store the seeds and proclivities produced by past actions. For Wŏnhyo, the storehouse consciousness is the foundation of all other forms of consciousness: "within the consciousnesses that are constantly active, the eighth, [i.e., *ālaya-vijñāna*] is the foundational [consciousness]."[28] Yet the storehouse consciousness cannot do the soteriological work because it is still the source of defilements. When the *sūtra* says that "existence is void and nonexistent," Wŏnhyo comments that this is "a reiteration of the aspect of leaving behind characteristics" (*ibid.*). But when the *sūtra* also says that "nonexistence is void and nonexistent," Wŏnhyo suggests that this reiterates the aspect of leaving behind nature. From this, Wŏnhyo infers, "[t]he One Mind leaves behind both characteristics and nature" and goes on to claim that there is in fact "an aggregation of immeasurable meritorious qualities" (*ibid.*). What he means is that there must be a ninth consciousness, which he calls "*amala-vijñāna* (immaculate consciousness)," and its task is to help human beings achieve enlightenment.[29] Wŏnhyo then identifies the *amala-vijñāna* with the *original enlightenment*,[30] going beyond the doctrinal confines of the early Indian *Yogācāra* school.

It follows that, for Wŏnhyo, One Mind, in its true nature, is empty of self-nature and thus expresses nothingness. Since the whole world depends on the mind, the whole world is also intrinsically enveloped in nothingness. Our mind then must be simultaneously deluded and yet enlightened. Sentient beings could be originally enlightened and yet still have to progress through a process of *acquired enlightenment*. The true nature of the mind, that is, *tathāgatagarbha*, is not merely a passive mechanism closeted behind the veils of defilements but also an active potency that conceals the principle (which is to say, *dharmakāya*, the true body of reality). Therefore, the *tathāgatagarbha* works at revealing its own principle to the adept through the process of "acquiring" his or her enlightenment.[31]

In the final analysis, then, enlightenment for Wŏnhyo turns out to be nothing other than a rediscovery of one's true nature, hidden within. When ordinary beings finally realize enlightenment, they find that "their ordinary state of mind is nothing more than *pon'gak*, i.e., the *original enlightenment* that has always been present."[32] In other words, they realize enlightenment when they realize nothingness in their nature, that is, when they realize they are no more than nothingness. In the end, all the different stages on one's journey to Buddhahood are simply the development of one and the same mind, *pon'gak*, that operates on itself. Epistemically, the students of Buddhism discover and cultivate the seed of enlightenment (*tathāgathagarbha*) through a gradual process, but ontologically, the fruit of enlightenment has been with them all along, for the students innately possess *pon'gak*. The moment the seed in the mind is discovered, the true nature of reality (*pŏpsin*/*dharmakāya*) is fulfilled.

Chinul

Let us now move onto our second philosopher, Chinul, an eminent *Sŏn* (禪) master and a reformer of the Korean s*angha* in the Koryŏ dynasty. He rejected the practical principle of uninhibited action (*muae haeng*) implied by Huayan idealism, yet his mature thought clearly and unmistakably manifests his sustained reflection on nothingness as found in the Chan traditions as well as in the *Avataṃsaka* doctrines. Chinul's leading motto may be presented as: "mind *is* Buddha."

While Buddhism was well established within Korea by the time of Chinul, there were strong divisions between the *Kyo* (教, doctrinal studies) schools and the *Sŏn* schools. Chinul almost single-handedly set the Korean *Sŏn* tradition firmly in place as he attempted to bridge the division between the two forms of Buddhism with his quintessentially ecumenical approach. He also systematized *Sŏn* teachings, using the *sūtras* revered by the *Kyo* schools for the sake of authenticating the *Sŏn* approach. In addition to this work in systemization and reconciliation, Chinul was a tireless reformer as well, introducing and regulating meditative practices that later became integral parts of *Sŏn* and, eventually, all of Korean Buddhism. As a result, the *Sŏn* school has dominated Korean Buddhism since then. Even when his style of *Sŏn* was eclipsed by later developments, many of his practices and teachings remained in wide use. A key innovation of his within *Sŏn* was his introduction and elaboration of *kong'an* (公案, the public case records) or rather the practice of its key component called "*hwadu* (話頭)" originating from Chinese Chan. To this day, his method of *hwadu* is still practiced as the key feature of *Sŏn* monasticism within Korean temples.

Now, what exactly is the difference between the *Sŏn* tradition and the doctrinal schools in Korean Buddhism, and what was Chinul's way of synthesizing them? The *Sŏn* school is most distinctively oriented to practice. The *Sŏn* here primarily refers to the conjoined practice of *samādhi* (*concentration*) and *prajñā* (*wisdom*). Already in early works such as *Encouragement to Practice* and *Secrets on Cultivating the Mind*, Chinul emphasizes the need to "cultivate *concentration* and *wisdom* in tandem." *Concentration* here means a mental absorption. As the student of Buddhism turns his or her attention away from the world of sensible things and brings it to bear on what is internal, he or she engages in meditation to obtain unmovable peace within himself or herself. In the process, the student exercises pure mental absorption with a resulting state of calmness. This is *concentration*. Furthermore, as this concentration naturally creates the energy of mental penetration, the mind is now directed to make inquiries into the nature of the world and that of the self, thereby generating a sweeping insight. This is *wisdom*—it is transcendental understanding of the nature of the world and the self in it, with a resulting state of alertness. *Sŏn* then combines the merits of both *concentration* and *wisdom*, eventually leading to the discovery of the source of all sentient beings, indeed, the whole world. With respect to the true nature of the mind, *wisdom*, which aims at alertness, refers to awakening to this source. *Concentration*, which aims at calmness, refers to the cultivation of this awakening.[33]

However, Chinul does not think that *concentration* and *wisdom* are two ontologically separate things—rather, they are two different aspects of the same self-nature. They may have different characters and expressions, but they are one and the same in their root. *Concentration* is the essence of the self-nature and is characterized by calmness. *Wisdom* is the function of that same self-nature and is characterized by alertness. Thus, *concentration* is actually the essence of *wisdom*, and *wisdom* is the functioning of *concentration*.[34] As conditioned in the phenomena, they may play a different role, but as unconditioned (i.e., as part of the unconditioned self-nature), they are identical.[35]

In his *Straight Talk on the True Mind*, Chinul calls the unconditioned reality of the world "the True Mind (*chinsim*, 真心)."[36] This is the same as Buddha-nature or mind-ground (*simji*).[37] "True" here means the absolute lack of falsehood, or in his words, "to leave behind the false." "Mind" means the source of reality that is a numinous mirror. In particular, it is not meant to be the mental faculty of an individual human being. The True Mind is then contrasted with false minds. Note also that in Chinul's usage the True Mind is not opposed to body or matter.[38] Chinul is not saying that everything in the world is mental, and we should not take him to be an idealist.[39] The True Mind is also not a subject as opposed to the object. Therefore, we should not construe the True Mind as a subject of cognition or action. Rather, as the genuine foundation of reality, the True Mind refers to the source of all beings in the world, including the Buddha, as well as the various phenomena. It is none other than the ultimate reality, whose intrinsic nature may be characterized as "nothingness" if we employ the language of the *Mādhyamaka* school.[40]

However, in *Secrets on Cultivating the Mind*, Chinul points out that this nature of the True Mind can also be characterized more positively by means of the concept of numinous awareness (*yŏngchi*, 靈知).[41] The True Mind is void, and calm in a way that is immutably alert. As Chinul puts it, "[t]his pure, void and calm mind is that mind of outstanding purity and brilliance of all the Buddhas of the three time periods; it is that enlightened nature which is the original source of all sentient beings."[42] Chinul places the highest emphasis on the positive element in the thought of nothingness. "Voidness (i.e., nothingness) is fundamentally nonvoid" as he sometimes puts it paradoxically,[43] for the former is not a pure absence or absolute lack but an infinitely rich source of reality in the world. There is thus "only the *tathāgata* [i.e., the Buddha's]'s bright, clear mind of complete enlightenment . . . [which] contains, without exception, the minds of all sentient beings."[44] The mind of Buddha, that is, the True Mind, is not something separate and independent from the ordinary minds but intrinsically embedded in the latter. Finally, because of this reason, Chinul suggests that "there the ignorant, discriminative minds of all sentient beings are empty and bright and have the same wisdom-sea and the same *dharma*-nature as all the Buddha of the ten directions" (*ibid.*). We ordinary beings are then, in effect, Buddhas.

This True Mind has both essence and function according to the Mahāyāna tradition.[45] In its essence, the True Mind is immutable in a way that is calm and void, expressing its *concentration*. This is its absolute aspect. Further, in this respect, the mind has numinous awareness (*yŏngchi*, 靈知), which expresses its *wisdom* as the function of the essence of the True Mind. The sudden awakening, the defining moment in one's long and arduous journey to Buddhahood, consists in understanding the voidness and calmness in the self-nature of the True Mind. It is to realize that "I am a Buddha inherently." This absolute aspect of the True Mind remains immutable. On the other hand, the same mind is also adaptable to external environment and thus changeable. It can adapt in infinitely many ways to worldly prodding. This is the aspect of *function* in the nature of the mind. For example, in the presence of arising desires and rampant temptations, one may remain unperturbed, consistently maintaining one's nature. In this case, one's numinous awareness preserves the state of thoughtlessness. Alternatively, one may fall victim to them, succumbing to the worldly defilements, which are like reflections on a jewel. But underneath all these various transactions lies the True Mind. In particular, one's numinous awareness may be expressed even in ignorance and defilements. On Chinul's view, all *dharmas* in and out of the world are nothing but manifestation of the True Mind. One's spiritual practice, that is, *bodhisattva* practice, then, must focus on preserving the essential calmness of the thoughtless state until Buddhahood is achieved in its actuality in the end.

Chinul calls this ultimate reality "a mind" because this identification is based on *Avataṃsaka*'s only-mind thesis. The *Avataṃsaka Sūtra* speaks of the three worlds as *cittamatra* (only-mind). It is clear that the mind here is not a psychological category but an ontological category—a metaphysical mode of existence. It is what makes all things what they are. It is then the *dharmadātu* of all beings. It transcends all beings yet it is inherent in them. Everyone is, accordingly, endowed with the Buddha-nature, and everyone's mind is intrinsically filled with all meritorious qualities. For Chinul, the rich conception of nothingness in its calm and luminous awareness can succinctly characterize the essential nature of the True Mind in a way that reconciles the duality of the "noumenon and phenomena, nature and characteristics, sentient beings and Buddhas, oneself and others, stained and pure, etc."[46]

How, then, do we realize this true nature of the mind within the confines of our finite embodied conditions? Chinul suggests that we adopt what he calls the method of the *hwadu*, which literally means 'head of speech' or 'the limit of speech.' Since speech presupposes the discriminating mode of the mind, the *hwadu* works as an agent of transcending the discriminations of the discursive mind and thought. In the *Dharma Collection*, Chinul suggests that *hwadu* produces the "cleaning of knowledge and understanding." He then approvingly gives the quintessential *hwadu*: "A monk asked Zhaozhou, 'Does a dog have the Buddha-nature or not?' Zhaozhou replied, 'Mu! [無, No!].'" It is common sense in Mahāyāna Buddhism that all living beings have Buddha-nature. So, why is the monk asking what is an obvious and absurd question, and why is Zhaozhou giving a paradoxical answer? In discussing this *hwadu* and instructing his students how to work with it, Chinul suggests that *Mu* is "the weapon which destroys wrong knowledge and wrong understanding."[47] Zhaozhou's "*Mu*" here does not mean an affirmative answer nor a negative one. The student of *Sŏn* here then should not consider it in relation to a doctrinal theory—one only needs to "be concerned about keeping this question before [one] and [one's] attention always focused."[48] In this way, when the student of *Sŏn* follows the tortuous yet fruitful path of *hwadu* patiently, "unexpectedly, in an instant, the student activates one moment of realization in regard to the tasteless, elusive *hwadu*, and the *dharmadhātu* of the one mind becomes utterly evident and clear."[49] The *hwadu* method then enables the students to realize the true inner nature of the mind—the intrinsic nothingness of Buddhahood—and to enter into the realm of *nirvāṇa*.

Yet despite his emphasis on the *hwadu* method, Chinul believes that a doctrinal study is a vitally important component of the Buddhist cultivation. It is well known that each of his three awakening experiences in life came in connection with the contemplation of a passage in a Buddhist text. This is in stark contrast to the typical case of awakening experience due to the so-called "mind-to-mind transmission" between a teacher and a student as characterized in the usual *Sŏn* school.

Now, there is still a lingering question in Chinul's *Sŏn* project that urgently needs to be answered: If we obtain an awakening by means of the *hwadu* method, what should we then do from that point on? What else is there remaining to do to become a Buddha? In his mature period, Chinul clearly suggests that we must start with a sudden awakening and this should be followed by gradual cultivation.[50] The awakening to the true nature of the mind is sudden and immediate. We ordinary people usually believe that we are a composite of mind and body, where the mind is frequently in the process of thinking and the body is a physical entity occupying a region in space. But we may suddenly discover that "in the original forms, our body is actually the true *dharma*-body of all the Buddhas and our mind is actually the void and calm, numinous awareness of the true mind."[51] We then realize that we are inherently Buddhas.

To be sure, this initial state of awakening is not created out of nothing—it does not arise out of the blue. This must assume a proper understanding of (and faith in) the nature and function of the mind. Meditations are needed, spiritual training must be engaged in, and the study of *sūtras* is to be conducted. In other words, a spiritual novice must first learn about the course and goal of practice by means of scriptural investigations and the engagement with conceptual means. But these discriminative devices alone will never get the student from the realm of the conditioned to the unconditioned, as was pointed out. A meditation by way of the *hwadu* can provide such an impetus. But the crucial question here is: how do you sustain the momentum of sudden awakening thus achieved? After all, we are mere sentient beings with a less than perfect capacity for wisdom. We still make a lot of mistakes in thought and action, and we are still in the grip of burning desires for worldly goods. Thus we stand in urgent need of the continual process of cultivation. As is clear now, gradual cultivation cannot begin unless there is a sudden awakening. Yet we still need judgment and guidance from the *sūtras* in order to facilitate understanding of the true nature of practice. It is one thing to obtain a sudden initial awakening and it is another to develop the full range of meritorious virtues, which can be provided only by the process of cultivation. In other words, we still need discriminating descriptions of the non-dual nature of the reality and the proper course of practice. They will serve nicely as a necessary tool for attaining a complete and full-fledged enlightenment. In sum, the understanding of the non-dual nature of the mind is obtained suddenly but the complete eradication of practical evils is achieved only gradually.

In the *Dharma Collections*, Chinul points out that there are two aspects to this process of sudden awakening and gradual cultivation.[52] To begin with, awakening has two aspects: the initial awakening and the realization-awakening. The initial awakening is a relative awakening in which we enter into the ten faiths. We are not quite *bodhisattvas* but we are on the road to a completely new realm, one that has been hidden from us because of the defiled state of mind. The realization-awakening is the ultimate awakening. This takes place after the gradual process of cultivation is completed. One then becomes a *bodhisattva*.

Gradual cultivation also has two aspects: absolute and relative. The absolute cultivation is performed by means of thoughtlessness. This happens when the mind shows unity with its nature, or when the undifferentiated and non-dual nature of the mind leads the process. When this happens, the mind does not proceed in a discriminative mode. Rather it operates in thoughtlessness and remains in it. On the other hand, the relative aspect of cultivation consists in fighting the defilements of the mind and nurturing meritorious qualities. The mind does not remain ever in thoughtlessness but rather deals with the objects of the senses with noumenal calmness. The mind actively engages the non-dual nature to curb worldly attachments. All together, gradual cultivation must perform the function of keeping the state of awakening alert and dynamic. Without such cultivation, the state will become obtuse and dull, ending with nihilism about the sufferings of the world. Awakening then derives constant impetus from cultivation.

This approach of Chinul is contrasted with the doctrine of mere sudden awakening. On this view, since the mind is already inherently Buddha, once its true nature is truly laid bare by awakening, there is no further need to engage in additional practices of meditation, character development, virtuous action, and so on, which is to say, gradual cultivation. Nothing remains to be cultivated because there is nothing after all. At the moment of true awakening, all the meritorious qualities of the Buddha seem to have been achieved. There is simply nothing more to do. We can just let ourselves go with the flow in the rest of the world without any more artificial contrivances on our part. But this perpetuates the kind of nihilism about Buddhist practices that Chinul is constantly on guard against. This nihilist attitude entails that we do not need those practices anymore because we are already Buddhas once we realize our inherent nature. The reform-minded Chinul simply could not accept this consequence because it would have condoned the corrupt state of the Koryŏ *sangha* instead of remedying it.[53] In the final analysis, he believed that the vast majority of the practitioners of Buddhism are average Joes with limited capacity for understanding. But there is no reason to believe that awakening is accessible only to the spiritually advanced minority—instead, it can be maintained by anyone through ongoing cultivation.

T'aego Pou

We now turn to the last figure in our study. In his *Recorded Sayings*, T'aego Pou, also from the Koryŏ period, employs the *kanhwasŏn* (看話禪) practice of observing the *hwadu* (話頭) method for meditation originally derived from Chinul. Initially, he was under the sway of Chinul's way of thinking in addressing the issue of practice and study of the Buddhist writings as a practitioner of both sudden awakening and gradual cultivation.

Yet T'aego Pou soon came to realize the limits of *sūtra* studies and immediately returned to the intense practice of *Sŏn*. His mature career suggests a delicate yet clear penchant for the sudden awakening/sudden cultivation doctrine, despite his basic orientation in Chinul's line. In other words, T'aego Pou established the new system of *kanhwasŏn* and unified the *Sŏn* and doctrinal approaches to Buddhism based on subitism.

One of the lasting contributions he made for the Korean *sangha* at the time was to settle some of problems that had arisen in the various schools of the Korean Buddhist community. In particular, he made a decisive contribution to the *kanhwasŏn* tradition in Korea with a focus on '*Mu*':

> The word 'Mu' means neither 'non-existence' of 'existing or not existing,' nor 'nothingness.' If this is so, then what is it? In this questioning state, the practitioner doesn't think of anything at all, not even the thought of not thinking! When a person does not think and does not even have consciousness of thinking, then a state of great calm and emptiness is reached. Do not think too much.[54]

Here, the question "What is it?" increases the level of doubt and leads to Master Zhaozhou's "Mu *kong'an* (公案)." According to T'aego Pou, the word '*Mu*' is neither relative nor absolute: it means neither 'nonexistence' of 'existing or not existing,' nor the absolute real 'nothingness'. Then how do you grasp the content of this '*Mu*'? Arriving at this questioning, a *Sŏn* practitioner must stop thinking about one's body and stop doing anything artificial at all. In this way, T'aego Pou advocated the non-duality (不二) of everything including mind and body, life and death, substance and manifestation, even being and nonbeing, and so on. When one also can stop thinking about one's non-doing then one will reach a plane of great calmness and nothingness. Thus T'aego Pou's articulation of nothingness builds on the works of Wŏnhyo and Chinul, yet develops their ideas further in the direction of concentrated practice, paving the way for the subsequent works of various *Sŏn* masters during the Chosŏn dynasty.

The main thrust of T'aego Pou's thought is aimed at unifying various tendencies in Buddhism into a harmony based on *Sŏn*. First of all, he deepened the unification process of the *Sŏn* and *Kyo* schools. He thought that the understanding of the *sūtras* was not in opposition to the practice of *Sŏn*. Since the Buddhist community had become confused and corrupt at the time especially because of the reform-minded, slave-turned-radical cleric *Sin Ton's* (1322–1371 CE) rise to power at the royal court, T'aego Pou not only consolidated *Sŏn* and *Kyo* schools, but also brought Pure Land and other philosophies into an accord with *Sŏn* practice as well. For instance, he taught that reciting the name Amitabha Buddha is not designed for the purpose of enabling rebirth in the Western Paradise through the power of the *mantra*, but reminds us of the nature of Amitabha's characteristics.[55] When the name of Amitabha Buddha is chanted for a whole day, the mind and the chanting become one. Our 'True Nature,' he believes, can be found through this practice. This formulation of the reason for chanting or recollecting the Buddha is not the same as what is usually taught in Pure Land Buddhism, but it is similar to the investigation of the *kong'an*. Its purpose is to go beyond the discriminative thought process and usher us into the realm of nothingness. In T'aego Pou's view, the nature of Amitabha is our true nature. He further proposed that different Buddhist practices could be fused in the *Sŏn* method. By expanding the horizon of the *kanhwasŏn*, T'aego Pou tried to embrace a variety of Buddhism ideas. In practice, he did not live a life removed from the world in a hermitage—he made constant efforts to spread Buddhism and to help all human beings achieve enlightenment. Far from practicing the kind of nihilism that the Neo-Confucians cried foul about, his *Sŏn* practice was the diametric opposite of nihilism.

By way of introducing the *Linji* school to the later, stagnant Koryŏ Buddhism through the cultivation of One Mind, T'aego tried to merge varying Buddhist sects within the boundaries of the *Sŏn* School. Thus, his way of practicing *kanhwasŏn* played a key role in transmitting the lamp of the patriarchs and served as the cornerstone of the major tradition in Korea, especially in the *Chogye* (= Jogye) Order.[56] Even though it clearly developed under the sway of Chinul's way of thinking in addressing the issue of practice and study in its inception, it indubitably went beyond it. Later, this line of *Sŏn* meditational practice was continued by Sŏngch'ŏl (1912–1993), the well-known master from Haeinsa temple. Revolting against Chinul's sudden awakening/gradual cultivation approach, Sŏngch'ŏl claims that monks must practice sudden awakening/sudden cultivation instead of the gradual one.[57] It is no surprise that the *hwadu* of *Mu* was at the focal point of this effort as well. We may then say that T'aego Pou's thought laid the foundation for all of these later developments.

Conclusion

All in all, even though the *Mādhyamaka* school never became the major one in Korean Buddhism, we can see that the concept of nothingness in one form or another played a large role in the development of the most influential Buddhist movements in Korea. In Wŏnhyo's thought, nothingness is fundamentally understood from the logic of interfusion which enables him to embrace and harmonize different strands of Buddhism without forsaking the substance of them. Chinul's *Sŏn* philosophy is developed in the scheme of sudden awakening to our true nature under the guise of nothingness, followed by a gradual cultivation via the practice of nothingness. Finally, nothingness in T'aego Pou is emphasized as a quintessentially practical notion where both awakening and cultivation are fully realized in one fell swoop. As a corollary, we can now clearly see that the Neo-Confucian attack on nothingness is in this respect unfounded. The concept of nothingness simply does not entail nihilism conceived as expressing a fatalistic stance about forces of nature (including human nature) with a strong implication for inaction and despair. Thus, this polemic on the part of the Neo-Confucians turns out to be little more than a straw-man argument, largely motivated by political considerations.[58]

Notes

1 Chŏng Tojŏn, *Sambong chip* (Collected Works of Chŏng Sambong) (Seoul: Kuksa p'yŏnch'an wiwŏnhoe, 1961), 446–463.

2 Ibid., 464–470.

3 For a detailed analysis of these arguments, or rather this family of arguments, see Ja-kyoung Han, "A Critical Study on Chŏng Tojŏn's Critique of Buddhism concerning the Ontological Status of the Human Mind in Cosmos" [in Korean], in *Pulkyohak Yŏn'gu* [Buddhist Studies], Vol. 6 (2003): 72–104.

4 Kwŏn Kŭn, "Preface to 'The Three Treatises on the Mind, Ki Force and the Principle' (Simkiri sampyŏnsŏ)," in *Yangch'on chip* [Collected Works of Kwŏn Yangch'on] (Seoul: Minjok munhwa ch'ujinhoe, 1979). Vol. 16.

5 Mark Siderits, *Buddhism as Philosophy: An Introduction* (Aldershot, England : Ashgate; Indianapolis, IN: Hackett Publishing Company, 2007), 180.

6 David F. Burton, *Emptiness Appraised: A Critical Study of Nāgārjuna's Philosophy* (Surrey: Curzon, 1999), 45.

7 Ibid., 87.

8 Wŏnhyo's various works represent the first major systematic inquiry into the fundamental metaphysical reality of the world on the Korean peninsula. His major writings include *Exposition of the Vajrasamadhi-Sūtra*, in Robert E. Buswell, Jr. (ed. and trans.), *Cultivating Original Enlightenment: Wŏnhyo's Exposition of the Vajrasamadhi-Sūtra* (Honolulu: University of Hawaii Press, 2007) and *Autocommentary on the Awakening of Mahāyāna Faith (Daesŭng kisillonso pyŏlki)*, in Ki-yong Rhi (Yi) (ed. and trans.) *Hankukŭi Pulkyosasang* (Seoul: Samsung, 1981). Other writings of his, such as *Arouse Your Mind and Practice* [Palsim suhaeng jang], *The Treatise on the Ten Ways of Resolving Controversies* [Simmun hwajaeng non], *System of the Two Hindrances* [Yijang ŭi], *Commentary on the Discrimination between the Middle and the Extremes* [Chungbyŏn punbyŏllon so], and the *Critical Discussion on Inference* [P'an piryang non] are found in A. Charles Muller and Cuong T. Nguyen (eds.), *Wŏnhyo's Philosophy of Mind* (Honolulu: University of Hawaii Press, 2012).

9 Wŏnhyo, *Exposition of the Vajrasamadhi-Sūtra*, 76–77.

10 Wŏnhyo, *Autocommentary on the Awakening of Mahāyāna Faith*, 101.

11 Wŏnhyo, *Exposition of the Vajrasamadhi-Sūtra*, 170 (translation modified).

12 Ibid.

13 Wŏnhyo, *Exposition of the Vajrasamadhi-Sūtra*, 254.

14 Wŏnhyo, *Exposition of the Vajrasamadhi-Sūtra*, 284.
15 Ibid. In *Mahāyāna* Buddhism, the six perfections (*pāramitās*) refer to generosity (布施波羅蜜), virtue (持戒波羅蜜), patience (忍辱波羅蜜), diligence (精進波羅蜜), concentration (禪定波羅蜜), and wisdom (智慧波羅蜜).
16 Wŏnhyo, *Exposition of the Vajrasamadhi-Sūtra*, 285.
17 Wŏnhyo's original term is "hwajaeng," which is usually translated as harmonization or reconciliation; since this term, as A. Charles Muller and Cuong T. Nguyen point out (*Wŏnhyo's Philosophy of Mind*, 24), carries the sense of an emotional resolution of a personal squabble among members of the *sangha*, I have used "interfusion" instead to emphasize the objective, methodical dimension of it.
18 See Yoshita Hakeda (trans.), *The Awakening of Faith* (New York: Columbia University Press, 1967), 31 et passim.
19 Ibid.
20 Pak Chong-hong, "Wŏnhyo ŭi chŏrak sasang," in *Han'guk sasangsa* [History of Korean Thought] (Seoul: Ilsinsa, 1972); see also Buswell's English translation, "Wŏnhyo's Philosophical Thought" in Lewis R. Lancaster and C. S. Yu (eds.), *Assimilation of Buddhism in Korea* (Berkeley, CA: Asian Humanities Press, 1983), 64.
21 Ibid.
22 Wŏnhyo, "The Great Vehicle Repentance for Indulgence in the Six Faculties," in A. Charles Muller, (ed.) *Wŏnhyo: Selected Works* (Seoul: Jogye Order of Korean Buddhism, 2012), 270 (translation modified).
23 Wŏnhyo, *Autocommentary on the Awakening of Mahāyāna Faith*, 97–98.
24 Rhi (Yi), Ki-yong, "Wŏnhyo and His Thoughts," in The Korean National Commission for UNESCO (ed.), *The Main Currents of Korean Thought* (Seoul, Korea: The Si-sa-yong-o-sa Publishers, Inc.,1983), 14–25.
25 Wŏnhyo, *Autocommentary on the Awakening of Mahāyāna Faith*, 97.
26 Wŏnhyo, *Autocommentary on the Awakening of Mahāyāna Faith*, 79.
27 Robert E. Buswell Jr., *Cultivating Original Enlightenment*, 6.
28 Wŏnhyo, *Exposition of the Vajrasamadhi-Sūtra*, 284.
29 Wŏnhyo, *Exposition of the Vajrasamadhi-Sūtra*, 157.
30 Wŏnhyo, *Exposition of the Vajrasamadhi-Sūtra*, 205. The concept of *amala-vijñāna* also appears in the work of Paramārtha (499–569 CE).
31 Buswell, *Cultivating Original Enlightenment*, 6–7.
32 Ibid., 5.
33 Buswell, *Tracing Back the Radiance: Chinul's Korean Way of Zen* (Honolulu: University of Hawaii Press, 1991), 64.
34 Chinul, *Secrets on Cultivating the Mind*, in *The Korean Approach to Zen. The Collected Works of Chinul*, trans. and ed. Robert E. Buswell (Honolulu: University of Hawaii Press, 1983), 150.
35 Conceived thus, *samādhi* (*concentration*) and *prajñā* (*wisdom*) here are then not just instruments, nor are they merely convenient media for fighting ignorance and defilements on the road to the enlightenment. They are an integral part of the true underlying reality—they are part of the self-nature. The whole phenomenal world, then, must be the product of the operation of both *samādhi* (*concentration*) and *prajñā* (*wisdom*) in the originally unconditioned self-nature. Chinul calls this "*samādhi* (*concentration*) and *prajñā* (*wisdom*) of the self-nature (chasŏng chŏnghye" (in contrast to relative *samādhi* (*concentration*) and *prajñā* (*wisdom*)). Chinul, *The Secrets on Cultivating the Mind*, 150–151.
36 Chinul, *The Straight Talk on the True Mind*, in *The Korean Approach to Zen: The Collected Works of Chinul*,163.
37 It is also alternatively called "bodhi," "dharmadhātu," "tathāgatha," "nirvana," "tathatā," "dhamakāya," "sambhogakāya," "nirmahakāya," "buddhadhātu," "dharani," and "tathāgatagarbaha" (ibid.).

38 Hee-Sung Keel, *Chinulŭi Sŏnsasang* [The Sŏn of Chinul] (Seoul: Sonamu, 2001), 113.
39 Ibid., 116.
40 Ibid., 113.
41 Chinul, *Secrets on Cultivating the Mind* in *The Korean Approach to Zen: The Collected Works of Chinul*, 145, 147; See also *Excerpts from the Dharma Collection*, in *The Korean Approach to Zen*, 332 inter alia.
42 Chinul, *Secrets on Cultivating the Mind* in *The Korean Approach to Zen*, 147.
43 Ibid. 121.
44 Ibid.
45 In particular, this distinction is due to the *Awakening of Faith.*
46 Chinul, *Complete and Sudden Attainment of Buddhahood* in *The Korean Approach to Zen. The Collected Works of Chinul*, 203.
47 Chinul, *Resolving Doubts about Observing the Hwadu* in *The Korean Approach to Zen. The Collected Works of Chinul*, 240.
48 Ibid., 245.
49 Ibid., 246.
50 However, as Jin Y. Park notices, even in *Resolving Doubts about Observing the Hwadu*, one can unmistakably notice that Chinul puts a great emphasis on the direct path of obtaining final enlightenment by way of the *hwadu* (especially the so-called 'live words' *hwadu*) at the expenses of any doctrinal studies. See Park, "Zen Language in Our Time: The Case of Pojo Chinul's *Huatou* Meditation," *Philosophy East & West*, vol. 55, no. 1 (January 2005), 84–88.
51 Buswell, *Tracing Back the Radiance*, 58.
52 Chinul, *Excerpts from the Dharma Collection*, in *The Korean Approach to Zen. The Collected Works of Chinul*, 287.
53 Buswell, "Introduction: The Life and Thought of Chinul," in *Tracing Back the Radiance*, 61.
54 T'aego Pou, *The Recorded Sayings of T'aego*, in J. Jorgensen (ed.), *Seon Dialogues* (Seoul: Jogye Order of Korean Buddhism, 2012), 352.
55 Ibid., 360–362. See also "Analects" in J. C. Cleary (ed.) *Buddha from Korea* (Boston and Shaftesbury: Shambala, 2001), 108–111.
56 This is the main sect in Korean Buddhism.
57 See, e.g., Sŏngch'ŏl, *Sŏnmunchŏngno* (Haeinsa Paekryŏnam, Korea: Changkyŏnggak, 1987).
58 I would like to thank Professors Chaehyun Chong, Yunho Cho, Seung-Taek Lim, Jin Y. Park, and Hee-Sung Keel for comments on this paper. I am also grateful to the audience at my lecture on the same topic delivered at Osaka University for their responses, especially to Professors Yukio Irie and Narifumi Nakaoka for arranging the lecture there and also for their constructive comments. Finally, my sincere thanks go to the editors of this volume, JeeLoo Liu and Doug Berger.

17 Zen, Philosophy, and Emptiness

Dōgen and the Deconstruction of Concepts

Gereon Kopf

Introduction[1]

In the second half of the twentieth century, a tendency among English language scholars of comparative theology and philosophy emerged in portraying Buddhist philosophy, and Japanese Zen 禪 Buddhist philosophy in particular, as a "philosophy of nothingness." In *Zen and the Western World*, Masao Abe (阿部正雄 1915–2006) makes the claim that the Kyoto school developed a philosophy based on a (in Abe's words, "the") Buddhist perspective and contributed to world philosophy the concept of "absolute nothingness" (*zettai mu*, 絕對無) (1985, 128, 158–159). Leaving aside the fact that the prevalent East-West rhetoric has become completely untenable and that Buddhist philosophy and even the philosophy of the Kyoto school are not monolithic, Abe still makes a valuable observation. Two of the three main thinkers of the Kyoto school, Kitarō Nishida 西田幾多郎 (1870–1945) and Keiji Nishitani 西谷啓治 (1900–1990), did indeed develop philosophical systems based on the conceptions of "absolute non-being" (*zettai mu*, 絕對無)[2] and "emptiness" (*kū*, 空), respectively. Both claimed that the sources for these philosophical conceptions lay in the Buddhist tradition, particularly in the texts of the *Prajñāpāramitā* literature, and the Chan as well as Zen Buddhist traditions. In addition, they agreed that a philosophy that takes "absolute non-being" or "emptiness" as its basic paradigm is well suited to solve some of the fundamental problems created by Cartesian dualism. However, there are also differences between them: Nishitani suggested that "emptiness" is the better suited concept for the paradigm of a philosophy that eschews the traps of dualism, including the dualism between "being" and "non-being." Nishida, on the other hand, argued that a monistic philosophy that resolves the tension between the opposites constitutes an implied dualism. Using a phraseology that connects opposites with the character for *soku* 即, literally "is," but more appropriately translated as "and-yet," he expresses an existential ambiguity and suggests that while difference should not be essentialized, it should not be abolished either.[3] Both philosophers identify as their inspiration a variety of Buddhist texts and especially the writings of Zen Master Dōgen 道元禪師 (1200–1253). I believe that Dōgen provides the blueprint for such a non-dualistic philosophy. In this paper, I will attempt to demonstrate how Dōgen's overall non-dualistic worldview affects his philosophies of language and practice.

In *The Treasury of the True Dharma Eye* (*Shōbōgenzō* 正法眼藏), Dōgen develops what some of the Kyoto school philosophers will later call a "philosophy of nothingness" based on his examination of the records of the Chinese Chan masters and other Buddhist texts. However, Dōgen, like Nishitani later, seems to privilege the term "emptiness" over "non-being." The term "emptiness" constitutes the central concept of Madhyamaka Buddhist philosophy while Chan thinkers tend to employ the terms "nonbeing," "being-and-nonbeing (*youwu*, 有無)," or various derivations thereof. The reason for this is that, while many Mahāyāna Buddhist philosophers that emphasize "emptiness," also known as *śūnyatāvāda*, critique the dualistic structures inherent in conceptual language from a third perspective, many Chan Buddhist texts directly aim at the deconstruction of language itself. This deconstruction can be linguistic or non-linguistic and performative in nature. Dōgen inherits from the Chan tradition a deep distrust of conceptual structures and from *śūnyatāvāda*, a method to destabilize language. This paper will read Dōgen's conceptions of "nothingness" and "emptiness" in the context of his predecessors in order to explore in what way his philosophy can shed light on the nature of language and its relationship to non-verbal communication.

The Conception of "Emptiness" in the *Prajñāpāramitā Sūtras*

At this point in the book, the reader will be quite familiar with the philosophies of the Madhyamaka school, especially with that of Nāgārjuna. The philosophy of emptiness emerged around two thousand years ago in the *Prajñāpāramitā* (*Perfected Wisdom*) literature. According to Paul Williams (1989), "wisdom" (*prajñā*, 般若) "is said to be a state of consciousness which understands emptiness (*śūnyatā*), the absence of self or essence, even in *dharmas*" (43). This wisdom, however, is depicted in the large and philosophically diverse body of the *Prajñāpāramitā* literature as either "conceptual" or "non-conceptual" (44). The *Heart Sūtra* (*Mahā-prajñāpāramitā-hṛdaya-sūtra*, 般若波羅蜜多心經) (T 8.253), which is falsely identified as the nutshell version of what is mistakenly held to be the shared teaching of the vast body of the *Prajñāpāramitā* literature by texts in the Japanese Buddhist tradition, gives us, nevertheless, a quick glimpse at the key concepts of *śūnyatāvāda*.

The *Heart Sūtra*, portrayed as a dialogue between the Bodhisattva Avalokiteśvara and Śāriputra, roughly divides into two sections: a litany of negations of everything important to the teaching of early Buddhism and a section that introduces the mantra "*gate gate pāragate pārasaṃgate bodhisvāhā*" as the means to "unsurpassed awakening" (*anuttarā-samyak-saṃbodhim*, 阿耨多羅三藐三菩提, 無上菩提). Huayan thinkers will later classify "unsurpassed awakening" as the highest of the "five kinds of enlightenments" (*wuputi*, 五菩提) (T 35.1733.412). A closer look, however, reveals that this extremely short text, which has become famous for its formula "form is emptiness, emptiness is form" (*sejishikong kongjishise*, 色即是空, 空即是色) (T 8.253.849), introduces three basic usages of "emptiness." In short, "emptiness" 1) negates all essences; 2) rejects the major early Buddhist teachings such as the "four noble truths" (*āryasatya*, 四聖諦), the "five aggregates" (*pañcaskandha*, 五蘊), the "eighteen sense worlds" (*āyatanadhātu*, 十八界), as well as the notion of a transcendent world of bliss, *nirvāṇa* (*niepan*, 涅槃), conceived of in contrast to an immanent world of suffering, *saṃsāra* (*shengsi*, 生死); and 3) implies that detachment functions as a soteriological means. The phrase "form is emptiness, emptiness is form, form is not different from emptiness, emptiness not different from form" (T 8.253.849) expresses these three dimensions of "emptiness": because "form" (*rūpa*, 色) and "emptiness" (*śūnyatā*, 空) do not have an essence, they are not essentially different from each other. Therefore, any ideology privileging one over the other is meaningless, and attachment to either one is a trap that obstructs wisdom. This threefold *dictum* of no essence, no ideology, no attachment, while still in a rather rudimentary form in the *Heart Sūtra*, provides the basis for the "theory of emptiness" in Mahāyāna Buddhist thought.

Two of the *śūnyatāvāda* texts that are important to the current discussion are Nāgārjuna's (second/third century CE) *Mūlamadhyamakārikā*, and the *Diamond Sūtra* (*Vajracchedikā-prajñāpāramitā-sūtra* 金剛般若波羅蜜經) (T 8.235). In the former, Nāgārjuna introduces his tetralemma as the method, literally a "medicine,"[4] to destabilize the conceptual language of early Buddhist discourses, while the latter constitutes the bridge between *śūnyatāvāda* philosophy and Zen thought. The twenty-fifth chapter of the *Mūlamadhyamakārikā* argues that "there is no distinction between *saṃsāra* and *nirvāṇa*. There is no distinction between *nirvāṇa* and *saṃsāra*." This is so because *nirvāṇa* is neither an "existent" (*bhāva*), nor an "absence" (*abhāva*), nor "both an existent and an absence," nor "neither an existent nor an absence" (Siderits 2013, 293–302). Nāgārjuna suggests here that, since *saṃsāra* and *nirvāṇa* are devoid of "self-existence" (*svabhāva*), the difference between them cannot be essential either. The method he employs systematically reveals the inability of conceptual language to express reality in a sufficient and appropriate way.

The *Diamond Sūtra* picks up the same theme of the insufficiency of conceptual language even though its context is a soteriological project rather than philosophical discourse. The text is constructed as Śākyamuni's answer to Subhūti's question inquiring how to walk on the bodhisattva path. In his response, Śākyamuni elaborates on the notion of "wisdom" (*prajñā*). Even though the *Diamond Sūtra*'s full name identifies it as a member of the wisdom literature, the text itself uses the term "wisdom" rather sparsely and, even then, mostly in the two compounds "eye of wisdom" (*prajñācakṣus*, 慧眼) and "perfected wisdom" (*prajñāpāramitā*, 般若波羅蜜). The term "emptiness" (*śūnyatā*, 空) does not occur at all.[5] Rather, the goal of *Diamond Sūtra* is to juxtapose various sets of opposites in order to question the sufficiency of conceptual language as a guide to religious practice. Kumārajīva's (鳩摩羅什

344–413 CE) translation (and for the discussion of "emptiness" in Zen Buddhism, the Chinese translation is of more relevance than the Sanskrit original) facilitates this juxtapositions by what D. T. Suzuki 鈴木大拙 (1870–1966) will later call the "logic of *sokuhi*" (*sokuhi no ronri* 即非の論理). As Suzuki has pointed out, Kumārajīva's translation of the *Diamond Sūtra* uses the Chinese phrase "is not" (*jifei* 即非) to construct phrases of the form "A is not A." The full formal expression of this logic of *sokuhi* Suzuki provides us with is, "We call A 'A'; however, A is not A; therefore we call it A" (SDZ 1968–1971, 5: 380–1). While many scholars, such as Shigenori Nagatomo (2000), follow Suzuki's suggestion and interpret these phrases to indicate a "logic of the religious experience,"[6] Rein Raud (2003) and I (Kopf 2005) believe that the intent of these kinds of phrases is to destabilize conceptual language and to suggest that the method for bodhisattvas to "control their thoughts" is non-conceptual.

As I have discussed elsewhere (Kopf 2005), it is possible to identify five kinds of conceptual constructions using the phrase "*jifei*" (is not) in Kumārajīva's translation of the *Diamond Sūtra*. The prototypes of these five formulations are 1) "Buddha said 'the perfected wisdom is not the perfected wisdom'" (T 8.235.750); 2) "the world-honored one said 'the views of self, person, sentient being, and life are not these views; therefore, we call them the views of self, persons, sentient beings, and life'" (T 8.235.752); 3) "what we call the Buddha *dharma* is not the Buddha *dharma*" (T 8.235.749); 4) "what we call 'all *dharma*s' is not all *dharma*s, therefore we call them 'all *dharma*s'" (T 8.235.751); and 5) "the Tathāgatha said 'totality is not totality, therefore we call it totality; Subhūti, totality is incomprehensible'" (T 8.235.752). If we were to translate these phrases into formulas the way Suzuki did, they would read as follows: 1) "A is not A"; 2) "A is not A, therefore we call it A"; 3) "what we call A is not A"; 4) "what we call A is not A, therefore, we call it A"; 5) "A is not A, therefore we call it A, because A is incomprehensible." It is really important to note that, for the most part, these phrases do not establish a logical contradiction, but rather contrast concepts with reality.[7] In the two instances where the formula could be interpreted to indicate a contradiction (prototypes one and five), the terms in question constitute concepts signifying transcendence, "perfected wisdom" and "totality," and not particular objects. Both are, by definition, beyond opposition and thus beyond contradiction. The point Kumārajīva's translation of the *Diamond Sūtra* seems to make is that concepts and positions do not have a one-to-one correspondence with the reality they suggest and are thus insufficient. The wisdom of the *bodhisattva*s is nonconceptual, and its attainment requires a systematic deconstruction, as we would say today, of conceptual language. It is for these reasons that the *Diamond Sūtra*, and more specifically Kumārajīva's translation thereof, enjoyed quite some popularity among Chan thinkers and practitioners.

The *Platform Sūtra* (*Liuzudashifabaotanjing*, 六祖大師法寶壇經) (T 48.2008), which is attributed to the sixth Chinese patriarch of Chan Buddhism, Huineng 慧能, directly takes up the legacy of the *Diamond Sūtra*. Huineng's name roughly translates into "the possibility of wisdom" and the main theme of the *Platform Sūtra* is "wisdom." Not only is Huineng himself said to have decided to join the Buddhist community (*sangha*) upon hearing a recitation of the *Diamond Sūtra*, but also the *Platform Sūtra* declares explicitly that "the heart of anyone who hears or explains the *Diamond Sūtra* will open up to awakening" (T 48.2008.350). Most of all, however, the text takes "wisdom" (*bore*, 般若) as its central focus. The well-known poetry competition, the focal point of Huineng's biography that opens the *Platform Sūtra*, introduces his teaching as the "medicine of emptiness" that negates the sense of reification if not essentialism in Shenxiu's 神秀 poem: "The body is the bodhi tree/the mind is like a standing, clear mirror/always keep on wiping it/do not allow the dust to cling" by responding with "the bodhi is not a tree/neither does the clear mirror stand/originally there is not a single thing/where to should the dust cling" (T 48.2008.348). Huineng's poem accomplishes nothing short of a thorough negation of Shenxiu's statements. Philosophically, it aims to reject any kind of essentialism. Accordingly, the text defines "wisdom" (*bore*, 般若) negatively as "no-thought" (*wunian*, 無念) (T 48.2008.351) and positively as *prajñā* (*zhihui*, 智慧), that is, the knowledge that "all is one and one is all" (*yiqiejiyi yijiyiqie*, 一切即一, 一即一切). While "the deluded person explains, the wise person practices. There even are deluded people who quietly sit with a heart of emptiness." And again, "the deluded person utters a thought, the practitioner practices wisdom" (T 48.2008.350). Finally, "having no thoughts is correct, having thoughts is evil" (Y 48.2008.355).

"Emptiness" and the Rhetoric of Silence

This somewhat lengthy discussion of the role of "emptiness" in the *Prajñāpāramitā* literature and its continuation in the *Platform Sūtra* has identified the main themes that will become formative for Chan ideology as it developed in late Tang and mostly Song China: 1) a distrust of conceptual language as an adequate means to attain awakening but even to describe reality; 2) a relatively systematic destabilization of language; 3) the use of what can be called a dialectical method to break out of a dualistic framework of language and thought; and 4) an emphasis on practice over words. These themes become the building blocks for the Chan discourse that favors a rhetoric of silence and immediacy over what was referred to as doctrinal Buddhism. This rhetoric of silence is most visible in the four principles of Chan and the so-called flower sermon. The four principles of Chan, as introduced by the *Records of Linji* (*Zhenzhou linji huizhao chanshi yulu*, 鎮州臨濟慧照禪師語錄) (T 47.1985), summarize the teaching of Chan Buddhism as follows: "There is a tradition outside of the scriptures; it does not rely on letters and words, just point to the heart of the person, see your nature and become a Buddha" (T 47.1985.495). Here, Linji explicitly juxtaposes "doctrinal" (*jiao*, 教) and "meditation" (*chan*, 禪) Buddhism and identifies introspection and self-awareness as the sole methods for becoming a Buddha. The phrase "see your own nature" (*jianxing*, 見性) later becomes the key slogan for many Japanese Rinzai Zen Buddhist teachers.

The sixth case of the *Gateless Barrier* (*Wumenguan*, 無門關) (T 48.2005) introduces the rhetoric of silence in a narrative from. Written in the Song dynasty, it recalls a story from the Buddha's life that had not made it into the scriptures in the first 1,500 years of Buddhism. When the disciples gathered around Śākyamuni on Vulture Peak, he simply held up a flower and his student Mahākāśyapa smiled. Asked by his students to explain, he famously replied,

> I possess the treasury of the true dharma eye; it is the heart of *nirvāṇa*, and the mysterious *dharma* gate without form. It does not rely on letters or words but constitutes is a special tradition outside of the scriptures. I have just transmitted it to Mahākāśyapa (T 49.2005.293).

This quote is important for our present discussion because it locates the first two of the four principles of Chan Buddhism in the life of Buddha and thus provides the highest possible authority for the rhetoric of Chan, which permeates a lot of Chan teaching and especially the Zen thought of D. T. Suzuki, who popularized Zen Buddhism in the English language.

On the other hand, Chan texts inherit the Mahāyāna conception that "*saṃsāra* is not different from *nirvāṇa* and *nirvāṇa* is not different from *saṃsāra*." This non-dual position is expressed in sayings such as "this mind is the Buddha" (*jixinshifo*, 即心是佛) (T 48.2005.296). The *Wumenquan* locates this phrase in a conversation between Daoyi Mazu 馬祖道一 (709–788 CE) and Damai Fachang 大梅法常 (752–839 CE). It is one of many Chan phrases, including Linji's infamous "[t]he Buddha dharma is not useful nor does it accomplish anything; it constitutes nothing but the everyday and the ordinary; have a shit take a piss; put on your clothes, eat and drink, retire when tired" (47.1985.498) that collapse the distinction between the Buddha and sentient beings. These kinds of sayings are iconoclastic, on the one side, and deeply philosophical, on the other, since they leave, as I will argue below, no room for either dualism or monism. I cite Mazu's phrase here because Dōgen wrote a commentary on it and Nishida quoted it to develop his concept of the "self-identity of absolute contradictories" (*zetai mujunteki jiko dōitsu*, 絕對矛盾的自己同一) (NKZ 8: 516). Even the *Platform Sūtra* declares, despite its clear distinction between those adhering to words and those engaging in practice, "ordinary people are Buddhas, desire is the awakened mind" (T 48.2008.350) and thus collapses the carefully constructed distinction between the "deluded mind" (*wangxin*, 妄心) (T 48.2008.354) of ordinary people and the "no mind" (*wuxin*, 無心) of "wisdom" (T 48.2008.357).

This tension between the rhetoric of silence that permeates the Chan Buddhist traditions and the non-dualism of immanence and transcendence, "this mind" and the Buddha, enabled thinkers in the Sŏn and Zen traditions to come up with a creative solution to how to reconcile these seemingly opposite positions. Pojo Chinul 普照知訥 (1158–1210) facilitated a synthesis between doctrinal and meditative Buddhism to make his Chogye 曹溪宗 order the strongest Buddhist force in the Chŏson dynasty in Korea.[8] To Chinul, *samādhi* (*sanmae*,

三昧), the highest meditative state, constitutes the function and *prajñā* the essence of the mind. In short, *samādhi* and *prajñā* are two paths to and descriptions of the same cognitive state. As Robert Buswell explains,

> *Samādhi*, in its guise of calmness, accords with the noumenal voidness; it is used to counter distraction. *Prajñā*, in its guise of alertness, accords with phenomenal plurality; it is used to stimulate the mind out of its occasional dullness, which obscures its natural penetrative quality. In their relative forms, *samādhi* and *prajñā* are instruments for counteracting ignorance and defilements; they are used until enlightenment is achieved (1983, 63).

Soseki Musō 夢窓疎石 (1275–1351) sees doctrines and meditation equally as the cure for the "illusion and ignorance" (2000, 110). However, he approaches the division between doctrinal (*kyō*, 教) and meditative (*zen*, 禪) Buddhism as an abnormal state and considers it pathological. He even uses the terms "doctrinal sickness" (*kyōbyō*, 教病) and "meditative sickness" (*zenbyō*, 禪病) to describe this state of dissociation:

> In the original place of people the pathological aspects of delusion and awakening, ordinary being and saints, do not exist. The *dharma* gate corrects teachings and mediation. Therefore, if you start with the pathological aspects, there will be many kinds of suffering based on inaccuracies. . . . If people unearth illusion and ignorance, they will not see the reincarnation of birth-and-death, past-and-future. There is no distinction between ordinary people and saints, delusion and awakening (109–110).

This passage is saturated with concepts and imagery. What is important for us, however, is that, like Chinul, Musō also sees doctrinal and meditative Buddhism as two means to the same goal. In addition, Musō suggests that the difference between delusion and awakening, words and silence, is not one of essence but, as Nishida would say, "only one of degree." Specifically, Nishida says, "if we think about it thoroughly, in the end even unity and non-unity are but different by degree" (NKZ 1: 16). To Nishida, "pure experience" (*junsui keiken* 純粋経験) and the "impure" (*fujunsui*, 不純粋) are not essentially different from each other. For thinkers like Chinul and Musō, neither are words and silence, study and meditation, different in essence. So how do both accomplish the same goals? The answer to this question, I believe, lies in Dōgen's deconstruction of the mainstream interpretation of the *flower sermon*.

The fascicle in which Dōgen explores Śākyamuni's famous, albeit not necessarily historical, flower sermon at Vulture Peak is the fascicle "Esoteric Words"[9] (*Mitsugo*, 密語) in his collection *The Treasury of the True Dharma Eye* (*Shōbōgenzō*, 正法眼藏).[10] In this fascicle, Dōgen uses the term "esoteric words (*mutsugo*, 密語)," a term used in Mahāyāna texts such as the *Mahāparinirvāṇa Sūtra* (*Da banniepan jing*, 大般涅槃經) (T 12.374) and the *Avataṃsaka Sūtra* (*Dafangguang fo huayan jing*, 大方廣佛華嚴經) (T 10.278–279) to refer to the teaching of Śākyamuni not explicated in the *sūtras*. Specifically, Dōgen interprets the flower sermon through the lens of Chan Master Yunju's 雲居禪師 (?-902 CE) observation that "if you don't get it, you possess the World-honored-One's 'secret explanations', if you do get it, you manifest Kāśyapa's not keeping things to himself" (SBGZ 4: 146). As hinted at above, traditionally, thinkers such as Zenkei Shibayama 柴山全慶 (1894–1974) declare that only ignorance misunderstands the "[t]alk of no talk" (1974, 61), the "transmission of the untransmittable," and the "ever unnamable" as "secret talk" (62), while the awakened mind realizes it as the "true *dharma*," the "*dharma* of as-it-isness," and the "truth that transcends space and time" (63). Shibayama adds that even Śākyamuni's explanation, "I posses the treasury of the true dharma eye, it is the heart of *nirvāṇa*, and the mysterious *dharma* gate without form. It does not rely on letters or words but constitutes a special tradition outside of the scriptures. I have just transmitted it to Mahākāśyapa," falls short of describing the "talk of no talk."

Dōgen radically disagrees with this position when he sarcastically remarks that "if The-World-honored-One hated using words but loved picking up flowers, he should have picked up a flower at the latter time [instead of his explanation] too." And he adds, "how could Kāśyapa not understand, how could the people not hear?" (SBGZ 4: 153) Dōgen emphasizes that Śākyamuni used words to explain "picking up flowers" and asks rhetorically "are these words, or are these not words" (SBGZ 4: 153). Dōgen's reasons for emphasizing the linguistic character of Śākyamuni's explanation are threefold. First, Dōgen argues that delusion is not to be understood in terms of "esoteric words" but as ignorance about "esoteric words." As Musō suggested, this ignorance is caused by a dualistic worldview that distinguishes between "others" who "don't know" and the "self" that "knows," between "people who don't know" and "people who know" (SBGZ 4: 155). Such a worldview attributes "esoteric words" (*mitsugo*, 密語) to the "unlearned" (*gakugyō naki mono*, 學業なきもの) and claims that "*dharma* eyes" (*hōgen*, 法眼) and "*dharma* ears" (*hōji*, 法耳) are devoid of "secrets." Dōgen corrects this position and asserts that, "at the time of the Buddha-patriarchs, secret words and secret actions are presenced" (*genjō* 現成). He further confirms this rejection of dualism when he observes that, "when I know myself, I know secret actions" (SBGZ 4: 155). Later he adds that "secret action does not exist in the place where self and other know each other but only the secret self knows itself, outside of the secret it is not known" (SBGZ 4: 156). These passages are reminiscent of Dōgen's observations in *The Mountain and Water Sūtra* (*Sansuikyō*, 山水經). In this fascicle, Dōgen explicates the epistemic problem of the dualistic attitude, which is symbolized as the attitude of "people outside the mountains" (*sangenin*, 山水外人), when he observes that "people outside the mountains do not experience. People, who don't have the eyes to see the mountains, do not experience, do not know, do not see, and do not hear" (SBGZ 1: 407). On the other hand, "in the mountains . . . there is not one person who meets another" (SBGZ 1: 427). Second, Dōgen argues that Śākyamuni's speech qua *mitsugo* comprises the non-dualism of individual and universal, form and formlessness. Dōgen reprimands those who follow the traditional interpretations of the flower sermon à la Shibayama. Śākyamuni's words do not comprise merely "form" (*meisō*, 名相) but simultaneously form and "formlessness" (*meisō naki koto*, 名相なきこと). Dōgen continues that both the "picking up of the flower" and the "words" equally constitute "formal" expressions of the formless. Third, similarly, Dōgen argues that both "knowledge" and "ignorance" constitute manifestations of the "secret," and thus both function as "paths" "to study the *buddha-dharma*."[11] Dōgen concludes that even "the moment when the *buddha-dharma* is not understood constitutes one aspect of secret talk" (SBGZ 4: 150).

In this way, Dōgen radically reinterprets the flower sermon as well as Master Yunju's commentary. Dōgen explains that the true *dharma* transcends the dichotomy between language and silence and encompasses both "secret words" and secret actions. The true *dharma* qua *mitsugo* remains transcendent and irrelevant and, subsequently, has to be manifested in a concrete form, in either language or silence. Even the "picking up of a flower" constitutes a form. The very term *mitsugo* indicates the non-dualism of linguistic and non-linguistic expression. Dōgen, however, goes one step further and implies, in words reminiscent of the phrase "this mind is the Buddha" that the *buddha-dharma* requires a non-dualism of, and subsequent manifestation in, both understanding and ignorance. This conclusion not only undermines the dichotomy between language and silence, ignorance and awakening inherent in the rhetoric of silence, but also discloses far-reaching implications for the conceptions of emptiness and language themselves. In the following sections, I will explore the conceptual framework for Dōgen's non-dualism and what its implications are for a philosophy of language and practice.

Dōgen's Hermeneutics of "Emptiness"

Today, Dōgen is seen as one, if not *the*, representative of Japanese Buddhist philosophy in general. But that has not always been the case. Even though he was a contemporary to Thomas Aquinas (1225–1274) and was regarded the founder of Japanese Sōtō Zen Buddhism, his work remained in relative obscurity until he was "discovered" for the thinkers of the Sōtō school by Dōhaku Manzan 卍山道白 (1636–1715) as well as Zuihō Menzan 面山瑞方 (1683–1769) in the Edo period (1603–1867) and introduced to the larger intellectual community of, first, Japan and, then, the world by Tetsujirō Watsuji 和辻哲郎 (1889–1960) and Uno Kimura 木村卯之. What makes Dōgen a figure of interest for us is that he developed a philosophical non-dualism that is probably unrivalled in its consistency and took the core features of the "philosophy of emptiness" as introduced by the *Prajñāpāramitā* literature as well as the Madhyamaka philosophers to heart. In short, he followed this line of thought implied in *śūnyatāvāda* to its radical conclusion. As I have tried to show in the previous section, Dōgen applies the non-duality of *nirvāṇa* and *saṃsāra* expressed by the *Heart Sūtra's dictum* that "form is emptiness,

emptiness is form," and by Chan master Mazu's assertion that "this mind is the Buddha" to the rhetoric of silence pervasive in the Chan Buddhist traditions, and arrives at the conclusion that silence and discourse are equally instances in which Buddha's *dharma* is "presenced" (*genjō*, 現成). The keys to this conception are the four key characteristics of a philosophy of emptiness as discussed above: 1) a distrust of concepts; 2) a methodic destabilization of language; 3) a method that anticipates dialectics insofar as it engages playfully in the juxtaposition of opposites; and 4) the emphasis on practice. What distinguishes Dōgen from many of his predecessors, though, is that he actually makes room for what we could call today a "linguistic practice." It is this acknowledgement of the soteriological efficacy of linguistic practice that brings him closer to Jacques Derrida's (1930–2004) deconstruction than any of the other thinkers and texts discussed here. And as Derrida (1982) anchors his theory and practice of deconstruction in the term *différance* (11), Dōgen grounds his subversive philosophy in his own creative understanding of "emptiness."

Early in his career, Dōgen wrote one fascicle each on the *Heart Sūtra* and on Mazu's observation that "this mind is the Buddha." In the former fascicle, Dōgen reminds the reader of the non-duality as expressed in the *Heart Sūtra* in the formula "form is emptiness, emptiness is form." Concretely, he suggests that

> the five *skandhas* are body, perception, emotion, volition, and consciousness. They are the five aspects of *prajñā*. Their illumination[12] is *prajñā*. When these meanings are presenced and performed, form is emptiness, emptiness is form, form is form, emptiness is emptiness. There are one hundred leaves of grass, there are ten thousand phenomena." (SBGZ 1: 78)

Saṃsāra and *nirvāṇa* are not different from each other; they do not mark two separate realms. But they are also not identical. They each reside, as Dōgen says, elsewhere, in their own "*dharma*-position" (*hōi*, 法位). In his fascicle "Presencing the Kōan" (*Genjōkōan*, 現成公案), Dōgen observes that "*dharma*-positions" "cut off" and "possess" "before-and-after" (SBGZ 1: 96). This means that each *dharma*-position is at the same time individual as well as complete, and yet, each resides in a larger continuity and causal web of infinite *dharma*-positions. To put it differently, the relationship among individual *dharma*-positions is one of ambiguity: they are neither the same nor separate: they are without an essence.

The key to this understanding of reality is the notion of "emptiness." As Dōgen observes in the last paragraph of the fascicle on the *Heart Sūtra*: "Therefore, the Buddhas Bhagavats are perfected wisdom, perfected wisdom is all *dharma*s. All *dharma*s reveal the mark of emptiness. They neither appear, nor disappear; they are neither defiled nor pure; they neither increase nor decrease" (SBZG 1: 89). Each phenomena is devoid of an essence. Thus, it is unique, and yet interrelated with and reflective of the whole universe. Seven hundred years after Dōgen, Nishida will call upon Leibniz's *monads* to express this ambiguity of Dōgen's *dharma*-position, even though Leibniz's own substantialism prevents him from articulating the ambiguity of individual phenomena appropriately and sufficiently.[13] In the fascicle "This Mind is the Buddha," Dōgen gives us a glimpse of how this vision of reality can be conceived. Ranting against what he calls the "Senika heresy" (*senni gedō*, 先尼外道), Dōgen suggests that "the Buddhas pick up and throw away one hundred leaves of grass" and that "this triple world . . . is not mind-only, but that the mind constitutes fences and walls. . . . Therefore, practice 'this mind is the Buddha'"[14] (SBGZ 1: 141). Because emptiness is the fundamental nature of reality, each phenomenon, or as Dōgen says, each "*dharma*-position," constitutes an individual expression of the whole universe. As Dōgen famously says elsewhere: "to forget the self is to be actualized by the ten thousand *dharmas*" (SBGZ 1: 95).

The lesson to be learned here is a very important one. The theory of "emptiness" rejects the notion of essence, not the notion of existence. "Essence" or "self-nature" implies the causally independent existence of a permanent being. The theory of "emptiness" pronounces that reality is impermanent, interconnected and, most of all, ambiguous. To avoid the traps of essentialism and dualism, Dōgen devises a sophisticated conceptual strategy. In the good tradition of Buddhist philosophy, Dōgen provides his own heuristic device on how to interpret various philosophical positions as well as epistemic states during the process of self-cultivation. While his model is not as historically or doctrinally accurate as the *panjiao* 教判 systems of, for example, Fazang 法藏 (643–712 CE) and Kūkai 空海 (774–835 CE), it is not only conceptually precise and consistent but also continuous with the philosophical traditions of *śūnyatāvada* and Chan Buddhism. In this section, I will first examine Dōgen's heuristic model and then explore its implication for his theories of language and practice in the final section.

The prototype of Dōgen's heuristic model can be found in the opening paragraph of the fascicle "Presencing of the Kōan":

> When all *dharmas* have Buddha nature, there is delusion and awakening, there is practice, there is life, there is death, there are all buddhas, there are sentient beings. When neither *dharmas* nor self exist, there is neither delusion nor awakening, there are neither buddhas nor sentient beings, there is neither life nor death. Because the Buddha-way is originally beyond fulfillment and lack, there is birth and destruction, delusion and awakening, sentient beings. Nevertheless, flowers fall in regret, grass grows in dismay (SBGZ 1: 94).

To general readers, this passage can be confusing on a first reading, and even scholars do not necessarily agree on its interpretation. However, a second look clearly reveals a fourfold structure. Each line commences with a condition, a description of a mental or cognitive state, which is followed by a position or belief characteristic of this particular state. The positions described in the second half of each sentence are about Buddhist themes such as delusion, awakening, life, death, sentient beings, and buddhas. This passage, then, seems to imply that, even in Buddhism, there are a variety of beliefs about these rather central matters. At stake is the process of progressing from delusion to awakening and the relationship between these stages. While he does not identify the various beliefs by schools or thinker as Fazang and Kūkai do, this passage does imply a ranking of these beliefs, and hence a subtle criticism of certain positions within Buddhism. As a reading of his fascicle "This Mind is the Buddha" reveals, his main target is the so-called Senika heresy, which he accuses of advocating the "belief in a permanent self" (*ātmavāda*, 計我論). In the same fascicle, he also accuses certain interpretations of Mazu's "this mind is the Buddha" and by implication certain theories of "buddha-nature," also referred to as the *tathāgatagarbha* doctrine, of essentialism. The first line of the passage reiterates this criticism. But what does this passage aim at? How can these positions be interpreted?

The first three lines are reminiscent of the famous Chan saying from the *Record of the Transmission of the Lamp* (*Xu zhuangdeng lu*, 續傳燈錄) (T 51.2077):

> Thirty years ago, when I had not yet started meditation, I saw that mountains were mountains, waters were waters. After I had begun meditating and gained some knowledge, I saw that mountains were not mountains, waters were not waters. But now as I have achieved a place free of desire, I see that mountains are just mountains and waters are just waters (T 51.2077.614).

The similarities between both models are striking, and Dōgen's reference to this saying in the "Mountain and Water *Sūtra*" indicates that he had knowledge of it. The structure of the three levels introduced in the first three lines of Dōgen's "Presencing the Kōan," and the famous saying from the *Records of the Transmission of the Lamp* is *affirmation*, *negation*, and what D.T. Suzuki calls "*higher affirmation*" (Suzuki 1964, 66). Dōgen adds to this structure three elements: First, while the *Records of the Transmission of the Lamp* locates the various cognitive stages in the very process of meditation itself, Dōgen assigns to them ideological positions: a) positivism, that is, the belief that "*dharma*s have a nature"; b) nihilism, that is the belief that there are "neither *dharma*s nor self"; and c) a third position, best called "non-dualism," that is beyond easy juxtapositions and describes the primary condition, literally, "originally" (*motoyori*, もとより) of any kind of knowledge. Dōgen also structurally distinguishes the third position from the former two, and seems to indicate that the third position mediates between the first two, especially since it said to be "beyond dichotomies." The first two lines commence with the phrase "when there are (not) *dharma*s," while the third one starts with the phrase "because" and implies an "original" standpoint. Second, Dōgen is definitely interested in the interplay between dualities in addition to the aspects of affirmation and negation. Finally, and most importantly, Dōgen added a fourth line.

How are we to understand Dōgen's heuristic model? He very clearly incorporates aspects of the "two truths" (*erdi*, 二諦) developed in Madhyamaka philosophy, "mundane truth" (*saṃvṛti-satya*, 世俗諦) and "ultimate truth" (*paramārtha-satya*, 勝義諦), as well as Zhiyi's 智顗 (538–597 CE) "three truths" (*sandi*, 三諦): "emptiness" (*kong*, 空), "provisionality" (*jia*, 假), and the "middle" (*zong*, 中). However, in some sense Dōgen's model seems to have more in common with Nāgārjuna's tetralemma.[15] Let us recall Nāgārjuna's discussion of *nirvāṇa* where he rejects the notion that *nirvāṇa* constitutes being, nonbeing, both, or neither. Similarly, Dōgen suggests, not with regard to a term, but to the relationship between two terms, that there is a duality, there is no duality, there is the coexistence of both terms of the duality, and the duality disappears. This comparison lacks in four obvious ways: 1) Nāgārjuna talks about terms, Dōgen about the relationship between opposites; 2) Dōgen does not actually say that the duality both exists and does not exist, but rather hints at this predicament by expressing that phenomena exist in relationship to their opposites and, thus, opposites are, simultaneously, separate and connected; 3) Dōgen avoids the phraseology of the fourth line of the tetralemma altogether by employing poetical terminology; 4) Nāgārjuna rejects the four possibilities of being, nonbeing, both, and neither, while Dōgen seems to affirm them by locating them in different epistemic contexts. What makes this analogy interesting, however, is that the quarternity of "is," "is not," "both," and "neither" actually informs Dōgen's model if it is applied to the relationship between opposites rather than to terms themselves.

The most helpful key to his heuristic model, however, comes from Dōgen's fascicle "Buddha-Nature" (*Busshō*, 佛性), where he reinterprets the famous line from the *Mahāparinirvāṇa Sūtra* that "all sentient beings have buddha-nature" (T 12.374.522). What is of interest for the current discussion is not Dōgen's re-reading of this line, but rather his reinterpretation of the notion of "buddha-nature" (佛性) as what has been called "being-buddha-nature" (有佛性) (SBGZ 2: 206), "non-being-buddha-nature" (無佛性) (SBGZ 2: 223), "emptiness-buddha-nature" (空佛性), and "impermanence buddha-nature" (*mujōbusshō* 無常佛性).[16] Dōgen creates the term "non-being buddha-nature" by means of a playful reading of the *Records of the Transmission of the Lamp*. This text recalls the first meeting between the fifth and sixth patriarchs of Chan Buddhism, also recorded in the *Platform Sūtra* (T 48.2008.348). However, the *Records of the Transmission of the Lamp* cites the fifth patriarch as saying "people from the South do not have Buddha-nature" (T 51.2076.222). Dōgen re-reads "not having buddha-nature" (無佛性) as "non-being-buddha-nature" (無佛性). In the fascicle "Buddha-Nature," Dōgen himself only uses the terms "being-buddha-nature" and "non-being-Buddha-nature" as nouns, and, after an idiosyncratic analysis of anecdotes from the "*Zen Records*" (*Chanyulu*, 禪語錄) and central Mahāyāna *sūtra*s, he concludes that "Buddha nature is originally non-existent" (*foxingbenwu*, 佛性本無) (48.2008.348), "Buddha-nature is empty" (佛性空) (T 31.1589.70), and "Buddha-nature is impermanent" (*busshōmujō* 佛性無常), literally, "impermanence is buddha-nature" (SBGZ 2: 228; T

48.2008.359). It is, of course, no coincidence that Dōgen identifies "being" and "nonbeing" as nouns, and "empty" and "impermanence" as adjectives. Like Nāgārjuna, Dōgen uses the "medicine of emptiness" to avoid the conclusion that either "Buddha-nature" or "nonbeing" constitutes or possesses an *essence*. And just in case anyone is tempted to essentialize "being empty" as "emptiness," Dōgen drives home the point that, "no," "buddha-nature is impermanent."

Finally, Dōgen urges the reader to "always practice" (*gyōji*, 行持) (SBGZ 3: 33–192). This exhortation indicates an inherent openness and it reflects his commitment to the doctrine of impermanence. In some sense, Dōgen seems to indefinitely defer "attainment," be it cognitive, moral, or spiritual.

Conclusion

How are we to understand a worldview without essences? What is the relationship between individual and Buddha-*dharma*, between self and other in such a world? The probably most often cited quote of Dōgen is a passage from the fascicle "Presencing the Kōan," in which Dōgen suggests that meditation is about self-awareness. He famously says, "[t]o study the Buddha-way is to study the self, to study the self is to forget the self, to forget the self is to be actualized by ten thousand *dharma*s" (SBGZ 1: 95). In some sense, this is just a description of meditation as a process of self-awareness. But on a closer look, it is obvious that Dōgen's fourfold hermeneutical model applies: 1) "to study the self" constitutes an affirmation of the self; 2) "to forget the self" suggests its negation; 3) "to be actualized by ten thousand *dharma*s" takes the practitioner beyond the dichotomies of self and no self, individual and the totality, and suggests that in its practice the self "expresses"[17] the world; 4) this "expression" is beyond the dualities of self and other, body and mind. Of course, this does not completely correlate to the notion of impermanence in the fourfold model. We have to read it in the context of Dōgen's overall exhortation of "continuous practice." In Dōgen's view, even one moment of "seated meditation" (*zazen*, 坐禪) can actualize "all *dharmas*" (SBGZ 1: 35).

This brings us back to Dōgen's philosophy of language. To explain how "esoteric words and esoteric actions are presenced" (SBGZ 4: 155), Dōgen utilizes a "commonplace expression" (Kim 1987, 67) (*dōtoku*, 道得). The compound comprises the Chinese characters for "way" and "to say" (*dō*, 道), and "accomplishment" (*toku*, 得). Hee-Jin Kim suggests that "[t]he term signifies simultaneously what is said and what can be said—expression and expressibility; at the same time, it means the Way's appropriation, making and expression, the embodiment of the Way" (67). Dōgen defines "expression" as the activity of "all buddhas": "all buddhas constitute verification" (SBGZ 3: 384) and "all buddha-patriarchs constitute expression" (SBGZ 3: 366).

At the same time, however, he points out the necessary dialectic between "expression" and "non-expression" (*fudōtoku*). Dōgen explains that

> [w]hen we express expression we do not express non-expression. Even when we recognize expression in expression, if we do not verify the depth of non-expression as the depth of non-expression, we are neither in the face of the buddha-ancestors nor in the bones and marrow of the buddha-ancestors. . . . In me, there is expression and non-expression. In him, there is expression and non-expression. In the Way, there is self and other and in the non-Way, there is self and other (SBGZ 3: 368–369).

Here, Dōgen makes three fundamental observations. First, language is highly ambiguous: expressions, linguistic and non-linguistic, usurp the space between language and silence as demonstrated in the analysis of "esoteric words." Similarly, expressions themselves imply, if not necessitate, their opposites, non-expressions, since "[e]ven when we recognize expression in expression, if we do not verify the depth of non-expression as the depth of non-expression, we are neither in the face of the buddha-ancestors nor in the bones and marrow of the buddha-ancestors." Second, "expressions" and "non-expressions," language and silence, presuppose the intersubjective space between self and other and thus point toward the dialogue between the master and the disciple: "In the Way there is self and other and in the non-Way, there is self and other."

In his fascicle "Tangled Vines" (*Kattō*, 葛藤), Dōgen elaborates on this psychic interwovenness of self and other exemplified as master-disciple when he exhorts the practitioner, "[y]ou should know that there is 'you are attaining me', 'I am attaining you', 'attaining me and you', and 'attaining you and me'" (SBGZ 4: 15). Similarly, he observes in his *Mountain and Water Sūtra* that " '[t]he person sees Decheng' means that there is Decheng, while 'Decheng touches the person' means that there is the person" (SBGZ 1: 431). Third, expressions are indeterminate insofar as they presuppose a minimum of four possibilities: the expression of expression, the expression of non-expression, the non-expression of expression, and the non-expression of non-expression. This multiplicity of possibilities discloses the ultimately volatile and ambiguous nature of language as well as of non-linguistic expression. Every single moment of "seated meditation" and any other activity fully "expresses" the buddha-*dharma*. At the same time, it constitutes a non-expression, as it fails to "express" an infinite amount of other expressions. Therefore, "seated meditation" constitutes an open-ended process that is never complete. This is "the paradox of meditation," for it "expresses the Buddha-dharma fully but not completely."[18]

As we have seen, in his writings, Dōgen uses a plethora of heuristic strategies. He employs creative readings of phrases from the Buddhist canon, as in the case of "no (non-being)-buddha-nature." He juxtaposes opposites such as "delusion" (*mayoi*, 迷い) and "awakening" (*satori*, 悟り). He creates tripartite heuristic models that expand on the juxtaposition of "being" and "nonbeing" by including "emptiness," to preclude any forms of dualism, as well as the fourfold models discussed above, which incorporate the moment of impermanence to ward off essentialism. With the tripartite models in particular, Dōgen introduces a deconstructive method to destabilize conceptual language that has been used by Zen thinkers in general, as well as modern and contemporary philosophers, to 1) map out the process of self-cultivation; 2) establish a phenomenology of self-cultivation; and 3) develop a modern day *panjiao* system.

To sum up Dōgen's theory of emptiness: it is a rejection of positivism, annihilationism, dualism, and monism; in short, it is a rejection of any form of essentialism. This is why Dōgen rejects not only the rhetoric of silence, what Noriaki Hakamaya (1990) calls "*dhātuvāda*" (63), the *tathāgatagarbha* doctrine, but also even the "doctrine of emptiness" itself. It is not so much that these positions are wrong as they are insufficient and provide ample opportunities for attachment. To ward off the possibility of attachment, Dōgen systematically subverts the concepts in questions, since the simple negation of the *Heart Sūtra* may lead to annihilationism while Nāgārjuna's tetralemma logic may land us in the rhetoric of silence. Dōgen is equally critical of his predecessors in the Chan tradition if their slogans fall either into the positivistic or the annihilationistic trap. Even non-dual philosophies are not immune to essentialism. This is why Dōgen always emphasizes "continuous action." Philosophy is a practice, and an open-ended one at that. The three stages as outlined in the first three lines of the fascicle "Presencing the Kōan," can thus be understood as three stages of the process of self-cultivation à la Takuan, as three levels of a phenomenological reduction, as Thomas Kasulis suggests, or, following Nishida, as three epistemic modalities. All these approaches can be considered extensions of Dōgen's thought as long as one remembers his warning: "Nevertheless, flowers fall in regret, grass grows in dismay."

Notes

1 I would like to thank Luther College for my sabbatical leave, Saitama University for my research affiliation, and the Nanzan Institute for Religion and Culture for their hospitality. This paper would have not been possible without the support of these three institutions. I would also like to thank the online resource of CBETA and the *Digital Dictionary of Buddhism*, without which this paper would have been a lot harder to complete.

2 Abe distinguishes between "non-being," which is conceived of as opposed to "being," and "nothingness," which transcends this duality. Here, I follow Nishida's lead and call the former "relative non-being" (*tairitsuteki mu* 對立的無) (NKZ 1988, 4: 219) and the latter "absolute non-being" (*zettai mu* 絕對無) (5: 176).

3 For a detailed argument on how to understand Nishida's use of "*soku*" as deconstruction, see Maraldo (2003) and Kopf (2010a).

4 In verse 52 of his *Acintyastava*, Nāgārjuna writes that "[t]he Ultimate truth is the teaching that things are without own-being. This is the unsurpassed medicine for those consumed by the fever of *svabhāva*" (Lindtner 1986, 29).

5 Kumārajīva's translation of the *Diamond Sūtra* shows two occurrences of "empty space" (虛空). For a more detailed discussion of this term, see Section 2 ("Emptiness" and the Rhetoric of Silence) of this paper.

6 Michiko Yusa (2014) makes this suggestion in her discussion of D. T. Suzuki's philosophy that will appear this year in the *Dao Companion to Japanese Buddhist Philosophy*. Suzuki believed that Mahāyāna Buddhist thinkers developed this "logic of *sokuhi*" to express the intersection of the transcendent and the immanent in the

religious experience (SDZ 1968–1971, 6: 14–15). In his *Essays in Zen Buddhism*, he suggests that

> perhaps our so-called logic is only the ultimate utilitarian instrument wherewith we handle things belonging to the superficialities of life. The spirit, or that which occupies the deepest part of our being, requires something thoroughly non-conceptual, i.e., something immediate and far more penetrating than mere intellection. The latter draws its materials from concepts. The spirit demands immediate perceptions (Suzuki 1976, 270).

7 Despite obvious similarities, this classification does not correspond to Ferdinand de Saussure's (1857–1913) distinction between "signifier" (*signifiant*) and "signified" (*signifié*), which conceptualizes the relationship between sign and meaning.
8 Editors' note: see Chapter 16 by Halla Kim for a detailed discussion on Chinul.
9 Thomas P. Kasulis (2011, 16) employs the same translation of "*mitsugo*."
10 The origin of the title to this collection of Dōgen's essay is not clear. Since his departure from China preceded the distribution of the *Gateless Barrier*, he probably did not know of its sixth case. A possible source is Zonggao Dahui's 大慧宗杲 (1089–1163) kōan collection with the same title.
11 Here I paraphrase Dōgen's famous "to study the Buddha-way" (SBGZ 1: 95).
12 Dōgen employs the term, "*shōken*" (照見) (T 1961, 8.253.849, 8.254.850, 8.255.850) used in most Chinese translations of the *Heart Sutra*.
13 Nishida explains that

> Spinoza goes so far as to deny the individual and arrives at a timeless world. When we get to Leibniz, we see that he thinks being in the direction of many individuals. He introduces the notion of expressive action to account for the relationship between the one and the many. From there we have to proceed to the contradictory identity of that which expresses and that which is expressed. However, Leibniz stops at the standpoint of pluralism (NKZ 1988, 10:490–491).

14 Actually, Dōgen suggest five different character combinations of "this mind is the Buddha," all of which should be practiced.
15 Editors' note: see Chapter 3 of this volume by Jay Garfield for a detailed discussion on Nāgārjuna's tetralemma.
16 As I will explain below, Dōgen only uses the first two terms in this form but describes the two latter terms in such a way that even these formulations are warranted.
17 I borrow the term "expression" (*hyōgen*, 表現) from Nishida, who uses it to describe how the individual is determined by the world that surrounds her and, at the same time, "creates" (*tsukuru*, 作る) the future world through her actions.
18 I have mapped out this dynamics of expression in my "Ambiguity, Diversity, and an Ethics of Understanding: What Nishida's Philosophy Can Contribute to the Pluralism Debate" (Kopf 2011).

18 Anontology and the Issue of Being and Nothing in Kitarō Nishida

John W. M. Krummel

Undeniably the concept of the nothing or nothingness (*mu*, 無) stands out as one of the most important concepts in NISHIDA Kitarō's (西田幾多郎) philosophical oeuvre. Its importance for the rest of the Kyoto School can be attested to in the way that it was inherited, critiqued, and developed by his contemporaries and successors. What did Nishida mean by *mu*? In this chapter, I will explicate what Nishida meant by the term and trace its development from its pre-Nishidian origins through his appropriations of the concept during the various periods of his philosophical career from the 1910s to the 1940s. I will also provide my own reading of Nishida's concept of the nothing in terms of what I call *anontology*. But in order to comprehend what Nishida generally meant by *nothing*, a grasp of his sense of the accompanying term of *being* (*yū*, 有) would be in order. I shall thus begin with a short summary of how he understands the two contrasting terms of being and nothing.

Being and Nothing, Form and Formlessness

Nishida often characterizes the distinction between being and nothing in terms of the cultural contrast of West and East. In the preface to *Hatarakumono kara mirumono e* (『働くものから見るものへ』); From the working to the seeing) of 1927, he contrasts the "brilliant development of Western civilization that takes form as being" and "the root of Eastern culture that harbors within itself that which sees the form of the formless and hears the sound of the soundless" (Z3: 255)[1]—a formlessness that has nurtured the traditions of the East. The distinction he makes here between West and East is that between form (*keisō*, 形相; *katachi*, 形) and formlessness. Being (*yū*) corresponds to form and the nothing corresponds to the formless. Beings accordingly are what are present in *determinate form*, contrasted and differentiated from one another. In *Tetsugaku no konpon mondai* (『哲學の根本問題』; Fundamental problems of philosophy) of 1933–1934, Nishida reiterates this contrast by stating that the thought of being is at the root of Western culture while the thought of the nothing is at the root of Eastern culture (Z6: 348). Here as well, reality for the West is grounded in *being qua form*, while reality for the East is grounded in *the nothing as formless*. Because the European tradition conceives the root of reality to be being (*yū*) or the "possession of form (*yūkei*, 有形)," it prioritizes "the form-possessing [*katachiarumono*, 形あるもの], the determinate [*genteiseraretamono*, 限定せられたもの], as reality [*jitsuzai*, 實在]" (Z6: 335–336). On the premise that "something cannot be born from nothing" (*ex nihilo nihil fit*), the ancient Greeks came to conceive of the source of all beings in terms of a constant and unchanging primordial being. The prime example here would be the Platonic *ideas* serving as principles of the actual world, and among which the ultimate source would be the "*idea* of the Good."[2] The Platonic concept of the *idea* (ἰδέα) etymologically means "form" (*eidos*, εἶδος), which also literally means the "look" of a thing, and hence that which can be objectified in its visibility to the eye, or by extension, its intelligibility. In Nishida's view, the ancient Greek philosophy that became the source of Western culture took form in this sense as the ground of what is real. By contrast, the Eastern tradition takes a certain formlessness or non-substantiality—as in the Buddhist sense of the emptiness of substance (Skt. *śūnyatā*, Jp. *kū*, 空; Skt. *nihsvabhāva*)—to be the source of everything. Nishida makes the same contrast in 1940 in *Nihon bunka no mondai* (『日本文化の問題』; The problem of Japanese culture) when he speaks of Western antiquity as conceiving the root of reality to be being (*yū*) and the formed (*yūkei*, 有形), and Eastern antiquity as conceiving the root of reality to be the nothing (*mu*) and the formless (*mukei*, 無形) (Z9: 60).

This division of the globe that reduces its hemispheres into distinct metaphysical categories of form and formlessness appears simplistic. Nishida ignores aspects of Presocratic thought that might exemplify his sense of an originary formlessness, for example, Anaximander's *apeiron*—even though Nishida does mention it, it is only to reduce it to the sense of a self-contained circle—or Hesiod's *chaos* that was also a kind of void. An outright exclusion of any sort of philosophical understanding of nothingness for the West would be unfair. Counterexamples to such reduction nevertheless would all fall outside of the main current of the Western tradition. Nishida was primarily reacting to the mainstream of Western philosophy. His stance is not without significance as a response to what he found in that current: substantialism and dualism. In consequence, Nishida announces his project of what came to be called "Nishidian philosophy" (*Nishida tetsugaku*, 西田哲學) in the following manner: to provide a philosophical grounding for the demand to seek after *the formless* hidden at the root of Eastern culture (Z3: 255).

To understand what Nishida means by *nothing* (*mu*), we need to keep in mind what he means by *being* (*yū*). It is clear from the above that Nishida understands by *being* that which is determined, distinguished, or differentiated from others, that is, a *thing* with determinate properties, having form. *The nothing* by contrast is the formless and undifferentiated potential for such formations and differentiations. *Nothing* in Nishida's sense, while meaning *to not have form*, cannot mean utter nothingness or that there is nothing existing. More precisely, Nishida takes *nothing* to be a dynamism that perpetually forms itself while remaining essentially formless—it is that which every being qua formed must presuppose. In his 1926 *Basho* (『場所』; "Place") essay, Nishida states that "to be" is "to be implaced" (Z3: 415). What he means is that to be determinate, formed, or differentiated is to stand in relation to others, and this in turn presupposes a place wherein things can be differentiated but also related. This leads him to his notion of the nothing as a kind of an opening, which envelops and makes room for the determinate and mutually distinct or differentiated beings. In other words, the ground is a place that is an abysmally open *un*ground. According to Nishida, the ground of being cannot be conceived in terms of what has form in that we will be forced to inquire after the cause of that form and the cause of its cause, *ad infinitum*, since every form in itself is determinate and hence determined.[3] We avoid this problem by conceiving the ground as an unground, an undelimited place providing space for the causal interactions between things with form. Only the formless can envelop forms, only a no-thing can envelop things. And so, rather than partaking in the philosophical search for an "absolute being" that would ground all beings—a metaphysical principle whether it be *idea*, God, or reason or subjectivity that would secure their rationale—Nishida chooses to plumb the depths beneath being to face that abyss, un/ground, which he designates "absolute nothing (*zettai mu*, 絶對無)." But before we follow the unfolding of his philosophy of absolute nothing, let me touch briefly upon possible sources of his conception.

Sources from East and West

In looking for the sources of Nishida's conception of the nothing, the easiest route would be to simply take his own dichotomization between East and West for granted and to assume that his idea of *mu* is nothing but Eastern in origin. The most obvious source from the East would be Buddhism, since *mu* (Ch. *wu* 無) itself is one of the principle concepts of Japanese Zen. Japanese Zennists often emphasize the term "nothing" or "no" (*mu*) and related phrases like "no mind (*mushin*, 無心)" and "no self (*muga*, 無我)." The use of this notion however was made pivotal in the famous dialogue between Chan[4] master Zhaozhōu (Jp. Joshū, 趙州) (778–897 CE) and a monk. The dialogue was made into a *kōan*,[5] often called "Zhaozhōu's dog" (or "Joshū's dog," 趙州狗子) and recorded in the thirteenth-century collection of *kōans*, *Wumenguan* (Jp. *Mumonkan* 『無門關』; Gateless gate) as its first *kōan*. In the dialogue, the monk asks Zhaozhōu whether a dog has buddha-nature, and Zhaozhōu replies "no[thing]." It is well known that Nishida undertook Zen meditation practice from his late twenties through his thirties and also undertook *kōan* training. It is significant that one of the culminating points of his *kōan* training was his passing of this *kōan* of *mu* under his Zen teacher. This was when he was thirty-four years old, two years before he began drafting his first major philosophical work (*Zen no kenkyū* 『善の研究』; Inquiry into the good, 1911). In turn, this Zen notion of *mu* can be traced to the Daoist influence upon Chinese Chan. Nishida's understanding of being as being-formed thus can be traced to Chinese Daoism as well. According to A.C. Graham, the Chinese graph for being (Jp. *yū*, Ch. *yǒu*, 有) has the sense of either being a possessor of properties or being itself a property belonging to something.[6] Its opposite, *not to have* or *not to be had*, means "to be without distinction or determination" for the ancient Chinese. For ancient Daoist texts such as the *Daodejing*, indistinction or indeterminateness is *the nothing* (*wu*), which also serves as the potentiality for becoming something. The Daoists characterized the *dao* (Jp. *dō*, 道) that is the oneness and source of all reality in such terms as a *nothing* (*wu*), a formless and nameless empty vessel, the chaos preceding distinctions between *this* and *that*, *yes* and *no*.[7] Nishida's fondness for the Daoist classics (the *Laozi* or *Daodejing* and the *Zhuangzi*) is evident in his diary.[8] Another interesting point in regard to this ancient Chinese concept of *wu* is that originally it referred to a cleared opening made in what was previously covered by thick vegetation.[9] Nishida himself was probably unaware of such ancient etymological significances or pre-philosophical meanings of the term. Nevertheless, it is interesting to note this ancient association of the sense of a nothing with an open space in light of Nishida's own development of the concept in terms of place.

Within Zen, the Daoist sense of *wu* historically became intermingled with the Mahāyāna theme of emptiness (Jp. *kū*, Ch. *kong*, 空). The Daoist sense of nondistinction became associated with the Mahāyāna motif of the middle way that escapes reduction to being on the one hand and nonbeing on the other, an idea traceable to the *Heart Sutra*'s equation that "form is emptiness and emptiness is form." Nishida appears to walk that middle path of Mahāyāna with his understanding of a primal nothing that not only negates substantialism (being) but also its opposite (nonbeing). The source for Nishida's frequently used metaphor for the nothing as an empty mirror that mirrors itself might be found in the Buddhist classic *The Awakening of Faith in the Mahāyāna*.[10] In his later works, Nishida makes frequent and explicit references to other Buddhist ideas, including emptiness, in association with his concept of the absolute nothing. For example, in his 1940s piece *Kūkan* (『空間』; "Space") he speaks of "the true emptiness of Buddhism" (*bukkyō no shinkū*, 真空) (Z10: 157), and in 1939 he speaks of his interest in the vision of emptiness (*kūkan*, 空観) hidden in the depths of Eastern culture and upon which he would like to build his philosophy.[11]

Yet it would be misleading to ignore Western sources of influence on Nishida's concept of the nothing, to which Nishida himself refers. The Neo-Kantian notion of validity as nonbeing is significant in this regard. In brief, the Neo-Kantians, inheriting Hermann Lotze's dichotomy, dualistically distinguished the realm of validity (*Geltung*), for example, "truth," as a realm of nonbeing (*Nichtseiende*, *Nichtsein*), from the realm of being (*Sein*), what-is, confined to the realm of the sensible material. The two, validity and being, are distinct but related. *Being* can be predicated of the sensible matter of perception or cognition, for example, "The desk I see in front of me *exists*." *Validity*, on the other hand, constitutes a distinct realm and involves value (*Wert*). Values—for example, truth, beauty, goodness—while not falling under the domain of what-is (being), provide the ultimate meaning or intelligibility behind what-is. What we can say of them is not that they exist but that they are valid. While a being "is" (*Seiendes ist*), values "are valid" (*Werte gelten*).[12] However, "the last" Neo-Kantian, Emil Lask, who had a profound influence on the development of Nishida's theory of place during the 1920s, viewed validity qua intelligibility as inseparable from beings in our pre-thematic "immediate intuitable lived experience" (*unmittelbare anschauliche Erleben*). That is to say, we encounter things as already imbued with meaning prior to making judgments about them.[13] Meaning or intelligibility here is the context one lives through, and within which the thing is experienced prior to its thematization. I believe that this Laskian sense of validity that is *not being* gave Nishida a clue to developing his own notion of *the place of nothing*, within which objects thematized (i.e., beings) belong. Nishida makes it his project to bridge the dichotomy he inherits from Neo-Kantianism, and in that respect repeatedly refers to Lask in the period when he is formulating his theory of place. For the Neo-Kantians, what determines being to provide it with intelligibility is validity qua nonbeing; for Nishida, it is the nothing that does the same. The difference here is that in Nishida—radicalizing Lask's sense of the inseparability of being and validity (meaning)—the nothing is *self-forming*. He aimed to show that that duality in its inseparability cannot be traced to two distinct entities—subject and object—but must have its source in a self-forming dynamic whole. It is this holistic dynamism that Nishida will conceive in terms of *the place of nothing*, as that *wherein* each pole of a dichotomy—such as subject and object—can have its rightful place relative to one another.

The hylomorphism in Neo-Kantian epistemology can be traced in turn to Plato. But Plato's hylomorphism, in reverse to that of the Neo-Kantians, takes the transcendent *ideas*, and not their matter of formation, to be true being. By contrast, the receptacle of that formation by *ideas* is a kind of nothing, an indeterminate space that Plato called *chōra* (χώρα). In Nishida's initial formulation of the concept of the nothing in terms of a primal place (*basho*), he did refer to Plato's *chōra* (see Z3: 415). But Nishida reverses the Platonic hierarchy of *idea-chōra* by developing the Laskian collapse of the Neo-Kantian dichotomy in terms of an abyssal place that is *self*-determining rather than being the mere receptacle of determination.

A third Western source—in addition to Plato and Neo-Kantianism—for Nishida's *nothing* is the mystical tradition. Nishida frequently refers to mystics like Pseudo-Dionysius, Nicholas of Cusa, Meister Eckhart, and Jacob Böhme, and their notions of a "dazzling obscurity" or *das Nichts* (the nothing) that is at the same time the divine source of creation but is reached *via* negation. We see this already in *Zen no kenkyū*, wherein he refers to the thirteenth century mystic Nicholas of Cusa and his idea that God transcends both being and nonbeing while at the same time God is also both being and nonbeing (Z1: 151). One could argue that this sense of a transcendence of *both* being and nonbeing, together with the East Asian notion of nothing (both Jp. *mu* and Ch. *wu*) as the nondistinction of opposites, is an important contributor to what I shall call Nishida's *anontological* sense of the nothing. Aside from Cusa, Nishida in his first book also refers to Jakob Böhme's notions of God as an "unground" or "without ground" (Jp. *mutei*, 無底; Ger. *Ungrund*), "stillness without anything" (*Stille ohne Wesen*), and "will without an object" (*Wille ohne Gegenstand*); and Meister Eckhart's notions of God as "Godhead" or "Godhood" (Jp. *shinsei*, 神性; Ger. *Gottheit*) and his idea that the true God is where even God has been lost (Z1: 148, 151, 153).[14] All of this is significant for Nishida's own development of his concept of God (*kami*, 神) and the absolute (*zettai*, 絕對) or absolute one (*zettaisha*, 絕對者) that he seems to equate with, or at least associate with, his notion of the absolute nothing (*zettai mu*). In his final essay, *Bashoteki ronri to shūkyōteki sekaikan* (『場所的論理と宗教的世界觀』; The logic of place and the religious worldview) of 1945, immediately after stating that the true God is what the Western mystics called *Gottheit*, Nishida adds that this "is the emptiness of the *Prajñāpāramitā*" (*hannya no kū*, 般若の空) (Z10: 104–105). But we also cannot understate the significance of the Biblical idea of *kenosis*, or "self-emptying," that appears in Paul's Letter to the Philippians (Phil. 2: 6–8) for Nishida's explication of the self-negating act of the nothing. In other words, we cannot deny that there is a Christian element within Nishida's thoughts concerning the nothing, even if he gives it his own distinct coloring.

Now that we have touched upon some of the background sources from both Western and Eastern traditions that informed Nishida's formulations about the nothing, we are ready to look into the evolution of his own theory.

Nishida's Formulations of the Nothing: Plumbing the Depths of Being From Inner Self to Outer World

Nietzsche once stated: "When you gaze into an abyss, the abyss also gazes into you."[15] According to Nishida, the abyss looking back does so from the bottomless depths of one's own self. In the early stages of his oeuvre, Nishida expressed the formless source of forms in a series of formulations that make the inward-directedness of his approach conspicuous: "pure experience," "self-awareness," "absolute free will," and so forth. In all these formulations, the nothing is explicitly non-dual because it ontologically and phenomenologically precedes the subject-object duality. However, Nishida places the focus on the introspective. His project to uncover this formless source of forms began as an epistemological one to bridge the seemingly insurmountable gap recognized in Western epistemology between the knowing subject and the known object. Nishida arrives at a solution to the dichotomy through a kind of phenomenological introspection: the primal nondiscrimination of subject-object in one's concrete immediacy, entailing a rejection of the entire debate between materialism and idealism that has occupied much of the history of Western philosophy. As the formless potential for realities—both material and mental—the nothing refuses reduction to either. On this basis, Nishida can take the self-formation of the formless as *also* a kind of *self-seeing* or *self-mirroring* that unfolds in the depths of the individual's self. Thus, from the 1910s to the 1920s, Nishida takes an introspective approach to the nothing that grounds reality. This is in contrast to the more outward-looking approach that he later takes in the 1930s. For the convenience of the reader I will subdivide this section into subsections corresponding to important phases in Nishida's thought.

Pure Experience and Absolute Will (1911–1920s)

As just stated, one of Nishida's primary concerns during those early years was epistemological: How does the knowing subject cross the gap of otherness in order to know the object? The solution for Nishida lay in their pre-cognitive primal nondistinction. The very distinction between subject and object unfolds only through the self-differentiation or determination of that primal nondistinction. In the early teens in *Zen no kenkyū*, Nishida expresses that sense of an originary nondistinction in terms of pure experience (*junsui keiken*, 純粋經驗). By this he meant one's most immediate experience before the advent of reflection that would dichotomize the event in terms of subject ("I") and object ("it"). In pure experience, one is absorbed in the act, "at one" with the experience itself. Distinction is only latent to permit its unfolding, "after the fact," through reflection and judgment. Yet this significance of pure experience for Nishida was neither only epistemological nor a subjective state of mind. Pure experience bears ontological significance in its subsequent unfolding. In harboring the potential for differentiation and diversification, pure experience is also taken to be the infinite and unifying force of cosmic reality itself. Nishida named the foundation of that infinite activity of the cosmos, "God (*kami*, 神)." But he also characterized it as "the nothing (*mu*, 無)" in its indeterminateness, whereby he claimed, "God is completely nothing" (*mattaku mu*, 全く無) (Z1: 81). In other words, the nondistinction in the individual's pure experience mirrors, or is nondistinct with, the nondistinction at the root of the cosmos, God as nothing. In his later works, Nishida goes on to speak of the absolute one mirroring itself or manifesting itself through the interactivities of many individuals. But already at the initiation of his career, Nishida equated God and the nothing, both as the root of reality and of the self—an equation that he would return to and develop in detail in his final essay of 1945.

In the series of works following *Zen no kenkyū*, from *Jikaku ni okeru chokkan to hansei* (『自覺に於ける直觀と反省』; Intuition and reflection in self-awareness) of 1917 to *Ishiki no mondai* (『意識の問題』; The issue of consciousness) of 1920, Nishida inquires after that fundamental reality by plumbing through the interior depths of the self. In the 1917 work, he takes what he calls the "absolute free will" (*zettai jiyū ishi*, 絕對自由意志) to be not only the root of our self-awareness (*jikaku*, 自覺), but also the creative act of the cosmos (*uchū no sōzō sayō*, 宇宙の創造作用), transcending the individual's will. Again, just as he did with the concept of pure experience (*junsui keiken*), he broadens the significance of the will (*ishi*, 意志) beyond its ordinary meaning to something cosmic and ontological. The will that operates in the depths of one's soul is, in some sense, not distinct from the will in its cosmic significance. Combining Fichte's sense of the "fact-act" (*Tathandlung*) and Rickert's notion of the “ought” (*Sollen*; Jp. *tōi*, 當為) that precedes being, Nishida takes the will (*ishi*) to be the driving force of the activity of differentiation and identification. He tells us that the will as such is the creative source of being precisely at the point where “being is born out of nothing” and where “the will comes from, and returns to, the creative nothing [*sōzōteki mu*, 創造的無]” (Z2: 217, 264). This sense of the will may seem novel and strange to those unfamiliar with the history of European philosophy. But before Nishida there was a whole tradition within German thought of treating the will in this impersonal and cosmic sense, the prime exemplars being Nietzsche, Schopenhauer, and Schelling. Even prior to the nineteenth century, we can point to Böhme. Nishida has inherited, and develops further, their conception of the will.

Theory of Place (1926)

Nishida’s treatment of the nothing as the root of self-awareness as well as of the cosmos’ reality reaches a significant stage of development in the mid-1920s with the formulation of his philosophy of place (*basho*, 場所) in his *Basho* essay. As mentioned above, he wanted to solve the epistemological issue of how the subject-object dichotomy is bridged. But he also wanted to avoid the apparent psychologism of his earlier formulations. This led him to the notion of *place* in the sense of an ultimate context that embraces and envelops both the knower and the known in a formless nondistinction preceding their differentiation. This would precisely be the place where the will emerges from a creative nothing. Because this ultimate place in its nondistinction is unobjectifiable, escaping assertion, Nishida characterizes it as the transcendent predicate pole (*chōetsuteki jutsugomen*, 超越的述語面), “the predicate that cannot be made into a grammatical subject” (Z3: 325, also see 405, 467, 502; Z6 186ff). He intends to contrast his metaphysics of the predicate to Aristotle’s metaphysics, which is founded upon the notion of substance (*ousia*) or substratum (*hypokeimenon*) that “becomes the grammatical subject but never a predicate” (Z3: 325, 405; Z6: 186; Z7: 221). In *Torinokosaretaru ishiki no mondai* (『取殘されたる意識の問題』; “The unsolved issue of consciousness”) of the same year, Nishida states that his attempt is to initiate a new sort of metaphysics that could ground epistemology in the direction of the predicate rather than seeking for the ground of being in the direction of the grammatical subject (Z7: 224). By “predicate (*jutsugo*, 述語),” he means the unobjectifiable concrete immediacy that contextualizes the grammatical subject. As such, it escapes reduction to the grammatical subject and thus cannot be treated in terms of realism or idealism or any sort of dualism. Expanding its sense beyond its grammatical significance, Nishida is thus using the notion of predicate here as a heuristic device to defocus our attention *away* from *being qua object*—the grammatical subject—that normally lies on the foreground of our attention. The point is to turn us toward the set of conditions constituting the thing and ultimately to its contextual *background*. The ultimate context of contexts, however, as a predicate not subsumed under further predicates and transcending all possible grammatical subjects, would have to be a *nothing* enveloping things objectifiable as possible subjects of assertion. The nothing in that absolute sense—absolute nothing (*zettai mu*, 絕對無)—thus is that ultimate contextual place assumed by any predicative determination or ontological differentiation.

The movement away from the object and toward that ultimate contextual place proceeds through a series of "implacements."[16] By "implacement," I mean the state of occupying a place. Every object, in virtue of being the subject of a statement, belongs to a determining context. That context is its place. But if we turn to that place and objectify it, turning it into a subject of another statement, we find that it belongs to a broader place. Each determining place is thus further determined by a broader horizon that is in turn determined by an even broader horizon. This series of "implacements" can go on and on, but Nishida argued that the final place would have to be indeterminate, a nothing embracing all determinations. Nishida sought to overcome classical dualism by reformulating the various dichotomies—subject-predicate, object-subject, particular-universal, matter-form, noema-noesis, content-act, determined-determiner, and so on—in terms of the relationship of implacement between the implaced (*oitearumono*, 於いてあるもの) and the place of implacement (*oietaru basho*, 於いてある場所) (see Z3: 390, 464–465, 498; 4: 81). In the reverse direction, he saw implacement to involve individuation through self-differentiation (see Z3: 347–348, 391, 400, 402–403, 431, 465, 517). In other words, rather than starting with the premise that the terms of a dichotomy are ontologically independent and discrete entities, he begins with the premise that the terms or poles form an integral whole from the start. That is to say that place and implaced fit together as a whole that only subsequently are differentiated, abstracted and articulated as distinct things. But that whole itself, qua whole, cannot be articulated because it embraces the very process of articulation. For physical things, the force field would be their *place*. Once they are objectified as objects of consciousness, their place would be the field of consciousness (*ishiki no ba*, 意識の場) serving as the matrix for the interrelations of phenomena and acts of consciousness. That field of consciousness is termed "relative nothing" (*sōtai mu*, 相對無) in that it is in relation to those objectified beings that it determines.[17] Once our focus of attention shifts from the object of consciousness to its (epistemological) subject, consciousness itself becomes objectified to be potentially determined as a grammatical subject of the statement, "I think X." This is also why for Nishida consciousness is only a relative nothing or an oppositional nothing (*tairitsuteki mu*, 對立的無), but not the absolute nothing. Consciousness itself is determined and contextualized upon a further receding background, the concreteness of which is no longer objectifiable. The ultimate unobjectifiable and unsayable horizon would be the holistic situation that precedes the subject-object dichotomy and serves to root and envelop it along with all oppositions. That holistic situation is the absolute or the true nothing (*shin no mu*, 真の無) (Z3: 424, 432).

Nishida qualifies the term "nothing" here with "absolute (*zettai*, 絕對)" to convey the sense that it is free of—in the sense of being cut-off from—(*zetsu-*, 絕) opposition (*-tai*, 對). This is similar to how the Western term *absolute* has its etymological meaning in the sense of being *absolved* of anything that would relativize it. The point is that there is no longer anything beyond to delimit it, to oppose it, or to determine it, since there is no more "outside." Absolute nothing is undelimited, undetermined, and in that sense *no-thing*. Beings are all *within* its embracing context. Nishida calls it "the place of true nothing" (*shin no mu no basho*, 真の無の場所) or "the place of absolute nothing" (*zettai mu no basho*, 絕對無の場所) (see Z3: 467, 482), as it is the ever-implicit horizonless horizon that contextualizes and makes possible every determination of being as well as their negation, that is, the basic opposition between being and non-being. What Nishida means by *place* (*basho*) here, at its most concrete level, eludes positive description. As it slips from any attempt to make it into a subject of judgment, one cannot state that it *is* or *is not*. In other words, it cannot be predicated as *being* or *not being* (Z3: 424, 503). Rather, it is that which must be presupposed by any such utterance, as that which makes room for those things determined, enveloping them as their place (see Z3: 415, 421). Eluding both the ontological (what pertains to being) and the meontological (what pertains to the negation of being), while encompassing both being and nonbeing and permitting their very opposition, we might characterize this place as *anontological*. But this negativity is simultaneously the positivity of its self-determination that inverts its nothingness into being. As a nothing, the only attribute it can have is negation. The absolute nothing is perpetually involved in the act of negating itself, whereby it gives birth to beings within itself as its own self-determinations. The nothing negates itself to give rise to beings. Or put differently, the undifferentiated differentiates itself into the many. In other words, Nishida is arguing that its creativity is a consequence of its negativity. As a living creativity, the place of nothing is thus *self*-forming. It forms itself into those beings it environs. Beings are thus expressions of this nothing in its self-forming formlessness. We can see that by "true nothing" or "absolute nothing" here, Nishida does not mean a literal nothingness. Like the Mahāyānists before him, he wants to avoid any nihilistic tendency just as much as he wants to avoid reifying being. But as such, it is also the dimension where one encounters in the depths of one's self the existential nullity environing and finitizing one's being. That is to say, when one intuits the absolute nothing mirroring itself in the abysmal depths of one's self-awareness, one sees a contradiction inherent to one's existence. The contradiction is of being and nonbeing, or life and death. Nishida's point seems to be that one is *neither necessarily* being *nor necessarily* nonbeing, but rather is finite and contingent. One lives a precarious existence. He calls the concrete place of this intuition, "the place of generation-and-extinction" (*shōmetsu no basho*, 生滅の場所) (Z3: 423), borrowing the term "generation-and-extinction" (*shōmetsu*) from Japanese Buddhism, wherein it had been used to refer to the Indian concept of *samsāra*, the "wheel of birth-and-death," or more generally to refer to impermanence. In other words, one intuits in the absolute nothing one's non-substantiality preceding the bifurcation of ideal and real, self and world. One's self is constituted out of the absolute nothing to face the world. It is the place of an amorphous nothing that opens the space for things—including one's self—determined and differentiated from one another.

Nishida views judgments to be articulations or amplifications, even abstractions, of a fundamental (self-)intuition (*chokkan*, 直觀) of that primal nonduality, the place of absolute nothing, in its self-differentiating self-mirroring self-awareness. He characterizes that intuition in terms of the self-seeing of the absolute nothing, explaining its self-formation as a self-mirroring that occurs within the abysmal depths of each of our individual selves. But since what lies there is unobjectifiable and undeterminable, its seeing is a "seeing without seer" (*mirumono nakushite miru*, 見るもの無くしてみる) (Z3: 255). Nishida explains that "to see the self itself . . . [means] to see that the self seen disappears, that the self becomes absolutely nothing. Hence we conceive of the true self to be where we have truly forgotten the self itself" (Z4: 297). In other words, true self-awareness is not simply of the individual self, but of the absolute nothing seeing itself by mirroring itself within the individual. It means simultaneously the self-awareness of the place of absolute nothing *and* our own self-awareness of the nothingness of our selves.[18] In addition to being the ultimate contextual horizon or place, the nothing for Nishida then has the character of seeing or awareness.[19] The nondistinction of the nothing includes the non-duality of mind and matter, or seeing and formation.

In the following years, Nishida moves to characterize this self-seeing in terms of the "self-determination of the universal (*ippansha no jikogentei*, 一般者の自己限定)" or "the self-aware determination of the nothing (*mu no jikakuteki gentei*, 無の自覺的限定)." In the 1930s, he further developed this notion in terms of the self-determination of the world (*sekai no jikogentei*, 世界の自己限定). By the 1940s, he returned full circle to the notion of a self-mirroring self-awareness with the sense of the world's self-mirroring in each individual as its microcosmic mirror.

The Dialectic of the World (1930s)

Nishida became aware of a problem in his own characterization of the place of absolute nothing as the transcendent predicate pole, and this spurred a shift in his attention to the outer world. His focus on the predicate corresponds to his focus on the pole of subjectivity, or, in metaphysical terms, the focus on the universal or the ideal. Some of his contemporaries thus criticized him for ignoring the real world of historical events and concrete individuals. The tendency in his theory of place formulated in the late 1920s was toward some sort of idealism or subjectivism, harboring the potential for misunderstanding the place of absolute nothing as a universal substance hidden in the depths of transcendental subjectivity.[20] Nishida thus wanted to show the concrete reality of the absolute nothing as it manifests itself in historical events. His solution was to conceive of the place of nothing as the very *medium* for the interaction between subject and predicate, individual and universal, object and subject. And that medium is the world. To avoid falling into idealism or subjectivism, Nishida turned his attention 180 degrees, from the standpoint of consciousness that looks within to the standpoint of the world that looks outward. The content—the non-dual nothing—remains the same, but he unfolds its significance beyond the epistemological or judicative framework to speak of *place* more explicitly as the contextual whole of what he calls the "dialectical world" (*benshōhōteki sekai*, 辯證法的世界), that is, a world consisting of, and constituted by, interrelationships and unfolding historically through these interrelations. Within this world we interact with one another and with the environment to take part in the world's self-formation.

Nishida initiates this move in his 1932 *Mu no jikakuteki gentei* (『無の自覺的限定』; The self-aware determination of the nothing), wherein the self, instead of being privileged, is analyzed in its relation with its *other* in the "I-thou (*watashi to nanji*, 私と汝)" relationship operating in co-determination with the environing socio-historical world (*shakaiteki rekishiteki sekai*, 社會的歷史的世界). The absolute nothing as manifest in the world envelops "I and thou" as their ultimate context of contexts necessary for their meaningful interaction. And yet, precisely as that context, sinking into the background, it escapes intelligibility or appropriation. In this regard Nishida calls it the "absolute other (*zettai ta*, 絕對他)" (Z5: 305ff). In other words, the absolute nothing that negates each individuality qua substance is *also* the absolute other in that it cannot be rendered into a subject of a statement. *Alterity* in this sense is paradoxically non-duality. In other words, the non-dual nothing uncovered within the interiority of the self is non-dual with the world's own abyssal ground. Having taken this move, Nishida thus follows the unfolding of the absolute nothing from the side of the historical world throughout the 1930s. With this shift from the inner to the outer, the self-formation of the formless that was described earlier in terms of the self-seeing or the self-awareness of the absolute nothing within the self takes on a world-historical significance as unfolding in the events of the world.

Moreover, this is described in a conspicuously dialectical manner as that which involves the interrelationships and interactivities of individuals. In turn, Nishida views the acting individuals as participating in the world's self-determination. Since that world of determinations is ultimately founded upon the nothing, "seeing without a seer" now becomes "determination without a determiner" (*genteisurumono naki gentei*, 限定するものなき限定) (Z7: 8, 8: 9), another way of rendering the "forming of the formless." The nothing as such is the ultimate context of the world as the dialectical medium (*benshōhōteki baikaisha*, 辯証法的媒介者) wherein individuals interact. In other words, the nothing serves as an open space for the interactivities and relations of individuals that in their dialectic constitutes the world. This concentration on the dialectical world becomes pronounced in his *Tetsugaku no konpon mondai* of the mid-1930s, whereby the place of absolute nothing that in 1926 was a predicate place (*jutsugoteki basho*, 述語的場所) discovered in the depths of the self now opens up as a place of mediation (*baikaiteki basho*, 媒介的場所), relating man and world.[21]

As Nishida unfolds the dialectic of the world during this period, one important feature of the dialectical world that he highlights is the pervasive function of mutual self-negation (*jiko hitei*, 自己否定) that permits relationships and interdeterminations in general. In the dialectic between organism (or life: *seimei*, 生命) and environment (*kankyō*, 環境) in his *Ronri to seimei* (『論理と生命』 "Logic and life") of 1936, for example, the environment conditions the individual, and conversely the individual acts upon the environment to alter those conditions. Each negates the other for the sake of self-affirmation (Z8: 58). Yet Nishida points out that such negation of the other cannot happen without *self*-negation. One must also negate one's self vis-à-vis the conditions delimiting one's state of being. In order to get from point A to point E, one must traverse the terrain of points B, C, and D, even if one does not want to. In terms of relationships, in order to receive, one must give. In order to enjoy the joys of friendship or intimacy, one must be willing to sacrifice one's self to a certain degree. We may recall how in Mahāyāna Buddhism, the codependent origination of things means the emptiness of their *own* (independent) being. Likewise for Nishida, the co-relative determination of things involves their mediation through mutual self-negation (see Z8: 19). Otherwise, their mutual independence (i.e., self-assertion) would obstruct their relationship. Mutual self-negation inverts independence into interdependence and correlativity (Z8: 13) to enable self-determination and hence self-affirmation. Paradoxically, we cannot determine ourselves without being determined by others, and we cannot affirm ourselves without negating ourselves. Nishida calls such negation of negation that de-substantializes negation itself (a self-negation that negates a one-sided negation of the other) "absolute negation" (*zettai hitei*, 絕對否定) (Z6: 18, 68-69, 273). Such self-negation occurs not only on the part of individuals, but also on the part of the universal embracing them. Nishida means by "universal (*ippansha*, 一般者)," in this context, the world. The universal as the world, instead of asserting itself over the individuals it embraces, negates itself to make room for the interrelationships and interactivities of individuals. As we mentioned above, what he means by universal qua world, then, is an extension of his earlier concept of place (*basho*). At the same time, as it makes room for the individuals, the universal is differentiating itself into these individuals (see Z8: 13, 91).[22] Through such self-negation, the one becomes the many to establish a world of individuals. But Nishida also calls the universal in this function "the dialectical universal (*benshōhōteki ippansha*, 辯證法的一般者)" because the world is constituted by the complex interrelationships of its individuals. It historically unfolds through these interrelations involving mutual self-negation in manifold directions: amongst individuals and between universal and individuals.

The entire dialectic involves a complex *chiasma* of vertical and horizontal lines of interrelations: the self-negation of the dialectical universal on the vertical plane, making room for the many individuals, simultaneously means the mutual self-negation among individuals on the horizontal level. And in turn, that mutual self-negation among individuals constitutes the universal (qua world). What this means is that the self-determination of the universal is at the same time the self- and mutual determination of individuals within the world. Self-negation mediates the dialectic on all levels, as a dialectic of, within, and upon the nothing as its place. The dialectic on all levels is made possible through mutual self-negation and implacement within the absolute nothing. One could also say that the self-negation of each term is therefore the activity or process of the place of true nothing as the non-substantial medium of the worldly sphere. Through self-negation, the absolute nothing ontologizes itself, affirms itself, into beings. The world thus is the self-formation of the formless.

Religion and Self-Awareness (1940s)

Coming full circle from the dialectic of the world, Nishida later returned to his concept of self-awareness. In 1943 (*Jikaku nit suite* 『自覺について』; "On self-awareness"), he discusses the world's self-formation in terms of the world's own self-awareness and states, "when the world is self-aware, our self is self-aware; when our self is self-aware, the world is self-aware. Each of our self-aware selves is a contextual center of the world" (Z9: 528). Moreover, during the 1940s, his notion of self-awareness came to possess an explicitly "religious" significance in a Nishidian sense. This is so especially in his final essay, *Bashoteki ronri to shūkyōteki Sekaikan* of 1945, where he speaks of the absolute nothing in terms of "the absolute one" (*zettaisha*, 絕對者) or the creator God (*kami*, 神) who relates to the world through kenotic self-negation. In this final essay, Nishida applies Suzuki Daisetsu's logic of *soku-hi* (or: "is/is not") (*sokuhi no ronri*, 即非の論理)[23] to his understanding of God in order to explain the meaning of the absolute (*zettai*). Nishida claims that God's self-identity as a true absolute is mediated by absolute negation in a dialectic expressed by the *soku-hi* logic of the *Prajñāpāramitā sūtras*[24] (Z10: 333). An utterly transcendent God without reference or relation to anything else, which is independent in self-identity, is no true God. Yet the absolute, by definition, cannot stand opposed to anything that would relativize it. Standing unopposed, the *absolute*—in its etymology as Nishida already noted in the 1920s (and as we discussed above)—is beyond all opposition (*zetsu-tai*, 絕-對), *ab-solved*, cut-off (*zetsu*, 絕) from all opposition (*tai*, 對) from without. In being opposed by nothing, God is absolute being (*zettai yū*, 絕對有), but in being undelimited by anything, God is the absolute nothing (*zettai mu*, 絕對無). The absolute thus possesses the contradictory self-identity (*mujunteki jikodōitsu*, 矛盾的自己同一) of being and nothing (see Z10: 315–316, 335). Nishida's God here is thus a dialectical God. Undetermined by anything, its determination occurs only through *self*-negation. Through self-negation, it contains all oppositions within. As an "immanent transcendence (*naizaiteki chōetsu*, 內在的超越)," the absolute perpetually negates itself in self-inversion to make room for co-relative and finite beings. Its nothingness is the background for the foreground of beings. Nishida takes this to be the true meaning of *agape* and *kenosis* in Christianity. In other words, Nishida interprets what in Christianity is God's self-giving love that embraces the world and God's self-emptying that redeems the world in his own terms. He understands them in terms of his own notion of the absolute nothing that negates itself to give rise to the world of many, and at the same time envelops those many individuals as their *place*.

In Nishida's philosophical development, we thus witness the turn from interiority to exteriority and a return back to the inner dimensions of the self. In the interior depths of the self, where one encounters the abyssal nothing that deconstructs any sense of self-sufficient or self-righteous egoity, one meets God, the absolute. The absolute is encountered only in utter self-negation, ego-death (see Z10: 315, 325; 13: 235). Self-negation in this case means the awareness of one's finitude or powerlessness, a recognition of sin or evil within one's self. This amounts to self-awareness of an interior contradiction that culminates in the self's "vanishing point" (*shōshitsuten*, 消失點) (Z10: 356), birthing what Nishida calls the "religious mind" (*shūkyōshin*, 宗教心) (Z10: 312–313). This is equivalent to the realization of the nothing in the depths of one's self in self-awareness. In this realization one dies to one's ego—the self believed to be a self-subsistent entity—in what Nishida calls the self's "eternal death" (*eien no shi*, 永遠の死). In this process, the true self—the self that has awakened to the nothing from which it emerged, the self as non-substantial—is authenticated in its finite existence.

Nishida equates this realization with what Zen calls "seeing into one's nature" (*kenshō*, 見性) (Z10: 352–353). Nishida repeatedly quotes Dōgen's (道元) statement from the *Genjōkōan* (『現成公案』) that "to study the Buddha way is to study the self; to study the self means to forget the self, and to forget the self means to be authenticated by the ten thousand *dharmas*" (Z10: 336; see also 8: 512, 514; 10: 326). Nishida finds such "religious" self-awareness evident not only in Dōgen's Zen but also in the True Pure Land (*Jōdoshin*, 淨土真) Buddhist idea of relying on other-power (*tariki*, 他力) as well (Z8: 514). In both Dōgen's "forgetting oneself" and Shinran's (親鸞) "relying on other-power," one discovers true self-identity in self-negation. And in such self-negating self-awareness—awareness of one's contingency, conditionality, non-substantiality—one faces one's ultimate *other*, the absolute (see Z10: 314–315). In the death of ego and owning up to finitude, one realizes one's true nature as the self-negation of the absolute, a mirror image of God. In other words, one realizes that one is sustained as being through the self-negating act of the absolute nothing that perpetually gives rise to the world of beings, which translated theistically means the self-seeing of God.[25] Nishida thus understands "salvation" to be an event of co-respondence of self-negation on the part of finite and infinite, relative and absolute, man and God: self-doubt and ego-death on the part of the saved, sacrifice on the part of the savior. Just as the dialectic of individual and world developed through the 1930s was predicated upon mutual self-negation, here the dialectic of religious encounter operates through the mutual self-negation of man and absolute—what he now calls their inverse correspondence (*gyakutaiō*, 逆對應).

In Christian terms, God meets man in kenotic grace symbolized in the figure of Christ (i.e., God's incarnation and death as man), and man meets God in his own death (and thus resurrection) (see Z10: 325–326). Nishida discovers the same motif in the Pure Land notion of Amida's infinite compassion (*jihi*, 慈悲) expressed in his vow to save all, including the most sinful, and man's corresponding faith in Amida's vow expressed in *nenbutsu* (念仏)[26] (see Z10: 345). Nishida thus takes these religious doctrines to be sectarian expressions acknowledging our existential implacement within a non-substantiality that has some sort of sacred significance. Inverse correspondence is thus predicated asymmetrically—in the mutual fit between place and implaced—upon the absolute's own nature as a de-substantializing nothing. Religiosity for Nishida means the realization of that implacement or non-substantiality.

Concluding Remarks

Let me first provide a short summary of Nishida's philosophical development before discussing the final picture of his thought. Nishida had begun his analysis of reality by looking inward into the depths of the self, which in 1911 led him to his notion of pure experience and in the 1920s led him to the notion of the absolute will. Both, in preceding the subject-object distinction, were characterized in terms of a nothing. Moreover, that same nondistinction on the cosmic scale was identified with the source of the universe of many. With the formulation of his theory of place in 1926, he was able to reconceive this in terms of a place of absolute nothing that differentiates itself to encompass the manifold it implaces. While his discussion of place in 1926 was still focused on the realm of consciousness that gives rise to cognition and permits the subject-object relationship, in the 1930s he turns his attention to the external world. He focuses on the world and its dialectical structure encompassing the interactivities of individuals and takes the latter to be the self-differentiation—or self-negation—of the place of absolute nothing into the manifold. And then in his final essay of 1945, he connects this theory of place qua world-dialectic with the religious or existential themes informed by Christianity and Buddhism. But running through all of these phases is the motif of the nothing (*mu*), indicating the primal undifferentiatedness or nondistinction that precedes and gives rise to the many. Moreover, the absolute nothing as such is often identified with, or its term used interchangeably, with God, the true self, and, after 1930, the world, or at least its *ground*. Hence it seems to have an overall significance for Nishida as the primal reality in a variety of levels.

The final picture that Nishida leaves us of his concept of the nothing is inseparable from his philosophy of place (*basho*). We might summarize Nishida's mature standpoint as involving a multi-layered structuring or horizon of meaning that constitutes an environment wherein one finds oneself *always already*. Each particular horizon—a place—in being itself limited, implies a "beyond" that constitutes its condition.[27] The "beyond" of each horizon implies further horizons as the ultimate horizon continually recedes into the dark and the unknowable. That indeterminable determining condition is what Nishida calls *mu* (nothing). Yet to acknowledge it is itself an act of "self-awareness" (*ji-kaku*), since it is one's deepest non-substantiality. Especially in his last writing this is shown to have a kind of religious significance. In his attempt to construct a complete system of self-awareness that would surmount the gap of Kantian dualism, Nishida had ingeniously allowed for the impossibility of its completion as an aspect integral to his account.[28] Nishida's theory of place is then an attempt to construct a theoretical system that is inherently irreducible to thought in virtue of its unreifiable concrete source, the un/ground, or nothing, an open horizon. That place of absolute nothing in his philosophical works after 1930 takes on the significance of a *trans-temporal* and *trans-spatial* space, enfolding and unfolding its dialectic. Our being-in-the-world involves our implacement within the world that, in turn, is implaced within that open horizon or what he calls a "sphere without periphery" (Z10 340–41).[29] The absolute nothing designates that abyss wherein self, world, and beings are implaced and unfold in mutual distinction as the self-differentiation of the nothing itself—a primal sphere preceding the bifurcations between ideal and real, experience and reality, subjective and objective. At the same time, it is the most concrete level of human awareness-*cum*-existence, where life meets death and from which we emerge in birth and into which we sink in death. For Nishida to intuit this nothing in one's depths—a seeing where there is neither seer nor seen—is to be self-aware of one's selflessness, a self-realization as the nothing from out of which one's self is constituted to face the world in self-differentiation.

Questions have been raised, however, whether the way in which Nishida treats this nothing (*mu*) as the absolute—even if groundless—ground implies a form of substantialism or harbors a tendency toward its substantialization, or at least the danger of its being misunderstood in such terms as some sort of a metaphysical substance. Nishida had criticized the philosophies of the West as "philosophies of being [*yū*]" (see Z6: 335ff) founded upon the groundless assumption of metaphysical principles. But some of his contemporaries[30] suggest that Nishida's notion of the nothing carries the danger of becoming a new metaphysical principle in its own right or being reduced to another form of "being." Does the nothing that was to negate every metaphysical principle in the end turn out to be a new metaphysical principle?[31] This concern especially applies to his view during the late 1920s when he first formulated his philosophy of place. Amongst the paired opposites of subject-predicate, particular-universal, object-subject, the nothing was generally taken to lie on the latter side. The place of nothing as the transcendent predicate pole was to be reached through introspection into the depths of consciousness. But the consequence was that it could easily be mistaken for some sort of a universal substance belonging to a quasi-Platonist ideal realm, some sort of a static and eternal being transcending the world of change.[32] As we already discussed above, Nishida was not unaware of this issue and he attempted to clarify the dynamic function of the nothing by underscoring its endless self-negation, which constitutes the manifold in a radicalized dialectic of the world beyond the subjective realm but immanent to the world itself. Yet some may still find a metaphysical tendency lingering in the explicitly "religious" character of his final essay—with its use of ontic notions like the absolute one (*zettaisha*) or God (*kami*).

To be fair to Nishida, however, we need to remember that for him this "religious" character means the very opposite of a substantialism in that it involves de-substantialization (i.e., self-negation). What I find particularly interesting in Nishida is his development of the notion of place, and of *nothing* as a space that encompasses oppositions and distinctions, as well as his analysis of human existence in those terms. His general theory of a place of nothing escapes the charge of substantialism. A substance is something distinct and discrete with its own properties, whereas Nishida's absolute nothing is non-substantial in its nondistinction and amorphousness. The nondistinction is such that it even escapes categorization as being or its opposite, nonbeing. This is why he used the designation "absolute nothing," while he called the opposite of being "relative nothing," in the sense that it is *relative to*, opposed to, being. So whenever he speaks of "God" or the "absolute one," we need to keep in mind this qualification that he means, the absolute nothing. Intrinsic to Nishida's notion of absolute nothing is its movement of negating all apparent being, substance, principle, or ground. Moreover, in self-negation, that negation encompasses and negates the opposite of being as well. What Nishida means by absolute nothing then is truly abysmal; it cannot be reduced to either being or its opposite, nonbeing. We might underscore this aspect in Nishida's thought as what escapes any reductive tendency. The Greek term for Aristotle's substance, *ousia* (οὐσία), is also the abstract noun form for the verb *einai* (εἶναι), "to be." In contrast to the Aristotelian *ontology* that is an *ousiology*, a "logic of substance," Nishida's "logic of place" (*basho no ronri*, 場所の論理), one might argue, is an *an-ontology*. By *anontology* I am referring to Nishida's structure of double negation that negates both being and nonbeing. To use Greek terminology, Nishida's place of absolute nothing enfolds and unfolds both *on* (being) and its opposite, *mēon* (nonbeing). In Japanese, this would be *yū* (being) and *sōtai mu* (relative nothing). The Greek *anon* in *anontology* thus refers to what Nishida calls *zettai mu* or "absolute nothing" as what is reducible to neither *on* nor *mēon* while enveloping them as their place (*basho*).[33] Nishida's absolute nothing is the anontological place embracing the *chiasma* that unfolds being and nonbeing—as the very space making contradictory and oppositional relations possible in the first place. As such, it perpetually slips away from any principle or law of contradiction that would reduce it to exclusively being or nonbeing.[34]

To recapitulate, by "true nothing" or "absolute nothing," Nishida does not mean that there is literally nothing existing. Nishida wanted to avoid any nihilistic tendency that would reify negation into utter nothingness. To him, "nothing" signifies the fundamental non-duality of reality that is the most concrete and immediate in experience. It is at the same time undelimitable, indeterminable, unobjectifiable in its undifferentiatedness—reducible neither to the merely material nor to the merely ideal, neither to being nor to nonbeing, and preceding any sort of dichotomy. As the ultimate place, it *enfolds* all, and as a self-forming formlessness it *unfolds* all, determining and mirroring itself—through endless self-negations—in the *manifold*. In that capacity as an all-encompassing amorphous place, it gives rise to things (i.e., objects) through self-determination, and to awareness (i.e., subjects) through self-mirroring. The absolute nothing as such is non-dual with being, in non-differentiation prior to its self-determination in beings. Nishida's move in a certain sense then takes off from the Mahāyāna notion of the middle path or the emptiness of emptiness (*śūnyatāyāh śūnyatā*) that avoids the reductive extremes of utter nothing in nihilism (*uccheda*) and of substantial being in eternalism (*śāśvata*). But he develops this into his own creative position in a stance that Ueda Shizuteru has called a "dynamic non-foundationalist multi-dimensionalism"[35] and what I call *anontology*.

Today when worlds are merging into one big mega-world under the phenomenon of globalization, when we find ourselves prone to fall into conflict amidst the confusion of this phenomenon, it may do us well to lend an ear to Nishida's non-foundationalist and multi-dimensional anontology that refuses the reificiation or hypostatization of positions, as well as nihilism. The acknowledgment of an absolute nothing that opens a space for our being-in-the-world and inter-being reminds us of our own finitude and contingency, the fragility our being in its very concreteness. It encourages humility vis-à-vis the *other*. It calls upon us to bear in mind the indefinite and irreducible expanse of the nothing, *wherein we all are* in *co-implacement* amidst mutual *difference*—a place we must share.

Notes

1 All references to Nishida's works are from the latest edition of *Nishida Kitarō zenshū* [Collected works of Nishida Kitarō], multiple volumes (Tokyo: Iwanami shoten, 2002). They will be identified in the text with a Z followed by the volume number and page number.

2 See Kosaka Kunitsugu, *Nishida Kitarō no shisō* (Tokyo: Kodansha, 2003), 56.

3 See Kosaka, *Nishida Kitarō no shisō*, 60–61.

4 Chan is the Chinese word for what in Japanese is *Zen*.

5 A *kōan* (Ch. *gongan*, 公案) is a kind of a riddle or puzzle used in Zen for practitioners to meditate on, formulated in a way that intellectual reasoning alone cannot solve.

6 Thus in Japanese, for example, the same graph that means "being" when pronounced *yū* can also mean "to have" when taking on an additional phonetic ending and pronounced *yūsuru* 有する.

7 See A. C. Graham, *Disputers of the Tao: Philosophical Argument in Ancient China* (LaSalle, IL: Open Court, 1989), 411.

8 On this see Lothar Knauth, "Life is Tragic—The Diary of Nishida Kitarō," *Monumenta Nipponica* vol. 20, no. 3/4 (1965): 335–358, 349.

9 See Reinhard May, *Heidegger's Hidden Sources: East Asian Influences on His Work*, trans. Graham Parkes (London and New York City: Routledge, 1996, 1989), 32. May here cites Morohashi Tetsuji, *Dai kan-wa jiten* [Chinese-Japanese dictionary], 13 vols. (Tokyo: Taishukan, 1986), entry no. 19113, also 49188, 15783, 15514.

10 See David Dilworth, "Nishida Kitarō: Nothingness as the Negative Space of Experiential Immediacy," *International Philosophical Quarterly* vol. XIII, no. 4 (December 1973): 463–483, 474; and *The Awakening of Faith Attributed to Aśvaghosha*, trans. Yoshito S. Hakeda (New York City: Columbia University Press, 1967), 42f.
11 The latter is in a letter in the old edition of Nishida's *Zenshū* [Collected works], vol. 19 (Tokyo: Iwanami, 1980), 90.
12 See Hermann Lotze, *Drei Bücher: Vom Denken, Vom Untersuchen, und Vom Erkennen* (Leipzig: S. Hirzel, 1874); in English: *Logic in Three Books: Of Thought, of Investigation, and of Knowledge*, trans. Bernard Bosanquet (Oxford: Clarendon Press, 1888). Also see his *Metaphysik: Drei Bücher der Ontologie, Kosmologie und Psychologie* (Leipzig: S. Hirzel, 1879), e.g., p. 27; in English: *Metaphysic in Three Books: Ontology, Cosmology, and Psychology*, 2 vols., trans. Bernard Bosanquet (Oxford: Clarendon Press, 1887), 32. Or from the Baden school of Neo-Kantianism, see Heinrich Rickert, *Der Gegenstand der Erkenntnis: Einführung in die Transzendentalphilosophie* (Tübingen: J.C.B. Mohr [Paul Siebeck], 1928), ix, 232, 274, 300.
13 See Emil Lask, *Die Logik der Philosophie und die Kategorienlehre* (Tübingen: J.C.B. Mohr (Paul Siebeck), 1911), 33–34, 55, 70, 98–99, 192, 215ff; and his *Die Lehre vom Urteil* (Tübingen: J.C.B. Mohr (Paul Siebeck), 1912), 127.
14 Eckhart himself characterized what he meant by *Gottheit* as a "nothing" (*Nichts*) or a "desert" that precedes the personal creator God. Meister Eckhart (c. 1260–c. 1327) and Jakob Böhme (1575–1624) were both German mystics. While Eckhart lived before the Protestant Reformation, Böhme belonged to the Lutheran tradition.
15 Friedrich Nietzsche, *Beyond Good and Evil: Prelude to a Philosophy of the Future*, trans. Walter Kaufmann (New York City: Random House, 1966), 89, §146. Altered translation.
16 I use the spelling *implacement* as opposed to *emplacement*, although both forms of spelling can be found in scholarly works. I use this spelling because I first became aware of the concept in that spelling in the late 1990s while reading Ed Casey's *Fate of Place: A Philosophical History* (Berkeley, CA: University of California Press, 1997).
17 This is perhaps akin to how Jean-Paul Sartre conceived consciousness as a nothing in relation to its objects.
18 See Kosaka Kunitsugu, *Nishida Kitarō o meguru tetsugakusha gunzō* (Kyoto: Mineruva shobō, 1997), 13.
19 Ibid., 15, 109.
20 See, for example, Tanaka Kyūbun, *Nihon no "tetsugaku" o yomitoku: "mu" no jidai o ikinukutameni* (Tokyo: Chikuma shobō, 2000), 44–45.
21 Ibid., 54.
22 This is Nishida's development of Hegel's concrete universal.
23 The term '*soku-hi*' connotes the dialectical inseparability and biconditionality between contradictories, that is, affirmation and negation, *is* and *is-not*, via mutual reference and interdependence, founded upon the Mahāyāna notion of emptiness (i.e., the absence of ontological independence; non-substantiality). Suzuki developed his notion in his own reading of the *Prajñāpāramitā sūtras*, especially the *Diamond Sūtra*. See Suzuki Daisetsu, *Kongōkyō no zen* [The Zen of the Diamond Sūtra] in *Suzuki Daisetsu zen senshū* [*Selected Works of Suzuki Daisetsu*] (Tokyo: Shunshūsha, 1991), pp. 3-228.
24 In particular, Nishida has in mind the paradoxical formulations of the *Diamond Sūtra*, such as that X is not X, therefore it is X. He was influenced by D. T. Suzuki's interpretation of this as expressing a particular sort of logic that Suzuki called the logic of *soku-hi*. See the previous note on this topic.
25 Nishida has in mind here the conception of God of the medieval mystics and negative theologians, for whom God creates the world in order to see himself.

26 Hence Nishida treats the word "Buddha" as understood by the Pure Land Buddhists in their worship of Amida Buddha, which is in much the same way as he understands the Christian "God." In both cases God or Buddha serves as a personification of the absolute, and it is precisely in that sense that Nishida uses these terms—Buddha and God—interchangeably in his last essay.

27 Shizuteru Ueda, "Pure Experience, Self-Awareness, Basho," *Etudes phénoménologiques*, vol. 18 (1993): 80.

28 On this and the following, see Yoko Arisaka, "System and Existence: Nishida's Logic of Place," in Augustine Berque (ed.), *Logique du lieu et dépassement de la modernité* (Brussels: Ousia, 1999), 44.

29 For example, Ueda characterizes this in terms of the world's implacement in an "unrestricted openness." See Ueda, "Pure Experience," 78–79.

30 A prime example is Tanabe Hajime.

31 See Tanaka, *Nihon no "tetsugaku" o yomitoku*, 10–11, 65–66.

32 See ibid., 44–45; Kosaka, *Nishida Kitarō o meguru tetsugakusha gunzō*, 111. Also see Tanaka, *Nihon no "tetsugaku" o yomitoku*, 65–66 on the following.

33 Since *mē* is still a conditional adverb (e.g., "I think *not*. . . "), the designation *meontology* would not do justice to Nishida's system of non-system.

34 That is to say that for the same reasons it is anontological, it is an-archic (in preceding *archai*, principles).

35 Ueda, "Pure Experience," 67.

19 Tanabe's Dialectic of Species as Absolute Nothingness

Makoto Ozaki

Introduction

Hajime Tanabe (1885–1962), one of the so-called Kyoto School philosophers of modern Japan, explores his own unique Triadic Logic of Species in the form of the dialectic as the foundation of his whole system of thought. He creates a new synthesis of Western and Eastern philosophy on the basis of the traditional Buddhist notion of Emptiness or Absolute Nothingness, the latter of which was first used by his mentor Kitaro Nishida (1870–1945), under whose influence Tanabe develops his ideas in a different way. Nishida's system of thought focuses upon the concept of ultimate Place or *Topos* as Absolute Nothingness, which encompasses everything in the world. Tanabe is very critical of this seemingly static logic of Place as dichotomic in character, and further develops his own logic in the form of the Triadic Dialectic of the three parties: the genus, or universal; the species, or particular; and the individual. Tanabe's Triadic Logic or Trinity, however, is different from the ancient Christian doctrine of the Trinity in that the latter occurs in the eternal dimension of God, whereas the former takes place in the historical realm in which human activity plays a central role. Tanabe stands by practical action, without resorting to any type of contemplation of truth, and his goal is to bring about the self-realization or self-manifestation of eternity in history through the mediation of free human subjective action. His philosophy aims at constructing a kind of philosophy of history.

The distinctiveness of Tanabe's thought does not lie in its being a guide for individual subjects to attain or ascend toward an eternal truth, but in his analysis of how eternal truth may be realized in the actual world. In this regard, the emphasis is shifted from the eternal God to the historical man, who can make mistakes and be evil because of the twin possibilities of acting from either goodness or evil. This is the problem of radical evil as it has been understood since Kant, and Tanabe was entangled with it.

In this chapter, we will situate Tanabe in the context of modern understanding of the contingency of human existence, within the limits of historical freedom. In the light of modern interpretations of the free subjectivity of contingent human beings, Tanabe's way of thinking points out the vivid dynamic activity of the historical dimension on the stage of human ideas.

Nishida and Tanabe on Absolute Nothingness

Even though Tanabe derived his idea of Absolute Nothingness from his teacher Nishida, he rejected Nishida's version of Absolute Nothingness. It may be argued that Tanabe is successful in establishing the modernization of the traditional Buddhist notion of Emptiness from the perspective of Western philosophy, while Nishida fails to do so. Nishida remains committed to the Chinese philosopher Laozi's idea of Nothingness, which is very similar to Neo-Platonist Plotinus's concept of the One as standing beyond being, from which the world is produced and to which it eventually returns. This is not the same as the Indian Buddhist's notion of Emptiness, which is based on the concept of codependent origination. The authentic meaning of the Buddhist notion of Emptiness excludes any substantial nature, and instead points the non-substantiality of being. On account of its own non-substantiality, everything in the phenomenal world can arise codependently. We might even argue that the shift of ideas from Nishida to Tanabe parallels what happened in the ancient Chinese historical situation, in which the Daoist notion of Nothingness as ultimate reality from which everything in the world arises and to which it returns was merged with the earlier Buddhist notion of Emptiness as codependent origination.

The Neo-Platonist Plotinus's idea of the One was perhaps formulated in the light of the Upanishadic or Vedantic idea of *Brahman* as ultimate reality, and Nishida, too, is affected by Plotinus's theory of emanation. On this point, Tanabe attacks Nishida's tendency toward the theory of emanation, which is diametrically opposed to Absolute Nothingness. Tanabe accuses Nishida in the final analysis of regressing into the affirmation of Absolute Being. According to Tanabe, Nishida's concept of Absolute Self-Identity in Contradistinction implies the self-identity of Being without the inner moment of self-negation. For Tanabe, Nishida's final concept of Place or *Topos* as Absolute Nothingness has the connotation of the self-identical Being, despite its ostensible ring of Nothingness. Tanabe's criticism of Nishida should be reviewed and analyzed from the perspective of Japanese intellectual history, in which a diversity of ideas arising from different origins coexists with each other in rich complexity. A deeper analysis of the subtle distinction between Nishida and Tanabe with regard to their fundamental principles of Absolute Nothingness may result in a fertile development in comparative thought.

Tanabe's Triadic Logic of Species

Tanabe distinguishes between two different kinds of universal: one, the absolute universal, and the other, the relative universal. In addition, universality corresponds to eternity, and particularity corresponds to time or history in which individuality takes action. For Tanabe, the relation of eternity to time or history through the mediation of the individual action is crucial in articulating the triad structure of universality, particularity, and individuality, just as in the case of Hegel, who recognizes that the truth of human existence lies in its action.

Tanabe's Triadic Logic of Species refers to the distinction between the absolute universal as the genus and the relative universal as the species. He thinks this logic may contribute to the analysis of social entities, such as the political state and a possible higher union of the world, which modern existentialism fails to grasp in its entirety due to its own individualistic tendency. Tanabe's construction of the philosophy of history is an existential and historical one, which avoids both an individualistic type of existentialism, devoid of socio-historical extension in the space-time dimension, and a relativistic type of historicism that never reaches beyond relativity, which is merely immanent in the historical horizon, without the eternal dimension.

Tanabe's Logic of Species was motivated by the fact that he was inevitably involved in the surrounding circumstances of his time, during which the state was committed to both World War I and World War II, and consequently he undertook the theoretical task of justifying the state's existence from a philosophical standpoint. However, this historical fact does not render his thought invalid in the contemporary context. Instead, we find in Tanabe's works a shift of emphasis from the state to cultural-civilizational typology that attains absolute universality beyond specific particularities of different cultural patterns or zones. This is because there is no culture *as such* apart from each particular culture, such as Asian, European, American, or others. Culture as such in the sense of universality only appears in the different forms of particularity such as the various cultural forms or patterns in world history. This view on culture might echo Hegel's assertion that there is no philosophy apart from the history of philosophy; and in Tanabe's thought, this would mean that each specific philosophy represents the spirit peculiar to its own period. In this way, Tanabe's triadic logic of universality, particularity, and individuality might be applicable and convertible to the typology or topology of cultures as well.

Next, we will see how this logic is applied to time.

Eternity and Time

Tanabe identifies Absolute Nothingness as eternity. For him, eternity is not only beyond time in the sense that it is non-generative and without beginning, but is also made to become immanent in time at every present to realize itself as the result of self-limitation. His reason is that if eternity is somehow generated, then it must be generated in time with a beginning, and hence would be limited by time and be subject to time. But such a thing would entail a denial of eternity. Time is not merely the immanent dynamics contained in eternity, but also cooperates with eternity to disrupt eternity in and through negation in succession. In other words, eternity to Tanabe is not a "static transcendence" beyond the change and becomings of time; it is not a self-subsisting realm that embraces the dynamic time. Eternity is not a self-identical being, but a continual conversion through negation—continual negation of the past and continual conversion of the present into the past.

However, what is the subject of the conversion of eternity from transcendence into immanence? According to Tanabe, the subject is none other than the self as the individual existence, which acts freely in mediating between eternity and time. The self's free subjective action at every present is the driving force that enables eternity to be immanent in time and to move from the past to the future in order to realize its eternal essence in actuality. The past cannot be expressive of eternity, which is without beginning or further generation. Eternity is restricted by the uncertainty of the future and is thus renewed and resurrected at every present. The past is re-opened and recurs in a higher cycle. The repetition is thus the symbol of eternity in a spiral movement. Time, participating in eternity without generation and beginning in the direction of the past, is characterized by the uncertainty of the future and yet retains the finitude of the past, but in its persistence it is endless and imperishable as it continues into the future. In other words, Tanabe takes eternity to be renewed, through the mediation of the subjective free action of the individual existence, at every present in the continuous process of ever-higher repetition. Eternity, in self-negation, becomes real and successive in time in and through *the present*, in which both the past and the future are negated by each other, so that the past is converted into the occurrence of a new future. Eternity is repetition in such a way that the self freely acts as the subject of the self-consciousness of Absolute Nothingness, wherein the opposition between the past and the future is cancelled out and at the same time conserved in a higher dimension of time. As a result, according to Tanabe, eternity does not stand outside of our actuality. It is always mediated, through our action and our consciousness, to return to time. This is what he means by "the transcendent is mediated to the immanent through conversion" (Tanabe 1963a, 117).

In this way, although eternity as such is both non-generative and without beginning in character, it becomes immersed in time through self-negation, and in doing so, comes to the end of time and constantly begins anew at each present. Time cannot be included simply in eternity, but eternity, in self-negation, is the origin of time, and realizes it in the indefinite openness of the future. While the endurance of the past and the creation of the future negate each other in the present, declining into the bottom of Nothingness, their negative tension becomes the mediating moving power in the end, and a reformative action is to be realized toward the future. As a movement of negation against the nontemporal totality of space, the contemporaneity of each present is apprehended by the differential vibration, in which the end is identical with the beginning, and is superimposed in repetition into the integral cooperative system. As a symbol of eternity, the present contemporaneity, which is realized in the existing individual, is infinitely extended, deepened, and even lifted up in the double form of the contemporaneity of contemporaneity, with eternity as its ground.

In terms of the structure of time, the movement of each present, as a contemporary negative mediation of a future-oriented action, is a unity of the past and the future at the present in which action arises. At the same time, the repetition in eternity from moment to moment attempts to realize the transcendent unity of the dynamic connection of locality and nonlocality. The cooperation in opposition of individual existences and their contemporariness in time is mediated to repeat their cooperation as a dynamic symbol of eternity. Metaphorically speaking, the differential corresponds to death as perishing, whereas that state in which it is negated and positively repeated up to a symbol of eternity qua Absolute Nothingness is the resurrection. Thus, eternity means the return of the eternal to itself by repetition in time. This basic structure may not be concretely apprehended other than by means of the dialectic of existential cooperation. The future is not an immediate existence immanent in time, but a mediative existence that stands in the negative mediation of the action in the present. Absolute Nothingness is thereby converted into action in time. For a subjective self, the future will always be a creative content of the self's action, though it is at the same time a manifestation of the Absolute.

Absolute Nothingness qua Conversion into Being: the State versus the Individual

According to Tanabe, human existence on the level of being is tenable only in so far as it is mediated by the transcendental principle of Absolute Nothingness in the form of Nothingness qua being. The absolute mediation that is accompanied by the returning movement from the transcendental to the historical realm permeates into the root of human existence as "radical evil." We may prove our salvation only to the extent that we are perpetually converted by acts of faith and repentance. The Absolute is thus mediated in and through the relative movement of returning love to others, whereby they are inevitably involved in the reciprocal cooperation of edification with each other.

The returning character of the Absolute requires *being* as the mediation of Absolute Nothingness. This is applicable to the relation of religion and politics, in that religion as the faith in the Absolute is to be mediated by the state's existence as the content of political practice based upon the social substratum. The purpose of practice is to participate in the salvific edification of other individual existences in cooperation with the nurturing love of God or the mercy of the Buddha. While the affirmative phase of practice is the returning activity, the negative one is the sociopolitical practice. Both phases constitute the content of practice in their mutual mediation. This is the practical mediation of religion and politics. The return of religious love and inter-existential cooperation of mutual edification is the principle of social existence. Hereby Tanabe stresses the important role of the Buddhist notion of the *Bodhisattva*, who mediates between the Buddha and human beings, that is, the enlightened and unenlightened. In other words, in order to attain Buddhahood, the Bodhisattva must refrain from attaining Buddhahood and instead cooperate with others who have not yet attained Buddhahood. This practice of the Bodhisattva implies the mutual edification of people in terms of the inter-existential structure of human society, rejecting ego-centrism and isolation.

Since Absolute Nothingness necessarily mediates being and never emanates it, absolute mediation does not emanate a relative state society as self-determination; instead, it mediates the species-like substratum of a state society. This fact can be manifested in the primitive society in which religion is sociopolitical in character. When such a religiosity of the primitive society is disintegrated, however, its negativity is further negated and converted by the religious geniuses from the mundane world into the transcendental pure land or the Kingdom of God. This disintegration of religiosity leads to the separation of religion and politics along with the revolution from monarchy to democracy. Here, however, separation does not necessarily mean self-estrangement or self-alienation. On the contrary, Tanabe argues, the dialectic demands mediation amid separation. In other words, today's politics should be mediated by the returning love of the world religion to participate in the political salvation of humankind. This, of course, never implies that we should reduce politics to religion as a consequence of a direct determination of politics by religion.

According to Tanabe, the mundane social institution is to be determined according to the historical actuality. As the positive practical aspect of actuality is determined through the negation of its historical particularity in the form of absolute actuality-qua-ideality, it is untenable apart from the religious principle of Absolute Nothingness. Through the practice in terms of Absolute Nothingness, the spontaneous freedom of an individual person is grounded in religion and is then subjectified with the attainment of a mutual identification of the individuality and the totality. Hereby the universality of humankind is realized and manifested in the form of cultural phenomena. The state goes beyond its species-like particularity and participates in the universality of humanity. On the relationship between the state and the individual, Tanabe criticizes Hegel's dialectical logic because it, in Tanabe's judgment, still clings to the self-identity of being. For Tanabe, if the subjectivity of the state, which is to be mediated by individual freedom, were directly unified with the subjectivity of God, and there were no *conversion in negation* of the individual and hence no need of the mediation of the Other-power, but only the self-effort of the individual, then the state could be merely a finite God on earth as a self-limitation of God, and never signify the negative mediation of the revelation of God. For Tanabe, Hegel's view of history seems to be optimistically a linear progression. It lacks a serious repentance for sin and evil that inherently lurks in the ground of human existence. Tanabe sees that, for Hegel, the subject of history is God and not the human individual, and history is the predicate of God as the subject. Even though Hegel converts God from the substance into the subject, human individuality is not yet taken as the subject of history with full seriousness. This implies that the state is the outcome of God's self-manifestations in history, a self-identical being without the moment of self-negation within itself. Under Hegel's view, according to Tanabe, the state is regarded as the Kingdom of God realized on earth without the full mediation of the human individual subjective action of freedom. This is implied by Hegel's famous phrase: "What is rational is actual, and what is actual is rational" (Hegel, 1989, 24, my trans.).

Even though Tanabe once accepted this hasty identification of God and the state, he later modified his view to claim that even the state is able to commit sin and evil. Tanabe thinks that the state therefore stands in need of a repentance that is activated by the Other-power, or the Absolute. This reformulation by Tanabe bore the influence of both Buddhism and Christianity. Unlike Hegel, Tanabe places his emphasis on the aspect of human individuality, which is the subject of free action in history, rather than on a transcendent being like God, as if God emanated Himself in history via a linear development of some self-identical being.

Even so, however, Tanabe admits the Other-power, which is beyond human self-power, for the salvation of human beings as the interaction between human self-effort and a transcendental divine operation akin to grace. It is impossible for human beings to attain Buddhahood or redemption only by means of their own action of self-effort without the help of the transcendental power of the Absolute Other. The negation of its finitude, together with the negation of the finitude of the individual spirit, would preserve and retain the content of the world, but at the cost of leaving us with an optimistic representation of the world's *status quo*.

According to Tanabe, the construction of the state is negative in character, as the state exists as an expedient, and only in so far as it is constantly renewed in reformative practice can it be made to exist in action through the mediation of the individual. In other words, without the individuals and their actions, the state does not exist. The individual existence is based upon the principle of Absolute Nothingness, whereas the state existence is the dynamic balance between the negation resulting in a constant renewal in reformation and the affirmation retained by the past tradition. The former is the revelation of the subjectivity of God, whereas the latter is the mediating manifestation of the substratum of God. God as Absolute Nothingness becomes manifest and present through conversion in negation of both of the state and the individual.

Tanabe identifies God as Absolute Nothingness in a traditional Asian context. For him, the Christian personal God should be demythologized in terms of Emptiness, and the historical character of Christianity should be taken into Buddhism as well. The concept of God as Absolute Nothingness, for him, has a double character: one is subjectivity, and the other a substrative nature. In this regard, Tanabe differs from Hegel: for Tanabe, the Absolute is subjective as well as substrative, while for Hegel it is not only the substance but also the subject. Tanabe introduces the concept of substratum, which is on the level of species in relation to the genus and individuality, and this concept of substratum is applied to social entities such as the state. So Tanabe aims at a dialectical unification of Buddhism and Christianity as a historical development in relation to the integral political action in the modern world.

For Tanabe, the state is not a self-subsisting subject that manifests God. Instead, the existence of the state on the level of species-like society is a mere substratum, on the basis of which the individual is to be negated. The state is an expediency, as it mediates between the individual and the substratum on which the mutual love among individuals is communicated, and is made to exist as far as it is to be renewed in conformity with its historical mission by the constant practical action of the individual. It is so as a moment of negation within Absolute Nothingness as the expedient. The state is not a specific being subsumed under the universal God, according to the self-identical logic as in the case of Hegel.

For Hegel, in Tanabe's view, there is no mediation of the state between the individual and the universal genus; rather, the individuals are subsumed under both the species and the genus. In other words, individuals should be negated to a genus by the state, and this negation, though it is ascribed to Nothingness owing to its self-negation, yet stands in opposition to the universal divine goodness which is the ground of its existence. In the later Plato, in particular in his *Nomoi*, according to Tanabe's interpretation, Absolute Goodness arises from the practical mediation of Absolute actuality-qua-ideality as the second order, and in doing so, the species comes to terms with absolute unity solely through the negative mediation of the state. For Hegel, God is the subject of history, and history is the predicate; in other words, world history is none other than the self-manifestation or development of God Himself. As a result, human individuals tend to disappear from the historical horizon in Hegel's system. But for Tanabe, the Absolute never emanates Itself in the manner of a self-identical being, but on the contrary, is made to become real and actual only in and through the mediation of free individual human subjective action. Tanabe also follows and further develops the later Platonic dialectic in that the eternal ideality should be converted into the human world in order to realize itself in the form of the second order, that is, as a dialectical unification of the eternal ideality and historical actuality, though without the full realization of ideality as actuality at once. Even so, however, Tanabe believes Plato's limitation as still confined within the rational standpoint of contemplation, never deepening our insight into unavoidable human bondage to radical evil and needing religious redemption from it, never going beyond the teleology of the art. Tanabe sees that Plato's dialectic should be combined with the Christian doctrine of the resurrection from death as the dialectic of conversion in its full development.

Tanabe's notion of species is, on the other hand, much more directly influenced by Hegel's dialectical logic of socio-historical existence. Tanabe aims at depicting the legal system of the state as a perpetual realization of universal genus-like truth in the actual world of human beings. In other words, the state has the dual structure of oscillating between the universal genus, that is, good, and its regression into self-estrangement, that is, bad.

There is no practice without a sociopolitical substratum. On this point, Tanabe criticizes Hegel for formulating a dangerous emanationist logic of self-identity in terms of contemplation. If one neglects the self-negating mediation of a socio-material entity on the level of species, and overlooks concrete political practice from the standpoint of idealism, then one betrays the state's religious functions. The state would then easily fall back into a status quo, bound up with self-satisfactory egoism and inertial radical evil. This view leads to an extreme materialism as the result of the absence of religion. The mistake lies in overlooking the significance of the material moment within a larger practical dialectic. The species-like substratum as a moment of practice is not social material as such; it is rather a negative mediation between the genus and the individual. It cannot fulfill the full destiny of the self-manifestation of Nothingness in and by itself. On the contrary, it is, so to speak, a relative Nothingness and a mediation toward Absolute Nothingness. It is not the completion of self-mediation, but rather in pursuit of an infinite realization as a possibility.

The state can transcend its own particular definiteness on the level of species and go a step further to participate in the universality of humankind, as long as it is a being mediated by the religious principle of Absolute Nothingness, or a negative existence in the form of being-qua-nothingness. In other words, the state is an expedient or balanced being between genus-like universality and individuality. The state is not just an assembly of an infinite number of individual persons. It further aims at a unification of all other states, that is, a world unity, as the self-manifestation of the religious principle of Absolute Nothingness. Through the practice of absolute negation of the particularity of the state, a world unity is achieved.

Universality and Individuality

One aspect of the species-like entity, that is, society, the highest level of which is the existence of the state, is capable of being the realization of universality, whereas the other aspect of it is the self-estrangement from the realized universality. Universality in itself does not appear but in a particular, specific form through the mediation of the individual action. For Hegel, eternal truth is not a static being beyond our world, but is to be realized in history through the negative activities of human beings. Tanabe appears to be much influenced by Hegel, but he modifies and transforms Hegel's dialectical thinking on the basis of the principle of Absolute Nothingness. In Tanabe's conception, the state is not the final objective of the realization of the universality or eternal truth, but rather is "on the way," never reaching its finality. As a result, the ontological status of the state is on the level of particularity, that is, it is not the genus but the species. This suggests the duality of realization of the universal eternal truth and the self-estranged form from it, and this duality depends on the individual's activity, which plays the role of self-negation. If the self-negating activity of the individual person is lost, then the state, once it realized universality, would degenerate into a foregoing inactive, objective being that no longer possesses its subjectivity. This may be akin to A. N. Whitehead's concept of process in which, upon reaching the goal, the subjective act of becoming in the present is terminated and transformed into objective being as the past. So, the present activity of the individual to negate the present situation as status quo does not work in the form of individual freedom, and may regress into the past inertia.

For Aristotle, the individual as a substance cannot exist apart from the particular species, which is to say, the social community of the state. Politics aims at enabling the individual to realize his potential to achieve the common human good. The individual's free active participation in a specific form of the political state is essential for a good human life. Tetsuro Watsuji (1889–1960), a colleague of Tanabe, also distinguishes between an absolute totality and a relative totality in such a way that the absolute totality is to be realized in the form of the relative totality, that is, the social community, leading to the state as the highest form, in and through the self-negating activity of absolute negativity that is identical with the absolute totality in the historical process of self-development. The absolute totality as absolute negativity cannot be fully realized in history, but rather step by step only in the form of the relative totality. This relative totality may correspond to Tanabe's concept of species as the relative universality, and the absolute totality to absolute universality. In any case, the absolute universality or totality cannot be exhausted by any specific particular form of relative universality in the temporal process of history.

The individual, who is made to return and resurrect through an absolute conversion from self-negation as death, cannot directly possess its self-identical continuity. Self-identity is feasible only for wise men, not for ordinary people. The existence of the state is mediated through the individual action based upon the Absolute Other into an Absolute Nothingness or Totality on the level of genus in the form of their practical unification. In short, the genus-like universalization of the state is mediated by the individual's political practice. On the one hand, the state as a species-like substratum possesses its expedient character of being in the form of being-qua-nothingness, which is negatively mediated by the individual, and on the other, it is also possible for the state to arrogantly mistake itself to be the absolute substratum in which the individual is wholly negated as a consequence of the denial of its own negativity. Consequently, the state is inevitably destined to perish and disappear from history due to God's judgment of the world. The state stands in opposition to God, which results in what Tanabe calls "radical evil" (Tanabe 1963b, 363). If the state, in regard to God as Absolute Nothingness, is not negatively mediated by individual practice, then it cannot escape from being denied by God.

The individual as a free existence, too, cannot escape from the bondage of radical evil, which tends to stick to its own being in opposition to God. It is only by means of repentance that the individual can be taken into the love of God. Through repentance, the individual can be mediated to God in and through his political practice of the reformation of the state. Only insofar as the state is mediated through the practical action of the individual, the state is permeated by the religious principle of Absolute Nothingness as the expedient being, and is recognized as the substratum in relation to the ever-negating practice of the individual in the form of being-qua-nothingness.

In terms of the particular state in space and time, whereas space is always limited and confined, time refers to an intended unification through conversion in history, brought about by the politically constructive practice of the state, or a union of states, mediated by limited space. A union of many states is directed toward a unification of the world from the religious standpoint of Absolute

Negation. This requires concrete practice through which politics and religion are to be unified through conversion in negation in a higher dimension.

The state is only negatively mediated to the universality of humankind as the content of its politico-religious practice, and hence can retain its existence as a balance between being and nothingness, arising from conversion at each moment. It may maintain its negative mediation in the form of relativity-qua-absoluteness, that is, solely in its reformed shapes continuously renewed in practice. Even so, however, the state needs to be a juridical state, so that it may be governed according to the universal norms of laws in order to preserve its relative absoluteness. In analogy to the mediating role of species tending toward universalization in objective being as the eternal Idea or Form, the state moves toward universalizing itself through its legal system as the affirmative aspect of its negative mediation.

Based upon the principle of negativity in the form of being-qua-nothingness realized through mediation, the state cannot help but tend to become a substratum, a self-identical being of its own. It does so in its tendency toward its own juridical perpetuation, that is, as meant by the possibility of degeneration into an unmediated existence, in spite of its negative mediating nature. This is because the state on the level of species, too, is deeply involved in radical evil, clinging to its own self-identity of being apart from its perpetually self-negating conversion in action, just as in the case of individual persons. This is the reason why the state as such can be evil from the religious perspective. It, like human beings, is inevitably involved in evil. Therefore, the state may also acquire its mediating being in the form of the relative-qua-the absolute only through religious redemption, which is to say, through repentance for its radical evil. The state and religion are set in opposition to each other; nevertheless, they are mutually converted in negation and dialectically unified through mediation. The relation of the state to religion should be, as Tanabe famously puts it, "metanoetically" (Tanabe 1963b, 364) understood as a paradox. In this connection, it is important to understand Tanabe's conception of radical evil and his view of the role of repentance.

Radical Evil and Repentance

The notion of radical evil comes from Kant, according to whom human nature has the irrevocable tendency toward evil, inherently lurking at the ground of human existence. This might, in Kant's articulation, be the secularized version or hidden influence of the Christian myth of original sin. Tanabe seriously takes it to be of fundamental importance for analyzing human nature as well as the sociopolitical entity of the state, while further appropriating the influences of Fichte's and Schelling's ideas of evil as inertia and nature within God respectively.

Contrary to Hegel, who regards the state's existence as the Kingdom of God realized in history, Tanabe asserts that the state's existence is inevitably involved in radical evil. As we have seen above, for Tanabe, the state is not the realization of eternal truth in the actual world, but is, in its authentic form of realized universality, sustained through the individual's subjective action mediated by Absolute Nothingness. In his view, radical evil is inherently lurking in the individual as well as in the state, and is to be negated and purified by religious practice based upon Absolute Nothingness. Absolute Nothingness, however, does not directly operate through the individual, but only through the mediation of the state. The state's existence as such is not absolute, but is relative in the form of the mediating balance between the ideal and the real, or between the universal and the individual. The state's existence qua the species-substratum has the duality of the realization of the genus-like universality and the self-estrangement from it. Insofar as the state is perpetually renewed in and through its reformative practice, it can be made to exist only through the mediation of the individual's act of repentance for evil. Hence, repentance, in Tanabe's philosophy, plays a crucial role in the realization of Absolute Nothingness.

Tanabe proposes a new idea of the relationship between religion and politics in terms of the triadic logic of species that is motivated by the religious moment of repentance. Even the state's existence, as in the case of the individual person, inherently possesses radical evil, due to its duality of the species-level of being. The state's existence is on the way to the actualization of genus-like universality, but it always involves a regression into the past substrative being, which prevents it from realizing its own universality. In other words, the state's existence is not absolute as such, but is rather a balance between ideality and reality, absolute and relative. Since the state is perpetually struggling with radical evil, politics is in need of perpetual reformation in connection with the religious act of repentance for sin. Evil deeply lurks in human beings from time immemorial, and only repentance can save human beings.

Tanabe says that without repentance, there can be no act bearing upon Nothingness. Repentance is the indispensable basic moment of human action. However, repentance in Tanabe's conception is not a special religious act, but rather the utterly necessary condition and universal moment in which action returns from the transcendental realm, and in which ordinary people, laden with deep sin and inescapably bound up with radical evil, are made to participate in absolute mercy and cooperate with its saving activity. Without it, there can be no religious practice. Since human beings are primordially entangled with radical evil from time immemorial, they are further in need of renunciation from it. In the reverse side of the practical conversion from Nothingness to being, a human subject is strained by species-like inertia in the form of self-alienation, and hence requires a moment of repentance, for redemption from it as the negative mediation of the act by which a mutual identification of the individuality and the totality is to be brought about.

Tanabe acknowledges the fact that human beings are primordially involved in radical evil from time immemorial, and he is the first major philosopher in modern Japan to seriously take sin and evil to be fundamentally constitutive of human existence. On that basis, he takes up the problem of the relation of religion and politics in general. His deep insight into repentance might be derived from the Buddhist tradition in which the triadic factors of precept, meditation and wisdom play the central role in attaining Buddhahood. So, it may have been no accident for Tanabe to take into consideration repentance as the indispensable element of the negative mediation and integration via mutual suppression of religion and politics or the state. In this regard, his philosophy is profound in its religious significance.

Tanabe's Philosophy in Today's World

Tanabe anticipated the coming of the dialogue and mutual transformation of world religions in connection with the political action of the state in terms of the Logic of Species more than fifty years ago, at a time when almost nobody had predicted such a situation in the near future. This reveals Tanabe's deep insight into the ideal state of world religions in the coming era. Immediately after World War II, he revised the Logic of Species according to which Japanese Buddhism, Christianity, and Marxism should be unified in the form of a world religion that would be the product of a second religious reformation. And further, this new kind of world religion should also be negatively mediated (by being partially suppressed and partially transformed) in world politics for the purpose of practically realizing the unity of humankind as a whole. He intended to integrate Japanese Buddhism, Christianity, and Marxism with a view toward reformulating them in a higher stage of world religion. He was neither satisfied with Zen Buddhism nor with Pure Land Buddhism, but rather aimed to reform them in such a way that both types of Japanese Buddhism could be integrated with the historical character of Christianity, though the Christian idea of a personal God should at the same time be demythologised in terms of the Buddhist principle of Emptiness or Absolute Nothingness, as well as with Marxist social and historical practice.

Tanabe may have been influenced by Marxist socio-historical practice, oriented toward the reformation of the state to stress sociopolitical action rather than contemplation. After World War II, Tanabe regarded the Japanese emperor as the symbol of Absolute Nothingness, and this might be critically seen as an affirmation of the given actuality. The propensity for the affirmation of historical actuality is the foremost distinction of the Tendai Buddhism's conception of Original Enlightenment in medieval Japan, according to which all phenomena are nothing but the self-manifestations of truth, appearances expressing truth itself without any negative mediation. The propensity for the affirmation of actuality is thus the distinguishing characteristics of Tendai Buddhism's idea of Original Enlightenment in medieval Japan. The Buddhist logic of the non-duality of actual fact and eternal truth culminates in the doctrine of so-called Original Enlightenment, in which the distinction between actual fact and eternal truth disappears and results in their non-duality as the ultimate self-identity of the phenomenal world and principle, that is, Absolute Nothingness. This turns into a full affirmation of the phenomenal world without any self-negation within itself. All phenomena in the actual world are positively affirmed as the self-expression of eternal truth itself, and relative actuality is none other than the self-manifestation of the absolute principle. Actual facts are directly identified with eternal truth itself, without the mediating moment of conversion in negation between them. This is the immediate and direct identification of actuality and ideality, in which self-negating activity does not operate any more. But this standpoint only adopts the perspective of contemplation, not of action. The tendency toward the affirmation of historical actuality belongs to the Chinese way of thinking, and this might be reflected in Tendai's interpretation of the reciprocal self-identity of appearance and truth. This tendency is further deepened in the Japanese Tendai School, which teaches that human beings are originally all buddhas, being identical to each other, without any moment of self-negation within themselves.

The tendency to affirm actuality might be also reflective of the general mentality of Japanese people, and Tanabe is not exempt from that tendency. Therefore, there is some ambivalence in Tanabe: on the one hand, he aims at self-negating action in the reformation of actual society, and on the other hand, he is still bound up with the traditional mentality of affirming actuality. This may be seen as a prime example of Nishida's concept of the "absolute self-identity in contradistinction." (Nishida 1995, 7–84).

In contrast to the Indian way of thinking, oriented toward eternal ideality, Chinese and Japanese tend to shift focus to the affirmation of socio-historical actuality. Emptiness turns out to be actuality in reverse. In terms of its essential nature, Emptiness must not be confined to any stage of self-development, but further continue its self-negating activity. This is because Emptiness must always maintain itself as Emptiness throughout. This entails ever self-emptying activity in an endless process, never reaching finality. Emptiness must be emptied again and again, retaining itself without regressing onto the level of being that is to be emptied. Once something is emptied, it must be further emptied, without stopping at any point or stage of its empting activity.

On the whole, Tanabe attempts to synthesize Eastern and Western ideas in a higher level of harmony in correspondence with the contemporary historical situation, and his thought might be seen as an eclecticism or a sort of creative syncretism, as pointed out by some Marxist critics such as Jun Tosaka and Kanichi Kuroda. For example, he identifies Absolute Nothingness with God or the Absolute Other, despite the varying cultural and historical origins of these ideas. However, he was not alone in this tendency. Nishida also undertakes the same project, and this may be reflective of a characteristics of very traditional Japanese habits of syncretism in which, in earlier periods, Buddhism and Shinto were mixed and compromised. Even in Chinese intellectual history, the three different religions of Confucianism, Daoism, and Buddhism are regarded as three teachings manifesting ultimately the same truth. Within the ambit of Buddhism, the *Lotus Sutra* is estimated to be the most comprehensive synthesis of different teachings. In the Japanese Tendai School, the founder Saicho takes the *Lotus Sutra* as the integral and unifying fundamental principle of all *sutra*s and various teachings. Shinran and Dougen, by whose thought Tanabe is immensely influenced, are not excluded from this tendency, and their interpretations are much affected in Tanabe's estimation by the thought of the *Lotus Sutra*. So even though Tanabe does not explicitly mention or refer to the *Lotus Sutra*, his thought may be considered in accord with the syncretism of the Japanese intellectual tradition.

From such a perspective, it might not be a surprise that Tanabe attempts a synthetic unification of Japanese Buddhism, Christianity, and Marxism as the second religious reformation, and also aims at negative mediation, which is to say, inclusion with suppression, of these world religions and political practices designed for the global salvation of humankind. A higher unification of world religions and world politics through their mutual mediation in negation is still an ideal reflective of the post-war world situation, insofar as it envisages a triadic dialectic of genus, species and the individual aiming toward global unity.

What is highly significant in Tanabe's philosophy for today's world may be the relationship of religion and politics in terms of negative mediation and the act of repentance for evil and sin, as we are now standing at the crossroad of negation within the mediating unification of religion and politics. In the advanced countries of the contemporary world, religion and politics are legally separated from each other. Tanabe's new proposal is not, in the present light, an anachronism, but instead, a prediction of a future possibility of the relationship between religion and politics that is based on his view of the dialectical development of history. In this context, however, it must not be forgotten that the moment of repentance for sin and evil is necessarily indispensable for further historical developments and the realization of the human common good in terms of the deep triadic structure of universality, particularity and individuality.

For Hegel, a religious truth such as freedom should be realized through politics in the state. Originally, religion and politics were unified with one another, and in the modern era they are separated from each other. However, Tanabe does not stop there but goes a step further to synthesize two historical religions, Buddhism and Christianity, in the direction of a higher unification in relation to politics on the world scale, anticipating the ideal unity of a world government. This anticipation resulted from Tanabe's own reflections on our inescapable involvement in the given historical situation, and on this basis, he advocates a calm struggle to overcome the crises facing the world.

In the end, Tanabe asserts that today's politics on a worldwide scale should participate in the salvation of humankind through the mediation of the rewarding love of the world's religions, which could be ideally realized as a result of a mutual transformation of Buddhism and Christianity. Here, Tanabe proposes a new idea of world religion that is neither Buddhism nor Christianity, but rather a creative dialectical unification of them in the direction of ongoing historical development. Even Hegel already predicted the coming of a third religion as a new development of Christianity. Today, the American process theologian John Cobb also hypothesizes a mutual transformation of Buddhism and Christianity in terms of the Whiteheadian conception of process. Although Cobb regards the Amida Buddha as a possible Christ, because of the deficiencies of the historical development of Pure Land Buddhism, he sees Christianity as historically superior. Tanabe's envisaged unfolding of religious and political tendencies includes Marxism as well, as a necessary element of socio-historical practice devoted to reforming the given historical actuality, itself ultimately wedded to the Christian conceptions of progress, informed by the Buddhist standpoint of Emptiness. The relation of religion and politics is essential for Christianity; the coming of the Kingdom of God in which Jesus's return is postponed and expected in the eschatological future. In terms of the triadic structure of social existence oscillating between universality and individuality, Tanabe anticipates that religion and politics are in a negative mediation through conversion toward a higher unification in the historical development of the world.

20 Nishitani on Emptiness and Nothingness

Yasuo Deguchi

> A deep and bottomless valley lies within the endless sky. Likewise, nihility lies within emptiness. But in this case, the sky is not only something that stretches far and wide over the valley, but also something within which the earth, we, and countless stars exist and are moving about. It lies under our feet, at a further depth of the bottom of the valley. If the residence of the omnipresent God is heaven, then heaven should also lie at a further depth of bottomless hell. So heaven is a depth for the hell. In the same way, emptiness is a depth for the nihility.[1]
>
> —Keiji Nishitani, *What Is Religion?* 1961/1987a, 110f.

Introduction

Emptiness (空, *kū*) and Nothingness (無, *mu*) are among the most important philosophical terms in East Asian thoughts. Emptiness, as a philosophical term, has an Indian origin; it is *śūnyatā* in Sanskrit, and was formulated in Mahāyāna Buddhism, particularly in the *Paramīta sūtras* and the Mādhyamaka school. On the other hand, nothingness came from Chinese Daoism, especially the doctrine of reverence for nothingness (貴無論, *ki mu ron*) in Neo-Daoism (玄學, *gen gaku*).

When the Mahāyāna idea of emptiness was introduced into China, it was sometimes translated and explained as nothingness.[2] Since then, these terms have been largely taken as synonyms in Buddhist philosophical discourse. But some have challenged this common wisdom, and claimed that in certain contexts the two ideas are distinct. For instance, a prominent scholar in the history of Zen Buddhism wrote that nothingness in the Zen tradition had nothing to do with emptiness in the *Paramīta* texts (Yanagida 1984, 196). We thus have cause to ask ourselves the following questions: do emptiness and nothingness differ from each other in meaning, and if so, what is the difference between them, and what significance does this difference have?

These problems become particularly pressing when we examine the philosophy of Keiji Nishitani (1900–1990), the most influential postwar Kyoto school philosopher. He changed the key term of his thought from *absolute nothingness*, an expression he inherited from Kitarō Nishida (1870–1945), the founder of the Kyoto school, to *emptiness*, in the middle of one of his major works, *What Is Religion?*(1961/1987a). Despite this apparent shift, however, he didn't explain explicitly whether the two terms were synonymous, why he changed his key term, and what significance this shift had. Naturally, his silence has led some scholars of Nishitani to ask themselves the questions asked above (e.g., Ueda 2004; Hanaoka 2004).[3] In this chapter, I will raise these questions, and try to answer them in my own way.

Let me outline my answer to begin. Nishitani didn't articulate any substantial difference between emptiness and nothingness in *What Is Religion?*. The terms are used interchangeably and employed as an *existential category*, as I called it. In other words, the only difference between them still remains nominal in this early work. A substantial difference between the meanings and significance of the difference can only be identified in one of his latest and most important works, "Emptiness and That-Is-Ness" (1982/1987b). But the philosophical importance of this difference cannot be fully understood without taking into account Nishitani's idea of *emotional reconciliation with nihilism* in his essay "On Bashō" (1962/1991a). As this back and forth movement of my arguments from one to the other text suggests, the difference and its significance are not completely spelled out by Nishitani himself. Rather, they are major open questions that he left to us.

Nishitani as a Mahāyāna Existentialist

In *What Is Religion?* Nishitani tried to establish his own version of existentialism that incorporated traditional ideas of Mahāyāna Buddhism, or *Mahāyāna existentialism*, as I call it, contrasting it with older versions of existentialism found in Kierkegaard, Nietzsche, the early Heidegger, and Sartre.[4] In so doing, he reformulated a Mahāyāna idea, *emptiness*, as an existential category. By existential category, I mean both an ontological and epistemological mode of ourselves and our world; that is, a mode of how we and our world exist, and how we know ourselves and the world.

Then what is existentialism? Like Sartre in *Question de méthode* (Sartre 1960/1985, 1), existentialists usually reject any attempt to define their own positions. Nishitani is no exception; he didn't define existentialism. But he roughly characterized it as a philosophical position that puts its "emphasis on subjectivity" (Nishitani 1987a, 64). This characterization qualifies him as an existentialist because he also emphasizes "fundamental subjectivity" (82). Furthermore, from his critical comments on the earlier versions of existentialism, we can extract his ideas of what existentialism ought to be (63ff). According to him, existentialism has to be aware of nihility as the basis of human existence and the world as a whole, or in other words, to acknowledge the meaninglessness of our existence, our lives, and the entire world, and nevertheless tries to construct its own view of ourselves and the world, as opposed to the scientific objectifying views on them. This is exactly what Nishitani aimed to do in *What Is Religion?*[5] He tried to attain this aim by contrasting three views, "standpoints," or existential categories: the category of reason or consciousness; the category of nihility or *karma* (業, *gou*); and the category of emptiness. According to Nishitani, the first category is represented by classical modern Western philosophies, such as Cartesianism and Kantianism, with science as their output. He takes the second category to correspond to the views of Western existentialists such as Nietzsche, the early Heidegger, and Sartre. Since Nishitani takes these existentialists to also be nihilists (108), he takes the second category as the nihilistic worldview. Finally, the third category represents his own position, which is characterized by Mahāyāna ideas such as emptiness.

Why are Mahāyāna ideas taken to exemplify the *third* category? An obvious reason is that Nishitani takes the Mahāyāna worldview to be the truest and most profound one in comparison with the first two, in the sense that those two categories are made possible only on the basis of the Mahāyāna category. At the same time, he cautiously avoided giving a privileged position to Mahāyāna Buddhism by writing that the same category can be seen "to be implied by, not only Buddhism, but all genuine religious lives" (Nishitani 1987a, 289). In his view, these "religious lives" include those of Christians such as Paul (31, 67ff), Eckhart (70–78, 102, 112, 120) and Francesco d'Assisi (310f, 313f). But he also adds that the worldview represented in the third category is "manifested most straightforwardly" (288) or "in a clearer manner" (102) in Mahāyāna Buddhism, and especially in the Zen tradition. So he does give a special status to certain kinds of religious worldviews, and reserves just a relative advantage for Mahāyāna Buddhism.

We can identify yet another reason for Nishitani's appeal to Mahāyāna ideas. This reason has to do with his strategy for overcoming the older forms of existentialism or nihilism by means of his new version. Any new version of existentialism must be distinct from, and, at least in a sense, superior to the older ones, but at the same time, it should share the same spirit with them. In other words, the new version of existentialism has to criticize some aspects of the older ones while retaining some of their virtues. Nishitani's appeal to Mahāyāna is appropriate for carrying out this twofold task.

Though having a history of almost two millennia, Mahāyāna Buddhism is a relatively new addition to the Buddhism movement. In its inception, to establish itself as a new and better version of Buddhism, it had to criticize some aspects of an older tradition of Buddhism, Hīnayāna or Theravāda, while accepting its other aspects. In other words, Mahāyāna was established as a dialectical *antithesis* to Hīnayāna. Many Mahāyāna ideas, such as emptiness, were designed to surpass some core ideas of Hīnayāna without violating the original spirit of Buddhism. In this way, Mahāyāna's relation to Hīnayāna as its archrival is analogous to Nishitani's stance to the older forms of existentialism. Against this background, Nishitani appropriated Mahāyāna's position into his own version of existentialism, and consigned Hīnayāna's thought to the older versions. This amounts to affixing the label "new and superior" to his version of existentialism, while assigning the label "old and inferior" to its previous versions. On the basis of this strategic labeling, the Mahāyāna idea of emptiness was elevated. In this way, emptiness and other Mahāyāna ideas play a strategically crucial role in his philosophical project, which is to propose a "new and better" version of existentialism that overcomes nihilism.

Nishitani's strategy also belongs to an established tradition of the Kyoto school; that is, to construct an alternative philosophical position to one or another Western counterpart by means of Mahāyāna ideas, especially those of Zen Buddhism. Nishitani applied this strategy to existentialism, proposing his Mahāyāna existentialism as an alternative to the older versions of existentialism. In effect, he formed an existentialist's version of Kyoto school philosophy, or, to wit, *existentialized* Kyoto school thought. This *existentialization* of the Kyoto school was so popular among later generations of Kyoto school philosophers that it made Nishitani the most influential postwar Kyoto school figure.

Three Existential Categories

We shall now sketch Nishitani's three existential categories. The idea of existential categories had been continuously developing from the earliest chapter to the final one in *What Is Religion?*, and the contents of these categories had steadily grown richer as the chapters advanced. Take an example of this snowballing effect by citing both the earliest and a later description of the category of emptiness. Here is the earliest one.

> 'Emptiness' is the place where we, as concrete human beings, that is, whole individuals, including not only our personalities but also our bodies, realize ourselves as we are, and where everything that surrounds us realizes itself as it is. (Nishitani 1987a, 102)

Next is a description from the latest chapter:

> In the place of emptiness, *Dasein* returns to its original phase of "non-Twoness of self and other," by breaking through "ignorance" as an entire closure-within-self, stands on the basis of non-ego rather than nihility, and is "non-action" by departing from its infinite drive. In this sense, the place of emptiness is the place of absolute transcendence from time, space and causal necessity, and as a result, the linkage of the "world". But this absolute transcendence is at the same time an absolute immanence. Within the life-and-death-that-is-enlightenment is real life-and-death and real enlightenment, as noted above, the absolute other side realizes itself only as absolute this side. The place of true emptiness realizes and manifests itself as being united with that dynamic linkage of "being" – "doing" – "becoming" that takes place in "time", or rather is "time" itself. That is why I said that true *Dasein* is "self" as an emergence from non-ego. *Dasein* is non-"being-in-the-world" while "being-in-the-world," and it is "being-in-the-world" since it is non-"being-in-the-world." (292f)

At the beginning, the emptiness category was only about a special manner of human existence and the world's existence; both exist in a way that they realize their original or authentic nature. At the end, however, emptiness had also come to be about the relation of the self or *Dasein*,[6] to other self, action, time, space, causation, and the world. In addition, as an existential category is about the relation of the world to the self, and all that is other than the self. Nishitani wrote that *Dasein*, or the self, "comes into existence as being united with the endless world linkage" (293). Due to this unification, what holds for the self also holds for the world.

Although Nishitani's existential category is about many things, it can be summarized as being about the self and the world, and more specifically, their ontological modes (i.e. how the self and the world exists) and their epistemological modes (i.e. how the self knows itself and the world). By and large, Nishitani's explanations of epistemological modes are based on the ontological ones. For Nishitani, ontology precedes epistemology in the order of explanation.

1. The Category of Reason or Consciousness

Ontological mode: The self, as a rational person or an ego, confronts the world as an independent object (Nishitani 1987a, 18). This mode of self is well formulated as the Cartesian cognitive agent, *Cogito*, that doubts everything but itself (18) as well as the Kantian autonomous moral agent that has its ground and aim in itself (301).

Epistemological mode: The self as a subject knows itself and the world by representing them as objects, and gives them meaning and significance from its standpoint (Nishitani 1987a, 18, 122). So the subject-object dichotomy holds here. Self-consciousness reveals the self as self-contained and being free of fetters from any other authority, including God (42). The self also tries to know the essence of everything, including itself, as self-identical being (22, 129).

2. The Category of Nihility

Ontological mode: The self, the world and even God are nullified. In other words nihility is realized; everything losses its meaning, significance, and even its reality (Nishitani 1987a, 108, 122). Being determined to choose nihility (62, 99), the self willingly makes itself a nihility or non-self (108), or in other words, the self as a person or an agency is dissolved into pure volition (Nietzsche) or desire (Sartre) (99). As pure volition or desire, we come to be totally free (42).

Epistemological mode: There is neither a knowing subject nor an object to be known (Nishitani 1987a, 123), so the subject-object dichotomy fails to hold here (126). Being without meaning, significance, or existence, everything becomes something strange to us, a pure "question mark" that cannot, in principle, be answered (99, 126). Unlike Cartesian doubt, doubt here is cast even upon oneself. However, only in these negative ways, we, as pure activities, directly encounter or experience ourselves and the world as nihility (108).

3. The Category of Emptiness

Ontological mode: The term *realization* (リアリゼーション, *ri a ri zē shon*; or 現成, *gen jō*) is a key component of this category. It was given a double-meaning: manifestation and understanding (Nishitani 1987a, 9). Manifestation is an ontological term, and means that something manifests itself as it is or returns to its authentic, original and fundamental condition (80). On the other hand, understanding is obviously an epistemological term. So in this category, the ontological and epistemological modes are just two sides of the same coin. But for the moment let us focus on the ontological aspect.

According to Nishitani, the ontological realization or manifestation of the self and that of the world are also merely two aspects of one and the same event. This sameness is often rephrased in apparently contradictory expressions such as "the self and the world are absolutely two and absolutely one" (120). Thus, the ontological picture here is *not* simply a monistic or unitary one according to which, while things are different on a superficial level, they are depicted as united in their authentic states. This contradictory or dialetheic nature of things in this category can also be identified in Nishitani's characterization of this category's counterpart of the essence of things in the category of reason—non-own-nature (無自性, *mu ji shō*). For instance, while the essence of fire is burning, its non-own-nature is burning *and* non-burning (132f). In addition, everything including the self has apparently contradictory properties, for example, death-that-is-life (死即生, *shi soku sei*). In this context, death and life mean pure materiality and personality respectively (106). This doesn't mean that the self, for instance, is matter in some respect, and a person in another respect. Rather, the self is said to have only apparently inconsistent properties by being both a material thing and being a person. For Nishitani, these apparently contradictory characters reflect the double nature of reality (58f, 202).

The realization of this contradictory nature is also described as a return to, or reappropriation of the original state of affairs (Nishitani 1987a, 102). Unlike the other two categories, only this category of emptiness is approved to be the authentic and fundamental mode of existence of the self and the world. So, the self is not dissolved into the world, but restores its original mode of being, that is, being contradictorily united with the world.

In contrast with the category of nihility, where every being is nullified, in this category nihility itself is nullified or *emptified* (Nishitani 1987a, 80). This nullification or *emptification* of nihility means, of course, the reappropriation of originality; or the this-side-ness (此岸性, *hi gan sei*) in Nishitanian terms. While admitting a nihilistic turn from being to nothingness, Nishitani proposes a return from nothingness to being by introducing the emptiness category (78). He calls the category "the standpoint that transcends the subjective nihility further towards this side" (110). Similarly, in the place of a nihilistic thesis of non self (which is to view the self as empty), Nishitani claim that emptiness or non-self *is* the self (156), implying a restoration of the self as something that has an apparently contradictory non-own-nature, or own-ness (自體, *ji tai*), as Nishitani calls it, in contrast to substance (實體, *jittai*).

Epistemological mode: In this mode, another meaning of realization, or understanding, is central. The understanding in this category is rephrased as "bodily recognition (體認, *tai nin*)" (Nishitani 1987a, 24) or "apprehension (會得, *e toku*)" (183). Citing a phrase of a Japanese Zen master, Dōgen (1200–1253), "everything comes to confirm the self by practice" (Dōgen 1931, 23), Nishitani explained this cognitive mode as follows.[7]

> The reality, that is realizing itself as [a Japanese word] *koto* (that has a double meaning of thing and word) transfers itself, as it is and in its essence, to human existence, and human transfers himself to the reality. (Nishitani 1987a, 200f)

Here Nishitani seems to mention a joint practice between human beings and the reality or world, which is to say, *mutual transference*. As one of the above characterizations has it, bodily recognition suggests that the understanding at issue can be taken to be a certain sort of somatic or embodied knowledge that is attained in the course of this joint practice. It is also characterized as *samādhi*, a traditional Buddhist idea for mental concentration in meditation (24, 185). So we can call this cognitive mode *samādhi cognition.*

Samādhi cognition is also dubbed "the knowing of non-knowing" (Nishitani 1987a, 174). But this Socratic phrase is meant to refer to the non-cognitive nature of cognition, which is different from its original sense of awareness of ignorance. So cognition in this category also has an apparently contradictory nature as its non-own-nature.

Like many other types of somatic knowledge, it doesn't make sense to distinguish the knowing subject from the object of knowledge. So the subject-object distinction doesn't hold here. Furthermore, *samādhi* cognition doesn't employ any representation of things whatsoever. Being nonobjective and non-representational, *samādhi* cognition is distinct from the epistemic mode of the category of reason.

Samādhi cognition can also close the question that nihilism left open, which is, what are the self and the world? The self and the world are now understood as joint practitioners or mutual transferrers that share an apparently contradictory non-own-nature. This closure of the question is a crucial point that distinguishes between nihilistic cognition and *samādhi* cognition.

Remaining Problems

These three categories remain problematic, nevertheless. In particular, the third one, which represents the worldview of Nishitani's Mahāyāna existentialism, is not sufficiently explicated. For instance, his characterization of *samādhi* cognition depends too heavily on metaphorical terms such as "interference". It requires further conceptual clarification in order to lift the mystic fog surrounding the idea of *samādhi.*

Furthermore, this brand of Mahāyāna existentialism cannot decisively clear itself of the suspicion that its alleged contradictions are spurious. As shown above, a distinctive feature of the emptiness category is that at least some contradictions are taken as true and real. Indeed, Nishitani clearly and unconditionally affirms some contradictions as true—especially ones with regard to two opposing concepts such as life and death.[8] But at least some of those contradictions seem to be dissoluble when we examine them carefully. Take an example of the apparently contradictory non-own-nature of fire: burning and non-burning. It seems quite possible to cancel the apparent contradiction by introducing a parameter, which is to say, a distinction of objects' being burned: the fire doesn't burn itself while it burns something else. Then, we can parameterize away the apparent contradiction. Nishitani takes into account the possibility of this parameterization. His discussion of the non-own-nature of fire began from the remark that mentions the distinction of objects. But he tries to call off the distinction by rephrasing the original remark, so as to come up with a sentence that implies a flat contradiction. It seems that here he is attempting *reverse*-parameterization, as it were.

Unfortunately, Nishitani's attempt doesn't seem to be successful. We can still identify a crucial leap or a lack of argumentation from a contradiction-free sentence to a contradictory one.[9] However, it would be too hasty to declare, based merely on those shortcomings, that Nishitani's entire philosophical project has come to a dead end. Just as the issue of how to differentiate emptiness from nothingness, these are among the main problems that he left for us to solve. We can thus take his unfinished tasks as our own.[10]

Mahāyāna Overcoming Nihilism

Nishitani advocates the third category as being superior to and more profound than the first two. In so doing, he tries to overcome earlier forms of existentialism or nihilism, as these are found in the second category, with his own version of existentialism. To establish the superiority of the category of emptiness, ideas of Buddhism, especially those of Mahāyāna Buddhism, are mobilized. The category of reason is dismissed as a non-Buddhism standpoint, while that of nihility in both its non-Buddhist and Hīnayāna Buddhism forms is found wanting. The ultimately superior category of emptiness is described as the worldview of Mahāyāna Buddhism.

In the category of reason, the self is regarded as self-contained in the sense that it pretends to ground its own existence as a Cartesian ego, and to give the ultimate aim to itself as a Kantian moral agent does. From the Buddhist point of view, Nishitani re-characterized this self-contained nature of the self in a negative manner: "being caught in one's own trap" (Nishitani 1987a, 38), "self-centeredness" (19, 116), "closure-within-the-self" (15), and so on. This category is then curtly dismissed as "attachment to the self" (20, 116). Moreover, in this category, the objects of recognition, that is, the self and the world, are represented and objectified by the self. Even in these apparently indifferent representation and objectification of cognition, Nishitani finds symptoms of greed for, or attachment to, objects (140, 170). This is because, in his view, by representing something as an object, a cognitive agent is already attracted to, or is drawn by it (140).

In a nutshell, Nishitani regards the category of reason as a position of "attachment to self and being" (Nishitani 1987a, 116). In the Buddhist terminology, this means ignorance or delusion (無明, *mu myō*), roaming in life-and-death (生死, *sho ji*), or *saṃsāra*, which is quite opposite of enlightenment (涅槃, *ne han*) or *nirvāṇa*. So he dismisses this category as taking the standpoint of a non-Buddhist who is yet to be enlightened.

By contrast, in the category of nihility, the self and the world are nullified, and the cognitive dichotomy of subject and object is abandoned. So the attachment to the self and the world appears to vanish from this category. However, Nishitani still senses here a trace of attachment. In this category, the self is dissolved into pure desire or volition. Nishitani rephrases it as "infinite compulsion " (Nishitani 1987a, 244, 260, 270, 275) or "self-will" (275, 276), and characterizes it, by using another Buddhist term, *karma* (業, *gou*), a sinful and fateful act (243, 244, 260, 276). Then he found in the infinite compulsion or karma a vestige of the self, and judged that even this second category was not entirely free from self-centeredness or closure-within-the-self (266, 280, 282). Accordingly, pure volition or desire is also characterized negatively as a product of attachment (271, 280) and ignorance or delusion (274, 280, 282). In this respect, Nishitani finds no substantial difference between the categories of reason and nihility. The latter is thus also dismissed as remaining at a non-Buddhist level.

On the other hand, however, this category does acknowledge the nihility for the self and the world. The self and the world are deprived even of their reality, and therefore are neither subjectified nor objectified any longer. This is definitely progress from the non-Buddhist standpoint. Nishitani's criticism of the resulting standpoint is directed to its attitude toward nihility rather than the self and the world. He wrote:

> [T]here nihility is still seen from the side of self-existence as a "no-groundness" (*Grundlosigkeit*) that lies at the bottom of self-existence. This means that nihility is seen outside the self's existence, and therefore seen as something other than "existence" or something that can be other than "existence." (Nishitani 1987a, 108)

So, in Nishitani's eyes, the earlier existentialists or nihilists such as Nietzsche, Heidegger, and Sartre made a crucial mistake in taking nihility as an object, or more precisely, in speaking of a nonexistent object. To Nishitani, though free from the objectification of the self and the world, these earlier existentialists were still confined to an objectification of nihility, and therefore were "captured by nothingness" (109).

Nishitani takes the nihilists' attitude to nihility as analogous to Hīnayāna Buddhists' regard for nirvāṇa that had been criticized by Mahāyāna as being "attached to emptiness" (Nishitani 1987a, 39). He continued to say that "the self that set up nothingness, is, in so doing, chained to nothingness and attached to nothingness. In the disguise of the negation of self-attachment, it is, in fact, a hidden and empowered self-attachment" (39). To him, Hīnayāna Buddhism is not a full-fledged Buddhism. It is an impure alloy between Buddhism and non-Buddhism. This is also his judgment of the nihilistic category as a whole.

Now finally the category of emptiness as articulated by Mahāyāna is elevated above the earlier two categories.

> We are usually grounded in the standpoint that sees being merely as being, and is captured by being. Once that standpoint is destroyed and negated, nihility emerges. The standpoint of nihility is also the standpoint that sees nothingness merely as nothingness, and is captured by nothingness. That is to say, it is a standpoint that is to be negated again. Then "emptiness," as the standpoint that disposes such a double capture, and is totally non-attached, comes to emerge. (Nishitani 1987a, 109)

In contrast to the earlier two categories, the emptiness category is affirmed as being free from any attachments to the self and the world, as well as to nihility, nothingness or emptiness. The self is described as being free from self-attachment, self-centeredness and closure-within-the-self (119, 275). As for emptiness or nothingness, it is taken as emptying the standpoint that represents emptiness as something empty (108), advocating "absolute emptiness" that empties emptiness (40), or implying that "there is no such thing as nothing or true or absolute nothingness" (80). As shown above, the freedom from all sorts of attachments is also described as the restoration of or return to everything's original states of affairs or its absolute this-side-ness (40, 110, 119).

Among these characterizations of the category of emptiness, we have already been able to identify echoes of Mahāyāna Buddhist terms: emptying emptiness (空空, *kū kū*) and the return to the origin (本源に還る, *hon gen ni kae ru*). In addition, Nishitani characterized these categories by using more explicitly Mahāyāna labels for non-Buddhist, Hīnayāna, and Mahāyāna Buddhist ideas (Nishitani 1987a, 40, 81, 300). For instance, the categories of reason, nihility, and emptiness are said to be the place of life-and-death, enlightenment, and life-and-death-that-is-enlightenment (300).

None of these Buddhist terms is value-free. They incorporate the idea that non-attachment is valuable, and it is on that basis that Mahāyāna is taken to be the highest category, Hīnayāna comes second, and non-Buddhism is ranked at bottom. But, of course, we are not obligated to endorse the Mahāyāna values. So Nishitani needs to provide us some independent reason for the superiority of his own category. He seems to have two reasons, a practical and a theoretical one.

According to Nishitani, the categories of reason and nihility have given rise to severe problems for the modern world; they jointly have threatened human values in various ways. Why? First, the category of reason gave birth to, among other things, scientism, according to which only science can provide us with *the* true picture of the world, while philosophy, religion and art cannot (Nishitani 1987a, 88). The scientific picture of the world is purely mechanistic and totally indifferent to human values (69). In consequence, the grounds of those latter values are severely undermined. On the other hand, the category of nihility dissected the rational self, which was thought to be a source of human values, into an agent of pure desire. Then, once we obtain technology that has been enhanced by science, we tend to "overdose on it," so to speak, to meet our desires. As a result, the science and technology driven by our restless desire has over-mechanized human life, society and our culture, making them meaningless, alienating many individuals, and threatening human values (96, 97ff, 100). Consequently, to root out those practical predicaments, we need to overcome or at least modify those categories through the category of emptiness, which, according to Nishitani, does not threaten human values.

Nishitani also has a theoretical reason for preferring his category of emptiness to the other two. He wrote:

> The place of nihility greatly transcends the place of consciousness, where the confrontation between materialism and idealism holds. Needless to say, the place of emptiness is the only one where the depth of nihility can be found at all. Hence, neither the place of consciousness nor that of nihility can be realized if it is alienated from that of emptiness. Everything is, in emptiness, in its truly original and profound phase, prior to its phase of being objectified as external existence and prior to its more profound phase of being nullified. At the place of emptiness, things are truly as they originally are. And at the same time, at emptiness as the absolute this side, truly original and profound knowledge takes place, prior to the consciousness of objects and prior to the cognition of existence on the basis of nihility. (Nishitani 1987a, 123f)

Here, Nishitani seems to claim that the emptiness category makes the other two possible, and is therefore more fundamental than they are. But why? His answer might be that the emptiness category expresses the original and profound states of affairs while the others do not. But this is obviously a poor answer because it leads him to asserting a tautology—since the emptiness category is profound, it must be profound. However, we can rescue him from this tautology by appealing to the virtue of the Mahāyāna category of emptiness—non-attachment or detachment. Take the two opposing concepts that are mentioned in the above citation: *the material* and *the ideal*. Both of them commonly presuppose a more universal concept: say, *being*. Or, we might say, each member of the opposing pair is one specification of the universal concept. The material is a certain sort of being, specifically, a spatiotemporal being, while the ideal is another sort of being, specifically, a non-spatiotemporal being. Conversely, the universal concept itself is unspecified or undetermined with respect to the choice between those specifications. In terms of the Mahāyāna virtue, it is detached from, or not attached to, the choice between the opposing pair. Then here is a crucial thesis that is implicit in Nishitani's passage: the pair is obtained or generated *only* through the specifications of the non-attached concept, and in this sense the latter makes the former possible, and therefore is more fundamental. The most unspecified, and totally detached concept is *emptiness*, or *absolute emptiness*. So it makes other key concepts of the earlier categories possible. Therefore, the emptiness category is the most profound among the three. Of course, the thesis is highly contentious. But it is, I think, one of Nishitani's important insights that are inspired by Mahāyāna ideas. And by making it explicit, we can save him from postulating the above tautology since he provides a theoretical reason for the superiority of the emptiness category.

Even though the category of emptiness is practically more preferable and theoretically more profound than the other two, Nishitani doesn't dismiss the latter two as simply false. In contrast, he admits that those two categories also express how things are and how they come to be known. He wrote that we could occasionally adopt one category or another, or shift our worldview from one to another (Nishitani 1987a, 300). So he doesn't take eliminative reductionism according to which the other two categories should be abandoned or reduced to the emptiness category. Rather, his approach is pluralistic in that each category is our genuine view of the self and the world.

Mahāyāna Backgrounds of Emptiness

Nishitani's emptiness has various Mahāyāna backgrounds. Among them, as he admitted, influences from Zen texts, especially Dōgen's *Shōbōgenzō*, are dominant (Nishitani 1987a, 288). But we can also find that many other Mahāyāna sources were used to characterize one or another aspect of his emptiness. Those include Nārgārjunarian terms such as *non-own-nature* and Tientai terms such as *life-and-death-that-is-enlightenment*. Nishitani borrowed some phrases for the contradictory character of *non-own-nature* such as "since the fire is not fire, therefore it is fire" from the *Diamond Pramīta Sūtra* (133). He also referred to Huayan terms such as "one is all, and all is one," "the net of Indra," and "intercommunion (回互, *ego*)" to describe the relation between the self and the world. (114, 168f, 184).

Notably, Nishitanian emptiness has Sanlun flavors. Sanlun combined emptiness with another Mahāyāna idea, *Buddhahood* (佛性, *busshō*), that had been interpreted in terms of Daoism as *the original state of affairs*. So for Sanlun, emptiness means *the return to, or reappropriation of, the original state of affairs* (Jizang 1927, 35). Also in a Sanlun text, we can find one of the clearest expressions of the idea of *emptying emptiness* (Jizang 1926, 326). Furthermore, another Sanlun text, *Da Sheng Xuan Lun* (大乘玄論), mentioned double contradictions such as "non-Being and non-Nothingness and Being and Nothingness" (Jizang 1927, 18). Thus there are remarkable similarities between Sanlun's and Nishitani's ideas. Though he didn't mention Sanlun at all, it is a hidden but significant source of Nishitani's emptiness. In any case, Nishitani's emptiness has diverse Mahāyāna backgrounds that form a gently gathered constellation rather than a tightly united system.

The Nominal Difference between Emptiness and Nothingness

Let us go back to the problem of the difference between emptiness and nothingness. In *What Is Religion?*, the term "nothingness" appeared first, and the term "emptiness" entered the stage later. But references to the latter eventually outnumbered those to the former. So we can witness a shift in the key term in this text. Despite of this apparent change, these two words continue to be used interchangeably throughout the text. Take some examples. "The standpoint of absolute nothingness" was used as a synonym for "the standpoint of emptiness" (Nishitani 1987a, 107, 144). The term "absolute emptiness" was mentioned in place of "absolute nothingness" (137). So, in *What Is Religion?*, in which emptiness made its debut as the key word of Nishitani's philosophy, its difference from nothingness still remains merely nominal rather than substantial.

Then why did Nishitani prefer 'emptiness' to 'nothingness' in the later part of *What Is Religion?* The answer seems rather obvious. Throughout the book, he intended to contrast the category of emptiness with that of nihility. So he needed to make clear the difference between emptiness/nothingness and nihility. But the term nihility originated from a Latin word for nothingness, *nihil*. To avoid possible confusions between his stance and that of nihilists, he gradually shifted his key term from nothingness to emptiness.

Before leaving *What Is Religion?*, let me summarize what emptiness/nothingness means in this text. As the above discussion suggests, Nishitani didn't define these terms clearly while characterizing them in various ways. This is not a symptom of Nishitani's lack of intellectual clarity. Rather, we should understand that "emptiness" is used in a way that renounces any attempt at precise definition. It is a symbolic name for, rather than an accurate description of, his own existential category, that is, his ontological and epistemological worldview. As with any other worldview, Nishitani's category of emptiness is so comprehensive that it has many aspects. By focusing on one or another aspect, we can summarize the category with one or another term or phrase such as realization, non-own-nature, the original state of affairs or intercommunion. Which term is to be used depends on which aspect one wants to highlight. So there is no single optimal way to characterize or summarize the category. Then why was "emptiness" rather than the other terms selected as its symbolic name? A possible answer is that the category was inspired, mainly or in a relatively conspicuous manner, by emptiness as formulated in traditional Mahāyāna thought. But the historical sources of Nishitanian emptiness are again so diverse and rich that they cannot be summarized in a single characterization without doing harm to their multiplicity. The best we can do is, as we have tried, to enumerate his characterizations of the category of emptiness.

Two Sorts of Emptiness in a Later Work

In searching for a substantial difference between Nishitanian emptiness and nothingness, let us now turn to one of his latest and most important works,

"Emptiness and That-Is-ness" (or *E&T*) (1982/1987b). In this work, Nishitani introduced an important distinction into his idea of emptiness: doctrinal emptiness (法義の空, *hougi no kū*) and emotive/volitional emptiness (情意的空, *jōi teki kū*), from which, I shall claim, we can find a clue for thinking of a substantial differentiation between emptiness and nothingness.

Before examining these two kinds of emptiness, let us undertake a brief overview of the general feature of Nishitani's final position in *E&T*. As before, Nishitani set up three existential categories here: the category of science, of art, and of religion, as I call them. Each of those categories represents the scientific, the artistic, and the religious worldview respectively. While the first one corresponds to the category of reason in *What Is Religion?*, the latter two can be seen as new versions of the category of emptiness. Specifically, in *E&T*, while the category of emptiness splits off into two layers, the former category of nihility disappears. This means that nihilism and any attempt to overcome it appear to vanish out of Nishitani's sight. Actually he didn't even mention nihility or nihilism in this culminating paper at all.

Now let us turn to these two kinds of emptiness in *E&T*. Doctrinal emptiness should be understood as the doctrinal formulations of emptiness in the history of the Buddhist philosophical traditions (Nishitani 1987b, 113). Nishitani didn't specify which ideas these were, but they should coincide with the Mahāyāna sources for the category of emptiness outlined above. On the other hand, emotive/volitional emptiness is also called emptiness as it is experienced in emotion and volition (情意, *jōi*), and is said to be the artistic *image* that is a counterpart expression of the doctrinal emptiness. Nishitani takes these artistic images to be typically represented in Chinese and Japanese art forms such as painting and poetry (112, 113).

Although the typical examples of emotive/volitional emptiness can be found in artistic works, Nishitani seems to maintain that its archetypical instance or prototype is our visual image of the sky (Nishitani 1987b, 111f). For instance, he wrote that even in a classical Chinese poem that describes the tranquil atmosphere of a Zen monk's villa, we could still appreciate the reflections on or associations made with the image of the sky (113). Nishitani's thought can be understood as meaning that we originally obtained images (rather than ideas or concepts) of emptiness from viewing the sky, and then either those images permeate one or another artistic work, or, in other words, we project one or another image of emptiness that is prototypically produced by the sky unwittingly onto some paintings or poems.

But why the sky? Nishitani seems to appeal to a linguistic fact that the Chinese word for emptiness, 空 (*kū*), has a double-meaning: emptiness (or being empty) and the sky. This double-meaning is not to be taken as a case of a homonym in which two meanings just accidentally share the same pronunciation or character. Rather, it is an example of polysemy in which two meanings have a common etymological origin, "hole" in this case. However, this shared origin between emptiness and the sky is more or less a local linguistic phenomenon. It doesn't hold for, among other languages, Sanskrit, Japanese, and English. While the Sanskrit word for empty is *śūnyā*, the one for the sky or air is *ākāśa*, for instance.[11] So among the major languages in which Mahāyāna Buddhism has long established itself, the double-meaning between emptiness and the sky is limited to Chinese only. But in the Sinosphere, which includes Japan and Korea, this double-meaning is widely recognized and accepted.[12] In any case, Nishitani's identification of the image of the sky as the archetype of emotive/volitional emptiness relies on this local linguistic phenomenon.

A Historical Source of the Emotive/Volitional Emptiness

The term 'sky' has been traditionally used as a metaphor or even a synonym for emptiness. We can find its eye-catching example in the chapter on the sky (虚空, *kokū*) in Dōgen's *Shōbōgenzō*. The whole chapter was inspired by a poem of Dōgen's mentor, Rú Jìng (如淨), a Chinese Zen master. In his verse, Rú Jìng mentioned a wind-bell, whose entire body looked like a mouth, hanging in the sky. Dōgen modified his master's phrase describing this bell as "the entire body of the sky hanging in the sky (虚空ノ渾身ハ虚空ニカカレリ, *kokū no unshin wa kokū ni kakareri*)" (Dōgen 1931, 259). Through this rephrasing, he seems to mean not only that the wind-bell hangs against the background of the sky, but also that the wind-bell itself is the sky. For Dōgen, this is also the case for everything else, including the self and all that is other than the self. The self and everything else is the sky. Obviously, he used the word "sky" as a metaphor or, more straightforwardly speaking, a synonym for emptiness. So by talking about the sky, Dōgen effectively meant that everything was empty. But on the other hand, he clearly distinguished the sky from the Mahāyāna ideas or doctrines of emptiness (258). For him, the poetic image of the sky connotes emptiness, but emptiness is not to be reduced to its doctrinal dimensions. Here we can find a germ for Nishitani's idea of emotive/volitional emptiness that is expressed in artistic works such as poems, originating from the image of the sky, and which is to be distinguished from doctrinal emptiness.

Curiously, Nishitani never mentioned either Rú Jìng's poem or Dōgen's chapter on the sky. But it seems obvious that he followed the Rú Jìng–Dōgen tradition when he occasionally evoked metaphors of the sky in *What Is Religion?* (Nishitani 1987a, 164, 240) Among them is the epigraph that opened this chapter. While it is a metaphor for his idea that emptiness is more profound than nihility, from its key insight that the sky exists everywhere, enveloping everything within itself, we can clearly hear an echo of the sounds that the wind-bell of Rú Jìng and Dōgen still makes.

Nishitanian Image as an Integrated Representation

Nishitani imputed a special meaning to *image*. As he wrote that image is "originally inseparable from what is visible" (Nishitani 1987b, 156), we may take visual perception to be the origin or at least an essential element of image. But the Nishitanian image has many other elements; it is considered to be an integrated representation that consists of common sense, emotion and volition. By "common sense," Nishitani draws on an Aristotelian idea, the *sensus communis*, which mixes different forms of sense perception. For example, a common sense of cicadas combines the acoustic perceptions of their chorus with the visual perceptions of their shapes (153f). Furthermore, the Nishitanian image is not emotionally and volitionally transparent or neutral, but is painted with emotion and volition. Image always has emotional and volitional dimensions (159). So the image of cicadas involves not only the above-mentioned common sense but also an emotion together with volition, for example, lamenting for another passing summer and willing idly to stop the lapse of time. Indeed, the compound word emotion/volition means a unification of emotion and volition. This means that the archetypical emotive/volitional emptiness, the image of the sky, should also be an integrated representation, and have its emotional and volitional elements as well as synthetic perceptual ones.

We may ask: What synthetic sense perception does the image of the sky contain? The answer would vary with weather and climate. By characterizing the sky as a "space that has an interminable expanse and an unlimited depth" (Nishitani 1987b, 111), Nishitani obviously was thinking of the crystal clear sky. So this should give us a combination of a bright, deep blue visual image, a refreshing somatic feeling for breathing fresh air, and so on. Then what emotion and volition does the image of the clear blue sky provoke in us? Letting its volitional element aside for the time being, let us explore what emotion or feeling is associated with the sky? According to Nishitani, it provokes in us, on the one hand, some negative feelings such as those of futility, vanity and despair at the transient (114). On the other hand, citing Chinese and Japanese poems that, for him, reflect the image of the sky, Nishitani tries to read between the lines a breathtaking feeling for a panoramic view, a relaxed feeling in an open space (144), a relief from suffering, and even a feeling of mutual understanding and cooperation between correspondents (117). These associations are definitely not negative. Rather, they are positive, having a tint of pleasantness, pleasure and joy. So, in Nishitani's eyes, the image of the sky stirs mixed feeling in us that have both negative and positive sides. As mixed, they are far from either plainly negative feelings such as grief, sorrow or rage or clearly positive ones such as zeal, enthusiasm, or rapture. The accumulated feeling is rather calm and stabilized. Though calm, its overall tone is still not totally balanced between negative and positive feelings. It slightly inclines toward the positive side: warm rather than cold, bittersweet rather than simply bitter. So let us call this mixed feeling a *warm* feeling.

On the image of the sky, Nishitani wrote:

> The sky [as an image] appears in sensations, perceptions and feelings in everyday life as a momentum that determines them, gives certain specific characterizations to the sensuous and the emotive/volitional. (Nishitani 1987b, 117)

In his conception, the image of the sky is not only the prototype of a certain sort of artistic images, but also of a certain sort of image in general that we experience in everyday occasions. It is the origin of a particular kind of combined representation that consists in, among other things, the warm feeling mentioned above. Although having the warm feeling in common, those artistic and everyday images vary with each other in one or another way. They can have different sense perceptions and volitions. But at any rate they have the image of the sky as their archetype. Or they are variations upon the archetype as their theme.

Let us then redefine emotive/volitional emptiness as a certain sort of artistic and everyday life image that shares the warm feeling and are variations of the image of the sky as their prototype.

A Substantial Difference between Emptiness and Nothingness

We are now ready to make explicit a substantial distinction between *emptiness* and *nothingness* that Nishitani implies; that is, while there is emotive/volitional *emptiness*, there is no such a thing as emotive/volitional *nothingness*. Let me outline an argument for this contrast between emptiness and nothingness, by using Nishitani's ideas about the emotive/volitional emptiness.

1. The term "emptiness" means the sky. The sky is directly visual and invokes the warm feeling.
2. So for emptiness, there is something visual and the warm feeling invocative that can be the origin of its prototypical image— here, the image of the sky.
3. On the other hand, the term "nothingness" doesn't have a meaning that signifies anything directly visible and the warm feeling invocative.
4. So for nothingness, there isn't something directly visual and the warm feeling invocative that can be the origin of its prototypical image—that is, there is no counterpart of the image of the sky.
5. Therefore, there are no such things as prototypical images of nothingness and an emotive/volitional nothingness that might originate from the prototype.
6. There is thus a substantial difference between emptiness and nothingness: emptiness has its proper image, that is, emotive/volitional emptiness, whereas nothingness does not.

In *What Is Religion?* Nishitani made no substantive difference between emptiness and nothingness as existential categories. Why? An easy speculation is that he didn't discern any significant difference between the traditional Mahāyāna ideas of emptiness and nothingness. The traditional concept or idea of emptiness corresponds to the doctrinal emptiness in *E&T*. Also, we can rephrase the traditional idea of nothingness as *doctrinal nothingness*.

Consequently, for him there should be no substantial difference between doctrinal emptiness and doctrinal nothingness. They can be used interchangeably. The difference between emptiness and nothingness lies only at the level of the image, but not at the level of ideas or concepts.

Let me sum up Nishitani's view of the difference between emptiness and nothingness. At the level of traditional ideas or concepts, there is no difference between them. Whenever he talks about doctrinal emptiness, he should also mean doctrinal nothingness because they are taken as simply equivalent. On the other hand, while we have emotive/volitional emptiness, that is, the image that shares one or another warm feeling and has, among others, one or another volition, there is no such thing as emotive/volitional nothingness, because while we have a prototypical image of the former in the image of the sky, we lack a prototypical image for the latter. This crucial asymmetry at the image level, however, relies on a local linguistic fact that the Chinese words for emptiness and for sky have the same etymology. So this difference between *emptiness* and *nothingness* holds only locally in the Sinosphere.

The Calligraphy of the Circle

One might challenge the above argument by appealing to some artistic works that appear to represent the image of nothingness, which can therefore be counted as examples of representations of emotive/volitional nothingness. A typical instance in the Zen tradition is the Chinese ink painting or calligraphy of the circle (円相, *en sou*) (Figure 1). This work of calligraphy appears to be designed to provide us with an image of nothingness. Let us first try to explain the image-making process of this picture, without taking into account the image of the sky or emptiness.

The main device for the image-production here, I claim, is a double *Gestalt* switch with an intellectual guidance. At the outset, when we face the painting, we plainly have a visual perception of a circle, but not of nothingness. Then, we are invited to undergo a double *Gestalt* switch, one of which is visual and the other emotional. The visual *Gestalt* switch is a shift in the objects of our visualization from the black ink circle to the blank space inside it. This shift is usually triggered or guided by one or another verse that is typically affixed to the circle. As its example, we can read in Figure 1 a part of a commonly cited phrase from Sū Dōng Pō (蘇東坡), an eleventh century Chinese Zen poet: "Having-nothing contains unlimited things that include a flower, a moon, and a tower."[13] This phrase directs the viewer to recognize that the space inside the circle or the absence of black ink in that space is meant to be a symbol of nothingness.

The emotional *Gestalt* switch is a change of the objects of our emotion from the circle to the inner space. The round shape of the circle and its deliberately naïve brush strokes are intended to provoke an agreeable and heartwarming feeling within us. Then this positive feeling is transported, to the inner space. Consequently, we begin to entertain a positive feeling toward it. In this way,

Figure 1. Calligraphy of a circle (円相, *en sou*) by a Kyoto school philosopher, Shinichi Hisamatsu (1889–1980). Copyright: Hisamatsu Shinichi Memorial Museum

we come to have an integrated image of nothingness that consists of, among other things, a visual perception of the absence of black ink and this new, positive feeling.

However, this explanation is unsatisfactory. For instance, it is not clear why and how the emotional *Gestalt* switch takes place. It remains unexplained why we can so readily transport our positive feeling for the circle to the inner space. Even though we feel the circle as agreeable, we have no reason or motivation to feel the *nothingness* as agreeable. The visual perception of the absence tells us nothing about its emotional aspects. Furthermore, the intellectual guidance doesn't have any implications for our feeling for the nothingness that contains everything within it. In contrast to the Nishitanian integrated image, a mere perception or thought is not integrated, and does not convey any information about our emotion or feeling for the objects.

So we need another factor, missing in the above explanation, that can provide us with information about not only the perceptual but also the emotive side of the object. What is this factor? Nishitani's answer is the image. To make the emotional *Gestalt* switch work, we need an image that is at our disposal prior to the switch. In other words, the production of an image requires a prior image. In Nishitani's own words, "The image should have its own independent mode of being, its own inherent origin" (Nishitani 1987b, 158).

This consideration would lead us to an infinite regress, however, unless there is at least one original image to stop the regress. The image of the sky can be this regress-stopper. We can entertain it without any prior image whenever we look up to the clear sky. That is why it is archetypical. So the image of the sky (or one or another images of emptiness that have been produced by it) should be mobilized to allow the picture of the circle to produce the image of nothingness. In other words, in this picture of the circle or any other artistic works that appear to produce the image of nothingness, the image of the sky or another image of emptiness is smuggled into, or we are invited to project one or another image of emptiness onto, those artistic works. The agreeable feeling that we have for the inner space is a warm feeling originated from the image of the sky. The image we obtain from the calligraphy of the circle is nothing but one of variations of the image of the sky. Shortly, it is a disguised image of emptiness rather than the image of nothingness.

But there still remains a problem: Why is the image of sky projected into the picture of the circle so readily and so smoothly? Nishitani might answer this question by appealing to the equivalence between doctrinal emptiness and doctrinal nothingness. As noted above, in *What Is Religion?*, he didn't make any substantial distinction between emptiness and nothingness and gave no explicit reason for this conflation. An easy speculation is that he didn't discern any substantial difference between the traditional Mahāyāna ideas of emptiness and nothingness. In other words, for him, doctrinal emptiness and nothingness are interchangeable.

Since the traditional ideas of emptiness and nothingness are interchangeable, the term "nothingness" that appears in the verse can be easily be read to mean "emptiness" by those within the Mahāyāna tradition. Now the intellectual guidance for taking the inner blank space as a symbol of nothingness is recast as one for taking it as a symbol of emptiness. We are ready to project onto the picture of the circle the prototypical image of the sky that we have already acquired.

Nishitani could also remind us that in the Zen tradition the circle was originally associated with the sky. In one of its oldest texts, *Faith Mind Inscription* (信心銘, *shin jin mei*), that is conventionally ascribed to the third patriarch of Chinese Zen tradition, Sēng Càn (僧璨), the circle was mentioned as a property of the sky, or precisely speaking, a common property of the sky and our mind (Sēng Càn 1928, 376).[14] So, Nishitani could continue, the sky image could be more readily projected onto the calligraphy of the circle by anyone who was familiar with this historical episode. At any rate, in his view the circle is actually a "window to the sky," and through the round window people look up and feel the sky whenever they appreciate the calligraphy.

Emotive/Volitional Reconciliation with Nihilism[15]

The difference between emptiness and nothingness turns out to be of philosophical significance when we take into account Nishitani's emotional reconciliation, as I call it, with the nihilism or the older versions of existentialism. It can be found in his essay "On Bashō" (1962/1991a), and we can take this work to represent an alternative to his attempt of overcoming nihilism in *What Is Religion?*[16]

In my view, Nishitani's emotional reconciliation takes place in three stages. In the first stage, nihility is emotionalized or volitionized, so to speak. In this essay, Nishitani suggests that nihility has two aspects. One is the aspect that can be articulated in ideas or concepts such as groundlessness and transience. The other is the aspect that can be expressed as 'moods' (Nishitani 1991a, 71, 74), 'senses' (73, 74), or such feelings as 'bottomlessness,' 'vain,' and 'sorrow.' (74) But moods, senses, or feelings mentioned here are not to be taken as mere "emotions." They also have to incorporate "a sort of resolution . . . [or] decision to accept the transient thoroughly as it is" (78). The mood is nothing but an emotion that is united with the volition not to escape from the transient or nihility. What Nishitani emphasizes here is to come to grips with nihility as an emotion/volition, as experienced in such things as the feeling of bottomlessness, or in other words, to entertain deliberately an emotion/volition of nihility rather than to have merely "concepts" of nihility. What happens here can be described as the emergence of nihility as an emotion/volition or the emotionalization/volitionalization of nihility. This is not, however, the objectification of nihility which Nishitani condemned the nihilists for committing. Rather, the nihility here becomes a genuine aspect, which is to say, the emotive/volitional aspect of our existence.

On the insights of Bashō, a great master of Haiku, into the transient, Nishitani wrote, "something like affection as well as a deep feeling of sorrow, or shortly warmth, adds to the bottomless transient." As a result, he continued, "the feeling of deep sorrow and the feeling of affection are connected in an inseparable manner." And this brings about, he said, "an attitude to genuinely accept as *it is* even what cannot really be affirmed [such as nihility or the transient]" (Nishitani 1991a, 74) or "an attitude to accept and comply with the transient being as it is, and to give affection to it" (73).

What Nishitani wrote here can be summarized as a two-staged conversion of emotion/volition that corresponds to our second and third stages. The second is the stage at which we deliberately combine the emotion/volition of nihility in such feelings as bottomlessness or sorrow with one or another positive emotion/volition such as affection or mercy. And finally, at the third stage, a new emotion/volition will emerge from the combination or fusion of these two sorts of emotion/volition. Since the additional emotion/volition is a positive one rather than a negative one, such as hatred and hostility, the combined or fused emotion/volition has a character of reconciliation or amicable settlement with nihility or the transient. So let us call this emotion/volition that is the end product of this conversion process a *reconciling* one. As this reconciling emotion/volition occupies our minds, we come to be inclined to accept or comply with nihility.

This is a process of the conversion of emotion/volition from that of nihility to that of reconciliation. But it can also be interpreted as a way of dealing with nihilism or the older forms of existentialism. In this manner of dealing with nihilism, nihility is firstly made an emotion/volition, then by being fused with a positive feeling, it is transformed into a reconciling one, and finally we come to be ready to comply with nihilism. What happens here is not a conceptual analysis or argumentation, but rather a progression or deepening of our emotion/volition. Furthermore, what is attained here is reconciliation with nihilism rather than overcoming it. So let us call this final dealing with nihilism an emotive/volitional (or in short, emotional) reconciliation with nihilism.

As Nishitani admitted, in *What Is Religion?*, he approached emptiness only from the intellectual point of view, setting aside its emotional or emotive/volitional aspect.[17] Thus his strategy for overcoming nihilism or the earlier forms of existentialism is, as shown above, purely intellectual. It is nothing but a manipulation of ideas; labeling the Mahāyāna ideas his own position while affixing the tags of Hīnayāna and non-Buddhist thought to nihilism. So, though not fully explored by him, the emotive/volitional reconciliation with nihilism in "On Bashō" is quite distinct from what he attempted in *What Is Religion?*, and has its own significance.

The Mature Stage of Nishitani's Existentialism

We can resolve the reconciling emotion/volition into its emotional and volitional aspects; emotion or feeling of friendliness and volition to reconcile. The feeling of friendliness here is not a simply positive emotion such as that of unconditional cordiality. Instead it has to be a slightly positive feeling because it is about amicable settlement or reconciliation with *the irreconcilable*. So it is an example of the warm feeling mentioned earlier. Since the warm feeling is the hallmark of the image of emptiness, we can say that the reconciling emotion/volition is nothing but one of many variations of the image of the sky or a variant of emotive/volitional emptiness mentioned in *E&T*. This means that the volition for reconciliation is a nice example of volition that can be associated to the image of the sky and its variations.

Being put in the context of how to deal with nihilism, the prototypical image of the sky can function as a powerful tool for reconciliation with nihilism. By fostering the image of emptiness or emotive/volitional emptiness in our minds, we are enabled to attend decisively to nihilism with mercy and affection, and to attain an emotional reconciliation with it, rather than to refute or repudiate it. In other words, we can embrace nihilism with the image of the sky or emptiness.

At the time of the composition of *E&T*, Nishitani had already achieved the emotive/volitional reconciliation with nihilism. This may explain why reference to nihility and nihilism disappeared altogether in this work. Possibly he felt no need to overcome it any longer, so left it simply unmentioned.

The emotive/volitional side of emptiness is crucial for Nishitani's final attitude toward nihilism or the older existentialisms. Since, as shown above, nothingness lacks an emotive/volitional side, it can play no part in the emotional reconciliation. The reconciliation can be attained only by emptiness, and not by nothingness. Here we can identify a decisive difference between them.

In comparison to the overcoming of nihilism, the emotional reconciliation can have two kinds of significance, if not advantages over it. First, the human being is a being with emotion and volition. So as far as existentialism aims to provide a view on how human beings and their world are, it is obliged to take into account our emotional and volitional depths and our emotive and volitional attitudes toward the world. Actually, a number of existentialists have discussed those issues. But, as mentioned above, in *What Is Religion?*, Nishitani only talked about our cognition and cognitive stance toward the world. In this respect, his Mahāyāna existentialism suffered an obvious omission in comparison to its predecessors. His ideas of emotive/volitional emptiness and emotional reconciliation with nihilism can plug up this philosophical hole, by adding emotional and volitional dimensions to his existentialism. In brief, they can make Nishitani's Mahāyāna existentialism more fully fledged than it otherwise would be.

In his retrospective essay on his adolescence, Nishitani allegorized himself as "a large elm tree that was injected with poison," and suggested that he had shared "the melancholy of the tree that was stung to its very core by a poisonous needle, and the solitude of the tree that fought with the fatal liquids that were poured into its blood vessels" (Nishitani 1950/1990, 179). By the poison mentioned here, Nishitani meant nihility or nihilism. For the young Nishitani, nihilism had been an abominable threat that could only be properly compared with poison. In his wording, "overcoming nihilism," we can read a nuance of a showdown with nihilism that is rooted in his personal aversion to it.

By contrast, in emotive/volitional reconciliation, such a confrontational attitude vanishes. Nihility or nihilism has come to be taken as a partner in reconciliation. We can imagine that elder Nishitani had been modifying or weakening his longstanding hatred of nihilism. Like an old person who feels attachment, as a part of his body, even to a nidus that has tormented him for a long time, Nishitani had come to take a conciliatory attitude toward nihilism after lifelong attempts to overcome it. From his texts such as "On Bashō" and *E&T*, we can possibly imagine that in his final years, Nishitani had come to reconcile with nihilism or embrace it rather than aiming to overcome it.

Now the second significance of the emotional reconciliation should become clear. The emotional reconciliation could relieve Nishitani's hatred of nihility or nihilism, or more properly speaking, release him from his lifelong hatred of or obsession with it. This release from obsession can be achieved only by emptiness, rather than nothingness.

Let us sum up. The emotional reconciliation with nihilism, rather than the intellectual overcoming, can make Nishitani's position more full-fledged than otherwise and can free him from his enduring hatred of or obsession with nihilism. These two fruitions can be regarded as signs of his philosophical and personal maturity. These maturities can only be attained by the emotional reconciliation with nihilism, rather than the intellectual overcoming of nihilism. They are accomplished only by emptiness, which can have its emotive/volitional sides thanks to the prototypical image of the sky, and not by nothingness, which lacks an emotive/volitional side. The significant difference between emptiness and nothingness for Nishitani, in the final analysis, is that full existential maturity can be attained through the former, but not the latter.

Conclusion

Nishitani changed his key term from nothingness to emptiness in the course of his philosophical career. But it took him decades to substantiate the difference between them. Only after he analyzed the distinction between doctrinal and emotive/volitional emptiness was he able to make a substantial distinction between emptiness and nothingness. The crucial difference lies in the fact that emptiness has its prototypical image in the sky while nothingness doesn't. Due to this difference, only emptiness, but not nothingness, could gain a new dimension, that is, an image that consists of, among others, one or another warm feeling and one or another volition such as that for reconciliation, and play a decisive role in his emotional reconciliation of nihilism and effectively bring about his philosophical and personal maturities. This is the philosophical significance of the key shift of central terms in Nishitani.

However, the above differences are derived from a rather local and accidental linguistic phenomenon that the Chinese terms "emptiness" and "sky" have the same etymology. So the above points might be taken to hold only in the tradition of the Sinosphere, and therefore to be culturally relative and to have a limited significance. I don't think, however, that this is the case. The local and accidental linguistic fact might have provided Nishitani just an occasion to entertain a rather more universal insight that the image, as an integrated representation that has, among other things, emotional and volitional dimensions, can play an important role in our understanding of ourselves and the world. In particular, the image of the sky can rescue us from our desperate feelings of the meaninglessness of our lives and the entire world. How can the image of the sky do so? By presenting itself to us as an amicable meaninglessness. It can do this only because it is an emotion-laden representation rather than an emotion-free idea or concept.

In conclusion, thanks to an accidental linguistic phenomenon, this importance of the image and particularly that of the sky has been more readily acknowledged by those with philosophical acumen in the Sinosphere, such as Rú Jìng and Dōgen, than those in different linguistic and cultural traditions. With his acute philosophical abilities, Nishitani also could detect this importance, but didn't have enough time or occasions to develop his insights. Instead, he left its full development a task for generations to come, dropping hints here and there. I am always struck by such an idea whenever I read his beautiful metaphor of the sky that is cited as the epigraph that began this chapter.

Notes

1 All translations of non-English texts are mine.

2 For example, Kumārajīva translated emptiness or *śūnyatā* as nothingness in a famous passage of Nārgārjuna's *Mulamadhyamikakarika*; see for example verse 18 of Chapter 24 of Nārgārjuna (1926, 33).

3 Hanaoka and Ueda apparently assumed that Nishitani's and Nishida's nothingness were equivalent. But this seems dubious. So, though admitting they provide us valuable insights, I will approach those questions from a different perspective.

4 Nishitani didn't explicitly declare himself an existentialist. But he characterized his philosophical position as "the standpoint of the existence of non-self (無我, *mu ga*)" (Nishitani 1987a, 276, 309), and a conversion from Nietzsche's, the early Heidegger's, or Sartre's stance to his own stance as "an existential turn" (80f) or "existential self-awareness" (277), for instance. Nishitani criticized Heidegger's ideas in *Sein und Zeit* (1926/2006), and *Was ist Metaphysik* (1931/1977b) (Nishitani, 1987a, 121). But he suspended his final judgment on the late Heidegger's philosophy, taking it as approaching his own stance (78).

5 Nishitani described his aim as "to shed light on the essence and reality of 'existence' and human being" (Nishitani 1987a, 3), "to inquire into the essential aspect of reality and 'human existence' singlehandedly" (288), and so on.

6 Nishitani took this Heideggerian concept, *Dasein*, as the "self as an emergence from non-ego (Nishitani 1987a, 293).

7 The source of the citation is in the *Genjōkōan* chapter (現成考按) of Dōgen's *Shōbōgenzō*. The original passage is "while it is a delusion to carry the self to confirmation, by practice, of everything, in enlightenment, everything proceeds to confirm, by practice, the self" (Dōgen 1931, 23).

8 For instance, Nishitani wrote unreservedly that the reality is life and death, and at the same time neither life nor death (Nishitani 1987a, 59). This remark can be rephrased as that the reality is life, and is not life, and also it is death, and is not death. Representing the propositions that the reality is life, and that the reality is death as A and B respectively, this phrase can also be formalized as $(A \wedge \neg A) \wedge (B \wedge \neg B)$. Then we have a double contradiction.

The list of Nishitanian double contradictions is quite long. It includes those between the itself and the not-itself (Nishitani 1987a, 168), the natural surroundings (or mountains and rivers (山河, *san ga*)) and the self (187), life-and-death and *nirvāṇa* (200), and inside and outside (Nishitani 1967/1991b, 97f).

9 Nishitani began with the distinction of the objects of burning and of non-burning, and concluded with sentences that imply flat contradictions; that is, that burning is non-burning, and this is fire and not fire (Nishitani 1987a, 131ff). But what he really could arrive at from the distinction is the claim that the burning of fire is not reflective, and this non-reflectiveness is a necessary condition for its burning of firewood. This doesn't imply any contradiction. So he made an illicit leap from here to contradictory conclusions.

10 I have tried to secure the genuineness of Nishitanian contradiction (Deguchi, 2006, 2008a, 2008b, 2012, and forthcoming). My approach differs from his reverse-parameterization. I tried to construct a non-classical logical system that can incorporate Nishitanian double contradictions. By showing that the system is logically and philosophically meaningful, I attempted to demonstrate those contradictions as genuine and true. This move is also an extension of Nishitani's efforts to construct an alternative logic that he called a logic of that-is/non (即非, *soku hi*) or of existence (Nishitani 1987a, 211), the *logos* of being (214, 217), the *logos* of 'thing' in 'emptiness' (217), or the *logos* of the boundary-less-ness between *ri* and *ji* (理事無礙, *ri ji mu ge*) (Nishitani 1982/1987b, 131).

11 The Japanese word for 'empty' is '*kara*', while its word for 'sky' is '*sora*'.

12 For instance, the Japanese interlocutor featured in Heidegger's dialogue, *Aus einem Gespräch von der Sprache, Zwischen einem Japaner und einem Fragenden*, mentioned the double-meaning between empty and sky (Heidegger 1959, 102).
13 The original Chinese phrase is: 無一物中無盡藏, 有花有月有樓臺. Only the first seven characters are written in Figure 1.
14 It reads: "[The mind is] as circular as the great hollow." The 'great hollow (大虛, *dà xū*)' means sky.
15 This section is based on Deguchi (2009).
16 The main theme of the essay is Nishitani's interpretations of the works of Bashō Matsuo (1644–1694), a great master of Japanese Haiku.
17 Citing one of Bashō's Haiku, Nishitani wrote that the poem allowed him to "restrict problems [for discussions] only with respect to the place of emptiness as knowledge, for the time being" (Nishitani 1987a, 182).

Bibliography

AS *Arthasaṅgraha*. (1934). *The Arthasaṅgraha of Laugākṣī Bhāskara*. Translated by A. B. Gajendragadkar and R. D. Karmarkar. Delhi: Motilal Banarsidass.

BBh. (1971). *Bodhisattvabhūmi: A Statement of Whole Course of the Bodhisattva (Being Fifteenth Section of Yogācārabhūmi)*. Edited by Unrai Wogihara. Tokyo: Sankibo Buddhist Book Store.

JDZL. *Jue ding zang lun* 決定藏論. Translated by Paramārtha, CBETA, T30, no. 1584.

NKC. (1986–1995). 『西谷啓治著作集』 [Collected works of Keiji Nishitani]. 26 vols. Tokyo: Sōbunsha.

NKZ. (1988). 『西田幾多郎全集新版』 [Complete works of Kitarō Nishida]. 20 vols. Tokyo: Iwanami Shoten.

NZG. (1977–1981). 『日本禅語録』 [Collected Zen records of Japan]. 20 vols. Tokyo: Kōdansha.

SBGZ. (1993–1994). 『正法眼蔵』 [Treasury of the true dharma eye]. 6 vols. Edited by Kōshirō Tamaki (玉城康四郎). Tokyo: Daizōshuppan.

SDZ. (1968–1971). 『鈴木大拙全集』 [Complete works of Daisetsu Suzuki]. 32 vols. Tokyo: Iwanami Shoten.

T. (1961). 『大正新修大藏經』 [*Taishō Shinshū Daizōkyō*]. Edited by Junjirō Takakusu and Kaigyoku Watanabe. Tokyo: Taishō Shinshū Daizōkyō Kankōkai.

VP. (1974a). *The Vākyapadīya of Bhartṛhari: Chapter III, Pt. II*. Translated by K.A. Subramania Iyer. Delhi: Motilal Banarsidass.

———. (1974b). *The Vākyapadīya of Bhartṛhari: Chapter II*. Translated by K.A. Subramania Iyer. Delhi: Motilal Banarsidass.

———. (1977). *Vākyapadīya*. Part III: *Padakāṇḍa: Vṛttisamudeśa*. With Helārāja's Prakāśa and Raghunātha's Ambākartṛ Commentaries. Varanasi: Sampurnananda Sanskrit University.

VSM. (1977). *Vaiyākaraṇasiddhāntamañjūṣā of Nāgeśa Bhaṭṭa*. Varanasi: Sampurnananda Sanskrit University.

YBhc. *Yujia shidi lun* 瑜伽師地論. Chinese translation of the *Yogācārabhūmi* by Xuanzang, CBETA, T30, no. 1579.

YBhs. (1957). *The Yogācārabhūmi of Ācārya Asaṅga: The Sanskrit Text Compared with the Tibetan Version*. Edited by Vidhushekhara Bhattacharya. Calcutta: University of Calcutta.

YBht. *rNal 'byor spyod pa'i sa rnam par gtan la dbab pa bsdu ba*. Tibetan translation of the *Viniścayasaṃgrahanī* section of the *Yogācārabhūmi* by Prajñāvarman, Surendrabodhi, and Ye shes sde, Derge 4038, sems tsam, zhi1a1-zi127a4.

Abe, Masao. (1985). *Zen and Western Thought*. Edited by William LaFleur. Honolulu: University of Hawaii Press.

Ames, Roger T., and David L. Hall (trans.). (2003). *Dao De Jing: A Philosophical Translation*. New York: Ballantine Books.

Anscombe, G.E.M. (1971). *An Introduction to Wittgenstein's Tractatus*. London: Hutchinson University Library.

Appelfeld, Aharon. (2005). "Always, Darkness Visible." *New York Times*, January 27.

Arisaka, Yoko. (1999). "System and Existence: Nishida's Logic of Place." In Augustine Berque (ed.), *Logique du lieu et dépassement de la modernité*. Brussels: Ousia. 41–65.

Aristotle. (1941). *Metaphysics*. In Richard McKeon (ed.), *The Basic Works of Aristotle*. New York: Random House. 689–934.

———. (1984). "Metaphysics." In Jonathan Barnes (ed.), *Complete Works of Aristotle*. Vol. 2. Princeton, NJ: Princeton University Press. 1552–1729.

Arnold, Dan. (2010). "Nāgārjuna's 'Middle Way': A Non-Eliminative Understanding of Selflessness." *Revue Internationale de Philosophie* 64(3): 367–395.

Aśvaghoṣa (traditionally attributed). (1967). *The Awakening of Faith*. Translated by Yoshita Hakeda. New York: Columbia University Press.

Austin, Scott. (1986). *Parmenides: Being, Bounds, and Logic*. New Haven, CT: Yale University Press.

Barrett, Timothy Hugh. (1992). *Li Ao: Buddhist, Taoist, or Neo-Confucian?* Oxford: Oxford University Press.

Bhattacharya, K. C. (1976). *Search for the Absolute in Neo-Vedanta*. Edited with introduction by J. B. Burch. Honolulu: University of Hawai'i Press.

———. (1983). *Studies in Philosophy*. Delhi: Motilal Banarasidass.

Baumer, Bettina. (2011). *Abhinavagupta's Hermeneutics of the Absolute Anuttaraprakriya*. Delhi: D. K. Printworld.

Beardsworth, Richard. (1996). *Derrida and the Political*. London: Routledge.

Beijing Daxue Chutu Wenxian Yanjiusuo (BJDX). (2012) *Beijing Daxue cang Xihan Zhushu* No. 2 北京大學藏西漢竹書(貳). Shanghai: Shanghai guji chubanshe.

Bergson, Henri. (1911). *Creative Evolution*. Translated by Arthur Mitchell. New York: The Modern Library.

Bernasconi, Robert, and Critchley, Simon (eds.). (1991). *Re-Reading Levinas*. Bloomington: Indiana University Press.

Bhattacharya, Kamaleswar. (1986). *The Dialectical Method of Nāgārjuna*. Delhi: Motilal Banarsidass.

Bilimoria, Purushottama. (2008). "Abhava: Negation in Logic, Real Non-Existent, and a Distinctive Pramana in the Mimamsa." In M. K. Chakraborty, B. Lowe, M. Nath Mitra, and S. Sarukkai (eds.), *Logic, Navya-Nyaya and Application: Homage to Bimal Krishna Matilal*. London: College Publications. 43–64.

Bocking, Brian. (1995). *Nāgārjuna in China: A Translation of the Middle Treatise*. Lewiston: The Edwin Mellen Press.

Bradley, Francis H. (1922). *The Principles of Logic*. London: Oxford University Press.

Burton, David F. (1999). *Emptiness Appraised: A Critical Study of Nāgārjuna's Philosophy*. Surrey: Curzon.

Bu-ston. (1931). *The History of Buddhism in India and Tibet*. Translated by E. Obermiller. Heidelberg.

Buswell, Robert E., Jr. (1983). "The Life and Thought of Chinul." In Robert E. Buswell Jr. (ed. and trans.), *The Korean Approach to Zen: The Collected Works of Chinul*. Honolulu: University of Hawaii Press. 1–95.

Candrakīrti. (1970). *Prasannapadā Madhyamakavṛtti*. Edited by Louis de la Vallée Poussin. Mūlamadhyamakakārikās (Mādhyamikasūtras) de Nāgārjuna, avec la Prasannapadā commentaire de Candrakīrti. St. Petersburg: Bibliotheca Buddhica IV, 1903–1913. Reprint, Osnabrück: Biblio.

Cardona, George. (1967). "Negations in Pāṇinian Rules." *Language* 43(1): 34–56.

Carus, A. W. (2004). "Sellars, Carnap, and the Logical Space of Reasons." In Steve Awodey and Carsten Klein (eds.), *Carnap Brought Home: The View from Jena*. Chicago: Open Court. 317–355.

Casati, Roberto, and Varzi, Achille C. (1995). *Holes and Other Superficialities*. Cambridge, MA: MIT Press.

Casey, Ed. (1997). *Fate of Place: A Philosophical History*. Berkeley: University of California Press.

CBETA. (2011). *Chinese Electronic Tripiṭaka: Taishō Edition, vols. 1–55, 85*. Taipei: Chinese Buddhist Electronic Text Association (www.cbeta.org).

Chakrabarti, Arindam. (1997). *Denying Existence*. Dordrecht, Netherlands: Kluwer Academic Publishers.

Chan, Alan K. L. (2003). "Zhong Hui's *Laozi* Commentary and the Debate on Capacity and Nature in Third-Century China." *Early China* 28: 101–159.

———. (2009). "Wuqing yu changkuang: lun *Zhuangzi* zhong wuqing de liangzhong quanshi 無情與猖狂: 論莊子中無情的兩種詮釋." *Zhongguo zhexue yu wenhua 中國哲學與文化*. Edited by Xiaogan Liu. Chinese University of Hong Kong. 6:243–258.

———. (2011). "Harmony as a Contested Metaphor and Conceptions of Rightness (*Yi*) in Early Confucian Ethics." In R.A.H. King and Dennis Schilling (eds.), *How Should One Live? Comparing Ethics in Ancient China and Greco-Roman Antiquity*. Berlin: De Gruyter. 37–62.

———. (2013). "Laozi." In Edward N. Zalta (ed.), *Stanford Encyclopedia of Philosophy*. http://plato.stanford.edu/entries/laozi/.

Chan, Wing-tsit (ed.). (1973). *A Sourcebook in Chinese Philosophy*, 4th ed. Princeton, NJ: Princeton University Press.

Chen, Lai (陳來). (2005). *Song-Ming liuxue* 宋明理學 [Song-Ming Neo-Confucianism], 2nd ed. Shanghai: East China Normal University Press.

Chen, Shou (陳壽). (1982). *Sanguo zhi* 三國志. Beijing: Zhonghua shuju.

Cheng, Hsueh-li. (1984). *Empty Logic: Mādhyamika Buddhism from Chinese Sources*. New York: Philosophical Library.

Cheng, Yishan (程宜山). (1986). 中國古代元氣學說 [The Chinese Ancient *Yuanqi* Theory]. China: Wubei Renmin Chubanshe.

Chinul. (1983). *The Korean Approach to Zen: The Collected Works of Chinul*. Translated and edited by Robert E. Buswell Jr. Honolulu: University of Hawaii Press.

———. (1991). *Tracing Back the Radiance: Chinul's Korean Way of Zen*. Translated and edited by Robert E. Buswell Jr. Honolulu: University of Hawaii Press.

———. (2012). *Condensation of the Exposition of the Avatamsaka*. In Robert E. Buswell Jr. (ed.), *Chinul: Selected Works*. Seoul: Chogye Order of Korean Buddhism. 355–366.

Chŏng, Tojŏn. (1961). *Sambong chip* [Collected Works of Chŏng Sambong]. Seoul: Kuksa p'yŏnch'an wiwŏnhoe.

Clayton, Barbra R. (2006). *Moral Theory in Śāntideva's Śikṣāsamuccaya: Cultivating the Fruits of Virtue*. Abingdon, UK: Routledge.

Coward, Harold, and Kunjuni Raja. (1990). *Encyclopedia of Indian Philosophies. Volume V: The Philosophy of the Grammarians*. Delhi: Motilal Banarsidass.

Cowherds, The (eds.). (2011). *Moonshadows: Conventional Truth in Buddhist Philosophy*. New York: Oxford University Press.

Cox, Collett. (1988). "On the Possibility of a Nonexistent Object of Consciousness: Sarvāstivādin and Dārṣṭāntika Theories." *Journal of the International Association of Buddhist Studies* 11(1): 31–87.

Csikszentmihalyi, Mihaly. (1990). *Flow: The Psychology of Optimal Experience*. New York: Harper and Row.

Cuneo, Terence. (2007). *The Normative Web: An Argument for Moral Realism*. Oxford: Oxford University Press.

Davis, Gordon. (2013). "Traces of Consequentialism and Non-Consequentialism in Bodhisattva Ethics." *Philosophy East and West* 63(3): 275–305.

Deguchi, Yasuo. (2006). "Neo-Nishitanian Dialetheic Monism." In *Humaniora Kiotoensia: On the Centenary of Kyoto Humanities*. Graduate School of Letters, Kyoto University, Kyoto. 53–77.

———. (2008a). "Shin Mujyun Shugi Teki Ichigen Ron 真矛盾主義的一元論" [Dialetheic Monisim]. Part 1. *Das Tetsugaku Kenyu*, 1:585, 36–80.

———. (2008b). "Shin Mujyun Shugi Teki Ichigen Ron 真矛盾主義的一元論" [Dialetheic Monisim]. Part 2. *Das Tetsugaku Kenyu*, 1:586, 24–56.

———. (2009). "Nihilizumu Wo Daki Shimete ニヒリズムを抱きしめて" [Embracing Nihilism]. *Nihon No Tetsugaku* [Japanese Philosophy] 10: 67–83.

———. (2012). "Kū No Shisō No Rogosu 空の思想のロゴス" [Logos of Philosophy of Emptiness]. *Risō* 689: 144–160.

———. (Forthcoming). "Constructing Logic of Emptiness: Nishitani, Jizang, and Paraconsistency." In Yasuo Deguchi, Jay Garfield, Graham Priest, and Koji Tanaka (eds.), *The Moon Points Back*.

De Meyer, Jan. (2006). *Wu Yun's Way: Life and Works of an Eighth-Century Daoist Master*. Leiden: Brill.

Derrida, Jacques. (1974). *Of Grammatology*. Baltimore: Johns Hopkins University Press.

———. (1978). "Violence and Metaphysics." In Jacques Derrida (ed.), *Writing and Difference*. Chicago: The University of Chicago Press. 79–153.

———. (1982). *Margins of Philosophy*. Translated by Alan Bass. Chicago: University of Chicago Press.

Descartes, René. (2003). *Discourse on Method and Meditations*. Mineola, NY: Dover.

De Silva, Padmasiri. (2007). "Buddhist Ethical Theory." In Purushotamma Bilimoria, Joseph Prabhu, and Renkula Sharma (eds.), *Indian Ethics: Classical and Contemporary Challenges*. Aldershot, UK: Ashgate. 229–245.

Dilworth, David. (1973). "Nishida Kitarō: Nothingness as the Negative Space of Experiential Immediacy." *International Philosophical Quarterly* 13(4): 463–483.

Dōgen. (1931). *Shōbōgenzō* (正法眼蔵) [The Tashiō Shinshū Daizōkyō]. Vol. 82. Tokyo: The Taishō Issai-Kyo Kanko Kwai.

Dreyfus, Georges. (1997). *Recognizing Reality*. Albany: State University of New York Press.

Duerlinger, James. (2009). "Vasubandhu's *Abhidharmakośa*." In William Egelglass and Jay L. Garfield (eds.), *Buddhist Philosophy: Essential Readings*. New York: Oxford University Press. 286–296.

Dummett, Michael. (1981). *Frege: Philosophy of Language*, 2nd ed. Cambridge, MA: Harvard University Press.

Edgerton, Franklin. (1986). *The Mīmāṃsānayaprakāśa*. Delhi: Satguru Publications.

Eifring, Halvor (ed.). (2004). *Love and Emotions in Traditional Chinese Literature*. Leiden: Brill.

Eklund, Matti. (2008). "The Picture of Reality as an Amorphous Lump." In Theodore Sider, John Hawthorne, and Dean Zimmerman (eds.), *Contemporary Debates in Metaphysics*. Oxford: Blackwell. 382–396.

Falk, Harry. (1982). "The Three Groups of Particles in the 'Nirukta'." *Bulletin of the School of Oriental and African Studies* 45(2): 260–270.

Fang, Xuanling (房玄齡) (ed.). (1982). *Jin shu* 晉書. Beijing: Zhonghua shuju.

Foucault, Michel. (1984). "On the Genealogy of Ethics: An Overview of Work in Progress." In Purushottama Rabinow (ed.), *The Foucault Reader*. New York: Pantheon Books. 340–372.

———. (1988). *The History of Sexuality. Volume II, The Use of Pleasure*. Translated by Robert Hurley. Harmondsworth: Penguin Books.

Fox, Alan. (1996). "Reflex and Reflectivity: *Wuwei* in *the Zhuangzi*." *Asian Philosophy* 6(1): 59–72.

Fraser, Chris. (2008). "Psychological Emptiness in *the Zhuangzi*." *Asian Philosophy* 18(2): 123–147.

———. (2011). "Emotion and Agency in *the Zhuangzi*." *Asian Philosophy* 21(1): 97–121.

———. (2013). "Landscape, Travel, and a Daoist View of the 'Cosmic Question'." In Hans-Georg Moeller and Andrew Whitehead (eds.), *Landscape and Travelling East and West: A Philosophical Journey*. London: Bloomsbury Academic Publishing. 211–222.

———. (Forthcoming). "Wandering the Way: A Eudaimonistic Approach to *the Zhuangzi*." In *Dao: A Journal of Comparative Philosophy*.

Frege, Gottlob. (1967). "The Thought: A Logical Inquiry." In P. F. Strawson (ed.), *Philosophical Logic*. Oxford: Oxford University Press. 17–38.

Fu, Charles Wei-Hsun. (1973). "Lao Tzu's Concept of Tao." *Inquiry* 16(4): 367–394.

Furley, David. (1989). "Notes on Parmenides." In *Cosmic Problems*. Cambridge: Cambridge University Press. 27–38.

Furth, Montgomery. (1968). "Elements of Eleatic Ontology." *Journal of the History of Philosophy* 6: 111–132.

Gallop, David. (1984). *Parmenides of Elea: Fragments*. Toronto: University of Toronto Press.

Garfield, Jay L. (1995). *The Fundamental Wisdom of the Middle Way: Nāgārjuna's Mūlamadhyamakakārikā*. New York: Oxford University Press.

———. (1996). "Emptiness and Positionlessness: Do the Mādhymika Relinquish All Views?" *Journal of Indian Philosophy and Religion* 1(1): 1–34.

———. (2002a). *Empty Words: Buddhist Philosophy and Cross-Cultural Interpretation*. New York: Oxford University Press.

———. (2002b). "Vasubandhu's Treatise on the Three Natures." In *Empty Words: Buddhist Philosophy and Cross-Cultural Interpretation*. New York: Oxford University Press. 128–151.

Garfield, Jay L., and Graham Priest. (2003). "Nāgārjuna and the Limits of Thought." *Philosophy East West* 53: 1–21. (Reprinted as ch. 5 of Jay L. Garfield. (2002). *Empty*

Words. Oxford: Oxford University Press; and ch. 16 of Graham Priest. (2002). *Beyond the Limits of Thought*, 2nd ed. Oxford: Oxford University Press.)

———. (2009). "Mountains are Just Mountains." In Mario D'Amato, Jay L. Garfield, and Tom J.F. Tillemans (eds.), *Pointing at the Moon: Buddhism, Logic, Analytic Philosophy*. New York: Oxford University Press. 83–100.

Gillon, B. (1997). "Negative Facts and Knowledge of Negative Facts." In P. Bilimoria and J.N. Mohanty (eds.), *Relativism, Suffering and Beyond: Essays in Memory of Bimal K. Matilal*. Oxford: Oxford University Press. 127–147.

Girardot, Norman J. (2008). *Myth and Meaning in Early Daoism*. Magdalena, NM: Three Pines Press.

Goodman, Charles. (2002). "Resentment and Reality: Buddhism on Moral Responsibility." *American Philosophical Quarterly* 39(4): 359–372.

———. (2009). *Consequences of Compassion: An Interpretation and Defense of Buddhist Ethics*. New York: Oxford University Press.

Graham, A.C. (1981). *Chuang-tzu: The Inner Chapters*. London: George Allen & Unwin.

———. (1989). *Disputers of the Tao*. La Salle, IL: Open Court.

Griffith, Ralph T. H. (tr.). (1896). *RgVeda*. www.sacred-texts.com/…/rigveda/rv10129.

Guo, Qingfan(郭慶藩) (ed.). (1985). 莊子集釋 [*Collected Annotations on Zhuangzi*]. Edited by Xinbian Zhuzi Jicheng 新編諸子集成, 4 vols. China: Zhonghua Shuju.

Hakamaya, Noriaki (袴谷憲昭). (1990). 批判佛教 [*Criticizing Buddhism*]. Tokyo: Daizō Shuppan.

Han, Ja-kyoung. (2003). "A Critical Study on Chŏng Tojŏn's Critique of Buddhism concerning the Ontological Status of the Human Mind in Cosmos" [In Korean]. In *Pulkyohak Yŏn'gu* [Buddhist Studies] 6: 72–104.

Han, Wei (韓巍) (ed.). (2012). *Laozi—Beijing Daoxue cang Xi Han zhushu* 老子—北京大學藏西漢竹書. Vol. 2. Shanghai: Shanghai guji chubanshe.

Hanaoka, N. (2004). "Emptiness and 'That-Is-ness' in the Philosophy of Emptiness" [kū no tetsugaku ni okeru kū to soku,空の哲學における「空と即」]. *Nihon No Tetsugaku* [Japanese Philosophy] 5: 87–101.

Hansen, Chad. (1992). *A Daoist Theory of Chinese Thought*. New York: Oxford University Press.

He, Yan (何晏). (1963). *Lunyu jijie* 論語集解 [Collected commentary to *Lunyu*]. In Huang Kan 皇侃 (488–545 CE), *Lunyu jijie yishu* 論語集解義疏. Taipei: Shijie shuju.

Hegel, G.W.F. (1989). *Grundlinien der Philosophie des Rechts*. Frankfurt a.M.: Suhrkamp.

Heguanzi (鶡冠子). (2004). *A Complete Correction and Annotations of Heguanzi* [Heguanzi Huijiao Jizhu]. China: Zhonghua shuju.

Heidegger, Martin. (1959). *Aus einem Gespräch von der Sprache, Zwischen einem Japaner und einem Fragenden*. In *Unterwegs zur Sprache*. Verlag Günter Neske. 83–155.

———. (1969). *Identity and Difference*. Chicago: The University of Chicago Press.

———. (1977a). "Letter on Humanism." In David Farrell Krell (ed.), *Martin Heidegger: Basic Writings from* Being and Time *(1927) to* The Task of Thinking *(1964)*. New York: Harper & Row. 215–266, 229.

———. (1977b). "What Is Metaphysics?" In David Farrell Krell (ed.), *Martin Heidegger: Basic Writings from* Being and Time *(1927) to* The Task of Thinking *(1964)*. New York: Harper & Row. 91–112.

———. (2006). *Sein und Zeit*. Tübingen: Max Niemeyer Verlag.

———. (2010). *Being and Truth*. Bloomington: Indiana University Press.

Henricks, Robert G. (trans.). (1989). *Lao-Tzu Tao-Te Ching: A New Translation Based on the Recently Discovered Ma-wang-tui Texts*. New York: Ballantine Books.

——— (trans.). (1991). *Lao-Tzu Te-Tao Ching: A Translation of the Ma-wang-tui Manuscripts*. London: Rider.

——— (trans.). (2000). *Lao Tzu's Tao Te Ching: A Translation of the Startling New Documents Found at Guodian*. New York: Columbia University Press.

Hirakawa, Akira. (1990). *A History of Indian Buddhism: From Śākyamuni to Early Mahāyāna*. Honolulu: University of Hawai'i Press.

Ho, Chien-hsing. (2006). "Saying the Unsayable." *Philosophy East and West* 56(3): 409–427.

Horn, Laurence R. (1989). *A Natural History of Negation*. Chicago: University of Chicago Press.

Huang, Zongxi (黃宗羲). (1966). *Song Yuan xue'an* 宋元學案. Taipei: Shijie shuju.

Hung, William. (1956). *Zhuangzi yinde* 莊子引得 [*A concordance to Zhuangzi*]. Harvard-Yenching Institute Sinological Index Series, Supplement no. 20. Cambridge, MA: Harvard University Press.

Ivanhoe, Philip J. (trans.). (2002). *The Daodejing of Laozi*. Indianapolis, IN: Hackett Publishing Company.

Ives, Christopher. (2009). "In Search of a Green Dharma: Philosophical Issues in Buddhist Environmental Ethics." In John Powers and Charles S. Prebish (eds.), *Destroying Māra Forever*. Ithaca, NY: Snow Lion. 165–185.

Iyer, K. A. Subramania. 1974. *The Vākyapadīya of Bhartṛhari*. Chapter III, pt. 2. English Translation. Delhi: Motilal Banarsidass.

———. (1992). *Bhartṛhari: A Study of the Vākyapadīya in the Light of the Ancient Commentaries*. Pune: Deccan College.

James, Simon P. (2007). "Against Holism: Rethinking Buddhist Environmental Ethics." *Environmental Values* 16(4): 447–461.

Jha, Ganganatha. (1999). *Nyaya Sutras*. Delhi: Motilal Banarsidass.

Jizang. (1926). *Rén Wáng Bān Ruò Jīng Shū* 仁王般若經疏. *The Tashiō Shinshū Daizōkyō*. Vol. 33. Tokyo: The Taishō Issai-Kyo Kanko Kwai. 314–359.

———. (1927). *Dà Shèng Xuán Lùn* 大乘玄論. *The Taishō Shinshū Daizōkyō*. Vol. 45. Tokyo: The Taishō Issai-Kyo Kanko Kwai. 15–77.

Jochim, Chris. (1998). "Just Say 'No' to 'No Self' in *Zhuangzi*." In Roger Ames (ed.), *Wandering at Ease in the Zhuangzi*. Albany, NY: SUNY Press. 35–74.

Kahn, Charles H. (1968/1969). "The Thesis of Parmenides." *Review of Metaphysics* 22: 700–724.

Kalupahana, David J. (1986). *Mūlamadhyamakakārikā: The Philosophy of the Middle Way*. Albany, NY: SUNY Press.

Kamalaśīla. (1955–1961). *Sarvadharmaniḥsvabhāvasiddhi*. Tibetan Tripiṭaka, Peking Edition. Tokyo-Kyoto: Tibetan Tripiṭaka Research Institute.

Kang, Zhongqian (康中乾). (2003). *Youwu zhibian* [*Discerning Being and Nothingness*]. Beijing: Renmin University Press.

Kanterian, E. (2007). *Wittgenstein*. London: Reaktion Books.

Kassor, Constance. (2013). "Is Gorampa's 'Freedom from Conceptual Proliferations' Dialetheist? A Response to Garfield, Priest, and Tillemans." *Philosophy East and West* 63(3): 399–410.

Kasulis, Thomas P. (1981). *Zen Action: Zen Person*. Honolulu: University of Hawaii Press.

———. (trans.). (2011). "Esoteric Words." In James W. Heisig, Thomas P. Kasulis, and John C. Maraldo (eds.), *Japanese Philosophy: A Sourcebook*. Honolulu: University of Hawaii Press. 160–161.

Katsura, Shōryū. (2011). "From Abhidharma to Dharmakīrti: With a Special Reference to the Concept of *svabhāva*." In Helmut Krasser, Horst Lasic, Eli Franco, and Birgit Kellner (eds.), *Religion and Logic in Buddhist Philosophical Analysis: Proceedings of the Fourth International Dharmakirti Conference Vienna, August 23–27, 2005*. Vienna: Austrian Academy of Sciences Press. 267–275.

Keel, Hee-Sung. (2001). *Chinulŭi Sŏnsasang* [The Sŏn of Chinul]. Seoul: Sonamu.

Kellner, Birgitt. (2006). "Negation in Indian Philosophy." In Donald Borchert (ed.), *Encyclopedia of Philosophy*, 2nd ed. Detroit: Macmillan Reference. 530–533.

Kim, Hee-Jin. (1987). *Dogen Kigen—Mystical Realist*. Tucson: University of Arizona Press.

Kim, Kun-su. (2012). "Funerary Inscription and Epitaph for the State Preceptor Puril Pojo of the Society for Cultivating Son on Chogye Mountain." In Robert E. Buswell Jr. (ed.), *Chinul: Selected Works*. Seoul: Chogye Order of Korean Buddhism. 367–386.

Kimura, Uno (木村卯之). (1941–1942). 『道元と日本哲学』 [*Dōgen and Japanese Philosophy*]. Kyoto: Chōjiya Shoten.

Knauth, Lothar. (1965). "Life is Tragic—The Diary of Nishida Kitarō." *Monumenta Nipponica* 20(3/4): 335–358.

Kohn, Livia, and Michael LaFargue (eds.). (1998). *Lao-tzu and the Tao-te-ching*. Albany, NY: SUNY Press.

Kong, Yingda (孔穎達). (1963). *Liji zhengyi* 禮記正義, *Shisanjing zhushu buzheng* 十三經注疏補正 ed. Taipei: Shijie shuju.

Kopf, Gereon. (2001). *Beyond Personal Identity: Dōgen, Nishida, and a Phenomenology of No-Self*. Richmond, UK: Curzon Press.

———. (2005). "Critical Comments on Nishida's Use of Chinese Buddhism." *Journal for Chinese Philosophy* 32(2): 335–351.

———. (2010a). "Language Games, Selflessness, and the Death of God; A/Theology in Contemporary Zen Philosophy and Deconstruction." In Bret Davis, Brian Schroeder, and Jason Wirth (eds.), *Continental and Japanese Philosophy: Comparative Approaches to the Kyoto School*. Bloomington: Indiana University Press. 160–178.

———. (2010b). "The Self-Identity of the Absolute Contradictory What?—Reflections on How to Teach the Philosophy of Nishida Kitarō." In David Jones (ed.), *Teaching Texts and Contexts: The Art of Infusing Asian Philosophies and Religions*. Albany, NY: SUNY Press. 129–148.

———. (2011). "Ambiguity, Diversity, and an Ethics of Understanding: What Nishida's Philosophy Can Contribute to the Pluralism Debate." *Culture and Dialogue* 1(1): 2–25.

———. (2012). "Meditation as Moral Training: Reading Dōgen's 'Shoakumakusa' in the Light of His Meditation Manuals." In Charles Willemen and Ven. Khammai Dhammasamai (eds.), *Buddhist Meditation: Text, Tradition and Practice*. Mumbai: Somaiya Publication. 341–352.

Kosaka, Kunitsugu. (1997). *Nishida Kitarō o meguru tetsugakusha gunzō* [The philosophical milieu surrounding Nishida Kitarō]. Kyoto: Mineruva shobō.

———. (2003). *Nishida Kitarō no shisō* [The thought of Nishida Kitarō]. Tokyo: Kodansha.

Krell, David F. (1977). *Martin Heidegger: Basic Writings*. New York: Harper & Row.

Kriegel, Uriah. (2008). "The Dispensability of (Merely) Intentional Objects." *Philosophical Studies* 141(1): 79–95.

Kūkai (空海). (2011). "Esoteric and Exoteric Teachings." Translated by David L. Gardiner. In James W. Heisig, Thomas P. Kasulis, and John C. Maraldo (eds.), *Japanese Philosophy: A Sourcebook*. Honolulu: University of Hawaii Press. 52–59.

Kumārajīva. (trans.). Longshu pusa zhuang 龍樹菩薩傳 [Biography of Bodhisattva Nāgārjuna]. T. 50.2047.

———. Tipo pusa zhuang 提婆菩薩傳 [Biography of Bodhisattva Āryadeva]. T.50.2048.

Kupperman, Joel. (1999). *Learning from Asian Philosophy*. Oxford: Oxford University Press.

Kwok, Man-Ho, Martin Palmer, and Jay Ramsay (trans.). (1993). *The Ilustrated Tao Te Ching*. Shaftesbury: Element Books.

Kwŏn, Kun. (1979). *Yangch'on chip* [Collected works of Kwŏn Yangch'on]. Seoul: Minjok munhwa ch'ujinhoe.

Lao, Siguang (勞思光). (2003). *Xujing yu Xiwang* 虛境與希望 [*Delusion and Hope*]. Hong Kong: CUHK Press.

Lask, Emil. (1911). *Die Logik der Philosophie und die Kategorienlehre*. Tübingen: J.C.B. Mohr (Paul Siebeck).

———. (1912). *Die Lehre vom Urteil*. Tübingen: J.C.B. Mohr (Paul Siebeck).

Lau, Din Cheuk. (1983). *Tao Te Ching*. Hong Kong: Chinese University of Hong Kong Press.

——— (trans.). (2001). *Tao Te Ching: A Bilingual Edition*. Hong Kong: Chinese University of Hong Kong Press.

Levinas, Emmanuel. (1969). *Totality and Infinity*. Pittsburgh: Duquesne University Press.

Lewis, David, and Stephanie Lewis. (1970). "Holes." *Australasian Journal of Philosophy* 48: 206–212.

Li, Ao (李翱). (1990). *Fuxing shu* 復性書. In *Quan Tang wen* 全唐文, vol. 3. Shanghai: Shanghai guji chubanshe. 2849–2851.

Liji zhengyi (禮記正義). (1963). Commentary by Kong Yingda 孔穎達B (574–648). Shisanjing zhushu edition. Taipei: Shijie shuju.

Lindtner, Christian. (1986). *Master of Wisdom*. Berkeley, CA: Dharma Publishing.

Liu, JeeLoo. (2006). *An Introduction to Chinese Philosophy*. Malden, MA: Blackwell Publishing.

Liu, Ming-wood. (1994). *Madhyamaka Thought in China*. Leiden, Netherlands: E. J. Brill.

Liu, Xiaogan (劉笑敢). (1997). *Laozi: Niandai Xinkao yu Sixiang Xinquan* 老子: 年代新考與思想新詮 [Laozi: A new textual study and interpretation of its thought]. Taipei: Dongda tushu gongsi.

———. (2006). *Laozi Gujin* 老子古今. Beijing: Zhongguo shehui kexue chubanshe.

———. (2008–2009). "Orientational Issues in Textual Interpretation: Essays by Liu Xiaogan." In Carine Defoort (ed.), Topical issue of *Contemporary Chinese Thought* 40(2).

———. (2009a). "Daoism: Laozi and the Daodejing." In Bo Mou (ed.), *A History of Chinese Philosophy*. London: Routledge. 209–236.

———. (2009b). *Quanshi yu Dingxiang* 詮釋與定向 [Hermeneutics and orientation]. Beijing: Commercial Press.

———. (2010). *Zhuangzi Zhexue jiqi Yanbian* 莊子哲學及其演變 [Zhuangzi's philosophy and its evolution]. Revised and expanded edition. Beijing: Zhongguo Remin University Press.

Liu, Youming (劉又銘). (2009). "The Philosophical Paradigm of Ming-Qing Confucian Naturalistic *Qi*-Ontology" [Mingqing rujia ziran qi-ben-lun de zhexue dianfan].

National Chengchi University Philosophical Journal [*guoli zhengzhidaxue zhexue xuebao*] 22: 1–36.

Lotze, Hermann. (1874). *Drei Bücher: Vom Denken, Vom Untersuchen, und Vom Erkennen*. Leipzig: S. Hirzel.

———. (1879). *Metaphysik: Drei Bücher der Ontologie, Kosmologie und Psychologie*. Leipzig: S. Hirzel.

———. (1887). *Metaphysic in Three Books: Ontology, Cosmology, and Psychology*, 2 vols. Translated by Bernard Bosanquet. Oxford: Clarendon Press.

———. (1888). *Logic in Three Books: Of Thought, of Investigation, and of Knowledge*. Translated by Bernard Bosanquet. Oxford: Clarendon Press.

Lou, Yulie (樓宇烈). (1980). *Wangbi ji Jiaoshi* 王弼集校釋 [Critical edition of the works of Wang Bi with explanatory notes]. Beijing: Zhonghua shuju.

Lynn, Richard John (trans.). (1999). *The Classic of the Way and Virtue: A New Translation of the Tao-te Ching of Laozi as Interpreted by Wang Bi*. New York: Columbia University Press.

Ma, Lin. (2008). *Heidegger on East-West Dialogue: Anticipating the Event*. New York: Routledge.

Makeham, John. (2003). *Transmitters and Creators: Chinese Commentators and Commentaries on the Analects*. Cambridge, MA: Harvard University Asia Center.

Maraldo, John. (2003). "Rethinking God: Heidegger in the Light of Absolute Nothing, Nishida in the Shadow of Onto-Theology." In Jeffrey Bloechl (ed.), *Religious Experience and the End of Metaphysics*. Bloomington: Indiana University Press. 31–49.

Mather, Richard (trans.). (1976). *Shih-shuo Hsin-yu: A New Account of Tales of the World*. Minneapolis: University of Minnesota Press.

Matilal, B. K. (1968). *Navya Nyaya Doctrine of Negation*. Cambridge, MA: Harvard University Press.

———. (1971a). *Epistemology, Logic, and Grammar in Indian Philosophical Analysis*. The Hague: Mouton.

———. (1971b). "The Navya-Nyaya Doctrine of Negation: The Semantics and Ontology of Negative Statements in Navya-Nyaya Philosophy." *Indo-Iranian Journal* 13: 199–205.

———. (2002). "A Critique of the Mādhyamika Position." In Jonarden Ganeri (ed.), *Mind, Language and World: Philosophy, Religion and Culture*. New Delhi: Oxford University Press. 203–212.

May, Reinhard. (1996). *Heidegger's Hidden Sources: East Asian Influences on His Work*. Translated by Graham Parkes. London: Routledge.

McBride, Richard, II. (2003). *The Domestication of Dharma*. Honolulu: University of Hawaii Press.

McCagney, Nancy. (1997). *Nāgārjuna and the Philosophy of Openness*. Lanham, MD: Rowman & Littlefield.

McDowell, John. (1996). *Mind and World: With a New Introduction*. Cambridge, MA: Harvard University Press.

Meyer, Robert, and J. Michael Dunn. (1972). "A Semantics for Relevant Logic." *Journal of Philosophical Logic I:* 53–73.

Meyer, Robert, and Richard Routley. (1972). "Classical Relevant Logic I." *Symbolic Logic* 32: 51–68.

———. (1973). "Classical Relevant Logic II." *Symbolic Logic* 33: 183–194.

Morohashi Tetsuji. (1986). *Dai kan-wa jiten* [Chinese-Japanese dictionary], 13 vols. Tokyo: Taishukan.

Mourelatos, Alexander. (1976). "Determinacy and Indeterminacy, Being and Non-Being in the Fragments of Parmenides." In Roger A. Shiner and John King-Farlow (eds.), *New Essays on Plato and the Pre-Socratics*. Guelf, Ontario: Canadian Association for Publishing in Philosophy. 45–61.

———. (1979). "'Nothing' as 'Not-Being': Some Literary Contexts That Bear on Plato." In Glen W. Bowersock, Walter Burkert, and Michael C. Putnam (eds.), *Arktouros*. Berlin: de Gruyer. 319–329.

Muller, A. Charles, and Cuong T. Nguyen (eds.). (2011). *Wŏnhyo's Philosophy of Mind*. Honolulu: University of Hawaii Press.

Murti, Mulakaluri Srimannarayana. (1997). *Bhartṛhari the Grammarian*. Calcutta: Sahitya Academy.

Musō, Soseki (夢窓疎石). (2000). 『夢中問答集』 [The collection of questions and answers in a dream]. Edited by Kasume Kawase (川瀬一馬). Tokyo: Kōdansha.

Nāgārjuna. (1903–1913). *Mūlamadhyamakakārikā*. In Louis de la Vallée Poussin (ed.), *Mūlamadhyamakakārikās (Mādhyamikasūtras) de Nāgārjuna, avec la Prasannapadā commentaire de Candrakīrti*. St. Petersburg: Bibliotheca Buddhica IV. (Reprint; Osnabrück: Biblio, 1970. http://indica-et-buddhica.org/repositorium/nagarjuna/mulamadhyamakakarikas-sanskrit-digital-text).

———. (1978). *Vigrahavyāvartanī*. In E.H. Johnston and Arnold Kunst (eds.) and Kamaleswar Bhattacharya (trans.), *The Dialectical Method of Nagarjuna: (Vigrahavyavartini)*. Delhi: Motilal Banarsidass.

———. (1983). *Madhyamashastram* with prasannapadā by Chadrakirti, p. 117. Edited by Swami Dwarikada. Bauddha Bharati: Varanasi.

Nagatomo, Shigenori. (2000). "The Logic of the Diamond Sutra: A Is Not A, Therefore It Is A." *Asian Philosophy* 10(3): 213–244.

Nakamura, Jeanne, and Mihalyi Csikszentmihalyi. (2009). "Flow Theory and Research." In C.R. Snyder and Shane J. Lopez (eds.), *Oxford Handbook of Positive Psychology*, 2nd ed. Oxford: Oxford University Press. 195–206.

Nārgārjuna. (1926). *Mulamadhyamikakarika* 中論. Translated by Kumārajīva. *The Taishō Shinshū Daizōkyō*. Vol. 30. Tokyo: The Taishō Issai-Kyo Kanko Kwai.

Newland, Guy. (2011). *Introduction to Emptiness*. Ithaca, NY: Snow Lion Publications.

Nietzsche, Friedrich. (1966). *Beyond Good and Evil: Prelude to a Philosophy of the Future*. Translated by Walter Kaufmann. New York: Random House.

Nishida, Kitarō. (1995). "Zettai Mujunteki Jikodouitsu." In Ueda Shizuteru (ed.), (「絶対矛盾的自己同一」上田閑照編『西田幾多郎哲学論集 III』), Absolute Self-Identity in Contradistinction. *The Philosophical Essays of Kitaro Nishida,* Vol. III. Tokyo: Iwanami. 7–84.

———. (2002). *Nishida Kitarō zenshū* [Collected works of Nishida Kitarō], multiple volumes. Tokyo: Iwanami shoten.

Nishijima, Gudo, and Chodo Cross (trans.). (1994–1997). *Master Dogen's Shōbōgenzo*. Vols. I–IV. Woods Hole, MA: Windbell Publications.

Nishitani, K. (1987a). Shūkyō Towa Nanika 宗教とは何か [*What Is Religion?*]. *Keiji Nishitani's Collected Works*. Vol. 10. Tokyo: Sōbunsha.

———. (1987b). Kū To Soku 空と即 [Emptiness and That-Is-ness]. *Keiji Nishitani's Collected Works*. Vol. 13. Tokyo: Sōbunsha. 111–160.

———. (1990). Watashi No Seishun Jidai 私の青春時代 [My Adolescence]. In *Keiji Nishitani's Collected Works*. Vol.20. Tokyo: Sōbunsha. 175–184.

———. (1991a). Bashō Ni Tsuite芭蕉について [On Bashō]. In *Keiji Nishitani's Collected Works*. Vol. 19. Tokyo: Sōbunsha. 67–96.

———. (1991b). Zen Bunka No Sho Mondai禪文化の諸問題 [*Some Problems from Zen Culture*]. In *Keiji Nishitani's Collected Works*. Vol. 19. Tokyo: Sōbunsha. 97–118.

O'Leary, Timothy. (2002). *Foucault and the Art of Ethics*. London: Continuum.

Orenstein, Alex. (1995). "How to Get Something from Nothing?" *Proceedings of the Aristotelian Society* (New Series) 95: 93–112.

Oshima, Harold. (1983). "A Metaphorical Analysis of the Concept of Mind in the *Chuang-tzu*." In Victor Mair (ed.), *Experimental Essays on Chuang-tzu*. Honolulu: University of Hawaii Press. 63–84.

Owen, G.E.L. (1971). "Plato on Not-Being." In G. Vlastos (ed.), *Plato 1: Metaphysics and Epistemology*. Garden City, NY: Doubleday. 223–267.

———. (1982). "Eleatic Questions." In Schofield and Nussbaum (eds.), *Language and Logos*. Cambridge: Cambridge University Press. 1–25.

Pak, Chong-Hong. (1972). "Wŏnhyo ŭi chŏrak sasang." In *Han'guk sasangsa* [History of Korean thought]. Seoul: Ilsinsa.

———. (1983). "Wŏnhyo's Philosophical Thought" [Wŏnhyo ŭi chŏrak sasang]. In Lewis R. Lancaster and C. S. Yu (eds.), *Assimilation of Buddhism in Korea*. Berkeley, CA: Asian Humanities Press. 47–105.

Pang, Pu (龐樸). (1995). *Yifenweisan* 一分为三 [The tripartite one]. Shenjun, China: Haitian Chubanshe.

Park, Jin Y. (2005). "Zen Language in Our Time: The Case of Pojo Chinul's *Huatou* Meditation." *Philosophy East & West* 55(1): 84–88.

Parmenides. (1986). "On Nature." In Henry Sider and David E. Johnstone (eds.), *The Fragments of Parmenides*. Bryn Mawr.

Plato. *Phaedo*. Available at classics.mit.edu/Plato/phaedo.html.

Plumwood, Val, and Richard Routley. (1982). "The Inadequacy of the Actual and the Real: Beyond Empiricism, Idealism and Mysticism." In Werner Leinfeller (ed.), *Language and Ontology*. Vienna: Holder Pichler-Tempsky. 49–87.

Priest, Graham. (2002). *Beyond the Limits of Thought*, 2nd ed. Oxford: Oxford University Press.

———. (2005). "The Limits of Language." In K. Brown (ed.), *Encyclopedia of Language and Linguistics*, Vol. 7, 2nd ed. Dordrecht: Elsevier. 156–159.

———. (2008a). "Jaina Logic: A Contemporary Perspective." *History and Philosophy of Logic* 29(3): 263–278.

———. (2008b). *Introduction to Non-Classical Logic: From If to Is*. Cambridge: Cambridge University Press.

———. (2010a). "Two Truths: Two Models." In The Cowherds (eds.), *Moonshadows: Conventional Truth in Buddhist Philosophy*. New York: Oxford University Press. 13–14, 213–220.

———. (2010b). "The Logic of the Catus.kot.i." *Comparative Philosophy* 1(2): 32–54.

———. (2014). "Plurivalent Logics." *Australasian Journal of Logic* 11.: article 1. http://ojs.victoria.ac.nz/ajl/article/view/1830

Putnam, Hilary. (1982). "Why There Isn't a Ready-made World." *Synthese* 51(2): 141−167.

Quine, W.V.O. (1948). "On What There Is." *The Review of Metaphysics* 2(5): 21–38. (Reprinted in Quine, W.V.O. (1961). *From a Logical Point of View*. Cambridge, MA: Harvard University Press.)

———. (1957). "Speaking of Objects." *Proceedings and Addresses of the American Philosophical Association* 31: 5–22. (Reprinted in *Ontological Relativity and Other Essays*. New York: Columbia University Press, 1969.)

———. (1963). *From a Logical Point of View*. New York: Harper and Row.

Ramanujatatacharya, N. S. (1999). *Chaturdasalaksani of* Gangeśa *Updhāyaya-Didhiti Gadadhari*. Commentary by *Vivarana*. Tirupati, India: Rashtriya Sanskrit University.

Raud, Rein. (2003). "The Genesis of the Logic of Immediacy." *Asian Philosophy* 13(2/3): 131–143.

Reischauer, Edwin O. (1995). *Ennin's Travels in Tang China*. New York: The Ronald Press Company.

Rhi (Yi), Ki-yong. (1983). "Wonhyō and His Thoughts." In The Korean National Commission for UNESCO (ed.), *The Main Currents of Korean Thought*. Seoul: The Si-sa-yong-o-sa Publishers. 14–25.

Rhys Davids, T. W. (trans.). (1890). *The Questions of King Milinda*. Oxford: The Clarendon Press.

Rickert, Heinrich. (1928). *Der Gegenstand der Erkenntnis: Einführung in die Transzendentalphilosophie*. Tübingen: J.C.B. Mohr [Paul Siebeck].

Robinet, Isabelle. (1999). "The Diverse Interpretations of the *Laozi*." In Mark Csikszentmihaly and Phillip J. Ivanhoe (eds.), *Religious and Philosophical Aspects of the Laozi*. Albany, NY: SUNY Press. 127–160.

Rorty, Richard M. (1992). *The Linguistic Turn: Essays in Philosophical Method*. Chicago: University of Chicago Press.

Royal Swedish Academy of Sciences. (2011). "Written in the Stars." *The Nobel Prize in Physics 2011: Information for the Public*. Accessed January 24, 2014. http://www.nobelprize.org/nobel_prizes/physics/laureates/2011/popular-physicsprize 2011.pdf.

Russell, Bertrand. (1904). "Russell to Frege 12.12.1904." In Gottfried Gabriel, Hans Hermes, Friedrich Kambartel, Christian Thiel, and Albert Verrart (eds.), *Philosophical and Mathematical Correspondence*. English translations edited by B. McGuinness and translated by H. Kaal. Chicago: University of Chicago Press [1980]. 166–170.

———. (1956). *Logic and Knowledge*. London: Unwin Hyman Unlimited.

———. (1971). *Introduction to Mathematical Philosophy*. New York: Touchstone.

———. (1980). *Inquiry into Meaning and Truth*. London: Unwin Hyman Unlimited.

———. (1994). "The Nature of Truth." In A. Urquhart (ed.), *The Collected Papers of Bertrand Russell, Volume 4: Foundations of Logic*. London: Routledge [1905]. 490–506.

Śabdakalpadruma. (Eds.) *Varadaprasada and Haricarana Vasu*. Varanasi: Chaukhamba Sanskrit Series, 1967.

Sanguo zhi (三國志). (1982). Beijing: Zhonghua shuju.

Śankara Miśra. (2003). *Bhedaratnam, "The Jewel of Difference."* Varanasi: Samparnanand Sanskrit University.

Sartre, Jean-Paul. (1960). *Critique de la raison dialectique: précédé de question de method. Tome I*. Paris: Gallimard.

Sellars, Wilfrid. (1963). *Empiricism and the Philosophy of Mind*. London: Routledge & K. Paul.

Sēng Càn (僧璨). (1928). *Faith Mind Inscription* [xìn xīn míng or shin jin mei, 信心銘]. *The Tashiō Shinshū Daizōkyō*, Vol.48. Tokyo: The Taishō Issai-Kyo Kanko Kwai. 376–377.

Sengzhao (僧肇). (1961a). *Zhaolun* 肇論. [The treatise of Sengzhao]. T.45.1858.

———. (1961b). *Zhu Weimojiejing* 注維摩詰經 [A commentary on the Vimalakīrtinirdeśa Sūtra]. T.38.1775.

Sextus Empiricus. (1935). *Against the Logicians* (*Adversos Mathematicos*). Trans. R. G. Bury. Vol. 291. Cambridge: Loeb-Harvard University Press.

———. (1949). *Against the Professors*. Loeb Classical Library No. 382. Cambridge, MA: Harvard University Press.

Shakespeare, William. (1996). *The Collected Works of William Shakespeare*. Ware, UK: Wordsworth Editions.

Shastri, Dwarika Das. (1985). *The Nyāyabindu of Acharya Dharmakirtti with the commmentaries by Arya Vinitadeva & Dharmottara & Dharmottara-tika-tippani*. Dharmakīrti Nibandhawali, Vol. 3 Bhauddha Bharati Series Varanasi, Vol. 18. Varanasi: Bauddha Bharati.

Shibayama, Zenkei. (1974). *Zen Comments on the Mumonkan*. New York: Harper and Row.

Shulman, David. (2012). *Beyond Reality: A History of the Imagination in South India*. Cambridge, MA: Harvard University Press.

Sider, David. (1986). "Commentary." In David Sider and Henry E. Johnstone (eds.), *The Fragments of Parmenides*. Bryn Mawr.

Siderits, Mark. (1989). "Thinking on Empty: Madhyamaka Anti-Realism and Canons of Rationality." In Shlomo Biderman and Ben Ami Scharfstein (eds.), *Rationality in Question*. Leiden: E.J. Brill. 231–249.

———. (2003a). *Personal Identity and Buddhist Philosophy: Empty Persons*. Aldershot, UK: Ashgate.

———. (2003b). "The Soteriological Significance of Emptiness." *Contemporary Buddhism* 4(1): 9–23.

———. (2007). *Buddhism as Philosophy: An Introduction*. Aldershot, UK: Ashgate.

———. (2008). "Paleo-Compatibilism and Buddhist Reductionism." *Sophia* 47(1): 29–42.

———. (2013). "Does a Table Have Buddha-nature?" *Philosophy East and West* 63(4): 373–386.

Siderits, Mark, and Shōryū Katsura (trans.). (2013). *Nāgārjuna's Middle Way: Mūlamadhyamakārikā*. Sommerville Wisdom Publication.

Sŏngch'ŏl. (1987). *Sŏnmunchŏngno* (Haeinsa Paekryŏnam, Korea: Changkyŏnggak).

Sorensen, Roy. (2009). "Nothingness." In Edward N. Zalta (ed.), *Stanford Encyclopedia of Philosophy*. Available at http://plato.stanford.edu/entries/nothingness/.

Sprung, Mervyn. (1979). *Lucid Exposition of the Middle Way: The Essential Chapters from the Prasannapadā of Candrakīrti*. Boulder, CO: Prajñā Press.

Staal, Johan Frederick. (1962). "Negation and the Law of Contradiction in Indian Thought: A Comparative Study." *Bulletin of the School of Oriental and African Studies* 25(1/3): 52–71.

———. (1988). *Universals: Studies in Indian Logic and Linguistics*. Chicago: The University of Chicago Press.

Strawson, Peter. (1974). "Freedom and Resentment." In *Freedom and Resentment and Other Essays*. London: Methuen. 1–28.

Suzuki, D. T. (1964). *An Introduction to Zen Buddhism*. New York: Grove Press.

———. (1976). *Essays in Zen Buddhism, Third Series*. New York: Samuel Weiser.

——— [as Suzuki Daisetsu]. (1991). *Kongōkyō no zen* [The Zen of the Diamond Sūtra]. In *Suzuki Daisetsu zen senshū* [Selected Works of Suzuki Daisetsu]. Tokyo: Shunshūsha.

———. (2000). "Zen of Diamond Sūtra" [kongō kyō no zen, 金剛經の禪]. In *Daisetsu Suzuki's Complete Works*. Vol. 5. Tokyo: Iwanami Shoten. 363–455. (Originally published as a part of *Japanese Spirituality* [nihon teki rei sei, 日本的靈性], in 1944.)

T'aego Pou. (2001). "Analects." In J.C. Cleary (ed.), *Buddha from Korea*. Boston: Shambala. 79–168.

———. (2012). *The Recorded Sayings of T'aego*. In J. Jorgensen (ed.), *Seon Dialogues*. Seoul: Jogye Order of Korean Buddhism.

Takuan Sōhō (沢庵宗彭). (1970).『不動智神妙録』[The mysterious records of unmovable wisdom]. Edited and translated by Ikeda Satoshi (池田諭). Tokyo: Tokuma Shoten.

Tanabe Hajime. (1963a). "Eien rekishi koui." In Tanabe Hajime Zenshuu (ed.),「永遠·歴史·行為」『田辺元全集』[Eternity/History/Action, *The Collected Works of Hajime Tanabe*, Vol. 7]. Tokyo: Chikuma. 117.

———. (1963b). "Shu no ronri no benshouhou." In Tanabe Hajime Zenshuu (ed.),「種の論理の弁証法」『田辺元全集』[The Logic of Species as the Dialectic, *The Collected Works of Hajime Tanabe*, Vol. 7]. Tokyo: Chikuma. 251–372.

Tanaka, Kyūbun. (2000). *Nihon no "tetsugaku" o yomitoku: "mu" no jidai o ikinukutameni* [Reading the philosophy of Japan: Living through the era of nothingness]. Tokyo: Chikuma shobō.

Tang, Yong-tong (湯用彤). (1983). *Tang Yong-Tong Xue Shu Lun Wen Ji* 湯用彤學術論文集 [*Collection of Tang Yong-Tong's Academic Articles*]. Beijing: Zhonghua Press.

———. (2001). *Wei-Jin Xuan Xue Lun Gao* 魏晉玄學論稿 [*Essays on Wei-Jin Philosophy*]. Shanghai: Guji Chubanshe.

Taylor, Richard. (1952). "Negative Things." *Journal of Philosophy* 49(13): 433–449.

———. (1953). "Ayer's Analysis of Negation." *Philosophical Studies*: 49–55.

Tillemans, Tom. (2010). "How Far Can a Mādhyamika Buddhist Reform Conventional Truth?" In The Cowherds (eds.), *Moonshadows: Conventional Truth in Buddhist Philosophy*. New York: Oxford University Press. 151–165.

Tillich, Paul. (1987). *The Essential Tillich: An Anthology of the Writings of Paul Tillich*. Edited by F. Forrester Church. New York: Collier Books.

Timalsina, Sthaneshwar. (2009a). "The Brahman and the Word Principle (*Śabda*): Influence of the Philosophy of Bhartṛhari on Maṇḍana's Brahmasiddhi." *Journal of Indian Philosophy* 373: 189–206.

———. (2009b). "Bhartṛhari and Maṇḍana on Avidyā." *Journal of Indian Philosophy* 37(4): 367–382.

Tsongkhapa. (2000). *Great Exposition of the Path to Enlightenment*. Translated by the Lamrimchenmo Translation Committee. Ithaca, NY: Snow Lion Press.

———. (2006). *Ocean of Reasoning: A Great Commentary on Nāgārjuna's Mūlamadhyamakakārikā.i*. Translated by Geshe Ngawang Samten and Jay L. Garfield. New York: Oxford University Press.

———. (2009). dBu ma dgongs pa rab gsal. Sarnath: Gelugpa Student Weslfare Committee.

Ueda, Shizuteru. (1993). "Pure Experience, Self-Awareness, Basho." *Etudes phénoménologiques* 18: 63–86.

———. (2004). "Mu To Kū Wo Megutte 「無と空」をめぐって [Concerning "Nothingness and Emptiness"]". *Nihon-no-Tetsugaku [Japanese Philosophy]* 5: 3–18.

Various authors. (2013). "Buddhism and Contradiction." Special issue, *Philosophy East and West* 63(3).

Venkateshananda, S. (1985). *The Concise Yoga Vaishistha*. New York: SUNY Press.

Vyasa. *The Mahabharata*. Available at www.sacred-texts.com/hin/maha.

Wagner, Rudolf G. (2000). *The Craft of a Chinese Commentator: Wang Bi on the Laozi*. Albany, NY: SUNY Press.

———. (2003). *A Chinese Reading of the Daodejing: Wang Bi's Commentary on the Laozi with Critical Text and Translation*. Albany, NY: SUNY Press.

Walleser, Max. (1922). "The Life of Nāgārjuna from Tibetan and Chinese Sources." In *Asia Major: Hirth Anniversary Volume*, 421–455.

Wang, Bi (王弼). (1980). *Wangbi ji jiaoshi* 王弼集校釋 [Annotations to Wang Bi's Collected Works]. Edited and annotated by Lou Yulie (樓宇烈). Beijing: Zhonghua Shuju.

Wang, Bo. (2011). "The Discovery and Establishment of *Wu*." *Contemporary Chinese Thought* 43(1): 9–29.

Watson, Burton (trans.). (1968). *The Complete Works of Chuang Tzu*. New York: Columbia University Press.

———. (trans.). (1997). *The Vimalakīirti Sūtra*. New York: Columbia University Press.

Watsuji, Tetsujirō (和辻哲郎). (1987).『車紋道元』[The monk Dōgen]. Tokyo: Ryūbunkan.

Watts, Alan. (1957). *The Way of Zen*. New York: Random House.

Wei, Zheng (魏徵). (1982). *Sui shu* 隋書. Beijing: Zhonghua shuju.

Wenzel, Christian. (2003). "Ethics and Zhuangzi: Awareness, Freedom, and Autonomy." *Journal of Chinese Philosophy* 30(1): 115–126.

Westerhoff, Jan. (2009). *Nagarjuna's Madhymaka: A Philosophical Introduction*. Oxford: Oxford University Press.

———. (2010). *Nāgārjuna's Madhyamaka: A Philosophical Analysis*. New York: Oxford University Press.

Wilhelm, Richard, and Cary F. Baynes (trans.). (1977). *The I Ching: Book of Changes*. Princeton, NJ: Princeton University Press.

Williams, Paul. (1980). "Some Aspects of Language and Construction in the Madhyamaka." In *Journal of Indian Philosophy* 8(1): 1–45.

———. (1989). *Mahāyāna Buddhism: The Doctrinal Foundations*. London: Routledge.

———. (1998). *Altruism and Reality: Studies in the Philosophy of the Bodhicaryāvatāra*. Curzon Critical Studies in Buddhism. Richmond, UK: Curzon Press.

Wŏnhyo. (1981). *Autocommentary on the Awakening of Mahāyāna Faith (Daesŭng kisillonso pyŏlki)*. In Ki-yong Rhi (Yi) (ed. and trans.), *Hankukŭi Pulkyosasang* [The Buddhist Thoughts of Korea]. Seoul: Samsung publishing. 53–167.

———. (2007). *Exposition of the Vajrasamadhi-Sūtra*. In Robert E. Buswell Jr. (ed. and trans.), *Cultivating Original Enlightenment: Wŏnhyo's Exposition of the Vajrasamadhi-Sūtra*. Honolulu: University of Hawaii Press. 100–560.

———. (2012). "The Great Vehicle Repentance for Indulgence in the Six Faculties." In A. Charles Muller (ed.), *Wŏnhyo: Selected Works*. Seoul: Jogye Order of Korean Buddhism. 269–280.

Wood, Thomas. (1994). *Nāgārjunian Disputations: A Journey Through an Indian Looking-Glass*. Honolulu: University of Hawai'i Press.

Wu, Yun (吳筠). (1992). *Zongxuan xiansheng wenji* 宗玄先生文集. Shanghai: Shanghai guji chubanshe.

Xenophanes of Colophon. (2001). *Fragments: A Text and Translation with a Commentary*. Edited and translated by J.H. Lesher. Toronto: University of Toronto Press.

Xu, Zhen-e (徐震堮). (1987). *Shishuo xinyu jiaojian* 世說新語校箋. Hong Kong: Zhonghua shuju.

Yanagida, Seizan. (1984). "*Muji No Ato Saki*無字のあとさき" [Before and After Muji]. *Risō* 610: 183–196.

Yang, Bojun (楊伯峻). (1980). *Liezi jishi* 列子集釋. Beijing: Zhonghua shuju.

———. (1984). *Mengzi yizhu* 孟子q譯注. Hong Kong: Zhonghua shuju.

Yao, Zhihua. (2004). "Dignāga and Four Types of Perception." *Journal of Indian Philosophy* 32(1): 57–79.

———. (2008). "Some Mahāsāṃghika Arguments for the Cognition of Nonexistent Objects." *Journal of Indian Council of Philosophical Research* 25(3): 79–96.

———. (Forthcoming). "Dārṣṭāntika Arguments for the Cognition of Nonexistent Objects."

Yasua, Yasuo. (1999–2006). *Complete Works* (湯淺泰雄全集) [YYZ]. 17 vols. Tokyo: Hakua Shobō.

Yearley, Lee. (1983). "The Perfected Person in the Radical Chuang-tzu." In Victor Mair (ed.), *Experimental Essays on Chuang-tzu*. Honolulu: University of Hawaii Press. 125–139.

Yusa, Michiko. (2014). "D.T. Suzuki and the 'Logic of *Sokuhi*,' or the 'Logic of *Prajñāpāramitā*'." In Gereon Kopf (ed.), *The Dao Companion to Japanese Buddhist Philosophy*. Dordrecht: Springer.

Zhang, Zai (張載). (2006). *Zhang Zai Ji* 張載集 [*The Complete Works of Zhang Zai*]. Beijing: Zhonghua shuju.

Zhiyi (智顗). (1927). *Māhē Zhǐguàn* [ma ka shi kan, 摩訶止觀]. *The Taishō Shinshū Daizōkyō*. Vol. 46. Tokyo: The Taishō Issai-Kyo Kanko Kwai.

Zhou, Dunyi (周敦頤). (1975). *Zhouzi Quan Shu* 周子全書 [*The Complete Works of Master Zhou*]. Taipei: Guanxueshe Chubanshe.

The *Zhuangzi* (莊子). (1961). *Collected Annotations on Zhuangzi* (莊子集釋 *Zhuangzi Jishi*). Edited by Guo Qingfan. Beijing: Zhonghua shuju.

Ziporyn, Brook (trans.). (2009). *Zhuangzi: The Essential Writings*. Indianapolis, IN: Hackett Publishing Company.

Zongbao (宗寶) (ed.). Liuzu dashi fabao tanjing 六祖大師法寶壇經 [The Platform Sūtra of the Dharma Treasure of the Master of the Sixth Patriarch], T.48.2008.

Index

abhāva (nonexistence) 4, 36, 145, 178, 248
Abhidharma xv, 56, 57, 58, 59, 64, 66, 67, 68, 74, 75, 76n1, 81, 89n6, 129, 134, 137; cowboy metaphysics 69
Ābhidharmikas xv, 56, 57, 58, 59, 64, 65, 74, 76n1, 81
abrāhmaṇa: Bhartṛhari 26, 31, 33, 34, 35, 36–7, 38, 43n28; Patañjali 32
absence of: active striving xxv, 214; affective activity 222, 224; a cup on a table 15; desire xxv, 214 (*see also wu yu*); a feeling 21; agency xvii; all things 4; anything 202; any *x* can always be reduced to the presence of some *y* 10; black ink 317, 318; the chairman 10, 11; color in air 6, 9; the compound term 40; conceptual differentiation and structuring 112; definition and determination184; desire xxv; detectable measurements 184; determination xxi; discernible characteristics 214; distinctions and discrimination 187; the doer and doing xvii; emotions xxv; essence 81; everything 4; existence xvii, 187; external reference 36; fixed forms xxiv; food 7; information 122; intrinsic existence 49; intrinsic nature xvii; a jar 42n8; milk 12; ontological independence 282n23; pain xiii; particularity and determination 184; the prover property15; qualification 187; religion 292; self-independence xxvi; pain xiii, 5; self xvii, 247; self-nature 231; self-independence xxvi; something 16, 34, 48; a symmetrical pattern 32; things in certain places xii
absences 4–5, 8–12; bare locus theory 10–2; as contents of negative introspective reports 20–3; heterologous 15–7; real xiii, 9, 16; repulsion theory 12–5; subjective 10
absolute emptiness 128, 309, 311, 312
acquired enlightenment 232, 234, 235
Advaita Vedantins 42n8
affectless xxv; sage 213–29
affective oblivion 221–3
Ai Tai Tuo 197
Amida Buddha 283n26, 299
anontology xxviii; and the issue of being and nothing in Kitarō Nishida 263–83
Appelfeld, Aharon 78
Aquinas, Thomas 76n1, 254
Aristotle xx, 91, 126; *Metaphysics* 119; metaphysics 270; substance 280, 292
Āryadeva xvii, 79
asat 3, 4
Ascombe, G. E. M. 6
asīt 3
āyatana (sense spheres) 136
Auschwitz 78
Avataṃsaka Sūtra 236, 238, 252
The Awakening of Faith in the Mahāyāna 233, 245n45, 266

bare locus theory 10–2
Berger, Douglas L. xii, xxiii–xxiv, 41n1, 119n25, 166–80, 212n9, 227n1, 245n58
Bergson, Henri xiii, 3, 5, 17, 22, 23
Bhartṛhari: compounds with negative particles and the metaphysics of negation 31–40; negation xiv, 25–43; from Patañjali to Bhartṛhari 26–7; sentential negation 27–31; *Vākyapadīya* 25, 29, 30, 31, 42n14
Bhattacharya, Gopinath xiii; *The Category of Negation* 6
Bhattacharya, K. C. 5, 21, 22